Handbook of Research on Multimedia Cyber Security

Brij B. Gupta
National Institute of Technology, Kurukshetra, India

Deepak Gupta
LoginRadius Inc., Canada

A volume in the Advances in Information Security,
Privacy, and Ethics (AISPE) Book Series

Published in the United States of America by
    IGI Global
    Information Science Reference (an imprint of IGI Global)
    701 E. Chocolate Avenue
    Hershey PA, USA 17033
    Tel: 717-533-8845
    Fax: 717-533-8661
    E-mail: cust@igi-global.com
    Web site: http://www.igi-global.com

Library of Congress Cataloging-in-Publication Data

Names: Gupta, Brij, 1982- editor. | Gupta, Deepak, 1983- editor.
Title: Handbook of research on multimedia cyber security / Brij B. Gupta
   and Deepak Gupta, editors.
Description: Hershey PA : Information Science Reference, [2020] | Includes
   bibliographical references and index. | Summary: "This book explores
   recent and future advancements in multimedia security and processing. It
   also presents new and recent algorithms in various emerging areas for
   copyright protection, content authentication, ownership authentication,
   and identity theft"-- Provided by publisher.
Identifiers: LCCN 2019043843 (print) | LCCN 2019043844 (ebook) | ISBN
   9781799827016 (hardcover) | ISBN 9781799827023 (ebook)
Subjects: LCSH: Multimedia communications--Security measures. | Biometric
   identification. | Database security.
Classification: LCC TK5105.15 .H3585 2020 (print) | LCC TK5105.15 (ebook)
   | DDC 006.7--dc23
LC record available at https://lccn.loc.gov/2019043843
LC ebook record available at https://lccn.loc.gov/2019043844

This book is published in the IGI Global book series Advances in Information Security, Privacy, and Ethics (AISPE) (ISSN: 1948-9730; eISSN: 1948-9749)

British Cataloguing in Publication Data
A Cataloguing in Publication record for this book is available from the British Library.

For electronic access to this publication, please contact: eresources@igi-global.com.

Advances in Information Security, Privacy, and Ethics (AISPE) Book Series

Manish Gupta
State University of New York, USA

ISSN:1948-9730
EISSN:1948-9749

MISSION

As digital technologies become more pervasive in everyday life and the Internet is utilized in ever in-creasing ways by both private and public entities, concern over digital threats becomes more prevalent.

The **Advances in Information Security, Privacy, & Ethics (AISPE) Book Series** provides cutting-edge research on the protection and misuse of information and technology across various industries and settings. Comprised of scholarly research on topics such as identity management, cryptography, system security, authentication, and data protection, this book series is ideal for reference by IT professionals, academicians, and upper-level students.

COVERAGE

- Cyberethics
- IT Risk
- Access Control
- Privacy Issues of Social Networking
- Device Fingerprinting
- Technoethics
- Security Classifications
- Computer ethics
- Tracking Cookies
- Network Security Services

IGI Global is currently accepting manuscripts for publication within this series. To submit a pro-posal for a volume in this series, please contact our Acquisition Editors at Acquisitions@igi-global.com or visit: http://www.igi-global.com/publish/.

Titles in this Series

For a list of additional titles in this series, please visit:
http://www.igi-global.com/book-series/advances-information-security-privacy-ethics/37157

Cyber Security of Industrial Control Systems in the Future Internet Environment
Mirjana D. Stojanović (University of Belgrade, Serbia) and Slavica V. Boštjančič Rakas (University of Belgrade, Serbia)
Information Science Reference • © 2020 • 374pp • H/C (ISBN: 9781799829102) • US $195.00

Digital Investigation and Intrusion Detection in Biometrics and Embedded Sensors
Asaad Abdulrahman Nayyef (Sultan Qaboos University, Iraq)
Information Science Reference • © 2020 • 320pp • H/C (ISBN: 9781799819448) • US $235.00

Handbook of Research on Intrusion Detection Systems
Brij B. Gupta (National Institute of Technology, Kurukshetra, India) and Srivathsan Srinivasagopalan (AT&T, USA)
Information Science Reference • © 2020 • 400pp • H/C (ISBN: 9781799822424) • US $265.00

Applied Approach to Privacy and Security for the Internet of Things
Parag Chatterjee (National Technological University, Argentina & University of the Republic, Uruguay) Emmanuel Benoist (Bern University of Applied Sciences, Switzerland) and Asoke Nath (St. Xavier's College, University of Calcutta, India)
Information Science Reference • © 2020 • 315pp • H/C (ISBN: 9781799824442) • US $235.00

Internet Censorship and Regulation Systems in Democracies Emerging Research and Opportunities
Nikolaos Koumartzis (Aristotle University of Thessaloniki, Greece) and Andreas Veglis (Aristotle University of Thessaloniki, Greece)
Information Science Reference • © 2020 • 200pp • H/C (ISBN: 9781522599739) • US $185.00

Quantum Cryptography and the Future of Cyber Security
Nirbhay Kumar Chaubey (Gujarat Technological University, India) and Bhavesh B. Prajapati (Education Department, Government of Gujarat, India)
Information Science Reference • © 2020 • 343pp • H/C (ISBN: 9781799822530) • US $235.00

Impact of Digital Transformation on Security Policies and Standards
Sam Goundar (The University of the South Pacific, Fiji) Bharath Bhushan (Sree Vidyanikethan Engineering College, India) and Vaishali Ravindra Thakare (Atria Institute of Technology, India)
Information Science Reference • © 2020 • 300pp • H/C (ISBN: 9781799823674) • US $215.00

701 East Chocolate Avenue, Hershey, PA 17033, USA
Tel: 717-533-8845 x100 • Fax: 717-533-8661
E-Mail: cust@igi-global.com • www.igi-global.com

This book is dedicated to my wife Varsha Gupta and daughter Prisha Gupta for their constant support during the course of this handbook - B. B. Gupta

This book is dedicated to my family for their constant support during the course of this handbook - Deepak Gupta

Editorial Advisory Board

List of Contributors

Table of Contents

Detailed Table of Contents

Data compression is the process of encoding data using a representation that decreases the overall size of data, where this reduction is possible when the original dataset contains some type of redundancy. Data compression, also called compaction, is the process of reducing the amount of data needed for storage or transmission of a given piece of information, typically using encoding techniques. Multimedia compression is employing tools and techniques to reduce the file size of various media formats, taking up less space. Both downloading and uploading a compressed file takes a lot less time. Data compression is one of the factors that contributed most to the great growth of information and communication technologies. Without compression, most consumer and entertainment technology products, which are today commonplace, would never have come into existence. This chapter provides an updated review of multimedia compression, showing and approaching its success relationship, with a concise bibliographic background, categorizing and synthesizing the potential of both technologies.

Continuous authentication systems allow users not to possess or remember something to authenticate themselves. These systems perform a permanent authentication that improves the security level of traditional mechanisms, which just authenticate from time to time. Despite the benefits of continuous authentication, the selection of dimensions and characteristics modelling of user's behaviour, and the creation and management of precise models based on Machine learning, are two important open challenges. This chapter proposes a continuous and adaptive authentication system that uses Machine Learning techniques based on the detection of anomalies. Applications usage and the location of the mobile device are considered to detect abnormal behaviours of users when interacting with the device. The proposed system provides adaptability to behavioural changes through the insertion and elimination of patterns. Finally, a proof of concept and several experiments justify the decisions made during the design and implementation of this work, as well as demonstrates its suitability and performance.

Chapter 3

Sadiq J. Almuairfi, Prince Sultan University, Saudi Arabia
Mamdouh Alenezi, Prince Sultan University, Saudi Arabia

Cloud computing technology provides cost-saving and flexibility of services for users. With the explosion of multimedia data, more and more data owners would outsource their personal multimedia data on the cloud. In the meantime, some computationally expensive tasks are also undertaken by cloud servers. However, the outsourced multimedia data and its applications may reveal the data owner's private information because the data owners lose control of their data. Recently, this thought has aroused new research interest on privacy-preserving reversible data hiding over outsourced multimedia data. Anonymous Authentication Scheme will be proposed in this chapter as the most relatable, applicable, and appropriate techniques to be adopted by the cloud computing professionals for the eradication of risks that have been associated with the risks and challenges of privacy.

Chapter 4

Avinash Kaur, Lovely Professional University, Phagwara, India
Parminder Singh, Lovely Professional University, Phagwara, India
Anand Nayyar, Duy Tan University, Da Nang, Vietnam

The data transmission on network channel has increased tremendously in the past few decades. Watermarking is a process to add watermark as a digital signal, label, or tag into a cover media. The primary requirements of multimedia watermarking are robustness and embedding capability. The robustness is defined as the strength of an algorithm to repel the noise. However, it is challenging to achieve both at the same time. The numerous characteristics of watermarking are very imperative in the multimedia watermarking system. The researchers are using watermarking schemes in various applications such as military, digital forensics, medical, and so on. Attacks of these watermarking harm or uncover the secret information carried in the watermark. Potential researchers have been presented various techniques for balancing or improving these concerns. This chapter reviews the recent multimedia watermarking techniques on the basis of robustness and embedding capability. The characteristics, applications, and attacks on multimedia watermarking techniques are introduced.

Chapter 5

Brij B. Gupta, National Institute of Technology, Kurukshetra, India
Somya Rajan Sahoo, National Institute of Technology, Kurukshetra, India
Prashant Chugh, National Institute of Technology, Kurukshetra, India
Vijay Iota, National Institute of Technology, Kurukshetra, India
Anupam Shukla, National Institute of Technology, Kurukshetra, India

In global internet usage, increasing multimedia message, which includes video, audio, images, and text documents, on the web raised a lot of consequences related to copyright. For copyright protection, authentication purpose and forgery detection digital watermarking is the robust way in social network content protection. In this technique, the privacy information is embedded inside the multimedia content like image and video. The protected content embedded inside multimedia content is called watermark-enabled information. To make more effective the process of watermarking, the content encrypted before embedding to the image. Basically, the digital watermarking embedded process implemented in two different domains called spatial and frequency domain. In spatial domain digital watermarking, the watermark information is embedded in the least significant bit of the original image on the basis of bit plane selected and on the basis of the pixels of image, embedding, and detection is performed.

Chapter 6

Poonkuntran Shanmugam, Velammal College of Engineering and Technology, Madurai,
India
Manessa Jayaprakasam, Independent Researcher, India

This chapter presents an integer transform-based watermarking scheme for digital fundus image authentication. It is presented under multimedia applications in medicine. The chapter introduces image authentication by watermarking and digital fundus image. The key requirements in developing watermarking scheme for fundus images and its challenges are identified and highlighted. Authors describe a proposed watermarking scheme on integer transform. The experimental results emphasize the proposed scheme's ability in addressing key requirements and its attainment. The detailed results are summarized.

Chapter 7

Phuc Do, University of Information Techonology (VNU-HCM), Vietnam
Trung Hong Phan, University of Information Techonology (VNU-HCM), Vietnam

In this chapter, Image2vec or Video2vector are used to convert images and video clips to vectors in large multimedia database. The M-tree is an index structure that can be used for the efficient resolution of similarity queries on complex objects. M-tree can be profitably used for content-based retrieval on multimedia databases provided relevant features have been extracted from the objects. In a large multimedia database, to search for similarities such as k-NN queries and Range queries, distances from the query object to all remaining objects (images or video clips) are calculated. The calculation between query and entities in a large multimedia database is not feasible. This chapter proposes a solution to distribute the M-Tree structure on the Apache Spark framework to solve the Range Query and kNN Query problems in large multimedia database with a lot of images and video clips.

Kirti Raj Bhatele, Rustamji Institute of Technology, India
Shivangi Jain, Rustamji Institute of Technology, India
Abhishek Kataria, Rustamji Institute of Technology, India
Prerana Jain, Rustamji Institute of Technology, India

This chapter simply provides a brief introduction to the various fundamentals and concepts that are related to the digital forensics. The overview of the digital forensics comprises the life cycle of the digital forensics with different stages, i.e., the preparation, collection, analysis, and reporting. The evaluation of the digital forensics tools comprises the encase forensic, The FTK(forensics tool kit), and The Helix digital forensic tool with their benefits and limitations. The digital forensics tools and techniques examination comprises the digital examination techniques, along with the live forensics analysis and the recovery of window registry, and the comparison of the digital forensics tools, and also focuses on the ACPO guidelines for digital forensics analysis.

Jia Lu, Auckland University of Technology, New Zealand
Wei Qi Yan, Auckland University of Technology, New Zealand

With the cost decrease of security monitoring facilities such as cameras, video surveillance has been widely applied to public security and safety such as banks, transportation, shopping malls, etc. which allows police to monitor abnormal events. Through deep learning, authors can achieve high performance of human behavior detection and recognition by using model training and tests. This chapter uses public datasets Weizmann dataset and KTH dataset to train deep learning models. Four deep learning models were investigated for human behavior recognition. Results show that YOLOv3 model is the best one and achieved 96.29% of mAP based on Weizmann dataset and 84.58% of mAP on KTH dataset. The chapter conducts human behavior recognition using deep learning and evaluates the outcomes of different approaches with the support of the datasets.

Maria Rodriguez, University of Melbourne, Australia
Rajkumar Buyya, University of Melbourne, Australia

Containers are widely used by organizations to deploy diverse workloads such as web services, big data, and IoT applications. Container orchestration platforms are designed to manage the deployment of containerized applications in large-scale clusters. The majority of these platforms optimize the scheduling of containers on a fixed-sized cluster and are not enabled to autoscale the size of the cluster nor to consider features specific to public cloud environments. This chapter presents a resource management approach with three objectives: 1) optimize the initial placement of containers by efficiently scheduling them on existing resources, 2) autoscale the number of resources at runtime based on the cluster's workload, and 3) consolidate applications into fewer VMs at runtime. The framework was implemented as a Kubernetes plugin and its efficiency was evaluated on an Australian cloud infrastructure. The experiments demonstrate that a reduction of 58% in cost can be achieved by dynamically managing the cluster size and placement of applications.

Chapter 11

Chaoran Liu, Auckland University of Technology, New Zealand
Wei Qi Yan, Auckland University of Technology, New Zealand

Gait recognition mainly uses different postures of each individual to perform identity authentication. In the existing methods, the full-cycle gait images are used for feature extraction, but there are problems such as occlusion and frame loss in the actual scene. It is not easy to obtain a full-cycle gait image. Therefore, how to construct a highly efficient gait recognition algorithm framework based on a small number of gait images to improve the efficiency and accuracy of recognition has become the focus of gait recognition research. In this chapter, deep neural network CRBM+FC is created. Based on the characteristics of Local Binary Pattern (LBP) and Histogram of Oriented Gradient (HOG) fusion, a method of learning gait recognition from GEI to output is proposed. A brand-new gait recognition algorithm based on layered fu-sion of LBP and HOG is proposed. This chapter also proposes a feature learning network, which uses an unsupervised convolutionally constrained Boltzmann machine to train the Gait Energy Images (GEI).

Chapter 12

Avila Jayapalan, SASTRA University (Deemed), India

With the advent increase in growth of wireless technology Orthogonal Frequency Division Multiplexing (OFDM) gains popularity in recent years. OFDM forms the fundamental backbone of many currently used wireless transmission standards. It is a multicarrier modulation scheme which overcomes the need for equalizer to mitigate ISI caused due to multipath propagation. In this work, an OFDM based transceiver has been developed utilizing various modules like Source Coding, Channel Coding, IFFT-FFT, scrambler, cyclic prefix, and signal mapper. To ensure secure data transmission, Hadamard matrix is XORed with the data. This provides a low level of protection to the image which is transmitted. LabVIEW has been used as the processing tool to develop the transceiver and the prototype developed has been tested using Universal Software Radio Peripheral (USRP).

Chapter 13

Amany Sarhan, Department of Computers and Control Engineering, Faculty of Engineering,
Tanta University, Egypt
Ahmed Ramadan, Department of Computer and Control Engineering, Faculty of
Engineering, Tanta University, Egypt

Nowadays, touchscreen mobile devices make up a larger share in the market, necessitating effective and robust methods to continuously authenticate touch-based device users. A classification framework is proposed that learns the touch behavior of a user and is able afterwards to authenticate users by monitoring their behavior in performing input touch actions. Two models of features are built; the low-level features (stoke-level) model or the high-level abstracted features (session-level) model. In building these models, two different methods for features selection and data classification were weighted features and PCA. Two classification algorithms were used; ANN and SVM. The experimental results indicate the possibility of continuous authentication for touch-input users with higher promises for session-level features than stroke-level features. Authors found out that using weighted features method and artificial neural networks in building the session-level model yields the most efficient and accurate behavioral biometric continuous user authentication.

Chapter 14
Rui Hu, Auckland University of Technology, New Zealand
Wei Qi Yan, Auckland University of Technology, New Zealand

Although our communities are paying extensive attention to the blockchain technology, it is still far away from realistic applications. Thus, this red-hot technology could be understood and employed for visual applications. Authors focus on online videos that collect sufficient user clicks owning to the high demand every day. When people watch the videos of TV drama episodes in an online website, they often need to exactly organise the playlists in ascending or descending order. However, video websites such as YouTube can't provide this service due to multiple reasons. This chapter creates a private blockchain for these video websites and applies Merkle tree to store the sorted videos in the chain. A sorted playlist has been created in the video website. Getting out of the box of video search so as to provide a quick video ranking solution is authors' main task. Sorting results are evaluated by using edit distance.

Chapter 15
Chen Xin, Auckland University of Technology, New Zealand
Minh Nguyen, Auckland University of Technology, New Zealand
Wei Qi Yan, Auckland University of Technology, New Zealand

Identifying fire flames is based on object recognition which has valuable applications in intelligent surveillance. This chapter focuses on flame recognition using deep learning and its evaluations. For achieving this goal, authors design a Multi-Flame Detection scheme (MFD) which utilises Convolutional Neural Networks (CNNs). Authors take use of TensorFlow in deep learning with an NVIDIA GPU to train an image dataset and constructed a model for flame recognition. The contributions of this book chapter are: (1) data augmentation for flame recognition, (2) model construction for deep learning, and (3) result evaluations for flame recognition using deep learning.

Chapter 16
Ahmad Al-Qerem, Zarqa University, Jordan
Bushra Mohammed Abutahoun, Princess Sumaya University for Technology, Jordan
Shadi Ismail Nashwan, Computer Science Department, Jouf University, Saudi Arabia
Shatha Shakhatreh, Princess Sumaya University for Technology, Jordan
Mohammad Alauthman, Zarqa University, Jordan
Ammar Almomani, Department of Information Technology, Al-Huson University College, Al-Balqa Applied University, Jordan

The spread of IoT devices is significantly increasing worldwide with a low design security that makes it more easily compromised than desktop computers. This gives rise to the phenomenon of IoT-based botnet attacks such as Mirai botnet, which have recently emerged as a high-profile threat that continues. Accurate and timely detection methods are required to identify these attacks and mitigate these new threats. To do so, this chapter will implement a network-based anomaly detection approach for the Mirai botnet using various machine learning and feature selection algorithms. Authors use Multiphase Genetic Algorithm section methods and PSO to select the best subfield of features capable of producing good overall classification results, and with this Feature Selection Algorithm, Random forest algorithm can detect all anomaly behavior with 100% accuracy.

This study technically analyses the maximum number of combinations for common passwords up to 12 characters long. A maximum storage size necessary for the creation of a data base that holds all possible passwords up to 12 characters is also presented along with a comparison against the publicized cost of storage from popular cloud storage providers and the national budget for intelligence and defense activities of a nation. Authors prove that it is technically possible that any password could be computed within seconds with nothing more than currently commercially available components. The study concludes that it is possible that nation states or even combined nation states working in collaboration could or already have bought private citizens' and businesses' passwords revealing that it may already be an age where the password may not be a legitimate defense for privacy anymore.

Preface

Noticeable increase can be seen in the data production sources as a result of enhancements in high-end data streaming devices, and technological paradigms like Internet of Things (IoT), Wireless Sensor Networks (WSNs), Cloud Computing, and so forth. Multimedia has seen a major breakthrough in the field of Information and Communication Technology (ICT). It is accompanied with bulk of information being generated and transmitted among the computing devices across the Internet. Consumer applications, entertainment, healthcare, and smart cities are some of the application areas where multimedia aspects are playing a crucial role. These applications are accompanied with higher mobility and interactivity among the participating entities. However, this information including Credit card information and business secrets, is usually of confidential nature and requires high-end protection from the mischievous users or adversaries. Cyber-attacks have become a crucial concern for the individuals and organizations across the globe as they can cause huge losses in terms of finance and other aspects. Unsecured channels make this information vulnerable to attacks including identity theft, copyright and ownership violation, breach of confidentiality, and so forth. Exposure of confidential information to the malicious users across different applications is a significant concern. Hence, it has become inevitable to establish adequate security measures to safeguard the sensitive information, and to identify and evaluate the security challenges.

Therefore, the Handbook of Research on Multimedia Cyber Security provides a comprehensive solution to understand the latest advancements and research findings in the field of multimedia security. Additionally, this handbook will likewise present the essentials of cyber security as the initial move towards figuring out how to protect confidential multimedia information from adversaries. This handbook will turn out significant to the readers in terms of the concepts covered, open research challenges, various solutions and research insights. It emphasizes on focusing attention towards the fast-evolving and critical cyber world, and to develop potential solutions to deal with the security challenges associated with it. The subject matter of the book presents fundamentals, techniques, challenges, and applications of multimedia cyber security. It illustrates the underlying concepts using examples, models, and terminologies that would fascinate readers towards the highly informative content. In addition, the book covers current trends and future research directions in the domain. This handbook is suitable for faculties scientists, researchers, scholars and professionals who are seeking to carrying out work in the field of Cyber Security, Multimedia Security, IT Security, Incidence Response, Network Administration, and so forth.

This handbook contains chapters dealing with different aspects of multimedia cyber security. These include multimedia encryption, multimedia compression, multimedia watermarking, multimedia forensics, authentication in multimedia mobile devices, anonymous authentication for privacy preserving of multimedia data in Cloud, security of multimedia contents embedded on Online Social Networks (OSNs), medical image authentication, multimedia database, multimedia applications in medicine, multimedia security in cloud computing environments, multimedia security for consumer applications, soft computing techniques for multimedia, human behavior recognition, container orchestration with cost-efficient autoscaling in Cloud computing, deep learning for Gait recognition, USRP based secure data transmission, user authentication, design and implementation of visual blockchain with Merkle tree, flames recognition, network-based detection of Mirai botnet, password security. This handbook is organized into 17 chapters.

Chapter 1 aims to provide an updated review of multimedia compression, showing and approaching its success relationship, with a concise bibliographic background, categorizing and synthesizing the potential of both technologies. In chapter 2, authors propose a continuous and adaptive authentication system that uses Machine Learning techniques based on the detection of anomalies. Applications usage and the location of the mobile device are considered to detect abnormal behaviours of users when interacting with the device. The proposed system provides adaptability to behavioural changes through the insertion and elimination of patterns. Finally, a proof of concept and several experiments justify the decisions made during the design and implementation of this work, as well as demonstrates its suitability and performance.

Cloud computing technology provides cost-saving and flexibility of services for users. With the explosion of multimedia data, more and more data owners would outsource their personal multimedia data on the cloud. In the meantime, some computationally expensive tasks are also undertaken by cloud servers. However, the outsourced multimedia data and its applications may reveal the data owner's private information because the data owners lose control of their data. Recently, this thought has aroused new research interest on privacy-preserving reversible data hiding over outsourced multimedia data. Anonymous authentication scheme is proposed in Chapter 3 as the most relatable, applicable, and appropriate techniques to be adopted by the cloud computing professionals for the eradication of risks that have been associated with the risks and challenges of privacy. In Chapter 4, the recent multimedia watermarking techniques are reviewed on the basis of robustness and embedding capability. Further, this article introduces the characteristics, applications and attacks on multimedia watermarking techniques.

In order to make more effective the process of watermarking, the content is encrypted before embedding to the images. The selected image passes through low and high pass filter based on the axis selection i.e. X-direction and Y-direction. On the basis of the method selection, the overall band of the images is divided into four different decompositions called LL, LH, HL and HH. Where low- low (LL) is having the lowest frequency and high-high (HH) is having the highest frequency component of any image. In the approach presented in chapter 5, the LL is also decomposed into four different regions and again it decomposed the LL of level 2. DWT provides the watermarking at level 3. To evaluate and identify the effectiveness of watermarking process, authors evaluate the PSNR (Peak Signal Noise Ratio) and MSE (Mean Square Error) values in the proposed model. Another effective scenario i.e. NCC (Normalized Correlation Coefficient) is used for matching the extracted watermark with the original watermark. By applying this process, the image copyright protection is done with the help of DWT. Authors also implemented similar applications for video content that are shared in the social network platform by breaking the video content into number of different frames. Chapter 6 presents an integer transform based watermarking scheme for digital fundus image authentication. It is presented under multimedia applications in medicine. This chapter starts with an introduction to image authentication by watermarking and digital fundus image. The key requirements in developing watermarking scheme for fundus images and its challenges are identified and highlighted. The chapter describes a proposed watermarking scheme on integer transform. The experimental results emphasize the proposed scheme's ability in addressing key requirements and its attainment. Also, the detailed results are summarized.

In Chapter 7, Image2vec or Video2vector are used to convert images and video clips to vectors in large multimedia database. The M-tree is an index structure that can be used for the efficient resolution of similarity queries on complex objects. M-tree can be profitably used for content-based retrieval on multimedia databases provided relevant features have been extracted from the objects. In a large multimedia database, to search for similarities such as k-NN queries and Range queries, distances from the query object to all remaining objects (images or video clips) are calculated. The calculation between query and entities in a large multimedia database is not feasible. This chapter also proposes a solution to distribute the M-Tree structure on the Apache Spark framework to solve the Range Query and kNN Query problems in large multimedia database with a lot of images and video clips. In addition, this chapter also presents experimental results on creating both local and distributed. Chapter 8 provides a brief introduction of various fundamentals and concepts that are related to the digital forensics. The overview of the digital forensics comprises of the life cycle of the digital forensics which includes different stages i.e. the preparation, collection, analysis and reporting. The evaluation of the digital forensics tools comprises of The encase forensic, The FTK (forensics tool kit) and The Helix digital forensic tool with their benefits and limitations. The digital forensics tools and techniques examination comprises of the digital examination techniques along with the live forensics analysis and the recovery of window registry, the comparison of the digital forensics tools and also focuses on the ACPO guidelines for digital forensics analysis.

In chapter 9, authors used public datasets Weizmann dataset and KTH dataset to train their proposed deep learning models. The contribution of this chapter is to conduct human behavior recognition using deep learning in first time and evaluate the outcomes of different approaches with the support of the datasets. Four deep learning models were investigated in this chapter for human behavior recognition. Obtained results show that YOLOv3 model is the best one and achieved 96.29% of mAP based on Weizmann dataset and 84.58% of mAP on KTH dataset. Chapter 10 presents a resource management approach with three objectives: i) optimize the initial placement of containers by efficiently scheduling them on existing resources, ii) autoscale the number of resources at runtime based on the cluster's workload, and iii) consolidate applications into fewer VMs at runtime. The framework was implemented as a Kubernetes plugin and its efficiency was evaluated on an Australian cloud infrastructure. The experiments demonstrate that a reduction of 58% in cost can be achieved by dynamically managing the cluster size and placement of applications.

In Chapter 11, a deep neural network CRBM+FC is created. Based on the characteristics of Local Binary Pattern (LBP) and Histogram of Oriented Gradient (HOG) fusion, a method of learning gait recognition from GEI to output is proposed. A brand-new gait recognition algorithm based on layered fusion of LBP and HOG is proposed. This chapter also proposes a feature learning network, which uses an unsupervised convolutionally constrained Boltzmann machine to train the Gait Energy Images (GEI). In Chapter 12, an OFDM based transceiver has been developed utilizing various modules like Source Coding, Channel Coding, IFFT-FFT, scrambler, cyclic prefix and signal mapper. To ensure secure data transmission, Hadamard matrix is XORed with the data. This provides a low level of protection to the image which is transmitted. LabVIEW has been used as the processing tool to develop the transceiver and the prototype developed has been tested using Universal Software Radio Peripheral (USRP).

In Chapter 13, a classification framework is proposed that learns the touch behavior of a user and is able afterwards to authenticate users by monitoring their behavior in performing input touch actions.

Two models of features are built; the low-level features (stoke-level) model or the high-level abstracted features (session-level) model. In building these models, two different methods for features selection and data classification were; weighted features and PCA. Two classification algorithms were used; ANN and SVM. The experimental results indicate the possibility of continuous authentication for touch-input users with higher promises for session-level features than stroke-level features. As overall conclusion, it is found out that using weighted features method and artificial neural networks in building the session-level model yields the most efficient and accurate behavioral biometric continuous user authentication. In Chapter 14, authors created a private blockchain for video websites and applied Merkle tree to store the sorted videos in the chain. Finally, a sorted playlist has been created in the video website. Getting out of the box of video search so as to provide a quick video ranking solution is the main task. Finally, the sorting results are evaluated using edit distance.

Identifying fire flames is based on object recognition which has valuable applications in intelligent surveillance. The focus of Chapter 15 is on flame recognition using deep learning and its evaluations. For achieving this goal, authors design a Multi-Flame Detection scheme (MFD) which utilizes Convolutional Neural Networks (CNNs). Authors use TensorFlow in deep learning with an NVIDIA GPU to train an image dataset and constructed a model for flame recognition. The contributions of this chapter are: (1) data augmentation for flame recognition, (2) model construction for deep learning, and (3) result evaluations for flame recognition using deep learning.

Chapter 16 presents a network-based anomaly detection approach for the Mirai botnet using various machine learning and feature selection algorithms. Authors use Multiphase Genetic Algorithm section methods and PSO to select the best subfield of features capable of producing good overall classification results. With this feature selection algorithm, Random forest algorithm can detect all anomaly behavior with 100% accuracy. Chapter 17 presents a study which analyses the maximum possible number of combinations for common passwords up to 12 characters long. A maximum storage size necessary for the creation of a data base that holds all possible passwords up to 12 characters is also presented along with a comparison against the publicized cost of storage from popular cloud storage providers and the national budget for intelligence and defense activities of a nation. Authors prove that it is technically possible that any password could be computed within seconds with nothing more than currently commercially available components. The study concludes that it is possible that nation, states or even combined nation states working in collaboration, could or already have bought private citizens' and businesses' passwords revealing that we may already live in an age where the password may not be a legitimate defense for privacy anymore.

Acknowledgment

Many people have contributed greatly to this Handbook of Research on Multimedia Cyber Security. We, the editors, would like to acknowledge all of them for their valuable help and generous ideas in improving the quality of this handbook. With our feelings of gratitude, we would like to introduce them in turn. The first mention is the authors and reviewers of each chapter of this handbook. Without their outstanding expertise, constructive reviews and devoted effort, this comprehensive handbook would become something without contents. The second mention is the IGI Global staff, and the development team for their constant encouragement, continuous assistance and untiring support. Without their technical support, this handbook would not be completed. The third mention is the editor's family for being the source of continuous love, unconditional support and prayers not only for this work, but throughout our life. Last but far from least, we express our heartfelt thanks to the Almighty for bestowing over us the courage to face the complexities of life and complete this work.

Brij B. Gupta
National Institute of Technology, Kurukshetra, India

Deepak Gupta
LoginRadius Inc., Canada
December 5, 2019

Chapter 1

A Review on the Technological and Literary Background of Multimedia Compression

Reinaldo Padilha França

State University of Campinas (UNICAMP), Brazil

Yuzo Iano

State University of Campinas (UNICAMP), Brazil

Ana Carolina Borges Monteiro

State University of Campinas (UNICAMP), Brazil

Rangel Arthur

Faculty of Technology (FT), State University of Campinas (UNICAMP), Brazil

ABSTRACT

Data compression is the process of encoding data using a representation that decreases the overall size of data, where this reduction is possible when the original dataset contains some type of redundancy. Data compression, also called compaction, is the process of reducing the amount of data needed for storage or transmission of a given piece of information, typically using encoding techniques. Multimedia compression is employing tools and techniques to reduce the file size of various media formats, taking up less space. Both downloading and uploading a compressed file takes a lot less time. Data compression is one of the factors that contributed most to the great growth of information and communication technologies. Without compression, most consumer and entertainment technology products, which are today commonplace, would never have come into existence. This chapter provides an updated review of multimedia compression, showing and approaching its success relationship, with a concise bibliographic background, categorizing and synthesizing the potential of both technologies.

DOI: 10.4018/978-1-7998-2701-6.ch001

INTRODUCTION

Internet users are consuming more and more multimedia content. It is estimated that the audiovisual format will account for 80% of online content by 2020. However, files are often heavy and may not run easily on all devices, so it is essential to understand what audio and video compression are (Kaplan et al., 2014).

Data compression is the process of encoding data using a representation that reduces the overall size of data. This reduction is possible when the original dataset contains some type of redundancy. Data compression, also called compaction, the process of reducing the amount of data needed for the storage or transmission of a given piece of information, typically by the use of encoding techniques. Multimedia compression is employing tools and techniques in order to reduce the file size of various media formats. Compression consists of reducing the physical size of blocks of information. A compressor uses an algorithm that serves to optimize the data by taking into account considerations specific to the type of data that will be compressed. Therefore, it is necessary to decompress to reconstruct the original data thanks to the algorithm opposite that used for compression (Sayood, 2017).

The compression method depends intrinsically on the type of data to be compressed, that is, it does not compress an image in the same way as an audio file. It is reducing a large amount of data in a file so that it takes up less space in the memory of a device or requires less of the broadband transmission. It can happen with or without loss, although most eliminate some almost imperceptible details. However, the greater the compression of audio and video, in general, results in lower quality, when compressing sound files, it reduces or simplifies bit repetition and eliminates data considered imperceptible to the human ear (Sayood, 2017; Uthayakumar et al., 2018).

Modern techniques explore the perception of the human ear and provide a compression that has apparently suffered no loss. The most popular is FLAC (Free Lossless Audio Codec: lossless compression) unlike most, it does not delete any information from the sound file but can reduce it by up to 50% in size. Despite the decrease, it can be up to ten times heavier than the MP3 format; ALAC (Apple Lossless; no loss): audio data compression produced by Apple; MP3 (MPEG-1/2 Audio Layer 3 with loss) the most popular audio compression format decreased file size considerably and still maintained its quality. It was officially discontinued in 2017, but is still very popular; Ogg Vorbis (lossy) an audio format that offers lower bitrates and higher quality than MP3. It is divided into two parts, Ogg, responsible for the metadata of the file, and Vorbis, encoder that compresses the songs; AAC (lossy) designed to be the successor to MP3, AAC is the standard format for playing audio on devices such as iPhone, iPad and PlayStation (Uthayakumar et al., 2018; Siegert et al., 2016; Firmansah et al., 2016; Ahmed et al., 2018; Hennequin et al., 2017; Hennequin et al., 2017).

Like audio, video compression involves reducing the size of the file, but in this case removing the parts that have already been projected. When it occurs without loss, no part of the data is discarded from the image. In lossy compression, the bits are selectively discarded. One of the ways to do this is to reduce the number of frames, which is usually the same as the TV (30 per second). Some of the most popular compression formats are MKV (Matroska Video) widely used for high-resolution video, MKV offers an effective compression and maintains quality. For this to occur, the codec encapsulates the audio, video, and subtitle tracks into a single container; MPEG (Moving Picture Experts Group) defined by ISO as the standard video compression format, it can vary between MPEG-1 (for VCD), MPEG-2 (DVD) and MPEG-4; AVI (Audio Video Interleave) like MKV, AVI encapsulates audio and video in a single container. With this, both are played synchronously. As it was produced by Microsoft, the format is easily run on Windows and recognized by DVD and Blu-Ray players that are compatible with the DivX codec (Sayood, 2017; Chalmers et al., 2016).

In addition to taking up less space, both downloading and uploading a compressed file takes a lot less time. This makes it much easier when you want to post some video files on social networks. Audio and video compression also allows streaming to be viable. Without that, many streaming platforms and social networks would not have the popularity and profitability they currently have. Thus, data compression is one of the factors that contributed most to the great growth of information and communication technologies. Without compression, most consumer and entertainment technology products, which are today banal, would never have come into existence (Burroughs, 2019).

In fact, multimedia compression technologies allow you to represent information more efficiently, reducing the large volumes of storage space you occupy and therefore the bandwidth you consume to transmit on the networks and on the Internet. Therefore, this chapter aims to provide an updated review of multimedia compression, showing and approaching its success relation, with a concise bibliographic background, categorizing and synthesizing the potential of both technologies.

METHODOLOGY

This study was based on the research of 66 scientific articles and books that address the theme of the present work, exploring mainly a historical review and applicability of techniques related to Multimedia and Multimedia Compression. These papers were analyzed based on the publication date of fewer than 5 years, with emphasis on publications and indexing in renowned databases, such as IEEE and Scholar Google

RESULTS

The amount of information transmitted and stored (such as images, voice, and video) grows with technological advances and popularization of products such as mobile phones, tablets, and computers. Therefore, the bandwidth and/or storage capacity requirements of communications networks need to be minimized. In view of this, signals need to be encoded efficiently to suit transmission channel limitations and storage memory limitations. The technological development of high-speed information and communication systems has led to the emergence of new applications in the field of distributed systems. One of the main trends in this context is the integration of different types of media such as text, voice, images, and videos into a wide range of distributed computing applications (e.g. teleteaching, electronic publishing, cooperative work, and currently the spread of entertainment) (Hashem et al., 2015; Jeschke et al., 2017).

Multimedia is one of the most used terms in this decade, such terminology is at the crossroads of five major computer, telecommunications, advertising, audio and video device consumers, television and film industries. This great interest in these powerful industries contributed to the great evolution of multimedia. Multimedia is also considered the Area concerned with computer-controlled integration of text, graphics, images, videos, animations, sounds, and any other medium where all kinds of information can be represented, stored, transmitted and digitally processed. A multimedia system is one capable of handling at least one discrete media type and one continuous media type in digital form synchronously. Already captured media is information captured from the real world such as images, videos and sounds;

where in contrast the synthesized media is the information synthesized by the computer as text, graphics, and animations. Where both types of media are multimedia applications, being audio, video, and images natural means of communication. Multimedia systems have applications in all areas where these media need to be used, communicated and shared, be it education/training, entertainment, medicine, health, media-on-demand, e-commerce or even e-government, among many others (Hanjalic, 2017; Alvi et al., 2015).

It is important to note that in multimedia thematic there are discrete media which are static (or block) media, composed of information items independent of time. These are media with uniquely spatial dimensions such as text, images, graphics, where time is not part of the semantics of information, and downloading is the operation of recovering discreet media, such as its bursty traffic. Just as continuous media are dynamic (or time-dependent) media, where time or temporal dependency between information items is part of the information itself, they are media with temporal dimensions such as audios, videos, and animations, and time does. If semantic dependence is not respected, its meaning can be changed, and streaming is a term used to indicate that a continuous medium is being sent and presented directly to the destination as it is received (in time), where your traffic can be CBR (Constant Bitrate) or VBR (Variable Bitrate) (Kaae, 2017; Baroňák et al., 2017).

Multimedia data has a temporal dimension, i.e. it must be transmitted, processed and presented at fixed rates, its processing and communication must meet real-time requirements, and it's multimedia applications use multiple media types, temporal and spatial relationships between media must be maintained. Multimedia data is large in volume, where it must be compressed, high-speed networks and powerful computers are required. Although multimedia data lacks obvious syntax and semantics, conventional databases do not effectively support multimedia data, so it is necessary to index, retrieve and recognize multimedia information techniques. In general, in today's modern world, multimedia is strongly encountered in interactive Internet applications and entertainment applications, such applications requiring encoding, storage, and manipulation of unconventional objects, long object manipulation, continuous data transfer, and high data rates. as well as synchronized access to data (Ohm, 2015).

Data Compression

A file on your computer has a size expressed in Bit, Byte, Kilobyte, Megabyte, Gigabyte, and currently, a terabyte is common (all multiples of 1024). Typically, text files are much smaller than those of images, videos, and sounds because the latter, in their original format, is very heavy. Once created, we have to store them, either for local printing or transportation, where there should be suitable media for this purpose, such as CDs and DVDs. But images and videos require a large amount of data to represent/ store and a large bandwidth to transmit. Thus, data compression is essential for information to take up acceptable disk space and to be transmitted over the network at reasonable transmission rates. There would be no multimedia today without the drastic progress that has occurred in recent years in compression algorithms and their implementations (Sayood, 2017; Cato, 2015).

Another issue is to prepare this data for use on the Internet, where it needs to travel at a certain speed and with a minimum of performance, especially in the case of video, where we want to have the perception that we see it in real-time, being one of the most widely used solutions is data compression. As the word implies, compressing or compressing a file means shrinking it, making it lighter, and to make it possible, we have to use techniques to eliminate redundancy. Multimedia (audio and video) compression is the technology that makes it possible to play and store multimedia files on PCs, mobile phones and tablets. We can note a part of the immense importance of compression in the lives of any user of multimedia applications, including some contemporary and widely used over the Internet, usually dependent on some streaming system, or even digital game players. Despite the expansion of communication and computing capabilities, the demand for new multimedia applications is growing rapidly, and the cost of transmission and storage tends to be reduced. However, the slow speed of storage devices still limits time-dependent media presentations (especially video), where it is necessary to set standards to facilitate interoperability and hardware implementation (ZainEldin et al., 2015; Berres et al., 2017).

Data compression is a way of encoding a certain set of information so that the generated code is smaller than the source. The use of compression techniques is clearly essential for multimedia applications. There are two principles, **compression**, which refer to encoding a data set to generate a final code smaller than the source; and the principle of **data redundancy** (or correlation) removal, where we take advantage of how man interprets data, that is, adjacent audio samples, silence removal, similarity between scanned or sampled lines in the digital image, similarity between regions in a video. Because multimedia objects may require unavailable network bandwidth, that is, because of the amount of data transmitted (or connection time), the least amount of data sent on the network, the lower cost. Multimedia data compression techniques basically explore two factors: data redundancy and the properties of human perception (Gupta et al., 2016; Wu et al., 2017).

Data Redundancy concerns subsequent audio and image samples (for video) not entirely different. Accordingly, digital audio is a series of sampled values; a digital image is an array of sampled values (pixels), and a digital video is a sequence of images presented at a certain rate. Since neighboring values of a series or matrix are generally somehow related. This correlation is called redundancy. Removing this redundancy does not change the meaning of the data, there is only elimination of data replication (Wu et al., 2017; Terplan & Morreale, 2018).

Temporal Redundancy consists in taking advantage of the similarity between successive frames that form a dynamic image. A practical example would be the image of a golfer pulling a ball, where after serving the difference between successive frames would be only the position of the ball at any given time. In this way, the algorithm would send the information of a full-frame plus the effectively dynamic image shift-vector. Motion compensation is based on similarities between subsequent images and allows only differences to be transmitted. This method can be understood as the subtraction of an image by its predecessor (Wu et al., 2017; Wien, 2015).

Spatial Redundancy, on the other hand, spatial redundancy or spatial frequency consists of the similarity of the adjacent pixels of an image. A possible analogy is a plane passing in the cloudless sky, where the relevant information to be transmitted is the plane, and the background is the part of the blue image whose image content is practically uniform. Based on this physical concept that high frequencies can be eliminated without causing noticeable degradation in the image (Wu et al., 2017; Rasch et al., 2018).

Although the word compression does not mean loss, however, a process in which the pressure on a system is increased by the action of external agents, in computer science, this expression is used.

In **Entropy Reduction,** algorithms are used that are in charge of finding the best solution, that is, removing as many bits as possible, to preserve what one "wants to show". In this type of compression, the quality is usually compromised, since bits are taken from the original file and the author applies a compression ratio as needed and can reach up to 1: 200. It is the most used type of internet compatibility; a very common example is the JPG format (Sikora, 2018; Wang & Yao, 2016; Wu et al., 2015).

In **Redundancy Reduction,** however, the data is only compressed, where the algorithms eliminate redundancy. They are used when quality is to be maintained, i.e. data is rearranged, returning to its original form. These algorithms work by rearranging the bits, where "*zzzzzzzz*" (8 equal bytes) exists, is now stored as 8z (2 bytes). Compression ratios are between 1: 2 and 1: 4, so files don't shrink much, practical applications are in ZIP format (Wang & Yao, 2016; Joshi et al., 2017).

Compression Techniques

Compression is basically the change in the representation of some data to reduce its size, without loss of quality, or even if it exists, is minimal. Thus, when data reduction causes loss of information, some techniques are used for specific signals such as image, audio, and video; Where Compression Perceptually Lossless Humans Don't Realize (MP3). Lossy compression seeks to enable the retrieval of a version of the original data that is perceived by the user to be sufficiently similar to the original, as the human eye and ear cannot perceive a slight loss of signal quality. If the information, after its compression, can be accurately reconstructed, the compression technique is said without loss. This technique must be used to compress legal or medical programs and documents. Lossless compression techniques are not new ideas, they are widely used. These techniques only exploit data statistics (data redundancy) and the compression ratio is usually low. An example of this type of compression is replacing successive space characters or zeros with a special flag and the number of occurrences (Gregor et al., 2016).

Examples of lossless techniques include Arithmetic coding, Huffman coding, and Run-length coding. Lossy compression techniques are used for audio, image and video compression where errors and losses are tolerable. These techniques are usually based on data statistics and properties of human perception. With it, high compression ratios can be obtained. As an example of Lossless Techniques (Used in Audio and Video encoding) is Run-Length, which is basically a row of symbols of equal value; Huffman being an algorithm for compressing files, especially text files, assigning smaller codes to more frequent symbols and larger codes to less frequent symbols, remembering that code is a set of bits; Lempel-Ziv, being a variation of Lempel-Ziv developed by Terry Welch and implemented in GIF format for image storage (Hidayat et al., 2018).

As an example of Lossy Techniques, it has Wavelets, being a function capable of decomposing and describing or representing another function (or data set) originally described in the time domain (or another or several independent variables, such as space), so that we can analyze this other function at different frequency and time scales; Vector Quantization that can be seen as an extension of scalar quantization in a multidimensional space, is based on Shannon's Versus Rate-Distortion Theory, according to which better performance is obtained by coding sample blocks (i.e. vectors). instead of individual (i.e. scalar) samples, where quantization is a relevant technique in signal compression systems. Its aim is to digitize the sample values of a signal. Similarly, users of networks charged for the amount of data transmitted (or amount of connection time) would benefit from the decreased amount of data sent on the network (Chui, 2016; Pagès, 2015).

Domain Reduction, simply discards a few samples, one application example is digital video standards, with 4: 2: 2, 4: 2: 0 formats, where luminance information is more important than chrominance, so the number of chrominance samples may be smaller; similarly compression in images decreases geometric resolution by increasing pixel size; also being applied in digital video standards.

Reduction of quantization space, reduces the amount of bits per sample, having practical application in image compression, where an original image with 24 bits per pixel (16 million colors) can be compressed with 8 bits per pixel (256 colors) making a match between the codes (Onggosanusi et al., 2015).

Differential Coding or relative coding, where the amplitude of a sample is large, but the amplitude difference between successive samples is relatively small, rather than encoding the value of each sample, encodes the difference between its value and the previous one, using fewer bits and more. get the same error. With practical transmission applications such as Differential Pulse Code Modulation (DPCM) and Adaptive Differential Pulse Code Modulation (ADPCM) (Wu & Rao, 2017).

Sub-Band Coding is the division of the signal passing band into several distinctly coded sub-bands, handling the most important sub-bands of the signal more accurately. For example, voice signals, such as Hz (quality and timbre and 8 bits per sample, low information being 2 bits per sample, with recognition and intelligibility and greater content information such as metallic voice, 3 bits per sample) (Aydin & Foroosh, 2017).

Transform Coding, where they transform data to another mathematical domain where a compression technique is best applied, i.e., Fourier transform transforms time-domain signals to the frequency domain. However, there must be an inverse transform, where Data-Reducing Effective Transforms are DCT - Discrete Cosine Transform (JPEG) and FFT - Fast Fourier Transform (MPEG-audio) (Sikora, 2018).

Vector Quantization, builds a table (or uses a predefined one) containing the set of values that appear most often (default values), for each block, the table is queried to find the most similar pattern, so each block is encoded with the index of the vector and the decoder must know the same table and use the indices to generate an approximation of the original data stream (Guo et al., 2017).

Most files that are used in multimedia have repeated information, and compression does nothing more than organizing and eliminate these redundancies. The main goal of multimedia data compression is to reduce storage space as well as reduce transmission time.

Audio

In many cases, adjacent audio sampling is similar, where the future sample is not completely different from the past, the next value can be predicted based on the current value. The compression technique that takes advantage of this audio feature is called predictive coding. Predictive compression techniques are based on the fact that it is possible to store the previous sample and use it to help build the next sample. In the case of a digital voice, there is another type of redundancy, assuming that you do not talk all the time. Between bursts of information, there are moments of silence. This period of silence can be suppressed without loss of information, knowing that this period is maintained. These compression techniques are called Silence Removal (Gibson, 2016).

Once the sound is filtered, sampled, and quantized, it is in a digital format and, moreover, humanly audible, so it is often referred to as audio. The sampling process observes the original (analog) sound signal at a frequency known as the Sampling Frequency, which determines how many (equally spaced) observations will be made over a 1-second interval. Such a process discretizes the x-axis with equally spaced values. Following the Nyquist-Shannon Sampling Theorem says that for a sampled signal to be perfectly reconstructed, the sampling frequency must be equal to or greater than twice the highest frequency that makes up the original signal. Since the humanly audible spectral region is between 20 Hz and 20 kHz, this sampling frequency must, therefore, be at least 40 kHz so that signals originally limited to this spectral region can be perfectly reconstructed. And using this principle the CD uses 44100 Hz, and in this medium, this condition is respected. Pointing out that the higher the sampling frequency, the larger the memory space to store this signal. Thus, the quantization process, in turn, discretizes the y-axis, thus adopting a limited set of possible values to be assumed by each audio sample. What defines the amount of different possible values is the depth of resolution bits; 2 bits allow 4 distinct values to be used; 3 bits allow 8 values, 4 bits allow 16 values… going sequentially (Sayood, 2017; Chion, 2019; Sanders, 2017).

In the case of CD, 16 bits are used, i.e., each sample has a range of 65536 different values that can be assumed. Still considering 44100 Hz sampling frequency with 16-bit depth, 705,600 bits (or 88200 bytes) will be required for a single second of a single channel audio signal. For a 5-minute song (or 300 seconds), the total will be 26,460,000 bytes, i.e., for each audio channel about 25.2 Megabytes will be consumed. Since the CD has 2 audio channels (i.e. Stereo), one song will occupy 50.4 MB. If we want to analyze based on bit rate, whose unit of measure for this purpose is usually given in kbps, and considering the consumption ratio between kilobits per 1 second of this audio, results in 705.600 bits per second for each audio track. the bit rate, in this case, will be about 1411 kbps. Pointing out that the bit rate interferes with the quality of the audio to be heard, and this measure is related to the quality of the user experience when listening to the audio (Sayood, 2017; Chion, 2019; Sanders, 2017).

Streaming services are fully related to this illustrated scenario, where free plan users who have access to music with about 128 kbps bit rate, while paying users usually have access to 256 kbps, 320 kbps or up to 1411 kbps. However, for the vast majority of non-audiophile users, music at 128 kbps is already good enough to be heard and enjoyed. It should be noted that the minimum theoretical bandwidth to ensure streaming service operation must be higher than the audio bitrate. Extra bandwidth (which goes beyond the service bitrate) is required to properly use Buffer, and the more available extra bandwidth (also respecting server limits), the faster it will fill up the buffer. MP3 is not the only existing compressed music format, but it is undoubtedly the most famous since many years ago. If the same 5-minute white noise Stereo audio is compressed using MP3 at a constant rate of 128 kbps, the result will be a small file of just over 4.5 MB. Based on the 50.4 MB space occupied by the WAV file, this MP3 version resulted in approximately 91% efficiency compression. From the point of view of computer networks, looking at the bit rate can make it easier to understand and the importance of this compression (Sayood, 2017; Chion, 2019; Sanders, 2017).

Digital music has evolved immensely over time. MP3 files are the most used audio files but there are more formats that are becoming more popular such as FLAC, WAV, and AAC. Among these files are lossy formats, where are files in which data is lost when ripping from the CD to the computer. The benefit of this compression process is the shrinking of the file. MP3 and ACC are examples of this type of category. And the lossless formats, being those formats that do not show quality loss compared to the CD. However, the file size occupies on average four times more space. Also, iPod and MP3 players do not support major audio formats in this category (FLAC and WAV) (Dittmar, 2017; Kim & Rafii, 2018).

MP3 is the main audio file on the internet and is supported by all music players. Although it is a file with data loss if the MP3 file has a bit rate of 224-320 kbps or 192 kbps, you can hardly distinguish this file from the CD. AAC (Advanced Audio Coding) has been gaining popularity thanks to Apple. Although iPod and iPhone support MP3, they have the default AAC format. Like the MP3 format, AAC format also has data loss. The differences between MP3 and AAC mean that the MP3 format has a sampling frequency of 16 to 48 kHz, while AAC is between 8 to 96 kHz. The number of channels is also higher in AAC, 48 versus 5.1. The compression ratio in AAC also results in higher quality and smaller files (Britanak & Rao, 2018).

FLAC is an acronym for Free Lossless Audio Codec, which as its name implies, is a lossless audio format. This format has become popular, it is used by users who want to keep their CD collection on their computer. There are already portable players that support this type of file. Flac can be used freely by anyone. WAV was created by the company Microsoft for some time, but is also compatible with the Macintosh. It contains the same quality as FLAC but is a little-used format as it is on average twice larger than an FLAC file. MPEG 1 (3 layers) was created by the Fraunhofer IIS institute and corresponds to a three-layer compression scheme. There are many losses with the compression of audio data, limited only by the intended quality of the human ear. The default compression is 10: 1. HD-AAC is the succession of AAC, which gives quality to ripped audio files. This format provides new music storage capabilities because it has less compression and is supported by iPods and mobile phones. This format also provides better quality than CDs (recorded with 16-bit compression and 44.1 kHz sampling rate). This format is superior in that it preserves all bits of information from the original song, thanks to a 96-bit sampled 24-bit compression. WMA is an acronym for Windows Media Audio created by Microsoft. It allows you to create files up to 50% smaller than MP3, but with a slight loss of quality (Britanak & Rao, 2018; Rai & Sathuvalli, 2017).

MPEG-2 is an Advanced Audio Coding format, MPEG's newest perceptive sound coding standard. It uses a complex coding system that involves numerous techniques, among them, are Huffman coding; Quantization and scaling; M/S Matrixing; Intensity Stereo; Coupling channel; Backward adaptive prediction; Temporal noise shaping; Modified discrete cosine transform; Gain control and hybrid filter bank (polyphase quadrature filter) (Britanak & Rao, 2018; Rai & Sathuvalli, 2017; Cardozo et al., 2018).

Just like the VQF format you need a faster computer for encoding and decoding than mp3. Transform-domain Weighted Interleave Vector Quantization (VQF) or TwinVQ (VQF) is a proprietary audio compression format from YAMAHA, where the final file size is smaller than a similar quality MP3 file due to the high compression ratio of the VQF format. being about 30% smaller than 128kbps bit rate encoded MP3 files. Of the 3 formats, however, it has the best final quality (closest to the original). However, one of its biggest problems is the existence of several versions of the pattern, directly incompatible with each other (significant coding difference). Despite the lower quality, the greater popularity of mp3 is linked to the greater amount of music and software available (Britanak & Rao, 2018; Rai & Sathuvalli, 2017; Cardozo et al., 2018).

The audio codec is the coder junction with a decoder (compressor/decompressor), represent high-quality audio signals with minimal bit quantity, which reduces storage space and bandwidth. In some contexts, audio codec refers to the hardware implementation of a sound card. When used in this way, audio codec designates the device that encodes an analog audio signal. Similarly, to the type of compression, there are Lossy Audio Codecs, which encode the sound, resulting in a loss of quality to achieve higher compression ratios. Many of these codecs have negligible quality loss acting on MP3, AC3 and WMA files. And the lossless audio codecs that encode the sound, compressing the file without changing the quality. This type of codec generates encoded files that are 2 to 3 times smaller than the original files. They are generally used by radios acting on Flac, Shorten, Wavpack files (Hennequin et al., 2017, March).

Image

An image can be understood as an array of pixels, and considering an RGB (Red, Green, and Blue) pattern, each pixel can be represented by a 3-position vector, where each position corresponds to the value of a layer. by heart; It is common to use an 8-bit bit depth, which means that integer values between 0 and 255 will be accepted for each of the 3 color layers in each Pixel. In digital images, neighboring samples on a scan line and neighboring samples on adjacent lines are similar. This similarity is called spatial redundancy. It can be removed, for example using predictive or other coding techniques. A conventional monitor nowadays works with what is popularly called Full HD (or FHD) with 1920x1080 resolution. This resolution indicates the size of such a matrix of pixels, being 1920 columns and 1080 rows. Multiplying the number of rows by the number of columns shows that a Full HD image has 2,073,600 pixels. Since 8 bits are being considered to represent the value of each color layer, i.e., 1 byte, we can say that each pixel of the image requires 3 bytes; on a full HD image, this means 6,220,800 bytes, or about 6 MB for a single image (Wu & Rao, 2017; Stearns & Hush, 2016).

JPEG (Joint Pictures Expert Group) is the best format for anyone who wants to email images. It emerged in 1983 and eventually became one of the most popular Internet standards. A JPEG (or JPG as it is also called) file is small in size compared to other formats, making it easy to store and distribute. It compresses the data to be much smaller, but this causes a loss in image quality, is most commonly used when file size is more important than the maximum image quality (e.g., web pages, blogs, email, camera memory cards, among others) (Wu & Rao, 2017; Stearns & Hush, 2016; Kaur & Choudhary, 2016).

GIF (Graphics Interchange Format) is another very common format on the Internet. It is a light file and famous for motion photography, animated gifs. It is recommended for those who need to spread a lot of images on the internet, because it generates small files, and for those who are not concerned with sending low color images, since GIF only works with 256 color scheme (8 bits), so it is not. It is very common in photographs. Created in 1987, GIF was designed by CompuServe in the early days of 8-bit computer video, even before JPG, for viewing at dial-up modem connection speeds. It's bad for 24-bit color photos, so don't use GIF for today's color photos, the color is very limited. But GIF is still very good for web graphics (with a limited number of colors). Although this format seems limited due to the low number of colors it works with, GIF is widely used by some of its features. Its use is greater in icons, illustrations (mainly in black and white) and small animations. It also allows saving files with transparent background and compression without loss of quality (Wu & Rao, 2017; Stearns & Hush, 2016; Kaur & Choudhary, 2016).

Portable Network Graphics (PNG) Unlike GIF, PNG supports more colors. It is a competitor of GIF. It emerged in 1996 and has features that made GIF so well accepted: animation, transparent background, and lossless compression, even with constant file saves, supports millions of colors, not just 256 colors, making it a great choice for photos. An additional feature in PNG is transparency by 24-bit RGB images. Usually, PNG files are slightly smaller than TIF (both TIF and PNG use LZW for lossless compression of different types), but PNG is perhaps a bit slower to read or write. It is still less widely used than TIF or JPG, but is another good option for lossless quality work (Wu & Rao, 2017; Stearns & Hush, 2016; Kaur & Choudhary, 2016).

The bitmap can support millions of colors and preserve details but make files extremely large as they do not use compression. If you want to send photos to your friends, forget about Bitmap. The format makes sending images on the Internet slow as these files are not compressed. BMP is a historical format because it came up with the Windows operating system. BMP images can range from black and white (1 bit per pixel) up to 24 color bits (16.7 million colors) (Wu & Rao, 2017; Stearns & Hush, 2016; Kaur & Choudhary, 2016).

Tagged Image File Format (TIFF) is most commonly used by image professionals. It is the preferred file type for most graphic designers for editing and printing. They have little or no compression and do not lose any details, although the files can be quite large. TIF is the most versatile except web pages, as some browsers do not display TIF images. It is also widely used in scanning (scanner and fax). It offers a large amount of color and excellent image quality, making the size of your files large. It also allows the use of layers (as in the original photoshop PSD files) and supports transparent background (Wu & Rao, 2017; Stearns & Hush, 2016; Kaur & Choudhary, 2016).

RAW is a standard on some digital cameras, but it is not a required format and you can choose between JPG or PNG standards. It is "raw" because it contains no effects or adjustments. Because of this, it offers high image quality and greater color depth. Since the files in this pattern are "pure", the editor is free to use the image the way it was captured and apply its own effects or adjustments, usually generating very good photos (Wu & Rao, 2017; Stearns & Hush, 2016; Kaur & Choudhary, 2016).

Exchangeable image file format (EXIF) is a file standard similar to the JFIF format with TIFF extensions, which is incorporated into the JPEG writing software used on most cameras. Its purpose is to record and standardize metadata exchanges between digital camera images and their editing and viewing software. Metadata is recorded in individual images and includes things like camera settings, date and time, shutter speed, exposure, image size, compression, camera name, and color information. When images are viewed or edited by image editing software, all of this information may be displayed (Wu & Rao, 2017; Stearns & Hush, 2016; Kaur & Choudhary, 2016).

SVG (Scalable Vector Graphics) is a vector image file. It is an open format, developed by W3C and which emerged in 2001. Instead of being based on pixels, ie the "dots" that make up images, it uses XML language to describe what the file should look like. Fits both static and animated images. As a vector, images can be enlarged or reduced without causing quality loss. The same is the case with CDR images (coming from the CorelDraw program) (Wu & Rao, 2017; Stearns & Hush, 2016; Kaur & Choudhary, 2016).

WebP is a new image format that uses lossy compression. It was designed by Google to reduce image file size to speed up web page loading: its main purpose is to replace JPEG as the main format for web photos. WebP is based on VP8 intra-frame coding and uses a RIFF-based container (Wu & Rao, 2017; Stearns & Hush, 2016; Kaur & Choudhary, 2016).

Video

A video is a set of images, for example, bitmap (frames) passed in sequence at a certain speed, to convey the idea of movement. The number of images that are passed each second is commonly referred to as the frame rate or number of frames per second (nfs). In the case of video, there are a lot of moving images and you can have audio. Where in a video that is in Full HD and 24 FPS (frames per second) standard, which is often used in movies. This is equivalent to every 24 seconds of video being displayed in an equal interval sequence. Illustrating an uncompressed scenario and assuming that each image occupies 6 MB along with a WAV audio bitrate is 0.2 MB for every second of Stereo audio. For a 2-hour movie (or 7200 seconds), 172,800 images will be displayed. Only the images will consume 1,036,800 MB (close to 1 Terabyte). The audio will consume 1440 MB alone. It is noted that, in relation to space demanded, the audio is negligible. Either way, a movie would require about 1TB of storage space (or traffic if viewed via Streaming) (Kaur & Choudhary, 2016; Owens, 2017).

If via Streaming, not even a 1 Gbps connection would be sufficient to ensure that the video would play uninterrupted, meaning that no ordinary end-user would be able to enjoy such a service, even if it was a movie hosted on a local server, given that end-user NICs are typically limited to 1 Gbps (or even 100 Mbps for older models still on the market). Still, services like Netflix, YouTube and Twitch have probably enjoyed higher resolutions and even higher frame rates than those cited in the example, where a key element of this is precisely the compression used, ensuring very good image quality and high movement fluidity, allowing users not to rely on an incredibly powerful connection (Kaur & Choudhary, 2016; Owens, 2017).

Compressed Video Formats

Video compression refers to Redundancy Reduction, where some areas of the frame have the same color that spans more than one pixel (spatial redundancy); and when the scene or part of it contains predominantly vertically oriented objects, two adjacent lines are very likely to be the same (spatial redundancy); similarly images where some pixels repeat over several frames (temporal redundancy). Standard definition video has a maximum of 480 viewable lines as opposed to high definition video up to 1,080 lines. High definition videos are clearer especially when viewed on large screens (Bovik, 2010; Wu et al., 2018; Wu et al., 2018; Baraniuk et al., 2017).

ISO developed the Motion Picture Experts Group (MPEG) to develop standards for digital video, created in 1988. Compression takes place in both Video and audio, with rates ranging from 1.5 Mbps to 60 Mbps (MPEG1, MPEG2, and MPEG3 (later discarded)). Displays videos from 30 frames / s up to 60 fps. MPEG-1 is the standard used for VCD drafting, with 352 x 240 resolution, slightly lower quality than videotapes. MPEG-2 is the standard DVD with 720 x 480 resolution or 1280 x 780, excellent quality, is the most popular method for use in Digital TV. The basic principle of the MPEG2 process is to use techniques that imperceptibly reduce image quality, along with techniques that do not affect image quality, primarily by using the process of eliminating information redundancies. MPEG-4, unlike MPEG-1/2 linear audio and video encoding, is that audio-visual scenes are encoded based on objects such as a moving car, a dog photograph, as well as an image or an audio object, such as an instrument or a sound, so I work with Visual Audio objects. It is the current standard for authoring, multimedia, games, video conferencing, mobile communication, interactive graphics applications, and WWW. It has good quality and widely used in narrowband (Shree, 2016; Paikray et al., 2018).

VCD (Video Compact Disc) created in 1993 by a consortium formed by Philips, JVC, Matsushita, and Sony, uses MPEG1 standard and can be played on CR-ROM and DVD players, for read-only standards and single-sided recording. Holds 70 minutes (for normal movie time 2 discs are required). Features 350 x 240 NTSC and 352 x 288 PAL resolution, similar in quality to videotapes. SVCD (Super Video CD) was developed in 1998 by the China National Committee of Recording Standards, uses MPEG2 standard and can be played on CR-ROM and DVD players in read-only mode and burns only to one side on CD media., 70 minutes (for normal movie time 2 discs are required). From 1988, a standard called Chao Ji VCD was established in China, where players of this type should be able to play CVD, SVCD, VCD 1.1, VCD 2.0 and CD-Audio. With variable bitrate MPEG2 resolution, 5.1 surround sound, being worse than DVD and better than VCD, 480 x 480 in NTSC and 480 x 576 in PAL (Shree, 2016; Paikray et al., 2018).

DivX is made up of two software, DeCSS, which extracts content, breaking encryption that prevents DVD files from being copied to your computer, and a Microsoft-made version of MPEG-4 (codec avi) software. video compression standard built into Windows Media Tools. Divx can put a DVD into a CD, with the same resolution as MPEG4. Seen full screen on computers over the Internet, similar in quality to normal TV broadcasts, good quality. Xvid is the same Divx, but free code, with its resolution depending on the video, played, being better than Divx and good quality. (Shree, 2016; Paikray et al., 2018; Zhang & Mao, 2019).

WMV (Windows Media Video) is Microsoft's format, working at 1.3–2 Mbps, with 480 to 1280 resolution and excellent quality. Matroska (MKV - Matroska Video and MKA - Matroska Audio) is not a video codec, but a container that allows you to insert a combination of video, audio, and subtitles into a single file. You can combine a DivX movie with a subtitle package, it also works with audio-only. Matroska is an open-source project with good quality and equal resolution as MPEG4 (Batubara & Ariani, 2016).

Digital Games

The situation of those who enjoy playing digital games for long hours, especially in the case of competitive gamers who are keen to play at rates up to 240 FPS, or even Gamers who, while not necessarily making such high fees., love high resolutions, like the increasingly used 4K (3840x2160), equals 4 Full HD screens in a 2x2 matrix. Media compression is directly proportional to this reality. Illustrating a scenario likely to exist today, a 4K game at 240 FPS using a 10-bit RGB standard, each 4K image would be equivalent to 8,294,400 Pixels, where if each pixel required 30 bits, that would amount to 248,832. .000 bits (close to 237 MB) per image. At 240 frames per second, then a single second would require 56,880 MB (close to 56 GB) of information processing. For illustration purposes only, a single match in a game such as League of Legends or FIFA that lasts about 30 minutes (1800 seconds) would require processing 100,800 GB (close to 98 TB) of information, not including talk between players. Where access to such content ranging from more modest mobile devices to equipment designed to perform such scenarios clearly illustrates the importance of multimedia compression (Redi et al., 2015; Eliseo & Silva, 2016).

Audio Coding and Compression

Audio compression is employed to decrease the bandwidth (measured by frequency band, in hertz of the signal) and/or physical space of the audio file. Prior to the appearance of audio compression, the digital data from a good quality audio file took up a huge amount of disk space. An illustration of this is CD-quality music, with 44.1 kHz stereo (2 channels) with 16 bits per sample meaning about 10 megabytes per minute of audio. In this context, audio coding is synonymous with audio compression because only through these concepts is it possible to reduce the size of audio files. Thus, current file formats (MP3) exploit the capabilities of human hearing to acquire a decrease in the size of an audio file without a noticeable loss of quality (Thompson, 2018; Winer, 2017).

Audio compression is divided into two points: encoding, that is, transforming audio file data stored in an uncompressed file into a compressed file (within a structure called a bitstream), and decoding, which analyzes bitstream and re-expand it. What you get after decoding is not the same as the original file, all unimportant information has been deleted. However, the file still sounds the same (more or less) depending on the file compression ratio. Normally, the lower the compression, the better the file quality will be, since bitrate refers to the compression force, it denounces the average number of bits that in a second will bring the compressed bitstream (Thompson, 2018; Winer, 2017).

File Encoding and Decoding - CODEC

The word CODEC is formed by the junction of COder and DECoder, encoding and decoding, or, Compression and DECompression, compression and decompression. As previously mentioned in some cases, a common example of this technique is a compressed video, without the proper CODEC to "decode that file format in which the video was saved, the image will not appear on the screen but a message from reporting the absence of a specific CODEC. Nowadays it is common to "download" or save files

Table 1.

Bitrate	Bandwidth	Quality (Equal/Better)
16 kbps	4.5 kHz	Shortwave radio
32 kbps	7.5 kHz	AM radio
96 kbps	11 kHz	FM radio
128 kbps	16 kHz	next CD
160-180 kbps	20 kHz	perceptive transparency
256 kbps	22 kHz	Sound studio

in "compression formats", so-called in the common language of internet users such as the famous MP3, AIFF, AAC, MIDI, AVI, WMA, MPEG, MPEG2, DivX, and more. H.263 recently, as are the programs that run all existing CODECs, such as images, videos, and sounds (Khan et al., 2017).

Performance Parameters

A coding achieves the best compression rates, because it compresses the data, be it audio, image or video, and then decompresses it to retrieve its content or view it, also having characteristics of data loss. part or not of the quality of this media. However, there are some metrics that help to estimate the quality of compression performance of this media as well as its transmission by a certain medium (Winer, 2017; Khan et al., 2017; Dubin et al., 2018).

The compression ratio is the ratio of the original data size to the data size after compression. In the case of lossless techniques, the higher the compression ratio the better the compression technique. For lossy compression techniques, the quality of the returned media should also be considered. The quality of the reconstituted media can be measured in SNR (Signal/Noise Ratio). This parameter is applicable for lossy techniques only. In choosing a lossy compression technique, a compromise between a high compression ratio and the desired quality for the developing application should be chosen. Implementation complexity and compression speed are generally related to the more complex the technique, the lower the compression speed. For real-time applications such as videoconferencing, these parameters should be considered. This is because compression/decompression must be performed in real-time. In the case of information gathering and presentation applications, compression speed is not very important, but decompression speed is important (Winer, 2017; Khan et al., 2017; Dubin et al., 2018).

TRENDS

Innovations and technological breakthroughs are becoming faster and more frequent, transforming society and businesses where we see the direction the world is taking for a future where the world will be intersected by high-capacity fiber optic data networks, connecting all our increasingly ubiquitous devices. The future is mobile from the point that portable media is transforming the world, since, in the beginning, the communication industry and the media were electronic, today they are digital, and in the process, they have become multimedia and then increasingly more will become interactive. And mobility is that. Modern devices are electronic, also being considered multimedia, from all the aspects presented in this chapter, but not yet so good at interactivity. The Internet is great at this, but not yet everywhere with traditional devices. Mobility is, then, the transformation that is happening and will happen more and more through mobile devices we make people's communication. As long as you do something interesting, register at that moment in a photo, and for a mobile device use the internet to upload, or upload games or read some news. From that point on, it acquires interactivity functions, from that moment on, becoming a multimedia communication device (AlZu'bi et al., 2019; Zhang et al., 2018; Li et al., 2018; Li et al., 2019; Wang et al., 2018; Gupta, 2018; Gupta et al., 2016; Tian et al., 2019; Hai et al., 2018; Li et al., 2018; Panjanathan & Ramachandran, 2017).

Similar to the emergence of new technologies such as collusion security of LUT-based client-side watermark embedding, compressed ciphertext length scheme using multi-authority CP-ABE for hierarchical attributes, efficient employment of internet of multimedia things, self- annotation via label correlation mining, watermarking-based authentication and image restoration in multimedia sensor networks, new Authorization Scheme for Multimedia Social Networks Under Cloud Storage Method, enhanced low latency queuing algorithm with active queue management for wireless applications, among many others that which will facilitate and provide better quality of life and technological interactions for people (AlZu'bi et al., 2019; Zhang et al., 2018; Li et al., 2018; Li et al., 2019; Wang et al., 2018; Gupta, 2018; Gupta et al., 2016; Tian et al., 2019; Hai et al., 2018; Li et al., 2018; Panjanathan & Ramachandran, 2017).

CONCLUSION

Data compression is the act of reducing the data space occupied by a given device. This operation is performed through various compression algorithms, reducing the amount of bytes to represent a given data, which is an image, a text, or any file. Compressing data is also intended to remove redundancy on the grounds that too much data contains redundant information that may or may need to be deleted in some way. This form is through a rule, called a code or protocol, which then eliminates redundant bits of information in order to decrease its size in files. In addition to eliminating redundancy, data is compressed for a variety of reasons. The best-known ones are saving space on storage devices such as hard drives, or gaining performance (decreasing the time these transmissions happen) on transmissions.

Although they may seem synonymous, data compression and compression are distinct processes. Compression, as seen, reduces the amount of bits to represent some data, while compression has the function of joining unjoined data. Today In the 21st century the main keywords related to technology are optimization and low memory consumption. Therefore, the creation of new methodologies and investments in research of this nature will lead to the development of lighter and more compact telecommunication devices and channels, which allow the flow of data with more fluidity and low computational consumption, paving the way for an era of greater ease of use. data sharing as well as communication from home, medical, industrial, social and educational devices.

REFERENCES

Ahmed, R., Islam, M., & Uddin, J. (2018). Optimizing Apple Lossless Audio Codec Algorithm using NVIDIA CUDA Architecture. *International Journal of Electrical & Computer Engineering (2088-8708), 8*(1).

Alvi, S. A., Afzal, B., Shah, G. A., Atzori, L., & Mahmood, W. (2015). Internet of multimedia things: Vision and challenges. *Ad Hoc Networks, 33*, 87–111. doi:10.1016/j.adhoc.2015.04.006

AlZu'bi, S., Hawashin, B., Mujahed, M., Jararweh, Y., & Gupta, B. B. (2019). An efficient employment of internet of multimedia things in smart and future agriculture. *Multimedia Tools and Applications*, 1–25.

Aydin, V. A., & Foroosh, H. (2017, September). Motion compensation using critically sampled dwt subbands for low-bitrate video coding. *Proceedings 2017 IEEE International Conference on Image Processing (ICIP)* (pp. 21-25). IEEE. 10.1109/ICIP.2017.8296235

Baraniuk, R. G., Goldstein, T., Sankaranarayanan, A. C., Studer, C., Veeraraghavan, A., & Wakin, M. B. (2017). Compressive video sensing: Algorithms, architectures, and applications. *IEEE Signal Processing Magazine, 34*(1), 52–66. doi:10.1109/MSP.2016.2602099

Baroňák, I., Čuba, M., Chen, C. M., & Beháň, L. (2017, November). Traffic Management by Admission Control in IMS Networks. *Proceedings of the 3rd Czech-China Scientific Conference 2017*. IntechOpen.

Batubara, H. H., & Ariani, D. N. (2016). Pemanfaatan Video sebagai Media Pembelajaran Matematika SD/MI. *Muallimuna, 2*(1), 47–66. doi:10.31602/muallimuna.v2i1.741

Berres, A. S., Turton, T. L., Petersen, M., Rogers, D. H., Ahrens, J. P., Rink, K., ... Bujack, R. (2017, June). Video compression for ocean simulation image databases. In *Workshop on Visualisation in Environmental Sciences (EnvirVis)*.

Bovik, A. C. (2010). *Handbook of image and video processing*. Academic Press.

Britanak, V., & Rao, K. R. (2018). Audio Coding Standards, (Proprietary) Audio Compression Algorithms, and Broadcasting/Speech/Data Communication Codecs: Overview of Adopted Filter Banks. In *Cosine-/Sine-Modulated Filter Banks* (pp. 13–37). Cham, Switzerland: Springer. doi:10.1007/978-3-319-61080-1_2

Burroughs, B. (2019). A cultural lineage of streaming. *Internet Histories, 3*(2), 147–161. doi:10.1080/24701475.2019.1576425

Cardozo, D., Campo, S., Manjarres, J., & Percybrooks, W. (2018, November). Sub-band coding for audio signals using Matlab. [IOP Publishing.]. *Journal of Physics: Conference Series, 1126*(1). doi:10.1088/1742-6596/1126/1/012029

Cato, A. (2015). A Bit of Bytes: The Anatomy of Size and Memory. *Austl. L. Libr., 23*, 33.

Chalmers, A., Campisi, P., Shirley, P., & Olaizola, I. G. (Eds.). (2016). *High dynamic range video: concepts, technologies, and applications*. Academic Press.

Chion, M. (2019). *Audio-vision: sound on screen*. Columbia University Press. doi:10.7312/chio18588

Chui, C. K. (2016). *An introduction to wavelets*. Elsevier.

Dittmar, T. (2017). *Audio Engineering 101: A Beginner's Guide to Music Production*. Routledge. doi:10.4324/9781315618173

Dubin, R., Hadar, O., Dvir, A., & Pele, O. (2018). Video quality representation classification of encrypted http adaptive video streaming. *TIIS*, *12*(8), 3804–3819.

Eliseo, M. A., & Silva, L (2016). Desenvolvimento de Jogos em Ultra-Alta Definição (UHD-4K).

Firmansah, L., & Setiawan, E. B. (2016, May). Data audio compression lossless FLAC format to lossy audio MP3 format with Huffman shift coding algorithm. *Proceedings 2016 4th International Conference on Information and Communication Technology (ICoICT)* (pp. 1-5). IEEE. 10.1109/ICoICT.2016.7571951

Gibson, J. (2016). Speech compression. *Information*, *7*(2), 32. doi:10.3390/info7020032

Gregor, K., Besse, F., Rezende, D. J., Danihelka, I., & Wierstra, D. (2016). Towards conceptual compression. In Advances In Neural Information Processing Systems (pp. 3549-3557).

Guo, Y., Ding, G., & Han, J. (2017). Robust quantization for general similarity search. *IEEE Transactions on Image Processing*, *27*(2), 949–963. doi:10.1109/TIP.2017.2766445 PMID:29757738

Gupta, B., Agrawal, D. P., & Yamaguchi, S. (Eds.). (2016). *Handbook of research on modern cryptographic solutions for computer and cyber security*. IGI Global. doi:10.4018/978-1-5225-0105-3

Gupta, B. B. (Ed.). (2018). Computer and cyber security: principles, algorithm, applications, and perspectives. Boca Raton, FL: CRC Press.

Gupta, R., Kumar, M., & Bathla, R. (2016). Data Compression-Lossless and Lossy Techniques. *International Journal of Application or Innovation in Engineering & Management*, *5*(7), 120–125.

Hai, H., Qing, X. D., & Ke, Q. (2018). A watermarking-based authentication and image restoration in multimedia sensor networks. *International Journal of High Performance Computing and Networking*, *12*(1), 65–73. doi:10.1504/IJHPCN.2018.093846

Hanjalic, A. (2017). Multimedia Research: What Is the Right Approach? *IEEE MultiMedia*, *24*(2), 4–6. doi:10.1109/MMUL.2017.31

Hashem, I. A. T., Yaqoob, I., Anuar, N. B., Mokhtar, S., Gani, A., & Khan, S. U. (2015). The rise of "big data" on cloud computing: Review and open research issues. *Information Systems*, *47*, 98–115. doi:10.1016/j.is.2014.07.006

Hennequin, R., Royo-Letelier, J., & Moussallam, M. (2017, March). Codec independent lossy audio compression detection. In *2017 IEEE International Conference on Acoustics, Speech and Signal Processing (ICASSP)* (pp. 726-730). IEEE. 10.1109/ICASSP.2017.7952251

Hennequin, R., Royo-Letelier, J., & Moussallam, M. (2017, March). Codec independent lossy audio compression detection. In *Proceedings 2017 IEEE International Conference on Acoustics, Speech and Signal Processing (ICASSP)* (pp. 726-730). IEEE. 10.1109/ICASSP.2017.7952251

Hidayat, T., Zakaria, M. H., Pee, A. N. C., & Naim, A. (2018). Comparison of Lossless Compression Schemes for WAV Audio Data 16-Bit between Huffman and Coding Arithmetic. *International Journal of Simulation-Systems, Science & Technology, 19*(6).

Jeschke, S., Brecher, C., Meisen, T., Özdemir, D., & Eschert, T. (2017). Industrial internet of things and cyber manufacturing systems. In *Industrial Internet of Things* (pp. 3–19). Cham, Switzerland: Springer. doi:10.1007/978-3-319-42559-7_1

Joshi, G., Soljanin, E., & Wornell, G. (2017). Efficient redundancy techniques for latency reduction in cloud systems. *ACM Transactions on Modeling and Performance Evaluation of Computing Systems, 2*(2), 12. doi:10.1145/3055281

Kaae, J. (2017). Theoretical approaches to composing dynamic music for video games. In *From pac-man to pop music* (pp. 75–91). Routledge. doi:10.4324/9781351217743-6

Kaplan, A. M., & Haenlein, M. (2014). Users of the world, unite! The challenges and opportunities of Social Media. *Business Horizons, 53*(1), 59–68. doi:10.1016/j.bushor.2009.09.003

Kaur, R., & Choudhary, P. (2016). A Review of Image Compression Techniques. *International Journal of Computers and Applications, 975*, 8887.

Khan, M. U. K., Shafique, M., & Henkel, J. (2017). *Energy Efficient Embedded Video Processing Systems: A Hardware-Software Collaborative Approach*. Springer.

Kim, B., & Rafii, Z. (2018, September). Lossy audio compression identification. *Proceedings 2018 26th European Signal Processing Conference (EUSIPCO)* (pp. 2459-2463). IEEE. 10.23919/EUSIPCO.2018.8553611

Li, C., Zhang, Z., & Zhang, L. (2018). A Novel Authorization Scheme for Multimedia Social Networks Under Cloud Storage Method by Using MA-CP-ABE. *International Journal of Cloud Applications and Computing, 8*(3), 32–47. doi:10.4018/IJCAC.2018070103

Li, D., Deng, L., Gupta, B. B., Wang, H., & Choi, C. (2019). A novel CNN-based security guaranteed image watermarking generation scenario for smart city applications. *Information Sciences, 479*, 432–447. doi:10.1016/j.ins.2018.02.060

Li, J., Yu, C., Gupta, B. B., & Ren, X. (2018). Color image watermarking scheme based on quaternion Hadamard transform and Schur decomposition. *Multimedia Tools and Applications, 77*(4), 4545–4561. doi:10.100711042-017-4452-0

Ohm, J. R. (2015). *Multimedia signal coding and transmission*. Springer. doi:10.1007/978-3-662-46691-9

Onggosanusi, E., Li, Y., Rahman, M. S., Nam, Y. H., Zhang, J., Seol, J. Y., & Kim, T. (2015, June). Reduced space channel feedback for FD-MIMO. *Proceedings 2015 IEEE International Conference on Communications (ICC)* (pp. 3873-3878). IEEE. 10.1109/ICC.2015.7248928

Owens, J. (2017). *Video production handbook*. Routledge. doi:10.4324/9781315530574

Pagès, G. (2015). Introduction to vector quantization and its applications for numerics. *ESAIM: proceedings and surveys, 48*, 29-79.

Paikray, B., Mallick, C., Sundaram, R. M., Sharma, R., Sengupta, S., Mishra, S. S., ... & Pradhan, D. C. (2018). *Introduction to Multimedia*. Academic Press.

Panjanathan, R., & Ramachandran, G. (2017). Enhanced low latency queuing algorithm with active queue management for multimedia applications in wireless networks. *International Journal of High Performance Computing and Networking, 10*(1-2), 23–33. doi:10.1504/IJHPCN.2017.083197

Rai, R., & Sathuvalli, S. (2017). Five Key Criteria for Choosing the Right Audio Codec Implementation.

Rasch, J., Kolehmainen, V., Nivajärvi, R., Kettunen, M., Gröhn, O., Burger, M., & Brinkmann, E. M. (2018). Dynamic MRI reconstruction from undersampled data with an anatomical prescan. *Inverse Problems, 34*(7), 074001. doi:10.1088/1361-6420/aac3af

Redi, J., D'Acunto, L., & Niamut, O. (2015, June). Interactive UHDTV at the Commonwealth Games: An Explorative Evaluation. *Proceedings of the ACM International Conference on Interactive Experiences for TV and Online Video* (pp. 43-52). ACM. 10.1145/2745197.2745203

Sanders, A. (2017). *Multimedia Signals: Image, Audio, and Video Processing*. NY: Research Press.

Sayood, K. (2017). *Introduction to data compression*. Morgan Kaufmann.

Shree, M. (2016). *Zoom Detection in Video Sequences* (Doctoral dissertation).

Siegert, I., Lotz, A. F., Duong, L. L., & Wendemuth, A. (2016). Measuring the impact of audio compression on the spectral quality of speech data. *Elektronische Sprachsignalverarbeitung, 81*, 229–236.

Sikora, T. (2018). MPEG digital video coding standards. In Compressed Video over Networks (pp. 45–88). Boca Raton, FL: CRC Press.

Stearns, S. D., & Hush, D. R. (2016). Digital signal processing with examples in MATLAb. Boca Raton, FL: CRC Press. doi:10.1201/9781439837832

Terplan, K., & Morreale, P. A. (2018). Video Communications. In The Telecommunications Handbook (pp. 344-411). Boca Raton, FL: CRC Press.

Thompson, D. M. (2018). *Understanding audio: getting the most out of your project or professional recording studio*. Hal Leonard Corporation.

Tian, F., Shang, F., & Sun, N. (2019). Multimedia auto-annotation via label correlation mining. *International Journal of High Performance Computing and Networking, 13*(4), 427–435. doi:10.1504/IJHPCN.2019.099266

Uthayakumar, J., Vengattaraman, T., & Dhavachelvan, P. (2018). A survey on data compression techniques: From the perspective of data quality, coding schemes, data type and applications. *Journal of King Saud University-Computer and Information Sciences*.

Wang, H., & Yao, X. (2016). Objective reduction based on nonlinear correlation information entropy. *Soft Computing, 20*(6), 2393–2407. doi:10.100700500-015-1648-y

Wang, Y. G., Xie, D., & Gupta, B. B. (2018). A study on the collusion security of LUT-based client-side watermark embedding. *IEEE Access: Practical Innovations, Open Solutions*, 6, 15816–15822. doi:10.1109/ACCESS.2018.2802928

Wien, M. (2015). High efficiency video coding. Coding Tools and specification, 133-160.

Winer, E. (2017). *The audio expert: everything you need to know about audio*. Routledge. doi:10.4324/9781315223162

Wu, C. Y., Singhal, N., & Krahenbuhl, P. (2018). Video compression through image interpolation. *Proceedings of the European Conference on Computer Vision (ECCV)* (pp. 416-431).

Wu, C. Y., Zaheer, M., Hu, H., Manmatha, R., Smola, A. J., & Krähenbühl, P. (2018). Compressed video action recognition. *Proceedings of the IEEE Conference on Computer Vision and Pattern Recognition* (pp. 6026-6035).

Wu, H., Miao, Z., Wang, Y., Chen, J., Ma, C., & Zhou, T. (2015). Image completion with multi-image based on entropy reduction. *Neurocomputing*, *159*, 157–171. doi:10.1016/j.neucom.2014.12.088

Wu, H. R., & Rao, K. R. (Eds.). (2017). Digital video image quality and perceptual coding. Boca Raton, FL: CRC Press. doi:10.1201/9781420027822

Wu, H. R., & Rao, K. R. (Eds.). (2017). Digital video image quality and perceptual coding. Boca Raton, FL: CRC Press. doi:10.1201/9781420027822

ZainEldin, H., Elhosseini, M. A., & Ali, H. A. (2015). Image compression algorithms in wireless multimedia sensor networks: A survey. *Ain Shams Engineering Journal, 6*(2), 481-490.

Zhang, T., & Mao, S. (2019). An Overview of Emerging Video Coding Standards. GetMobile. *Mobile Computing and Communications*, *22*(4), 13–20.

Zhang, Z., Li, C., Gupta, B. B., & Niu, D. (2018). Efficient compressed ciphertext length scheme using multi-authority CP-ABE for hierarchical attributes. *IEEE Access: Practical Innovations, Open Solutions*, *6*, 38273–38284. doi:10.1109/ACCESS.2018.2854600

Chapter 2
Machine Learning as an Enabler of Continuous and Adaptive Authentication in Multimedia Mobile Devices

José María Jorquera Valero
Universidad de Murcia, Spain

Pedro Miguel Sánchez Sánchez
Universidad de Murcia, Spain

Alberto Huertas Celdran
https://orcid.org/0000-0001-7125-1710
Waterford Institute of Technology, Ireland

Gregorio Martínez Pérez
Universidad de Murcia, Spain

ABSTRACT

Continuous authentication systems allow users not to possess or remember something to authenticate themselves. These systems perform a permanent authentication that improves the security level of traditional mechanisms, which just authenticate from time to time. Despite the benefits of continuous authentication, the selection of dimensions and characteristics modelling of user's behaviour, and the creation and management of precise models based on Machine learning, are two important open challenges. This chapter proposes a continuous and adaptive authentication system that uses Machine Learning techniques based on the detection of anomalies. Applications usage and the location of the mobile device are considered to detect abnormal behaviours of users when interacting with the device. The proposed system provides adaptability to behavioural changes through the insertion and elimination of patterns. Finally, a proof of concept and several experiments justify the decisions made during the design and implementation of this work, as well as demonstrates its suitability and performance.

DOI: 10.4018/978-1-7998-2701-6.ch002

1. INTRODUCTION

Continuous authentication systems provide a higher level of security (Gupta, Yamaguchi, & Agrawal, 2018) than traditional authentication systems. This is due to traditional systems rely on passwords, patterns or PINs, which can be lost, forgotten or discovered by an attacker. Additionally, many times, users use the same authentication credentials to different services, which is a security problem in case of being stolen. In this sense, continuous authentication systems allow users not to possess or remember something to authenticate themselves in a device or system. This feature improves the user's quality of experience because it allows performing certain operations that require a prior authentication in a faster and easier way. This is because continuous authentication systems are responsible for performing authentication without requiring new credentials. Apart from the different traditional security techniques provided by current mobile devices, the fact of being able to authenticate continuously a user provides a higher level of security. Besides, it allows users to interact with applications, which require the previous authentication, in a more simple, agile and enjoyable fashion.

Multimedia mobile devices (Jararweh et al., 2017) are one of the most important subjects where continuous authentication can be applied. The use these devices has become a daily activity for the majority of the population of industrialized countries, for example, there are 2.71 billion smartphone users in the world today (2019) (Deyan, 2019). Within this wide range of multimedia mobile devices, there is a huge variety in terms of usage, from a private and personal usage such as social networks, take pictures or videos, online banking or entertainment, to a professional usage as the generation of invoices or consult customer data. The sensitive information stored in the multimedia devices and its usage is extremely important (Huertas, Gil, García & Martínez, 2016) so several knowledge managements measures must be taken. The private information should be protected, so, most users restrict access to this information by controlling the access to the device. For that, it is necessary to make use of authentication mechanisms.

The idea of using the authentication mechanisms based on users' actions (behavioural biometrics) arose as a potential solution to improve the security (Gupta, 2018) of multimedia mobile devices. These mechanisms allow analysing continually the behaviour pattern of the owner of the device. After modelling the user's behaviour, the authentication system creates a behaviour profile associated with this conduct or conducts. Finally, in real time the authentication system evaluates the current behaviour of the mobile device with the stored profile of the owner. According to the numeric output of this evaluation, the system decides if the person using the device is the owner or not. This mechanism is passive, and it does not need any change in the interaction between the user and the device. Note that if processing is done in an external cloud, extra measures should be taken to preserve users' privacy (Olakanmi & Dada, 2019).

Despite continue authentication systems provide a lot of benefits, as previously highlighted, they also present some open challenges that should be solved to have complete and effective systems. Among these open challenges, we highlight the next ones:

- Selection of dimensions and characteristics that allow modelling the user's behaviour accurately and effectively. The combination and selection of both the different device input sources, and dimensions, from which the authentication system obtains information about the user's behaviour, as well as the features that compose these, are one of the main pillars for the correct evaluation of the user's behaviour.

- Creation and management of models that shape the user's behaviour. Once the dimensions that will be part of the modelling of the user's behaviour have been selected, the characteristics must be chosen for each of the dimensions. The set of features of each dimension will be stored in a dataset. In this context, another important decision that must be made is to determine the moment in which the content of the dataset must be updated with new features to model the user's behaviour. It will ensure the system adaptability.
- Usage of Machine Learning (ML) techniques that accurately authenticate the owner of the mobile device without forgetting critical aspects such as limited use of resources. ML algorithms based on anomaly detection and not on the classification of vectors concerning users should be used.

With the goal of improving the previous challenges, this book chapter proposes a ML-based adaptive and continuous authentication system for multimedia mobile devices based on the users' behaviour. The proposed system is able to create users' behaviour profiles according to the location of the mobile device and the usage of multimedia applications. Once the profile is created, the proposed solution uses a ML technique based on anomaly detection to measure in real time the level of similarity between the current usage of the mobile device and the well-known behaviour, modelled by the profile. The proposed continue authentication system is sufficiently generic to be adapted in different environment of real life. A pool of experiments is presented to demonstrate the suitability and performance of the proposed solution.

The rest of this chapter is structured in the following way. Section 2 reviews previous works in the same field, focusing attention on solutions that obtained good results in terms of accuracy. Section 3 explains the methodology of the proposed solution, putting the focus on different existing ML techniques. This section also details the design and implementation details of the proposed solution. Section 4 discusses the proposed solution with regard to the existing one. Then, Section 5 demonstrates the usefulness of the proposed solution through a pool of tests. Finally, Section 6 summarizes the work carried out and also proposes different future steps to continue with the development of the system.

2. LITERATURE REVIEW

In the state of the art, we can find multiple works dealing with continuous authentication on mobile devices. In this sense, (Bo, Zhang, Li, Huang & Wang, 2013) identified a user through the use of the touch screen and the sensors of the device. Regarding the dimension of the sensors, authors make use of the accelerometer and gyroscope by carrying out different experiments with users where they obtain information about the device such as rotation and vibration when interacting with the screen, the pressure and the duration that the user exerts on the screen, and values on the sensors mentioned above (see Figure 1). Experiments were carried out while the user remained static as when he was walking. The union of the patterns generated by a user when pressing on the screen together with the patterns obtained when walking allows the user to be identified by a non-intrusive technique and with a false negative rate (FRR) of less than 1%.

Figure 1. Overview of the authentication process
(Bo, Zhang, Li, Huang and Wang, 2013)

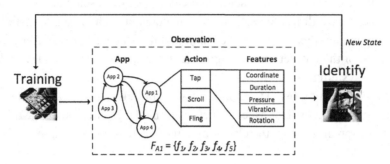

On the other hand, (Patel, Chellappa, Chandra & Barbello, 2016) analysed the dimensions related to facial recognition, user's gestures, touch screen, movements of the device, applications, and location. The authors performed various tests with ML classifier algorithms such as SVM (Ng, 2003), Decision Tree (Gilles, 2014), Bayes Net (Ben-Gal, Ruggeri, Faltin & Kenett, 2007) and K-NN (Sutton, 2012). According to their results, different conclusions can be obtained such as the high computational cost generated by the use of the SVM algorithm, which would be a negative factor to deploy the prototype in the owner's device.

The work published by (Ehatisham-ul-Haq et al., 2017) presents a solution based on the use of the accelerometer, gyroscope and magnetometer to identify a user's interaction with the device. Based on everyday habits, the authors decided to create five positions in which the device is located. The proposed framework uses a combination of three device motion sensors, the accelerometer, gyroscope and magnetometer, as an input data source for activity recognition and user's authentication. The authors generated different features for each sensor by applying formulas such as maximum, minimum, average, variance, peak to peak distance for the coordinates obtained from each of the sensors. After generating the vectors with the corresponding features, the user's behaviour is classified based on a training dataset. The training dataset is composed of different users' vectors that contain the results returned by the functions for each sensor and the possible positions in which the device can be found. The vectors will be classified in different user's profiles that will allow having a higher or lower level of privileges (see Figure 2). A distinction is made between the authenticated user, who obtains full access to the device, subsidiary user, which obtains similarities in behaviour to the authenticated user and has restricted access, and an unauthenticated user, whose privilege level is zero. The authors used different classifying algorithms like SVM (Ng, 2003), Bayes Net (Ben-Gal, Ruggeri, Faltin & Kenett, 2007), K-NN (Sutton, 2012), Decision Tree (Zhu, 2018). After getting the results, it can be concluded that SVM obtains a successful result when classifying the user with an average percentage of 99.18% followed by Bayes Net with an average percentage of 97.38. It should be noted that despite obtaining a lower success rate, Bayes Net has a computational cost five times lower than SVM, reaching a computational cost of 25 seconds to classify a user's vector against the 5 seconds of Bayes Net average.

Figure 2. Proposed methodology for continuous authentication on devices
(Ehatisham-ul-Haq et al., 2017)

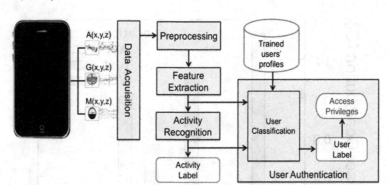

Another interesting work was presented by (Fridman, Weber, Greenstadt & Kam, 2017) which considers very different characteristics, which are evaluated separately to later be combined and obtain the desired result. The authors considered the text written by the user, the location, the applications used, and the visited web pages. The performed experiments have been completed by 200 subjects, each using their mobile device with Android operating system, for at least 30 days. Authentication systems achieved an equal error rate (ERR) of 0.05 (5%) after 1 minute of user's interaction with the device, and an EER of 0.01 (1%) after 30 minutes. After 1 minute of interaction with the device, it can be seen how the location dimension is the one that contributes the most to classify the user's behaviour in a short time, doubling and even tripling the contribution with the rest of the dimensions. After the location dimension, the contribution of the other dimensions, which provide better results, to classify user's behaviour is web pages, applications used and user's writing (see Figure 3).

The project carried out by (Bala, 2017) is based on different combinations of features and algorithms of ML to generate a user's profile that is able to identify the user from the dynamics of keystrokes. The main reason for selecting pulse dynamics as a method to identify user's behaviour is because such a technique is considered more reliable, less expensive and faster than other biometric methods. The objective of this project is to show the evaluation result after completing the training phase where vectors composed of some irrelevant features have been stored and the subsequent impact after selecting only the features that are considered relevant. The process of removing features from the data set that are irrelevant reduces overfitting, improves accuracy and reduces training time. To make the selection of relevant features of the dataset, we use the Weka tool (Weka 3, 2019) which allows you to observe the values of the features that make up the dataset through various graphs and select which features you want to remove from the entered dataset. In addition, different ML algorithms are used to check which combination of features obtain the best results and display the evaluation values before and after the selection of the relevant characteristics.

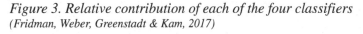

Figure 3. Relative contribution of each of the four classifiers
(Fridman, Weber, Greenstadt & Kam, 2017)

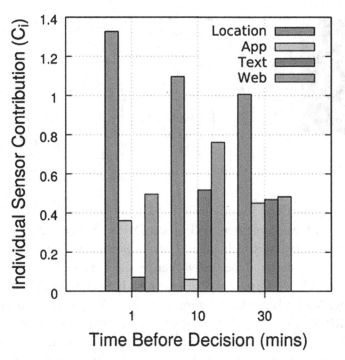

Another related article was published by (Centeno, van Moorsel & Castruccio, 2017), which aims to detect the anomalous behaviour of a user only through the sensors of the device and more specifically through the accelerometer data. Unlike the rest of the articles and projects found, in this case, the data processing is not performed on the device but is carried out on a server (Gupta & Agrawal, 2019) of the company, which receives the data by sending the vectors periodically generated in the device. The effectiveness of the system in real-world scenarios has been shown to achieve 2.2% EER for an evaluation time of 20 seconds. To meet the intrinsic requirements of mobile platforms, the detection process is based on a small number of characteristic biometric data which are sent to the cloud for data processing. The time elapsed to process an authentication user's request is insignificant (approximately five milliseconds), and the time to train the model that achieves the highest accuracy rate is approximately equal to 72 seconds. (Jorquera et al., 2018) proposed an intelligent and adaptive continuous authentication system for mobile devices. The proposed system enabled real-time users' authentication by considering statistical information from applications, sensors and Machine Learning techniques based on anomaly detection. Several experiments demonstrated the accuracy, adaptability, and resources consumption of their solution. Finally, there was proposed an online bank application as proof of concept, which allows users to perform different actions according to their authentication level. (Nespoli et al., 2019) proposed the PALOT framework, which leverages IoT to provide context-aware, continuous and non-intrusive authentication and authorization services. Specifically, the authors proposed a formal information system model based on ontologies, representing the main source of knowledge of the framework. Furthermore, to recognize users' behavioural patterns within the IoT ecosystem, they introduced the confidence manager module. The module is then integrated into an extended version of their early framework architecture,

IoTCAF (Nespoli et al., 2018), which is consequently adapted to include the above-mentioned component. (Sánchez, Huertas, Fernández, Martínez & Wang, 2019) proposed a continuous and intelligent authentication architecture oriented to Smart Offices. The architecture was oriented to the cloud computing paradigm and considers ML techniques to authenticate users according to their behaviours. Some experiments demonstrated the suitability of the proposed solution when recognizing and authenticating different users using a classification algorithm.

Several companies have been found that offer a continuous authentication service to users. Among them, (BehavioSec, 2019) is currently the private company that offers the best product on the market in the field of continuous authentication on devices with Android and iOS operating systems. BehavioSec is a company formed in Sweden in 2006. Through the use of behavioural biometrics techniques, they obtain features belonging to the user's behaviour of dimensions such as key dynamics, movements and gesture patterns, to later be combined to guarantee the user a precise detection of anomalous behaviours through of the use of ML techniques. The product offered provides transparent and adaptable security techniques through the use of an algorithm that is kept up to date with user's behaviours and abilities, so that as they change and improve, so does the security layer, reducing false positives. The central algorithm is continuously improved to verify the legitimate user, providing risk intelligence for an automated and dynamic risk assessment.

Veridium (Veridium Ltd., 2019) is a company which provides an SDK for mobile devices, available for Android and iOS, which allows biometric authentication to be incorporated into any business or consumer application. To carry out the identification of the user's behaviour, he uses the camera, sensors, the flash of the device and multiple biometric factors such as pressure and touches on the screen of the device. In addition, this product makes use of visual cryptography to protect the user's biometric data. This type of cryptography consists of the encryption by the SDK and the division of the captured biometric vectors. One piece is stored on the server, while the other remains on the device. For user's identification, the pieces are recombined and decrypted for comparison during authentication. Veridium allows the SDK to be configured so that the data storage of the event occurs on your back-end server or in the device memory. In the case of storing the data on a back-end server, the communication between the device and the server is sent through a secure two-way SSL connection.

The company Aware (Aware, 2019) based in Bedford, Massachusetts, provides a market product capable of authenticating the user through behavioural and physiological biometrics, although not continuously as the previous proposals. This product makes use of voice recognition, facial recognition, keystroke dynamics and fingerprint recognition. The product called Knomi, performs a biometric authentication through a collection of biometric SDKs that run on mobile devices (Android or iOS) and a server that, together, allows strong, multi-factor and password-free authentication from one device mobile that uses biometric data. Knomi software components can be used in different combinations and configurations to enable a server-centric architecture or a device-centric implementation. Another company that provides a product based on continuous authentication is Zighra (Zighra, 2019) that offers a platform for continuous authentication and threat detection powered by artificial intelligence (Romero, Dafonte, Gómez & Penousal, 2007), both for mobile devices (Android and iOS) and for the web. Its product, called SensifyID, combines knowledge of generative behaviour models and biological systems to train faster, dynamically adapt and accelerate threat detection compared to the AI approaches (Kok, Boers, Kosters, Van der Putten, & Poel, 2009) used today. More specifically, it makes use of dimensions such as location, user's writing techniques, networks and sensors. This product is composed of task-based authentication techniques, through which the user is asked to perform a specific action to demonstrate whether the person who is currently using the device is the rightful owner. In addition, to identify user's behaviour, they use proprietary ML and AI algorithms, capable of continuously learning user's behaviour and, above all, quickly using 15 user's interactions with the device.

3. METHODOLOGY

3.1 Available Machine Learning Techniques for Continuous Authentication

ML algorithms are distinguished into two main categories: supervised and unsupervised. Supervised learning algorithms (Patel, Chellappa, Chandra & Barbello, 2016) aim to determine a function capable of obtaining the desired result from the input data based on the training dataset. For this reason, the training dataset vectors are labelled, that is, the training data will be vectors divided into two parts: input data and expected outputs, also called classes. In this sense, from a set of training vectors, the algorithm determines the function that, from a certain input, will result in the output that best fits said input data. Unsupervised learning algorithms are designed to detect anomalies or cluster data vectors. This kind of algorithms has been present on the state of the art for many years but nowadays they have gained more impact. If the output is a number, the algorithm will be regressive (Domingos, 2012). In contrast, if the output is a value within a known set, the algorithm will be a classifier (Domingos, 2012). Some examples of this type of algorithms are Support Vector Machines (SVM) (Carmona, 2014), Bayesian Networks (Ben-Gal, Ruggeri, Faltin & Kenett, 2007), Decision trees (Quinlan, 1986), Neural Networks (Adeli, 1999), or k nearest neighbours (k-NN) (Peterson, 2009).

Next, the main algorithms used to perform anomaly detection (Jiang, Fu, Gupta, Lou, Rho, Meng, & Tian, 2018) will be analysed, and from them, the one that best fits into the continuous authentication system will be selected by comparing the characteristics of each of these algorithms in terms of accuracy and performance.

3.1.1 One-Class SVM (Support Vector Machines)

Although SVM is a supervised learning algorithm, there is a special case that conforms to the continuous authentication system and allows us to detect anomalies on user-generated vectors. This case is the one that complies that in the training dataset all vectors have the same output, that is, all training vectors are of the same class. This situation is called SVM of a single class or One-Class SVM (Vlasveld, 2013).

The operation of SVM is based on the representation of training vectors as points within a multidimensional space (as many dimensions as values have the vector), so the algorithm tries to build a set of hyperplanes (Hyperplane, 2019) that separate these points based on the class indicated by the vector. So, there will be a set of points separated from the rest for each possible kind of result. If the training vectors have a single class, the algorithm will behave as an unsupervised learning algorithm, generating correlations between the data but being unable to predict the output, since the generated hyperplane will group all the points in the same division of space. Thus, One-Class SVM is able to evaluate a vector to determine if when placed in space it falls within or outside the coordinates delimited by the generated hyperplane. If the vector is placed next to other points within the set delimited by the hyperplanes, the vector will be treated as a normal vector. On the other hand, if the vector falls outside the set, the vector will be treated as an anomaly and thus will be shown by the algorithm.

Figure 4. Graphical representation of One-Class SVM with two-variable vectors
(Zhu, Yang, Gao, Xu, Ye, & Yin, 2016)

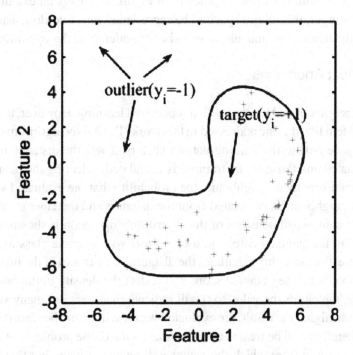

Figure 5. Graphic representation of the k-NN algorithm functioning
(Ömer, 2019)

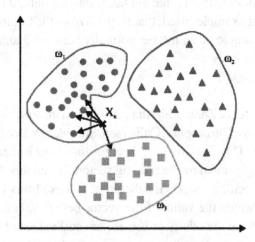

In this case, the algorithm's output will be 1 or -1, indicating the value 1 that the vector is normal and -1 that the vector is an anomaly. One of the disadvantages of this type of output is that it is not known how strange a vector is if it is anomalous, it is only known whether or not it is anomalous. Another counterpart of this algorithm is its computational complexity, since the training has an order between O (n2m) and O (n3m) (Abdiansah & Wardoyo, 2015), depending on the implementation, where n is the number of training vectors and m the number of fields of each of these vectors. The operation of the One-Class SVM algorithm is shown graphically in Figure 4. This is an example in which vectors will have two fields as input, this allows space to be represented on a two-dimensional graph so that it is understandable to the human eye and allows us to better understand the operation of the algorithm.

3.1.2 K-NN to Detect Anomalies

The K-NN (k nearest neighbours) algorithm is also supervised learning. However, it can be adapted for an anomaly detection system like the one addressed in this work. The K-NN algorithm classifies the vectors by placing them in space next to the training dataset vectors. Then, the distance in the space between the vector to be evaluated and those of the training is calculated, selecting the nearest k neighbours to perform the evaluation. From these neighbours, the probability that the evaluated vector belongs to the class of each of the k neighbours is calculated from the distance and the class to which they belong. A graphical representation in two dimensions of the algorithm's operation is shown in Figure 5.

The k-NN algorithm for anomaly detection uses vectors with a single class as in the case of One-Class SVM. In this case, the algorithm calculates the distance (k-distance) of the instance to be evaluated with its closest neighbours k. The obtained score will reflect the density in the point space around the evaluated point. Thus, the closer the value to 0 will indicate that there are many vectors similar to the one evaluated, while the higher the result, the evaluated vector will be further from the concentrations of points in space and therefore will be treated as an anomaly. One of the problems of using this algorithm is that there is no fixed score from which the vector will be an anomaly, but that this depends on the training dataset. For example, in some cases, a k-distance of 4 may represent an anomaly while in other cases, it may not. The k-NN algorithm for anomaly detection is also called Local outlier factor (LOF), and in some cases it can be seen in the literature. The algorithm k-NN has an order of complexity O (nkd), where k is the number of neighbours that are taken into account, d the number of dimensions of the vectors used, the number of examples used, that is, the size of the training dataset. This order can be reduced to O (nd) since k is going to be an integer normally between 3 and 10.

3.1.3 Isolation Forest

Isolation Forest (Liu, F., Ming, K., & Zhou, Zhi-Hua., 2008) is an unsupervised learning algorithm based on Random Forest (Svetnik, Andy, Christopher, Culberson, Sheridan, & Bradley, 2003) specially designed to perform anomaly detection. The objective of this algorithm is to isolate the instances evaluated by random divisions of the space generated by the training vectors. To do this, first, the algorithm randomly selects a characteristic of the vector. Next, divide the set of values of this variable also randomly. After division, the set of values in which the value of the vector being evaluated is chosen, check whether the value has been separated from the others or if there are still values of other training vectors in the set. This process is repeated as many times as necessary until the instance is completely isolated, thus generating a tree with the different divisions made on the set of values of each characteristic.

Isolation Forest randomly selects one of the characteristics of the vector to create a tree with different recursive divisions of the sampling space. However, this process is not performed only once, by default, the algorithm generates 100 trees since this number achieves a balanced performance between accuracy and resource consumption. Like the sampling size, this number can be determined manually when executing the algorithm to improve the results obtained. Through the process described above, the algorithm is able to give a vector a value that represents its anomaly concerning the training dataset. This value is between 0 and 1. So the higher the value (closer to 1), the more anomalous the vector will be (See Figure 6). To calculate the value, the algorithm counts the number of divisions that have been necessary to isolate the value. A small number of divisions indicates an anomalous value while a high number of divisions shows that the vector is within a large cloud of points, indicating that this vector is within normality.

Figure 6. Graphical representation of the anomaly value granted by Isolation Forest
(Liu, F., Ming, K., & Zhou, Zhi-Hua., 2008)

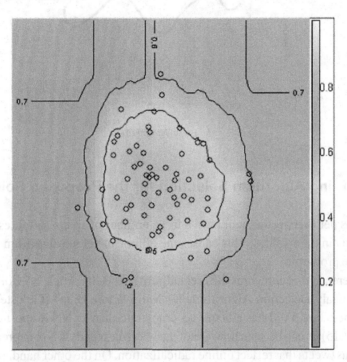

The algorithmic complexity of Isolation Forest is O (tvlog (v)) in the training phase and O (ntlog (v)) (Liu, F., Ming, K., & Zhou, Zhi-Hua., 2008) when executing it, being n the number of instances to evaluate, t the number of trees generated, v the sampling size. Taking the default values t = 100 and v = 256, the complexity of the algorithm remains as O (100256log (256)) + O (n100log (256)). Thus, since the constants have no weight in the orders of complexity, we have left that the complexity of the algorithm is practically O (n).

3.1.4 Elliptic Envelope

The elliptic envelope algorithm (Rousseeuw, & Driessen, 1999) also allows finding anomalies within a dataset. This algorithm generates an ellipse around the point space that represents the dataset vectors. Subsequently, to evaluate an instance, it will be placed in space and given a score depending on whether it falls within the ellipse or not and its proximity to this ellipse. This algorithm yields good results when the data that make up the dataset follows a Gaussian distribution. However, the performance of the algorithm decreases when vectors have numerous fields and do not follow a Gaussian distribution. A Gaussian distribution is one in which the graph of its density function has a flared shape (See Figure 7), that is, the most repeated numerical values are concentrated around a point in the domain of values.

Figure 7. Gaussian (blue) vs non-Gaussian (black) distribution

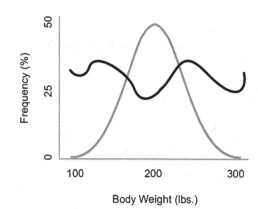

3.2 Machine Learning Algorithm Selection for the Proposed Solution

It is important to consider that vectors will have a large number of fields and foreseeably will not have a Gaussian distribution in their values. This causes the elliptic envelope algorithm to be discarded from a first approach to the problem.

An interesting reference that compares different algorithms is the article "A Comparative Evaluation of Unsupervised Anomaly Detection Algorithms for Multivariate Data" (Goldstein, & Uchida 2016), which shows how One-Class SVM has a better accuracy rate than k- NN in most cases. In addition, in (Agarwal & Sureka 2015). it can be seen how One-Class SVM exceeds k-NN in precision when it comes to detecting anomalous tweets that reflect online radicalization. On the other hand, in (Agarwal & Sureka 2015). it is also shown that the execution time of One-Class SVM is much greater than k-NN, this is very reasonable since the complexity order of SVM is greater than k-NN, since O (nd) <O (n2d) where n is the number of instances in the training dataset and d the number of dimensions of each instance.

One-Class SVM is chosen between One-Class SVM and k-NN as a better option because it has better accuracy than k-NN. To solve the performance penalty, it is proposed to keep the algorithm pre-trained during the evaluation phase so that it is not necessary to retrain it for each execution that is carried out when determining whether a vector is an anomaly or not. Now, One-Class SVM is going to be compared to Isolation Forest to determine which of these two algorithms will have better accuracy and speed of execution. As we can see in Figure 8 (Novelty and Outlier detection, 2019), Isolation Forest has greater precision when it comes to detecting anomalous vectors. In addition, as mentioned above, its order of algorithmic complexity is less than that of One-Class SVM (O (n2d)> O (n)).

For that, it is decided that the anomaly detection algorithm used in this work will be Isolation Forest since it offers better results with a lower resource consumption than One-Class SVM or LOF.

Figure 8. Comparison of anomaly detection algorithms
(Novelty and Outlier detection, 2019)

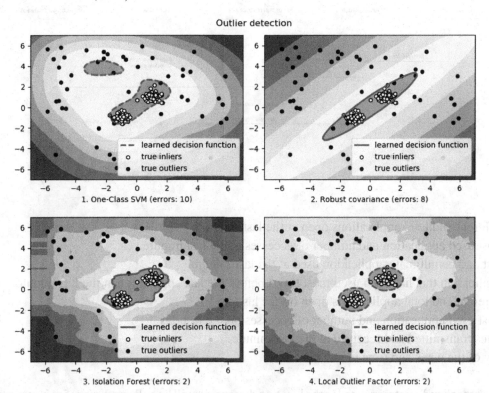

3.3 Design and Implementation of the Adaptive and Continuous Intelligent Authentication System

The proposed continuous authentication system is based on modelling the profile of the owner device to compare it with the current usage and evaluate the level of similarity between them. To model a user's profile, it is necessary to generate one or more datasets containing the user's behaviour while using the device. Regarding the implementation, we have decided to create a proof of concept of the previous solution because currently there are more users with Android devices (Android Developers, 2019), specifically around 2.3 billion, compared to its main rival iOS, it has been decided to develop our solution in Android. In addition, we use a version equal to or greater than API 21, which corresponds to version 5.0, because it is the version of more than the 84% of devices having Android.

The dimensions from which the features that will form the vectors are obtained are the usage statistics of the applications and the location. The vectors generated by both dimensions will be stored in different datasets to later generate the user's behaviour profile. On the one hand, the dimension of application usage statistics generates vectors every minute. The vectors related to the applications will only be collected when the device is unlocked, which allows us to make the necessary readings to collect the information without producing a high energy cost. These vectors are composed of the following features:

Figure 9. UML diagram of application main actions

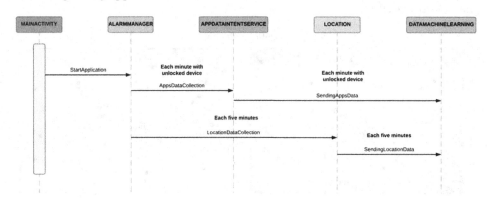

- Different and total applications open at the last minute.
- Most used application and number of accesses at the last minute.
- Last and penultimate application used at the last minute.
- Application that has been used most times before the last application at the last minute.
- Different and total applications open on the last day.
- Most used application and number of accesses on the last day.
- Bytes transmitted and received at the last minute.
- Day of the week and time in seconds.

On the other hand, vectors related to the location dimension will be collected every 5 minutes regardless of whether the user's device is locked or unlocked. These vectors are composed of the following features:

- Latitude.
- Longitude.
- Day of the week.
- Time in seconds.

Once the features that will form the vectors of both dimensions have been determined, the next step is to design and implement an Android application with the necessary classes to collect this information, which will be stored in different datasets during the training and evaluation phase. In our application, the *AlarmManager* class is one of the most important because it allows managing the launch of the services for collecting application usage and location statistics through scheduled alarms. Due to alarms are paused automatically if our device remains idle for some time, it is necessary to make additional use of the *BootReceiver* class that extends from *BroadcastReceiver*. This class is responsible for receiving the event that occurs when the device is turned on and schedules the necessary alarms.

Another important class is *IntentService*, which is provided by Android libraries. This class has the functionality of allowing asynchronous execution in the background of the operations necessary to obtain the data that will form the vectors. This class is used both in the *DataApssIntentService* class and in the Location class to periodically collect the characteristics of each dimension. In addition, this class, together with the alarms programs (*AlarmManager*), allow obtaining the information of the features when the device keeps in the background the application that implements the collection of sensors or is even closed.

The *DataApssIntentService* class is responsible for periodically collecting all the features related to application usage statistics. This process is carried out every minute, allowing the obtaining of application data through the use of the classes provided by the *Android.app.usage* library, which allows extracting data on application use, such as opening order, time of use, or first usage. Once the features of the application usage statistics are collected, they will be sent to the *DataMachineLearning* class to generate the vector of that dimension and store it in the corresponding dataset. The Location class collects the location of the device periodically (every 5 minutes). To do this, it makes use of the Google Play Services location API, which allows adding location detection to an Android application producing energy savings in the use of the application. After collecting the features, this class will be in charge of sending the collected values to the *DataMachineLearning* class where it will be stored in the corresponding dataset.

The *DataMachineLearning* class implements the functionality necessary to obtain the characteristics from which the vectors of each dimension and stored in the datasets will be generated from the *Localization* and *DataApssIntentService* classes. In addition, this class is responsible for performing the Isolation Forest algorithm training and the evaluation of the vectors generated in real-time by the user after the training phase, which lasts for two weeks. Figure 9 shows the diagram with the previous steps.

As previously indicated, we use Isolation Forest to identify anomalies and authenticate the owner of the device. The most used library that provides the necessary methods to configure the Isolation Forest algorithm is Scikit-learn (Scikit-learn developers, 2019). After choosing the appropriate library to use IF, the next decision that had to be made was the duration of the training phase. The estimated duration to obtain a training phase that provides optimal results is 14 days.

During the training phase, the features related to application usage statistics are collected every minute through the *DataApssIntentService*. In contrast, features related to the dimension of the location are obtained periodically every 5 minutes through the Location class. Each dimension will generate a vector independently that will be stored in different files, which the Isolation Forest algorithm will use to train.

Once the training phase is over, the evaluation phase begins where the IF algorithm will have learned the owner behaviour. The data collection services will follow the same periodic process, with the difference that every minute the device is unlocked, the generated vectors are evaluated. Because the user's evaluation process is carried out every minute and the location feature collection service are activated every 5 minutes, if a new location vector has not been generated at the time of evaluating the user, the algorithm uses the last vector generated.

The Isolation Forest algorithm performs the separate evaluation of each vector to be evaluated, in this case, a vector for application usage statistics and another for location statistics. The evaluation of each vector provides a value between 0 and 1. It is decided to carry out a weighting of the vectors that make up the dataset of each dimension used.

$$GA = 0.5 * Uva + 0.5 * Uvl$$

Where GA is the degree of authentication whose value is between 0 and 1, this score is calculated as 1-anomaly of the evaluated vector. *Uva* corresponds to the last feature vector of the applications, *Uvl* is the last feature vector of the location. If the evaluation result is close to 0 it means that the evaluated vectors are composed of features that the algorithm considers anomalous. In contrast, if we obtain an evaluation result close to 1 the user's behaviour will have a high similarity with that obtained during the phase of training.

Table 1. Comparison of the most current solutions

Proposal	Considered Dimensions	Adaptability	ML Techniques	Results
SilentSense (Bo, Zhang, Li, Huang and Wang, 2013)	Movement and touches on the screen	No	OneClass-SVM SVM	Accuracy: 72.36% FAR: 24.99%
(Ehatisham-ul-Haq et al., 2017)	Sensors accelerometer, magnetometer and gyroscope	No	SVM, Bayes Net (BN), Decision tree (DT), K-Nearest Neighbors (K-NN)	Accuracy: 99.18-93.30% depend on algorithm
SenGuard (Shi, Yang, Jiang, Yang & Xiong, 2011)	Movement, location, voice and touches on the screen	No	Bayesian Networks	Accuracy: 97-95%
(Fridman, Weber, Greenstadt & Kam, 2017)	Location, used applications, web navigation and writing	No	SVM	Accuracy: 95% EER: 5%
(Parreño, Moorsel & Castruccio, 2017)	Accelerometer	Yes	Autoencoder	Accuracy: 97.8% EER: 2.2%
(Li, Clarke, Papadaki and Dowland, 2011)	Calls, text messages and applications	Yes	Classification algorithm	EER: 5.4%, 2.2% y 13.5%, for each dimension, respectively
(Jorquera et al., 2018)	Applications' usage statistics and sensors	Yes	Isolation Forest	Precision: 77% Recall: 92%

Finally, note that the Isolation Forest algorithm used in this document has the ability to adapt to certain changes in the behaviour of the owner user. For this, once the training phase is over, the algorithm is re-trained with certain vectors which exceed a set threshold, from which it is considered that the user's behaviour is not anomalous. The purpose of re-training is to provide the authentication system with adaptability to possible changes in the owner's behaviour. Therefore, once the evaluation phase has begun, during which the user is continuously authenticated in real time, if the system considers that the evaluated vectors belong to the owner user, they will be added to the dataset generated in the training phase. The user's privacy is also preserved by not storing more data than is necessary for the system to work (Huertas, Gil, García & Martínez, 2014a, 2017, 2014b, 2016).

4. DISCUSSION

The system proposed in this chapter is a novelty in the state of the art since there is no other work that combines data from the applications and location. As can be seen in Table 1, despite the achieved advances by the previous solutions, these present a series of shortcomings. For example, most systems use classification ML algorithms instead of anomaly detection algorithms. This fact means that the systems cannot detect any intruder and only identify users whose data they have about their behaviour. In addition, those that perform anomaly detection do not have as good results as those that use classification algorithms.

Table 2. Authentication results using application data collected with the phone locked and unlocked

Evaluated User	Results
Legitimate user	~0.51 device locked
	~0.43 device unlocked
Illegitimate user	~0.35 device unlocked

In this sense, the proposed solution in this work seeks to improve existing solutions. To do this, it combines two dimensions, such as location and application usage, which are evaluated using unsupervised algorithms to detect anomalies. In addition, it is a system which adapts to changes in the user's behaviour, without forgetting a key aspect such as the consumption of mobile device resources.

(Bo, Zhang, Li, Huang and Wang, 2013) does not propose system adaptability to new behaviours and does not analyze the resource consumption. In (Parreño, Moorsel & Castruccio, 2017), mobile devices should be connected to the Internet and this is a situation that is not always met. In contrast, the proposed solution to this work can work offline as it is self-contained on the device. (Li, Clarke, Papadaki and Dowland, 2011) is the only work which provides information about energy consumption, being this consumption higher than the one on the present work.

Note that the work presented is based on (Jorquera et al., 2018) but using other dimensions, so the results are similar regarding the consumption of resources and the algorithms used. As practical implications, the developed system can be used to improve security on mobile devices, complementing traditional authentication systems and granting an extra level of users' privacy. The system is suitable for virtually any smartphone since the data used belongs to sources present in any modern device.

As system limitations, GPS coordinate location does not always work in all environments. Thus, in large cities with buildings that surround the user, the coordinates may be more inaccurate or difficult to determine. Besides, the use of motion sensors can cause the system to not work properly if the user is making unusual movements such as running or other sports.

5. RESULTS

In this section, the different experiments performed to determine the optimal set of features and dimensions will be explained. Through the different experiments, it is intended to achieve a continuous and adaptive authentication system capable of accurately evaluating user's behaviour, detecting anomalous behaviours.

Figure 10. Graphic representation of experiment 1 dataset

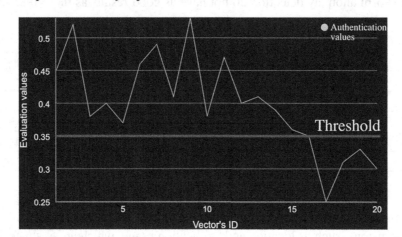

5.1 First Experiment

The aim of this first experiment is to collect as many features as possible to model a user's behavioural profile to detect anomalous behaviours. To carry out this experiment, a mobile application was implemented for Android in charge of collecting for 14 days the use of applications that the owner of the device made. The collection of data during the training phase, was done while the device was in a state of rest (locked) and while the owner made a daily use of the device (unlocked).

The characteristics that were compiled in each vector during the training phase are as follows:

- Different and total applications opened.
- Different and total applications opened at the last minute.
- Most used application, number of uses and average time of use.
- Most used application and number of accesses at the last minute.
- Last application used and average time of use.
- Penultimate application used and average time of use.
- Number of times that the penultimate application has been used before the last application.
- Application that has been used most times before the last application and number of uses.

After finishing the training phase, where the vectors generated by the user were collected every minute, regardless of whether the device was locked or unlocked, the behaviour of the user who owns the device is evaluated. Different assessments are made when the owner makes use of the everyday device and when the device is in standby mode. In addition, an external user, who has not made any use of the device during the training phase, uses the device as if he was the owner.

The mean of the standardised results obtained for the different tests carried out in the evaluation phase is shown in Table 2.

Next, a graph is shown (see Figure 10) which shows the evaluation of a set of vectors with respect to the training dataset that Isolation Forest has had. The red line of the graph (see Figure 10) represents the delimiter threshold between an anomalous and usual behaviour, and the yellow line represents the result of the evaluation of each one of dataset vectors. The evaluated dataset is composed of 20 vectors, of which the first 15 belong to the owner user and the last 5 to an anomalous user. In order to represent these values graphically, it has been necessary to normalize the result of the degree of authentication returned by the system in each of the vectors represented.

Figure 11. Graphic representation of experiment 2 dataset

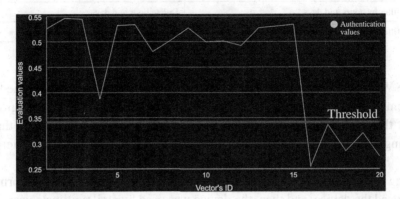

As can it be seen, the results obtained after this first experiment are not relevant enough to be able to differentiate an anomalous behaviour (vectors 16-20) in the use of the device. This is due to two factors:

- The algorithm provides a greater evaluation to the user when the device is in a locked state due to the fact that most time the phone is in standby mode, considering an anomalous behaviour in the use of the device.
- Some of the characteristics that have been collected in the vectors do not provide useful information to the algorithm to detect anomalies. Some features have been collected that increase linearly or vary very little even if the user's behaviour changes.

5.2 Second Experiment

The objective of this experiment is to select the most relevant features to determine with greater certainty an anomalous behaviour in the owner and to choose during which instances of time the features are collected. Specifically, the vector that represents the dimension of application usage statistics is composed of the following features:

- Different and total applications open at the last minute.
- Most used application and number of accesses at the last minute.
- Last and penultimate application used at the last minute.
- Application that has been used most times before the last application at the last minute.
- Different and total applications open on the last day.
- Most used application and number of accesses on the last day.
- Bytes transmitted and received at the last minute

Table 3. Authentication results of owner vectors using new features and selecting the training dataset vectors that will be used.

Usage of Applications and Localization			Score
Owner	Filter by hours and days	Delete hour and day	~0.83
	Filter by hours and days	No delete hour and day	~0.66
	No filter by hours and days	Delete hour and day	~0.89
	No filter by hours and days	No delete hour and day	~0.84

Thanks to the Weka tool (Weka 3, 2019), it was possible to detect the use of some features that did not provide information relevant to the algorithm. Through the visualization of the graphs where each of the features of the generated vectors were represented, it was possible to observe that some characteristics were being used that linearly increased their value without being a data of interest to model the user's profile.

After removing the features and inserting some new ones, different tests were performed in which the owner normally used the device, and then, the device was used by an illegitimate user. The normalized results obtained, between 0 and 1 showed a score of around 0.52 for the owner of the device and 0.34 for an anomalous user.

Figure 11 shows the evaluation of a set of vectors concerning the training dataset that Isolation Forest has had. The red line represents the bounding threshold between abnormal and usual behaviour, and the yellow line represents the evaluation result of each of the dataset vectors. The evaluated dataset is composed of 20 vectors, of which the first 15 belong to the owner user and the last 5 belong to an anomalous user. As it can be observed, the results obtained show an evaluation that distinguishes the anomalous behaviour in the use of the device

If we compare Figure 10 with the results of Figure 11, we can see how after doing the feature selection, the evaluation values of the vectors belonging to the owner are better (in this experiment the majority of values are around 0.5). However, we think that these results could be better if we consider an additional dimension. In this sense, next experiment shows the impact of adding a new dimension in the evaluation values.

5.3 Third Experiment

After the results obtained in the previous test, we investigated the fact of considering new dimensions and features that help to model the user's profile and increase the level of successes in the detection of anomalies. In this sense, we decided to add the following features of the geographical location dimension.

- Latitude.
- Length.
- Current time.
- Weekday.

Table 4. Results of anomalous vector authentication using new features and selecting the training dataset vectors that will be used

	Usage of Applications and Localization		Score
Anomalous user	Filter by hours and days	Delete hour and day	~0.282
	Filter by hours and days	No delete hour and day	~0.316
	No filter by hours and days	Delete hour and day	~0.238
	No filter by hours and days	No delete hour and day	~0.208

The goal of inserting the time and weekday lied in the idea of creating time ranges in which the owner of the device usually makes use of certain applications, and in most cases, is in the same location at certain times as a result of daily habits. Once the new dimension is specified and the characteristics that will form each vector have been chosen, a new training and evaluation phases are carried out.

This test was carried out both by removing the features related to the time and day of the week from the vectors and without eliminating them. The reason for eliminating these features is because IF selects some features randomly to determine how anomalous the user's behaviour is, and it may be the case that the time of day or day of the week is selected as a feature and not. In addition, the comparison of the results obtained will be performed in the case of filtering the training dataset by the hour and day, with the evaluation of the same vectors, but without applying any filter on the training dataset. The average of the normalized results obtained, between 0 and 1 as well as experiment 1, are those shown in Table 3.

The results obtained after this first test are contradictory with respect to the idea that was intended to be addressed with this experiment due to:

Figure 12. Graphic representation of experiment 3 dataset

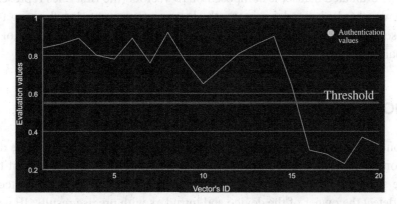

- The reduction of the dataset size, in most of the tests, performed to obtain the results shown in the table, the number of vectors that formed the datasets that were to be selected to train the ML algorithm and subsequently evaluate the user were lower to 200 vectors.
- The domain of values provided by the vectors that make up the datasets is smaller, which causes the ML algorithm to have to perform fewer divisions to isolate the value of a randomly selected feature.

- The user's behaviour during the training phase was not as repeated as predicted, negatively affecting the subsequent evaluation phase where the owner user does a daily behaviour.

Finally, it will be evaluated if the system is able to detect the anomalous behaviour of the device through the evaluation of different vectors not belonging to the owner user. In this case, as in the previous one, the evaluation of training datasets will be checked by applying a filter to obtain more specific and reduced datasets, in the case of obtaining two datasets without applying any filter to obtain the number of vectors reduced. The obtained results are shown in Table 4.

As can be seen, the system performs an accurate detection of anomalous vectors regardless of whether a filter is applied to training datasets to select only the collected vectors belonging to the same day and at the same time. The causes are:

- The time and day features of the week can be selected by Isolation Forest as the characteristics that will determine if the vector to be evaluated is anomalous. Therefore, the elimination of these characteristics allows the algorithm to randomly select other features which will have an anomalous value with respect to the training dataset vectors.
- The fact of not applying a filter from the time and day of the week provides a better result to detect anomalies due to the small size of the datasets. This implies that Isolation Forest has to perform a smaller number of divisions to isolate the values of the selected characteristics of the vector.

As a conclusion, it is decided to use a dataset for the location dimension and another for the application. Both datasets will not be filtered by time and day. In addition, the new features added, through which two specific training datasets were intended, are eliminated because Isolation Forest can select these characteristics from an anomalous vector.

Figure 12 shows the evaluation of a set of vectors with respect to the training dataset that Isolation Forest has had. The evaluated dataset is composed of 15 vectors (the first ones represented) belonging to the user who owns the device and 5 vectors (the last ones represented) belonging to an anomalous user. As you can see the threshold set in 0.55 allows us to differentiate the behaviour of a user owner of a user with anomalous behaviour.

6. CONCLUSION AND FUTURE WORK

In this work, a continuous and adaptive authentication system for multimedia mobile devices has been presented based on the collection of user's characteristics through the dimensions of the location and application usage statistics. A non-supervised ML technique based on anomaly detection such as IF has been used to detect the owner of the device and intruders with precise results. IF was chosen as the algorithm to be used due to the low energy and computational consumption associated with its use in mobile devices and the high level of precision it provides. After IF was trained with the profile of the device owner, the proposed solution was prepared to evaluate in real time the user's behaviour, allowing the adaptability of the algorithm with the insertion of new vectors to the dataset in case they meet certain characteristics. Finally, different experiments obtain valid results that allow accurately differentiating the behaviour of an unusual user and the device owner.

Among the future paths, we plan to move the computational calculations made by IF to the cloud to reduce the computational cost and the energy cost it generates in mobile devices. It is also intended to examine new dimensions that allow modelling a user's behaviour profile with greater certainty. Finally, we plan to use additional ML algorithms to test the efficiency in the detection of anomalies with the new improvements added.

ACKNOWLEDGMENT

This work has been funded by the Fundación Séneca - Agencia de Ciencia y Tecnología de la Región de Murcia, through the AUTHCODE (AUTHentication for Continuous access On DEvices) project (grant code 20549/PDC/18), and the Government of Ireland, through the IRC post-doc fellowship (grant code GOIPD/2018/466).

REFERENCES

Abdiansah, A., & Wardoyo, R. (2015). Time complexity analysis of support vector machines (SVM) in LibSVM. *International Journal of Computers and Applications*, *128*(3).

Adeli, H. (1999). Machine Learning-Neural Networks, Genetic Algorithms and Fuzzy Systems. *Kybernetes*, *28*(3), 317–318. doi:10.1108/k.1999.28.3.317.5

Agarwal, S., & Sureka, A. (2015). Using knn and svm based one-class classifier for detecting online radicalization on twitter. *Proceedings International Conference on Distributed Computing and Internet Technology*, 431-442. 10.1007/978-3-319-14977-6_47

Aware, Inc. (2019). Biometrics Software Solutions. - Fingerprint, Face, Iris, Keystroke Recognition. Retrieved October 29, 2019, from http://aware.com/biometrics-software-solutions/authentication-and-payments

Bala, J. D. (2017). *Application of Machine Learning in Feature Selection for Continuous Authentication*. Tennessee Tech University.

BehavioSec, Inc. (2019). Continuous Authentication through Passive Behavioral Biometrics. Retrieved October 29, 2019, from http://behaviosec.com

Ben-Gal, I., Ruggeri, F., Faltin, F., & Kenett, R. (2007). Bayesian Network.

Bo, C., Zhang, L., Li, X. Y., Huang, Q., & Wang, Y. (2013). SilentSense: Silent User's identification Via Touch and Movement Behavioral Biometrics. *Proceedings 19th Annual International Conference on Mobile Computing & Networking*, 187-190. 10.1145/2500423.2504572

Carmona, E. (2014). *Tutorial sobre Máquinas de Vectores Soporte (SVM)*. *Department of Intelligence Artificial, Universidad Nacional de Educación a Distancia*. Spain: UNED.

Centeno, M. P., van Moorsel, A., & Castruccio, S. (2017). Smartphone continuous authentication using deep learning autoencoders. *Proceedings 15th Annual Conference on Privacy, Security and Trust (PST)*, 147-1478. 10.1109/PST.2017.00026

Developers, A. (2019). Distribution Dashboard. Retrieved October 29, 2019, from https://developer.android.com/about/dashboards/

Deyan, G. (2019, March 28). 60+ Smartphone. *Stat, 2019*. Retrieved from https://techjury.net/stats-about/smartphone-usage/

Domingos, P. (2012). A Few Useful Things to Know about Machine Learning. *Communications of the ACM, 55*(10), 78–87. doi:10.1145/2347736.2347755

Ehatisham-ul-Haq, M., Azam, M. A., Loo, J., Shuang, K., Islam, S., Naeem, U., & Amin, Y. (2017). Authentication of Smartphone Users Based on Activity Recognition and Mobile Sensing. *Sensors (Basel), 17*(9), 2043. doi:10.339017092043 PMID:28878177

Fridman, L., Weber, S., Greenstadt, R., & Kam, M. (2017). Active Authentication on Mobile Devices via Stylometry, Application Usage, Web Browsing, and GPS Location. *IEEE Systems Journal, 11*(2), 513–521. doi:10.1109/JSYST.2015.2472579

Gilles, L. (2014). *Understanding Random Forest from Theory to Practice*. University of Liège.

Goldstein, M., & Uchida, S. (2016). A comparative evaluation of unsupervised anomaly detection algorithms for multivariate data. *PLoS One, 11*(4). doi:10.1371/journal.pone.0152173 PMID:27093601

Gupta, B. B. (2018). Computer and cyber security: principles, algorithm, applications, and perspectives. Boca Raton, FL: CRC Press.

Gupta, B. B., & Agrawal, D. P. (Eds.). (2019). *Handbook of Research on Cloud Computing and Big Data Applications in IoT*. IGI Global. doi:10.4018/978-1-5225-8407-0

Gupta, B. B., Yamaguchi, S., & Agrawal, D. P. (2018). Advances in security and privacy of multimedia big data in mobile and cloud computing. *Multimedia Tools and Applications, 77*(7), 9203–9208. doi:10.100711042-017-5301-x

Huertas, A., García, F. J., Gil, M., & Martínez, G. (2016). SeCoMan: A Semantic-Aware Policy Framework for Developing Privacy-Preserving and Context-Aware Smart Applications. *IEEE Systems Journal, 10*(3), 111–1124.

Huertas, A., Gil, M., García, F. J., & Martínez, G. (2014a). Precise: Privacy-aware recommender based on context information for cloud service environments. *IEEE Communications Magazine, 52*(8), 90–96. doi:10.1109/MCOM.2014.6871675

Huertas, A., Gil, M., García, F. J., & Martínez, G. (2014b). *What Private Information Are You Disclosing? A Privacy-Preserving System Supervised by Yourself* (pp. 1221–1228). Paris, France: IEEE Intl Conf on High Performance Computing and Communications.

Huertas, A., Gil, M., García, F. J., & Martínez, G. (2016). MASTERY: A multicontext-aware system that preserves the users' privacy. *NOMS IEEE/IFIP Network Operations and Management Symposium*, 523-528.

Huertas, A., Gil, M., García, F. J., & Martínez, G. (2017). Preserving patients' privacy in health scenarios through a multicontext-aware system. *Annales des Télécommunications*, *72*(9-10), 577–587. doi:10.100712243-017-0582-7

Hyperplane, W. (2019). Retrieved October 29, 2019, from https://en.wikipedia.org/wiki/Hyperplane

Jararweh, Y., Alsmirat, M., Al-Ayyoub, M., Benkhelifa, E., Darabseh, A., Gupta, B., & Doulat, A. (2017). Software-defined system support for enabling ubiquitous mobile edge computing. *The Computer Journal*, *60*(10), 1443–1457. doi:10.1093/comjnl/bxx019

Jiang, F., Fu, Y., Gupta, B. B., Lou, F., Rho, S., Meng, F., & Tian, Z. (2018). Deep learning based multi-channel intelligent attack detection for data security. *IEEE transactions on Sustainable Computing*.

Jorquera, J. M., Sánchez, P. M., Fernández, L., Huertas, A., Arjona, M., De Los Santos, S., & Martínez, G. (2018). Improving the Security and QoE in Mobile Devices through an Intelligent and Adaptive Continuous Authentication System. *Sensors (Basel)*, *18*(11), 3769. doi:10.339018113769 PMID:30400377

Kok, J. N., Boers, E. J., Kosters, W. A., Van der Putten, P., & Poel, M. (2009). Artificial intelligence: Definition, trends, techniques, and cases. *Artificial Intelligence*, 1.

Li, F., Clarke, N., Papadaki, M., & Dowland, P. (2011). Behaviour Profiling for Transparent Authentication for Mobile Devices. *Proceedings 10th European Conference on Information Warfare and Security, (pp. 307-314)*.

Liu, F., & Ming, K., & Zhou, Z.-H. (2008). Isolation forest. *Proceedings Eighth IEEE International Conference on Data Mining (ICDM)*, 413–422. Academic Press.

Nespoli, P., Zago, M., Huertas, A., Gil, M., Gómez, F., & García, F. J. (2018). A Dynamic Continuous Authentication Framework in IoT-Enabled Environments. *IoTSMS'18: Proceedings of the 5th International Conference on Internet of Things: Systems, Management, and Security*, Valencia (Spain). 10.1109/IoTSMS.2018.8554389

Nespoli, P., Zago, M., Huertas, A., Gil, M., Gómez, F., & García, F. J. (2019). PALOT: Profiling and Authenticating Users Leveraging Internet of Things. *Sensors. Special Issue on Sensor Systems for Internet of Things*, *19*(12), 2832.

Ng, A. Y. (2003). Support Vector Machines. CS229 Lecture notes, 5, 45-69.

Novelty and Outlier detection. Scikit-learn documentation. Retrieved October 29, 2019, from http://scikit-learn.org/stable/modules/outlier_detection.html

Olakanmi, O. O., & Dada, A. (2019). An Efficient Privacy-preserving Approach for Secure Verifiable Outsourced Computing on Untrusted Platforms. *International Journal of Cloud Applications and Computing*, *9*(2), 79–98. doi:10.4018/IJCAC.2019040105

Ömer Cengiz, Ç. E. L. E. B. İ. (2019). *Neural Networks and Pattern Recognition Using MATLAB*. Non-Parametric Techniques. Retrieved from http://www.byclb.com/TR/Tutorials/neural_networks/ch11_1.htm

Parreño, M., Moorsel, A., & Castruccio, S. (2017). Smartphone Continuous Authentication Using Deep Learning Autoencoders. *Proceedings 15th International Conference on Privacy, Security and Trust*, 147-1478.

Patel, V. M., Chellappa, R., Chandra, D., & Barbello, B. (2016). Continuous User's authentication on Mobile Devices: Recent Progress and Remaining Challenges. *IEEE Signal Processing Magazine*, *33*(4), 49–61. doi:10.1109/MSP.2016.2555335

Peterson, L. E. (2009). K-nearest neighbor. *Scholarpedia*, *4*(2), 1883. doi:10.4249cholarpedia.1883

Quinlan, J. R. (1986). *Machine Learning. Springer*, *1*(1), 81–106.

Romero, J. J., Dafonte, C., Gómez, A., & Penousal, F. (2007). Inteligencia artificial y computación avanzada. Santiago de Compostela: Fundación Alfredo Brañas, 10-15.

Rousseeuw, P. J., & Driessen, K. V. (1999). A fast algorithm for the minimum covariance determinant estimator. *Technometrics*, *41*(3), 212–223. doi:10.1080/00401706.1999.10485670

Sánchez, P., Huertas, A., Fernández, L., Martínez, G., & Wang, G. (2019). Securing Smart Offices through an Intelligent and Multi-device Continuous Authentication System. *Proceedings of the 7th International Conference on Smart City and Informatization*. Guangzhou, China: Springer Computer Science Proceedings.

Scikit-learn developers. (2019). Scikit-learn: machine learning in Python. Retrieved October 1, 2019, from http://scikit-learn.org/stable/index.html

Shi, W., Yang, J., Jiang, Y., Yang, F., & Xiong, Y. (2011). SenGuard: Passive user identification on smartphones using multiple sensors. *Proceedings IEEE 7th International Conference on Wireless and Mobile Computing, Networking, and Communications (WiMob)*, 141-148.

Sutton, O. (2012). Introduction to k Nearest Neighbour Classification and Condensed Nearest Neighbour Data Reduction. 10.

Svetnik, V., Andy, L., Christopher, T., Culberson, J., Sheridan, R., & Bradley, F. (2003). A Classification and Regression Tool for Compound Classification and QSAR Modeling. *Journal of Chemical Information and Computer Sciences*, *43*(6), 1947–1958. doi:10.1021/ci034160g PMID:14632445

Veridium Ltd. (2019). Biometric Authentication Technology - Fingerprint, Face, Camera, Sensors. Retrieved October 29, 2019, from http://veridiumid.com/biometric-authentication-technology/mobile-authentication

Vlasveld, R. (2013). Introduction to One-class Support Vector Machines. Retrieved October 29, 2019, from http://rvlasveld.github.io/blog/2013/07/12/introduction-to-one-class-support-vector-machines

Weka 3. (2019) Data Mining Software in Java. Retrieved October 1, 2019, from https://www.cs.waikato.ac.nz/ml/weka/

Zhu, F., Yang, J., Gao, C., Xu, S., Ye, N., & Yin, T. (2016). A weighted one-class support vector machine. *Neurocomputing, 189*, 1–10. doi:10.1016/j.neucom.2015.10.097

Zhu, J. (2018). *Machine Learning Decision Tree*. University of Wisconsin.

Zighra. (2019). Smart Identity Defense. AI-Powered Continuous Authentication and Fraud Detection. Retrieved October 29, 2019, from https://zighra.com/

Chapter 3
Anonymous Authentication for Privacy Preserving of Multimedia Data in the Cloud

Sadiq J. Almuairfi
iD https://orcid.org/0000-0002-7275-1677
Prince Sultan University, Saudi Arabia

Mamdouh Alenezi
iD https://orcid.org/0000-0001-6852-1206
Prince Sultan University, Saudi Arabia

ABSTRACT

Cloud computing technology provides cost-saving and flexibility of services for users. With the explosion of multimedia data, more and more data owners would outsource their personal multimedia data on the cloud. In the meantime, some computationally expensive tasks are also undertaken by cloud servers. However, the outsourced multimedia data and its applications may reveal the data owner's private information because the data owners lose control of their data. Recently, this thought has aroused new research interest on privacy-preserving reversible data hiding over outsourced multimedia data. Anonymous Authentication Scheme will be proposed in this chapter as the most relatable, applicable, and appropriate techniques to be adopted by the cloud computing professionals for the eradication of risks that have been associated with the risks and challenges of privacy.

INTRODUCTION

Authentication is a process of determining whether a particular individual or a device should be allowed to access a system or an application or merely an object running on a device. This is an important process which assures the basic security goals, viz. confidentiality and integrity. Also, adequate authentication is the first line of defence for protecting any resource. It is important that the same authentication technique may not be used in every scenario. For example, a less sophisticated approach may be used for accessing

DOI: 10.4018/978-1-7998-2701-6.ch003

a "chat server" compared to accessing a corporate database. Most of the existing authentication schemes require processing at both the client and the server end. Thus, the acceptability of any authentication scheme greatly depends on its robustness against attacks as well as its resource requirement both at the client and at the server end. The resource requirement has become a major factor due to the proliferation of mobile and hand-held devices. Nowadays, with the use of mobile phones, users can access any information including banking and corporate databases.

Anonymity is closely tied to confidentiality and privacy. A user should know that his online activity is secure and available only to him and a certain few authorized individuals from the service provider. That a user can have his entire browsing, purchasing activity accessed by others is unacceptable, and cloud service providers should ensure that this does not occur. Users should not have a fraudster accessing details of the online stores they visited, items purchased, frequency of visits and details of transactions.

The key to anonymity is the avoidance of the interception of the data being sent. If a user's cloud status cannot be ascertained, anonymity will be ensured, as third parties will not be able to tell whether a user is active or not, hence data interception will not occur. Users should have their anonymity guaranteed and no cookies should be allowed to monitor their activities, as cloud service deals with sensitive financial and personal data which could be used to detrimental ends if it fell into the wrong hands

Hiding one's real identity is important for users who do not like to share their personal or private information with others, for example, they may not want to share information regarding their meeting schedules with their business partners, which books they buy and read, how much money they have in their accounts, which transactions they execute, where they go, etc. In short, many users strongly prefer to remain anonymous as far as and whenever possible.

Since the revival of the 20th century, there is an enormous growth of mobile and wireless technologies. At present, a huge majority in the user of wireless devices, including mobile phones, for instance, notebooks, smartphones, PDAs, and so on, for accessing diverse online applications and services globally at any time. The services might include video conferencing, webinars, social networking, remote medical treatments, government services, VoIP, and net browsing. Yet, a limitation to these online services is the primary infrastructure of the public Internet, which permits an attacker to temper, interrupt, and spy on the transmitted messages amongst two trusted entities. Hence, it has become the most significant factor to ensure the transmitted messages' security, including the user's privacy. Further, the technology of advanced cloud computing has provided economical and flexible service to its users, making massive amounts of confidential multimedia data being outsourced on the cloud, leading to risks and privacy concerns associated with this data. The preservation of privacy has emerged to be one of the hot topics during a few years in the domains of cloud computing. Provided with the facts that, once the data of some user gets compromised, there could be several negative results. As a result, the construction of technologies linked to the preservation of privacy has emerged as a fundamental concern in the cloud computing domain.

Cloud computing technology provides cost-saving and flexibility of services for users. With the explosion of multimedia data, more and more data owners would outsource their personal multimedia data on the cloud. In the meantime, some computationally expensive tasks are also undertaken by cloud servers. However, the outsourced multimedia data and its applications may reveal the data owner's private information because the data owners lose control of their data. Recently, this thought has aroused new research interest on privacy-preserving reversible data hiding over outsourced multimedia data. Anonymous Authentication Scheme will be proposed in this chapter as the most relatable, applicable, and appropriate techniques to be adopted by the cloud computing professionals for the eradication of risks that have been associated with the risks and challenges of privacy.

MULTIMEDIA DATA CONCERNS IN CLOUD

With the provision of economic and flexible services by the advanced technology of cloud computing to users in combination with the multimedia data explosion on the cloud, has resulted in massive data outsourcing of private multimedia data by the owners on the cloud. Meanwhile, the cloud servers have adopted few expensive tasks of computation, yet the multimedia data, which has been outsourced, can reveal confidential information of the data owner due to the loss of control over data by the owner. During recent times, there is conductance of research on the hiding of "privacy-preserving reversible data" over the multimedia data which have been already outsourced. There are suggestions for multimedia data encryption for the preservation of privacy after the outsourcing of data as discussed by Xiong (2018).

The esteem of mobile gadgets in the daily lives of individuals has provoked a series of applications, particularly in the domain of mobile cloud computing. A common practice of any person, while reaching an unknown location is to upload pictures and check-in to that location. Then the next step is to search for a nearby place of residence or shopping. The "Location-based services (LBS)" are utilized for addressing such issues in which the user is sending queries to the LBS server cloud as mentioned by Wang (2017). During the ordering of this information, as per the time's and position's sequences might lead a person to threat in case of data leakage. For instance, it is a general marketing trend to encourage users to check-in and upload pictures while shopping at any brand store and gain discount vouchers, which can be done through several social networking applications, yet the point is that consistency of such check-ins might lead to massive disclosure probabilities of an individual; as it highlights where a person visits frequently, Peng (2017).

The social network integration into "vehicular ad-hoc networks" provide few innovative applications, majorly dedicated to entertainment and safety. For example, while considering an example of any driver receiving a message of warning related to some accident which occurred in some nearby place. Under such instances of emergency (like traffic congestion, fire, natural disaster, and so on), the communication of messages related to safety in vehicular ad-hoc networks can promote messages of early warning to vehicles. The multimedia messages, like video and audio, are effectual during vehicular communication, as they occur to be much illustrative, user-friendly, comprehensive, and descriptive in comparison to a plain text message.

In addition to this, with mobile devices recognition, multimedia messages like photos and videos, retargeting have occurred to be useful practice as mentioned by Ogundoyin (2018). For example, videos relating an accident have the capacity for providing live and precise clues, which could be helpful in making appropriate, accurate, and timely decisions. As per such précised and prompt information, vehicles have the capability for conveniently selecting suitable routes in the direction of safer and efficient driving. Conversely, trustworthy individuals who share similar trips, or neighbourhoods become capable of discussing their common interests. Hence, in the "vehicular ad-hoc networks", it can be priceless to offer, "Tailored access services to guarantee that the right messages can be delivered to the right vehicles", Xia (2017). As any leak of multimedia data can result in spam data that can result in a compromise of data privacy. During the distribution of multimedia data, disputes like a violation of copyright have emerged as a noteworthy challenge due to the illegal redistribution. During recent times, the cloud storage services, the major services of data outsourcing have been becoming much recognized. Yet during the outsourcing of data, there is also outsourcing of data control. Hence, threats associated with leakage of data have been becoming much serious. Zhen et al (2018) said that during the occurrence of any outsourced data leakage, the users are required to restore the provenance of data for the purposes of accountability.

Provided with the fact that the central data centres like cloud storage are not capable of managing massive data in a specified time, it has led to the introduction of a novel paradigm of computing, which is fog computing that has been offering low latency access to massive sets of data. In the environment of fog computing, the concerns associated with privacy in outsourced data occur to be more critical as it has complex innards of the system. Additionally, effective management of resources can be noted as one of the other significant criteria while focusing the pay-per-use application for commercial fog storage. Just like a further step to cloud storage, the majority of the service providers of fog storage opt to utilize techniques like data de-duplication for lessening of resource indulgence as explained by Wang et. al. (2017).

Simultaneously, the data holders may update or remove the data which has been outsourced in the remote storage for cost reduction. The existing literature has proposed the initial privacy conservation de-duplication protocols, which have the capacity of effective management of ownership while implementing fog computing. It attains compact access control through the introduction of the management of user-end keys and updated mechanisms. The "Data-invariant user-level private keys" make the data owners capable of maintaining a consistent amount of keys irrespective of the count of data files that have been outsourced. There is a dramatic reduction in communication overhead if the user-level public keys have been updated for the valid owners of data at the remote storage. The performance and security analysis illustrates the proposed scheme efficiencies in terms of management of keys and communication in the fog storage, Zhang (2018).

AUTHENTICATION SCHEMES

There are several authentication schemes available in the literature. They can be broadly classified as follows:

- What you know
- What you have and
- What you are

The traditional username/password or PIN-based authentication scheme is an example of the *"what you know"* type. Smartcards or electronic tokens are examples of the *"what you have"* type of authentication and finally, biometric-based authentication schemes are examples of the *"what you are"* type of authentication. Some authentication systems may use a combination of the above schemes.

Although traditional alphanumeric passwords are used widely, they have problems such as being hard to remember, vulnerable to guessing, dictionary attack, key-loggers, shoulder surfing, and social engineering as reported by Islam et. al. (2019). In addition to these types of attacks, a user may tend to choose a weak password or record his password. This may further weaken the authentication schemes. As an alternative to the traditional password-based scheme, the biometric system was introduced. This relies upon unique features that remain unchanged during the lifetime of a human, such as fingerprints, iris, etc. The major problem of biometrics as an authentication scheme is the high cost of additional devices needed for the identification process as mentioned by Pierce et al. (2005). The false-positive and false-negative rate may also be high if the devices are not robust. Biometric systems are vulnerable to replay attacks (by the use of sticky residue left by finger on the devices), which reduces the security and usability levels. Thus, recent developments have attempted to overcome biometric shortcomings by introducing token-based authentication schemes.

Token-based systems rely on the use of a physical device such as smartcards or an electronic key for authentication purposes. This may also be used in conjunction with a traditional password-based system. Ying et al. (2005) show that Token-based systems are vulnerable to man-in-the-middle attacks where an intruder intercepts the user's session and records the credentials by acting as a proxy between the user and the authentication device without the knowledge of the user. Thus, as an alternative, graphical-based passwords are introduced to resolve the security and usability limitations mentioned in the above schemes.

Graphical-based password techniques have been proposed as a potential alternative to text-based techniques, supported partially by the fact that humans can remember images better than text as reported by Wells et al. (2006). Psychologists have confirmed that in both recognition and recall scenarios, images are more memorable than text. Therefore, graphical-based authentication schemes have higher usability than other authentication techniques. On the other hand, it is also difficult to break graphical passwords using normal attacks such as dictionary attack, brute force, and spyware which have affected text-based and token-based authentication schemes as discussed by Takada and Hoike (2003). Thus, the security level of graphical-based authentication schemes is higher than other authentication techniques.

In general, graphical password techniques can be classified into two categories: recognition-based and recall-based graphical techniques.

Recognition-Based Systems

In recognition-based systems, a group of images is displayed to the user and an accepted authentication requires a correct image being clicked or touched in a particular order. Some examples of recognition-based systems are the Awase-E system, Pass-faces system, and AuthentiGraph, which are presented by Takada and Hoike (2003), Memon et al. (2007), and Wei-Chi and Maw-Jinn (2005) respectively.

An image password called Awase-E is a system, which enables users to use their favorite image as a "pass-image" instead of a text password for authentication purposes. There are two phases in the Awase-E authentication framework: image registration interface and notification interface. To register an image, a user needs to send the image with a few key clicks by email to the system. Then the user should choose the pass-image from the other images. The notification interface gives users a trigger to handle a threat practically. It notifies users of the occurrence of all kinds of events related to the authentication process. For example, Awase-E sends an email with a URL (Uniform Resource Locater) to the user who has registered a photo. The web page that is linked to that URL contains the photo that a user has just registered. A user can thus confirm the registered photo through a web page.

Even though the Awase-E system has higher usability, it is difficult to implement due to the storage space needed for images and also the system cannot tolerate replay attacks. Adding to this, a user may always tend to choose a well-known (or associated with the user through some relation, as son, wife or a place visited, etc.) image which may be prone to guessing attacks.

Dirik et al. (2007) studied a recognition-based scheme and concluded that users can still remember their graphical password with 90% accuracy even after one or two months. Their study supports the theory that humans remember images better than text. In addition, for example, the commercial system Passfaces uses images of human faces. In fact, working on such a scheme and concluded that a user's password selection is affected by race and gender. This makes the Passfaces's password somewhat predictable.

Although a recognition-based graphical password seems to be easy to remember, which increases usability, it is not completely secure. It needs several rounds of image recognition for authentication to provide a reasonably large password space, which is tedious as said by Wei-Chi and Maw-Jinn (2005). In addition, it is obvious that recognition-based systems are vulnerable to replay attack and mouse tracking because of the use of a fixed image as a password. Thus, we consider these drawbacks in our proposed system, described in the next chapter, which overcomes the problems of recall-based schemes too.

Recall-Based Systems

In recall-based systems, the user is asked to reproduce something that he/she created or selected earlier during the registration phase. Recall-based schemes can be broadly classified into two groups, viz: pure recall-based technique and cued recall-based technique.

In this approach, users need to reproduce their passwords without any help or reminder by the system. The draw-a-secret technique, Grid selection, and Passdoodle are common examples of pure recall-based techniques.

Towhidi et al. (2009) proposed the DAS (Draw-A-Secret) scheme, in which the password is a shape drawn on a two-dimensional grid of size G * G as in Figure 1. Each cell in this grid is represented by distinct rectangular coordinates (x, y). The values of touch grids are stored in the temporal order of the drawing. If exact coordinates are crossed with the same registered sequence, the user is authenticated. As with other pure recall-based techniques, DAS has many drawbacks. Birget and Dawei (2006) conducted a survey that concluded that most users forget their stroke order and can remember text passwords easier than DAS. Also, the password chosen by users is vulnerable to graphical dictionary attacks and replay attacks.

The Grid selection technique was proposed by Thorpe and Van Oorschot as mentioned by Renaud (2009) to enhance the password space of DAS. Their study showed the impact of stroke-count on DAS password space which decreases significantly with fewer strokes for a fixed password length. To improve the DAS security level, they suggested the "Grid Selection" technique, where the selection grid is large at the beginning, A fine-grained grid from which the person selects a drawing grid, a rectangular area to zoom in on, in which they may enter their password, is shown in Figure 2. This technique increases the password space of DAS, which improves the security level at the same time. Actually, this technique only improves the password space of DAS but it still contains the weaknesses and drawbacks of DAS, as mentioned above.

Passdoodle, which is discussed by Birget and Dawei (2006), is a graphical password of a handwritten drawing or text, normally sketched with a stylus over a touch-sensitive screen, as shown in Figure 3. They showed that users were able to recognize a complete doodle password as accurately as text-based passwords. Unfortunately, the Passdoodle scheme has many drawbacks. As mentioned by Renaud (2009) users were fascinated by other users' drawn doodles, and usually entered other users' passwords merely to draw a different doodle from their own. The author concluded that the Passdoodle scheme is vulnerable to several attacks such as guessing, spyware, key-logger, and shoulder surfing.

Figure 1.

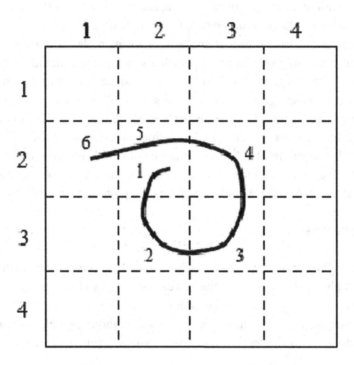

Draw a secret on a 4*4 Grid

Figure 2.

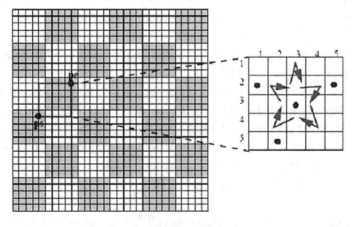

Grid Selection Method

Figure 3.

An example of a Passdoodle

Cued Recall-Based Technique

In this technique, the system gives some hints which help users to reproduce their passwords with high accuracy. These hints will be presented as hot spots (regions) within an image. The user has to choose some of these regions to register as their password and they have to choose the same region following the same order to log into the system. The user must remember the "chosen click spots" and keep them secret. There are many implementations, such as the Blonder algorithm and the PassPoint scheme.

In 1996, the Blonder algorithm designed a method where a pre-determined image is shown to the user on a visual display and the user should "click" on some predefined positions on the image in a particular order to be authenticated as in Figure 4. This method was later modified and presented as Passpoint as shown by Dawei et al. (2006) and Birget at el. (2005).

Figure 4.

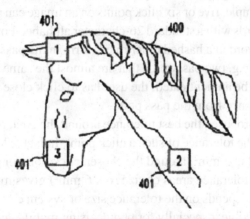

Example of Blonder Scheme

In 2005, the PassPoint scheme was created to be similar to Blonder's scheme while overcoming some of its main limitations. In Passpoint, the image can be an arbitrary photograph or painting with many clickable regions, as shown in Figure 5. This will increase the password space of the Passpoint scheme which, in turn, will increase the security level. Another source of difference is that there is no predefined click area with clear boundaries like the Blonder algorithm. The user's password could contain any chosen sequence of points in the image, which increases the usability level of this scheme.

Figure 5.

Example of a PassPoint System

The Passpoint system has a large password space, which improves the security level compared with other similar systems. For example, five or six click points on an image can produce more passwords than 8-character text-based passwords with a standard 26-character alphabet. For more security, the Passpoint system stores the image password in a hashed (encrypted) form in the password file. Moreover, hashing does not allow approximation e.g. two passwords that are almost the same but not fully identical will be hashed differently. In order to be authenticated, the user has to click close to the selected points, within some measured tolerance distance from the pass point.

Wiedenbeck et al. (2006) proposed the best tolerance around the click point in such an image. To log in, the user should click with the tolerance of such a click point. In fact, a larger password space leads to a smaller tolerance size e.g. (2 to 5 mm^2) around the chosen click point or pixel. For example, an image of size (330 x 260 mm^2) with tolerance areas of size (6 x 6 mm^2) gives more than 590 tolerance areas. It is clear that password space depends on the tolerance size or system choice. This enhancement makes the Passpoint system more flexible, especially for people using mobile devices.

The above-mentioned schemes are used for device-level authentication and application-level authentication. Unfortunately, they suffer from different problems as shown in the next section.

Table 1. Summary of authentication schemes

	Examples	Strength	Weakness
Text-Based	Alphanumeric	Easy to use, Not expansive, Easy to implement	Vulnerable to guessing and attacks such as dictionary attack, shoulder surfing, reply attacks, social engineering, and others
Token-Based	Cards, One-time Password token machine	Easy to use, Secured comparing with text-based	Additional cost for a token, Vulnerable to attacks such as Man-in Middle, lost and theft, and shoulder surfing.
Biometric-Based	Fingerprint, Voice, Facial, and Iris Recognition	Simple and easy, No need to memorize the password	Expensive to implement, Vulnerable to man-in-middle, reply attack, and internal recording attacks
Graphical-Based	Awase-E, AuthentiGraph, Passdoodle, Draw a secret	Easy to use and to remember.	Vulnerable to replay attack and shoulder surfing, Need additional hardware
Image-Based	Blonder, Passfaces, Passpoint	Easy to remember, more secure than other schemes.	Vulnerable to shoulder surfing and replay attacks

PROBLEMS WITH AUTHENTICATION SCHEMES

Traditional alphanumeric passwords are always vulnerable to guessing and dictionary attacks. There may even be a rogue program that may record the keystrokes and publish it on a remote website. In order to overcome key logger-based attacks, newer systems may show a graphical keyboard and the user has to press the correct password using "mouse clicks". This may also be defeated if the attacker uses a screen capture mechanism, rather than using a key logger. Since new video-codecs provide a higher compression ratio, an attacker may use a screen capture program and record a short video clip and send it to a remote server for publishing. So, as an alternative, a token-based authentication method may be used, either as a stand-alone authentication or used in addition to the traditional alphanumeric password. But this technology is not pervasive. The user may have to carry a trusted token card reader. With unknown token readers, a user may not be aware of whether they are using a trusted legitimate reader or using an un-trusted one that may clone the token (similar to the recent ATM card scam).

Although the image-based authentication systems reviewed above address most of the threats, still they suffer from the following attacks: replay, shoulder surfing, and recording the screen.

One may argue that a replay attack can be prevented using encryption and tamper-proof time stamps, and physical shoulder surfing may be known to the user as this process is invasive. However, due to the availability of high-bandwidth mobile devices and light-weight, high-efficient video codec, a rogue program may be able to capture the password and publish it remotely. Since all the image-based password schemes known to us use static passwords, a recorded movie may be replayed and with some human interaction, and the user's password may be decoded. In addition, using a fixed image or a static password is vulnerable to internal software recording e.g. Trojan horse software which could be controlled by remote hackers. A Trojan often acts as an undetectable backdoor, contacting a controller which can then have unauthorized access to the affected device. Thus, encryption and tamper-proof time stamps are not enough to prevent such a user from replay attacks and shoulder surfing. Table 1 summarizes the strengths and weaknesses of the authentication scheme.

ANONYMOUS AUTHENTICATION

The concept of anonymous authentication and privacy of location are divisible into three major categories.

Encrypting IMSI

The capturing of IMSI (International Mobile Subscriber Identity) has been addressed as a challenge of privacy in the authentication protocols of LTE (Long-Term Evolution) Networks. Hence, there exists a proposal of the self-certified scheme which is known as "SP-AKA" which is based on the cryptography of public keys for encryption of IMSI during the course of transmission. Yet connection amongst two transmitted identities is to date concern of privacy. Sanaa et al (2017), while studying the heterogeneous networks considered the anonymity and privacy of the location of a mobile node. They believed that the preservation of location privacy of some mobile node was a challenge that faced the trusted roaming through a heterogeneous network. Consequently, the authors proposed update schemes of "anonymous home building" for "mobileIPv6 wireless networking". The scheme comprised of achievement of mutual authenticity along with the sharing of symmetric keys amongst two anonymous networks. It was also unleashed in the existing literature that 4G networks accompany numerous challenges like multi-homing, location privacy, and mobility. Hence there was the introduction of a proxy protocol for modification, which was IPv6 protocol. In this scheme, virtual identities were utilized for the achievement of location privacy. Yet, these proxy protocols permitted home entities to entrust privileges to other entities to enter on behalf of them. Consequently, there is to date the existence of impersonating attack as discussed by Jabr (2017).

Dynamic Identity-Based Privacy

An Internet connection and AP (Access Points) were considered as non-trustworthy entities as states by Hamandi (2013). Thus, active and passive attackers might circulate via such through those non-trusted internet connections and APs for violating the user equipment's privacy. For the preserving of privacy of any user equipment, there is allocation of some dynamic identity rather than utilization of the conventional IMSI for the creation of pseudonyms "W-AKA". The "Home subscriber Server (HSS)" entities must have periodically or initially met during every procedure of authentication in this scheme, which causes massive overhead on the network. In addition to this scheme achieving further confidentiality, there is no achievement of backward confidentiality due to the upcoming pseudonyms being generated by the help of the prior ones. Also, there must be a transmission of IMSI in clear text during the procedure of registration, which results in building a link with the IMSI.

Likewise, an enhanced privacy method known as mutual-authentication, namely cryptography, has been proposed by Gier M. Koien. (2013), as he considered the user equipment privacy might getting violated through the tracing attack, as such attacks might like temporary identities sequence of any user equipment. Hence, the literature has provided with authors utilizing encryption of public keys by using dummy IMSI for the construction of temporary un-linkable identities withstanding the tracing attack.

Yet, the scheme uplifts the number of messages that are needed for the performance of authentication leading to the consumption of a noteworthy bandwidth of the network, Zaher (2013).

Pseudonyms-Based Privacy

Pseudonyms in the scheme of authentication (HSK-AKA) for the achievement of IMSI were proposed by Hamandi et. al. (2013), the scheme consumes the network bandwidth, given that the proposed scheme of authentication must reach the HSS. In addition to this, the entities of network, which are mobility and management entities and the user equipment, do not have the capability for checking the pseudonyms' accuracy. Hence, the malicious attacker remains a problem. The user equipment's permanent ID proposes a scheme of pseudonym-based authentication for the preservation of the IMSI privacy. On the other hand, the anticipated scheme of authentication must reach the HSS, which needs the consumption of more bandwidth. In addition to this, the proposed scheme depended on a novel function's set, which might be or might not be appropriate for the LTE network infrastructure. Also, a pseudonym for the preservation of the IMSI privacy in the LTE authentication scheme was utilized by Parne et al. (2019). The traceable attack remains a challenge provided that attackers have the capability to associate amongst two permanent pseudonyms as proved by Haddad (2017).

Above authentication, schemes are vulnerable to many threats such as:

- shoulder surfing
- replay attacks (internal or external recording)

In the next section, researchers propose an authentication scheme that is immune to the above-mentioned threats. The proposed authentication scheme, which we call the Implicit Password Authentication System (IPAS), belongs to the graphical-based techniques. IPAS is lightweight, easy to remember, and hard to break by common attack methods. Also, IPAS is suitable for mobile and non-mobile devices in a friendly and flexible manner.

IMPLICIT PASSWORD AUTHENTICATION SYSTEM (IPAS)

Authentication is the first line of defence against compromising confidentiality and integrity. Though traditional login/password-based schemes are easy to implement, they have been subjected to several attacks. As an alternative, the token- and biometric-based authentication systems were introduced. However, they have not improved substantially enough to justify the investment. Thus, a variation to the login/password scheme, viz. a graphical scheme was introduced, but it also suffered due to shoulder surfing and screen dump attacks. In this section, researchers introduce a framework called the Implicit Password Authentication System (IPAS) initiated by Almuairfi et al. (2011), which is immune to the common attacks suffered by other authentication schemes.

Overview

IPAS is similar to a graphical scheme with some fine differences. In every "what you know to type" authentication scheme of which we are aware, the server requests the user to reproduce the fact given to the server at the time of registration. This is also true in graphical passwords such as PassPoint. In IPAS, we consider the password as a piece of information known to the server at the time of registration and at the time of authentication, the user gives this information in an implicit form that can be understood only by the server. IPAS may also be implemented in any client-server environment, where we need to authenticate a human as a client (IPAS will not work in machine-to-machine authentication). The authors also assume that the server has enough hardware resources, such as RAM and CPU. This is not unrealistic as high-end servers are becoming cheaper day by day.

IPAS Implementation

The authentication system usually has both a client and server component. Each component facilitates the implementation of a standard interface function and an initialization function that registers the module with the system. In fact, the client-server model is a more scalable approach to client authentication than other models. Thus, the design model of IPAS is a client-server model where both ends must be trusted. Any client is authenticated when connected to the server (cloud) and trusted afterward. The authenticated user actions are checked against a specific access control policy that controls allowed or denied access.

IPAS Design Stage

A client device could be any portable device, such as a laptop or mobile phone. Mobile phones have become increasingly important in our daily lives. One main reason for this is that an increasing number of functions have been integrated within mobile phones, such as Internet browsing, mobile banking, and shopping. Some of the latest smartphones are similar in performance to the high-end desktop PCs of a decade ago. People are now paying much more attention to their mobile phones than they did before, which makes mobile phones relatively hard to lose, compared with devices that users do not care very much about, such as USB flash drives. However, having such an advantage in relation to security is not enough to prove that mobile phones are more suitable for online banking authentication than USB drives. Therefore, an in-depth inspection of mobile phones, malware and applications is desirable. IPAS has considered this issue by allowing users to access their accounts on the move, with a high level of security and usability. Our system does not require any high-end specialized software. The presence of a standard web browser with an Internet connection is enough to launch our application. Thus, our system may very well scale from a smartphone to desktop PCs.

On the other side, the server (at cloud) is the other entity of our design model in IPAS. However, we assume that the communication between client and server is secure and trusted through protocols like SSL (Secure Socket Layer) and IPSec against malicious intermediate nodes caching and making offline guesses. This only adds an extra layer of protection. However, the IPAS authentication process may still work without this assumption. The server(s) which is located at the cloud side, should be equipped with appropriate safety measures such as firewalls, intrusion detection systems and rapid recovery mechanisms to guarantee information security. The authentication server, which is one of the most important servers in our design model, should contain an Intelligent Graphical (IG) module to covert user information/answers into an image. This image, which implicitly represents the user's password, will be pushed to the client's device during the authentication process. The user will be authenticated only if he/she clicks on the right objects in the image that match the stored information. Moreover, a trusted link between the authentication server and the main image database server should take place for access control purposes of such an authentication level.

IPAS Development Model

In this stage, researchers provide the system requirements which are needed to reform IPAS. Client-server interactions start by defining the needs of each party. Therefore, we need to define the properties of the system which may be used by any organization or in any payment environment.

Image Database

The image database at the server-side is the heart of our authentication scheme. Depending upon the number of users, the image database may contain tens of thousands to millions of images. The system administrator and/or the user may add more images on a regular basis. Each image may have more than one "clickable" object. With each clickable-object, one or more text keywords are associated with it. Some objects within the image will be used as a decoy object to increase the security level of IPAS. The relation between the image objects and associated texts play a significant role in our authentication scheme, which is described later in this chapter.

Registration Phase

In this phase, the user's initial information will be collected to enable him/her to use the system. At the time of registration (either online or offline), a set of different topics is provided to the user, for example, *childhood memories, current hobbies, dream holidays,* etc. The user may have to choose *m* out of *n* topics (where *m* and *n* are the system parameters decided by the domain people).

For each chosen topic, the user has to provide a story with sufficient information (again, this is application and domain-dependent). If there is insufficient information, the system will prompt the user again to input more information. The stories provided by the user create a personalized information space for the user (similar to a static password).

Now authors demonstrate this feature through an example. Here, the user describes his/her childhood experience.

"When I think about it, I had a real good childhood. Believed in the things some kids are supposed to believe in like Santa Clause and the tooth fairy which made it exciting. Always had a good Christmas with toys laid out like Santa had been there and when I lost a tooth, when I put it under my pillow, I would get money for it. I enjoyed playing childhood games, playing with my cousin and the other kids. I was crazy about Barbie dolls and had a lot of them and Barbie houses. I had a bike and a scooter. I had the love and care of my family and knew it. I loved jumping on our trampoline and playing outside. Well, life was great back then when I was a kid! I could look any way I wanted to and had no real worries. I didn't have it hard; I had it good and easy. I hate ghosts and scary stories. I was always afraid of dark places and being alone."

Based on the given story, the system will extract keywords and information from every possible sentence or the system manager may extract the keywords from the given story. The following are the possible keywords and information:

- Santa
- Tooth fairy
- Jumping on *trampoline*
- hate *ghosts* and *scary* stories
- Afraid of *dark places* and *being alone.*
- Crazy about *Barbie dolls.* Had *Barbie houses.*
- Love to *play* with cousin and friends.

Based on this information, the system may either create or link with the existing image database. The keywords and the information will be embedded in an image and implicitly presented to the user during the authentication process. The user has to click the right object to represent his/her answer. It has been shown that this information is easy to remember than complex passwords.

Segmentation Phase

In this phase, the system works on creating a visualized image of a user's logged answers (keywords) which lead to an interface behavior. The tool used in visualization is geared towards improving the system design so that the technique realized within the system development is perfectly segmented.

As reported by Merch and White (2003), the image relationships functions are categorized into three sets: (A) functions expressing a far/distant relation to the text; (B) functions expressing a close relation to the text; and (C) functions going beyond the text. Applying these sets identifies the level of implicitly for each image. The semantic variants of this concept can be developed quickly and with little effort by the system developer. It is true, therefore, to state that implementing a new segment of technology will take specialized skills, time as well as many resources that many organizations do need to take into consideration.

The Authentication Phase

First, a user may request access to the system by presenting his user name and the level of access required. This may be sent as a plain text. Depending on the level of access required, the system might request k out of m areas chosen by the user during the registration process. For each chosen area, the server may pick a random keyword extracted from the user's story. For each keyword, the server may again pick a random image from the image database that contains an object which has the chosen text attribute.

Similar to Kerberos, a session key $S(Q_i)$ is derived from the correct clickable area through a function $f(I)$. The server will choose a random number p and then encrypt p with the session key $S(Q_i)$ and transmit (Image, $S(Q_i)[p]$, $f(I)$) to the mobile device. The client application then displays the image. Using the stylus or a mouse, the user needs to choose the correct "clickable area". Then, based on the function $f(I)$, the image I and the area the user clicked, the client will generate a key K. The function $f(I)$ is chosen in such a way that $S(Q_i) = K$ if and only if the user and the server have exactly the same area of interest in the image. The user then decrypts $S(Q_i)[p]$ to obtain the random number. He then transmits $p+1$ to the server for authentication and to the next level. In this way, the user is authenticated implicitly and no confidential information is exchanged over the network. When the server is executing the last question in the authentication process, instead of encrypting a pseudo random number, it will pick a session key and encrypt it with the derived key. When the client decrypts it, he receives an implicit message from the server to use this session key for transmission. This procedure not only authenticates a user implicitly, but also exchange a session key implicitly.

Figure 6 illustrates the IPAS Client/Server authentication process steps for registered users which are as follows:

1. The user sends an authentication (*Login*) request to the IPAS server using his/her mobile phone device or computer.
2. The server checks the user's registration status. If the user is not registered, then the authentication process fails (END); however, for registered users, it proceeds to the next step.
3. The system checks the user's access level according to the user's pre-set IPAS domains and the implicit level of an object in the image (in the case of a payment process, access control will check the payment amount in order to make a decision).
4. The IPAS authentication image is created and sent to the user according to the output of Step 3.
5. The user receives a response from the server with the IPAS image. If the user clicks an incorrect object to represent his/her password, then he/she needs to resend the authentication request (i.e. return Step 1). However, if the user clicks on the correct object in the IPAS image, the user will be authenticated (Login).

Figure 6.

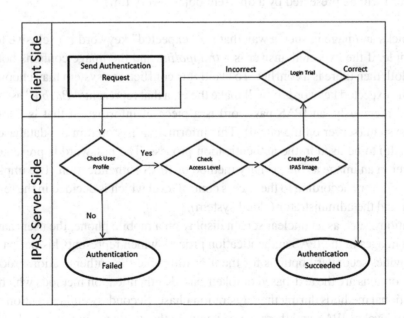

In this section, we presented the high-level flow chart of the IPAS authentication process between the user (client) and server (cloud). The above steps show the interaction architecture between client and server for authentication purposes. Our future directions will be focused on designing a detailed software architecture/prototype using UML (Unified Modeling Language) which will include software engineering and mathematical models. We consider IPAS to be a complex project with many stages; therefore, more scientific models and system processes will be left for future design, development, and implementation. In addition, a more analytical model of IPAS and its domains' performance indicators will be covered in later stages. Rapid developments in communication/network media and mobile device capabilities will help us to form future work of the remaining stages of IPAS.

Database and Image Characteristics

A user profile that contains personal information, account data, access control levels, and authentication questions and answers will be linked to the intelligent image server. Each authentication image may contain one or more "clickable objects" that represent the user's keyword(s) or information. For example, a "trampoline" represents one of the keywords which the user says she loves to jump on. For some other user, it represents a game he/she *hates* most; it may represent a *black color*; it may represent *gymnastics,* etc. Thus, an image may have the following characteristics:

- An image may contain one or more objects
- Each clickable area may have different keywords associated with it.
- Each object represents one answer at a time implicitly
- An object is clickable once
- There may some decoy objects within the image to increase the security level.
- Each keyword will be presented by a different object every time

The system picks an image in such a way that the "expected" keyword is exclusive to the presented image. For example, if the expected answer is a *trampoline* and the image contains both a trampoline and a "*Barbie*" doll, then there is a conflict. To avoid this conflict, the system may choose an image that has only one of the expected keywords or will make the area that represents "*Barbie*" as "non-clickable".

As mentioned previously, an IPAS password is a piece of information that is known by the user (client) and the system (server on the cloud). This information is stored in the database server (linked to the user's profile) to be used in the authentication process. The password is presented implicitly to the legitimate user in an image as the primary method of IPAS authentication. The implicit level of the presented object will vary according to the access control level which is decided in the registration phase between the user and the administrator (cloud system).

In some situations, such as an unclear screen display on a mobile phone, the user may have difficulties dealing with images in the IPAS authentication process which represents his/her password. In such a case, IPAS provides secondary options for the user to enable the authentication process to proceed. These secondary options are the text-based or token-based authentication methods which will be chosen by the user as optional methods during the registration phase. Secondary authentication options will not affect the security level of IPAS and there is no change in the user's anonymity level.

Figure 7.

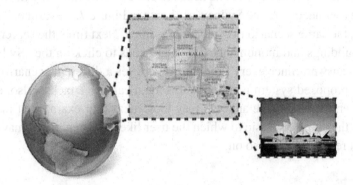

If the user has any difficulties dealing with the IPAS primary authentication image, he/she can switch to the text-based method. In this scenario, the user will type the password using the device's keypad instead of clicking on the object of the image. In the case of a failed password trial, the user can ask for another trial which involves another authentication request. The user types the password in an encrypted explicit form which represents the implicit object in the IPAS image. The next password is different from the previous password which eliminates any chance of the password being copied or recorded due to a replay attack or shoulder surfing hackers. Therefore, the security level will not be affected when the user switches to an IPAS secondary option.

In the token-based secondary option method, especially for a password in numeric form, the user can switch from the IPAS primary method to the secondary method, if needed. This scenario will not affect the IPAS security level and it is immune to any external or internal attacks. The user can use an OTP (One Time Password) token which represents his/her password in the IPAS authentication process. This password is changed every time which minimizes the chance of the password being copied or recorded. Nowadays, OTP soft tokens are available as an application for mobile phones which helps to eliminate the extra cost of hardware traditional tokens. Therefore, IPAS secondary authentication options are secure and immune to external and internal attacks. In addition, the secondary options show the dynamic characteristics of IPAS as a flexible and user-friendly authentication system.

As a result, the user can request another image in case he/she cannot identify the current image or switch to a text/token-based method at any time. Thus, IPAS provides a flexible authentication environment which increases the user-friendly aspect of the scheme and offers a high level of security as explained above.

Example Scenario of IPAS

For each keyword (password), the server may create an intelligent authentication space using images, where the answers to the particular keyword(s) for various users are implicitly embedded into the images. At the time of authentication, the server may randomly pick one or more keywords selected by the users at the time of registration (the number of keywords depends on the level of service requested). For each chosen keyword, the server may choose an image randomly from the authentication space and present it to the user as a challenge. Using the stylus or the mouse, the user needs to navigate the image and click the right answer. For example, the server may present the user with a picture of the globe. If Sydney is the city the user loves to visit or has visited, he needs to click on Australia. It will then enlarge Australia. Then on the map, the user needs to click Sydney, as shown in Figure 7. Next time, if the same keyword is chosen by the server, the same scenario may not be presented. Next time, the server may show an image containing famous buildings and monuments. The user needs to click on the "Sydney Opera house" to implicitly convey his answer. Since every time the server uses a different scenario and the answers are given implicitly, our proposed system is immune to screen capture attacks. Also, except for the server and the legitimate user, for others, the answers may look fuzzy. For example, if the user clicks "Opera house", it may mean the "type of music to which the user likes to listen", or it may represent his "place of birth", or "current residency" and so on.

IPAS Components

Most of the current schemes used to authenticate a user operate within a static process, such as a password or token, however, the flexibility of IPAS gives the user space and choices for the authentication process, depending on the access level needed for such an operation. Thus, the user can switch from an image-based to a text-based method at any time, using the same information, as explained in the next sub-section.

Intelligent Image-Based Authentication Option

Image-based authentication is the main component of IPAS where the user's answers are represented implicitly in an image during the authentication process. The system will choose the implicit level of the image depending on the requested access level as previously described in the segmentation phase. Therefore, the user needs to click on the correct objects within the image which represent his/her answers in order to be authenticated. Then, the access control module will allow the user to perform the required operations and actions.

Due to the dynamic and high flexibility of IPAS, the user can switch to a text-based method any time in case he/she successfully navigate an image-based method. Also, the user can ask for another image in case he/she faces difficulties with the current image.

Intelligent Text-Based Authentication Option

In the text-based method, the user will be allowed to type his/her answers using the keyboard. These answers (keywords) will represent the implicit objects in the given image. For example, the user can type "*apple*" or "*pillow*" if the image contains an implicit object of an apple or pillow. The user will be authenticated only if he/she types the correct answers to the given implicit image's objects. Then, the access control module will control the required actions.

Similar to the text-based method, the user can switch to a token-based "something you have" type of password, especially a numeric password. Therefore, if the user cannot respond correctly to an image-based method for some reason, he/she can switch to a token-based method at any time. For example, a one-time password (OTP) token, which is provided by certain banks, could be used for a numerical password in cases where the user cannot determine the numbers in an implicit image-based method.

For authentication purposes, it is desirable to rely on information the user already knows, rather than requiring him/her to memorize further information. In general, the system or registrar that collects user information should be aware of user privacy principles. Thus, the privacy, security, and usability of IPAS are major concerns.

IPAS Domains

IPAS provides another service which allows the system to be used in any client-server environment. IPAS's domain service makes IPAS flexible enough and suitable for any organization, regardless of location or size. The registered users can be categorized in relation to their interaction behaviour: Region/State domain and word space/distance domain.

Various kinds of users in a system can, at times, have a different perspective on their needs. For instance, the perception of someone who is in America may not be the same as someone who is in Australia. Therefore, the system will consider the area/region to which the user belongs during the creation of the user's password and link his/her information to the region domain. As a result, the objects in an authentication image will be related to the user's region. For example, if the keyword or the information is *Opera*, then users from Australia may easily recognize *Sydney Opera House,* whereas users from Europe may more easily recognize the *London Coliseum Theatre* than the *Sydney Opera house* (some may not even recognize it at all). Thus, the system under this domain will be country/region-dependent which should be considered during the production roll-out module.

Secondly, the space/distance domain will rely on the taxonomy of relationships between images and words that can be used for analyzing the way that images and text interact. Merch and White (2003) stated that the taxonomy identifies 49 functions that an image performs in relation to the relevant text. For example, let the chosen keyword be an *apple*. An image that contains an *apple pie* will represent a closer relation to the word *apple*, while an image that contains *Steve Jobs* will represent a more distant relation to the word *apple*. Therefore, the word space/distance domain can apply some of these functions, according to the required security level.

The aforementioned domains are critical components of IPAS because they improve their usability and security. The region domain, where the user is linked to his/her area, improves its usability and the user-friendly criteria of IPAS, while the distance domain, where the user chooses the implicit level between the keyword and image, enhances the security and anonymity levels of IPAS, as discussed below.

Criteria for IPAS Evaluation

As an aid to both the design and evaluation of IPAS, anonymity, security, and usability criteria are considered.

- **Anonymity:** In environments that use personal information, it should be common practice to follow recognized privacy principles. For example, collected personal user information should be used only for the authentication process. In addition, an answer to such a question should allow the user to access a particular level of his or her account.
- **Security:** Generally, the security of IPAS is concerned with protecting the user's account information and financial records. On the other hand, a comparison of IPAS with other authentication schemes, in the case of password space, shows the strength of IPAS in relation to the security criteria. Also, the difficulty of formal attacks breaking IPAS improves its security level over other schemes.

- **Usability:** IPAS usability is concerned with providing a user-friendly experience at the stage of answering a personal question that is picked from the user's previously given memorable stories. In fact, using information as a password could be an easy way for the user to remember his/her password during the authentication process. Moreover, IPAS is not used as a replacement of regular authentication in some cases, but rather, as an add-on factor. Thus, the user is allowed to switch back at any time to the normal authentication process, such as using a regular user name and password.

Strength and Limitations of IPAS

As can be easily seen, IPAS is immune to shoulder surfing and screen dump attacks. Also, the authentication information is presented to the user in an implicit form that can be understood and decoded only by the legitimate end-user. No password information is exchanged between the client and the server in IPAS. Since the authentication information is conveyed implicitly, IPAS can tolerate shoulder surfing and screen dump attack, neither of which the existing schemes can tolerate. The strength of IPAS lies in creating a good authentication space with a sufficiently large collection of images to avoid short repeating cycles. Compared to other methods reviewed in our study, IPAS may require human interaction and the careful selection of images and "clickable" regions. Traditional password-based authentication schemes and PassPoint are special cases of IPAS. The strength of IPAS depends greatly on how effectively the authentication information is embedded implicitly in an image and it should be easy to decrypt for a legitimate user and highly-fuzzy for a non-legitimate user.

In addition, IPAS provides an acceptable level of properties as below:

- **Correctness**: The results of each individual instance of authentication carried out should be correct. Only the legitimate user can easily proceed through the authentication steps to gain the correct access to the system.
- **User Anonymity and Privacy**: Completing the authentication process in IPAS is possible without the user's real identity being revealed or known by hackers.
- **Speed**: The IPAS authentication process is fast and flexible and can be implemented in any client-server environment and is suitable for mobile phones.
- **Attack Resistance**: IPAS provides strong resistance to common attacks such as replay attack, external discloser, guessing, communication eavesdropping, and host compromise.
- **Inexpensive**: Unlike the token-based authentication technique, IPAS does not need any additional device to be used for authentication purposes.
- **Universal**: Users in IPAS will use the same method of authentication in all services and everywhere, depending on their properties, by applying IPAS domains.

Resisting Attacks

IPAS is resistant to attacks such as brute force attacks, shoulder surfing attacks, dictionary attacks, and replay attacks.

- **Brute Force Attacks**: IPAS is protected against brute force attacks by having a large password space as it consists of text-based passwords or graphical-based passwords.

- **Dictionary Attacks**: It is very difficult to carry out a dictionary attack against IPAS as it contains a high degree of randomization.
- **Shoulder Surfing Attacks**: Shoulder surfing is basically watching over the shoulders of users to see or record their password with the help of a camera when a user is entering their password. IPAS is immune to this kind of attack by providing a new implicit object as a password at each time of authentication.
- **Replay Attacks**: Keylogging or key spyware cannot be used to break the IPAS scheme and mouse tracking software also cannot hack IPAS, as it is fully protected against them.

IPAS Limitations

Like any system, IPAS has certain limitations due to various components, such as network, human, and system hardware issues. The most common complexities which may be considered as a hindrance in the IPAS process and may influence system performance are:

- limited or short coverage of network and wireless communication in some locations where the user (client) cannot communicate with the server or service provider, especially in the payment authentication process.
- limited storage, a screen display or processing capabilities of the client's mobile device which may cause a delay in dealing with the IPAS image.
- frequent logins by users may result in an IPAS image being repeated on a particular level, for example, using IPAS to log in to a mobile phone with a one-minute auto-lock when the user logs in more than 30 times in one hour. This scenario requires many images to represent the user's password which may cause an overload on the server-side.
- some argue that even implicit objects can be guessed.

Researchers tried to minimize the above limitations by applying different solutions, which may help to stabilize the use of IPAS. The first solution is to provide optional secondary methods for users to switch to either text-based or token-based methods when they face difficulties dealing with the IPAS primary authentication method. The second solution depends on the IPAS domains, which help users to choose the implicit level of their objects within the IPAS image, as explained in the previous section. Finally, to avoid an image being repeated, the user can update his/her profile with real-time personal images (taken with his own camera) and change the keywords, which represent his/her password, from time to time. As we aim to introduce an authentication scheme that is immune to common attacks such as replay attacks (internal and external) and/or shoulder surfing, the above-mentioned solutions help to minimize the side effects of, but not remove, the above mentioned IPAS limitations.

SUMMARY

In this chapter, the authors presented IPAS and its applications, which solve the security drawbacks of other authentication schemes and provide an acceptable balance between security and anonymity for multimedia data in a cloud environment.

On the authentication side, IPAS has many features as follows:

- Immune to replay attacks and shoulder surfing, which are considered main problems in other authentication systems and graphical-based password authentication systems such as PassPoint by providing a new image at every time of authentication in an implicit form.
- Flexible compared with other graphical-based authentication techniques where the user can switch to a text-based password if they experience difficulties in dealing with the image by applying the intelligent text-based authentication option.
- Domains of IPAS provide different levels of security according to the user's needs.
- Can be implemented in mobile and non-mobile devices. In general, IPAS is a client-server authentication which works on personal computers and mobile phones.
- IPAS will improve the security level of Multimedia data in the cloud.
- IPAS is a fast and flexible authentication scheme for mobile users.
- The computation cost of the proposed scheme is acceptable and adjusts to different security levels.

CONCLUSION

Cloud computing technology provides cost-saving and flexibility of services for users. With the explosion of multimedia data, more and more data owners would outsource their personal multimedia data on the cloud. Privacy preserving is a hot topic in cloud computing in recent years. Once users' data are a leak, the negative impact can be huge. Therefore, the development of privacy-preserving technology is the key factor for cloud computing. IPAS can provide the first layer of protection and easy access for user's Multimedia data on the cloud environment. It is quite desirable and helpful in some sensitive applications such as mobile banking, multimedia data and online purchasing.

REFERENCES

Almuairfi, S., Veeraraghavan, P., & Chilamkurti, N. (2011). IPAS: Implicit Password Authentication System. *Proceedings 2011 IEEE Workshops of International Conference Advanced Information Networking and Applications (WAINA),* pp. 430-435, March 22-25, 2011 doi: 10.1109/WAINA.2011.36

Dirik, A. E., Memon, N., & Birget, J. C. (2007, July). Modeling user choice in the PassPoints graphical password scheme. *Proceedings of the 3rd symposium on Usable privacy and security* (pp. 20-28). Pittsburgh, PA: ACM.

Yang, Z., Huang, Y., Li, X., Wang, W., Wu, F., Zhang, X., ... & Li, W. (2018). Efficient, secure data provenance scheme in multimedia outsourcing and sharing. *Computers, Materials, & Continua, 56*(1), 1–17.

Geir, M. K. (2013, October). Privacy enhanced mutual authentication in LTE. *Proceedings 2013 IEEE 9th International Conference on Wireless and Mobile Computing, Networking and Communications (WiMob)* (pp. 614-621). IEEE.

Birget, J. C., Hong, D., & Memon, N. (2006). Graphical passwords based on robust discretization, *Information Forensics and Security. IEEE Transactions, 1*(3), 395–399.

Haddad, Z. J., Taha, S., & Saroit, I. A. (2017). Anonymous authentication and location privacy, preserving schemes for LTE-A networks. *Egyptian Informatics Journal, 18*(3), 193–203. doi:10.1016/j.eij.2017.01.002

Hamandi, K., Sarji, I., Chehab, A., Elhajj, I. H., & Kayssi, A. (2013, March). Privacy enhanced and computationally efficient HSK-AKA LTE scheme. *Proceedings 2013 27th International Conference on Advanced Information Networking and Applications Workshops.* (pp. 929-934). IEEE.

Wang, C., Zheng, W., Ji, S., Liu, Q., & Wang, A. (2018). Identity-based fast authentication scheme for smart mobile devices in body area networks. *Wireless Communications and Mobile Computing,* 2018.

Islam, A., Por, L. Y., Othman, F., & Ku, C. S. (2019). A Review on Recognition-Based Graphical Password Techniques. Proceedings *Computational Science and Technology* (pp. 503–512). Singapore: Springer. doi:10.1007/978-981-13-2622-6_49

Lashkari, A. H., Saleh, R., Towhidi, F., & Farmand, S. (2009, December). A complete comparison on pure and cued recall-based graphical user authentication algorithms. *Proceedings 2009 Second International Conference on Computer and Electrical Engineering* (Vol. 1, pp. 527-532). IEEE.

Masrom, M., Towhidi, F., & Lashkari, A. H. (2009, October). Pure and cued recall-based graphical user authentication. *Proceedings 2009 International Conference on Application of Information and Communication Technologies* (pp. 1-6). IEEE.

Merch, E. E., & White, M. D. (2003). A taxonomy of relationships between images and text. *The Journal of Documentation, 59*(6), 647–672. doi:10.1108/00220410310506303

(2018). Ogundoyin, Sunday Oyinlola. (2018). An autonomous lightweight conditional privacy-preserving authentication scheme with provable security for vehicular ad-hoc networks. *International Journal of Computers and Applications,* 1–16.

Parne, B. L., Gupta, S., & Chaudhari, N. S. (2019). PSE-AKA: Performance and security enhanced authentication key agreement protocol for IoT enabled LTE/LTE-A networks. *Peer-to-Peer Networking and Applications, 12*(5), 1156–1177. doi:10.100712083-019-00785-5

Peng, T., Liu, Q., Meng, D., & Wang, G. (2017). Collaborative trajectory privacy preserving scheme in location-based services. *Information Sciences, 387,* 165–179. doi:10.1016/j.ins.2016.08.010

Pierce, J. D., Wells, J. G., Warren, M. J., & Mackay, D. R. (2005). A Conceptual Model for Graphical Authentication. Paper presented in First Australian Information Security Management Conference. Perth, Australia, Sep. paper 16.

Renaud, K. (2009). On user involvement in production of images used in visual authentication. *Journal of Visual Languages and Computing, 20*(1), 1–15. doi:10.1016/j.jvlc.2008.04.001

Suo, X., Zhu, Y., & Owen, G. S. (2005, December). Graphical passwords: A survey. In 21st Annual Computer Security Applications Conference (ACSAC'05) (pp. 10-pp). IEEE.

Takada, T., & Koike, H. (2003). *Awase-E: Image-Based Authentication for Mobile Phones Using User's Favourite Images. Human-Computer Interaction with Mobile Devices and Services* (Vol. 2795, pp. 347–351). Berlin, Germany: Springer. doi:10.1007/978-3-540-45233-1_26

Wang, T., Zeng, J., Bhuiyan, M. Z. A., Tian, H., Cai, Y., Chen, Y., & Zhong, B. (2017). Trajectory privacy preservation based on a fog structure for cloud location services. *IEEE Access: Practical Innovations, Open Solutions*, *5*, 7692–7701. doi:10.1109/ACCESS.2017.2698078

Wei-Chi, K., & Maw-Jinn, T. (2005). A Remote User Authentication Scheme Using Strong Graphical Passwords. *Local Computer Networks, 30th Anniversary*.

Wells, J., Hutchinson, D., & Pierce, J. (2006). Enhanced Security for Preventing Man-in-the-Middle Attacks in Authentication, Data Entry and Transaction Verification. *Proceedings of the 6th Australian Information Security Conference*. [Online]. Edith Cowan University, Perth, Australia.

Wiedenbeck, S., Waters, J., Birget, J. C., Brodskiy, A., & Memon, N. (2005). PassPoints: Design and longitudinal evaluation of a graphical password system. [Special Issue on HCI Research in Privacy and Security]. *International Journal of Human-Computer Studies*, *63*(1-2), 102–127. doi:10.1016/j.ijhcs.2005.04.010

Wiedenbeck, S., Waters, J., Birget, J. C., Brodskiy, A., & Memon, N. (2006). Authentication using graphical passwords: Effects of tolerance and image choice. *Symposium on Usable Privacy and Security (SOUPS)*, Carnegie-Mellon University, USA.

Xia, Y., Chen, W., Liu, X., Zhang, L., Li, X., & Xiang, Y. (2017). Adaptive multimedia data forwarding for privacy preservation in vehicular ad-hoc networks. *IEEE Transactions on Intelligent Transportation Systems*, *18*(10), 2629–2641. doi:10.1109/TITS.2017.2653103

Xiong, L., & Shi, Y. (2018). On the privacy-preserving outsourcing scheme of reversible data hiding over encrypted image data in cloud computing. *Computers, Materials, & Continua*, *55*(3), 523–539.

Zhang, J., Sun, J., Zhang, R., Zhang, Y., & Hu, X. (2018, April). Privacy-preserving social media data outsourcing. *Proceedings IEEE INFOCOM 2018-IEEE Conference on Computer Communications* (pp. 1106-1114). IEEE. 10.1109/INFOCOM.2018.8486242

Chapter 4
Robust Multimedia Watermarking:
Characteristics, Applications, and Attacks

Avinash Kaur
Lovely Professional University, Phagwara, India

Parminder Singh
(iD) https://orcid.org/0000-0002-0750-6309
Lovely Professional University, Phagwara, India

Anand Nayyar
(iD) https://orcid.org/0000-0002-9821-6146
Duy Tan University, Da Nang, Vietnam

ABSTRACT

The data transmission on network channel has increased tremendously in the past few decades. Watermarking is a process to add watermark as a digital signal, label, or tag into a cover media. The primary requirements of multimedia watermarking are robustness and embedding capability. The robustness is defined as the strength of an algorithm to repel the noise. However, it is challenging to achieve both at the same time. The numerous characteristics of watermarking are very imperative in the multimedia watermarking system. The researchers are using watermarking schemes in various applications such as military, digital forensics, medical, and so on. Attacks of these watermarking harm or uncover the secret information carried in the watermark. Potential researchers have been presented various techniques for balancing or improving these concerns. This chapter reviews the recent multimedia watermarking techniques on the basis of robustness and embedding capability. The characteristics, applications, and attacks on multimedia watermarking techniques are introduced.

DOI: 10.4018/978-1-7998-2701-6.ch004

INTRODUCTION

During past, data transmission has increased among various channels and networks. As with the developing technologies, there is increase in growth and usage of transmission media. To avoid misuse and establish authenticity, watermarking techniques should be used to secure the multimedia data. The malevolent copying

and illegal dissemination of digital images is averted by digital watermarking by hiding the data ownership in host image (Ganic & Eskicioglu, 2004; Patel, Mehta, & Pradhan, 2011). Watermarking is designed as process of embedding dual/single watermark in terms of label, tag or digital signal. The process of watermark is defined on the basis of different groups and domains (Aslantas, 2008). The methods of watermarking are categorized into transform and spatial domain (Loukhaoukha, Nabti, & Zebbiche, 2014). The initially used methods are the spatial domain a technique in which watermarking embedding is performed by directly making a change in pixel. It exhibits the feature of accessibility for implementation and low computational cost. The important in this area is correlation based, spread spectrum and Least Significant bit (LSB). The potential example of transform domain is discrete Fourier transform (DFT), discrete wavelet transforms (DWT), singular value decomposition (SVD), discrete cosine transforms (DCT). The two different categories of digital watermark in context of visibility is invisible and visible. The classes of invisible watermark are fragile and robust (Aslantas, 2008). The detailed watermark classification is presented further in (Aslantas, 2008; Singh, 2017; Tsai, Huang, Kuo, Horng, 2012).

Watermark Embedding and Extraction Process

The complete process of watermark embedding and extraction is represented in Figure 1. In watermark embedding process, a secret key is generated. The method of watermark recovery is the function of watermarked original data/ watermarked image, test data and key. Similar kind of key is used in further processes as in Figure 2 and in Figure 3.

Figure 1. Detailed watermark extraction process

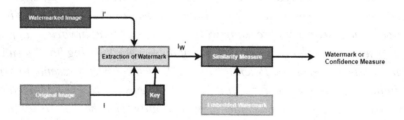

Classification of Watermark Systems

Watermark systems are classified into three different categories (Mathon, Cayre, Bas, & Mac, 2014; Singh, Dave, & Mohan, 2014; Singh, Kumar, Singh, & Mohan, 2017; Tsai, Jhuang, & Lai, 2012)as described below in Figure 3.

Figure 2. Watermark Embedding Process

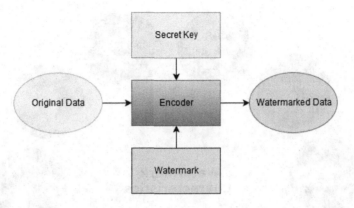

Figure 3. Watermark extraction process

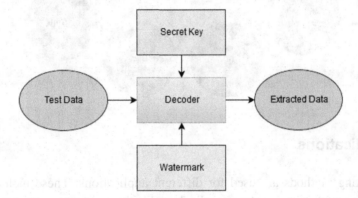

- **Blind Watermarking:** In this technique, the watermark is extracted by using a watermarked image. The applications are electronic voting system, copyright protection, health-care etc.
- **Non-Blind Watermarking:** In this technique, the original image and embedded watermark are copied during the extraction process. The applications are copyright protection and covert communication.
- **Semi-Blind Watermarking:** This technique works on non-blind watermarking system and is deprived of original data requirement for detection. Applications in this technique are CAD models, authentication etc.

Watermark Characteristics

It exhibits number of watermarking characteristics [106] depicted in Figure 4. Robustness is defined as algorithm capability to repel to noise. Security refers to difficulty in altering or removing the watermark without destruction of cover image. Data payload refers to the amount of contained information. The transparency of watermark is resultant of imperceptibility. The authentication framework is main focus area of fragile watermark. The total cost in revealing and enclosing the watermark is defined as computational watermark. The other important features are defined in Singh, Kumar, Singh, & Mohan (2017).

Figure 4. Various characteristics of watermark

Watermark Applications

Different watermarking methods are used for different applications. These include digital forensic, copyright protection, health care, military, medical applications etc. as represented below (Vallabha, 2003; Kumar, Singh, & Kumar, 2018).

1. **Copyright Protection:** The secret information is hided for providing the copyright protection to digital information.
2. **Broadcast monitoring:** It enables the proprietors to verify where, when and amount of time content is broadcast through satellite television and cable.
3. **Fingerprinting:** The source of illegal distribution is traced by this method as it contains the intended recipient's identification information.
4. **Medical Applications:** The method offers the confidentiality and authentication of medical data. It provides value added methods for health-care applications.
5. **Electronic Voting System:** As the evolution in computer network, Internet reached worldwide. It is the method of scheduling the elections by security preference during elections. Due to rapid internet usage in the fields of shopping, banking, secured transactions is an important factor.
6. **Remote Education:** Distance education is the most prevailing among villages. The smart technology needed for the remote education. Watermarking provided the authentication to distance learning data.
7. **Security on Cloud:** As number of increasing images, content based image retrieval is considered. Amount of storage taken by images is more as compared text. So, cloud storage is an example (Xia et al., 2016).

The authentication for sensitive images is to be performed before transferring to another place. So, unique watermark is inserted by cloud server before sending an encrypted image to server. The unauthorized user is outlined when illegal image is found.

Attacks on Watermarking

In the applications of watermarking, the data is treated in a way as it spreads the receiver of watermark (Sherekar, Thakare, & Jain, 2011). In the definition of watermarking, the attack is harming of unhidden secret information in the process of watermarking. Further, data attacked is described by watermarked data processed. The attacks are classified as:

1. **Active Attacks:** In this type of attack, the watermark is removed by the hacker and it is made undetectable. The main aim is to distort the embedded watermark so that it may not be recognized. Examples are copy control, finger printing, copyright protection etc.
2. **Passive Attacks:** The watermark is identified in passive kind of attack. The deletion or destruction is not performed. The play an important role in covert channels.
3. **Forgery Attacks:** The new watermark is inserted by the hacker instead of removing the old watermark.
4. **Collusion Attacks:** They are from active attacks. The number of instances of same information is used by the hacker where each instance consists of different marks, in order to build a duplicate copy without any mark.
5. **Simple Attacks:** It can also be said as noise attack or waveform attack. This is one of the simplest attack as it embedded watermark is harmed without recognizing a single watermark. Examples are waveform based compression, addition of noise, gamma correction etc.
6. **Ambiguity Attack:** This kind of attack confuse the user by generating fake original data or watermarked data. One of the example is inversion attack.
7. **Cryptographic Attack:** The main goal in this attack is to break the security method in techniques of watermarking and finding the mode for removing the information of already inserted watermark. This technique has limited application due to high computational complexity.
8. **Removal Attack:** Without hampering the security of watermark technique, watermarked data is completely removed (Voloshynovskiy, Pereira, Pun, Eggers, &Su, 2001). No key is used in embedding of watermark. It uses quantization and denoising.
9. **Geometric Attack:** The main goal is to synchronization of watermark detection with the inserted information without removing the inserted watermark.

REVIEW OF MULTIMEDIA WATERMARKING TECHNIQUES

Digital Watermarking Techniques

Digital watermark is composed of various methods for protecting the digital data from being modified and also the unauthorized access to data. The watermarking techniques are categorized into transform and spatial domain. The embedding of watermarks is performed in spatial domain and functionality is performed on pixel (Singh, Sharma, Dave, & Mohan, 2012). The pixel values are altered in this technique.

It mainly uses LSB technique for modification process. The main goal of transform domain technique is alteration of transform domain coefficient. The mainly used methods for watermarking in transform domain are DFT, DWT and DCT. The transform domain is much more effective then spatial domain technique due to security and robustness.

Spatial Domain Watermarking

This technique depicts an image as a combination of pixels. In order to attach the watermark, colour value of pixels and pixel intensity is modified. They consume less amount of time and also exhibit less complexity. Each and every operation in this technique is simple but have the higher computational speed. These are comparatively less robust to attacks. In the LSB technique (Neeta, Snehal, & Jacobs, 2006), the embedding of watermarks is performed in least significant bit of arbitrarily selected pixels. It can easily be implemented over the images and the quality of an image is not disrupted. The main disadvantage is that non robustness to signal processing operations leading to depletion of watermarks due to attacks of signal processing. It withstands against simple attacks like addition of noise and cropping.

Transform Domain Watermarking

In this method, no embedding of watermark is performed on cover image. In the first step, transformation of cover image is performed and then embedding of watermarks is performed to transformed image. In addition, for extraction of image inverse transform is calculated for manipulated coefficients (Akiyama, Motoyoshi, Uchida, & Nakanishi, 2006). These are robust against attacks such as JPEG compression. They are useful in robust watermarking for assuring the flexibility of watermark to most popular attacks of signal processing. Numerous transform watermarking techniques exist such as Singular Value Decomposition (SVD), Discrete Wavelet Transform (DWT), Discrete Cosine Transform (DCT) and Discrete Fourier Transform (DFT). These methods posses high imperceptibility, effective alterations to signal processing attacks and image alterations. The computation cost in this method is more in comparison to spatial domain based method.

- **Discrete Cosine Transform Base Watermarking Technique:** It obtains the frequency domain signal from the time domain signal. A two-dimensional matrix of coefficients is formed when DCT technique is applied on an image(Lin, Shie, &Guo, 2010). It is used in various applications of pattern recognition, data compression and also various fields of image processing. In method of DCT, the division of image is performed in to non-overlapping blocks of fixed dimension. It is applicable on every block of image. The criteria of block selection are applied for extracting the important blocks. Correspondingly, coefficients are selected as per the corresponding block selected. At the left corner of the coefficient matrix, low frequency components are situated and at the right corner high frequency components are situated. It fractions the image into pseudo frequency band. The embedding of watermarks is performed in middle frequency sub band. The watermarks can be hided if they are embedded between high frequency components. The coefficients are modified smoothly for inserting the watermark. At last, inverse DCT is applied over blocks of image.

For one dimension succession of length M, DCT is calculated as:

$$cal(v) = \alpha(v) \sum_{i=0}^{M-1} f(i) \cos\left[\frac{(2i+1)v\pi}{2N}\right] \tag{1}$$

Where V= 0,1, 2, 3 ..... M-1

Inverse DCT is calculated as

$$f(i) = \sum_{v=0}^{M-1} a(v) cal(v) \cos\left[\frac{(2i+1)v\pi}{2M}\right] \tag{2}$$

α (V) is described as

$$\alpha(v) = \left\{ \begin{array}{l} \sqrt{\dfrac{1}{n}}, v = 0 \\ \sqrt{\dfrac{2}{n}}, v \neq 0 \end{array} \right\} \tag{3}$$

On applying DCT on a block of image, it achieves two kinds of coefficients DC and AC (Kothari & Dwivedi, 2013). The coefficient matrix consist of only one DC coefficient and all other AC coefficients. The method of DCT withstands different kinds of attacks such as noising, sharpening, cropping and filtering. It also carries the excellent capacity to compute and also provides improved performance for reductions of bits. For the 2D transformation, DCT is defined as in equation.

$$cal(v,m) = \alpha(v)\alpha(w) \sum_{i=1}^{M-1} \sum_{j=1}^{M-1} \frac{f(i,j) = \cos\left[\dfrac{(2j+1)v\pi}{2M}\right]}{\cos\left[\dfrac{(2j+1)w\pi}{2M}\right]} \tag{4}$$

- **Discrete Wavelet Transform Based Watermarking Technique**: It generates multi-resolution image view that helps in understanding the formation of an image. Also, the observation of signals can be performed at multiple resolutions (Tao &Eskicioglu, 2004). The decomposition of image is performed in low frequency and high frequency components. In order to obtain the desired results, recursive decomposition of low frequency components is performed. On applying DWT on image, the decomposition of image is performed in four bands as in Figure 4. The four bands HH,HL, LH and LL consists of diagonal details, horizontal data, vertical data and approximation in the image respectively. The approximation subband consists of low frequency components of image appropriate for embedding watermark. The maximum information related to image is contained in subband. The Inverse Discrete Wavelet Transform (IDWT) is used to get back the original image. DWT is one of the most common technique in watermarking process due to the characteristics of multi resolution and localization. The embedded watermark on the section of image is recognized by spatial localization property. On applying DWT the image is decomposed into four non-overlapping multi resolution sets. The equations 5, 6, 7, 8 depicts the coefficients:

$$Z_{LL}^{P} = \sum_{i=0}^{M-1} \sum_{j=0}^{M-1} n(i)n(j)Z_{LL}^{P-1}(2v-i)(2w-j) \tag{5}$$

$$Z_{LH}^{P} = \sum_{i=0}^{M-1} \sum_{j=0}^{M-1} n(i)p(j)Z_{LL}^{P-1}(2v-i)(2w-j) \tag{6}$$

$$Z_{HL}^{P} = \sum_{i=0}^{M-1} \sum_{j=0}^{M-1} p(i)n(j)Z_{LL}^{P-1}(2v-i)(2w-j) \tag{7}$$

$$Z_{HH}^{P} = \sum_{i=0}^{M-1} \sum_{j=0}^{M-1} p(i)p(j)Z_{LL}^{P-1}(2v-i)(2w-j) \tag{8}$$

Where the decomposition level is P. $n(i)$ and $p(j)$ are the impulsive responses. The improved quality of visual images provided by DWT then DCT and it also provides better localization. The multi resolution description of host image is supported by DWT. The number of levels of image resolution can be shown raging from low to high. The limitations are high computation cost and high computation time. The example is explained in figure 5.

Figure 5. Image decomposition using DWT

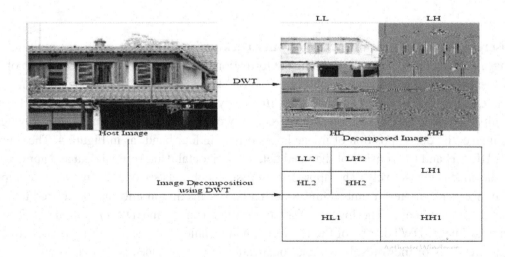

- **Discrete Fourier Transform Based Watermarking Technique:** This technique has a feature of pure frequency domain analysis and is one of the commonly used techniques. It withstands various attacks such as scaling, translation, rotation, cropping etc. The image is converted into sine and cosine forms on applying DFT. They are further categorized into Template based embedding and discrete embedding. In order to embed the watermark in direct embedding technique, DFT phase coefficients and magnitude are modified. Using the domain of DFT, transformation factor is estimated consisting of structure of template. During the process of image transformation searching of template is performed by estimating the transformation factor. For extraction of embedded spread spectrum watermark, detector is used. DFT is used for digital signals, periodic signals and also for discrete time function. It is calculated as in equation where period MP is:

$$F(v) = \sum_{i=0}^{MP-1} f(i)Q^{\frac{l2\pi vi}{MP}} \tag{9}$$

The Inverse Discrete Fourier Transform is calculated as:

$$f(i) = \frac{1}{MP} \sum_{v=0}^{MP-1} F(v)Q^{\frac{l2\pi vi}{MP}} \tag{10}$$

where v, i= 0, 1, 1, ..., MP-1. The computational dimensional formula for DFT is shown in equation 11 and 12.

$$F(v) = F(E + b.MP) \tag{11}$$

$$f(i) = f(i + b.MP) \tag{12}$$

In DFT, image is complex valued image and it is represented in the form of magnitude and phase. Low frequency component is one of the most important component of DFT and is also known as central component. It
works on the cropping attacks that leads to spectrum blurring. It does not require any synchronization of watermarks are embedded in the magnitude. The extracted signals discovered by correlation coefficient are amplified if the scaling is performed over image. It recuperates over the geometric attacks and is hence invariant to translation, scaling and rotations. The geometric distortions are difficult to recover in case of DFT and DWT. The main limitation of DFT is complex valued output. In the space time domain, positioning information is not produced.

- **Singular value decomposition based watermarking technique:** It originated from linear algebra and is used for reduction in dimensionality. On applying SVD over a matrix B, the matrix is decomposed into further three matrices. The first matrix produced is 'V' which is an orthogonal matrix, 'J' is transpose of another matrix and 'S' is a diagonal matrix. This method is able to expose the relationships between the variables clearly as it transforms correlated variables into sets of uncorrelated variables. A matrix of digital image consists of non negative scalar entries. Suppose 'B' is an image with size i x J. The SVD method can be used to decompose the SVD images as in equation 13.

$$B = VLJ^T \tag{13}$$

It is one of highly robust methods. During the process, the singular values produced helps conserve a watermark provided by the owner. The memory constraint is decreased and the accuracy is increased. Also, it is withstands attacks. The singular value represents the luminance of image layer.

TECHNIQUES FOR ROBUST WATERMARKING

The focus of research is watermarking algorithms robust to geometrical distortions (Elbafisi, 2012). The various methods to these kinds of problems include implicit synchronization, invariant domain, synchronization template/pattern and exhaustive search. The only variant of RST is mostly geometric transform invariant algorithms. The

criteria of geometrical distortion is also gaining importance. The effect of global align transform to watermarking algorithm performance have great effect. However, they are complex.

Exhaustive Watermark Search

One of the most popular method for cooperating with the problem of resynchronization (Kutter, Jordan, & Bossen, 1998). The detection of watermark is done on the sequence of training that consists of pilot geometrical inverse deformation. The searching of watermark is performed in every distortion parameter. It is difficult to analyze the parameters of deformation for absent original image (Alghoniemy & Tewfik, 2000;2006). There also exists high computational complexity. The parameters include the spaces to be explored. Hence, size limitation of search space degrades the perceptual quality. But there are unacceptable effects in search space (Lichtenauer, Setyawan, Kalker, & Lagendijk, 2003) that leads to synchronizer outcome error based. Also, there is proliferated false positive probability due to interpolation error and geometric distortion (FiAlvarez-Rodriguez & Perez-Gonzalez, 2002).

Template Based Approach and Self Synchronizing

The mostly use solution for attacks of synchronization are embedding periodic watermark pattern into the image or inserting of template along with the watermark (Herrigel, Perrig, &Ruanaidh, 1997; Stankovic, Djurovic, & Pitas, 2001). For the objective of resynchronization the additional templates are used as references for artificial embed. The information carried in them is insensitive. The template based technique accomplish the resynchronization pattern by compensating and estimating the geometric transformation and also asserting the presence of watermark (Lu, Lu, & Chung, 2006). Hence, the method of registration is identified and withstands geometric attacks (Bas, Chassery, & Macq, 2002).In this section, the template based algorithms introduced focuses on adaptive determination of strength of templates in order to constrain the search space. The search space contraction is suspect to system credibility. In between, number of synchronization points restricts the template leading to unaccepted false counter probabilities counter for estimating the parameters on applying affine transformation. The watermark detection method is reliable on precise template . The detection of error tolerance is unacceptable for detected position inaccuracy. In order to shrink the search space, unwarranted synchronization is performed . There is large progress in the field of template-based watermarking but in these the similarity between the watermarked and original image is ignored. The template and watermark insertion occur at position of embedding and carefully strengthen the account. It also maintains the restricted fidelity of original image leading to compromise in data payload.

Also the aspect of security is neglected as all these algorithms are vulnerable to template removal attacks (Dong & Galatsanos, 2002; Herrigel, Voloshynovskiy, & Rytsar, 2001; Bas, Chassery, & Macq, 2002). The exploitation of specific features can be performed for destructing the pattern of synchronization. The insertion of templates is performed as pseudo random noise patterns like filtering operators filters the local maxim out. Then by malicious attacks, applied templates are eliminated. Hence, it has the limitation of withstanding with risks of template attacks and threats. As the template-based methods, self-synchronizing watermarks (Kutter, 1999; Delannay & Macq, 2000) are suspect to estimation or removal attacks as attacker uses the knowledge periodic tiling of watermark for removing it. Also, the peaks can be removed in autocorrelation function by filtering in frequency or spatial domain hence making watermark vulnerable to geometric attack.

Invariant Domain

The other technique is embedding of watermark in geometrical invariant subspace. The histogram specification is suggested (Coltuc& Bolon, 1999) for hiding the watermark to geometrical distortions. Also watermarking s methods are proposed (Ruanaidh& Pun, 1998; Lin et al., 2001) based on Fourier-mellin transform (Lin & Brandt, 1993). A translation, scale and rotation invariant domain is obtained using the Fourier transform invariance properties and log polar mapping(LPM) to translations. This solution possesses a limitation of implementing after an image undergo local geometrical deformations. Additionally, approximation problems for discrete nature of images and also the reduced embedding space make watermark less resistant to lossy compression and low-pass filtering. There also exist another technique (Alghoniemy & Tewfik, 2000) where the space of watermarking is defined as normalized, canonical space based on moments in geometric image. This transforms the image into a form independent of scale, rotation and vertical/horizontal refection. The embedding of watermark is performed in this space and then inverse transformation technique is applied for obtaining the final watermarked image. In the phase of detection moment calculation is performed and normalization parameters are estimated. After the normalization, watermark on an image can be easily detected. Another technique of creating a self-similar watermark is proposed instead of embedding watermark in invariant space (Solachidis & Pitas, 2000). These watermarks are embedded into DFT domain and not effecting the magnitude of DFT. The identical sectors are used to create a watermark so it can easily be detected even after degree rotation. It also reduces the number of steps in frequency sampling where detection is only performed is image is scaled or cropped.

Features of Watermarking

Many algorithms are developed for feature-based watermarking over the years. In order to resolve the problem of watermark synchronization, the preferred method is feature-region detection for resisting against the local geometric distortions. The smain steps followed in content-based synchronization methods are:

1. Localization of detected feature points
2. pixels are eliminated by non-maxima suppression that are not local maxima
3. Determination of final set of features by threshold.
4. Applying the extracted features for identifying regions to insert watermark
5. Without the error of synchronization, feature points are detectable at the receiver side

These all have lead to development of various algorithms (Deng, Gao, Li, & Tao, 2009; Li & Guo, 2009; Lichtenauer et al., 2003; Seo & Yoo, 2004; Yu, Lu, Ling, & Zou, 2006; Yuan et al., 2006; Zheng, Liu, Zhao, & Saddik, 2007). The localized watermarking algorithms are used by feature point-based methods. The watermark is detected using a stable feature points in an image where the insertion of watermark is performed into corresponding local region (Kutter, 1999). Therefore, the process based on features is invariant to local geometrical deformations. It is one the best method for solving the problem of robustness against the geometrical deformations with blind detection. Also in another approach (Bas, Chassery, Macq, 2002) feature points are extracted using Harris detector and leading to production of Delaunay tessellation on stable feature group points. After that the watermark is inserted in every triangle of tessellation. But these points are not variant to scaling (Mikolajczyk & Schmid, 2002) and cannot withstands attack of scaling.

Further, Mexican Hat wavelet scale is introduced (Tang & Hang, 2003). The individual exploitation of image is performed to overlapping circles of an image with firm centre and radius at obtained points of features. Two 32 X 32 blocks are selected in each image circle for embedding the watermark (Li & Guo, 2009). It withstands robustness to major number of attacks but scaling transforms attacks can effect it as it alters the contents of block. Also another technique of Harris feature point is presented with a normalized scale and insertion of watermark is performed within each of the region of disk at firm radius and localized stalest harries points. The technique is resistant to global geometric transformations that include moderate translation, rotation and scaling. But this does into with stands cropping. Further scale invariant feature transform (SIFT) is introduced for producing the circular patterns as inserting modules(Gupta, Agrawal, & Yamaguchi, 2016). The transformation of rectangular watermark is performed to a polar mapped (Li, Yu, Gupta, & Ren, 2018) watermark. Inversely, before watermark insertion polar mapped for determination of insertion modules. The circular convolution is used for detection of watermark correspondence(Li, Deng, Gupta, Wang, & Choi, 2019). The translation feature of polar mapped circular pads is used for obtaining the invariant watermark of rotation. The technique of Harris Laplace is applicable for extraction of scale invariant feature points using the corner points of Harris (Lee, Kim, & Lee, 2006). As per the local characteristic scale of each feature point, the watermark is inserted after affine normalization. The scale of characteristic is defined by the scale where the maximum value is achieved by normalized scale-space representation of an image. The orientation characteristic relies on the angle of dominant axis of an image(Hai, Qing, &Ke, 2018).

The technique containing the local circular regions (LCRs) and Tchebichef moments combined is introduced (Deng, Gao, Li, & Tao, 2009). The shaping of LCRs is performed by Harris-Laplace detector and the global characteristics of LCRs are obtained by Tchebichef moments. Further, to detect the feature points affine invariant point detector is introduced (Li, Yu, Gupta, & Ren, 2018; Mikolajczyk& Schmid, 2002). For a specific feature point, an elliptical feature region is used and formed for inserting in spatial domain. According to the shape of region, before embedding the watermark is geometrically transformed into an elliptical pattern.

CONCLUSION

With the advancement in multimedia and rapid proliferation of global network, storage devices and economical digital recording enabled to construct a platform for transmitting, distributing, replicating, representing and acquiring the contents in digital formats with quality degradation. Also the manipulation is made possible. However, transmitting contents over the networks have made in insecure . The security feature is critical for some kinds of transmitted media data. Hence, we lead to introduction of digital watermarking, one of most popular research field. This method deals with process of embedding of information in some manner. Thus enabling the need of information security for various applications as copyright protection. In this chapter, different methods of watermarking are analyzed and reviewed. This is based on transform and spatial domain. Further the methods using the discrete wavelet transform and singular value decomposition is reviewed. Further, it can be concluded that various attack techniques are used for assessment of watermarking systems. Also, the algorithms of watermarking are robust against the geometrical distortions is the main focus. The different solutions to these problems includes synchronization template/pattern, exhaustive search, implicit synchronization and invariant domain using image features widely.

REFERENCES

Akiyama, T., Motoyoshi, F., Uchida, O., & Nakanishi, S. (2006). Hybrid digital watermarking for color images based on wavelet transform. Retrieved from https://www.researchgate.net/publication/267818801_HYBRID_DIGITAL_WATERMARKING_FOR_COLOR_IMAGES_BASED_ON_WAVELET_TRANSFORM

Alghoniemy, M., & Tewfik, A. H. (2006). Progressive quantized projection approach to data hiding. *IEEE Transactions on Image Processing*, *15*(2), 459–472. doi:10.1109/TIP.2005.860318 PMID:16479816

Alghoniemy, M., & Tewfik, A. H. (2000, May). Geometric distortion correction in image watermarking. In Security and Watermarking of Multimedia Contents II (Vol. 3971, pp. 82-89). International Society for Optics and Photonics.

Álvarez-Rodríguez, M., & Pérez-González, F. (2002). Analysis of pilot-based synchronization algorithms for watermarking of still images. *Signal Processing Image Communication*, *17*(8), 611–633. doi:10.1016/S0923-5965(02)00057-7

Aslantas, V. (2008). A singular-value decomposition-based image watermarking using genetic algorithm. *AEÜ. International Journal of Electronics and Communications*, *62*(5), 386–394. doi:10.1016/j.aeue.2007.02.010

Bas, P., Chassery, J. M., & Macq, B. (2002). Geometrically invariant watermarking using feature points. *IEEE Transactions on Image Processing*, *11*(9), 1014–1028. doi:10.1109/TIP.2002.801587 PMID:18249723

Coltuc, D., & Bolon, P. (1999). Robust watermarking by histogram specification. *Proceedings of 1999 International Conference on Image Processing*, 236-239. 10.1109/ICIP.1999.822891

Delannay, D., & Macq, B. (2000). Generalized 2-D cyclic patterns for secret watermark generation. *Proceedings of 2000 International Conference on Image Processing*, 77-79. Academic Press.

Deng, C., Gao, X., Li, X., & Tao, D. (2009). A local Tchebichef moments-based robust image watermarking. *Signal Processing*, *89*(8), 1531–1539. doi:10.1016/j.sigpro.2009.02.005

Dong, P., & Galatsanos, N. P. (2002). Affine transformation resistant watermarking based on image normalization. *Proceedings of the International Conference on Image Processing*, 489-492. 10.1109/ICIP.2002.1039014

Elbafisi, E. (2012). Robust mpeg watermarking in dwt four bands. *Journal of Applied Research and Technology*, *10*(2), 87–93.

Ganic, E., & Eskicioglu, A. M. (2004). Robust DWT-SVD domain image watermarking: embedding data in all frequencies. *Proceedings of 6th workshop on Multimedia & Security, MM & Sec*, p. 166-174.

Gupta, B., Agrawal, D. P., & Yamaguchi, S. (2016). *Handbook of research on modern cryptographic solutions for computer and cyber security*. Hershey, PA: IGI Global. doi:10.4018/978-1-5225-0105-3

Hai, H., Qing, X. D., & Ke, Q. (2018). A watermarking-based authentication and image restoration in multimedia sensor networks. *International Journal of High Performance Computing and Networking*, *12*(1), 65–73. doi:10.1504/IJHPCN.2018.093846

Herrigel, A., Perrig, A., & Ruanaidh, J. Ó. (1997). *A Copyright Protection Environment for Digital Images* (pp. 1–16). Berlin, Germany: Springer. doi:10.1007/978-3-322-86842-8_1

Herrigel, A., Voloshynovskiy, S. V., & Rytsar, Y. B. (2001). Watermark template attack. In Security and Watermarking of Multimedia Contents III (Vol. 4314, pp. 394-405). International Society for Optics and Photonics.

Kothari, A. M., & Dwivedi, V. V. (2013). Video Watermarking-Combination of Discrete Wavelet & Cosine Transform to Achieve Extra Robustness. *International Journal of Image Graphics and Signal Processing*, *5*(3), 36–41. doi:10.5815/ijigsp.2013.03.05

Kumar, C., Singh, A. K., & Kumar, P. (2018). A recent survey on image watermarking techniques and its application in e-governance. *Multimedia Tools and Applications*, *77*(3), 3597–3622. doi:10.100711042-017-5222-8

Kutter, M. (1999). Watermarking resistance to translation, rotation, and scaling. Proceedings Multimedia Systems and Applications (Vol. 3528, pp. 423-431). International Society for Optics and Photonics.

Kutter, M., Jordan, F. D., & Bossen, F. (1998). Digital watermarking of color images using amplitude modulation. *Journal of Electronic Imaging*, *7*(2), 326–333. doi:10.1117/1.482648

Lee, H. Y., Kim, H., & Lee, H. K. (2006). Robust image watermarking using local in variant features. *Optical Engineering (Redondo Beach, Calif.), 45*(3). doi:10.1117/1.2181887

Li, D., Deng, L., Gupta, B. B., Wang, H., & Choi, C. (2019). A novel CNN based security guaranteed image watermarking generation scenario for smart city applications. *Information Sciences, 479*, 432–447. doi:10.1016/j.ins.2018.02.060

Li, J., Yu, C., Gupta, B., & Ren, X. (2018). Color image watermarking scheme based on quaternion Hadamard transform and Schur decomposition. *Multimedia Tools and Applications, 77*(4), 4545–4561. doi:10.100711042-017-4452-0

Li, L. D., & Guo, B. L. (2009). Localized image watermarking in spatial domain resistant to geometric attacks. *AEÜ. International Journal of Electronics and Communications, 63*(2), 123–131. doi:10.1016/j.aeue.2007.11.007

Lichtenauer, J. F., Setyawan, I., Kalker, T., & Lagendijk, R. L. (2003). Exhaustive geometrical search and the false positive watermark detection probability. In Security and Watermarking of Multimedia Contents V (Vol. 5020, pp. 203-214). International Society for Optics and Photonics.

Lin, C. Y., Wu, M., Bloom, J. A., Cox, I. J., Miller, M. L., & Lui, Y. M. (2001). Rotation-, scale-, and translation-resilient public watermarking for images. *IEEE Transactions on Image Processing, 10*(5), 767–782. doi:10.1109/83.918569 PMID:18249666

Lin, F., & Brandt, R. D. (1993). Towards absolute invariants of images under translation, rotation, and dilation. *Pattern Recognition Letters, 14*(5), 369–379. doi:10.1016/0167-8655(93)90114-S

Lin, S. D., Shie, S. C., & Guo, J. Y. (2010). Improving the robustness of DCT-based image watermarking against JPEG compression. *Computer Standards & Interfaces, 32*(1-2), 54–60. doi:10.1016/j.csi.2009.06.004

Loukhaoukha, K., Nabti, M., & Zebbiche, K. (2014). A robust SVD-based image watermarking using a multi-objective particle swarm optimization. *Opto-Electronics Review, 22*(1), 45–54. doi:10.247811772-014-0177-z

Lu, W., Lu, H., & Chung, F. L. (2006). Feature based watermarking using watermark template match. *Applied Mathematics and Computation, 177*(1), 377–386. doi:10.1016/j.amc.2005.11.015

Mathon, B., Cayre, F., Bas, P., & Macq, B. (2014). Optimal transport for secure spread-spectrum watermarking of still images. *IEEE Transactions on Image Processing, 23*(4), 1694–1705. doi:10.1109/TIP.2014.2305873 PMID:24808340

Mikolajczyk, K., & Schmid, C. (2002). An Affine Invariant Interest Point Detector. In A. Heyden, G. Sparr, M. Nielsen, & P. Johansen (Eds.), Lecture Notes in Computer Science: Vol. 2350. *Computer Vision — ECCV 2002. ECCV 2002*. Berlin, Germany: Springer. doi:10.1007/3-540-47969-4_9

Neeta, D., Snehal, K., & Jacobs, D. (2006). Implementation of LSB steganography and its evaluation for various bits. *Proceedings of 1st International Conference on Digital Information Management*, 173-178.

Patel, S. B., Mehta, T. B., & Pradhan, S. N. (2011). A unified technique for robust digital watermarking of colour images using data mining and DCT. *International Journal of Internet Technology and Secured Transactions*, *3*(1), 81–96. doi:10.1504/IJITST.2011.039680

Ruanaidh, J. J. O., & Pun, T. (1998). Rotation, scale and translation invariant spread spectrum digital image watermarking. *Signal Processing*, *66*(3), 303–317. doi:10.1016/S0165-1684(98)00012-7

Seo, J. S., & Yoo, C. D. (2004). Localized image watermarking based on feature points of scale-space representation. *Pattern Recognition*, *37*(7), 1365–1375. doi:10.1016/j.patcog.2003.12.013

Seo, J. S., & Yoo, C. D. (2006). Image watermarking based on invariant regions of scale-space representation. *IEEE Transactions on Signal Processing*, *54*(4), 1537–1549. doi:10.1109/TSP.2006.870581

Sherekar, S., Thakare, V., & Jain, S. (2011). Attacks and countermeasures on digital watermarks: Classification, implications, benchmarks. *International Journal of Computer Science and Applications*, *4*(2), 32–45.

Singh, A. K. (2017). Improved hybrid algorithm for robust and imperceptible multiple watermarking using digital images. *Multimedia Tools and Applications*, *76*(6), 8881–8900. doi:10.100711042-016-3514-z

Singh, A. K., Dave, M., & Mohan, A. (2014). Wavelet based image watermarking: futuristic concepts in information security. *Proceedings of the National Academy of Sciences, India Section A: Physical Sciences, 84*(3), 345-359. 10.100740010-014-0140-x

Singh, A. K., Kumar, B., Singh, G., & Mohan, A. (2017). *Medical image watermarking: techniques and applications*. Cham, Switzerland: Springer. doi:10.1007/978-3-319-57699-2

Singh, A. K., Sharma, N., Dave, M., & Mohan, A. (2012). A novel technique for digital image watermarking in spatial domain. *Proceedings of 2nd IEEE International Conference on Parallel, Distributed, and Grid Computing*, 497-501. 10.1109/PDGC.2012.6449871

Solachidis, V., & Pitas, I. (2000). Self-similar ring-shaped watermark embedding in 2-DDFT domain. *Proceedings of 10th European Signal Processing Conference*, pp. 1-4. Academic Press.

Stankovic, S., Djurovic, I., & Pitas, I. (2001). Watermarking in the space/spatial-frequency domain using two-dimensional Radon-Wigner distribution. *IEEE Transactions on Image Processing*, *10*(4), 650–658. doi:10.1109/83.913599 PMID:18249654

Tang, C. W., & Hang, H. M. (2003). A feature-based robust digital image watermarking scheme. *IEEE Transactions on Signal Processing*, *51*(4), 950–959. doi:10.1109/TSP.2003.809367

Tao, P., & Eskicioglu, A. M. (2004). A robust multiple watermarking scheme in the discrete wavelet transform domain. Proceedings of 5601 International Society for Optics and Photonics, 133-144. doi:10.1117/12.569641

Tsai, H. H., Jhuang, Y. J., & Lai, Y. S. (2012). An SVD-based image watermarking in wavelet domain using SVR and PSO. *Applied Soft Computing*, *12*(8), 2442–2453. doi:10.1016/j.asoc.2012.02.021

Tsai, J. S., Huang, W. B., Kuo, Y. H., & Horng, M. F. (2012). Joint robustness and security enhancement for feature-based image watermarking using invariant feature regions. *Signal Processing, 92*(6), 1431–1445. doi:10.1016/j.sigpro.2011.11.033

Vallabha, V. (2003). Multiresolution watermark based on wavelet transform for digital images. Retrieved from https://www.mathworks.com/matlabcentral/mlc-downloads/downloads/submissions/3508/versions/1/download/pdf

Voloshynovskiy, S., Pereira, S., Pun, T., Eggers, J. J., & Su, J. K. (2001). Attacks on digital watermarks: Classification, estimation-based attacks, and benchmarks. *IEEE Communications Magazine, 39*(8), 118–126. doi:10.1109/35.940053

Xia, Z., Wang, X., Zhang, L., Qin, Z., Sun, X., & Ren, K. (2016). A privacy-preserving and copy-deterrence content-based image retrieval scheme in cloud computing. *IEEE Transactions on Information Forensics and Security, 11*(11), 2594–2608. doi:10.1109/TIFS.2016.2590944

Yu, Y., Lu, Z., Ling, H., & Zou, F. (2006). A robust blind image watermarking scheme based on feature points and RS-invariant domain. *Proceedings of the 8th international Conference on Signal Processing.* Academic Press.

Yuan, W., Ling, H., Lu, Z., Zou, F., & Yu, Y. (2006). Image Content-based Watermarking Resistant against Geometrical Distortions. Proceedings of the 8th international Conference on Signal Processing. Academic Press.

Zheng, D., Liu, Y., Zhao, J., & Saddik, A. E. (2007). A survey of RST invariant image watermarking algorithms. *ACM Computing Surveys, 39*(2), 5. doi:10.1145/1242471.1242473

Chapter 5
Defending Multimedia Content Embedded in Online Social Networks (OSNs) Using Digital Watermarking

Brij B. Gupta

National Institute of Technology, Kurukshetra, India

Somya Rajan Sahoo

National Institute of Technology, Kurukshetra, India

Prashant Chugh

National Institute of Technology, Kurukshetra, India

Vijay Iota

National Institute of Technology, Kurukshetra, India

Anupam Shukla

National Institute of Technology, Kurukshetra, India

ABSTRACT

In global internet usage, increasing multimedia message, which includes video, audio, images, and text documents, on the web raised a lot of consequences related to copyright. For copyright protection, authentication purpose and forgery detection digital watermarking is the robust way in social network content protection. In this technique, the privacy information is embedded inside the multimedia content like image and video. The protected content embedded inside multimedia content is called watermark-enabled information. To make more effective the process of watermarking, the content encrypted before embedding to the image. Basically, the digital watermarking embedded process implemented in two different domains called spatial and frequency domain. In spatial domain digital watermarking, the watermark information is embedded in the least significant bit of the original image on the basis of bit plane selected and on the basis of the pixels of image, embedding, and detection is performed.

DOI: 10.4018/978-1-7998-2701-6.ch005

INTRODUCTION

As in the social media perspective the pattern of communication with each other in social media has changed after mid-1990. Multiple online social networks like Facebook, Twitter, Instagram, and WhatsApp ease the distribution of user's real-time information between multiple users over the same and different networks. Due to multiple characteristics of online social networks like, ease of use, faster transformation and less expensive, it becomes the significant way of communication and information sharing. Nowadays, almost all the social network users access the news through online channels (Zhang et al., 2017). However, due to the increasing popularity of OSNs, the use of the Internet becomes an ideal way of communication and spreading of fake news. The spreading of fake news in the form of misleading content, fake reviews, fake rumours, advertisements, fake speech regarding politics, satires and many more through images. Currently, fake news is spread faster in social media rather than mainstream media (Sahoo & Gupta, 2020; Sahoo & Gupta, 2018). To protect the multimedia content like images, videos, texts and audios from attackers digital watermarking is the process to hiding and embedding certain information digitally to that content (Sahoo & Gupta, 2019). It is the effective way to protect the rights of the user/author of multimedia content and find whether the content misused/ manipulated by some unauthorized user on that network (Balan et al., 2017; Zedan et al., 2017; Sahoo & Gupta, 2019). The Digital Watermarking is related to the steganography technique in some extent. In that technique we hide the text message behind any multimedia content available. The processes of Digital Watermarking authenticate the status of the owner or author of that multimedia content. In past, different field uses Watermarking technique for protecting the similarity, i.e. watermarks were originally used in paper and subsequently in paper bills (Singh et al., 2012). The popularity of internet in past years has expanded rapidly due to the social networks and their contents like audio, video, images and other personal as well as professional content sharing method. Hence, copying the original content and altering the theme for malicious purpose becomes increases day by day and affect the normal users. Therefore, protecting multimedia content from unauthorized access, digital watermarking is the strongest way (Abraham et al., 2016). In Digital watermarking, the original multimedia content is embedded through signal or data (Li et al., 2019; Li et al., 2018; Gupta et al., 2015). The same principle also used to embed in audio, video and images also (Ansari et al., 2012). The embedded information in original multimedia content is known as watermarked content and that can be extracted and deleted with some specific predefined application and algorithms. The watermarked content may be in the form of image, audio and text etc. As per the digital signal presence in each and every unchanged copy of the original information or content, it behaves as a digital signature for all copies (Verma et al., 2006). The original multimedia content embedded with digital watermarking should be tenured, robust, unperceivable, and comprises of all information about multimedia content ownership. In order to accomplish maximal aegis, the watermark should have these properties 1) It must be protected and undeletable by hacker and attackers; 2) It should be undetectable if analyzed statistically, i.e. encrypted watermark 3) It should be tolerant to compression techniques like lossy 4) It should be tolerant to dissimilar varieties of operations that can be performed on that content; 5) It must be perceptually invisible. The process of Watermarking is categorized into two main categories. The two categories include the spatial domain watermarking and the frequency-domain watermarking (Patel et al., 2013). In spatial-domain watermarking techniques, on the basis of the pixels of image, embedding and detection is performed. Spatial domain watermarking method is a technique in which pixel values of original image are modified for embedding the watermark information in it. This technique is very easy to implement but are not robust against different types of attacks including compression and cropping (Cheng et al., 2004). In order to prevent from different attacks, the watermark is encrypted with some pseudo random noise before embedding it in the original image. The encrypted water-mark is embedded in the least significant bits of the original image on the basis whether the LSB of watermark pixel is set or unset. The LSB of the watermarked image get changed once the watermark is embedded in the original image and slight distortion of the original image take place after watermarking Zeki et al., 2011).Here the watermark is processed pixel by pixel and the LSB of the original image is set and unset according to the watermark image LSB. If it is set, then the LSB of the original image is set and make unset if watermark's bit is unset. The limitation of this technique is that here the watermark is not encrypted, so it can easily be attacked if encryption and decryption algorithm is known to attacker (Singh et al., 2012).The watermark is decomposed into RGB channels and the encrypted watermark is embedded in the original image block of 8 x 8 blocks i.e. block wise but the watermark that is used for watermarking is not partitioned (Zeimpekis et al., 2006). This technique provides the robustness against attacks like salt pepper noise and cropping attacks but it is not resistant to other attacks like compression attacks and other attacks, also the PSNR and MSE values are less good as compared to proposed technique. This technique is straight forward and the simplest method as far as implementation is concerned. It cannot sustain attacks like jpeg compression and low pass filtering. Here encoding and decoding requires less computational time. The pixel information of the image is distorted by small amount as it is manipulated according to the watermark image (Dougherty et al., 2009). On the other hand, frequency- domain techniques, works on the frequency representation of the image. Various transforms that are used are Discrete Cosine Transform, Singular Value Decomposition, Fast Fourier transform and time efficient Discrete Wavelet Transform. Also, Frequency-domain watermarking techniques are more robust as compared to the spatial domain techniques. On the basis of the visibility, Digital watermarking is classified into visible or invisible. In (Bianchi et al., 2013) the author describes invisible watermarking technique based on the spatial domain watermarking technique with encrypted watermark. The DWT is considered more computationally efficient as compared to other transform method which includes both DFT and DCT. Comparatively, frequency domain digital watermarking is more secure and robust than the spatial domain digital water marking due to the information spreading over the entire image (Almomani et al., 2013; Jiang et al., 2018) .Due to the robustness the high frequency portion of the image should not be used for watermark embedding process. In DWT, Digital Watermarking of the image is made up in frequency domain. It represents the entire image in form of different wavelets. Wavelet consisting of small wave having some particular frequency and determined duration. In this process the selected image filtered along a plane of X and y coordinate with high and low pass filters (Lowe et al., 2004). The method divides the entire image into four different bands called LL, LH, HL and HH. Where, LL contains lowest frequency and HH consisting of highest frequency component. Further, the lower bandwidths LL is dividing into four regions and continue up to level 3.To enhance the watermarking more robust the DWT improves with 2 more level i.e. level 2 and level 3.In this technique the overall image divided in to four different sub bands shown in table 1.

Table 1. DWT decomposing model of images

$(HL)_3$	$(LH)_3$	$(LH)_2$	$(LH)_1$
$(HL)_3$	$(HH)_3$		
$(HL)_2$		$(HH)_2$	
$(HL)_1$			$(HH)_1$

Every portion of the image i.e. sub band contains some information about the original image. Among all, $(LL)_1$ band contains maximum information of the image[7].For transformation of image, DWT based watermarking uses various filters like Haar wavelet filter, Morlet wavelets, Coiflets wavelets, Meyer wavelets and many more. The similar mechanism also required for the video content available in the internet and the user attraction is more in case of video content as compared to other. The video consisting of large number of frames group together and create some illusion and shown at fast speed. So in order to protect the video content by using digital watermarking, the entire video is divided in to various frames i.e. for 25 fps; there will be 25 frames per second in video. After dividing into frames, the technique is applied to one or more frames to protect the digital content. The selected image is first broken into number of sub bands based on their frequency components using the low and high pass filters along with the two coordinates X and Y (Kang et al., 2003). After successfully applying the watermarking to some portions of the video, we combined all the frames into a single video as a watermarked video (Gupta, 2018; Zhang et al., 2018; Chaudhary et al., 2016). The rest of the paper is organized as follows. In section 2, we describe various types of digital watermark on the basis of available content. In section 3, we describe literature survey related to digital watermarking principles. Also, we describe the embedding process of watermarking in various domains in section 4 and section 5. In section 6, we describe the robustness and various attack resistance related to watermarking. The flow of information and processing describes in section 7. Finally, we describe the various result analyses in section 8 with comparative analysis and conclude the overall execution of process in section 9.

TYPES OF WATERMARKING ON THE BASIS OF AVAILABLE CONTENT

On the basis of usage and content protection, the watermarking principle implemented with various multimedia contents like image watermarking, video watermarking audio watermarking and text watermarking. In image watermarking, the digital Watermarking content embedded into the images and to detect and extract the original content for the owner's ownership whenever necessary (Ruanidh et al., 1996). Also, the image watermarking principle can be implemented using various ways depicted below.

- **Visible Watermark:** In this type of watermarking principle, a logo or symbol is visible on the image. This watermarking principle used by TV channels and advertisement of products through banner representation.
- **Invisible Watermark:** it is Used to find ownership as well as prevention from unauthorized access of images by users. In this process, a watermark embedded inside an image but that image is not visible to other users.
- **Robust Watermark:** Robust watermarking principle used for sign copyright information for any digital work. It protects the content from unauthorized access and also resists the common edit process.
- **Fragile Watermark:** Fragile watermarking is one of the most sensitive watermarking principles used for integrity problem, which is very sensitive to the change of signals. It protects the content from tamper.

- **Semi Fragile Watermarking:** Semi fragile watermark is similar to fragile watermarks, but it is capable of tolerating some degree of the change to a watermarked image. In this approach the attacker can change some portion of the image such as addition of quantization noise to the original image.
- **Invisible Robust Watermark:** The invisible robust watermark implemented through the pixel value of any image. In this process the detection of watermark is too difficult to identify and it can be recovered through decoding process only.
- **Invisible Fragile Watermark:** it is A process similar to the fragile watermark with invisible concept. Due to the invisible nature it would not be tampered by ant user or threats.

In other hand in video watermarking, watermarking done under the features available with video contents. In this watermarking principle, the total frame divided into number of frames for embedding based on feature provision. It is the elaboration of the picture watermarking. In case of audio watermarking the advanced watermarking is dominant because of web music, MP3 and also for some other sound formats (Xianglin et al., 2006). Most commonly watermarking principle called text watermarking uses advanced watermarking of the PDF, .doc files and other documents available on the social structure. The information for uniquely identify is also added along with the content of document.

COVERING OF DIGITAL WATERMARKING

Various applications related to watermarking based on the content available in social network and there uses to protect against various threats by the attacker in OSN described as:

To protect the content that broadcasted using various TV channels, the owner of that content embedded copyright image inside the multimedia content. The watermark is embedded only to a certain image rather than all the available content to maintain the quality in the network or media (Hamadi et al., 2015). The other application called transaction tracking in digital watermarking. For example, the various variety of watermarking is embedded into some portion of the video that is received at the receiver end and record the receiver of every legal copy of a movie. If the content of the movie gets leaked in the internet, then the owner of the content easily identifies which receiver get leaked the content or the source of the spreading content (Ding et al., 2016).

- **Copyright Protection:** It will be those the most substantial preparation of the encouraged watermarking may be copyright protection from dissimilar unsanctioned client (Ansari et al., 2017).
- **Monitoring Broadcast**: This application checks the unauthorized broadcast station (Abraham et al., 2016) and analyse whether the content being aired by the authorised vendor or not. Tamper Detection is another application based on the fragile watermarks. If at any means the watermark is found to be destructed, then it depicts some tampering and therefore the digital content is no longer relied (Hu et al., 2011).
- **Verification of Authentication and Integrity**: The objective of the Digital Watermarking also includes protecting of the clients' content from unauthorised access. If someone used the legal copy of the user content and knowingly or unknowingly redistributes the content with other, then the detection of the content is easier by using watermarked content. At every transaction point the watermark is worked as a barrier between the sender and the receiver to protect the content.

By this process tracking of the unauthorized user is easier one (Tusi et al., 2008). Authentication based on fingerprints: the existing technique related to fingerprint is secure the user content. If someone lawfully create a duplicate product and distributed illegally over others, then the fingerprint authentication prevents this from unauthorised access. This principle also be used to track the entire transaction by embedding watermarking principle to the multimedia content over the network (Lu et al., 2000).

- **Content Description**: Marking and rendering multimedia content in watermark which is embedding process inside the host image. The size of the embedding image is as large as length of the original image and embedded into easily without any behavioural change. The selected method for watermarking need less robustness for this application. The size of the watermark is large as lengthy information is stored in the watermark and there is very less requirement of the robustness for this application.

- **Application Related to Medical**: To protect the medical information from unauthorized access, digital watermarking taking into action. This content includes patients report and other relevant document related to patent and hospital record (Tyagi et al., 2016). The security and verification of medical data is very significant due to frequent transformation of the multimedia content over the network.

WATERMARK EMBEDDING AND EXTRACTION PROCESS IN SPATIAL DOMAIN

Process of Embedding the Watermark

In the embedding process of the watermark, a private key which is secrete, is known to the author or proprietor of the multimedia content, is used to encrypt the water mark describes in figure 1. When the watermark has been encrypted to the original image or video then it is called embedded inside original image and the watermarked image is received (Huang et al., 2005). In the embedding process if the LSB of watermark image is set then the corresponding LSB of original image is set. The embedding process of digital watermark had shown in figure 2 and 3.

Figure 1. Embedding watermarking principle

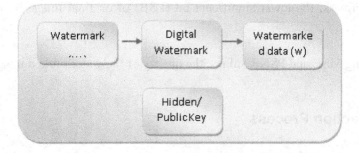

Figure 2. The random image encryption with watermark

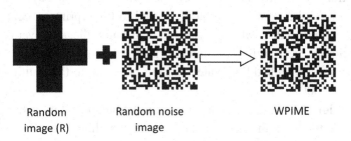

Random   Random noise   WPIME
image (R)   image

Algorithm

Step 1: Random image (R) of size 32 x 32 bit is created by using the random function of 0's and 1's where zero denotes black and 1 denotes white.

Step 2: The master watermarked image is encrypted with the random image available i.e. R doing XOR of least significant bits of the watermarked image and R. A new (32 x 32) bit image WPRIME is formed, which is the encrypted watermark.

Step 3: The original image divided into 4 equal regions i.e. (r1, r2, r3, r4)

$$W_1 = W(1+m, 1+n)$$

$$W_2 = W(1+m, 2+n)$$

$$W_3 = W(2+m, 1+n)$$

$$W_4 = W(2+m, 2+n)$$

Where, 'm' is represented as 0, 2, 4. . . (P/2–2) and 'n' is represented as 0, 2, 4. . (Q/2–2). P=Q=32

Now the region r1 of original image is embedded with region W1 of encrypted watermark image. Similarly, for other corresponding regions, embedding of watermark is done with original image. While embedding the watermark, the lower significant bit (LSB) of original image is set, if that bit of the watermark is set.

Step 4: By calculating MSE and PSNR values, the quality of the watermarked image is analyzed.

Watermark Extraction Process

In the process of extraction of watermark, the encrypted watermark is extracted from the LSB of the watermarked picture shown in Figure 4. The same process or secrete key also used for decryption process of watermark that is used in case of encryption (Kumar et al., 2016). The entire result of the process and data content shown in Figure 5.

Figure 3. Watermark embedding images

Original
Image

Encrypted
watermark

Watermarked
Image

Figure 4. Watermark Extraction process from embedded images

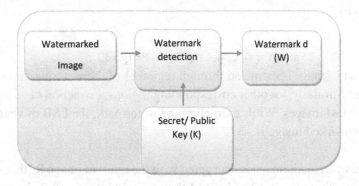

Figure 5. Extracted watermark without attack

Figure 6. Extracted watermark after cropping attack

Algorithm

Step 1: The original image divided into 4 equal regions i.e. (r1, r2, r3, r4)

$$W_1 = W(1+m, 1+n)$$

$$W_2 = W(1+m, 2+n)$$

$$W_3 = W(2+m, 1+n)$$

$$W_4 = W(2+m, 2+n)$$

Where m = 0, 2, 4. . . (P/2–2) and n = 0, 2, 4. . (Q/2–2). P=Q=32

W1 of the watermark image is extracted through region r1 of the watermarked image by comparing it with original image. Similarly, for other corresponding regions, extraction of watermark is done using original and watermarked images. While extracting the watermark, the LSB of watermark image is set, if that bit of the watermarked image is set.

Step 2: The obtained watermark image is decrypted with the random image R (that was used at the time of encryption) by taking the XOR of LSB of the obtained image and R shown in Figure 7.

Step 3: The quality of extracted watermark image is analyzed by calculating the NCC i.e. Normalized Correlation Coefficient.

Figure 7. Watermark extraction images

Watermarked Image

Watermarked Image after salt pepper

WATERMARK EMBEDDING PROCESS IN FREQUENCY DOMAIN (DWT)

The details of embedding watermark in frequency domain describes below.

Figure 8. Watermark encryption

Original Watermark   Encrypted Watermark Image

Algorithm for Embedding Images

1. For encrypting the watermark, a secret key or random binary string of 2000 bits is generated.
2. The row number or column number of the watermark image represents the bit position in the key. Initially the watermark is encrypted row wise i.e. entire row is rotate clockwise if the corresponding bit in key is set and for the others bit in secret key rotate counter clockwise.
3. In the next steps the image encrypted column wise i.e. the entire columns rotated upside down if the corresponding bit is set and counter clockwise for the unset bit.
4. For strong encryption step 2 and step 3 repeated several times. The entire process of DWT in the form of image i.e. watermark encryption shown in Figure 8, different band of signal shown in Figure 9 and the watermarked image shown in Figure 10.
5. Level 1 DWT is applied to the host image; this divides the entire image into four different sub bands LL_1, LH_1, HL_1, and HH_1. Again the DWT is applied on LL_1 and Level 2 DWT of LL_1 is obtained, LL_2 which is obtained by Level 2 DWT is again divided into LL_3, LH_3, HL_3, HH_3 after DWT application on LL2.
6. For watermarking the visibility factor F and the bands of image are changed according to F. For example, $WMKD\text{-}LL_3 = H\text{-}LL_3 + (F * W\text{-}LL_3)$.
   Where $WMKD\text{-}LL_3$ is the LL_3 for the watermark image, $H\text{-}LL_3$ is LL_3 of the host image and $W\text{-}LL_3$ is the LL_3 of the watermark image.
   Similarly, LL_2 of watermarked image is obtained by using the Inverse Discrete Wavelet Transform (IDWT) on the LL_3, LH_3, HL_3 and HH_3. Likewise, the LL_1, LH_1, HL_1, and HH_1 of the watermarked image are obtained by IDWT.
7. The quality of the watermark is analysed by using equation 1 and 2 depicted below.

$$M.S.E = \left[\sum_{i=1}^{n} \left(x_i - x_i^* \right)^2 \right] / N \qquad (1)$$

Figure 9. Different bands of the original image

Figure 10. Watermarked image

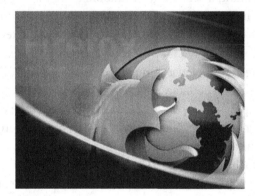

Figure 11. Watermark extraction

Encrypted extracted Watermark

Final Extracted Watermark

$$PSNR = 10 * \left(\log_{10}\left[MAX_I^2\right] / MSE \right) \tag{2}$$

Where, N is the Image Size and similar to(R*C) i.e. (ROW * COLUMN). x_i is the original watermark and watermarked image is x_i^*.MAX=255 for LSB embedding (Abraham et al., 2016).

8. For changing the random picture of the watermarked image, salt-pepper attack is also done as pixel value of white or black with calculated value of PSNR and MSE.

Algorithm for Images Extraction

The details of image extraction process from the embedded image describes below.

1. Level 1 DWT is applied to the watermarked image; this process divides the entire image into 4different sub bands LL_1, LH_1, HL_1, and HH_1. The same DWT is applied on the LL_1 and Level 2 DWT of LL_1 is obtained, LL_2 which is obtained by Level 2 DWT is again divided into bands LL_3, LH_3, HL_3, HH_3 after DWT application on LL_2.
2. Visibility factor F used for watermark embedding and the bands of image are changed. For example,

WMKD-LL_3 = H-LL_3 + (F * W-LL_3).

In order to find watermark band information from above equation, we find watermark bands as

W-LL_3 = (Wmkd-LL_3 - H-LL_3)/F.

Where, WMKD-LL_3 is the LL_3 for the watermark image, H-LL_3 is LL_3 of the host image and W-LL_3 is the LL_3 of the watermark image shown in Figure 11.

Similarly, for LL_2 of watermark image is obtained by using the IDWT (Inverse Discrete Wavelet Transform) on the LL_3, LH_3, HL_3, HH_3. Likewise, the LL_1, LH_1, HL_1, HH_1 of the watermark image are obtained by IDWT shown in Figure 12.

Figure 12. Watermarked images after noise addition

Watermarked Image with
saltPepper noise addition

Watermarked Image with
saltPepper noise in different

Figure 13. Extracted watermark

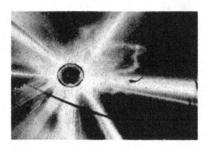

Extracted Watermark in encrypted
form

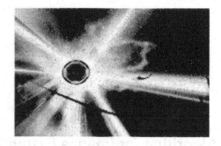

Extracted Watermark in decrypted
form

1. The encrypted watermark is obtained. So, to get the original content it must be decrypted. Row number or column number of the watermark image represents bit position in the secret key. Then decryption process starts with row wise and then column i.e. the whole row is rotated anticlockwise for set bits and counter clockwise for the unset bit shown in Figure 13.
2. Then the decrypted process applies to column wise downside up and upside down for set bit and unset bit.
3. Repeat Step 3 and Step 4 for better result (X, number of times as used while encrypting the watermark) to get decrypted watermark. Normalized Correlation Coefficient is calculated as

$$\text{NCC}=\frac{\sum_{a=1}^{m}\sum_{b=1}^{n}\left[W\left(a,b\right)W^{\prime}\left(a,b\right)\right]}{\sqrt{\sum_{a=1}^{m}\sum_{b=1}^{n}\left[W\left(a,b\right)\right]^{2}\sum_{a=1}^{m}\sum_{b=1}^{n}\left[W^{\prime}\left(a,b\right)\right]^{2}}} \tag{3}$$

Where, W = Original Watermark, W' = extracted watermark and (M * N) is original watermark size. The quality analysis of the extracted watermark represents by NCC.

Embedding Algorithm for Videos

The entire process of video watermarking with generated result shown in Figure 14 and Figure 15.

Figure 14. Encryption process

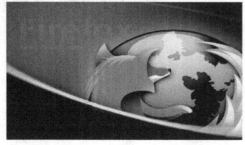

Original Watermark

Encrypted Watermark

Figure 15. Different frames of watermarked video

1. The total video divided into number of frames i.e. M.
2. Random permutation vector of the M is generated. For example, M=3, random permutation is [2, 3, 1].
3. We selected Specific number (N) of starting numbers from random permutation as f_1, f_2, f_3 ....f_N. i.e. [2, 3, 1] and for specific number 2, vector becomes [2, 3] or f_1=2, f_2=3.
4. All frames are extracted and the watermark is applied to frames f_1, f_2....f_N, using the embedding watermarking as DWT for images.
5. For analysing the quality, we calculated cumulative MSE and PSNR is calculated.

Extracting Algorithm for Videos

The result extracted as original from embedding images shown in figure 16.

Figure 16. Extracted watermark

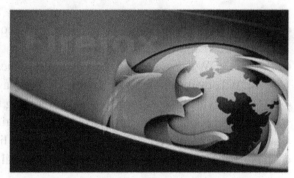

Encrypted watermark   Decrypted Watermark

1. The video divided into number of frames i.e. M.
2. Random permutation vector of the M is generated. For example, M=3, random permutation is [2, 3, 1].
3. We selected Specific number (N) of starting numbers from random permutation as f_1, f_2, f_3 ....f_N. i.e. [2, 3, 1] and for specific number 2, vector becomes [2, 3] or f_1=2, f_2=3.
4. All frames are extracted and the watermark is applied to frames f_1, f_2....f_N, using the embedding watermarking as DWT for images.

5. The encrypted watermark is obtained. So, to get the original content it must be decrypted. Row number or column number of the watermark image represents bit position in the secret key. Then decryption process start with row wise and then column i.e. the whole row is rotated anticlockwise for set bits and counter clockwise for the unset bit.
6. Then the decrypted process applies to column wise downside up and upside down for set bit and unset bit.
7. Repeat Step 5 and Step 6 for better result (X, number of times as used while encrypting the watermark) to get decrypted watermark.

NCC(Normalized Correlation Coefficient) is calculated as

$$NCC = \frac{\sum_{a=1}^{m}\sum_{b=1}^{n}\left[W(a,b)W`(a,b)\right]}{\sqrt{\sum_{a=1}^{m}\sum_{b=1}^{n}\left[W(a,b)\right]^2 \sum_{a=1}^{m}\sum_{b=1}^{n}\left[W`(a,b)\right]^2}} \tag{4}$$

Where, W = Original Watermark, W' = extracted watermark and (M * N) is original watermark size. The quality analysis of the extracted watermark represents by NCC.

ROBUST AND ATTACK RESISTANT DIGITAL WATERMARKING

To embed the watermark more securely following improvements are added to the existing methodologies.

-   Invisible Watermarking concept is applied in our proposed technique and depending on the condition the visibility factor can control.
-   Level3 DWT is used to protect the image, which is more robust as compared to the Level2 or Level 1 DWT, by maintaining the quality of the image.
-   We encrypted the watermark before applying to the original image due to more security. For encrypting content 2000 bits is used for encryption.
-   More Resistant over different types of attack like, salt-pepper and compression attacks.
-   For better analysis, we maintain the PSNR value of watermarked image.

To maintain quality of image, we embed watermark to the LL band of image due to less distortion and invisible in nature (Abraham et al., 2016). On the other hand, it protects the image securely by embedding the watermark to the original image. It is not easily extracted by the attacker and cannot be manipulated by malicious users in the network. So, it makes the watermarked image easy to verify but difficult to make changes to it (Sruthi et al., 2014). Different kinds of attack are affected the originality of image like, cropping attack, noise attack in the form of salt pepper etc. So this paper describes the protection of images from different attacks by possibly maintaining the PSNR value. Maintaining of the PSNR of original image is important due to maximum signal noise ratio in order to maintain the quality.

DATA FLOW DIAGRAM

Level 0 DFD

Level 0 DFD or context-level diagram displays the various exterior agents which act as the source, the interface connecting various system and data items. On the other hand structure graph shows the links with outer world and exhibited data flows (Devi et al., 2017). Here, to create the encrypted watermarked image, one copy of the original image and watermark image provided as input. The whole process of encryption is shown in Figure17.

Figure 17. LEVEL 0 DFD (Multistage watermarking)

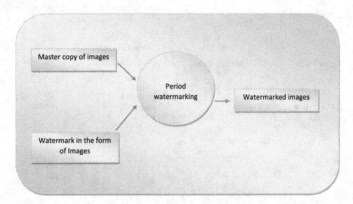

Level 1 DFD

Level 1 (DFD) is more detailed as compared to the level 0 DFD shown in Figure 18. It divides the main processes into different sub processes for the better understanding about the implementation of embedding watermark in to the image. Here we elaborate the encryption process in the sub process for the various security issues. The encrypted watermark is obtained. At last the watermarked image is obtainedby applying digital watermark in the form of image, video etc (Debas et al., 2013).

Figure 18. LEVEL 1 DFD (Multistage watermarking)

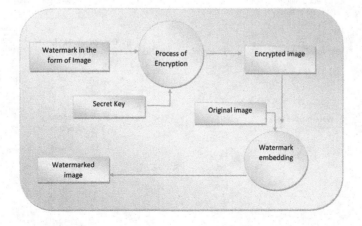

Level 2 DFD

A level 2 DFD provides the detail structure of the embedding watermark in image for protection by elaborating the processes that make up an information system as compared to level 1 shown in Figure 19 and Fig 20. It is used for planning or recording the specific makeup of the system (Devi & Singh, 2017). In level 2 DFD the process is deeply define for the random binary string. Random string is acting as the secret key for encrypting the watermark (Wu et al., 2017).

Figure 19. Level 2 DFD for spatial domain

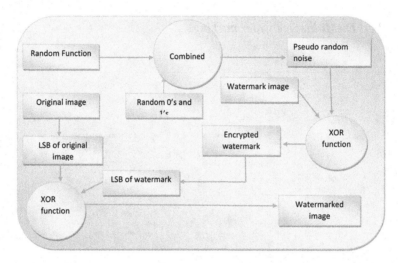

Figure 20. Level 2 DFD (Multistage watermarking) for frequency domain

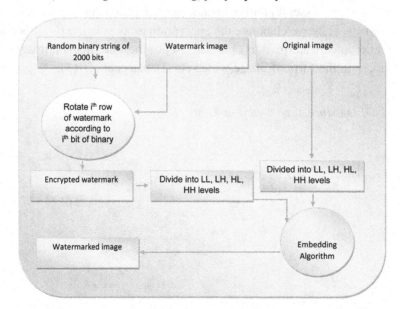

RESULTS AND EVALUATION

The character of generated watermarked image is measured by two metrics of the proposed algorithm, i.e. PSNR and MSE. PSNR is the Peak Signal to Noise Ratio described in (Abraham et al., 2016). This metric shows the actual content and the generated noise added in the process of watermarking. The original image should not get much distorted in the process of embedding the watermark. High PSNR value indicates good character of the watermarked image and it shows low level of distortion. PSNR and the MSE (Mean Squared Error) are computed for the watermarked image for calculating amount of distortion (Sruthi et al., 2014).

$$NCC = \frac{\sum_{a=1}^{m}\sum_{b=1}^{n}\left[W(a,b)W^{'}(a,b)\right]}{\sqrt{\sum_{a=1}^{m}\sum_{b=1}^{n}\left[W(a,b)\right]^2 \sum_{a=1}^{m}\sum_{b=1}^{n}\left[W^{'}(a,b)\right]^2}} \tag{5}$$

Where,

W = Original Watermark,
W' = extracted watermark and (M * N) is original watermark size (Kimpan, Lasakul, & Chitwong, 2004).

And the calculate PSNR and MSE shown in equation 6 and in equation 7.

$$M.S.E = \left(\sum_{i=1}^{n}\left(x_i - x_i^{*}\right)^2\right) / N \tag{6}$$

$$PSNR = 10 * \left(\log_{10}\left[MAX_I^2\right] / MSE\right) \tag{7}$$

Where, N is the Size of the Image and similar to (R*C) i.e. (ROW * COLUMN). x_i is the original watermark and watermarked image is represented as x_i^{*}. MAX=255 for LSB embedding.

We calculate the NCC and MSE by analyzing various images present and these are the input parameter of our proposed algorithm shown in table 2 and table 3. The MSE is calculated and it is found to be lesser value as compared to PSNR.

Table 2. MSE and PSNR Values according to stated algorithm of spatial domain

Image No.	MSE	PSNR	NCC
1	0.040	62.083	0.932
2	0.030	65.072	0.941
3	0.028	68.092	0.947
4	0.025	70.9	0.951

Table 3. MSE and PSNR Values according to stated algorithm of frequency domain

Image No.	MSE	PSNR	NCC
1	0.030	64.08	0.951
2	0.022	66.14	0.960
3	0.020	70.9	0.982
4	0.018	72.7	0.992

Table 4. Comparative analysis of our proposed method with other state of art techniques

Various Images	Our Result Spatial Domain		Our Result Frequency Domain		Sruthi et al., 2014		Hameed et al., 2016	
	MSE	PSNR	MSE	PSNR	MSE	PSNR	MSE	PSNR
Image 1	0.040	62.083	0.030	64.08	0.2310	51.1255	0.2810	52.69
Image 2	0.030	65.072	0.022	66.14	0.4196	51.9029	0.3269	46.23
Image 3	0.028	68.092	0.020	70.9	0.2679	51.9029	0.3252	52.52
Image 4	0.025	70.9	0.018	72.7	0.2619	51.1587	0.2012	50.94

As compared to the spatial domain, frequency domain achieved less distortion by our proposed method. As a result, the PSNR value of image 4 in frequency domain having higher as compared to others and less MSE value i.e. 0.018 for the same image. In some cases, the result of frequency domain is higher as compared to spatial domain due to the image quality and resolution. Also, some other factors like content on the image are very essential for embedding process. By analysing each image with their MSE and PSNR value, we conclude that the process of embedding watermarking principle by our proposed method achieve good accuracy as compared to other state of art techniques. the details of comparative analysis of our result with other state of art describes in section 8.1.

Comparative Analysis of Our Approach With Other State of Arts

Comparison of our framework with existing approaches is given in table 4. Therefore, our approach gives better result as MSE and PSNR as compared to other approaches. This is achieved by analyzing the features extracted from various images. In every image, our proposed method watermarked well as compared to other watermarking methods.

CONCLUSION

The proposed method describes the way to protect an image by embedding watermark image for security. Survival to attacks chances are enhanced as the watermark information is spread over wider areas. In this approach, we use certain random binary string to encrypt the watermark and it is applied to original image using DWT. The embedded bits (blue bits) are less distracting to the human eyes and makes it's less visible to the viewer. By applying this principle, we protect our image from various attacks like salt pepper noise attack and cropping attack by the attacker. The quality of the image after embedding the content is slightly distorted than the original one as compared to other techniques. To identify the effectiveness of our proposed method, we checked by using salt-pepper noise attack. The proposed algorithm is tested on number of images. The algorithm provided here delivers very high quality watermarked images that survive various attacks of images over network.

REFERENCES

Abraham, J., & Paul, V. (2016). An imperceptible spatial domain color image watermarking scheme. *Journal of King Saud University-Computer and Information Sciences*.

Abraham, J., & Paul, V. (2016). An imperceptible spatial domain color image watermarking scheme. *Journal of King Saud University-Computer and Information Sciences*.

Abraham, J., & Paul, V. (2016). An imperceptible spatial domain color image watermarking scheme. *Journal of King Saud University-Computer and Information Sciences*.

Advith, J., Varun, K. R., & Manikantan, K. (2016, February). Novel digital image watermarking using DWT-DFT-SVD in YCbCr color space. *Proceedings International Conference on Emerging Trends in Engineering, Technology, and Science*, (pp. 1-6). IEEE. 10.1109/ICETETS.2016.7603032

Almomani, A., Gupta, B. B., Wan, T. C., Altaher, A., & Manickam, S. (2013). Phishing dynamic evolving neural fuzzy framework for online detection zero-day phishing email. *arXiv preprint arXiv:1302.0629*.

Ansari, I. A., & Pant, M. (2017). Multipurpose image watermarking in the domain of DWT based on SVD and ABC. *Pattern Recognition Letters*, *94*, 228–236. doi:10.1016/j.patrec.2016.12.010

Ansari, R., Devanalamath, M. M., Manikantan, K., & Ramachandran, S. (2012, October). Robust digital image watermarking algorithm in DWT-DFT-SVD domain for color images. In 2012 International Conference on Communication, Information, & Computing Technology, (pp. 1-6). IEEE. 10.1109/ICCICT.2012.6398160

Balan, S., & Rege, J. (2017). Mining for social media: Usage patterns of small businesses. *Business Systems Research Journal: International Journal of the Society for Advancing Business & Information Technology (BIT)*, *8*(1), 43-50.

Bianchi, T., & Piva, A. (2013). Secure watermarking for multimedia content protection: A review of its benefits and open issues. *IEEE Signal Processing Magazine*, *30*(2), 87–96. doi:10.1109/MSP.2012.2228342

Chaudhary, P., Gupta, S., & Gupta, B. B. (2016). Auditing defense against XSS worms in online social network-based web applications. In *Handbook of research on modern cryptographic solutions for computer and cyber security* (pp. 216–245). IGI Global. doi:10.4018/978-1-5225-0105-3.ch010

Cheng, L. M., Cheng, L. L., Chan, C. K., & Ng, K. W. (2004, December). Digital watermarking based on frequency random position insertion. *Proceedings ICARCV 2004 8th Control, Automation, Robotics, and Vision Conference* (Vol. 2, pp. 977-982). IEEE. 10.1109/ICARCV.2004.1468975

Chu, W. C. (2003). DCT-based image watermarking using subsampling. *IEEE Transactions on Multimedia*, *5*(1), 34–38. doi:10.1109/TMM.2003.808816

Dabas, P., & Khanna, K. (2013). A study on spatial and transform domain watermarking techniques. *International Journal of Computers and Applications, 71*(14).

Devi, H. S., & Singh, K. M. (2017). A Novel, Efficient, Robust, and Blind Imperceptible 3D Anaglyph Image Watermarking. *Arabian Journal for Science and Engineering, 42*(8), 3521–3533. doi:10.100713369-017-2531-1

Ding, H. Y. (2016). Novel Efficient Image Watermark Algorithm Based on DFT Transform. International Journal of Signal Processing. *Image Processing and Pattern Recognition, 9*(10), 297–312.

Dougherty, G. (2009). *Digital image processing for medical applications.* Cambridge University Press. doi:10.1017/CBO9780511609657

Gupta, B. B. (Ed.). (2018). Computer and cyber security: principles, algorithm, applications, and perspectives. Boca Raton, FL: CRC Press.

Gupta, S., & Gupta, B. B. (2015). BDS: browser dependent XSS sanitizer. In *Handbook of Research on Securing Cloud-Based Databases with Biometric Applications* (pp. 174–191). IGI Global. doi:10.4018/978-1-4666-6559-0.ch008

Hameed, M. A., Aly, S., & Hassaballah, M. (2017). An efficient data hiding method based on adaptive directional pixel value differencing (ADPVD). *Multimedia Tools and Applications,* 1–19.

Hameed, M. A., Aly, S., & Hassaballah, M. (2018). An efficient data hiding method based on adaptive directional pixel value differencing (ADPVD). *Multimedia Tools and Applications, 77*(12), 14705–14723. doi:10.100711042-017-5056-4

Hamidi, M., El Haziti, M., Cherifi, H., & Aboutajdine, D. (2015, November). A blind robust image watermarking approach exploiting the DFT magnitude. *Proceedings 2015 IEEE/ACS 12th International Conference of Computer Systems and Applications* (pp. 1-6). IEEE. 10.1109/AICCSA.2015.7507124

Hu, Y., Wang, Z., Liu, H., & Guo, G. (2011). A Geometric Distortion Resilient Image Watermark Algorithm Based on DWT-DFT. *JSW, 6*(9), 1805–1812. doi:10.4304/jsw.6.9.1805-1812

Huang, P. S., Chiang, C. S., Chang, C. P., & Tu, T. M. (2005). Robust spatial watermarking technique for colour images via direct saturation adjustment. *IEE Proceedings Vision Image and Signal Processing, 152*(5), 561–574. doi:10.1049/ip-vis:20041081

Jiang, F., Fu, Y., Gupta, B. B., Lou, F., Rho, S., Meng, F., & Tian, Z. (2018). Deep learning based multichannel intelligent attack detection for data security. *IEEE Transactions on Sustainable Computing.*

Kang, X., Huang, J., Shi, Y. Q., & Lin, Y. (2003). A DWT-DFT composite watermarking scheme robust to both affine transform and JPEG compression. *IEEE Transactions on Circuits and Systems for Video Technology, 13*(8), 776–786. doi:10.1109/TCSVT.2003.815957

Kimpan, S., Lasakul, A., & Chitwong, S. (2004, October). Variable block size based adaptive watermarking in spatial domain. *Proceedings IEEE International Symposium on Communications and Information Technology* (Vol. 1, pp. 374-377). IEEE. 10.1109/ISCIT.2004.1412871

Kumar, S., & Dutta, A. (2016, February). Performance analysis of spatial domain digital watermarking techniques. *Proceedings 2016 International Conference on Information Communication and Embedded Systems* (pp. 1-4). IEEE. 10.1109/ICICES.2016.7518910

Li, D., Deng, L., Gupta, B. B., Wang, H., & Choi, C. (2019). A novel CNN based security guaranteed image watermarking generation scenario for smart city applications. *Information Sciences*, *479*, 432–447. doi:10.1016/j.ins.2018.02.060

Li, J., Yu, C., Gupta, B. B., & Ren, X. (2018). Color image watermarking scheme based on quaternion Hadamard transform and Schur decomposition. *Multimedia Tools and Applications*, *77*(4), 4545–4561. doi:10.100711042-017-4452-0

Lowe, D. G. (2004). Distinctive image features from scale-invariant keypoints. *International Journal of Computer Vision*, *60*(2), 91–110. doi:10.1023/B:VISI.0000029664.99615.94

Lu, C. S., Huang, S. K., Sze, C. J., & Liao, H. Y. M. (2000). Cocktail watermarking for digital image protection. *IEEE Transactions on Multimedia*, *2*(4), 209–224. doi:10.1109/6046.890056

Lu, W., Lu, H., & Chung, F. L. (2006). Robust digital image watermarking based on subsampling. *Applied Mathematics and Computation*, *181*(2), 886–893. doi:10.1016/j.amc.2006.02.012

Nasir, I., Weng, Y., & Jiang, J. (2007, December). A new robust watermarking scheme for color image in spatial domain. *Proceedings Third International IEEE Conference on Signal-Image Technologies and Internet-Based System* (pp. 942-947). IEEE. 10.1109/SITIS.2007.67

O'Ruanaidh, J. J., Dowling, W. J., & Boland, F. M. (1996). Phase watermarking of digital images.

Patel, M., Sajja, P. S., & Sheth, R. K. (2013). Analysis and Survey of Digital Watermarking Techniques. *International Journal of Advanced Research in Computer Science and Software Engineering*, *3*(10), 203–210.

Reddy, A. A., & Chatterji, B. N. (2005). A new wavelet-based, logo-watermarking scheme. *Pattern Recognition Letters*, *26*(7), 1019–1027. doi:10.1016/j.patrec.2004.09.047

Sahoo, S. R., & Gupta, B. B. (2018). Security Issues and Challenges in Online Social Networks (OSNs) Based on User Perspective. In Computer and Cyber Security (pp. 591-606). Auerbach Publications.

Sahoo, S. R., & Gupta, B. B. (2019). Classification of various attacks and their defence mechanism in online social networks: A survey. *Enterprise Information Systems*, *13*(6), 832–864. doi:10.1080/17517 575.2019.1605542

Sahoo, S. R., & Gupta, B. B. (2019). Hybrid approach for detection of malicious profiles in twitter. *Computers & Electrical Engineering*, *76*, 65–81. doi:10.1016/j.compeleceng.2019.03.003

Sahoo, S. R., & Gupta, B. B. (2020). Popularity-Based Detection of Malicious Content in Facebook Using Machine Learning Approach. *Proceedings First International Conference on Sustainable Technologies for Computational Intelligence* (pp. 163-176). Springer, Singapore. 10.1007/978-981-15-0029-9_13

Singh, A. K., Sharma, N., Dave, M., & Mohan, A. (2012, December). A novel technique for digital image watermarking in spatial domain. In *2012 2nd IEEE International Conference on Parallel Distributed and Grid Computing (PDGC),* (pp. 497-501). IEEE. 10.1109/PDGC.2012.6449871

Sruthi, N., Sheetal, A. V., & Elamaran, V. (2014, April). Spatial and spectral digital watermarking with robustness evaluation. *Proceedings 2014 International Conference on Computation of Power, Energy, Information, and Communication* (pp. 500-505). IEEE. 10.1109/ICCPEIC.2014.6915415

Sruthi, N., Sheetal, A. V., & Elamaran, V. (2014, April). Spatial and spectral digital watermarking with robustness evaluation. *Proceedings 2014 International Conference on Computation of Power, Energy, Information, and Communication* (pp. 500-505). IEEE. 10.1109/ICCPEIC.2014.6915415

Su, Q., & Chen, B. (2018). Robust color image watermarking technique in the spatial domain. *Soft Computing, 22*(1), 91–106. doi:10.100700500-017-2489-7

Su, Q., & Chen, B. (2018). Robust color image watermarking technique in the spatial domain. *Soft Computing, 22*(1), 91–106. doi:10.100700500-017-2489-7

Tsui, T. K., Zhang, X. P., & Androutsos, D. (2008). Color image watermarking using multidimensional Fourier transforms. *IEEE Transactions on Information Forensics and Security, 3*(1), 16–28. doi:10.1109/TIFS.2007.916275

Tyagi, S., Singh, H. V., Agarwal, R., & Gangwar, S. K. (2016, March). Digital watermarking techniques for security applications. *Proceedings International Conference on Emerging Trends in Electrical Electronics & Sustainable Energy Systems* (pp. 379-382). IEEE. 10.1109/ICETEESES.2016.7581413

Verma, B., Jain, S., Agarwal, D. P., & Phadikar, A. (2006). A New color image watermarking scheme. *INFOCOMP, 5*(3), 37–42.

Wu, M. L., Fahn, C. S., & Chen, Y. F. (2017). Image-format-independent tampered image detection based on overlapping concurrent directional patterns and neural networks. *Applied Intelligence, 47*(2), 347–361. doi:10.100710489-017-0893-4

Xianglin, C. R. W. Y. L. (2006). An Adaptive DFT Domain Digital Watermarking Scheme [J]. Computer Engineering and Applications, 10, 022.

Zedan, S., & Miller, W. (2017). Using social network analysis to identify stakeholders' influence on energy efficiency of housing. *International Journal of Engineering Business Management, 9.* doi:10.1177/1847979017712629

Zeimpekis, D., & Gallopoulos, E. (2006). TMG: A MATLAB toolbox for generating term-document matrices from text collections. In *Grouping multidimensional data* (pp. 187–210). Berlin, Germany: Springer. doi:10.1007/3-540-28349-8_7

Zeki, A. M., Abdul Manaf, A., & Mahmod, S. S. (2011). High watermarking capacity based on spatial domain technique. *Information Technology Journal, 10*(7), 1367-1373.

Zeki, A. M., Manaf, A. A., Ibrahim, A. A., & Zamani, M. (2011). A robust watermark embedding in smooth areas. *Research Journal of Information Technology, 3*(2), 123–131. doi:10.3923/rjit.2011.123.131

Zhang, Z., & Gupta, B. B. (2018). Social media security and trustworthiness: Overview and new direction. *Future Generation Computer Systems*, *86*, 914–925. doi:10.1016/j.future.2016.10.007

Zhang, Z., Sun, R., Zhao, C., Wang, J., Chang, C. K., & Gupta, B. B. (2017). CyVOD: A novel trinity multimedia social network scheme. *Multimedia Tools and Applications*, *76*(18), 18513–18529. doi:10.100711042-016-4162-z

Chapter 6
Integer Transform–Based Watermarking Scheme for Authentication of Digital Fundus Images in Medical Science:
An Application to Medical Image Authentication

Poonkuntran Shanmugam

(iD) https://orcid.org/0000-0002-2778-7937

Velammal College of Engineering and Technology, Madurai, India

Manessa Jayaprakasam

Independent Researcher, India

ABSTRACT

This chapter presents an integer transform-based watermarking scheme for digital fundus image authentication. It is presented under multimedia applications in medicine. The chapter introduces image authentication by watermarking and digital fundus image. The key requirements in developing watermarking scheme for fundus images and its challenges are identified and highlighted. Authors describe a proposed watermarking scheme on integer transform. The experimental results emphasize the proposed scheme's ability in addressing key requirements and its attainment. The detailed results are summarized.

DOI: 10.4018/978-1-7998-2701-6.ch006

INTRODUCTION

The advent of modern computing techniques and the explosion of the World Wide Web (WWW) are integrated together for providing instant information access to a large percentage of homes and businesses. The development of such integration has stimulated the use of information in the form of text, pictures, graphics, and integrated multimedia applications. Such information is acquired by converting a continuous signal into digital format and it can be viewed by using display devices such as computer monitors and projectors. This information is widely exchanged in digital visual format for its transmission, reception, storage, processing and display. The recent developments on the Internet with the inexpensive digital recording and storage devices have created an environment in which digital information can easily be accessed, replicated and distributed without any loss in quality. This has become a concern for information security. Thus, such information needs to be secured by an efficient method while it is being exchanged (Bovik, 2000) (Cole, 2003). Digital Image Processing (DIP) is a new technological advancement in the areas of digital computation and telecommunication. An image can be defined as two-dimensional function $f(x, y)$, where x and y are spatial coordinates and f is the amplitude at the spatial coordinate pair (x, y), known as grey value or intensity value at that location (x, y). If the spatial coordinates (x, y) and amplitude f are finite, discrete quantities, then the image is called a digital image. The term DIP refers to the processing of digital images by means of digital computers (Gonzalez & Woods, 2002). The DIP incorporates prior knowledge, identification of objects, interpretation of objects, description of objects, pattern classification and pattern recognition.

The applications of DIP acquire a broad spectrum of radiation as shown in figure 1. The ranges of image types can be derived from every type of radiation. The digital image acquisition methods are developed and improved by means of these radiations. For example, the recent developments in medical images come from new sensors that record image data from previously little-used sources of radiation, such as Positron Emission Tomography (PET) and Magnetic Resonance Imaging (MRI) (Bovik, 2000).

FROM CRYPTOGRAPHY TO WATERMARKING

Though security is a general term used in the literature, the way in which security is used in the daily lives of humans is extraordinary. It ranges from passwords that are used for entering the secure computers and electronic wallets, to fingerprint scanning technology that is used for personal identification. Thereby, the security measurements became a part of the daily lives of humans as telephones or automobiles. The human's daily lives are surrounded by a world of secret communication, where people of all types are transmitting information as innocent as an encrypted credit card number to an online store then and as dangerous as a hijacking plan to terrorists. Hence, secure secret communication became essential. The secret communication can be achieved by two techniques. They are cryptography and data hiding (also referred to as information hiding).

Figure 1. Applications of digital image processing (DIP)

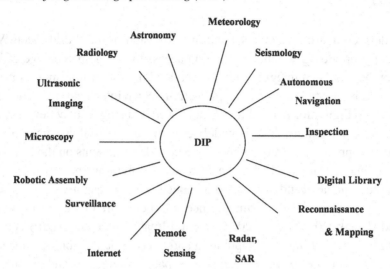

- **Cryptography:** It is the science that uses mathematics to encrypt and decrypt the sensitive information. Cryptography transmits sensitive information across insecure networks in an unreadable rubbish format, called *ciphertext*. Hence, the information cannot be read by anyone except the intended recipient. The information to be transmitted is called *plaintext* or *cleartext*. The *plaintext* can be read and understood without any actions. The *encryption* is a process that converts *plaintext* into *ciphertext*. It is used to ensure that the information is hidden from anyone for whom it is not intended, even those who can see the encrypted information. The process of reverting *ciphertext* to its original *plaintext* is called *decryption*. The *encryption* and *decryption* are illustrated in figure 2.

Figure 2. Encryption and decryption

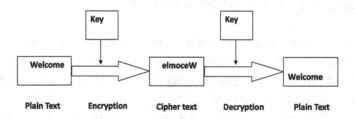

While cryptography techniques are used to prevent unauthorized access to digital information, it is clear that cryptography has its limitations in protecting intellectual property rights. Once the information is decrypted, there is nothing to prevent an authorized user from illegally replicating the information. Hence, another technique is needed to facilitate content authentication, protect ownership rights, track content usage, ensure authorized access and prevent illegal replication (Cox, Miller, Linnartz & Kalker, 1999).

- **Data Hiding or Information Hiding:** The data hiding or information hiding is a general term that encompasses two sub-disciplines. They are steganography and watermarking. Steganography is a process of transmitting the secret information hidden in innocent-looking cover medium so that its existence is undetectable. The secret information is always be hidden in an unseen manner. Watermarking is the process of imperceptibly altering the cover medium to embed the information about the cover medium. Watermarking is closely related to the steganography; however, there are differences between them. In the watermarking, the secret information is related to the cover medium. Steganography relates to secret point to point communications between the two parties where the secret information is not related to the cover medium. Watermarking has additional features. It must have resilience against the attacks that attempt to remove the hidden secret information. The steganography does not have the notion of attacks. Because the secret information is not related to the cover and it is not creating any suspicion to the attackers.

Figure 3. A general watermarking model

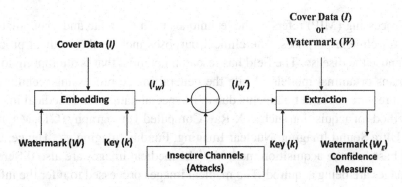

A general watermarking model is shown in figure 3. It involves two processes. They are *embedding* and *extraction*. In this model, the cover medium is referred to as *cover data* (*I*) and it can be text, audio, image and video. The embedding process inserts the secret information, referred to as *watermark* (*W*) inside the cover data in an encrypted form using the *key* (*k*). The key can be either secret or non-secret. The output of the embedding process will be composite data, referred to as *watermarked data* (I_w) containing the encrypted secret information inside the cover data. This watermarked data may be attacked by the hackers to destroy the watermark embedded inside it, to generate the hacked version of the watermarked data (I_w'). Once the watermarked data is hacked, the cover data becomes susceptible to all kinds of fraud. The extraction process separates the cover data and watermark from the watermarked data. The watermark removed from the watermarked data is known as *extracted watermark* (W_E), called a *confidence measure*.

It is used for the verification and validation of the cover data. The extraction process may be carried out with or without the knowledge of the cover data or watermark. Depends on the target application, the extraction process may either be lossy or lossless.

HISTORY OF WATERMARKING

The watermarking is not recent to this century. More than 700 years ago, the watermarking was employed in *Italy* for representing the paper brand and mills that produced it. In the 18th century, watermarking began to be used for anti-counterfeiting measures on money and other documents (Muharemagic & Furht, 2004). The term *watermark* was introduced at the end of the 18th century. Since the marks resemble the effect of water on the paper, the term *watermark* is chosen. In 1954, Emil Hembrook had filed a pattern for his identification towards digital watermarking in music. This was the first work carried out in digital watermarking and the same became an example. In 1988, Komatsu and Tominaga used the term *Digital Watermarking*, first time in the literature. Since 1995, the interest in the watermarking research started growing (Muharemagic & Furht, 2004; Cox, Miller, Linnartz & Kalker, 1999).

RELEVANCE OF WATERMARKING IN MEDICAL IMAGES

Medical Image Processing (MIP) refers to the techniques used to create and manipulate the images of the human body for clinical purposes. The clinical purposes include the medical procedures seeking to reveal and diagnose the disease. The field has research potential that is attempting to understand the processes in humans or animal models. While the general image processing techniques are used for medical images, it requires special treatments due to its special nature. The medical images are derived from different methods of acquisition such as X-Ray, Computed Tomography (CT), Magnetic Resonance Imaging (MRI), Ultra Sound Imaging, Nuclear Imaging, Fundus Imaging etc. Hence, the medical images are differed based on the acquisition methods. The medical images are also differed based on the subject whose images are being acquired. The medical images processed to infer the information about the volume under the skin. It is done exclusively to probe the anatomy of hidden objects below the skin. The medical images can be either as 2-D projection information or as full 3-D mapped information. Medical image protection and authentication are important in an e-healthcare environment where all the visual information and clinical records are stored and exchanged in digital form. Medical image watermarking is a process for enhancing information security, verification and fidelity. At the same time, it is necessary to preserve as much original information as possible in the image, to avoid performance loss for physicians.

SECURITY FEATURES OF MEDICAL IMAGES

The security of medical images is obtained from strict ethics and legislative rules which can be classified in three fixed characteristics: confidentiality, reliability, and availability (Dutta, Singh, Singh, Burget & Prinosil, 2015; Melkemi, Kamal, Singh & Golea, 2017; Hai, Dong Qing, &Ke, 2018; Sliwa, 2019).

- *Confidentiality*: It means that only the entitled users have access to the images in the scheduled system.
- *Reliability*: It is given by two features. i) Integrity: Ensuring that the images have not been modified by an unauthorized person. ii) Authentication: Ensuring that the image belongs indeed to the correct patient and is issued from the correct source.

- *Availability*: It is the capability of an image to be used by the entitled users in the normal scheduled conditions of access and exercise.

In the case of medical image security, the first two characteristics have mainly to be considered. The watermarking scheme has been recognized to control the image reliability by emphasizing its integrity and its authenticity (Coatrieux, Maitre, Sankur, Rolland& Collorec, 2000). A digital watermark is a secret key-dependent signal inserted into digital data and which can be later detected or extracted in order to make an assertion. In medical images, alterations due to the insertion process are not accepted by physicians for diagnosis. Therefore, the requirements in medical images have differed from multimedia applications (Amato, Cozzolino, Mazzeo & Romano, 2018; Wang, Ding & Gu, 2019; Karmakar & Basu, 2019; Bhatt, 2017) .

When the medical images are exchanged in public or private networks, two questions are mainly raised.

1. Whose image is that? It refers to the hospital which sends the image for the diagnosis and associated patient details.
2. Is the image received is genuine? It refers to the authentication of the image.
3. It checks that the image is received from the proper source and ensures that it is not modified.

These two questions can be answered using two different branches of application in watermarking schemes. They are copyright protection and authentication. Copy right protection protects the owner's intellectual property and traces the source of illegal copies of the content. Authentication checks that the received image has been altered or not and localize the tampered regions too. Authentication is the first and basic step in any security architecture whose success prevents other issues in the systems.

This chapter is focusing on developing a watermarking scheme for the authentication of Digital Fundus Image (DFI), a special class of medical images. The next few sections will be discussing on significance of DFI and its security.

DIGITAL FUNDUS IMAGE

The digital fundus images are one particular class of medical images. Ophthalmology is the branch of medicine which deals with the diseases and surgery of the visual pathways, including the eye, brain, and areas surrounding the eye, such as the eyelids. In ophthalmology, the fundus is the interior surface of the eye, including the retina, optic disc and macula. The fundus can be viewed with an ophthalmoscope. The fundus images are taken using a fundus camera. A fundus camera is a specialized low power microscope with an attached camera designed to photograph the interior surface of the eye as shown in figure 4. The optical design of the fundus camera is based on the principle of monocular indirect ophthalmoscopy. A fundus camera provides an upright, magnified view of the fundus. A typical camera views 30 to 50 degrees of retinal area, with a magnification of 2.5 x, and allows some modification of this relationship through zoom or auxiliary lenses from 15 degrees which provides 5 x magnifications to 140 degrees with a wide-angle lens which minimize the image by half. The optics of a fundus camera are similar to those of an indirect ophthalmoscope in that the observation and illumination systems follow dissimilar paths (Coatrieux, Lamard, Puentes& Roux, 2005).

Figure 4. A fundus camera
(Source: Creative Common, USA)

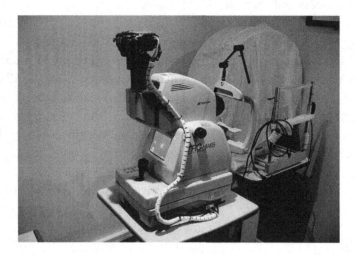

The observation light is focused via a series of lenses through a doughnut-shaped aperture, which then passes through a central aperture to form an annulus, before passing through the camera objective lens and through the cornea onto the retina. The light reflected from the retina passes through the un-illuminated hole in the doughnut formed by the illumination system. As the light paths of the two systems are independent, there are minimal reflections of the light source captured in the formed image. The image forming rays continue towards the low powered telescopic eyepiece. When the button is pressed to take a picture, a mirror interrupts the path of the illumination system allow the light from the flashbulb to pass into the eye. Simultaneously, a mirror falls in front of the observation telescope, which redirects the light onto the capturing medium. Because of the eye's tendency to accommodate while looking through a telescope, it is imperative that the exiting vengeance is parallel in order for an in-focus image to be formed on the capturing medium. The example of fundus images is shown in figure5. The fundus photography is usually taken using a green filter to acquire images of retinal blood vessels. Greenlight is absorbed by blood and appeared a darker color in the fundus photograph than the background and the retinal nerve fiber layer. Hence, the green channel of the fundus images possess valuable information for diagnosis than other channels (Hu, GuoHu, &Chen, 2005).

Importance of Digital Fundus Images in Medical Sciences

Fundus images are used by optometrists, ophthalmologists, and trained medical professionals for monitoring the progression of a disease, diagnosis of a disease. It can also be combined with retinal angiography for mass screening, where these images are analyzed first. Retinal fundus images are useful for the early detection of a number of ocular diseases-if left untreated, which can lead to blindness. Examinations using retinal fundus images are cost-effective and are suitable for mass screening. In this view, retinal fundus images are obtained in many health care centers and medical facilities during medical checkups for ophthalmic examinations. The increase in the number of ophthalmic examinations improves ocular health care in the population but it also increases the workload of ophthalmologists. Therefore, modern health care systems are developed with Computer-Aided Design (CAD) and networking for analyzing retinal fundus images and it can assist in reducing the workload of ophthalmologists and improving the screening accuracy. Such modern health care systems require highly secure communication techniques for exchanging information from one place to another (Wu & Liu, 2003).

Figure 5. Digital fundus image

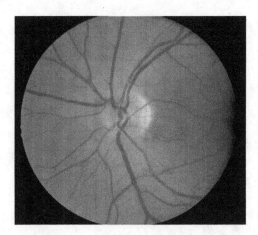

Developing user authentication is a challenging task for digital fundus images. Because, when images are sent through a network for getting suggestions and judgments from the medical science experts from various geographical locations, they must be secured against any form of external attacks.

Scope of the Research in Digital Fundus Images

Research on digital fundus image is an emerging area which is having a good scope in the medical sciences. Regular fundus examinations can detect the initial signs of various major diseases like diabetic retinopathy. Thereby, the actual treatment cost of such diseases in the later stages can be reduced drastically. In the security of medical images, the digital fundus images have not been studied in security. Hence, the theme of developing a security scheme for digital fundus image has been taken here.

KEY REQUIREMENTS FOR MEDICAL IMAGE AUTHENTICATION SCHEME

The following are key requirements used to design and develop an authentication scheme for any classes of medical images. The same requirements have been considered for digital fundus images. However, the behavior of the requirements will have differed from one class of images to another.

R1: Reversibility

Reversibility refers to the lossless watermarking scheme that retains the original image after the extraction process. The scheme is said to be irreversible if it is not able to produce the original image without loss of information after the extraction. Since the fundus images are used for diagnosis purposes, the watermarking schemes must be reversible. The loss of information in such cases may lead to an inaccurate diagnosis. Hence, the fundus images use only reversible watermarking schemes (Bovik, 2000; Muharemagic & Furht, 2004; Poonkuntran, Rajesh, & Eswaran, 2008).

Figure 6. Tradeoff among imperceptibility, fragility, and capacity

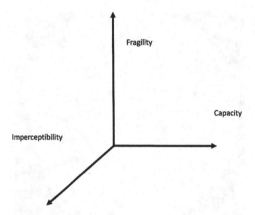

R2: Tamper Detection

The tamper detection is an essential feature in the authentication. It detects the unauthorized modifications done in the fundus images, while it is communicated over a network. This requirement can only detect the modifications on the fundus images, not localize the modifications (Bovik, 2000; Gonzalez & Woods, 2002).

R3: Tamper Localization

This is another feature in the authentication. It localizes the modifications in the fundus images. Based on this requirement (R3), the second requirement (R2) is measured. For a given fundus image, if there are no modifications, then the image is authentic. Otherwise, it is not authentic (Bovik, 2000; Gonzalez & Woods, 2002).

R4: Imperceptibility

Imperceptibility refers to the level of appearance of watermark in the fundus images under normal observation. Since the investigation is mainly done for authentication, it is to be invisible. The hidden watermark should not create any external artifacts in the images. The external artifacts may create rooms for suspicion to the hackers (Bovik, 2000).

R5: Capacity

The capacity is the amount of message to be embedded inside the fundus image. The capacity is measured in terms of the number of bits. The capacity will be in tradeoff with imperceptibility and fragility as shown in figure 6.

R6: Blind Detection

The extraction process in the watermarking can be done in two ways. They are blind and known detection. In blind detection, the watermark is extracted from the watermarked image without the knowledge of the original image. Only with the help of a secret or non-secret key, a watermark is extracted. In the known detection, the watermark is extracted with the knowledge of the original image. The need for the knowledge of the original image in the extraction process may degrade the security. Moreover, the knowledge of the original images may help the hackers to alter the images without altering the watermark. Thereby, the validity of the authentication process will be failed (Bovik, 2000; Gonzalez & Woods, 2002). Hence, it is decided to use blind detection in this research.

R7: Fragility

The fragility refers to the sensitiveness of the watermarking scheme to the attacks. The scheme must be sensitive to the attacks; thereby the watermark should easily be broken in order to authenticate (Bovik, 2000).

PROBLEM STATEMENT AND CHALLENGES

The primary objective of this work is to perform a detailed investigation of the design and development of watermarking schemes for digital fundus image authentication by satisfying the above mentioned all the key requirements (R1-R7). The second objective of this research is to propose and validate a mathematical based algorithmic scheme for fundus image authentication using watermarking. The proposed scheme will be quantitatively analyzed on a common testbed for the above-mentioned requirements (R1-R7) towards satisfying all the requirements.

From the above discussions, it is found that the digital fundus images have not been studied and analyzed on security in content authentication. It is also found that no specific investigation has been done for digital fundus image authentication by satisfying the above mentioned key requirements (R1-R7). Therefore, the detailed investigation has to be carried out in the design and development of digital fundus image authentication scheme by satisfying all the key requirements (R1-R7). The following are the challenging issues for designing such an authentication scheme.

Digital fundus images are one particular class of medical images. It is acquired through a fundus camera. The characteristics of the fundus images may limit the behavior of the scheme. Thereby, a few key requirements may not be satisfied. In the requirements, the capacity, imperceptibility and fragility are in tradeoff by nature. Complete study of all the requirements of the scheme is very difficult (Muharemagic & Furht, 2004). It is also very difficult to fix the optimal point where all the requirements will be satisfied at the possible maximum level (Muharemagic & Furht, 2004). Only a few works of literature are in the direction of the current area of research. The scheme should be designed with current available network bandwidth requirements. It should not seek the extra bandwidth requirements. (Poonkuntran, Rajesh & Eswaran, 2009a; Poonkuntran, Rajesh & Eswaran, 2009b; Poonkuntran, Rajesh & Eswaran, 2009c; Poonkuntran, Rajesh & Eswaran, 2009d).

PROPOSED SCHEME: MODIFIED INTEGER TRANSFORM WATERMARKING SCHEME

This section presents a Modified Integer Transform Watermarking Scheme (MITWS) for fundus image authentication. MITWS uses the color characteristics of the pixel and integer transform. It classifies the color values of the pixels in the image in to primary and secondary. The secondary colors are only used for embedding through the integer transform. MITWS improves the imperceptibility while increasing the capacity. MITWS could extract the watermark completely at the receiver side.

Related Works

The (Nammer &Emman, 2007) have proposed a High Capacity Steganography Scheme (HCSS) for color Bitmap (BMP) images. It hides the data into unwanted areas of the image that are identified with many color differences. It gives a high capacity rate and robust against visual and statistical attacks. The limitation of HCSS is irreversibility. The fundus image requires a reversible scheme which brings the originality of the image without any loss of information. Hence, the HCSS cannot be applied directly to the fundus image. (Tian, 2003) has proposed a Multiple Layer Data Hiding Scheme (MLDHS) for medical images. It uses the integer transform for embedding the secret data and produces the reversible solutions. It could not able to provide a reliable and confidential communication. The reason is that it generates high distortion when embedding takes place in multiple layers. The above mentioned two schemes cannot be applied to fundus images. As the first scheme HCSS is irreversible and second scheme MLDHS produces high distortion, these two schemes cannot suitable for digital fundus image. Through the literature survey, it is found that the use of color characteristics of pixels may improve the capacity with low distortion. Since the HCSS uses color characteristics for embedding and MLDHS is reversible, a new hybrid watermarking scheme using the HCSS and MLDHS is proposed. The proposed scheme mainly uses color characteristics of the pixels and integer transform. The integer transform in MLDHS uses a sequential pixel selection strategy and it is modified in the proposed scheme by introducing a new pixel selection strategy called "intra plane difference embedding" for reducing the distortion. Since the proposed scheme is given by a modified integer transform; it is called as "Modified Integer Transform Watermarking Scheme (MITWS)".

Color Characteristics of Pixels and Its Relevance to Watermarking

Information hiding inside the image is a popular technique nowadays.

An image with a secret message inside can easily be spread over the World Wide Web.

To hide a message inside an image without changing its visible properties, the cover image can be altered in "noisy" areas with many color variations. So that less attention is drawn to the modifications. The schemes in (Poonkuntran, Rajesh & Eswaran, 2009a; Poonkuntran, Rajesh & Eswaran, 2009b;

Poonkuntran, Rajesh & Eswaran, 2009c; Poonkuntran, Rajesh & Eswaran, 2009d) are most common schemes that are altering the images in the above-mentioned way for embedding. In true-color images, each pixel is given by red (R), green (G) and blue (B) components. These three components are referred to as a primary color or RGB color space. Here, each pixel is represented in 24 bits or 3 bytes. Each byte contains a number between 0 and 255. With these three bytes, the computer can generate 256×256×256 = 16777216 combinations. Such a combination is illustrated in figure 7 where R, G and B components are plotted in three different axes. It is very difficult to define a precise color by adjusting these three

Figure 7. RGB color space (cube model)

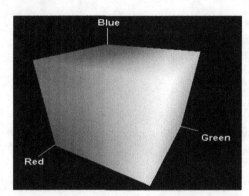

components.

When a 24-bit color image is used, a bit of each of red, green and blue color components can be used for embedding. In this case, a total of 3 bits of secret information is stored in each pixel. Thus, a 256 × 256 color image can contain a total amount of 524288 bits (65536 bytes). When a bit of each color plane of the pixel is used for embedding, the maximum capacity of the watermark is 196608 bits. It is found that the capacity can be improved if the color variations are used for embedding. It means that more than one bit of information can be embedded in a pixel without any external artifacts if the color variations in the image are vague. In a 24-bits or 3 bytes of RGB color, each byte contains two nibbles. The left nibble contains the highest value in the byte while the right nibble contains the lowest value in the byte. Any changes in the right nibble do not create much impact in a byte value and also minimizes embedding alterations. At the same time, a small change in the left nibble creates much impact in the byte value. The 3 bytes is composed of different proportions of three main colors. This proportion classifies these three main colors into primary and secondary. The color which dominates all other colors in a pixel is known as primary color and other colors are known as secondary color. The primary color plays an important role in making a particular color shade. The secondary colors are added with primary colors to create a particular color shade. It is found that if the secondary colors are modified, it improves the capacity with low distortion. Hence, the proposed MITWS is designed using color characteristics. The MITWS identifies the primary and secondary colors for each pixel of the image and the secondary colors are modified to embed the secret data inside the pixel.

Integer Transform Using Intra Plane Difference Embedding

Integer Transform

The integer transform is also called as integer Haar wavelet transform or S transform. The integer transform satisfies the property of reversibility (Tian, 2002). It works as follows. For an 8-bit grayscale pixel pair *(x, y)*, $0 \leq x, y \leq 255$ the integer transform is given by the pair *(m, d)*. Where *m* refers integer average and *d* refers to difference.

The *m* and *d* are calculated as follows.

$$m = \left\lfloor \frac{x+y}{2} \right\rfloor \tag{1}$$

$$d = x - y \tag{2}$$

The inverse transform is given by

$$x = m + \left\lfloor \frac{d+1}{2} \right\rfloor \tag{3}$$

$$y = m - \left\lfloor \frac{d}{2} \right\rfloor \tag{4}$$

Where $\lfloor \ \rfloor$ refers floor operation which rounds the value to nearest integer. In the integer transform, the difference *(d)* is modified based on the watermark bit *(b)* to hide the *b* into the pixel pair. The reversible integer transform provides one to one correspondence between *(x, y)* and *(m, d)*.

Here *(x, y)* and *(m, d)* are in integers that represent the pixels in the image.

The *(x, y)* is in the range of [0, 255]. The *(m, d)* should also be in the same range [0, 255] to prevent the overflow and underflow. It means that for a given pixel pair *(x, y)*, $0 \leq x, y \leq 255$ the *(m, d)* should satisfy the following condition.

$$0 \leq m + \left\lfloor \frac{d+1}{2} \right\rfloor \leq 255 \tag{5}$$

$$0 \leq m - \left\lfloor \frac{d}{2} \right\rfloor \leq 255 \tag{6}$$

The above inequalities are equivalent to

$$d \leq 2(255 - m) \tag{7}$$

$$d \leq 2m + 1 \tag{8}$$

By this, the following condition is made easily.

$$\begin{aligned} d &\leq 2(255 - m) \quad if\,128 \leq m \leq 255 \\ d &\leq 2m + 1 \qquad if\,0 \leq m \leq 127 \end{aligned} \tag{9}$$

Here the secret data bit (watermark) can be embedded by expanding the differences *(d)*. The expanded difference *(d')* is obtained by

$$d' = 2 \times d + b \tag{10}$$

The expanded difference should satisfy the overflow and underflow conditions. Therefore,

$$|d'| \leq \min\{2 \times (255 - m), 2 \times m + 1\} \tag{11}$$

The *(d')* is said to be expandable, if

$$2 \times d + b \leq \min\{2 \times (255 - m), 2 \times m + 1\}.$$

Where $b = \{0, 1\}$ represents the watermark (secret information). While these differences are being expanded, the integer average is not expanded. Therefore with this, a new pixel pair is made by using *(m, d')* through the equation 3 and 4.

From equation 10, it is found that the expanded difference is given by the sum of multiples of 2. Therefore, the expanded difference can be rewritten as

$$d' = 2 \times \left\lfloor \frac{d'}{2} \right\rfloor + LSB(d') \tag{12}$$

Where *LSB (d')* returns the least significant bit of integer *d'*. The following example explains how equation 10 is rewritten by equation 12.

Consider a difference *d=4* and the watermark *b=1*. Using equation 10, the *d=4* is expanded as follows. From equation 10

$$d' = 2 \times d + b \tag{13}$$

By applying $d=4$ and $b=1$ in equation 13

$$d' = 2 \times 4 + 1 = 9 \tag{14}$$

Now, d' is derived from the d' using equation 12 as follows.
From equation 12

$$d' = 2 \times \left\lfloor \frac{d'}{2} \right\rfloor + LSB(d') \tag{15}$$

By applying $d'=9$ in equation 15

$$d' = 2 \times \left\lfloor \frac{9}{2} \right\rfloor + LSB(9) = 9 \tag{16}$$

Thus, the expanded difference (d') is rewritten. The differences are first checked whether it is expanded or not. For the expandable differences, the expansion is done by the modification of LSB. After this modification, the expandable differences can be changed further to embed another bit of information. It is known as multi-layer embedding. The expanded differences are changed under the integer average value. The integer average value is not altered in the integer transform. With the help of this integer average value, the original pixel values are restored without any loss of information at the extraction process. Thus, the integer transform performs reversible embedding.

Modified Integer Transform using Intra Plane Difference Embedding

Tian (2003) proposed an MLDHS using the above-discussed integer transform. It is popularly known as the DE method. The scheme works as follows.

Step 1: Form the pixel pair from the consecutive pixels in the image and transform the pixel pair using integer transform. For example, consider the pixel pair (208,203). According to the above discussed integer transform

x=208 y=203

Mean (m) = floor ((208+203)/2) =205

Difference (d) =208-203=5.

Now, the pair (m, d) is obtained from the pair (x, y). It is known as a forward integer transform.

Step 2: Expand the difference for embedding watermark bit (b) inside the pixel pair (x, y). It is done by modifying the difference (d) with watermark bit (b). For example $b=1$, the modified difference (d') is obtained from equation 10 as follows.

$$d' = 2 \, X \, d + b = 2 \, X \, 5 + 1 = 11.$$

Step 3: Generate watermarked pixel using modified difference value. Apply inverse integer transform to get the modified pixel pair. For the example given in step1 and 2,

$$x'=m+ \text{floor} \, ((d'+1)/2) =205+ (12/2) =211.$$

$$y'=m-\text{floor} \, (d'/2) =205-(11/2) =200.$$

The modified pixel pair ($x'=211$ $y'=200$) is obtained. Thus, the watermark is embedded in the image. Now, this (x', y') is sent to the receiver.

Step 4: Once the receiver, receives the (x', y') repeat the step1 for $x=x'$ and $y=y'$. $x'=211$ and $y'=200$

Mean (m) $=$ floor $((211+200)/2) =205$

Difference (d) $=211-200=11$.

Step 5: Read the least significant bit of (d) to get the watermark information.

LSB (d) $=$LSB $(11) =1 \rightarrow$Watermark is extracted here.

Step 6: Retrieve the original pixel pair by modifying the d by $d/2$.

$$d'=\text{floor} \, (d/2) =\text{floor} \, (11/2) =5.$$

$$x=m+\text{floor} \, ((d'+1)/2) =205+\text{floor} \, ((5+1)/2) =208.$$

$$y=m-\text{floor} \, (d'/2) =205-\text{floor} \, (5/2) =203.$$

Thus, the watermark and original pixel pair are extracted without any loss of information. It is experimentally found MLDHS is not fragile for smaller size of watermarks. When this scheme is applied to fundus images with various sizes of watermarks, the scheme could make the changes in only one color plane. The rest of the color planes are untouched.

When MLDHS is applied to the fundus image, it changes only the Red color plane of the fundus image for the watermark size from 10000 to 100000 as shown in table 1.

Table 1. Fragility of MLDHS

MLDHS			
Size of the Watermark	PSNR at Red	PSNR at Green	PSNR at Blue
10000 bits	58.3826	100	100
20000 bits	49.4946	100	100
30000 bits	45.4838	100	100
40000 bits	43.2254	100	100
50000 bits	41.5407	100	100
60000 bits	40.2972	100	100
70000 bits	39.3442	100	100
80000 bits	38.6115	100	100
90000 bits	38.1254	100	100
100000 bits	37.6290	100	100

It does not change the other color planes. The watermark could not able to sense the modification done in the other color planes (green and blue). Thus, MLDHS is failed in fragility. However, the size (capacity) can be increased to make the scheme as fragile. Increasing capacity directly affects the imperceptibility. The literature survey shows that the fragility is decided by the way in which the locations of the image are chosen for embedding. Instead of ordered selection, if the locations are chosen randomly, fragility can be improved. This means that the locations are selected in a way by which when an attempt is made to tamper the image, the embedded watermark is also changed (Poonkuntran, Rajesh & Eswaran, 2009e). Therefore, a new location selection strategy has been brought in to the MITWS. It is known as intra plane difference embedding. It selects the pixel pair across the color planes rather than consecutive pixels in the single color plane. Thereby, the MITWS modifies two color planes to improve the fragility, while the watermark is being embedded. It is clearly shown in table 2. Thus, the newly introduced intra plane difference embedding strategy improves the fragility in MITWS.

The capacity, tamper detection, and tamper localization are other limitations found in MLDHS. For a given fundus image of size 256×256, the MLDHS can embed a maximum of 128×128 bits per layer. The reason is that it selects the pixel pair consecutively. In MITWS, the pixel pair is formed across the plane. So, the MITWS can embed a maximum of 256×256 bits per layer. Thus, the capacity is improved by the new pixel selection strategy in the MITWS. However, the tamper localization and detection is not yet addressed by the MITWS. The above-discussed color characteristics and modified integer transform with new pixel selection strategies are chosen as key techniques for the design of the proposed scheme MITWS presented in this chapter.

Table 2. Fragiity of MITWS using intra plane difference embedding

MITWS using Intra Plane Difference Embedding			
Size of the Watermark	PSNR at Red	PSNR at Green	PSNR at Blue
10000 bits	100	65.4757	74.9776
20000 bits	100	52.1807	52.5528
30000 bits	100	41.9646	42.0290
40000 bits	100	38.0520	38.0924
50000 bits	100	35.6311	35.6489
60000 bits	100	33.8596	33.8751
70000 bits	100	32.4007	32.4153
80000 bits	100	31.1363	31.1484
90000 bits	100	30.0566	30.0690
100000 bits	100	29.1001	29.1130

Modified Integer Transform Watermarking Scheme (MITWS)

The original fundus image (*I*) is given in 24-bits or 3 bytes of RGB color in MITWS. Each byte contains two nibbles. The left nibble contains the highest value in the byte while the right nibble contains the lowest value in the byte. Since, the nibble value is represented in 4 bits, yielding 16 different decimal values in the interval [0, 15].

This interval is used to identify the primary and secondary color of the pixels in the image. For a given pixel in RGB, the color index is calculated as

$$C_{index} = floor\left(\frac{ColorValue}{16}\right) + 1 \tag{17}$$

Where *Color Value* = {*Red, Green, Blue*}. The color which contains minimum index value is chosen as primary color and others are secondary colors. The primary color of the pixel is untouched and the rest colors of the pixels are taken to integer transform for embedding. The integer transform in MITWS work as follows. For an 8-bit gray scale pixel pair (x, y), $(x, y) \in Z$, $0 \leq Z \leq 255$, the integer average m and difference d are defined as follows:

m=floor ((x+y)/2) $\tag{18}$

Figure 8. Embedding process of MITWS

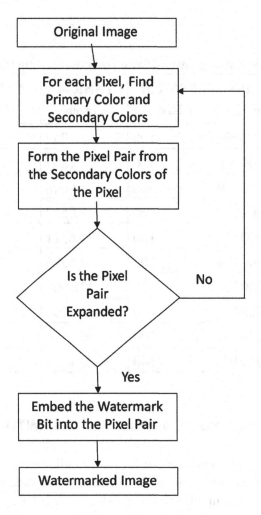

$d=x-y$ (19)

The inverse transform is defined as:

$x'=m+floor((d+1)/2)$ (20)

$y'=m-floor(d/2)$ (21)

The difference (d) is expanded by using watermark bit b to create an expanded difference (d').

$d'=2 \times d+b$ (22)

Where d' is modified difference after embedding the watermark bit (b).

The modified difference (d') is calculated by satisfying the following condition in order to prevent the overflow or underflow during the embedding process.

$$\left|d'\right| \leq 2 \times (255 - m)\, If\ 128 \leq m \leq 255$$

$$\left|d'\right| \leq 2 \times (m + 1)\, If\ 0 \leq m \leq 127 \tag{23}$$

If d' satisfies the equation 23, then d is expandable. Otherwise, d is unexpandable. An expandable difference can be used to hide secret information. If all the expandable differences are selected for data embedding, the capacity rate reaches its maximum limit. Let N and N_e denote the number of different and the number of expandable differences, respectively.

The hiding capacity of an image is defined as:

$$C = N_e / N \tag{24}$$

Therefore, the hiding capacity of the image is proportional to the number of expandable difference. Thus, the MITWS embeds the secret data into the original fundus image to create the watermarked image. The proposed embedding process is illustrated in figure 8.

The extraction process is reversible and it extracts the secret data and original image without any loss of information. For multilayer embedding, the same pixel pair is selected for further data embedding. Here some of the differences may not be expandable for a longer time (Tian, 2003). The extraction process requires information about the primary color of the pixel in the image. The reason is that the primary color of the pixel is not altered in the image for embedding. It means that no information is hidden inside the primary color of the pixel and it is untouched in the process. The secondary colors of the pixel are modified by the integer transform to embed the watermark into it. At this time, the actual color characteristics of the pixel are changed and it is restored at the extraction process after removing the watermark from the watermarked image. It is also difficult to classify the primary and secondary colors in the extraction process without prior information.

To avoid this problem, the Color Classification Map (CCM) is created separately and it is also sent with the watermarked image. The CCM contains binary values {0, 1}. The 0 refers that the color is primary which is not altered in the embedding process. The 1 refers that the color is a secondary color that is altered in the embedding process. For one pixel in the image, a 3-bit code is generated for each of the primary color planes red, green and blue. The expandable pixel pair in the image is also easily identified by this CCM. For non-expandable pixels, the CCM is 000.

Then, the extraction process becomes simple. The extraction process receives the watermarked image and CCM. CCM identifies the secondary colors of the pixel. These pixel values are given to the equation 18 and 19 to find the m and d. Then, the watermark or secret information embedded in the pixel pair is extracted by reading the LSB of a difference value between the pixels in the pixel pair. The other steps are done as discussed in section 4.4.2.

Thus, the embedding and extraction are done using intra plane difference embedding and color characteristics of the pixels in MITWS.

Figure 9. Test images used in the experiment

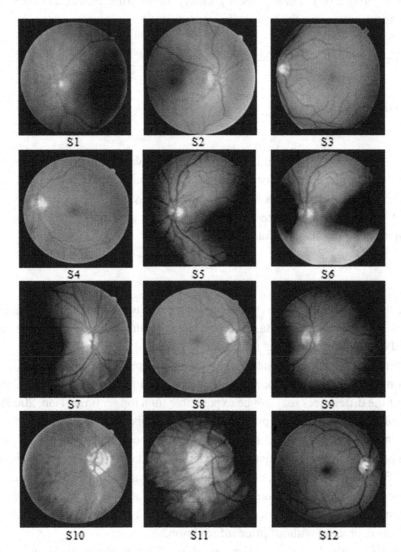

EXPERIMENTAL RESULTS AND ANALYSIS

The MITWS has been simulated using an exclusive common testbed that has been created in this research for the quantitative analysis of the proposed scheme. The details of the testbed are as follows.

- **Test Images:** The test digital fundus images were taken from two public research databases STARE and DRIVE (Poonkuntran, Rajesh & Eswaran, 2014). The database details are as follows.
  - Database Name: Structured Analysis of Retina (STARE)
  - Digital Retinal Images for Vessel Extraction (DRIVE)
  - Address: http://www.ces.clemson.edu/~ahoover/stare/
  - http://www.isi.uu.nl/Research/Databases/DRIVE/
  - Image Format: Tagged Image File Format (TIFF)

○ Size of the image: 565x584x3
○ Color Mode: RGB (Red, Green, Blue).

- **Image Formats:** The test images used in the experiments were given in the Tagged Image File Format (TIFF). Tagged Image File Format (abbreviated TIFF) is a file format for storing images, including photographs and line art. As of 2010, it is under the control of Adobe Systems. Originally created by the company Aldus and called "desktop publishing". The TIFF format is widely applied in medical image processing, image manipulation, publishing, scanning, faxing, word processing, optical character recognition and other applications. Adobe Systems, which acquired Aldus, now holds the copyright to the TIFF specification. The experiment uses 12 test images that are shown in figure 9. The secret message used for embedding is shown in figure 10.

Figure 10. Secret message used in the experiment

```
CAY34567 // IIN
SHANMUGAMPOONKUNTRAN
        // Digital Signature
EMBOLI //  Type of Manifest
0.45   // C/D ratio - Optic Disc
0.33  //  Maximum Vessel Width
0.22  //  Median  Vessel Width
0.44  //   Minimum Vessel Width
```

It consisting of 64 bits IIN (Image Identification Number), 160 bits digital signature, 48 bits manifest type that includes codes for various types of alterations in the retina (for example, emboli refers to emboli manifestation) and 128 bits vessel information that includes diameter of optic disc, Cup to Disc Ratio (C/D) and vessel width details. Finally, the total information came to 400 bits (Coatrieux, Maitre, Sankur, Rolland& Collorec, 2000) (Gonzalez & Woods, 2002). Thus, the watermark has been produced as cover independent. The experiments were carried out for all the key requirements mentioned in section 1. The results are analyzed and discussed in forthcoming sub-sections

Reversibility Experiment

To evaluate the reversibility of the MITWS quantitatively, Peak Signal to Noise Ratio (*PSNR*) in decibel (*dB*) between original image (*I*) and its extracted version image (I_E) were used as a parameter. The PSNR is given by

$$PSNR\ (I,\ I_E) = 10\ Log_{10}\ [(2^{depth}-1)^2/\ MSE] \tag{25}$$

Table 3. Imperceptibility of MITWS

Test Images	MITWS		
	PSNR at Red (in dB)	PSNR at Green (In dB)	PSNR at Blue(in dB)
S1	70.5785	59.8719	59.3724
S2	100.0000	59.5424	59.3338
S3	100.0000	74.0945	100.0000
S4	74.2004	60.2082	59.70214
S5	100.0000	59.1657	58.87464
S6	100.0000	59.2097	58.78281
S7	100.0000	61.7198	61.4854
S8	100.0000	74.0945	93.2853
S9	100.0000	78.0945	100.0000
S10	100.0000	76.3451	100.0000
S11	100.0000	74.0945	100.0000
S12	100.0000	74.0945	100.0000
Average for each plane	95.3982	67.5446	79.2363
Average for all Planes			80.7264

$$MSE(I, I_E) = \frac{\sum_{M,N}\left[I(i,j) - I_E(i,j)\right]^2}{M * N} \tag{26}$$

Where *MSE* is mean square error, *i=0* to *M-1 and j=0* to *N-1*. It is experimentally found that the MITWS is reversible for any size of watermark (capacity). The MITWS produces PSNR as 100% and thereby it guarantees reversibility. It confirms that the changes done in the original image for embedding is completely recoverable due to the integer transform.

Imperceptibility Experiment

The PSNR described above is again used here to measure the imperceptibility of the scheme. Here, the PSNR is taken between the original image (*I*) and its watermarked image (I_w). It is found from the experiment that MITWS produces 80.72% as an average PSNR for Imperceptibility. It means that 80.72% of the original images are not altered and it does not produce any external artifacts under normal vision. The lower PSNR will produce the artifacts. However, the imperceptibility is limited by capacity. When, the capacity increases, the imperceptibility decreases. The imperceptibility results are tabulated in Table 3.

Tamper Detection, Tamper Localization, and Fragility Experiment

For this experiment, 11 attacks have been chosen from the literature survey (Muharemagic & Furht, 2004; Poonkuntran & Rajesh, 2014). It includes jittering, geometrical and filtering attacks. These attacks have widely occurred against image authentication (Muharemagic & Furht, 2004). The attacks are explained as follows:

- **Jittering Attack:** The jittering attack is common to attack in any type of watermarking system. It modifies the pixel value of an image either by changing pixel value or duplicates in an unnoticeable manner. Hence, such an attack is not creating any suspicion externally. Under normal vision, these differences could not be noticed by humans. Jittering can be done on various levels. The levels were modeled as multiples of 5 from 5% to 95% in the experiment.
- **Average:** Returns an averaging filtered output of an image. The averaging can be done by using a mask of size (M x N). Where M refers to number of rows and N refers to the number of columns. The mask size of 3x3 is used in the experiment.
- **Disk:** Returns a circular averaging filtered output of an image. It is done by a mask and radius of the circle. The size of the mask is defined based on the radius of the circle used. If the radius of the circle is R, then the size of the mask is (2xR+1) x (2xR+1). The radius of the circle used in the experiment is 5.
- **Gaussian:** Returns a rotationally symmetric gaussian low pass filtered output of an image. It is done by using two parameters mask and sigma value. The mask size of 3x3 and the default value of sigma = 0.5 is used in the experiment.
- **Laplacian:** Operates the image with approximating the shape of the two dimensional Laplacian operator and returns the output. The approximated shape of Laplacian is controlled by the parameter called alpha. The mask of size 3x3 and the default value of alpha=0.2 were used in the experiment.
- **Log:** Returns a rotationally symmetric Laplacian of gaussian filtered output of an image. The size of the mask used in the experiment is 5×5. The default value of sigma =0.5 is used in the experiment.
- **Motion:** Returns the output of the motion filter. The motion filter approximates the convolved image with the linear motion of a camera by 1 pixels and an angle of theta degrees in a counterclockwise direction. The filter becomes a vector for horizontal and vertical motions. The default l is 9 and the default theta is 0, which corresponds to a horizontal motion of nine pixels. The default values of the filter are used in the experiments.
- **Prewitt:** Returns Prewitt edge Filtered output of images.
- **Sobel:** Returns Sobel edge filtered output of images.
- **Unsharp:** Returns a 3x3 Unsharp contrast enhancement filtered output of images.
- **Rotate** Rotates image by angle degrees in a counterclockwise or clockwise direction around its center point. The rotated image is calculated using bilinear interpolation. The final rotated image is cropped to fit in the original image size. The two angle values 25° and 75° are used in the experiment.

Table 4. MITWS: Results of jittering attack

Percentage of Modification in the Watermarked Image	MITWS	
	Number of bits Modified out of 400 bits of Secret Information	Percentage of Modification in the Watermark
5	40	10.00
10	73	18.25
15	91	22.75
20	108	27.00
25	125	31.25
30	116	29.00
35	160	40.00
40	164	41.00
45	175	43.75
50	161	40.25
55	186	46.50
60	172	43.00
65	190	47.50
70	177	44.25
75	189	47.25
80	188	47.00
85	203	50.75
90	177	44.25
95	217	54.25
Average		38.32

Table 5. MITWS: Results of Geometrical and Filtering Attacks

Name of the Attack	Number of bits modified in 400 Bits of Secret Information	Percentage of Modification in the Watermark
Average	168	42.00
Disk	171	42.75
Gaussian	150	37.50
Laplacian	163	40.75
Log	123	30.75
Motion	311	77.75
Prewitt	321	80.25
Sobel	154	38.50
Unsharp	167	41.75
Rotation by 25°	171	42.75
Rotation by 75°	104	26.00
Average		45.52

For all the above-mentioned attacks, the default values of the parameters are used in the experiment. The reason is that the default values are specifying the stable behavior of all the attacks. Moreover, these are the minimum requirements for the attacks.

If the scheme is fragile against the minimum requirements of the attack, it is sure that the scheme will be fragile for other levels of the requirements of attacks.

The first experiment is done for a jittering attack. In this, the watermarked image is modified from 5% to 95% in the multiples of 5. For the same, the number of bits changed in the corresponding watermark is also measured. From the results, it is found that MITWS changes around 38% at an average of the watermark to authenticate. The results are tabulated in Table 4.

The next experiment is done for geometrical and filtering attacks. It is experimentally found that MITWS changes around 45% of the watermark at an average for the geometrical and filtering attacks. The results are shown in figure 11 and table 5. It is also experimentally found that the MITWS could not detect and locate the tampering in the images. The reason is that the watermark in the MITWS is generated without the knowledge of the cover image.

Figure 11. MITWS: fragility against geometrical and filtering attacks

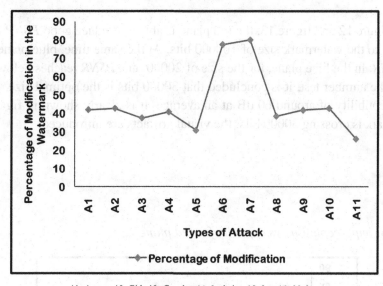

A1 - Average, A2 - Disk, A3 - Gaussian, A4 - Laplacian, A5 - Log, A6 - Motion,
A7 - Prewitt, A8 - Sobel, A9 - Unsharp, A10 - Rotation by 25°, A11 - Rotation by 75°.

Capacity Experiment

To identify the optimal size of the watermark with good imperceptibility, the experiment is conducted on a set of test fundus images in the size of 512×512×3 and the corresponding imperceptibility has been calculated using *PSNR* between original image *(I)* and watermarked image *(I$_w$)*. In this experiment, red and blue color planes of the fundus image are only considered for imperceptibility. The reason is that the green color plane of the fundus image is the primary color and it is not modified during embedding. Only red and blue color planes of the fundus images are modified for embedding.

Table 6. MITWS: imperceptibility vs capacity

Size of Watermark in Number of bits	PSNR at Red	PSNR at Blue
10000	81.46387	61.08983
20000	78.06911	50.1236
30000	76.30848	45.73024
40000	74.75822	41.48165
50000	72.99918	37.96801
60000	71.91828	36.63454
70000	70.92042	35.88567
80000	70.40995	35.31327
90000	70.08852	34.86395
100000	69.55787	34.45396

From table 6, figure 12 and figure 13, the red plane is able to produce good *PSNR* (around 70 dB at an average) values to the watermark size of 100000 bits. At the same time, blue planes are not able to produce good *PSNR*. In the blue plane, for the size of 20000 bits, *PSNR* reaches below 50 dB.

Therefore, by the number test, it is concluded that 30000 bits is the optimal size of the watermark with good imperceptibility of around 60 dB at an average. It is clearly shown in figure 14. When the size of the watermark is crossing 30000 bits, the visual artifacts are introduced.

Figure 12. MITWS: imperceptibility vs capacity for red plane

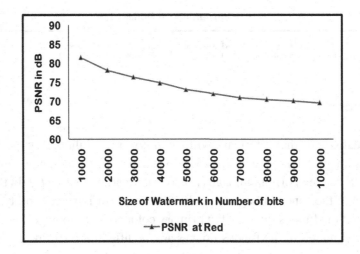

Figure 13. MITWS: imperceptibility vs capacity for blue plane

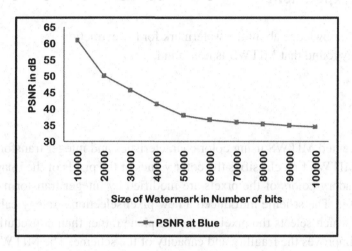

Figure 14. MITWS: imperceptibility vs capacity

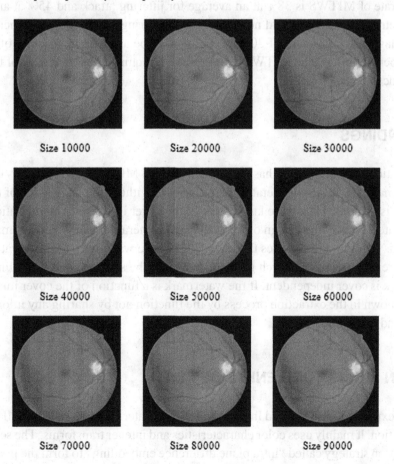

Size 10000   Size 20000   Size 30000

Size 40000   Size 50000   Size 60000

Size 70000   Size 80000   Size 90000

Blind Detection Experiment

The MITWS requires knowledge about the watermark for the extraction.

It is experimentally found that MITWS is non-blind.

OBSERVATIONS

This chapter has presented MITWS using color characteristics and integer transform for fundus image authentication. The MITWS first classifies the color values of the pixels of the image in to primary and secondary. The secondary colors of the pixels are modified by integer transform in order to hide the secret information in it. The scheme introduced a new pixel selection strategy called "intra plane difference embedding" which selects the pixel across the plane rather than consecutive pixels in the one plane. This strategy improves the fragility and capacity of the scheme. The MITWS is reversible since it uses the reversible integer transform for embedding. The reversibility is retained for any sizes of the watermark. The MITWS could produce imperceptibility of 80.72% at an average. The MITWS is fragile against jittering, filtering and geometrical attacks.

The fragility rate of MITWS is 38% at an average for jittering attack and 45% at an average for filtering and geometrical attacks. It could not detect the tampering and it could not locate the tampered regions in the images. A watermark of 30000 bits found to be an optimal capacity of MITWS with a good level of imperceptibility. The MITWS is non-blind. It requires the knowledge of the watermark at the extraction process.

CRITICAL FINDINGS

The tamper detection and localization has not been addressed MITWS. The reason is that the cover independent watermark, i.e. scheme generates the watermark without the knowledge of the cover image. If the watermark is generated using the knowledge of the cover image, any modification in the images can easily be located. Hence, the design of the watermark generation using a cover image is required.

The MITWS is non-blind. It requires the knowledge of the watermark at the extraction process. As per the key requirements of this research given in section 1, the scheme should be blind. The reason is that the watermark is cover independent. If the watermark is a function of the cover image, then the watermark can be known in the extraction process by the function not by sharing any information between the embedding and extraction.

CONCLUSION AND FUTURE ENHANCEMENT

This chapter has explained the Modified Integer Transform Watermarking Scheme (MITWS) for fundus image authentication. It mainly uses color characteristics and integer transforms. The scheme introduces a new pixel selection strategy called "intra plane difference embedding" to form the pixel pair by selecting the pixels across the color planes. The MITWS is reversible, fragile and imperceptible. It could not detect and locate the tampering in the images. The MITWS is non-blind. It requires the knowledge of the watermark at the extraction process. The tamper detection, tamper localization and blind detection are the major issues in the MITWS. If the watermark is generated as a function of the cover image, the two main issues mentioned above can easily be solved. For tamper detection and localization, any changes in the cover lead to change the response of the function used for generating watermark. If the image is tampered, then the watermark is also modified. So, the tampering can be easily detected and located. For blind detection, the function used to generate the watermark can be used to generate the reference watermark for the verification and validation during the extraction process. The actual embedded watermark can be extracted using an integer transform. Thus, the scheme can be designed as a blind scheme.

The future enhancement of this work is to generate watermark as cover dependent using non-linear functions such as chaotic models and hashing techniques. This step will bring tamper detection and localization in the proposed scheme. The marking spaces for embedding will be reviewed further using a pseudo-random process to make the scheme to do extraction in complete blind without the knowledge of the original and secret data.

REFERENCES

Amato, F., Cozzolino, G., Mazzeo, A., & Romano, S. (2018). Intelligent medical record management: A diagnosis support system. *International Journal of High-Performance Computing and Networking*, *12*(4), 391–399. doi:10.1504/IJHPCN.2018.096726

Bhatt, C. M. (2017). Data Protection and Security Issues in Social Media. In C. Bhatt, & S. Peddoju (Eds.), *Cloud Computing Systems and Applications in Healthcare* (pp. 135–162). Hershey, PA: IGI Global. doi:10.4018/978-1-5225-1002-4.ch008

Bovik, A. L. (2000). *Handbook of Image and Video Processing. Academic Press* (pp. 99–69120). Canada: Library of Congress Catalog Number.

Poonkuntran, S., & Rajesh, R. S. (2014). Chaotic model-based semi-fragile watermarking using integer transforms for digital fundus image authentication. *Multimedia Tools and Applications*, *68*. doi:10.100711042-012-1227-5

Coatrieux, G., Lamard, M., Lamard, W., Puentes, J., & Roux, C. (2005). A Low Distortion and Reversible Watermark: Application to Angiographic Images of the Retina. *Proceedings of the 27th IEEE Annual Conference on Engineering in Medicine and Biology,* pp. 1-4. Shanghai, China.

Coatrieux, G., Maitre, H., Sankur, B., Rolland, Y., & Collorec, R. (2000). Relevance of Watermarking in Medical Imaging. *Proceedings of the IEEE International Conference on Information Technology Applications in Biomedicine,* Arlington, TX, pp. 250-255, November 2000. 10.1109/ITAB.2000.892396

Cole, E. (2003). *Hiding in Plain Sight: Steganography and Art of Covert Communications*. USA: Wiley Publishing

Cox, I., Miller, M., Linnartz, J. P., & Kalker, T. (1999). A Review of Watermarking Principles and Practices. In K. K. Parhi, & T. Nishitani (Eds.), Digital Signal Processing in Multimedia Systems, pp. 461-485. Marcell Dekker Inc. doi:10.1201/9781482276046-17

Dutta, M. K., Singh, A., Singh, A., Burget, R., & Prinosil, J. (2015). Digital identification tags for medical fundus images for teleophthalmology applications. *Proceedings 2015 38th International Conference on Telecommunications and Signal Processing.* pp. 781-784. Prague, Czech Republic. DOI: 10.1109/TSP.2015.7296372

Gonzalez, R. C., & Woods, R. E. (2002). Digital Image Processing (2nd Ed.), Prentice-Hall Publishers, Upper Saddle River, NJ 07458.

Hai, H., Xie, D. Q., & Ke, Q. (2018). A watermarking-based authentication and image restoration in multimedia sensor networks. *International Journal of High-Performance Computing and Networking, 12*(1), 65–73. doi:10.1504/IJHPCN.2018.093846

Hu, Z., Guo, X., Hu, X., Chen, X., & Wang, Z. (2005). The Identification and Recognition Based on Ocular Fundus, Springer Link Lecture Notes in Computer Science, 3832, pp. 770-776.

Karmakar, R., & Basu, A. (2019). Implementation of a Reversible Watermarking Technique for Medical Images. In S. Bhattacharyya (Ed.), *Intelligent Innovations in Multimedia Data Engineering and Management* (pp. 1–37). Hershey, PA: IGI Global. doi:10.4018/978-1-5225-7107-0.ch001

Melkemi, K., & Golea, N. E. H. (2017). ROI-based fragile watermarking for medical image tamper detection. *International Journal of High-Performance Computing and Networking., 1*(1), 1. doi:10.1504/IJHPCN.2017.10013846

Muharemagic, E., & Furht, B. (2004). Survey of Watermarking Techniques and Applications, Department of Computer Science and Engineering Florida Atlantic University, 777 Glades Road, Boca Raton, FL 33431-0991, USA.

Nammer, N., & Emman, E. L. (2007). Hiding a Large Amount of Data with High Security using Steganography Algorithm. *Journal of Computer Science, 3*(4). pp. 223-232.

Poonkuntran, S., Rajesh, R. S., & Eswaran, P. (2009a). Reversible, Multilayered Watermarking Scheme for Fundus Images Using Intra-Plane Difference Expanding. *Proceedings of the IEEE International Advance Computing Conference,* pp. 2583-2587, Patiala, India.

Poonkuntran, S., Rajesh, R. S., & Eswaran, P. (2009b). Wavetree Watermarking: An Authentication Scheme for Fundus Images. *Proceedings of the IEEE Sponsored International Conference on Emerging Trends in Computing,* pp. 507-511. India.

Poonkuntran, S., Rajesh, R. S., & Eswaran, P. (2009c). A Robust Watermarking Scheme for Fundus Images Using Intra-Plane Difference Expanding. *Proceedings of the IEEE Sponsored International Conference on Emerging Trends in Computing. pp.* 433-436. India.

Poonkuntran, S., Rajesh, R. S., & Eswaran, P. (2009e). Analysis of Difference Expanding Method for Medical Image Watermarking. *Proceedings of 2009 International Symposium on Computing, Communication, and Control,* pp. 30-34. Singapore.

Poonkuntran, S., Rajesh, R. S., & Eswaran, P. (2009d). Imperceptible Watermarking Scheme for Fundus Images Using Intra-Plane Difference Expanding. *International Journal on Computer and Electrical Engineering, 1*(4). 1793-8198.

Shanmugam, P., Rajesh, R. S., & Perumal, E. (2008). A Reversible Watermarking With Low Warping: An Application to Digital Fundus Images. *Proceedings of the IEEE International Conference on Computer and Communication Engineering,* pp. 472-477.

Sliwa, J. (2019). Assessing complex evolving cyber-physical systems (case study: Smart medical devices). *International Journal of High-Performance Computing and Networking, 13*(3), 294–303. doi:10.1504/IJHPCN.2019.098570

Tian, J. (2002). Reversible Watermarking by Difference Expansion. *Proceedings of Workshop on Multimedia and Security: Authentication, Secrecy, and Steganalysis, pp.* 19-22.

Tian, J. (2003). Reversible Data Embedding using a Difference Expansion. *IEEE Transactions on Circuits and Systems for Video Technology, 13*(8), pp. 890-893.

Wang, B., Ding, Q., & Gu, X. (2019). A secure reversible chaining watermark scheme with hidden group delimiter for WSNs. *International Journal of High-Performance Computing and Networking, 14*(3). doi:10.1504/IJHPCN.2019.102126

Wu, M., & Liu, B. (2003). Data Hiding in Image and Video. I. Fundamental Issues and Solutions, *IEEE Transactions on Image Processing, 12*(6), pp. 685-695.

Chapter 7
A Distributed M–Tree for Similarity Search in Large Multimedia Database on Spark

Phuc Do

University of Information Techonology (VNU-HCM), Vietnam

Trung Hong Phan

University of Information Techonology (VNU-HCM), Vietnam

ABSTRACT

In this chapter, Image2vec or Video2vector are used to convert images and video clips to vectors in large multimedia database. The M-tree is an index structure that can be used for the efficient resolution of similarity queries on complex objects. M-tree can be profitably used for content-based retrieval on multimedia databases provided relevant features have been extracted from the objects. In a large multimedia database, to search for similarities such as k-NN queries and Range queries, distances from the query object to all remaining objects (images or video clips) are calculated. The calculation between query and entities in a large multimedia database is not feasible. This chapter proposes a solution to distribute the M-Tree structure on the Apache Spark framework to solve the Range Query and kNN Query problems in large multimedia database with a lot of images and video clips.

INTRODUCTION

Multimedia databases contain images and video clips (Guo, 2013; Riaz, Ashraf, & Aslam, 2014). Today, the volume of multimedia database contains a huge number of objects. In this we use Image2vec (Garcia-Gasulla, Béjar, Cortés, Ayguadé, & Labarta, 2015) or Video2vec (Hu, Li, & Li, 2016) to convert images and videos to vectors and store these vectors for more convenience in processing. To search for similarities such as kNN queries and Range queries in vector spaces (representing images and video clips), we need to calculate distances from the query vector to all remaining vectors. In a large multimedia database, the vector space with millions to billions of vectors. The calculation of distances

DOI: 10.4018/978-1-7998-2701-6.ch007

as above is not feasible. Therefore, we need a method to reduce the number of distance calculations in these problems. The M-Tree structure, which is a distance-based vector space indexing method, can effectively solve the Range queries and kNN queries (Ciaccia, Patella, & Zezula, 1997; Kouahla, 2011). Because the M-Tree structure is implemented on a local system, it only solves problems in small vector spaces, in which the set of vectors can fit into a computer. However, very large multimedia databases contain millions of vectors of image or video clip are very popular. The local M-Tree structure cannot meet the new needs to solve problems of similarity searching in large vector spaces, in which vectors must be stored distributedly across multiple computers. Therefore, in this article, we propose a solution to distribute the M-Tree structure on the Apache Spark framework (Assefi, Behravesh, Liu, & Tafti, 2018; Shanahan & Dai, 2019; Zecevic & Bonaci, 2017) to solve the kNN and Range Query problems in large vector spaces. In addition, we also present experimental results on creating both local and distributed M-Tree structures built from 64-dimentional vector sets with different scales. Finally, we present the experimental results on the kNN and Range queries on the built M-Tree structures of a multimedia database of image and video clips;

The main contributions of this article are as follows:

- Converting a multimedia objects as images and video clips to vectors using Image2vec and Video2vec.
- Proposing a solution to distribute the M-Tree structure to meet new needs in the era of big data.
- Solving kNN and Range Query problems based on the distributed M-Tree structure.
- Providing relevant experimental results.

The rest of this article is organized as follows. Section 2 is the related works. Section 3 introduces the knowledge base we use in this article. Section 4 is the methodology. Section 5 is the experiments. The final is the conclusion and future work

RELATED WORK

Beginning with a paper proposing the M-Tree structure as an effective method to search similarities (Ciaccia et al., 1997), there were many works to implement and develop the M-Tree structure, as well as develop similar indexing structures.

In 2010, Akrivi Vlachou proposed a framework for distributed similarity search, where each participating peer stored its own data that indexed locally by using M-Tree structures. In order to scalability and efficiency of search, they used a super-peer architecture, where super-peers were responsible for query routing. They also proposed the construction of metric routing indices suitable for distributed similarity search in metric spaces (Vlachou, Doulkeridis, & Kotidis, 2010).

In 2011, Z. Kouahla studied a variant of a metric tree data structure for indexing and querying data, and conducted experiments to compare his solution with techniques: MM-Tree and SliM-Tree. The author also provided the taxonomy of indexing techniques in metric spaces as shown in Figure 1 (Kouahla, 2011).

And most recently, in February 2019, Jörg Peter Bachmann proposed the SuperM-Tree structure as an extension of the M-Tree structure (Bachmann, 2019). This author introduced metric subset spaces as a generalized concept of metric spaces. Various metric distance functions can be extended to metric subset distance functions.

Most of the above works do not mention large vector spaces, in which data is stored distributedly in a computer cluster, except for works of Akrivi Vlachou. However, this author proposed a new framework for distributed similarity search. Here, we do not build a new framework but use the famous Apache Spark framework to distribute the M-Tree structure to solve problems of searching for similarities.

Figure 1. A simplified taxonomy of indexing techniques in metric spaces

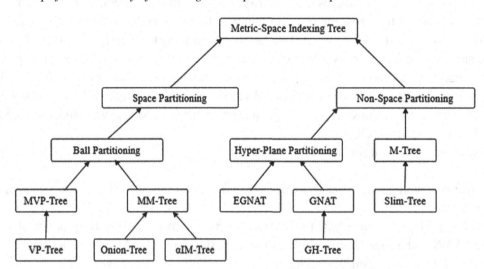

In the era of big data, word representations have been used in several reasearch areas. The famous model is word2vec model developed by Mikolov (Mikolov, Chen, Corrado, & Dean, 2013). Based on this model, we have graph2vec model, node2vec, topic2vec model… (Cai, Zheng, & Chang, 2018). Normally, these models used a pre-trained model to convert objects (word, graph node, topic of document) to vectors (Cai et al., 2018; Mikolov et al., 2013) (H. Cai V. W., 2018). Many authors have developed similar models to convert images to vectors. These models are named Image2vec (Garcia-Gasulla, 2016). Besides, we have Video2vec model (Hu et al., 2016) that can convert a video clip to vector. In this article, we don't discuss deeply in Image2vec or Video2vec, we just use this kind of models to generate Images or Video clip to vector. Then we feed these vectors to our proposed DM-Tree model.

PRELIMINARIES

Image to Vector

In this section, we will discuss how to convert image or Video clip to vector. Vector-space word representations include linguistic regularities, enabling semantic operations based on vector arithmetic. In linguistic research, we used a pre-trained model such as Word2vec or Glove2vec to convert a word into vector (Mikolov et al., 2013). Similarly, in this article, we used same method to obtain large and sparse vectors. The author used CNN to build a vector for each image. They used GoogLeNet pre-trained model available in the Caffe deep learning framework which was trained using the 1.2 Million images. This model is used to create vector of an image (Garcia-Gasulla et al., 2015). Beside of this, we can convert a video clip to vector. In this model, they use the Recurrent Neural Networks (RNN) to learn the temporal structure of video and embed semantic meanings to form a fixed length vector representation. This model is called Video2vec (Hu et al., 2016).

Metric Space and Euclidean Distance

In mathematics, a metric space is a set together with a metric on the set. The metric is a function that defines a concept of distance between any two members of the set, which are usually called points (Ciaccia et al., 1997; Kouahla, 2011). The metric satisfies the following properties:

- The distance from a point to itself is zero.
- The distance between two distinct points is positive.
- The distance from x to y is the same as the distance from y to x.
- The direct distance from x to y is less than or equal to the distance from x to y is via any third point z.

The following is definition formally of a metric space.

Definition 1: Metric Space

Given M is a non-empty set. A mapping $d : M \times M \to \mathbb{R}$ such that for any $x, y, z \in M$, the following holds:

1) $d(x, y) = d(y, x)$ (symmetry)

2) $0 < d(x, y) < \infty (x \neq y)$ and $d(x, x) = 0$ (non negativity)

3) $d(x, y) \leq d(x, z) + d(z, y)$ (triangle inequality)

then d is called a distance or a metric on M and an ordered pair (M, d) is called a metric space.

For example, we define a mapping $d : \mathbb{R}^n \times \mathbb{R}^n \to \mathbb{R}$ such that for any $x = (x_1, x_2, \ldots, x_n)$ and $y = (y_1, y_2, \ldots, y_n)$, $d(x, y) = \sum_{i=1}^{n} |x_i - y_i|$. We easily prove that d satisfies Definition 1, so d is a metric on $\mathbb{R}^n$ and a pair $(\mathbb{R}^n, d)$ is a metric space. d is known as Manhattan distance.

The metric space (M, d) is often written as M where d is understood implicitly when not confused.

There are many common distances such as Manhattan distance, Chebyshev distance, Euclidean distance… However, in this article, we only present the Euclidean distance.

Definition 2: Euclidean Distance

In, the Euclidean distance or Euclidean metric between points (or vectors) and is the length of the line segment connecting them and is given by the Pythagorean formula:

$$d(x,y) = \left[\sum_{i=1}^{n} (x_i - y_i)^2 \right]^{\frac{1}{2}}$$

For example, in $\mathbb{R}^3$, given $x = (1, -3, 4)$ and $y = (-2, 3, -8)$ then

$$d(x,y) = \sqrt{(1+2)^2 + (-3-3)^2 + (4+8)^2} \approx 13.75 \,.$$

Similarity Queries

There are two important types of similarity queries. They are the range query and the k nearest neighbors (kNN) query. The range query is used to find objects in a metric space such that the distance from them to the query object is less than or equal to a given radius. The k nearest neighbors query is used to find k objects closest to the query object in a metric space. The followings are definitions of them (Ciaccia et al., 1997).

Definition 3: Range Query

Given a metric space (M,d), a query object $Q \in M$ and a maximum search distance rQ. The range query $range(Q, rQ)$ selects all objects $O \in M$ such that $d(O,Q) \le rQ$.

Definition 4: K nearest Neighbors Query

Given a metric space (M,d), a query object $Q \in M$ and an integer k ≥ 1. The kNN query $kNN(Q,k)$ selects the k objects in M which have the shortest distance from Q.

M-Tree

The M-Tree is a method to index metric spaces. Structurally, the M-Tree is a balanced tree, able to process dynamic data files, so it does not require periodical rebuild. It partitions objects based on their relative distances measured by a specific distance function, and stores these objects into fixed-size nodes, which correspond to regions of the metric space.

One node of the M-Tree can store up to M entries, where M is the capacity of nodes. Internal nodes store entries of routing objects, whereas leaf nodes store entries of all indexed objects. Each entry of a routing object O_r has the following format:

$$entry\left(O_r\right) = \left[O_r, r_r, d\left(O_r, O_r^p\right), ptr\left(T_r\right)\right]$$

Where O_r is the routing object, $r_r \geq$ is the covering radius of O_r; $d\left(O_r, O_r^p\right)$ is the distance between O_r and O_r^p, the parent object of O_r; $ptr\left(T_r\right)$ is the pointer pointing to the root of sub-tree T_r, the covering tree of O_r. Whereas each entry of an indexed object O_i has the following format:

$$entry\left(O_i\right) = \left[O_i, d\left(O_i, O_i^p\right)\right]$$

Where O_i is the indexed object, and $d\left(O_i, O_i^p\right)$ is the distance between O_i and O_i^p, the parent object of O_i.

In summary, the components of the M-Tree include the following:

1. Routing objects: .
2. Indexed objects: .
3. Entries of routing objects. Each entry of a routing object $O_r \equiv entry\left(O_r\right)$ includes:

   a. The routing object: O_r.
   b. The covering radius of O_r: r_r.
   c. The pointer points to the covering tree, T_r, of O_r: $ptr\left(T_r\right)$.
   d. The distance between O_r and O_r^p, where O_r^p is the parent object of O_r: $d\left(O_r, O_r^p\right)$.

4. Entries of indexed objects. Each entry of an indexed object $O_i \equiv entry\left(O_i\right)$ includes:

   a. The indexed object: O_i.
   b. The distance between O_i and O_i^p, where O_i^p is the parent object of O_i: $d\left(O_i, O_i^p\right)$.

5. Internal nodes. Each internal node includes a set of entries of routing objects.
6. Leaf nodes. Each leaf node includes a set of entries of indexed objects.

Figure 2 is an example of an M-Tree with the capacity M = 3. The root node of the M-Tree (node 1) has two entries of two routing object O_1 and O_5. Consider $entry(O_1)$ in node 1, the covering radius of O_1 is 4.8. Because O_1 belongs to the root node (node 1), it means $O_1^p \equiv O_1$, so the distance between O_1 and O_1^p is 0.0. The entry of O_1 points to the sub-tree on the left, where the root node is node 2. And similar to above, node 2 has two entries of two routing object O_1 and O_8. The covering radius of O_1 is 2.5, and the covering radius of O_8 is 3.5. In node 2,

$$O_1^p \equiv O_8^p \equiv O_1\left(in\ node\ 1\right).$$

Figure 2. An example of an M-Tree with the capacity M = 3

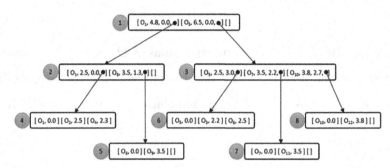

The distance between O_1 and O_1^p is 0.0, and the distance between O_8 and O_8^p is 1.3. And continue, the entry of O_1 points to a leaf node, node 4. Node 4 is full with three entries of three indexed objects O_1, O_2, and O_4. In node 4,

$$O_1^p \equiv O_2^p \equiv O_4^p \equiv O_1 \left(in\, node\, 2 \right);$$

$$d\left(O_1, O_1^p\right) = d\left(O_1, O_1\right) = 0.0,$$

$$d\left(O_2, O_2^p\right) = d\left(O_2, O_1\right) = 2.5,$$

and

$$d\left(O_4, O_4^p\right) = d\left(O_4, O_1\right) = 2.3.$$

The entry of O_8 points to a leaf node, node 5. Node 5 is not full with two entries of two indexed objects O_8 and O_9. In node 5,

$$O_8^p \equiv O_9^p \equiv O_8 \left(in\, node\, 2 \right);$$

$$d\left(O_8, O_8^p\right) = d\left(O_8, O_8\right) = 0.0$$

and

$$d\left(O_9, O_9^p\right) = d\left(O_9, O_8\right) = 3.5.$$

The remaining nodes are similar to above.

Table 1. Properties of the DM-Tree class

Properties	Types	Descriptions
CAPACITY	Int	The capacity of DM-Tree objects.
M-Trees	RDD[(Int, M-Tree)]	Storing M-Tree objects and the ids of them.

METHODOLOGY

To solve the problems of similarity search, we can calculate distances between the query vector and all other vectors in a vector space. However, we can only apply this method in small vector spaces. In large vector spaces, we must look for a method that can reduce the number of distance calculations. We have studied many methods and realized that M-Tree can help us do that. Therefore, we implemented the local M-Tree structure (running on one machine) in the Scala language. After that, we implemented the distributed M-Tree in the Scala language running on the Apache Spark framework. We also conducted a lot of experiments on the local and distributed M-Tree structures. The M-Tree structure was tested on a computer and the DM-Tree structure was tested on the Spark Cluster as shown in Figure 8. In the following are details of our solution.

We created the M-Tree class to represent the local M-Tree structure in Scala based on (Ciaccia et al., 1997; Kouahla, 2011). The M-Tree class has two important methods to search for similarities as follows:

- **def kNNSearch(Q: Entry, k: Int): ListBuffer[(Long, Double)]:** Execute a kNN Query and return k pairs (id, distance) of entries that are k nearest neighbors of the Q entry.
- **def rangeSearch(Q: Entry, rQ: Double): ListBuffer[(Long, Double)]:** Execute a Range Query and return pairs (id, distance) of entries that satisfy the distances from Q to them less than or equal to rQ.

We do not present these algorithms here because they have been described in (Ciaccia et al., 1997).

In the era of big data, we have large multimedia database with a lot of vectors representing images or video clips. To store large vector spaces, we use the HDFS distributed file system of the Hadoop framework (Zecevic & Bonaci, 2017). In addition to HDFS, we can also use other distributed file systems such as Amazon S3, Google File System… To solve the problems of searching similarities in large vector spaces we built a distributed M-Tree structure and named it DM-Tree.

We implement the DM-Tree structure by defining the DM-Tree class to combine with the M-Tree class. A DM-Tree object contains a set of M-Tree objects created from a vector space. The vector space is stored in the partitions of an RDD. We create an M-Tree object from each partition and use an RDD structure to store distributedly these M-Tree objects. Table 1 and Table 2 show properties and methods of the DM-Tree class.

The following are details of the algorithms applied in the DM-Tree class.

Table 2. Methods of the DM-Tree class

Methods	Descriptions
def createFrom(path: String, CAPACITY: Int): DM-Tree	
	Creating a DM-Tree object from HDFS files which contain vectors.
def save(path: String, dmtree: DM-Tree): Unit	
	Storing a DM-Tree object into HDFS.
def load(path: String): DM-Tree	
	Loading a DM-Tree object from HDFS.
def rangeSearch(Q: String, rQ: Double): ListBuffer[(Long,Double)]	
	Executing the Range Query.
def kNNSearch(Q: String, k: Int): ListBuffer[(Long,Double)]	
	Executing the kNN Query.

Creating the DM-Tree Structure

Figure 3. The process of creating the DM-Tree structure from a vector set

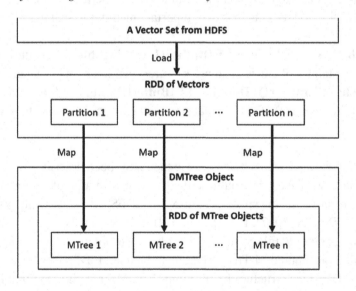

The process of creating the DM-Tree structure is shown in Figure 3. First, we load the set of vectors from the HDFS distributed file system of the Hadoop framework into an RDD structure in the Apache Spark cluster (Zecevic & Bonaci, 2017). Then, on each partition of the RDD structure, we create one M-Tree structure by using the Map transformation. The Map transformation is similar to the forEach loop but it executes tasks in parallel. The set of the M-Tree structures created from partitions of the RDD structure is the DM-Tree structure. Because we can configure the number of partitions of the RDD structure, the number of the M-Tree structures of the DM-Tree structure can also be configured. Algorithm 1 details the algorithm of creating a DM-Tree structure.

Storing the DM-Tree Structure

Algorithm 1. The algorithm creates a DM-Tree object from a vector set

```
- Input: 1) path: The path of HDFS files contains the vector set. 2) CAPACITY:
The capacity of M-Tree objects in the DM-Tree object.
- Output: a DM-Tree object.
1. Load HDFS files of the vector set into an RDD object in the Spark Cluster.
2. Create a new DM-Tree object with CAPACITY as the capacity of the M-Tree ob-
jects in the DM-Tree object.
3. Map each partition of the RDD object to an M-Tree object in the DM-Tree ob-
ject (It means creating an M-Tree object from each partition of the RDD object
in parallel).
4. Return the DM-Tree object.
```

Because creating DM-Tree structures is time-consuming, we need to store DM-Tree structures for reuse later. Further, vector spaces can be very large, so DM-Tree structures can also be very large. We cannot store DM-Tree structures in a local file system but must be stored in a distributed file system like HDFS. Algorithm 2 details the algorithm of storing a DM-Tree structure into HDFS.

Algorithm 2. The algorithm stores a DM-Tree object into HDFS

```
- Input: 1) path: The path of a directory in HDFS will store the DM-Tree ob-
ject. 2) dmtree: The DM-Tree object will be stored into HDFS.
- Output: none.
1. Store information of the DM-Tree object such as: the capacity of the DM-
Tree object, number of M-Tree objects in the DM-Tree object.
2. Map each M-Tree object in the DM-Tree object {
3. Store the M-Tree object into the directory in HDFS specified by the path.
4. }
5. Return.
```

Loading the DM-Tree Structure

When we need to search similarities in vector spaces effectively, we need to load DM-Tree structures from HDFS into Spark Cluster. Because a DM-Tree structure consists of a set of M-Tree structures, each executor should load an M-Tree structure to process effectively. Therefore, the number of executors should be equal to the number of M-Tree structures. Algorithm 3 details the algorithm of loading a DM-Tree object from HDFS.

Algorithm 3. The algorithm loads a DM-Tree object from HDFS

```
- Input: 1) path: The path of the directory in HDFS is storing the DM-Tree ob-
ject.
- Output: a DM-Tree object.
1. Load information of the DM-Tree object such as: the capacity of the DM-Tree
object, number of M-Tree objects in the DM-Tree object.
2. Create a new DM-Tree object with the capacity loaded.
3. From each executor, load M-Tree objects of the DM-Tree objects from files
in the directory specified by the path in parallel.
4. Return the DM-Tree object.
```

Executing a Distributed kNN Query

A distributed kNN Query is a kNN Query on a DM-Tree structure. Figure 4 shows the process of executing a distributed kNN Query. First, the driver program in the master node sends a request executing a kNN Query to the M-Tree objects in the worker nodes by using the Map transformation. Then, the driver program collects results from the workers to the master node and merges them into a single result by using the Reduce action. The result is sorted by distances in ascending order, and then the top k entries are extracted from the sorted result. Algorithm 4 details the algorithm of executing a distributed kNN Query.

Figure 4. The process of executing a distributed kNNSearch(Q, k)

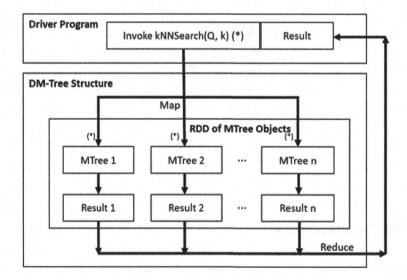

Algorithm 4 has successfully solved the problem of kNN Search. However, this algorithm still has a drawback that needs to be improved. That is, each worker sends k vectors to the master, then the master sorts and selects only k vectors closest to the query vector. As such, there are vectors sent to the master that are never used. This increases the amount of data that is transferred from workers to master in vain, which reduces the efficiency of the algorithm. However, improving this drawback is not simple. We need to do more research.

Algorithm 4. The algorithm executes a distributed kNN Query on a DM-Tree object

```
- Input: 1) Q: a query vector. 2) k: the number of nearest neighbors of the
query vector.
- Output: a list of pairs (id, distance), where id is the id of a vector, dis-
tance is the distance from Q to the vector.
1. Map each mtree object in the RDD of M-Tree objects of the DM-Tree object{
2. Set result = mtree.kNNSearch(Q, k)
3. }
4. Collect the results from the worker nodes to the master node
5. Set unionResult = union the collected results
6. Set sortedResult = unionResult.sortBy("distance", "ascending")
7. Return sortedResult.top(k)
```

Executing a Distributed Range Query

Figure 5. The process of executing a distributed RangeSearch(Q, rQ)

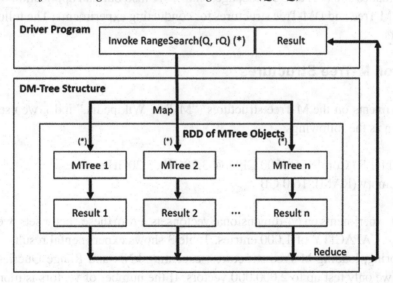

A distributed Range Query is a Range Query on a DM-Tree structure. Figure 5 shows the process of executing a distributed Range Query. First, the driver program sends a request executing a Range Query to the M-Tree objects in the worker nodes by using the Map transformation. Then, the driver program collects results from the workers to the master node and merges them into a single result by using the

Reduce action. For ease of observation, the result is sorted by distance in ascending order. Algorithm 5 details the algorithm of executing a Range Query on a DM-Tree structure.

Algorithm 5. The algorithm executes a distributed Range Query

```
- Input: 1) Q: the query vector. 2) rQ: the maximum distance.
- Output: a list of pairs (id, distance), where id is the id of a vector, dis-
tance is the distance from Q to the vector.
1. Map each mtree object in the RDD of M-Tree objects of the DM-Tree object{
2. Set result = mtree.rangeSearch(Q, rQ)
3. }
4. Collect the results from the worker nodes to the master node
5. Set unionResult = union the collected results
6. Set sortedResult = unionResult.sortBy("distance", "ascending")
7. Return sortedResult
```

EXPERIMENTS

In this section we present experiments on M-Tree and DM-Tree structures. The data we synthesized from the Yago knowledge base ("YAGO (database) Wikipedia," n.d.) downloaded from the Max Planck Institute for Informatics site ("YAGO Homepage," n.d.). We also built an application in Scala language to implement the M-Tree and DM-Tree structures for conducting experiments. The following are details of the experiments.

Experiments on M-Tree Structures

To conduct experiments on the M-Tree structures ("M-Tree Wikipedia," n.d.), we used one computer with configuration as the followings:

- Processor: Intel(R) Core™ i5-6500 CPU @ 3.20GHz 3.20GHz
- Installed memory (RAM): 16.0 GB

We conducted experiments on 64-dimensional vector sets. From these vector sets, we created M-Tree structures with the CAPACITY of 1,000 entries. Table 3 shows experimental results (in milliseconds) of creating & storing, loading M-Tree structures; executing kNN and Range Queries on the M-Tree structures. Here, we only test up to 2,000,000 vectors. If the number of vectors is more, it will exceed the capacity of our computer.

Figure 6 shows the chart compares the time (in milliseconds) of creating + storing and loading M-Tree structures. This chart shows that creating and storing M-Tree structures to local files is quite time consuming. However, loading M-Tree structures from local files is faster. For example, creating and storing the M-Tree of 2 million vectors takes 128,099 milliseconds (approximately 128 seconds), while loading the M-Tree takes 76,859 milliseconds (approximately 77 seconds).

Table 3. Experimental results (in milliseconds) of creating & storing, loading M-Tree structures; executing kNN and Range queries on the M-Tree structures

Number of Vectors	Creating & Storing	Loading	kNN Query	Range Query
0.1m	56,680	34,008	259	276
0.2m	58,093	34,856	527	481
0.3m	60,523	36,314	990	761
0.4m	65,132	40,679	1,341	1,022
0.5m	69,979	44,387	1,711	1,340
0.6m	75,091	45,055	1,882	1,628
0.7m	77,783	46,670	2,366	1,876
0.8m	81,062	48,637	2,503	2,165
0.9m	86,910	52,146	2,850	2,466
1.0m	91,837	55,102	3,190	2,814
1.1m	97,354	58,412	3,846	2,997
1.2m	102,286	61,372	3,861	3,289
1.3m	104,049	63,829	4,574	3,635
1.4m	110,409	66,245	4,620	3,903
1.5m	112,596	67,558	5,615	4,190
1.6m	114,304	68,582	5,567	4,620
1.7m	116,533	69,920	5,760	4,836
1.8m	118,344	71,006	6,220	5,233
1.9m	123,269	73,961	6,617	5,545
2.0m	128,099	76,859	7,823	5,649

Figure 6. The comparison of the time (in milliseconds) of creating+storing and loading M-Tree structures

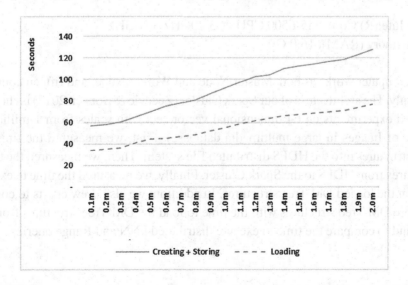

Figure 7 shows the chart that compares the time to execute kNN and Range queries on the M-Tree structures. This chart shows that executing queries is quite fast and kNN queries always take more time than Range queries. For example, executing a kNN query on the M-Tree of 2 million vectors takes 7,823 milliseconds (approximately 8 seconds), while executing a Range query on the M-Tree takes 5,649 milliseconds (approximately 6 seconds).

Figure 7. The comparison of the time (in milliseconds) of executing kNN and Range queries on the M-Tree structures

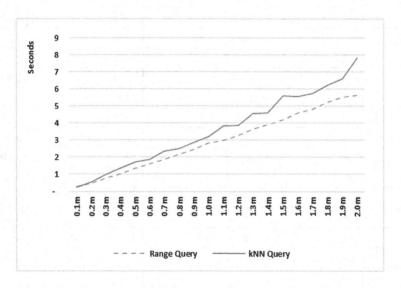

Experiments on DM-Tree Structures

To conduct experiments on the DM-Tree structures of multimedia database, we built a Spark Cluster including 16 computers with configuration as the followings:

- Processor: Intel(R) Core™ i5-6500 CPU @ 3.20GHz 3.20GHz
- Installed memory (RAM): 16.0 GB

Where, one computer works as both Master Node and Worker Node, and fifteen computers work as Worker Nodes only. The architecture of our Spark Cluster (Zecevic & Bonaci, 2017) is shown in Figure 8.

We conducted experiments on 64-dimensional vector sets with scales from 1 million to 6 million vectors (number of Images in large multimedia database). First, we measured the time to create and store DM-Tree structures into the HDFS distributed file system. Then, we measured the time to load the DM-Tree structures from HDFS to the Spark Cluster. Finally, we measured the time to execute kNN and Range queries on the loaded DM-Tree structures. In addition, we also drew charts to compare the time to create and store DM-Tree structures with the time to load the DM-Tree structures from HDFS to the Spark Cluster, and to compare the time to execute distributed kNN and Range queries.

Figure 8. The architecture of a Spark Cluster

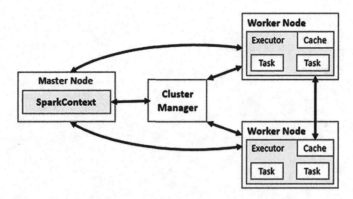

Table 4. Experimental results (in milliseconds) of creating & storing, loading DM-Tree structures; executing distributed kNN and Range queries on the DM-Tree structures

Number of Vectors	Creating & Storing	Loading	kNN Query	Range Query
1m	18,385	2,661	2,111	1,275
2m	21,920	5,593	2,845	1,649
3m	28,254	9,092	3,725	2,739
4m	41,215	12,002	4,769	3,217
5m	69,949	18,254	5,126	3,847
6m	98,066	25,883	6,483	5,190

Table 4 shows experimental results (in milliseconds) of creating & storing, loading DM-Tree structures; executing distributed kNN and Range queries on the DM-Tree structures.

Figure 9. Experimental results (in milliseconds) of creating + storing and loading DM-Tree structures

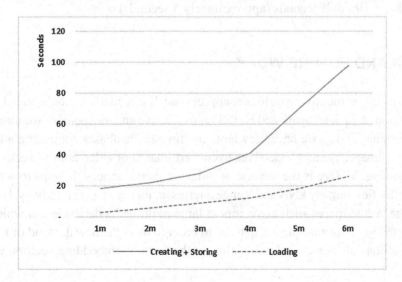

Figure 10. Experimental results (in milliseconds) of executing distributed kNN and Range queries on DM-Tree structures

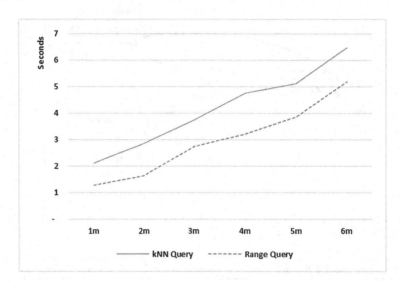

Figure 9 is the chart that compares the time to create and store DM-Tree structures with the CAPACITY of 10,000 entries into the HDFS file system with the time to load DM-Tree structures from the HDFS file system into the Spark Cluster. This chart shows that creating and storing DM-Tree structures is quite time consuming. However, loading DM-Tree structures is faster. For example, creating and storing the DM-Tree of 6 million vectors takes 98,066 milliseconds (approximately 98 seconds), while loading the DM-Tree takes 25,883 milliseconds (approximately 26 seconds) only.

Figure 10 is the chart that compares the time to execute distributed kNN and Range queries on DM-Tree structures. This chart shows that executing queries is quite fast and distributed kNN queries always take more time than distributed Range queries.

For example, executing a distributed kNN query on the DM-Tree structure of 6 million vectors takes 6,483 milliseconds (approximately 6,5 seconds), while executing a distributed Range query on the DM-Tree structure takes 5,190 milliseconds (approximately 5 seconds) only.

CONCLUSION AND FUTURE WORK

In the era of big data, old solutions are no longer appropriate. We need to distribute both data and processing. The combination of Apache Spark and HDFS is an effective and inexpensive solution for distributed storage and processing. Today, we have very large multimedia databases containing a lot of images or video clips. We use Image2vec and Video2vec to convert images or video clips to vectors for more convenience in processing. M-Tree is the method of indexing metric spaces. It helps to solve problems of searching for similarities, namely kNN and Range queries, in metric space effectively. However, M-Tree cannot index large vector spaces such as vectors in large multimedia databases, in which vectors must be stored distributedly across multiple computers. In order to meet the new demand of large multimedia databases with millions of images and video clips in the form of embedding vectors, we have studied and successfully implemented the distributed M-Tree structure on the Apache Spark framework called DM-Tree. We also presented some experiments on the DM-Tree structure to prove the performance of DM-Tree in searching the multimedia databases. In the future, we will continue studying to reduce the size of the DM-Tree structure and reduce communication costs between the master node and the worker nodes to search similarities in larger multimedia database more effectively.

In order to have a good distributed algorithm, it is important to note that the local processing algorithm must be good and the communication cost between workers and the master must be small. In fact, meeting both of these requirements is not simple.

ACKNOWLEDGMENT

This research is funded by Vietnam National University Ho Chi Minh City (VNU-HCMC) under the grant number B2017-26-02.

REFERENCES

Assefi, M., Behravesh, E., Liu, G., & Tafti, A. P. (2018). Big data machine learning using apache spark MLlib. *Proceedings - 2017 IEEE International Conference on Big Data, Big Data 2017.* 10.1109/BigData.2017.8258338

Bachmann, J. P. (2019). The SuperM-Tree: Indexing metric spaces with sized objects. *ArXiv*, 1–14. Retrieved from http://arxiv.org/abs/1901.11453

Cai, H., Zheng, V. W., & Chang, K. C. C. (2018). A Comprehensive Survey of Graph Embedding: Problems, Techniques, and Applications. *IEEE Transactions on Knowledge and Data Engineering*, 30(9), 1616–1637. doi:10.1109/TKDE.2018.2807452

Ciaccia, P., Patella, M., & Zezula, P. (1997). M-tree: An efficient access method for similarity search in metric spaces. *Proceedings of the 23rd International Conference on Very Large Databases, VLD.* Academic Press.

Garcia-Gasulla, D., Béjar, J., Cortés, U., Ayguadé, E., & Łabarta, J. (2015). Extracting Visual Patterns from Deep Learning Representations. *ArXiv:1507.08818 [Cs].*

Guo, C. (2013). Design and implementation of a multimedia database application system. *Journal of Theoretical and Applied Information Technology, 47(3).*

Homepage, Y. A. G. O. (n.d.). Retrieved January 21, 2019, from https://www.mpi-inf.mpg.de/departments/databases-and-information-systems/research/yago-naga/yago

Hu, S. H., Li, Y., & Li, B. (2016). Video2vec: Learning semantic spatio-temporal embeddings for video representation. *Proceedings - International Conference on Pattern Recognition.* 10.1109/ICPR.2016.7899735

Kouahla, Z. (2011). Exploring intersection trees for indexing metric spaces. *CEUR Workshop Proceedings.*

M-Tree Wikipedia. (n.d.). Retrieved March 15, 2019, from https://en.wikipedia.org/wiki/M-tree

Mikolov, T., Chen, K., Corrado, G., & Dean, J. (2013). Efficient Estimation of Word Representations in Vector Space. *ArXiv*, 1–12. Retrieved from http://arxiv.org/abs/1301.3781

Riaz, A., Ashraf, I., & Aslam, G. (2014). A Review On Multimedia Databases. *International Journal of Scientific & Technology Research*, 3(10), 186–191.

Shanahan, J. G., & Dai, L. (2019). Large scale distributed data science from scratch using apache spark 2.0. *Proceedings 26th International World Wide Web Conference 2017, WWW 2017 Companion.* 10.1145/3041021.3051108

Vlachou, A., Doulkeridis, C., & Kotidis, Y. (2010). *Peer-to-peer similarity search based on M-Tree indexing.* Lecture Notes in Computer Science Including Subseries Lecture Notes in Artificial Intelligence and Lecture Notes in Bioinformatics. doi:10.1007/978-3-642-12098-5_21

YAGO. (database) Wikipedia. (n.d.). Retrieved January 21, 2019, from https://en.wikipedia.org/wiki/YAGO_(database)

Zecevic, P., & Bonaci, M. (2017). *Spark in Action.* Manning Publications.

Chapter 8
The Fundamentals of Digital Forensics

Kirti Raj Bhatele
Rustamji Institute of Technology, India

Shivangi Jain
Rustamji Institute of Technology, India

Abhishek Kataria
Rustamji Institute of Technology, India

Prerana Jain
Rustamji Institute of Technology, India

ABSTRACT

This chapter simply provides a brief introduction to the various fundamentals and concepts that are related to the digital forensics. The overview of the digital forensics comprises the life cycle of the digital forensics with different stages, i.e., the preparation, collection, analysis, and reporting. The evaluation of the digital forensics tools comprises the encase forensic, The FTK(forensics tool kit), and The Helix digital forensic tool with their benefits and limitations. The digital forensics tools and techniques examination comprises the digital examination techniques, along with the live forensics analysis and the recovery of window registry, and the comparison of the digital forensics tools, and also focuses on the ACPO guidelines for digital forensics analysis.

INTRODUCTION

Digital forensics is a branch of science which deals with a collection of evidences, investigation and reverse engineering, which can determine that how the computer was compose. There are multifarious tools and methods which are available to work properly and to help investigators to authenticate and analyze the evidence (Bennett, 2012). The goal which comes under the prospects of digital forensics is to preserve any kind of digital evidence in the most primitive form. Digital forensic is based on perform-

DOI: 10.4018/978-1-7998-2701-6.ch008

ing structured research by collecting, identifying and validating the digital evidences or information for the major purpose of reimagining past events related to the cyber crime which took place on a victim's computer.

Despite this, there are Challenges which are faced by digital forensics investigators that are categorize into three parts:-

1. Technical challenge like encryption, stagnography, different media formats and analysis.
2. Legal challenge like privacy issue, lack of standardized international legislation and administrative issue.
3. Resource challenge like time taken for acquiring and analyzing forensic media.

Crimes occur and the investigations hit a dead end because there appears to be no witness or evidence—that is, until digital forensics comes into play. The FBI solved a case using computer forensics in 2008 where a Incident Response and Digital Forensics A case was received by the FBI govt in 2011 in which the two children being sexually abused at a hotel. Unfortunately, by the time the tip was received, the crime had occurred. At that time there was no evidence so that the charges can be imposed on the culprit until the computer of the accused was analyzed. The evidence on the computer, a deleted e-mail with directions to the hotel where the abuse occurred, was enough to charge three adults, who are now serving life sentences in prison. There are also times when you do not know a crime was committed until a forensic analysis is performed. Recall the situation described about the trade secret accessed by an executive after she quit and before she left to work for a competitor. The point is that an incident may appear to be innocuous or impossible to solve until the situation is analyzed. For example, in a situation where the server seemingly went off-line for no reason, after analyzing the log files, you may determine that the cause was malware installed after an intrusion. If a crime has been committed or is even suspected, it is of the utmost importance that the investigator has collected and documented the evidence in a forensically sound manner because the next step would be to hand all of the evidence off to law enforcement (Beebe, 2009).

There was another application for digital forensics is gathering of evidences for e-discovery—the pretrial phase where electronic evidence is collected. For example, a lawyer may want to prove a spouse's infidelity and may use a forensic analysis of e-mail files to prove the accusation. In evidence gathering, technique and accuracy are critical to ensure the authenticity of the data collected when an incident occurs. The forensic investigator needs always to keep in mind that he or she may be called on to defend the techniques utilized to gather the evidence. A case law is presented to demonstrate what can happen, when the law is not followed while collecting and preserving evidence. Handling digital evidence is a complex process that should be handled by a professional (Beebe, 2009). If not handled with care, it can be easily destroyed and rendered inadmissible if a court case ensues. There is some evidence that can be easily found but there may be some other evidence that have been hidden, deleted, or encrypted and cannot access by anyone. Adding to the complexity, if the evidence is not handled properly, it will be thrown out or the case will be lost.

LIFE CYCLES OF DIGITAL FORENSICS

There are four main stages of the digital forensics life cycle.

Preparation

Preparation is the first stage of digital forensics life cycle. In this we prepare for the forensics investigations which involve digital evidences that save our lot of time in the long run. This includes all the equipment's, tools which are needed and about the understanding of tool like how to use these tool efficiently to collect and analyze the evidences. There should be a secure place where we store our data or evidences which is stored securely to prevent contamination or data destruction. Today's there a lots of hardware and software that are used to perform forensics investigation. Some software like to duplicate evidences in a forensically sound manner that does not alter the evidences., some software to analyse the drive space that was duplicated and a write blocker to show that the disk copy did not modify the evidences. There are some other items which may be useful during an investigation like notebooks, evidences bags, taps, labels, pens, camera etc. This is not an exhaustive list of items, but it gives you an idea of what type of things needs to be considered when preparing for a digital forensics investigation (Chan, 2011).

Collection

Collection is the second stage of digital forensics. This includes documenting things like the model and make of the devices under investigation as well as photographing the surroundings. The investigator may take a photo of the screen to show what was happening when the scene entered. In addition, the investigator may also check out the task bar and take the photo of the maximized application running. Once the documentation was done the electronic data need to be dealt with. As we know in today's computing complexity is increasing the investigator response is not the same for every incident, sp powering it down right away may not be the best idea to avoid further damage. The reason that the computer should not be turned off is that volatile data (running process or network connections are lost). There is also a risk when a shutdown is detected the rogue application may start a malicious attack. Accordingly, there are a number of ways to respond alive data collection, focusing on the collection of the volatile data, collecting volatile data and log files or conducting a full investigation by collecting everything (where every bit of data is copied). The image is stored on the external drive, or we can send it over the network using a network utility such as netcat or crypcat. Netcat is a networking utility that reads and writes data across a network connection. Cryptcat is netcat with encryption. Remember that never use the suspect system to do any analysis if we are doing so then it will overwrite evidences. All of this digital evidences collected must be preserved to be suitable in court. Digital evidences are very fragile like footprints in snow or on the sand, because it is easily destroyed or changed. One way to preserve evidences is to transfer digital information onto a read only, non writable CD-ROM or uploading the data onto a source server and hashing the file to ensure the data's integrity.

Analysis

Analysis is the third stage of the digital forensics. After the data collection the data is analyzed. The image if the suspect machine needs to be restored so that the analysis of the evidences can begin. The image should be restored on a clean drive that is slightly larger or restore to a clean destination drive that was made by the same manufacture to ensure that the image was fit. After that the review process begins by using one of the forensics tools such as Encase (forensic toolkit). To recover deleted files, the unallocated space of the image needs to be reviewed. The investigator may find whole files or file fragments since files are never removed from the hard drive when the delete feature is utilized. What is deleted is the pointer the operating system used to build the directory tree structure. Once that pointer is gone, the operating system will not be able to find the file—but the investigator can! Keep in mind, however, that when new files are created, a memory spot is chosen, so there is a chance that the file is written over or at least part of the file. Here is why: All data are arranged on a hard drive into allocation units called clusters. A common investigation is an Internet usage analysis that monitors inappropriate usage at work where, for example, an employee is gambling or viewing pornography. Divorce lawyers may use this type of analysis to prove infidelity by showing evidence on a social networking site or proving a spouse was on a blog website looking for advice on how to get an easy divorce. An anonymous blog posting can be attributed to a spouse by showing that he or she made purchases with a credit card before and/or after the post on the blog. Web browsers store multiple pieces of information, such as history of pages visited, recently typed URLs, cached versions of previously viewed pages, and favourites. The challenge is also in showing that the accused was actually the one using that computer at the time of the incident. For example, if pornography was viewed on a particular employee's computer, the investigator has to make sure that employee was not on vacation or in meetings all day when the abuse occurred.

Reporting

The final stage in the digital forensics life cycle is reporting the results of the analysis in the previous stage as well as describing reasoning behind actions, tool choices, and procedures. NIST (2006) describes three main factors that affect reporting: alternative explanations, audience consideration, and actionable Information. Alternative explanations back up the conclusions of the incident by including all plausible explanations for what happened. In the Julie Amero case, she was convicted (later overturned) of viewing pornography on a school computer in front of minors. Had the investigators looked for alternative explanations, they would have figured out that the pornography websites viewed were caused by spyware. Instead, the clearly ignorant original investigators misled the jury by only presenting evidence in the temporary Internet files directory. They missed the alternative explanation and caused her to be unfairly convicted because their findings (temporary Internet files and firewall logs) do not demonstrate a user's intent. Some reanalysis was done by expert forensic investigators (Fowler, 2011), it was discovered that the antivirus software was an out-of-date trial version, that there was no antispyware software installed on the system, and that the spyware was definitely installed prior to the incident. The original investigators also misled the jury by informing them that spyware is not capable of spawning pop-ups (not true), that pop-ups cannot be in an endless loop (not true), and that the red *link* color used for some of the text on the porn website (that they showed the jury) indicated Amero clicked on the links (the link visits, whether intentional or not, are shown in the visited color, which they indicated was red). In this particular case, the link was red; however, if the original investigators had opened the browser preferences, they would have noted a few things: The links were selected to be green if a site was visited, and the html source code changed the font color to red. The investigators also misled the jury by telling them that the only way spyware is installed on a computer is by actually visiting a pornographic site (not true). There were multiple inconsistencies with the original investigation Reports on the results of a forensics analysis will vary in content and detail based on the incident. Thus, the level of detail of a forensic analysis report is determined by the audience who needs the report. If the analysis resulted in a noncriminal case, the executives or management may want a simple overview (Giustini, 2009).

EVALUATION OF DIGITAL FORENSICS TOOLS

In the digital forensics there are many steps and techniques for analysing and the investigation. In today life there are a lots of digital forensics techniques and corresponding tools are available for digital forensics investigation but few of them are popular and successful in market that provide accurate evidences and analysis. The steps involved across the digital forensics investigation and analysis are the major contribution for the efficiency of any digital forensics tools. There are many digital forensics popular tools like Encase, FTK (forensics tool kit) and helix is considered, but the major objective is to evaluate and compare these tools on different parameter. The advantages and limitations of each tool are discussed (Fowler, 2011).

Encase Digital Forensics Tools

As we know there are digital forensics tools and techniques but few of them are popular. Encase is one of the digital forensics tools. It is one of the widely used digital forensics tool that can be applicable anywhere or at every steps of digital forensics evidences, investigation, and analysis process. Encase has many new and different features and some inbuilt tools which can be used on digital data. There is also a advanced search option in Encase V7 that is used to investigate and analyze both the traditional computer and digital sources (Fowler, 2011).

Benefits of Encase Digital Forensics Tools

There are many advantages or the benefits of encase digital forensics tools.

- Encase digital forensics tool can be used to accomplished traditional computer and advanced digital forensics evidences, investigation and analysis.
- Encase digital forensics tool are helpful for Query processing and MLI (multiple language indexing) that can be accomplished easily against the process of digital source of evidence extraction and further investigation process.
- Encase digital forensics tool can be useful for the customization of programming language like C++, Java where the object-oriented programming languages are used.
- In Encase there is a simple reporting architecture when it is compared with another digital forensics tool.
- The key benefits of digital forensics tool is the production of binary duplicates where the examiners are provided with option of preview the evidence data in parallel to actual data.

Limitation of Digital Forensics Tool

There are some disadvantages and limitation of digital forensics tool.

- Encase has a problem with complex features in the user interface and designing phase.
- Encase has also a problem with time constraint in term of end user training and live search features when it is compared with other digital forensics tool like helix, and FTK.

FTK (Forensics Tool Kit)

FTK(forensics tool kit) has many advanced techniques, characteristics and some features are available when it is compared with another digital forensics tool. Access data is the basic techniques of forensics tool kit. Forensics tool kit provides the simplest way of scanning the digital evidences source like hard disk and memory. With the help of forensics tool kit the remove related information's like emails, password and other relevant text or string can be retrieve. In the digital forensics tool FTK image is one of the tool that can scan and retrieve the hard disk image in the form of single or multiple disk image. Calculation of complex MD5 can also be done with the help of FTk when it is compared with other tool. The most popular digital forensics tool that can be used in many investigation and cyber crime is the FTK (forensics tool kit).

Advantages of FTK

- FTK provides that the data packets of both the protocol like IPV4 and IPV6 can be processed, searched and recovered easily.
- With the help of FTK different file format can be read while the other digital forensics tools can't.
- The important advantages of FTK is the easy and fast recovery of ARP Ethernet frames when compared with other digital forensics tool like helix, encase.
- FTK provides the efficient network, memory and file management with the level of customization and user interface simplicity.
- Hash value calculation can be easily done bt the forensics tool kit.
- FTK provides the simple reading of multiple evidences source and the related files which include mobile, smart phone, tablets, PDA's laptop etc.

Limitation of Forensics Tool Kit

There are some limitations of FTK-

- FTK digital forensics tool has a problem with the response time against incidence analysis.
- In FTK there is a tedious and complex process is that integrating FTK with the third-party forensics tool where the configuration complexity limits the scope of tool level integration techniques.

Helix Digital Forensics Tool

Helix is built on the UNIX operating system. It is digitally oriented forensics tool and build on the Ubantu operating system architecture. The main goal of the helix digital forensics tool is to digitally investigate, analyze acquire the incident. The report of the incident is generated for both the traditional computer and digital forensics requirements. Helix easily run on the portable memory devices like CD, DVD. It also has the capability to work with the multiple operating system environments which includes other operating system like window, Linux and solarix etc. Helix is a forensically sound tool and it considered as host computer over the digitally forensics analysis process.

Benefits of Helix Digital Forensics Tool

There are some of the Benefits of digital forensics tool-

- The main benefit of the digital forensics tool is that it has the ability to run over the live CD.
- Helix makes the existing operating system inactive during the digital forensics process and acquires, analyze the source devices.
- With the help of the helix digital forensics tool the entire picture of the requires network can be gathered.
- Helix has the capability to run over on all the devices connected to the network and complex suspected network.
- Helix has the many key features like examination, investigation and analysis.
- It also has the key features of live network forensics acquisition.
- Helix tool provide the facility to generate the accurate digital forensics investigation report.

Limitations of Helix Digital Forensics Tool

There are some limitations of the helix digital forensics tool-

- The main limitation of helix digital forensics tool is User interface and complex command knowledge requirements.
- Live imaging and backup process is complex in nature.

COMPARISON OF DIGITAL FORENSICS TOOLS FTK, ENCASE AND HELIX

See Table 1.

DIGITAL FORENSICS TOOLS AND TECHNIQUES EXAMINATION

We have discussed in brief about the various tools with their techniques in the previous section. By comparing these tools we came to the conclusion that these tools have both the benefits and the limitations and they are applied over the various techniques. Across digital forensics data acquisition, examination, and investigation and analysis process and in general the respective source can be a simple computer, memory, laptop, Smartphone and tablets in all this the key role is played by the digital evidence source. This source of digital investigation also plays a key role in estimating the optimized conditions of the respective tools and techniques and the corresponding tools can be either be mobile, or memory or laptop (Huebner et al., 2009). The main step across the digital forensics analysis process is to gather the digital evidence, where it is important in this context to evaluate the overall performance of the digital forensics tools by the role of each of the tool that is mentioned in this report (Rocha, 2011). In this section we will discuss about the digital examination techniques of the respective tools like Encase, FTK and Helix and provided as below.

Table 1. Brief tabular comparison among the Encase, FTK (forensics tool kit), helix digital forensics tools

FTK (Forensics Tool Kit)	Helix Tool	Encase Tool
Digital forensics evidences sources are complex in nature when it compared with other digital forensics tool.	Examination, analysis live forensics acquisition is only possible with the help of this tool.	Investigation, analysis and digital forensics evidences acquisition are very easy and less configurable with encase comparison to other tools.
Data preview is very simple when compared with rest of the digital forensics tool but source media is complex with this tool.	In helix digital forensics tool both the source and data preview is complex compare to encase and FTK tool.	In encase digital forensics tool there is advantages of parallel processing with respect to data preview and source evidences.
The reporting structure of incident and digital forensics analysis are very simple and easy in comparison to other tools like helix and encase.	Helix digital forensics tool suffers from the live reporting of the respective digital forensics analysis process and also the level of complexity.	In encase the digital forensics analysis and respective reporting structure is simple when it compared with FTK and helix.
In FTK(forensics tool kit) simple live and offline search is possible.	In helix digital forensics live search is complex in nature but it takes very less search time compare to other forensics tools.	In Encase digital forensics tool there is a complexity of time-consuming live search.
In FTK digital forensics tool it can read multiple file format like NFTK this is the main benefits of FTK.	In helix digital forensics tools file reading of multiple file format is not possible.	In encase digital forensics tool there is a limitation of reading multiple file format.
With the help of FTk tool password recovery and registry recovery is possible very simply.	There is some difficulty in password recovery and registry recovery with the helix.	In Encase digital tool the password recovery and registry recovery is comparatively slow and complex.
The key benefits of FTK tool is complex functions and data integrity.	With helix the data integrity process is complex and sophisticated but the level of required functionality support is low compare to current tool.	In encase the data integrity process is not properly accomplished and it also suffers from hash function.
FTK digital forensics tool supports the object oriented and structured programming language.	UNIX programming language and shell scripting is supported by the helix digital forensics tool.	Encase also supports object oriented programming language like C++ and java.
In FTk simple query retrieval and processing function is possible when it compared with helix and encase.	The main benefits of helix is better query processing on live.	The main benefits of encase is of query processing and it also supports the MLI(multiple language indexing)

Digital Examination Techniques

The digital examination process involves many techniques. The Window registry recovery or reconstruction and live forensics are the key among them. The source being investigated over the analysis and examination process is responsible for the performance of the respective digital forensics tools (Rocha, 2011). The two techniques which are consider for the evaluation process and provided as below.

Live Forensics Analysis

The key process across the digital forensics examination process is the live forensics analysis and the steps of gathering the image of memory devices like hard disk over the live or offline environment are included in it. The corresponding live forensics analysis of a hard disk requires a minimum of 10 TB data and the respective process can be online, live or offline.

In general, making the image of hard disk or other memory sources at both the online and offline scenarios is included in a typical live forensics analysis. Few negative impacts with the live forensics analysis process are there which includes hash checks, timestamps, acquiring the required swap keys, gathering the registry entries and frequent memory checks.

With Encase the live forensics analysis becomes possible and there are the limitations with evidence gathering and the required hash checks. The required level of support of SH1 and respective encryption techniques is lacked by encase.

FTK support only the limited live search and forensics analysis options and suffer with the timestamp issues and failures and thus configuration is complex in nature.

As Helix runs over Live CD or USB so the live forensics support is provided across it, where little offline content is accessed against forensics analysis as well.

Recovery of Windows Registry

In general, the recovery process covers the windows registry recovery or the reconstruction includes the IIS and FTP event logs and the level of system security requirements. The key information related to all the installed programs, websites visited, recent documents processed are hold by the windows registry. The required windows registry is recovered by the digital forensics analysis and the investigation process and the reconstruction of the required windows directory is also possible (Pasupuleti, 2019).

The limitation in this context is that the required log files of the corresponding directory can't be maintained with Encase, that's why the windows registry reconstruction and recovery is accomplished with this tool. FTK digital forensics tool is the best possible way to recover and reconstruct the windows registry. Complex artefacts of windows registry like URL retrievals, log files and various documents with FTK tool can be searched in a simpler manner (Huebner et al., 2009).

The Helix runs purely over the UNIX operating system environment, so the main limitation with it is that, it can't reconstruct and recover the windows registry.

ACPO Guidelines for Digital Forensics Analysis

The digital forensics analysis process follows the following ACPO guidelines:

- **ACPO Guideline1:** The main source of the current ACPO guideline is the forensics investigation. In this context, the required responsibilities, authorities and the respective actions implemented over the cyber-crime investigation are purely with law and police and the forensic investigator has no significant role.
- **ACPO Guidelinie2:** Under the current ACPO guidelines all the activities with respective to forensics activities over the labs are covered. The forensics investigators or examiner's capability and ability should be considered over the digital forensics analysis. All the digital forensics techniques should be considered or not task is left in middle of the process, it is assumed.
- **ACPO Guideline3:** This ACPO Guideline 3 mainly in the digital forensics deals with the actual data records. In this context the top priority is given to the required audit roles and management.
- **ACPO Guideline4:** The main source of the current ACPO guideline is the forensics investigation and the respective information. Maintaining the required integrity and reliability is the responsibility of the forensics investor over the digital forensics analysis process.

CONCLUSION

To analyse and evaluate various digital forensics tools and techniques is the main goal of the current chapter. Encase, FTK and Helix are considered over the current analysis process, where at various level of digital forensics acquisition, examination and analysis process the respective tools are compared and evaluated. For each and every level the advantages and limitations are discussed over the current report and the required ACPO guidelines are discussed and explained.

From the entire analysis about the digital forensics it is clear that FTK, Encase and Helix digital forensics tools have their own limitations and features and can be applied with most of the digital forensics and critical network analysis.

Common Applications of Digital Forensics

By the term forensics we mean that against some nefarious offender in the court law, the digital forensics is used to recover the digital evidence which is true in many instances. Digital forensics is not just limited to the court of law. The digital forensics finds the evidence that either backs or disproves the assumption by some sort. Digital forensics is broke into five parts on the basis of those applications:

Identify

Identification is the starting of all he digital forensics. It is important to identify the data that is stored before anything. Nowadays, the data is stored on the hard drives of computer and servers, flash drives, network equipment.

Preserve

The crucial part of the digital forensics is Preservation. It largely rests on the shoulders of investigators. During investigation, another common practice is to create a forensic image of the data or device being examined.

Recover

There is some sort of recovery process in every case. Recovering deleted files from the normal OS processes, intentionally deleted files, password protected files and even damages or corrupted files are included in this process.

Analyze

The gut of the investigation is analysis. To look at the common artifact such as the memory, registry, event logs and browser history we use several apps and programs. A simple Google search is a good example for this. Whenever you search for something, It do not just logged in the browser history when we are searching for something, there is a coordinating registry artefact that points to that search.

Present

Once the examination is complete, it's the time to present the case report of our findings. It is a lot easier at the end as all the documentation that is recorded will create this report. And we reached to some definite conclusion from all the information that we have collected. The only thing that does matter in the digital forensics is preventing facts clearly and concisely.

REFERENCES

Angelopoulou, O. (2010). *Analysis of Digital Evidence in Identity Theft Investigations* (Doctoral dissertation). Available from the University of Hertfordshire Research database (5061154).

Beebe, N. (2009). Digital Forensic Research: The Good, the Bad and the Unaddressed. In *Advances in Digital Forensics V Digital Forensics 2009. IFIP Advances in Information and Communication Technology*. Berlin, Germany: Springer. doi:10.1007/978-3-642-04155-6_2

Bennett, D. (2012). The Challenges Facing Computer Forensics Investigators in obtaining the criminal investigation's information from the mobile devices. *Information Security Journal: A Global Perspective, 21*(3), 159-168.

Chan, E. M. (2011*). Philosophy in Computer Science* (Doctoral dissertation). Available from the University of Illinois at Urbana Champaign theses database (24365).

Cheong, C. W. V. (2008). *Data acquisition from volatile memory: A memory acquisition tool for Microsoft Windows Vista* (Doctoral dissertation). Available from the Naval Postgraduate School theses Archive Calhoun (10945/3795).

Fowler, S. (2011). An *Overview of small-scale digital forensics*. Available from the Eastern Michigan University Theses & Projects database (274).

Giustini, G. (2009). Open Source Live Distributions for Computer Forensics. In E. Huebner, & S. Zanero (Eds.), *Open source software for Digital* (pp. 69–82). US: Springer.

Huebner, E., Bem, D., & Cheung, H. (2010). Computer Forensics Education–the Open Source Approach. In *Open Source Software for Digital Forensics* (pp. 9–23). Boston, MA: Springer.

Pasupuleti, S. K. (2019). Privacy-Preserving Public Auditing and Data Dynamics for Secure Cloud Storage Based on Exact Regenerated Code. *International Journal of Cloud Applications and Computing, 9*(4), 1–20. doi:10.4018/IJCAC.2019100101

Poisel, R., & Tjoa, S. (2012). Discussion on the Challenges and Opportunities of Cloud Forensics. *Proceedings of the International Cross-Domain Conference and Workshop on Availability, Reliability, and Security (CDARES)*, Prague, Czech Republic. 10.1007/978-3-642-32498-7_45

Rocha, A. (2011). Current trends and challenges in digital image and video forensics. *ACM Computing Surveys, 25*(1), 111–116.

Chapter 9

Comparative Evaluations of Human Behavior Recognition Using Deep Learning

Jia Lu

Auckland University of Technology, New Zealand

Wei Qi Yan

Auckland University of Technology, New Zealand

ABSTRACT

With the cost decrease of security monitoring facilities such as cameras, video surveillance has been widely applied to public security and safety such as banks, transportation, shopping malls, etc. which allows police to monitor abnormal events. Through deep learning, authors can achieve high performance of human behavior detection and recognition by using model training and tests. This chapter uses public datasets Weizmann dataset and KTH dataset to train deep learning models. Four deep learning models were investigated for human behavior recognition. Results show that YOLOv3 model is the best one and achieved 96.29% of mAP based on Weizmann dataset and 84.58% of mAP on KTH dataset. The chapter conducts human behavior recognition using deep learning and evaluates the outcomes of different approaches with the support of the datasets.

INTRODUCTION

With the rapidly increasing number of surveillance cameras in various scenes, locating the region of interest (ROI) from thousands of surveillance videos has become one of the prominent problems. On the other hand, with continuous expansion of surveillance systems, a vast amount of video footages has been archived, which become more and more tough to find useful information from these large data, identifying a target is also less efficient. Therefore, how to make surveillance more efficiency in the environment with tremendous big visual data needs to be taken into consideration.

DOI: 10.4018/978-1-7998-2701-6.ch009

For traditional human behavior recognition, both low-level (without semantic understanding) and high-level processes (with semantic understanding) are needed to be considered. The low-level process helps to locate the region of interest and reduce the useless information from video footages; meanwhile, the high-level process will analyze these features to achieve the behavior recognition ultimately.

Nowadays, with the increasing capacity of computing devices, Deep Neural Networks (DNNs) obtained a massive attention to detect objects, which lead to a new era of computer vision (Lu et al., 2017). Deep learning models (Hinton et al., 2006) contain multiple hidden layers, pre-training methods are adopted to alleviate the troubles of local optimal solution, the hidden layers are up to many with the "depth", thus it is called "Deep Learning". The state-of-the-art methods mainly rely on artificial neural networks, such as Convolutional Neural Networks (CNNs or ConvNets), R-CNNs, Fast R-CNNs, Faster R-CNNs, Mask R-CNN, and SSD (Single Shot Multi-Box Detector). Moreover, deep learning has been implemented in both supervised or unsupervised models (Ji et al., 2013). Apparently, the work has clearly shown the difference between deep neural networks and shallow neural networks as well as conventional machine learning in various aspects (Liu et al., 2016).

In human behavior recognition, bounding box was proposed for deep neural networks to resample these proposed pixels. Because there are inherent local patterns in an image such as eyes, nose, mouth, etc., CNN is derived by combining digital image processing and artificial neural networks, which links the upper and lower layers through the convolution kernels. The convolution kernels are shared among all images, the images still retain the original position after the convolution operations. Compared to traditional approaches, deep learning conducted in an end-to-end process along with more higher classification probability which also shows an invariant to illumination, pose, etc. (LeCun et al., 2004). Moreover, region proposal methods and region-based convolutional neural networks (R-CNN) are more successful with high precision in pattern recognition (Ren et al., 2017). The selective Faster R-CNN (Uijlings et al., 2013) also carries out outperformance in a series of comparisons (Ren et al., 2017; He et al., 2016). Region proposal networks (RPN) were trained for the end-to-end purpose and generated the accurate location of the regions of interest. RPN and Fast R-CNN have been merged together into a single network which is able to accelerate the detection (Ren et al., 2017).

This book chapter is organized as follows. Literature review is presented at Section 2, our method is described in Section 3. Our results are demonstrated in Section 4, the conclusion is drawn in Section 5.

RELATED WORK

Human behavior understanding refers to analyze and recognize human motion patterns, and describe it with natural languages (Aggarwal et al., 1997). The motion sequence can be considered as the traversal process of static actions in different state nodes (Guo et al., 1994). The joint probability of traversal process is therefore calculated, its maximum value is taken into consideration for classification (Fujiyoshi et al., 2004).

Human behavior recognition is to identify the predefined behaviors automatically so as to reduce human labor effectively (Aggarwal et al., 1997). To recognize and analyze the periodic motions of human behavior, spatial-temporal model (Rui et al., 2000) and periodic model (Cutler et al., 2000) were proposed. Human behavior recognition can mainly split into twofold which contains template-matching-based methods and space-state-based methods.

Human behavior recognition can be implemented by using unsupervised learning which does not require pretrained data, in this case, the classes among the training data are unlabeled. The objective of unsupervised learning is to study the unlabeled training data so as to reveal the regular pattern of data for further data analysis. Clustering is the most typical method in unsupervised learning.

A multi-observation hidden Markov model (MOHMM) was proposed to detect abnormal activities which was much effective to noisy and sparse datasets (Xiang et al., 2005). Self-organizing map (SOM) is a unsupervised learning neural network, which can map high-dimensional input data onto low-dimensional space, maintain the topological structure of input data in high-dimensional space; it maps similar sample points in high-dimensional space to adjacent neurons in the output layer. SOM was adopted to detect rare events; a method for classifying new events using the gaussian mixture model (GMM) from SOM maps achieved abnormal behavior recognition (Petrushin et al., 2005). An unsupervised learning method was combined with the spatiotemporal words by extracting interest points to achieve human action categorizations, which can classify multiple actions with complex video sequences (Niebles et al., 2008).

In 2006, the concept of deep learning was put forward; specifically, the method of pretraining was used to alleviate the problem of local optimal solution, the hidden layer is increased to many, which realized the "depth" in real scenes. Moreover, the multilayer neural networks have better learning capability and its training complexity can be effectively alleviated by using layer-by-layer initialization (Hinton et al., 2006). Unlike the traditional approaches, deep learning which is inspired by the CNNs (ConvNets) leads to new era of modern computing. Although deep learning uses video frames as the input data directly, the images will be input into the network without feature extraction. Thus, the approaches are regarded as an end-to-end method, the feature maps are generated by themselves and integrated into the algorithm without human interventions; the input of the end-to-end method is original images, the output is the classes with their probabilities.

CNNs as one of the most popular methods at present have been applied to directly tackle the original images. There are inherent local patterns in the image such as mouth, eyes, etc.; therefore, the CNNs are regarded as the combination of digital image processing and artificial neural networks, it plays pivotal role in object recognition, image segmentation (Ciresan et al., 2012), and object detection (Farabet et al. 2013; Girshick et al., 2014; Krizhevsky et al., 2012). CNNs link both upper and lower layers together through using convolutional kernel; a "weight sharing" strategy can make fully use of a group of neurons with the same weights, which have taken great effect in the recognition (LeCun et al., 1995; LeCun et al., 1998). Figure 1 shows the example of typical CNNs, where the "Conv" means convolutional layer for feature extraction; "Pool" indicates "pooling layer" to reduce dimension, and FC represents "fully connected layer".

Figure 1. The example of a typical CNN

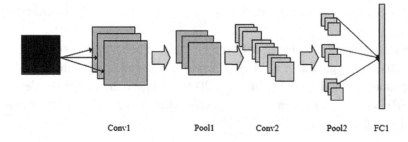

Conv1   Pool1   Conv2   Pool2   FC1

Compared to traditional methods, the convolution kernel in the convolutional layer can be used as feature map extractor. Despite each layer needs to be designed by itself, there are no additional operations that are required to obtain the feature map. The end-to-end learning method eliminates the need for data annotation before each individual learning task is performed.

In the end-to-end model, prediction results are acquired as the output. Compared to the predicted results and the ground truth, an error may be generated. This error will be minimized to each layer of the model by using backpropagation, the representation of each layer will be adjusted according to the errors until the model converges or the desired errors are reached. However, for conventional machine learning approaches, features extracted from the original data are particularly prominent in the image, because the number of image pixels is too large, the data dimension is very high, which will lead to the dimensional curse problem, while traditional machine learning requires several models which are serialized to each other. In Table 1, we summarize these two different methods with their advantages and disadvantages in human behavior recognition.

Table 1. Summary of two different methods for human behavior recognition

	Disadvantages	Advantages
Traditional methods	Easy to be implemented. Redundant features can be reduced before the training. Feature engineering (easy to explain and understand). It does not require GPU acceleration normally.	It cannot achieve the real-time recognition usually. It requires several models to work together. The results may be affected by external environments, less accurate.
Deep learning methods	It can achieve the real-time recognition. It can train the data without additional process of feature extraction. The results may not be affected by external environments, much accurate. It is adaptable and easy to convert (transfer learning).	It requires a large amount of data. It requires GPU acceleration. It requires more time for training. Black box (hard to be explained and understood).

A 3D neural network for human behavior recognition constructed spatiotemporal information for feature map extraction with an SVM classifier (Ji et al. 2013). Compared with 2D CNNs, no matter how many channels the 2D CNNs have, a convolutional kernel can only output one feature map, which means only the spatial relationship exists and the temporal relationship will be gone. For human behavior recognition, temporal information is also important to improve the classification. 3D Convolution operation is to stack multiple consecutive frames to form a cube and apply the 3D convolution kernel to the cube (Tran et al., 2015). In this structure, each feature map in the convolutional layer will be connected to multiple adjacent frames in the previous layer so as to capture the motion information. Fig. 2 shows the simple process of 3D Convolutional Neural Networks (3D-CNN).

The 3D convolution kernel can only extract one type of features from the cube, because the weight of convolution kernel in the whole cube is as same as the shared weights. Connected lines of the same color in Fig. 2 represent the same weight. We use multiple convolution kernels to extract the feature maps.

Szegedy et al. used deep neural networks and treated object detection as a regression (Szegedy et al., 2013). Girshick et al. proposed a region-based convolutional neural network (R-CNN), which used the region proposal (Sande et al., 2011) to obtain multiple local regions of the image; CNNs are utilized to obtain these features of each region so as to solve the object detection problem (Girshick et al., 2014). The region proposal is to find out the possible position of the target in the image, IOU (intersection-over-union) is guaranteed while selecting few candidate windows by using visual information, such as texture, edge, and color in the image. However, R-CNNs still have shortages such as the extracted local regions increase the storage of our disk space; moreover, most of the region proposals may overlap with others which make the extracted features from the overlapped portions repeating. Spatial pyramid pooling networks (SPP-Nets) were adopted to overcome the information loss and usage problems of R-CNNs by replacing it to the last pooling layer (He et al., 2015).

Figure 2. The simple process of 3D convolutional neural networks (3D-CNN)

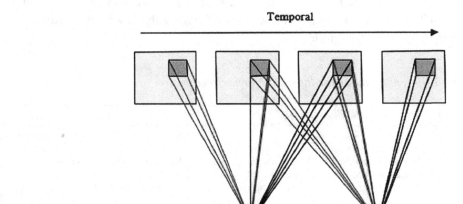

Fast R-CNN was proposed to improve the previous work of R-CNN which achieves higher mAP (average precision) of 66% on PASCAL VOC2012. Fast R-CNN has the ability to update the training process of all network layers using the ROI pooling layers by adopting the backpropagation. Fast R-CNN maps the region proposal directly on the feature map, the image only needs to be fetched once, which greatly reduces the time consuming. Faster R-CNN adopted the Region Proposal Network (RPN) to replace the selective search method in the Fast R-CNN so as to share the convolutional features of whole image (Ren et al., 2017). Fig. 3 shows the three types of R-CNNs with the processing steps.

Figure 3. The R-CNNs with its steps

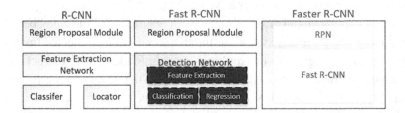

You Only Look Once (YOLO or Darknets) was proposed recently, which treated visual object detection as a regression problem based on the end-to-end neural networks. YOLO networks contain 24 convolutional layers and two fully connected layers (Redmon et al., 2016). The core idea of YOLO is to use the whole picture as the input and directly return to the position of the bounding box. The YOLO networks have the ability to train loss functions directly corresponding to the detection performance, which makes the entire model trained jointly. The YOLO algorithm is described as (1) a fixed 7×7 grid kernel is applied to the input image. If the center of the object falls on the corresponding grid, then the grid will respond to the regression of this object position. (2) Each grid prediction contains object position and its confidential information which is encoded as a vector. (3) The network output layer is the corresponding result for each grid, achieves the end-to-end training. However, the loss function was applied to the YOLO networks by utilizing the sum-squared error, which makes convergence worse; meanwhile, it cannot align with maximizing average precision correctly.

Our contribution of this book chapter is to adopt the end-to-end deep learning method for human behavior recognition. Moreover, a powerful GPU is used to accelerate the processing to achieve the time-efficiency. In this chapter, we implement four different deep learning models with the positive results.

METHODOLOGY

YOLO9000 (YOLOv2) was proposed to overcome the limitations of the initial version of YOLO, which can detect up to 9000 object categories in real time and improve the accuracy/recall of the object location. YOLOv2 used WordTree to conduct joint training of classification and detection, the joint training algorithm was proposed to train object detectors on both available classification and detection data (Redmon et al., 2017). It can also predict the bounding boxes of objects without box labelling with 9000 concepts in the dictionary. YOLOv2 introduced the idea of anchor box from Faster R-CNN instead of adopting the fully connected layers from the YOLO networks to predict the coordinates of each bounding box. The batch normalization was adopted to all convolutional layers, which normalizes the data of all layers to prevent gradient disappearance and gradient explosion by adopting batch normalization. Since there are only convolutional and pooling layers in the YOLOv2, the input of YOLOv2 is limited to fixed-size images. In order to enhance the robustness of this model, YOLOv2 adopted a multiscale input training strategy, specifically changed the input image size of the model after several rounds of iterations during the training process. Therefore, by adopting multi-scale training strategy, YOLOv2 is adaptive to images of various sizes and predict good results.

YOLOv3 was proposed to improve YOLOv2 networks, which used logistic regression to locate an object based on a bounding box; the logistic regression is used independently for each class; the binary cross-entropy loss is used to replace the softmax so as to increase the class prediction rates. The bounding box prediction is shown as:

$$b_x = \sigma\left(t_x\right) + c_x \tag{1}$$

$$b_y = \sigma\left(t_y\right) + c_y$$

$$b_w = p_w e^{t_w}$$

$$b_h = p_h e^{t_h}$$

where b_x, b_y, b_w, and b_h represent the predicted central coordinates x, y, w, h and t_x, t_y, t_w, t_h stand for predicted coordinates; c_x and c_y are the length between the top left corner of an image cell and the grid cell; p_w and p_h are width and height of the bounding box, σ is used to constrain its offset range.

There are a plenty of public datasets for human behavior recognition which are provided by multiple research groups, such as Weizmann dataset, KTH dataset, UCF dataset, CAVIAR dataset, CASIA dataset, and BEHAVE dataset. Table 2 shows a brief description of these datasets.

Table 2. A brief description of the different datasets

Dataset	Description
Weizmann	Single person behavior analysis with daily data, static camera.
KTH	Single person behavior analysis with daily data, static camera with different view angles.
UCF	Realistic action videos collected from the YouTube.
CAVIAR	Multi-person behavior analysis.
CASIA	Single/multiple person interaction data with different static camera angles.
BEHAVE	Multiagent interaction data.

In this chapter, all the experiments were based on the first two public datasets, namely, Weizmann dataset and KTH dataset. For Weizmann dataset, it contains ten classes, each of the classes were captured by a static camera, the dataset has nine participants in total. The resolution of the dataset is 180×144. For the KTH dataset, it includes a total of 2391 videos of six actions completed from 25 participants in four scenarios. The video samples in this dataset contain scaling, clothing, and lighting changes which were captured by using static cameras. The resolution of these images is 160×120. We mainly adopted two public datasets to achieve our experimental results. Moreover, there are 5667 video frames for KTH dataset; regarding Weizmann dataset, it contains 1500 video frames. All the experiments were operated with a single GPU (RTX 2080Ti) to reduce the time consuming while training.

To measure the models, cross validation was adopted in order to evaluate the performance of human behavior recognition. The primary purpose of this confusion matrix is to compare the ground truth with the classification results. Furthermore, the confusion matrix will not only provide the classification accuracy, but also show the relevant relationship of results and predicted classes.

EXPERIMENTAL RESULTS

In this chapter, we adopted four networks for our experiments which include YOLOv3, YOLOv2, ResNet, and DenseNet to achieve the results of human behavior recognition. Our focus is mainly on deep learning methods and how it can affect the outcomes. Fig. 4 shows the results of video frames of these results utilizing the two adopted datasets.

Figure 4. The video frames for the adopted datasets.

Four different deep learning models were adopted in this chapter; by utilizing these models, the accuracy was achieved up to 90%. YOLOv3 shows the highest accuracy (96.29%) and DenseNet has the lowest accuracy 92.62%. Fig. 5 shows the training loss of each proposed models and YOLOv2 achieved the lowest training loss of 0.96%. YOLOv3 has the highest training loss 1.81%.

Figure 5. The training loss via Weizmann dataset by adopting proposed models

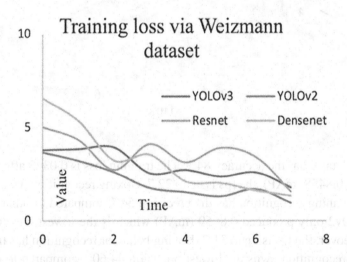

Pertaining to Weizmann dataset, YOLOv3 achieved the highest accuracy 96.29%, the overall accuracy of ResNet only reached 91.40% (He et al., 2016). The training loss is around 0.0181 after 44200 epochs. The test results of using YOLOv3 have 0.946 mAP. Jacking has the highest precision rate of 100% and that of the test FPS is up to 22.7. Moreover, the total accuracy achieved 96.29%. By adopting the YOLOv2, the overall accuracy is up to 92.71%. The test results by using YOLOv2 have 0.911 mAP; Jacking action has the highest recognition accuracy 100%, Running behavior recognition only achieved the lowest recognition 65.33%; the experiment has been carried out for behavior recognition at 31.3 frames per second (fps). The DenseNet was also utilized in the experiments, the total accuracy of human behavior recognition is 92.62%. The test result by adopting DenseNet has 0.953 (mAP), Jacking recognition has the highest one (100%), while the recognition of Running behavior only reached the lowest precision 90.83%, the fps is up to 30.3. ResNet has achieved the accuracy up to 91.40%. The test results of loss by adopting ResNet have the lowest one 0.888 compared with other three deep neural networks. The recognition of Jacking has the highest precision (100%) under this experimental condition, while the recognition of Running only achieved the precision at 82.05%. The frame rate of human behavior detection is up to 17.1 fps.

For KTH dataset, YOLOv3 achieved the highest mAP at 0.8458; YOLOv2 only has 0.8059 mAP which is the lowest one compared to others. Fig. 6 shows the training loss of each proposed models and DenseNet achieved the lowest training loss of 1.85%. ResNet has the highest training loss (3.92%).

Figure 6. The training loss via KTH dataset by adopting proposed models

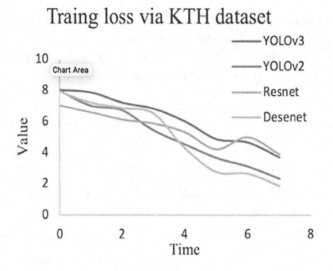

YOLOv3 in KTH dataset has the accuracy 84%. The training loss is 0.0373 after 28800 epochs. The test results reach up to 0.8458 (mAP), the fps is up to 22.7. Boxing recognition has the highest precision rate at 100%, while Running recognition has the precision 54% compared to other behaviors. The test result by using YOLOv2 only produced 0.8059 (mAP) which is the lowest one compared with other neural networks; moreover, the fps is up to 31.2. Boxing behavior recognition has the highest precision (100%), but Running recognition owns the lowest precision 44.60% compared to other behaviors. By adopting DenseNet in KTH dataset, it has the accuracy 86.63%, the average precision is 0.8446 (mAP) and the FPS is up to 32.3. Boxing behavior has the highest precision (100%) of recognition, while the Running behavior has the lowest one 63.46%. The network ResNet has the total accuracy 85.45% and the test result achieves 0.8383 (mAP), the fps is only 16.4. Boxing behavior has the highest precision (100%), Running behavior has the lowest precision (64.38%) compared to others.

Figure 7. Examples of incorrectly classified, the correct labels are: (a) Skip, (b) Run, (c) Jog, and (d) boxing

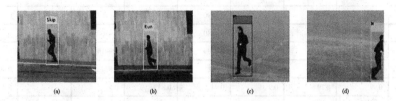

After these experiments, DenseNet has the highest accuracy 0.953 (mAP), YOLOv3 has the highest accuracy 96.29% by using Weizmann dataset, YOLOv3 has the highest mAP (0.8458) with KTH dataset. For Weizmann dataset, Jacking recognition has the highest precision and accuracy. Moreover, Boxing recognition using KTH dataset has the highest precision within all experiments. However, in Weizmann dataset, the precision and accuracy of Running and Skipping may not be robust, so do Running and Jogging recognition in KTH dataset. The reason why we obtain this low precision is that we are using video frames as the training dataset, these behaviors may have similarities. Thus, during the tests, the results got lower than the expected.

Table 4. The comparisons of machine learning and deep learning methods using Weizmann dataset

		Walk	Skip	Run	Jack	Jump	mAP	Accuracy	*fps*
Deep Learning Methods	YOLOv3	0.9916	0.9116	0.9066	1.00	0.9174	0.946	**0.9629**	23.3
	YOLOv2	0.9878	0.9699	0.6533	1.00	0.9428	0.911	0.9271	32.3
	DenseNet	0.9758	0.9552	0.9083	1.00	0.9250	0.953	0.9262	31.3
	ResNet	0.9313	0.8377	0.8205	1.00	0.8508	0.888	0.9140	17.0
	Modified YOLOv3	0.94	0.94	0.97	1.00	0.97	0.964	0.953	27.4
Machine Learning Methods	ANN	0.904	0.942	0.923	0.962	0.904	0.927	-	-
	Decision Tree	0.9615	0.8667	0.9808	0.9808	0.9231	0.942	-	-
	NNC	1.00	0.78	1.00	1.00	1.00	-	**0.956**	-
	SVM	1.00	0.67	1.00	1.00	1.00	-	0.934	-
Ensemble Learning Methods	AdaBoost + Naïve Bayes	1.00	0.956	0.927	1.00	0.895	-	0.9713	-
	AdaBoost + Random Forest	1.00	0.978	0.951	1.00	0.895	-	**0.9776**	-
	Bagging + Naïve Bayes	1.00	0.956	0.902	1.00	0.842	-	0.9617	-
	Bagging + Random Forest	1.00	0.911	0.951	1.00	0.978	-	**0.9776**	-

Table 5. The comparisons of machine learning and deep learning methods using KTH dataset

		Walk	Run	Box	Handclap	Jog	Handwave	mAP	Accuracy	*fps*
Deep Learning Methods	YOLOv3	0.9967	0.5400	1	0.8590	0.7323	0.9467	**0.8458**	0.8400	22.7
	YOLOv2	0.9727	0.4460	1	0.8280	0.6385	0.9500	0.8059	0. 8263	31.2
	DenseNet	0.9703	0.6346	1	0.8489	0.6220	0.9919	0.8446	**0. 8663**	32.3
	ResNet	0.9773	0.6438	1	0.8711	0.6628	0.8748	0.8383	0. 8545	16.4
	3D-CNN	0.97	0.79	0.9	0.94	0.84	0.97	-	**<u>0.902</u>**	22.7
Machine Learning Methods	LF+SVM	0.838	0.549	0.979	0.597	0.604	0.736	-	0.717	0.838
	Linear SVM+LTP	0.90	0.86	0.98	0.95	0.76	0.96	-	0.742	0.90
	Histograms of spatio-temporal gradients	0.969	0.969	0.938	1	0.781	1	-	**<u>0.942</u>**	-
	SVM+HOG	0.924	0.930	0.941	0.910	0.914	0.930	-	0.9248	-
	AdaBoost + C.45	0.850	0.780	0.960	0.838	0.820	0.690	-	0.823	-
Ensemble Learning Methods	AdaBoost + Naïve Bayes	0.998	0.882	1	0.992	0.948	1	-	0.9834	-
	AdaBoost + Random Forest	0.998	0.998	0.998	0.998	0.998	0.998	-	0.9871	-
	Bagging + Naïve Bayes	0.998	0.882	1	0.992	0.981	0.984	-	0.9861	-
	Bagging + Random Forest	0.998	0.855	1	1	0.975	1	-	**<u>0.9880</u>**	-

Table 4 and Table 5 compares traditional machine learning methods, deep learning methods and ensemble learning methods for human behavior recognition in two different public datasets. For YOLOv3, we achieved the highest accuracy 96.29%, the Nearest Neighbor Classifier (NNC) has shown the accuracy 95.6% by using the global spatiotemporal distributions of interest points (Bregonzio et al., 2009). Moreover, pertaining to the deep learning methods, it achieved the real-time recognition; meanwhile, traditional methods required the human behavior recognition frame by frame.

For KTH dataset, DenseNet achieved 86.63% of accuracy. With regard to 3D CNNs, it extracts spatiotemporal features by performing 3D convolutions which have the highest accuracy (90.2%) (Ji et al. 2013). Moreover, Ivan et al. proposed a histogram of gradients with a greedy matching method to recognize human behavior which achieved accuracy at 94.2% (Ivanov et al., 2000). Because some behaviors have the similar local spatiotemporal events, it leads to the misclassifications (Laptev et al., 2004). Moreover, Jagadeesh et al. implemented human behavior recognition with 92.48% accuracy by adopting SVM with HOG features (Jagadeesh et al., 2019). Furthermore, an ensemble learning-based method was proposed by using Weka 3 to combine these four models together, which gained more advanced results in human behavior recognition. In the experiments, we took use of two different ensemble learners to evaluate the results. For the Bagging classifier with random forest got 98.8% accuracy, which is 12.17% higher than single model recognition; by utilizing AdaBoost classifier with random forest which was able to have 98.71% accuracy with KTH dataset. By combining AdaBoost and Bagging ensemble learners with random forest with Weizmann dataset, the final accuracy has been achieved 97.76%.

The results show that both traditional machine learning methods and deep learning methods have succeeded for human behavior recognition. However, traditional machine learning methods may have the best accuracy on behavior recognition, but it requires preprocessing for ROI, segmentation, and feature extraction; it cannot achieve the real-time recognition. Ji et al. (Ji et al, 2013) proposed the 3D CNN model which has the highest accuracy 90.2%, the model used not only the spatial information of video frames, but also the temporal motion information which was also captured by using multiple adjacent frames. The 3D CNN model could be applied to realtime recognition in real scenarios.

CONCLUSION

Throughout our experiments, we implemented four deep neural networks to compare the outcomes. The previous studies were adopted by implementing the traditional approaches for human behavior recognition. Our study shows that deep learning can be improved in future. However, only the spatial information was considered at present, we do not consider the temporal information of the scenes. For our future work, we hope the temporal information will be taken into account so as to avoid the misclassification for the similar behaviors and make the model more suitable and more robust.

REFERENCES

Aggarwal, J. K., & Cai, Q. (1997) Human motion analysis: A review. *Nonrigid and Articulated Motion Workshop*, pp. 99-102.

Aggarwal, J. K., Cai, Q., Liao, W., & Sabata, B. (1997). Nonrigid motion analysis: Articulated and elastic motion. *Computer Vision and Image Understanding*, 142–156.

Bregonzio, M., Gong, S., & Xiang, T. (2009). Recognizing action as clouds of space-time interest points. *CVPR*, 1948–1955.

Ciresan, D., Giusti, A., Gambardella, L. M., & Schmidhuber, J. (2012). Deep neural networks segment neuronal membranes in electron microscopy images. *Advances in Neural Information Processing Systems*, 2843–2851.

Cutler, R., & Davis, L. S. (2000). Robust real-time periodic motion detection, analysis, and applications. *IEEE Transactions on Pattern Analysis and Machine Intelligence*, 22(8), 781–796. doi:10.1109/34.868681

Farabet, C., Couprie, C., Najman, L., & LeCun, Y. (2013). Learning hierarchical features for scene labeling. *IEEE Transactions on Pattern Analysis and Machine Intelligence*, 35(8), 1915–1929. doi:10.1109/TPAMI.2012.231

Fujiyoshi, H., Lipton, A. J., & Kanade, T. (2004). Real-time human motion analysis by image skeltonization. *IEICE Transactions on Information and Systems*, 113–120.

Girshick, R., Donahue, J., Darrell, T., & Malik, J. (2014). Rich feature hierarchies for accurate object detection and semantic segmentation. *CVPR*, 14, 580–587.

Guo, Y., Xu, G., & Tsuji, S. (1994). Tracking human body motion based on a stick figure model. *Journal of Visual Communication and Image Representation, 5*(1), 1–9. doi:10.1006/jvci.1994.1001

He, K., Zhang, X., Ren, S., & Sun, J. (2015). Spatial pyramid pooling in deep convolutional networks for visual recognition. *IEEE Transactions on Pattern Analysis and Machine Intelligence, 37*(9), 1904–1916. doi:10.1109/TPAMI.2015.2389824

He, K., Zhang, X., Ren, S., & Sun, J. (2016). *Deep residual learning for image recognition* (pp. 770–778). CVPR.

Hinton, G., Osindero, S., & Teh, Y. (2006). A fast learning algorithm for deep belief nets. *Neural Computation, 18*(7), 1527–1554. doi:10.1162/neco.2006.18.7.1527

Hinton, G. E., & Salakhutdinov, R. R. (2006). Reducing the dimensionality of data with neural networks. *Science, 313*(5786), 504–507. doi:10.1126cience.1127647

Ivanov, Y. A., & Bobick, A. F. (2000). Recognition of visual activities and interactions by stochastic parsing. *IEEE Transactions on Pattern Analysis and Machine Intelligence, 22*(8), 852–872. doi:10.1109/34.868686

Jagadeesh, B., Patil, C. M. (2019). Video based human activity detection, recognition and classification of actions using SVM. Transactions on Machine Learning and Artificial Intelligence, 22-34.

Ji, S., Xu, W., Yang, M., & Yu, K. (2013). 3D convolutional neural networks for human action recognition. *IEEE Transactions on Pattern Analysis and Machine Intelligence, 35*(1), 221–231. doi:10.1109/TPAMI.2012.59

Krizhevsky, A., Sutskever, I., & Hinton, G. E. (2012). ImageNet classification with deep convolutional neural networks. *Advances in Neural Information Processing Systems*, 1097–1105.

Laptev, I., & Lindeberg, T. (2004). Local descriptors for spatio-temporal recognition. *International Workshop on Spatial Coherence for Visual Motion Analysis*, pp. 91-103. Academic Press.

LeCun, Y., & Bengio, Y. (1995). Convolutional networks for images, speech, and time series. The Handbook of Brain Theory and Neural Networks.

LeCun, Y., Bottou, L., Bengio, Y., & Haffner, P. (1998). Gradient-based learning applied to document recognition. *Proceedings of the IEEE, 86*(11), 2278–2324.

LeCun, Y., Huang, F. J., & Bottou, L. (2004). Learning methods for generic object recognition with invariance to pose and lighting. *Proceedings of the 2004 IEEE Computer Society Conference on Computer Vision and Pattern Recognition.* (Vol. 2, pp. II-104). IEEE.

Liu, W., Anguelov, D., Erhan, D., Szegedy, C., Reed, S., Fu, C.-Y., & Berg, A. C. (2016). SSD: Single shot multibox detector. *ECCV*, 21–37.

Lu, J., Shen, J., Yan, W., & Bacic, B. (2017). An empirical study for human behavior analysis. *International Journal of Digital Crime and Forensics, 9*(3), 11–27. doi:10.4018/IJDCF.2017070102

Niebles, J. C., Wang, H., Li, F. (2008). Unsupervised learning of human action categories using spatial-temporal words. IJCV, 299-318.

Petrushin, V. A. (2005). Mining rare and frequent events in multi-camera surveillance video using self-organizing maps. *ACM Conference on Knowledge Discovery in Data Mining*, pp. 794-800. 10.1145/1081870.1081975

Redmon, J., Divvala, S., Girshick, R., & Farhadi, A. (2016). You only look once: Unified, real-time object detection. *CVPR, 2016*, 779–788.

Redmon, J., & Farhadi, A. (2017). YOLO9000: Better, faster, stronger. *CVPR, 2017*, 7263–7271.

Ren, S., He, K., Girshick, R., & Sun, J. (2017). Faster R-CNN: Towards real-time object detection with region proposal networks. *IEEE Transactions on Pattern Analysis and Machine Intelligence*, *39*(6), 1137–1149. doi:10.1109/TPAMI.2016.2577031

Rui, Y., & Anandan, P. (2000). Segmenting visual actions based on spatio-temporal motion patterns. *CVPR, 2000*, 111–118.

Sande, K., Uijlings, J., Gevers, T., Smeulders, A. (2011). Segmentation as selective search for object recognition. *ICCV 2011*, pp. 1879-1886.

Szegedy, C., Toshev, A., & Erhan, D. (2013). Deep neural networks for object detection. In Advances in Neural Information Processing Systems (pp. 2553-2561).

Tran, D., Bourdev, L., Fergus, R., Torresani, L., & Paluri, M. (2015). Learning spatiotemporal features with 3D convolutional networks. *Proceedings of the IEEE International Conference on Computer Vision*, pp. 4489-4497.

Uijlings, J., Sande, K., Gevers, T., & Smeulders, A. (2013). Selective search for object recognition. *International Journal of Computer Vision, 104*(2), 154-171.

Xiang, T., Gong, S. (2005) Video behavior profiling and abnormality detection without manual labelling. *Proceedings of the IEEE International Conference on Computer Vision*, pp. 1238-1245.

Chapter 10
Container Orchestration With Cost–Efficient Autoscaling in Cloud Computing Environments

Maria Rodriguez
University of Melbourne, Australia

Rajkumar Buyya
University of Melbourne, Australia

ABSTRACT

Containers are widely used by organizations to deploy diverse workloads such as web services, big data, and IoT applications. Container orchestration platforms are designed to manage the deployment of containerized applications in large-scale clusters. The majority of these platforms optimize the scheduling of containers on a fixed-sized cluster and are not enabled to autoscale the size of the cluster nor to consider features specific to public cloud environments. This chapter presents a resource management approach with three objectives: 1) optimize the initial placement of containers by efficiently scheduling them on existing resources, 2) autoscale the number of resources at runtime based on the cluster's workload, and 3) consolidate applications into fewer VMs at runtime. The framework was implemented as a Kubernetes plugin and its efficiency was evaluated on an Australian cloud infrastructure. The experiments demonstrate that a reduction of 58% in cost can be achieved by dynamically managing the cluster size and placement of applications.

INTRODUCTION

Containers, such as Docker (Docker, n.d.) and Linux Containers (LXC) (Bernstein, 2014), are stand-alone and self-contained units that package software and its dependencies together. Similar to Virtual Machines (VMs), containers are a virtualization technique that enable the resources of a single compute node to be shared between multiple users and applications. However, while VMs virtualize resources at the hardware level, containers do so at the operating system level. This makes them a lightweight

DOI: 10.4018/978-1-7998-2701-6.ch010

virtualization approach that enables application environment isolation, fast and flexible deployment, and fine-grained resource sharing.

Organizations are increasingly relying on containerization to deploy diverse workloads derived from modern-day applications such as web services, big data, and IoT applications. Container orchestration platforms, such as Kubernetes (Hightower et al., 2017), Docker Swarm (Naik, 2016) and Apache Mesos (Hindman et al., 2011), are responsible for the efficient orchestration of such applications in shared compute clusters. These platforms manage the lifecycle of containers as well as the usage of cluster resources and hence, one of their main goals is to (near) optimally place containerized applications on the available nodes. This scheduling problem is the focus of this chapter.

As applications are submitted for deployment, the orchestration system must schedule them as fast as possible on one of the available resources. This must be done while attempting to maximize the utilization of the cluster compute resources, as this is likely to reduce the operational cost of the organization. This placement should also be done while considering factors such as the capacity of the available machines, application performance and Quality of Service (QoS) requirements, fault-tolerance, and energy consumption among others. Although existing container orchestration platforms address these issues to an extent, further research is required in order to better optimize the use of resources under different circumstances and for different application requirements.

In cloud environments, containers and VMs can be used together to provide users a great deal of flexibility in deploying, structuring, and managing applications. In such cases, not only should the number of containers scale to meet the requirements of applications, but the number of available compute resources should also adjust to adequately host the required containers. At any given point in time, a cloud container orchestration system should avoid underutilizing VMs as a cost and energy controlling mechanism. It should also be capable of dynamically adding worker VMs to the cluster in order to avoid a degradation in the applications' performance due to resource overutilization. Therefore, autoscaling the number of VMs is essential to successfully meeting the performance goals of containerized applications deployed on public clouds and to reduce the operational cost of leasing the required infrastructure. This increases the complexity of the container placement and scheduling problem mentioned above.

Existing container orchestration frameworks provide bin-packing algorithms to schedule containers on a fixed-sized cluster but are not enabled to autoscale the size of the cluster. Instead, this decision is left to the user or to external frameworks at the platform level. An example of such a scenario is using Kubernetes for the placement of containers and Amazon's autoscaling mechanism to manage the cluster nodes. This approach may not only be impractical but also inefficient as external entities have limited information regarding the container workload.

Another optimization facet not considered by leading orchestration systems is related to rescheduling; in particular, rescheduling to reduce resource fragmentation and to reduce the size of the cluster. Regardless of how good the initial placement of these tasks is, the utilization of resources will degrade over time as the workload changes. Rescheduling applications that tolerate a component being shut down and restarted will enable the orchestration system to consolidate and rearrange tasks so that more applications can be deployed on the same number of nodes or some nodes can be shutdown to reduce cost or save energy. Similarly, if more nodes are added to the cluster, being able to reschedule some of the deployed applications on the new nodes may be beneficial in the long term.

As a result, the work on this chapter argues that a cloud-centric container orchestration framework capable of making all of the resource management decisions, including autoscaling and rescheduling, is essential in successfully optimizing the use of resources in cloud environments. The main contribution of this work is therefore a comprehensive container resource management framework that has three different objectives. The first one is to optimize the initial placement of containers so that the number of worker VMs is minimized and the memory and CPU requirements of the containerized applications are met. The second one is to autoscale the number of worker VMs based on the current cluster's workload. On one hand, scaling out will enable the current resource demand to be met while reducing the time it takes to place and launch containers. On the other hand, scaling in will enable applications to be relocated so that underutilized VMs can be shutdown to reduce the infrastructure cost. Finally, a rescheduling mechanism will further support the efficient use of resources by consolidating applications into fewer VMs when possible to avoid unnecessary scaling out operations and to encourage scale in operations.

The rest of the chapter is organized as follows. Section 2 presents existing container management platforms along other related scheduling algorithms. Section 3 discusses the application and resource models considered by our orchestration framework. The architecture of the proposed system and its realisation by leveraging Kubernetes is discussed in Section 4. The proposed autoscaling, rescheduling, and scheduling methods are discussed in Section 5. Section 6 presents the evaluation of our framework and the proposed algorithms on an Australian national cloud infrastructure. Finally, Section 7 concludes the chapter and identifies and discusses new research directions.

Related Work

There have been considerable attempts to build reliable and scalable container management platforms for clusters in the research and open-source communities (Rodriguez & Buyya, 2019). These systems are responsible for managing the deployment of general-purpose applications, usually packaged in either Docker or Linux cgroups-based containers. In this section, we briefly present related works in the context of software systems and resource management algorithms for container orchestration.

Software Systems

Kubernetes (Hightower, Burns, & Beda, 2017) is the leading open-source container management platform, which is derived from Google's in-house Borg (Verma et al., 2015). Kubernetes orchestrates and manages the lifecycle of heterogeneous containerized applications (such as services and batch jobs) in either virtualized or physical clusters. It provides a default scheduler that assigns each container group (or pod) to available cluster resources filtered by user-defined requirements and ranked based on individually defined application affinities. A detailed evaluation of Kubernetes can be found in (Medel, Rana, Bañares, & Arronategui, 2016).

Docker Swarm (Naik, 2016) is the native clustering solution for Docker containers. It provides discovery services and schedules containers onto hosts using predefined strategies and filters. By default, it supports two simple strategies: i) a spread strategy that favors running new containers on least loaded hosts, and ii) a bin packing strategy that favors the most loaded hosts that have enough resources to run the containers. Docker Swarm also employs a filtering mechanism to identify the qualified resources; users can define filters regarding host statuses, health check results, and container configurations (such as resource and file affinities and dependencies to other containers).

Apache Mesos (Hindman et al., 2011) enables cluster sharing among various applications. Different to Kubernetes and Swarm, Mesos can be viewed as a meta-platform that operates above them. It employs a two-stage scheduling approach. In the first stage, it divides the resources of the cluster and respectively provisions resources to each application via resource offers. Once an application accepts a resource offer, it can proceed to scheduling its tasks on the obtained resources using its own scheduling logic. After that, Mesos actually launches the tasks for the application on the corresponding hosts.

Apache Marathon (Marathon, n.d.) and Apache Aurora (DelValle, Rattihalli, Beltre, Govindaraju, & Lewis, 2016) are two popular general-purpose frameworks built on top of Mesos. Marathon is designed to orchestrate long-running services. Because of this, it focuses on providing applications with fault-tolerance and high-availability; Marathon will ensure that launched applications will continue to run even in the presence of node failures. Originally developed by Twitter, Aurora is a scheduler that enables long-running services, cron jobs, and ad-hoc jobs to be deployed in a cluster. Aurora specializes in ensuring that services are kept running continuously and as a result, when machine failures occur, jobs are intelligently rescheduled onto healthy machines. It is worthwhile mentioning that in terms of functionality, Marathon and Aurora are very similar products. However, there are a few differences. The main one is that Marathon handles only service-like jobs. Furthermore, setting up and using Marathon is considered to be simpler than doing so with Aurora; Marathon includes for example a user interface through which users can directly schedule tasks.

YARN (Vavilapalli et al., 2013) is a cluster manager designed to orchestrate Hadoop tasks, although it also supports other frameworks such as Giraph, Spark, and Storm. Each application framework running on top of YARN coordinates their own execution flows and optimizations as they see fit. In YARN, there is a per-cluster resource manager (RM) and an application master (AM) per framework. The AM requests resources from the RM and generates a physical plan from the resources it receives. Hence, YARN's two-level scheduling model is similar to Mesos, but instead of it offering resources to applications, applications request the needed resources from YARN.

Although most of the above systems are mature, the resource management optimization space can still be further explored. This is especially true in the era of cloud computing, as most existing frameworks ignore many of the inherent features of cloud platforms in favour of assuming a static cluster of resources. As a result, elasticity, pricing, and service heterogeneities are ignored. Rescheduling for defragmentation and autoscaling is another feature missing from the aforementioned systems. This work aims to address these gaps by exploring the benefits of considering autoscaling and rescheduling when managing the cluster's resources.

Resource Management Algorithms

This section discusses relevant works that focus on container-based scheduling algorithms. Xu et al. (Xu, Yu, & Pei, 2014) proposed a resource scheduling approach for container-based cloud environments to reduce the response time of requests and improve resource utilization, which can obtain an optimal mapping for containers to hosts by using stable machine theory. (Zhang et al., 2016) designed a novel video surveillance cloud platform based on containers, which applies future workload prediction to achieve fine-grained resource provisioning and ensure quality of service. (Kaewkasi & Chuenmuneewong, 2017) applied Ant Colony Optimization to allocate containers to hosts and aimed to balance the resource usage. (Kehrer & Blochinger, 2018) presented a two-phase deployment method for Apache Mesos to achieve a more flexible management of containers. (Guerrero, Lera, & Juiz, 2018) proposed a genetic algorithm for Kubernetes platform to optimize container allocation and elasticity management. Their algorithm can improve system performance and reduce network overhead. Contrary to the work presented in this chapter, the aforementioned approaches focus on the initial placement of containers (i.e., scheduling) and do not consider the rescheduling and autoscaling.

(Yin, Luo, J., & Luo, H., 2018) built a task-scheduling model by exploiting containers and developed a task-scheduling algorithm to reduce the completion time of tasks in fog computing environment. They also proposed a rescheduling approach to optimize task delays. However, the results are only validated in a simulated environment.

(Xu, Toosi,, & Buyya, 2018) proposed an approach based on containers and brownout, which can dynamically activate and deactivate optional containers to achieve an energy-efficient management of cloud resources while ensuring quality of service requirements are met. This approach applies autoscaling to reduce the active number of hosts but it doesn't consider the initial placement and rescheduling of containers.

Table 1 summarises the comparison of related works focused on resource management algorithms.

Table 1. Comparison of related algorithmic works

Work	Objective/Focus	Initial Placement	Rescheduling	Autoscaling	Platform
(Xu et al. 2014)	Reduce response time	√			Simulation
(Zhang et al., 2016)	Improve resource utilization	√			Docker
(Kaewkasi & Chuenmuneewong, 2017)	Balance resource usage	√			Docker
(Yin et al., 2018)	Reduce task delays	√	√		Simulation
(Guerrero et al., 2018)	Reduce network overhead	√			Kubernetes
(Kehrer & Blochinger, 2018)	Flexible management	√			Mesos
(Xu et al. 2018)	Reduce energy			√	Docker
Our work (this chapter)	Reduce cost	√	√	√	Kubernetes

Application and Resource Models

We consider a container orchestration framework that is deployed in a virtualized public cloud environment by either an organization or a platform as a service provider. Hence, the framework has access to an unlimited number of VMs that can be provisioned and deprovisioned on-demand. For the initial stages of this work, we assume homogeneous VMs, that is, VMs that have the same price and characteristics and are charged per billing period. The characteristics of VMs are defined in terms of their memory and CPU capacities.

The characteristics of the workload considered in this work are derived from the usage model of large-scale clusters in organizations like Google, Alibaba, and Fuji. To efficiently utilize resources, instead of running separate clusters of homogeneous containers, these organizations prefer to run different types of containerized applications on a shared cluster. We consider a workload that consists of two different types of continuously arriving containerized tasks. The first type of tasks are long-running services that require high availability and must handle latency-sensitive requests. Examples include user-facing web applications or web services. The second type of tasks are batch jobs. These have a limited lifetime and are more tolerant to performance fluctuations. Examples include scientific computations, data analytics, and map-reduce jobs.

We assume that all tasks define the amount of CPU and memory that they require (i.e., resource requests). In this way, tasks will only be deployed on nodes that have at least their required amount of resources available. Furthermore, long-running services may be defined by users as moveable. Moveable tasks are those that can tolerate being shut down and restarted on a different node for purposes of rescheduling and autoscaling. This may include stateless web applications or replicated web services.

From a high-level perspective, the problem being addressed in this work is divided in three phases:

- **Scheduling:** Place an incoming task on a cluster resource that has at least the amount of CPU and memory resources requested by the task available.
- **Rescheduling:** If there is an incoming task that is unschedulable (i.e., no node has the required amount of resources available), then the rescheduler will attempt to rearrange running tasks that are moveable in order to make room for the unschedulable task.
- **Autoscaling:** This problem is divided into two sub-problems: i) scaling out and ii) scaling in. On one hand, if after attempting to reschedule there is still an unschedulable task, the autoscaler should consider scaling out (provisioning a new VM) in order to increase the cluster's capacity. If there are unused VMs or the cluster resources are being utilized inefficiently, the autoscaler should consider shutting down unused VMs or consolidating tasks to increase the utilization of the cluster and deprovision unnecessary VMs.

The overall goal of this work is to emphasize and illustrate the need for a holistic resource management approach to container orchestration; that is, an approach that considers scheduling, rescheduling, and autoscaling. The proposed framework integrates these three processes and allows different policies to be seamlessly plugged in.

SYSTEM ARCHITECTURE

Figure 1 depicts the architecture of the system and its realisation by extending the Kubernetes (K8s) platform. The existing K8s components are shown in blue and the extended components are shown in green. In the rest of this section we first introduce Kubernetes and the key features relevant to this work followed by an overview of each of the proposed components.

Kubernetes

Kubernetes is a framework designed to manage containerized workloads on clusters. The basic building block in Kubernetes is a pod. A pod encapsulates one or more tightly coupled containers that are co-located and share the same set of resources. Pods also encapsulate storage resources, a network IP, and a set of options that govern how the pod's container(s) should run. A pod is designed to run a single instance of an application; in this way multiple pods can be used to scale an application horizontally for example. The amount of CPU, memory, and ephemeral storage a container needs can be specified when creating a pod. This information can then be used by the scheduler to make decisions on pod placement. These compute resources can be specified both as a requested amount or as a limit on the amount the container is allowed to consume.

The default Kubernetes scheduler ensures that the total amount of compute resource requests of all pods placed in a node does not exceed the capacity of the node. This even if the actual resource consumption is very low. The reason behind this is to protect applications against a resource shortage on a node when resource usage later increases (e.g., during a daily peak). If a container exceeds its memory limit, it may be terminated and may be later restarted. If it exceeds its memory request, it may be terminated when the node runs out of memory. Regarding the CPU usage, containers may or may not be allowed to exceed their limits for periods of time, but they will not be killed for this. On the other hand, containers and pods that exceed their storage limit will be evicted.

Other resources (called Extended Resources) can be specified to advertise new node-level resources, their resource accounting is managed by the scheduler to ensure that no more than the available amount is simultaneously allocated to pods.

From a technical perspective, Kubernetes allows for various types of container runtimes to be used, with Docker and rkt natively supported by the platform. More recently, the release of the framework's Container Runtime Interface (CRI) API has enabled Kubernetes to support other container technologies such as containerd (Containerd, n.d.) and frakti (Frakti, n.d.), a hypervisor-based container runtime. Furthermore, CRI-O (CRI-O, n.d.), an implementation of the CRI API, currently enables Kubernetes to support any OCI (Open Container Initiative) compliant container runtime such as runc (Runc, n.d.). Also, supporting Kubernetes in managing the cluster nodes and jobs is etcd (Etcd, n.d.), an open source, highly available, distributed key-value store. Specifically, etcd is used to store all of the cluster's data and acts as the single source of truth for all of the framework's components.

Overall, Kubernetes is a highly mature system; it stemmed from ten years of experience at Google with Borg and Omega (Schwarzkopf, Konwinski, Abd-El-Malek, & Wilkes, 2013) and is the leading container-based cluster management system with an extensive community-driven support and development base. It provides users with a wide range of options for managing their pods and the way in which they are scheduled, even allowing for pluggable customized schedulers to be easily integrated into the system. To conclude, although Kubernetes' performance and scalability may still not reach the levels of industry-based systems like Borg, as of version 1.10, Kubernetes is capable of supporting clusters of up to 5000 hundred nodes (Kubernetes, 2019), which suits the needs of many modern organizations.

Extended Components

This section discusses the additional components added to the Kubernetes framework as part of the implementation of the work proposed in this chapter.

A *Custom Scheduler* interacts with the Kubernetes API to continuously monitor the state of pods in the cluster. A pod corresponds to a single task, either long running or batch. Hence, the scheduler focuses on processing pending pods (i.e., those that need to be scheduled). For each pending pod, a set of suitable resources (i.e., Kubernetes workers) is filtered from the entire cluster pool. One of these resources is then selected and a binding between the pod and the resources is created. This binding leads to Kubernetes running the pod on the chosen node. Once again, it is worthwhile noting that different

Figure 1. Architecture of the prototype system

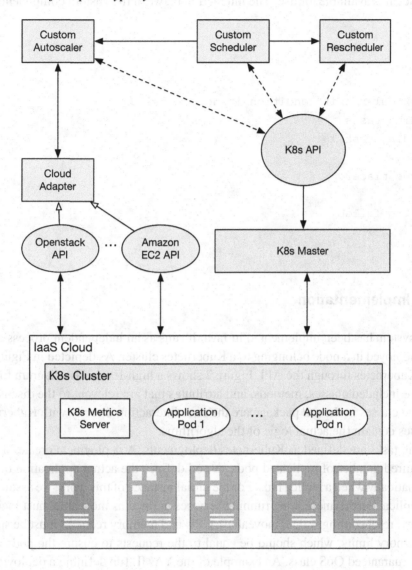

policies to select the set of suitable nodes and assign a task to one of them have been implemented and are easily pluggable into the system. These are described in detail in Section 5.

The *Custom Scheduler* interacts with the *Custom Rescheduler* whenever a pod cannot be placed. The rescheduler then attempts to consolidate moveable pods so that the incoming pod can be placed in an existing node. If the cluster is at capacity and there is no room for the incoming pending pod, then the *Autoscaler* component is invoked in order to determine whether a new VM should be provisioned to place the pod. The *Autoscaler* can then decides the number and type of VMs to launch and instructs the *Cloud Adapter* to create the new instances via the specific IaaS cloud provider API. In the meantime, the unschedulable pod can be left in the scheduling queue in a pending state so that it can be scheduled in a later cycle when the newly provisioned (or recently freed) resources become available. The pod can also be removed from the general scheduling queue so that it can be directly assigned to the newly created node once it is available for use. The interaction between the custom components is depicted in Algorithm 1.

Algorithm 1.

```
while the scheduler exit condition is not satisfied
get all pending tasks
for each pending task t
schedule t
if t cannot be placed
reschedule
if rescheduling failed
scale out
scale in
```

Design and Implementation

The prototype system has been implemented in Java. It runs as an independent process and hence does not need to be deployed in a node belonging to a Kubernetes cluster. As depicted in Figure 1, the system interacts with Kubernetes through the API. Figure 2 shows a high-level class diagram for the prototype system. We have included classes, methods, and attributes that are relevant to the discussion presented in this work. The classes in the *util* package are the ones interacting directly with Kubernetes while the rest of the classes contain the actual logic of the algorithms.

Long running tasks are defined as Kubernetes deployments. A deployment creates a replica set that spawns the required number of replicated pods. A pod defines the actual application or task. Pods are recreated automatically when a replica fails. For the initial instance of this work, we assume deployments with a single replica. Furthermore, long running services defined as moveable must include a label indicating this (key: rescheduling, value: moveable). CPU and memory requests must be specified as well as CPU and memory limits, which should be equal to the requests to ensure the pods are assigned to the Kubernetes guaranteed QoS class. An example of the YAML file defining a deployment of a single replica of an *nginx* service is shown in Figure 3.

The same rules regarding requests/limits and replicas apply to batch jobs. However, these are defined using Kubernetes jobs as opposed to deployments, which allow the definition of tasks that run to completion. Furthermore, jobs cannot be labeled as moveable and instead must be labeled with key type and value batch. A sample YAML defining a job is depicted in Figure 4.

Cost-Efficient Scheduling and Autoscaling Algorithms

This section describes the algorithms that were proposed and implemented in the prototype system. The design of the framework is flexible as it allows for any combination of scheduling, rescheduling, and scheduling to be used when launching the system.

Figure 2. Class diagram for the prototype system

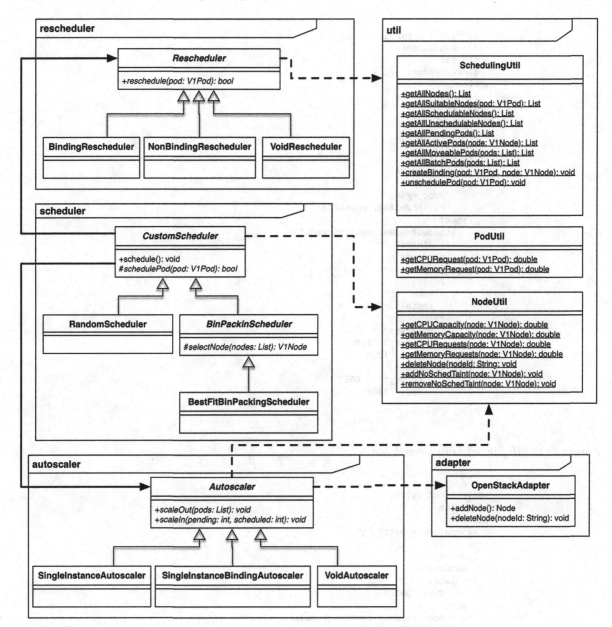

Scheduling

Best Fit Bin Packing Scheduler

The general bin packing problem can be defined as follows. Given n items of different weights and bins each of capacity c, assign each item to a bin such that number of total used bins is minimized. There are multiple greedy solutions designed to solve the online version of this problem, that is, instances where items arrive one at a time and must be placed in a bin before considering the next item. One of these

Figure 3. YAML file defining a deployment of a single nginx service replica

```
apiVersion: apps/v1
kind: Deployment
metadata:
  generateName: nginx-
spec:
  replicas: 1
  selector:
    matchLabels:
      app: nginx
  template:
    metadata:
      name: nginx
      labels:
        app: nginx
        rescheduling: moveable
    spec:
      schedulerName: customScheduler
      containers:
      - name: nginx
        image: nginx
        ports:
        - name: http
          containerPort: 80
        resources:
          requests:
            memory: "1.4Gi"
            cpu: "100m"
          limits:
            memory: "1.4Gi"
            cpu: "100m"
```

Figure 4. YAML file defining a batch job

```
apiVersion: batch/v1
kind: Job
metadata:
  generateName batch-
spec:
  template:
    metadata:
      labels:
        type: batch
    spec:
      schedulerName: customScheduler
      restartPolicy: Never
      containers:
        - name: batch-container
          image: busybox
          command: ['sh', '-c', ./batchJob']
          resources:
            requests:
              memory: "1Gi"
              cpu: "100m"
            limits:
              memory: "1Gi"
              cpu: "100m"
```

Algorithm 2. Best Fit Bin Packing Scheduler

```
Input: Pending pod p
Output: true if successful, false otherwise
nodes = getAllSuitableNodes(p)
node = node with least amount of available RAM in nodes
if node is not null
createBinding(node, p)
return true
return false
```

solutions is referred to as best fit, which places items in the fullest bin that can still accommodate an item without the bin capacity being exceeded.

For the scheduling problem addressed by this work, an item corresponds to a pod and a bin to a cluster node. Since pods are continuously arriving for execution, we consider the problem to be online as well. Hence, this scheduler places incoming pending pods in the node with the smallest amount of available resources that satisfy the pod requirements. This problem however is not one dimensional as pods require two different resources to be available, CPU and memory. We address this by first filtering nodes that have enough CPU available and then selecting from this list the node that has the least amount of available memory that is at least as large as the memory request of the incoming pod. The reason for this is two-fold. First, our goal is to keep the algorithm simple and capable of making fast decisions. Second, we consider CPU to be a compressible resource; that is, it's use can be throttled if the requested amount is exceeded or the node is overloaded. Memory on the other hand is non-compressible in that its use cannot be throttled. Stopping a pod from using excess memory can only be done by killing the pod and relieving memory pressure from an overloaded node can only be achieved by evicting pods currently deployed on the node.

Rescheduling

See Algorithm 3.

Void Rescheduler

The void rescheduler will simply ignore rescheduling request and hence is equivalent to a system without rescheduling capabilities.

Non-binding Rescheduler

This rescheduler aims to evict moveable pods from a node if and only if i) the moveable pods can be rescheduled somewhere else and ii) by evicting the moveable pods, the node now has enough resources to place an unschedulable pod. This is however only attempted if the unschedulable pod has been in a pending state for at least *max_pod_age*. This with the aim of reducing the number of unnecessary

Algorithm 3. Non-binding Rescheduler

```
Input: Unschedulable pod p
If age of p is greater than or equal to max_pod_age
nodes = getAllNodesWithEnoughCPU(p)
sort nodes descending based on available memory
for each node in nodes
if the node has moveable pods running
sort moveable pods descending based on requested memory
for each moveable pod
if the pod can be placed somewhere else
add pod to list of pods to evict
update freed memory
if enough memory has been freed
evict pods
success = true
break
if success
break
```

rescheduling and autoscaling decisions as it gives batch jobs the chance to complete and hence make room for the unschedulable pod.

Based on a best fit heuristic and on the same assumptions regarding compressible and non-compressible resources as the best fit bin packing scheduler, the non-binding rescheduler achieves its goals in the following way. First nodes are filtered to obtain only those that have enough available CPU to fit the unschedulable pod. These are then sorted ascendingly based on the amount of memory they have available. Then, for each of these nodes, if one or more moveable pods can be scheduled on a different node in the cluster and the amount of memory freed on the node is sufficient to execute the unschedulable pod, then the moveable pods are evicted and these and the unschedulable pod are left in the pending queue so that they can be placed by the scheduler in the next cycle (i.e., non-binding).

Binding Rescheduler

The binding rescheduler works in a similar way to the non-binding one. The only difference is that instead of leaving evicted and unschedulable pods in the pending queue, they are actually placed on their corresponding nodes by the rescheduler.

Autoscaling

Void Autoscaler

The void autoscaler will simply ignore the scale out and scale in requests and hence is equivalent to a system without autoscaling capabilities.

Algorithm 4. Binding Rescheduler

```
Input: Unschedulable pod p
If age of p is greater than or equal to max_pod_age
nodes = getAllNodesWithEnoughCPU(p)
sort nodes descending based on available memory
for each node in nodes
if the node has moveable pods running
sort moveable pods descending based on requested memory
for each moveable pod
if the pod can be placed somewhere else
add <pod, newNode> to map of pods to evict
update freed memory
if enough memory has been freed
evict moveable pods from node
for each pod in pods to evict
createBinding(pod, newNode)
success = true
break
if success
break
```

Simple Autoscaler

The simple autoscaler will consider launching a new instance of a predefined type whenever the scale out operation is invoked. The number of instances launched is capped to one every *provisioning_interval*. The motivation behind this limit is based on the following observation. Unschedulable pods are likely to be found in batches. That is, if there are insufficient resources to deploy one pod, there may be insufficient resources to deploy the next pending pod in the queue. Hence, scaling out requests are likely to be made several times during the same scheduling cycle. This may lead to an excessive number of instances being launched which may end up being underutilized as a single one may have sufficed to execute the unschedulable pods. In fact, we set the *provisioning_interval* based on an estimate of the instance provisioning delay (i.e., the time it takes for the VM to boot and join the K8s cluster) plus a small contingency value. Notice however that this parameter is configurable by users.

Regarding the scale in operation, it occurs only when the scheduling cycle was successful in placing all the pending pods in the queue. Also, only those nodes that were created dynamically (e.g., by scaling out) are considered to be shut down. If these conditions are met, firstly, any idle node with no pods running is deprovisioned. Secondly, any node that has only moveable pods that can be placed in any other node in the cluster is also shut down. Thirdly, any node that has a combination of moveable and batch pods is tainted as unschedulabe if all of its moveable pods can be placed on different nodes. If this is the case, moveable pods are evicted and left to be recreated by Kubernetes and placed by the scheduler in the next cycle. Because the node has been tainted as unschedulable, schedulers will avoid placing pods on the node unless strictly necessary (i.e., no other untainted node has sufficient capacity). In this way,

Algorithm 5. Simple Autoscaler – Scale Out

```
Input: Unschedulable pod p
if elapsed time since last instance launched >= provisioning_interval
launch new instance
update last instance launch time
else
ignore scale out operation
```

Algorithm 6. Simple Autoscaler – Scale In

```
if all pending pods were successfully scheduled in the last cycle
shutdown any nodes that are empty and were autoscaled
nodes = getAllSchedulableNodes()
for each node in nodes
if all pods are moveable
if all pods can be placed on other nodes
delete node
let Kubernetes recreate the pods
let the scheduler place the recreated pods
if some pods are moveable and some pods are batch jobs
if all moveable pods can be placed on other nodes
delete all moveable pods
let Kubernetes recreate the pods
let the scheduler place the recreated pods
taint the node as unschedulable
```

the node has the potential of becoming idle once the batch jobs running in it complete and hence should be deprovisioned on a subsequent scaling in cycle.

Single Instance Binding Autoscaler

The heuristic is similar to that of the single instance autoscaler. However, this autoscaler aims to address a key disadvantage of the non-binding autoscaler. When unschedulable pods are not bound or associated in any way to autoscaled nodes, multiple requests to autoscale triggered by the same unschedulable pod may be invoked. This may lead to multiple instances being launched unnecessarily.

This autoscaler keeps track of pods and the scaled-out nodes that have been launched for them. In fact, the autoscaler keeps a list of pods that could potentially run on a node that is being provisioned. Requests to scale out made for a pod that is already associated with a node that is in the process of booting up are ignored. Once the node has been provisioned and has joined the cluster, the autoscaler is notified so that the pod is no longer associated to any node. The scheduler is responsible then for placing the pod on an available node in the next cycle, this node is likely to be the newly provisioned one, but this is not mandatory. If the node was filled with other pending nodes by the scheduler, then a request to scale out for the pod will be triggered and the process repeated.

Algorithm 7. Simple Binding Autoscaler – Scale Out

```
Input: Unschedulable pod p
if pod has not been assigned to a provisioning node
if pod can fit in one of the nodes being provisioned
assign pod to provisioning node
else
launch a new node and assign the pod to the node
when new node is provisioned
unassign any pod associated to the node
remove node from list of provisioning nodes
let the scheduler place pods in the new node
```

To further prevent unnecessary nodes being launched, the binding autoscaler takes into consideration nodes that have been provisioned but have not joined the cluster yet when deciding whether to launch a new instance or not. When a request to scale out is made for an unschedulable pod, the autoscaler scans the list of nodes that are in the process of being provisioned. If there is still room in one of these nodes for the pending pod, then the pod is added to the list of pods that could potentially run on that node and no new instance is launched.

Table 2. Types of jobs used in the evaluation

	Name	Task	Memory Requests	CPU Requests
Batch Jobs	batch_small	sleep 5 min	0.3Gi	100m
	batch_med	sleep 10 min	0.6Gi	200m
	batch_large	sleep 15 min	0.9Gi	300m
Long-running Services	service_small	nginx server	1Gi	100m
	service_med	nginx server	1.4Gi	200m
	service_large	nginx server	2.359Gi	300m

PERFORMANCE EVALUATION

Testbed and Workload

To demonstrate the potential capabilities of the proposed framework and the benefits of autoscaling, we performed a set of validating experiments. We modelled synthetic workloads composed of batch jobs and long running services as presented in Table 2. Three different workloads with varying inter-arrival job times and combination of jobs and services were used as illustrated in Table 3. To generate these workloads, jobs were selected at random with equal probability and the delay between them was sampled from an exponential distribution with different means. For the bursty workload, a mean of 10 seconds was used, the aim is to simulate jobs arriving at a high rate. For the slow workload, a mean of 60 seconds was used. The mixed workload combines both a bursty and a slow job arrival rate. It was generated by splitting the workload into periods, each being either bursty or slow. The first period was chosen at random and subsequent ones were alternated. The number of jobs in each period was chosen at random with the minimum number of jobs in a period being 10.

The jobs do not actually use the requested resources; however, this does not affect the obtained results as the purpose of the requests is to validate the functionality and performance of the scheduler.

Table 3. Workloads used in the evaluation

Workload Name	Exponential Dist. Mean (sec)	Number of Batch Jobs			Number of Service Jobs			Total Batch	Total Service	Total
		Small	Med	Large	Small	Med	Large			
Bursty	60	10	8	5	6	12	9	23	27	50
Slow	10	17	11	4	6	7	5	32	18	50
Mixed	60 slow, 6 burtsy	6	7	9	7	11	10	22	28	50

The Kubernetes cluster was deployed on Nectar (Nectar, n.d.), an Australian research cloud based on Openstack. The VM specifications used to deploy the Kubernetes master and worker nodes are depicted in Table 3. The custom architectural components were deployed outside Nectar on a MacBook Pro with a 2.9 GHz Intel Core i7 processor and 8 GB of RAM and the Kubernetes version used was 1.10. Since Nectar does not charge for the use of resources, we estimate the cost of each approach based on the billing model of existing cloud providers. In particular, we assume a per-second billing of $0.011 for each worker based on Microsoft Azure's general purpose *B2S* instance type, with any partial use being rounded up to the nearest second. Although Microsoft bills per minute, we assume a per-second billing due to the nature and scale of the experiments without impacting the significance of the results. Table 4 depicts the values used for the algorithm-specific parameters.

Table 4. Master and worker nodes VM specifications

	VM Type	# of vCPUs	RAM	Operating System
Master	m2.medium	2	6 GB	Ubuntu 17.01
Worker	m2.small	1	4 GB	Ubuntu 17.01

Table 5. Algorithm-specific parameter values used in the evaluation

Parameter	Value	Algorithm
VM price per second	$0.011	N/A
max_pod_age	1 min	Rescheduler
provisioning_interval	1 min	Autoscaler

Results

First, we evaluate the performance of each of the rescheduling and autoscaling heuristics in terms of cost and scheduling duration. We define scheduling duration as the time elapsed from the moment the first job is submitted and the moment the last batch job completes its execution. The cost is estimated based on the amount of time each VM was provisioned for; that is, from the moment a request for provisioning was placed to the cloud provider until the moment a deprovisioning request was placed. For static nodes, the cost was estimated based on the total scheduling time of the workload. Finally, only the rescheduling and autoscaling policies vary throughout the experiments, the scheduler (best fit bin packing) is kept constant.

Figure 5. Cost and scheduling duration for the three different workloads and six different algorithms.

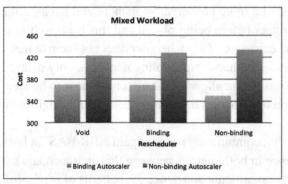 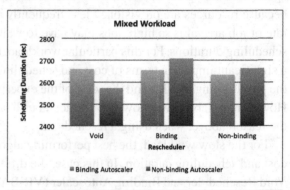

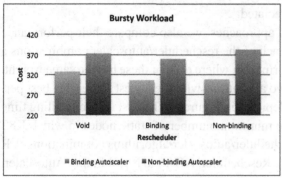 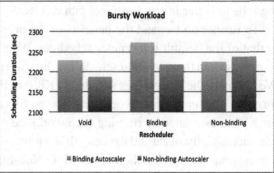

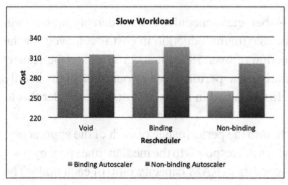 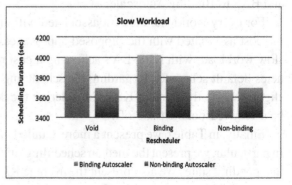

Figure 5 presents the cost and total scheduling duration for each of the scheduler/autoscaler combinations and each of the workloads. For the mixed workload, the lowest cost and scheduling duration is obtained by the Non-binding Rescheduler and Binding Autoscaler (NBR-BAS). In fact, the binding autoscaler combined with any of the rescheduler always leads to the lowest cost and in 2 out of 3 cases, to the lowest scheduling duration. This emphasizes on the importance of having heuristics in place that aim to avoid unnecessary scaling out operations. While the non-binding autoscaler blindly provisions a new instance if a pod cannot be placed, the binding autoscaler considers instances that are currently being provisioned as potential hosts for the incoming pod before provisioning a new node. As for the difference in performance between the binding and non-binding reschedulers, it seems to be a better option to allow the scheduler to place all pending pods as opposed to trying to replicate the job of the scheduler in the rescheduler.

The results in terms of cost for the bursty workload are similar to those of the mixed workload. Once again, the binding autoscaler leads to smaller number of resources used and hence lower costs. However, because resources are provisioned less frequently and in a more conservative manner and because the rate of job arrival is so high, jobs may have to wait longer before being placed and this leads to higher scheduling durations. For this particular workload, the existence of a rescheduler does not seem to make a significant impact in terms of cost and scheduling time. Perhaps rescheduling may have only delayed the provisioning of VMs and the scale of the experiments do not allow for the effects of these to be seen. However, in Table 5 we show how the actual utilization of resources does improve, although slightly for the reason above, when using a rescheduler.

For the slow workload, the best performing algorithm combination is once again NBR-BAS for both cost and scheduling duration. In this case, the difference in both metrics between this approach and the Void Rescheduler and Binding Autoscaler (VR-BAS) is significant and hence the benefits of rescheduling jobs to better utilize resources can be clearly appreciated.

To further understand the benefits of the proposed approaches, we also compare their performance to that of the default Kubernetes scheduler. We give each of the rescheduler/autoscaler combinations a score based on their cost and scheduling duration performance, where each of these has the same weight. We compare the Kubernetes scheduler (K8S) to the two algorithms with the lowest score (i.e., best performance) for each of the workloads. The results are depicted in Figure 6. The cost and scheduling time for K8S is estimated by running each workload on the minimum number of static nodes in which K8S can successfully place and execute all the jobs. In rescheduler/autoscaler algorithms combinations, VR corresponds to Void Rescheduler, NBR to Non-binding Rescheduler, NBAS to Non-binding Autoscaler, and BAS to Binding Autoscaler.

For every workload, the cost associated with the Kubernetes scheduler is considerably higher than the cost associated with the proposed approaches. The maximum reduction in cost is achieved for the slow workload, with NBR-BAS achieving a cost reduction of over 58% when compared to the Kubernetes default scheduler. Regarding the scheduling duration, the performance of our algorithms is only slightly worse than that of K8S. Considering the benefits obtained in terms of cost, we consider this to be a very reasonable trade-off.

Finally, in Table 6 we present a more detailed insight into the performance of each of the approaches. In particular, we present the median scheduling time, which corresponds to the median time spent by pods in a pending state. We also present the average RAM requests to RAM capacity ratio of each node. The average RAM requests of a node corresponds to the average of measurements taken every 20 seconds throughout the scheduling duration. These measurements are the sum of the memory requests of all the

Figure 6. Cost and scheduling duration for the k8s scheduler and the best performing rescheduler/autoscaler combinations for different workloads (mixed, bursty, and slow).

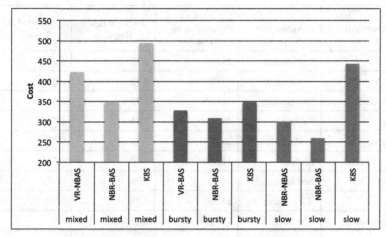

A. Cost of execution - default K8S vs others

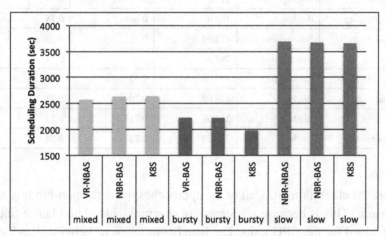

B. Scheduling duration - default K8S vs others

pods allocated to the node. The RAM capacity of a node is the maximum amount of memory that can be requested by all of the pods in the node. The average CPU requests to capacity ratio is also depicted in Table 5 and is estimated in the same way as the RAM ratio. The average number of pods deployed on a node is also shown.

The median scheduling time is the fastest for the slow workload and the NBR-NBAS. This is in line with what is expected of the algorithms as the non-binding autoscaler causes more resources to be provisioned and hence readily available for use as jobs arrive. Furthermore, a larger interarrival time between jobs means batch jobs can complete and hence space can be freed by the time a new job arrives. This is further supported by the large difference between the median times for the slow and bursty workloads. Jobs in the bursty workload have to wait for a considerably longer amount of time in pending state as resources cannot be provisioned fast enough. This due mainly to VM provisioning delays.

Table 6. Scheduling performance and resource utilization for each of the rescheduler/autoscaler combinations.

Workload	Rescheduler	Autoscaler	Median Scheduling Time (sec)	Average RAM Req/Cap	Average CPU Req/Cap	Average # Pods/ Node
Mixed	Void	Non-binding	**25.00**	0.72	0.68	2.03
	Binding	Non-binding	37.00	0.73	0.67	1.99
	Non-binding	Non-binding	111.00	0.79	**0.72**	2.22
	Void	Binding	49.50	**0.81**	**0.72**	2.20
	Binding	Binding	26.00	0.77	0.70	2.14
	Non-binding	Binding	112.50	0.80	**0.72**	**2.23**
Slow	Void	Non-binding	14.00	0.79	0.72	2.41
	Binding	Non-binding	11.50	0.78	0.70	2.33
	Non-binding	Non-binding	**10.00**	0.83	0.74	2.52
	Void	Binding	12.50	0.82	0.72	2.44
	Binding	Binding	17.50	0.84	0.74	2.49
	Non-binding	Binding	12.50	**0.86**	**0.76**	**2.62**
Bursty	Void	Non-binding	422.50	0.65	0.69	2.11
	Binding	Non-binding	**297.00**	0.67	0.71	2.24
	Non-binding	Non-binding	467.00	0.62	0.67	2.04
	Void	Binding	418.00	0.70	0.72	2.28
	Binding	Binding	354.00	0.71	0.73	2.31
	Non-binding	Binding	388.50	**0.73**	**0.74**	**2.36**

Regarding the RAM utilization ratio, all of the approaches using the non-binding autoscaler achieve the worst performance. This is because resources are overprovisioned and hence underutilized. Similar results were obtained for the CPU ratio. The benefits in terms of better utilization are clear for the NBR-BAS approach on the bursty workload, with it obtaining the highest ratios and average number of pods per node.

CONCLUSION AND FUTURE DIRECTIONS

In this work, we have proposed the integrated use of schedulers, autoscalers, and reschedulers as a mechanism to make container orchestration systems cloud-aware. In this, the scheduler optimizes the initial placement of containers, the autoscaler enables the current demand for resources to be met and underutilized or idle nodes to be shutdown improve the system's utilization and hence reduce cost, and finally the rescheduler allows for the initial placement of containers to be revised at runtime to reduce fragmentation and consolidate loads to encourage better resource utilization. A prototype system was developed as an extension to Kubernetes, a widely used open source container management system. Various rescheduling and autoscaling mechanism were proposed, implemented, and evaluated. Overall, we found rescheduling and autoscaling have clear benefits in terms of minimizing the cost of computation and enhancing the resource efficiency. We also identified and discussed future research directions.

There are various areas that could be further explored in order to better optimize the decisions made by the schedulers, reschedulers, and autoscalers. For instance, considering heterogeneous VMs could lead to a more efficient use of resources and decreased cost. This would enable for instance to dynamically provision resources with different pricing models to the virtual cluster in order to satisfy growing needs of the applications with minimum cost. For example, a customer-facing application should be placed on reserved instances that are leased for lower costs and longer periods of time while offering high availability. Batch jobs on the other hand could be placed on unreliable rebated resources, whose sudden termination will not disrupt the end user experience. The use of on-demand instances can be explored for applications with requirements in between where the availability is needed but they are not long-running services.

Implementing algorithms that are data-aware is another area worth exploring. This data-awareness may refer to either the container images or application data. Considering ephemeral storage as a resource in addition to memory and CPU can also further improve the proposed system and solutions. Extending the definition of moveable pods to a more robust one could also make the framework more appealing to users with more stringent requirements. For instance, containers may be defined as moveable if there are more than one replicas of a given pod currently running and the application can tolerate one of the replicas being shut down and restarted (e.g., stateless services or applications using persistent volumes).

Application QoS management is another improvement worthwhile exploring. Applications have specific QoS requirement, for instance, long-running services commonly have to serve a minimum number of requests per time unit or have stringent latency requirements. Batch jobs on the other hand can have a deadline as a time constraint for their execution or may need to be completed as fast as possible. For the first scenario, many systems offer a basic autoscaling mechanism. It monitors the CPU utilization of a service, and if a predefined threshold is exceeded, another instance of the service is launched. This however, is a baseline approach to autoscaling and integrating more sophisticated approaches to container-based management systems is required. For batch jobs, orchestrating them and assigning them to resources so that their QoS are met is another open research area. This feature is not present in any open source system and support for heterogeneous QoS constraints is still unexplored.

Resource consumption estimation can be used to predict and estimate the amount of resources a container consumes at different points in time, as opposed to relying simply on the amount of resources requested for a particular container. The reason is twofold. Firstly, resource requests are usually misestimated and overestimated by users. Secondly, the resource consumption of a task is likely to vary over time, with the peak consumption spanning only over a fraction of its lifetime. Both scenarios lead to resources that are reserved but are idle most of the time and hence lead to the cluster being underutilized. By monitoring and estimating the resource consumption of containers, better oversubscription and opportunistic scheduling decisions can be made by the system. In the proposed system prototype, this can be achieved by making use of Kubernetes metrics server, an InfluxDB to store the timeseries of the collected consumption data, and an online prediction algorithm designed for streaming data such as Hierarchical Temporal Memory (Cui, Ahmad, & Hawkins, 2016).

ACKNOWLEDGMENT

This work supported through a collaborative research agreement between the University of Melbourne and Samsung Electronics (South Korea) as part of the Samsung GRO (Global Research Outreach) program. We thank Minxian Xu for his help with improving the quality of this chapter.

REFERENCES

Bernstein, D. (2014). Containers and cloud: From lxc to docker to kubernetes. *IEEE Cloud Computing*, *1*(3), 81–84. doi:10.1109/MCC.2014.51

Containerd. (n.d.). Retrieved from https://containerd.io

CRI-O. (n.d.). Retrieved from http://cri-o.io

Cui, Y., Ahmad, S., & Hawkins, J. (2016). Continuous online sequence learning with an unsupervised neural network model. *Neural Computation*, *28*(11), 2474–2504. doi:10.1162/NECO_a_00893 PMID:27626963

DelValle, R., Rattihalli, G., Beltre, A., Govindaraju, M., & Lewis, M. J. (2016, June). Exploring the Design Space for Optimizations with Apache Aurora and Mesos. In *2016 IEEE 9th International Conference on Cloud Computing (CLOUD)* (pp. 537-544). IEEE.

Docker. (n.d). Retrieved from https://www.docker.com

Etcd. (n.d.). Retrieved from https://coreos.com/etcd

Frakti. (n.d.). Retrieved from https://github.com/kubernetes/frakti

Guerrero, C., Lera, I., & Juiz, C. (2018). Genetic algorithm for multi-objective optimization of container allocation in cloud architecture. *Journal of Grid Computing*, *16*(1), 113–135. doi:10.100710723-017-9419-x

Hightower, K., Burns, B., & Beda, J. (2017). *Kubernetes: up and running: dive into the future of infrastructure*. O'Reilly Media.

Hindman, B., Konwinski, A., Zaharia, M., Ghodsi, A., Joseph, A. D., Katz, R. H., . . . Stoica, I. (2011, March). Mesos: A platform for fine-grained resource sharing in the data center. In NSDI (Vol. 11, No. 2011, pp. 22-22).

Kaewkasi, C., & Chuenmuneewong, K. (2017, February). Improvement of container scheduling for docker using ant colony optimization. *Proceedings 2017 9th international conference on knowledge and smart technology (KST)* (pp. 254-259). IEEE. 10.1109/KST.2017.7886112

Kehrer, S., & Blochinger, W. (2018). TOSCA-based container orchestration on Mesos. *Computer Science-Research and Development*, *33*(3-4), 305–316. doi:10.100700450-017-0385-0

Kubernetes. (2019, June 12). Building Large Clusters. Retrieved from https://kubernetes.io/docs/setup/best-practices/cluster-large/

Marathon. (n.d.). Retrieved from https://mesosphere.github.io/marathon

Medel, V., Rana, O., Bañares, J. Á., & Arronategui, U. (2016, December). Modelling performance & resource management in kubernetes. *Proceedings 2016 IEEE/ACM 9th International Conference on Utility and Cloud Computing (UCC)* (pp. 257-262). IEEE. 10.1145/2996890.3007869

Naik, N. (2016, October). Building a virtual system of systems using Docker Swarm in multiple clouds. *Proceedings 2016 IEEE International Symposium on Systems Engineering (ISSE)* (pp. 1-3). IEEE. 10.1109/SysEng.2016.7753148

Nectar. (n.d.) Retrieved from https://nectar.org.au/

Rodriguez, M. A., & Buyya, R. (2019). Container-based cluster orchestration systems: A taxonomy and future directions. *Software, Practice, & Experience, 49*(5), 698–719. doi:10.1002pe.2660

Runc. (n.d.). Retrieved from https://github.com/opencontainers/runc

Schwarzkopf, M., Konwinski, A., Abd-El-Malek, M., & Wilkes, J. (2013). Omega: flexible, scalable schedulers for large compute clusters.

Vavilapalli, V. K., Murthy, A. C., Douglas, C., Agarwal, S., Konar, M., Evans, R., ... Saha, B. (2013, October). Apache hadoop yarn: Yet another resource negotiator. *Proceedings of the 4th annual Symposium on Cloud Computing* (p. 5). ACM. 10.1145/2523616.2523633

Verma, A., Pedrosa, L., Korupolu, M., Oppenheimer, D., Tune, E., & Wilkes, J. (2015, April). Large-scale cluster management at Google with Borg. *Proceedings of the Tenth European Conference on Computer Systems* (p. 18). ACM. 10.1145/2741948.2741964

Xu, M., Toosi, A. N., & Buyya, R. (2018). ibrownout: An integrated approach for managing energy and brownout in container-based clouds. *IEEE Transactions on Sustainable Computing, 4*(1), 53–66. doi:10.1109/TSUSC.2018.2808493

Xu, X., Yu, H., & Pei, X. (2014, December). A novel resource scheduling approach in container based clouds. *Proceedings 2014 IEEE 17th International Conference on Computational Science and Engineering* (pp. 257-264). IEEE. 10.1109/CSE.2014.77

Yin, L., Luo, J., & Luo, H. (2018). Tasks scheduling and resource allocation in fog computing based on containers for smart manufacturing. *IEEE Transactions on Industrial Informatics, 14*(10), 4712–4721. doi:10.1109/TII.2018.2851241

Zhang, H., Ma, H., Fu, G., Yang, X., Jiang, Z., & Gao, Y. (2016, June). Container based video surveillance cloud service with fine-grained resource provisioning. *Proceedings 2016 IEEE 9th International Conference on Cloud Computing (CLOUD)* (pp. 758-765). IEEE. 10.1109/CLOUD.2016.0105

Chapter 11
Gait Recognition Using Deep Learning

Chaoran Liu
Auckland University of Technology, New Zealand

Wei Qi Yan
Auckland University of Technology, New Zealand

ABSTRACT

Gait recognition mainly uses different postures of each individual to perform identity authentication. In the existing methods, the full-cycle gait images are used for feature extraction, but there are problems such as occlusion and frame loss in the actual scene. It is not easy to obtain a full-cycle gait image. Therefore, how to construct a highly efficient gait recognition algorithm framework based on a small number of gait images to improve the efficiency and accuracy of recognition has become the focus of gait recognition research. In this chapter, deep neural network CRBM+FC is created. Based on the characteristics of Local Binary Pattern (LBP) and Histogram of Oriented Gradient (HOG) fusion, a method of learning gait recognition from GEI to output is proposed. A brand-new gait recognition algorithm based on layered fu-sion of LBP and HOG is proposed. This chapter also proposes a feature learning network, which uses an unsupervised convolutionally constrained Boltzmann machine to train the Gait Energy Images (GEI).

INTRODUCTION

Biometrics is based on unique physiological or behavioral characteristics of individuals. Biometrics is not as easily transferred or stolen as physical documents such as ID cards, which is secure, reliable, and convenient (Ahonen, Hadid, & Pietikainen, 2006). Gait recognition is based on walking posture of a human body (Little & Boyd, 1998). Compared with fingerprint recognition, speech recognition, face recognition and other technologies, gait recognition has the advantages of easy collection, long distance, less contact, and difficult forge, which is a hotspot research topic in the fields of biometrics, computer vision, intelligent surveillance, and etc. (Cunado, *et al.* 1997).

DOI: 10.4018/978-1-7998-2701-6.ch011

Computer vision is one of the research fields including gait recognition. Given an image sequence containing one or many walking gestures, gait recognition in a broad sense can be divided into four main phases: pedestrian detection, pedestrian region segmentation, pedestrian tracking, and pedestrian recognition (Boykov & Jolly, 2001) (Bulat & Tzimiropoulos, 2016) (Cao, *et al.* 2017) (Tan, *et al.* 2006).

At pedestrian detection phase, it locates the position of a pedestrian in a single video frame and determines the image size (Liu & Payandeh, 2018). At the pedestrian segmentation stage, pixel-level segmentation is performed based on the detection result, background information in the video will be removed. The pedestrian tracking phase determines motion trajectory of the target object and distinguishes individuals from the video sequence (Foresti, 1999).

At the classification and recognition phase, it assigns one of class labels to the test gait samples, which is to identify the person (Kusakunniran, 2014). The process is to calculate the similarity between the test sample and the registered sample so as to complete the classification according to machine learning rules. This stage is often combined with feature extraction to identify a suitable class for classification. This type of methods can be divided into two categories according to gait features in a time-series way.

RELATED WORK

In general, gait recognition refers to pedestrian recognition (Sarkar, et al. 2005) (Shiraga, *et al.* 2016), which utilizes the features extracted from the pedestrian silhouette map to identify a person (Lam, *et al.* 2011) (Murase & Sakai, 1996)(Wang, *et al.* 2004). In recent years, with the development of deep learning, such as Mask Region-Based Convolutional Neural Network (Mask-RCNN), it is possible to apply gait recognition to practical complex scenes (He, *et al.* 2017) (Lee & Grimson, 2002).

Different from directly using the gait silhouette as an input to the deep neural network, Shiraga applied Gait Energy Images (GEI) as the input feature (Tao & Maybank, 2007). GEI is a gait model of static and dynamic information in a sequence of mixed gait silhouettes. The energy of each pixel in the model is obtained by calculating the average intensity of the silhouette pixels in a gait cycle.

The LBP is based on the values of grayscale image pixels. The HOG mainly uses gradient size and direction of the pixels (Dalal & Triggs, 2005). Therefore, after the first round of operations, there is still an image having grayscale intensity changes. In order to obtain pretty rich and useful texture information and edge shape information from the grayscale images, a hierarchical LBP and HOG can be generated in Figure 2.

Figure 1. The flowchart of general steps of gait recognition

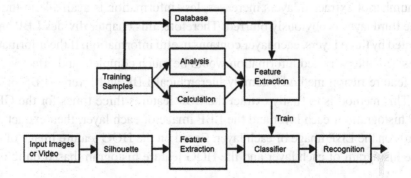

Figure 2. The hierarchical LBP and HOG features

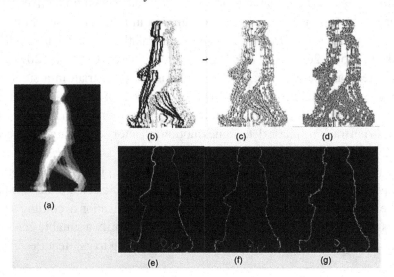

As shown in Figure 2, all of them include useful information for further process. Figure 2(b) clearly expresses strong texture information and contour information. Figure 2(e) apparently indicates the edge information of the human gait. Figure 2(c) and Figure 2(f) are weaker than Figure 2(b) and Figure 2(e), but there is still useful information that can be utilized. Therefore, the hierarchical structure can obviously provide more information.

Traditional gait recognition algorithms which extracted gait features are relatively simple (Niyogi & Adelson, 1994). Besides, due to the influence of occlusion, light, and other interference reasons, the gait recognition rate is usually very low. Therefore, information fusion theory is widely used in gait recognition. Han combined Platts analysis with elliptical Fourier descriptors to match human contours for gait recognition (Han, 2010). The method combines the temporal and spatial motion characteristics, statistical and physical parameters of human body to analyze the contour shape of gait. However, it ignores the internal features. Derlatka proposed a biometric system based on different gait data from human body, combining dynamic information (ground reaction) and static information (e.g., the width of trunk and buttocks, the length of thigh and height) (Derlatka & Bogdan, 2015). This method requires a cumbersome feature extraction process and complex information input, which leads to a complicated calculation process and cannot meet real-time needs. The combination method in this chapter can describe not only local texture information but also the edge contour information which is very simple and fast to calculate.

LBP and HOG features of the first two layers contain relatively clear texture features and contour edges. As the number of extracted layers increases, less information is available in the image. The information of the third layer is obviously blurred. Therefore, this chapter divides LBP and HOG feature images represented by three layers, each layer contains useful information. If the information of different layers is synthesized, the extracted information would be much complete and effective. Therefore, this chapter adopts feature fusion methods, namely hierarchical LBP and layered LBP-based hierarchical feature fusion. This method is to firstly extract the LBP features three times for the GEI map so as to obtain the LBP histogram of each layer and the LBP image of each layer, then extract the corresponding HOG features on the LBP image of each layer. Based on the HOG feature image of the LBP image, the LBP feature histogram of each layer and the HOG feature histogram based on the LBP image are sequentially connected to obtain a fusion feature histogram of each layer, and finally the three layers are fused. The feature histograms are sequentially cascaded to form the final fusion feature.

Gait recognition can be divided into two categories according to its objectives. One task is verification, the given samples and verification samples are judged according to a similarity index or a given threshold to identify the given objects; that is, given test samples, the research problem is how to find the samples with the same identity in the given dataset (Johansson, 1973).

The gait dataset includes a training dataset and a test set. The training set is used to train and generate a classification model, the test set is employed to evaluate the generalization performance of the classification model. The training set and test set maintain a mutually exclusive relationship; that is, the test samples should not appear in the training set (Zheng, *et al.* 2011). Usually, we train a model with the training datasets and evaluate the pros and cons of gait recognition methods based on the test sets. From a practical point of view, recognition rate is the performance indicator for measuring the gait recognition algorithm. Generally, the higher the recognition rate, the better the performance of the algorithm. In addition, cumulative recognition rates and ROC curves are often used to evaluate performance (Yu, *et al.* 2006) (Yu, *et al.* 2009).

METHODOLOGY

A feature that combined with HOG (Viola, et al. 2005) and LBP (Han & Bhanu, 2005)(Jeevan, *et al.* 2013) is adopted in this book chapter. Extracting feature from GEI for *m* times can obtain *m* levels LBP feature images (Derlatka & Bogdan, 2015)(Yan, *et al.* 2015). Fusing each level of the LBP feature with HOG feature could obtain the final fused feature. Sequentially concatenating all the features together (Wang, *et al.* 2003) provides the final feature of this GEI which is shown in Figure 2.

Deep neural network of this chapter consists of a convolutionally constrained Boltzmann machine and a fully connected layer network (Begg, Palaniswami & Owen, 2005). Different from the supervised learning method of convolutional neural networks (Tao & Maybank, 2007) (Yu, *et al.* 2006), the convolution-limited Boltzmann machine is an unsupervised learning model, which can learn the network parameters by comparing the divergence algorithm, and complete the feature extraction of the input image for identification and classification (Chen, *et al.* 2009) (Lee, *et al.* 2009). The network proposed in this chapter uses GEI+LBP+HOG feature as input and convolves it with 3×3 and 7×7 convolution kernels to obtain the asynchronous features at different scales (Xu, et al. 2011). Simultaneously, after the convolution-limited Boltzmann machine, the gait feature is obtained, the features acquired by the two

Figure 3. The Network Structure

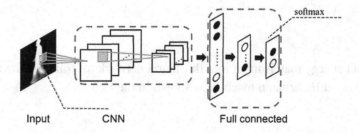

different convolution kernels are merged by using the fully connected network, the feature is used at the end of the fully connected network for classification and identification as shown in Figure 3.

First, the feature extraction is performed using a Convolutionally Restricted Boltzmann Machine (CRBM); the extracted gait features are trained by using a fully connected network and the features are finally classified using softmax function to obtain prediction results; then the predicted results are compared with the real results. The cross-entropy loss is calculated. Meanwhile, the backpropagation algorithm is used to optimize the network parameters.

Two convolution kernels of different sizes were set in the convolution-limited Boltzmann model training, which are 3×3 and 7×7 matrices, respectively; there are 32 convolution kernels of each size. Through this operation, how kernel size influences on the performance will be discovered.

EXPERIMENTAL RESULTS

The experiments were set to study the effectiveness of this proposed algorithm. In the experiments, walking posture of the training data is as same as the walking posture of the test data, and the set experiment (training set-test set) is denoted as (nm-nm), (bg-bg), (cl-cl). In the cross-state experiment, the walking posture of the training dataset is different from the test dataset, the experiment (training set-test set) includes (nm-bg) and (nm-cl). Four video sequences in the data set were used in training (nm-nm) and other data was used in the test. In (bg-bg) and (cl-cl), half of the data was used as a training set and half was used as a test set. In the cross-state experiments (nm-bg) and (nm-cl), four video sequences in nm were taken as training sets, and all data in bg and cl were used as test sets. Table 2 shows our experiment strategy.

Table 1 shows the databases that have been established for gait recognition. At present, these databases are lack of universality and wide applicability. The current largest gait database is the Soton Big Gait Database created by the University of Southampton in the UK, Multi-view gait database (CASIA-B) and infrared gait database (CASIA-C) created by the Institute of Automation, Chinese Academy of Sciences (CASIA), China. In addition, the CASIA-C database is currently the only publicly available large-scale infrared gait database. The USMT gait database is one of the few 3D gait libraries that is currently available.

Table 1. The existing gait recognition databases

Database	Subject Number	View Angel	Clothing Change	Carrying Change
OU-ISIR MVLP	10307	14	NO	NO
OU-ISIR LP	4016	4	NO	NO
OU-ISIR LP-Bag	2070	1	NO	YES
CASIA--B	124	11	YES	YES
USF	122	2	YES	YES

The calculated gait energy map is input into the neural network for training, the reconstruction error of the convolution-limited Boltzmann machine is shown in the Figure 6.

Figure 4. Final Fusion Features

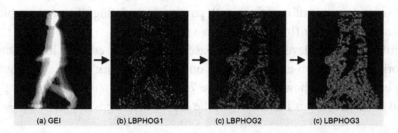

Figure 5. The Flowchart of Combination LBP and HOG Feature Extraction

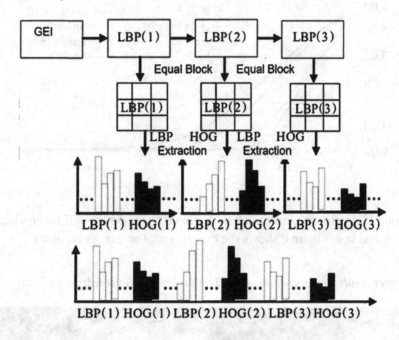

Figure 6. Reconstruction Error

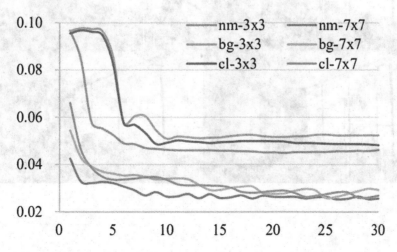

In Figure 6, the reconstruction error is large at the beginning because the parameters are randomly initialized. After several rounds of iterations with parameter updating, the errors rapidly decrease and gradually tend to a fixed value or fluctuates within a small range.

Training the fully connected layer network is based on the cross-entropy loss function to iteratively update the network parameters so as to obtain an optimized network model. During the training process, the training error curve is shown in the Figure 7. After the iterations, the training errors gradually decrease and tend to be stable, this indicates that the model converges.

Figure 7. Training Error Curve

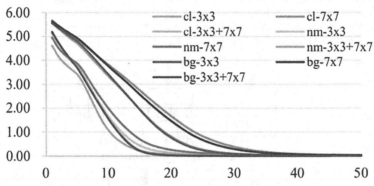

The verification of this proposed method has also been tested on the self-taken videos, we label the datasets for training and test. Figure 8 shows the experimental research outcomes.

Figure 8. The correct results are shown in single box and incorrect results are displayed in more boxes.

In this experiment, the recognition rates of the algorithm on the three gait data sets are compared under 2×4, 4×4, 4×8, 8×8, 8×16, 16×16, 16×32 blocks. The best block is obtained and the results are shown in Figure 9.

Figure 9. The Effect of Block Size on Accuracy

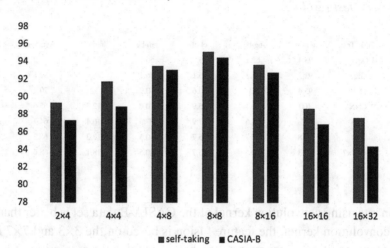

In Figure 9, the optimal block is 8×8. Larger or smaller blocks will affect the recognition rate because the oversized blocks cannot extract accurate and appropriate local features. Meanwhile, too small blocks are sensitive to image registration and human motion, the extracted global and local features inaccurate.

In this chapter, when evaluated the performance of the algorithm, the "Leave a Cross-Validation Method" is used to obtain an unbiased estimate of the Correct Classification Rate (CCR); that is, one sample sequence is reserved for each experiment as the test sample, the remaining sample sequence is used (Rida, *et al.* 2016). As a training sample of ANN, it is classified according to the similarity of training samples (Han, 2010). In order to compare the advantages of the fusion features of this chapter, the recognition rates of Original-GEI (Han & Bhanu, 2005), GEI+LBP+PCA (Sivapalan, *et al.* 2013), Bayes+HMM (Chen, *et al.* 2009), and Integrated-HOG (Viola, *et al.* 2005) were compared. The results are shown in Table 2.

Table 2. CCR of different feature extraction methods

Method	Correct Classification Rate
Original-GEI	74.89
GEI+LBP+PCA	83.68
Bayes+HMM	87.59
Intergrated-HOG	89.78
This Method	94.66

Besides, Cumulative Match Score is also applied to the evaluations. The CMS is defined as the cumulative probability of the actual category of a test metric between its previous rank value (e.g., Rank = 10). CCR is the cumulative recognition rate when Rank is equal to 1. The CMS for the five methods is shown respectively.

Table 3. The cross-state test results

Train-Test	nm-nm	bg-bg	cl-cl	nm-bg	nm-cl	Average
GPPE	93.4	62.2	55.1	56.1	22.4	57.8
GEnI	92.3	65.3	55.1	56.1	26.5	59.1
STIPs	95.4	73	70.6	60.9	52	70.4
CNN	100	89.1	95.9	30.6	12.3	65.6
3×3	97	84.5	87.9	37.5	16.4	64.7
7×7	97.8	89.7	95.7	40.5	17.2	68.2
3×3+7×7	98.3	90.5	95.7	40.5	18.1	68.6

The recognition rate using convolution kernel of the CASIA-B data set is better than the recognition result of the 3×3 convolution kernel, the feature fusion is based on the 3×3 and 7×7 convolution kernels. The subsequent recognition accuracy is better than or equal to the recognition accuracy of a single convolution kernel. At the same time, this chapter compares the proposed method with other existing methods GPPE, GEI, STIPs and CNN based methods. In Table 3, the proposed method is slightly lower than the existing deep learning-based methods in the same state experiments (nm-nm) and (cl-cl), because it used a deeper network. In the experiment of cross states, the method is better, it indicates that the method of this chapter is better than its robustness. In addition, the accuracy of cross states is lower than other existing methods, because traditional methods can be identified by using targeted design features, while deep learning requires more walking posture for training to increase the generalization ability of the network. However, only one kind of walking states lead to poor generalization ability of the network; thus, the experimental results of the cross states are not better than the existing methods.

CONCLUSION

In this chapter, the deep neural network CRBM+FC is created for human gait recognition. Based on LBP and HOG fusion, a method of end-to-end deep learning gait recognition from GEI to output is proposed. This paper also proposed an algorithm based on gait energy map for gait recognition. The method used the layering idea to overcome the shortcomings of gait energy map, which not only captures the local information of human body image, but also extracts its contour and shape information. The fusion of these information is based on the CASIA gait datasets. The recognition algorithm of this chapter has achieved a high recognition rate. It proposed a feature learning network consisting of a convolutionally constrained Boltzmann machine and a fully connected neural network. The network first uses feature-constrained Boltzmann machines with different convolution kernels to extract features from gait images; because convolution-limited Boltzmann machines are unsupervised, they can learn extensively and abundantly.

Although rich gait feature information is learned, there must be redundant and less useful information. Therefore, this paper used a supervised all-connected layer network to learn these features deeply.

In single scenarios, the detection and extraction of gait are relatively simple. However, in complex practical scenarios, the complexity of factors, e.g., background and multiple individuals, etc., makes it difficult to accurately acquire gait. Inaccurate gait information directly affects the final recognition efficiency and accuracy (Sivapalan, *et al.* 2013).

REFERENCES

Ahonen, T., Hadid, A., & Pietikainen, M. (2006). Face description with local binary patterns: Application to face recognition. *IEEE Transactions on Pattern Analysis and Machine Intelligence*, *28*(12), 2037–2041. doi:10.1109/TPAMI.2006.244 PMID:17108377

Begg, R. K., Palaniswami, M., & Owen, B. (2005). Support vector machines for automated gait classification. *IEEE Transactions on Biomedical Engineering*, *52*(5), 828–838. doi:10.1109/TBME.2005.845241 PMID:15887532

Boykov, Y. Y., & Jolly, M. P. (2001). Interactive graph cuts for optimal boundary & region segmentation of objects in ND images. *Proceedings IEEE International Conference on Computer Vision*. (*Vol. 1*, pp. 105-112). Academic Press.

Bulat, A., & Tzimiropoulos, G. (2016). Human pose estimation via convolutional part heatmap regression. *Proceedings European Conference on Computer Vision* (pp. 717-732). Springer. 10.1007/978-3-319-46478-7_44

Cao, Z., Simon, T., Wei, S. E., & Sheikh, Y. (2017). Realtime multi-person 2D pose estimation using part affinity fields. *Proceedings IEEE Conference on Computer Vision and Pattern Recognition* (pp. 7291-7299). 10.1109/CVPR.2017.143

Chen, C., Liang, J., Zhao, H., Hu, H., & Tian, J. (2009). Frame difference energy image for gait recognition with incomplete silhouettes. *Pattern Recognition Letters*, *30*(11), 977–984. doi:10.1016/j.patrec.2009.04.012

Cunado, D., Nixon, M. S., & Carter, J. N. (1997). Using gait as a biometric, via phase-weighted magnitude spectra. *Proceedings International Conference on Audio-and Video-Based Biometric Person Authentication* (pp. 93-102). Berlin, Germany: Springer. 10.1007/BFb0015984

Dalal, N., & Triggs, B. (2005). Histograms of oriented gradients for human detection. *Proceedings International Conference on Computer Vision & Pattern Recognition*, *1*, 886–893. IEEE.

Derlatka, M., & Bogdan, M. (2015). Fusion of static and dynamic parameters at decision level in human gait recognition. *Proceedings International Conference on Pattern Recognition and Machine Intelligence* (pp. 515-524). Springer. 10.1007/978-3-319-19941-2_49

Foresti, G. L. (1999). Object recognition and tracking for remote video surveillance. *IEEE Transactions on Circuits and Systems for Video Technology*, *9*(7), 1045–1062. doi:10.1109/76.795058

Han, J., & Bhanu, B. (2005). Individual recognition using gait energy image. *IEEE Transactions on Pattern Analysis and Machine Intelligence*, *28*(2), 316–322. doi:10.1109/TPAMI.2006.38 PMID:16468626

Han, X. (2010). *Gait recognition considering walking direction*. USA: University of Rochester.

He, K., Gkioxari, G., Dollár, P., & Girshick, R. (2017). Mask R-CNN. *Proceedings IEEE International Conference on Computer Vision* (pp. 2961-2969). IEEE.

Jeevan, M., Jain, N., Hanmandlu, M., & Chetty, G. (2013). Gait recognition based on gait pal and pal entropy image. *Proceedings IEEE International Conference on Image Processing* (pp. 4195-4199). IEEE. 10.1109/ICIP.2013.6738864

Johansson, G. (1973). Visual perception of biological motion and a model for its analysis. *Perception & Psychophysics*, *14*(2), 201–211. doi:10.3758/BF03212378

Kusakunniran, W. (2014). Attribute-based learning for gait recognition using spatio-temporal interest points. *Image and Vision Computing*, *32*(12), 1117–1126. doi:10.1016/j.imavis.2014.10.004

Lam, T. H., Cheung, K. H., & Liu, J. N. (2011). Gait flow image: A silhouette-based gait representation for human identification. *Pattern Recognition*, *44*(4), 973–987. doi:10.1016/j.patcog.2010.10.011

Lee, H., Grosse, R., Ranganath, R., & Ng, A. Y. (2009). Convolutional deep belief networks for scalable unsupervised learning of hierarchical representations. *Proceedings ACM Annual International Conference on Machine Learning* (pp. 609-616). 10.1145/1553374.1553453

Lee, L., & Grimson, W. E. L. (2002). Gait analysis for recognition and classification. *Proceedings IEEE International Conference on Automatic Face Gesture Recognition* (pp. 155-162). IEEE. 10.1109/AFGR.2002.1004148

Little, J., & Boyd, J. (1998). Recognizing people by their gait: The shape of motion. *Journal of Computer Vision Research*, *1*(2), 1–32.

Liu, X., & Payandeh, S. (2018). A study of chained stochastic tracking in RGB and depth sensing. *Journal of Control Science and Engineering*, 2018.

Murase, H., & Sakai, R. (1996). Moving object recognition in eigenspace representation: Gait analysis and lip reading. *Pattern Recognition Letters*, *17*(2), 155–162. doi:10.1016/0167-8655(95)00109-3

Niyogi, S. A., & Adelson, E. H. (1994). Analyzing gait with spatiotemporal surfaces. *Proceedings IEEE Workshop on Motion of Non-rigid and Articulated Objects* (pp. 64-69). IEEE.

Rida, I., Boubchir, L., Al-Maadeed, N., Al-Maadeed, S., & Bouridane, A. (2016). Robust model-free gait recognition by statistical dependency feature selection and Globality-Locality Preserving Projections. *Proceedings International Conference on Telecommunications and Signal Processing* (TSP) (pp. 652-655). 10.1109/TSP.2016.7760963

Sarkar, S., Phillips, P. J., Liu, Z., Vega, I. R., Grother, P., & Bowyer, K. W. (2005). The humanid gait challenge problem: Data sets, performance, and analysis. *IEEE Transactions on Pattern Analysis and Machine Intelligence*, *27*(2), 162–177. doi:10.1109/TPAMI.2005.39 PMID:15688555

Shin, J., Kim, S., Kang, S., Lee, S. W., Paik, J., Abidi, B., & Abidi, M. (2005). Optical flow-based real-time object tracking using non-prior training active feature model. *Real-Time Imaging, 11*(3), 204–218. doi:10.1016/j.rti.2005.03.006

Shiraga, K., Makihara, Y., Muramatsu, D., Echigo, T., & Yagi, Y. (2016). Geinet: View-invariant gait recognition using a convolutional neural network. *Proceedings International Conference on Biometrics (ICB)* (pp. 1-8). IEEE. 10.1109/ICB.2016.7550060

Sivapalan, S., Chen, D., Denman, S., Sridharan, S., & Fookes, C. (2013). Histogram of weighted local directions for gait recognition. *Proceedings IEEE Conference on Computer Vision and Pattern Recognition Workshops* (pp. 125-130). 10.1109/CVPRW.2013.26

Tan, D., Huang, K., Yu, S., & Tan, T. (2006). Efficient night gait recognition based on template matching. *Proceedings International Conference on Pattern Recognition* (Vol. 3, pp. 1000-1003).

Tao, D., Li, X., Wu, X., & Maybank, S. J. (2007). General tensor discriminant analysis and gabor features for gait recognition. *IEEE Transactions on Pattern Analysis and Machine Intelligence, 29*(10), 1700–1715. doi:10.1109/TPAMI.2007.1096 PMID:17699917

Viola, P., Jones, M. J., & Snow, D. (2005). Detecting pedestrians using patterns of motion and appearance. *International Journal of Computer Vision, 63*(2), 153–161. doi:10.100711263-005-6644-8

Wang, L., Ning, H., Tan, T., & Hu, W. (2004). Fusion of static and dynamic body biometrics for gait recognition. *IEEE Transactions on Circuits and Systems for Video Technology, 14*(2), 149–158. doi:10.1109/TCSVT.2003.821972

Wang, L., Tan, T., Ning, H., & Hu, W. (2003). Silhouette analysis-based gait recognition for human identification. *IEEE Transactions on Pattern Analysis and Machine Intelligence, 25*(12), 1505–1518. doi:10.1109/TPAMI.2003.1251144

Xu, D., Huang, Y., Zeng, Z., & Xu, X. (2011). Human gait recognition using patch distribution feature and locality-constrained group sparse representation. *IEEE Transactions on Image Processing, 21*(1), 316–326. doi:10.1109/TIP.2011.2160956 PMID:21724511

Yan, C., Zhang, B., & Coenen, F. (2015). Multi-attributes gait identification by convolutional neural networks. *Proceedings International Congress on Image and Signal Processing* (pp. 642-647). IEEE. 10.1109/CISP.2015.7407957

Yu, S., Tan, D., & Tan, T. (2006). Modelling the effect of view angle variation on appearance-based gait recognition. *Proceedings Asian Conference on Computer Vision* (pp. 807-816). Berlin, Germany: Springer. 10.1007/11612032_81

Yu, S., Tan, D., & Tan, T. (2006). A framework for evaluating the effect of view angle, clothing and carrying condition on gait recognition. *Proceedings International Conference on Pattern Recognition* (Vol. 4, pp. 441-444).

Yu, S., Tan, T., Huang, K., Jia, K., & Wu, X. (2009). A study on gait-based gender classification. *IEEE Transactions on Image Processing, 18*(8), 1905–1910. doi:10.1109/TIP.2009.2020535 PMID:19447706

Zhao, N., Zhang, L., Du, B., Zhang, L., Tao, D., & You, J. (2016). Sparse tensor discriminative locality alignment for gait recognition. *Proceedings International Joint Conference on Neural Networks* (pp. 4489-4495). 10.1109/IJCNN.2016.7727787

Zheng, S., Zhang, J., Huang, K., He, R., & Tan, T. (2011). Robust view transformation model for gait recognition. *Proceedings IEEE International Conference on Image Processing* (pp. 2073-2076). 10.1109/ICIP.2011.6115889

Chapter 12
USRP–Based Secure Data Transmission

Avila Jayapalan

SASTRA University (Deemed), India

ABSTRACT

With the advent increase in growth of wireless technology Orthogonal Frequency Division Multiplexing (OFDM) gains popularity in recent years. OFDM forms the fundamental backbone of many currently used wireless transmission standards. It is a multicarrier modulation scheme which overcomes the need for equalizer to mitigate ISI caused due to multipath propagation. In this work, an OFDM based transceiver has been developed utilizing various modules like Source Coding, Channel Coding, IFFT-FFT, scrambler, cyclic prefix, and signal mapper. To ensure secure data transmission, Hadamard matrix is XORed with the data. This provides a low level of protection to the image which is transmitted. LabVIEW has been used as the processing tool to develop the transceiver and the prototype developed has been tested using Universal Software Radio Peripheral (USRP).

INTRODUCTION

The development of wireless systems has opened the doors to connect globally because of its cheaper cost and ease of use. But, even with the presence of these perks, there is a need to combat a severe issue called multipath fading which leads to Inter Symbol Interference (ISI) or cross talk.

Orthogonal Frequency Division Multiplexing (OFDM) (Gouda, Hussien, Ragab, Anwar, & Gouda, 2017) solves the above said issue. It is a distinct type of FDM, where users are provided a set of subcarriers overlapping in frequency domain (Bartalwar & Deepa, 2017). However, these subcarriers are specially designed to be orthogonal to each other, which allow them to occupy the same bandwidth without any interference. This, in turn negates the use of guard bands. As a result, the subcarriers can be closely packed to increase the channel efficiency.

In OFDM, high speed data streams of large bandwidth are split into parallel, slower sub streams of lower bandwidth called subcarriers (Salwa & Eldin, 2017). These subcarriers are centred on carrier frequencies on both sides of Direct Current (D.C). As the bandwidth increases so does the number of

DOI: 10.4018/978-1-7998-2701-6.ch012

subcarriers in it. The subcarriers are placed in a manner that all the other sub carriers have zero components at the peak of one subcarrier. Such subcarriers are called orthogonal. Orthogonality is achieved by ensuring that all the subcarriers have same symbol duration Ts and the subcarrier is maintained at equal spacing of f=1/Ts.

In time domain these subcarriers will be represented as everlasting sinusoids at these carrier frequencies. However, in order to transmit data over these subcarriers they are loaded with modulation symbols that represent the constellation points of digital modulation schemes like Quadrature Phase Shift Keying (QPSK) and M-ary Quadrature Amplitude Modulation (QAM) (Sklar & Ray, 2001).

Image Acquisition

This work emphasises on transmitting only gray scale images (Saravanan,2010). Grayscale is one type of images where the value present in every pixel element represents only the amount of light present, i.e. the intensity. The levels of shades are given by 2^n, where n is the number of bits taken into account. Since the focus is on an 8 -bit gray scale image, there are 2^8 i.e. 256 levels ranging from 0 to 255.The input data considered is a 256*256 gray scale image.

Security

Encryption is the process of encoding the data such that only those with the encryption key can access the data (Balouch, Aslam, & Ahmed, 2017). At the transmitter end, the array elements are shuffled according to the encryption key while at the receiver end, the received data is reshuffled according to the same key thus restoring the originally transmitted data. To ensure a low-level security to the image which is transmitted through OFDM transceiver Hadamard sequences are XORed.

Hadamard matrix is a square matrix consisting of two values 1 and -1 having rows which are mutually orthogonal to each other. This can be explained in two basic terms. In geometric terms, each pair of rows is mutually perpendicular vectors whereas in combinatorial terms, it can be said that each pair of rows has exactly half matching elements. Certain Hadamard matrices are used as error correcting codes such as Hadamard codes. Hadamard matrices are also used for low scale encryption purposes as multiplication of an image with a similar size Hadamard matrix results in a scrambled image (Lee, Shahab, Kader & Shin, 2016).

USRP

The developed transceiver using LabVIEW tool is then implemented using USRP. The USRP Software Defined Radio Device is a tuneable transceiver (Nafkha, Naoues, Cichon, & Kliks, 2014). Any wireless system can be designed utilizing LabVIEW software tool and various parameters can be analysed by transmitting and receiving the signal using USRP.

This work aims at developing OFDM based transceiver which includes modules like source coding, channel coding, signal mapper, scrambler-descrambler, IFFT-FFT block with the aid of LabVIEW tool. The image is encrypted using Hadamard sequences and it is transmitted and received using USRP.

RELATED WORKS

In Serkin & Vazhenin (2013), the authors have discussed data transmission through USRP. FSK transmitter and receiver using simulink has been designed and analysed. In Jian Chen, Shengli Zhang, Hui Wang & Xiufeng Zhang (2013), two types of signal have been transmitted utilizing USRP. one is FM signal and other is the GPS signal. Both the signals are received and recorded. In Nagarjuna Telagam, Shailender Reddy, Menakadevi Nanjundan & Nehru (2018), OFDM based transceiver has been designed using LabVIEW tool and the signal is transmitted and received using USRP. In Rupali B. Patil, K. D. Kulat & A. S. Gandhi (2018), a real video signal has been transmitted and received through USRP. At the same time the video signal has been treated as primary user and the presence of white spaces has been detected using energy detection- based spectrum sensing. GNU radio has been used as the processing tool. Using USRP in Carsten Andrich, Alexander Ihlow, Julia Bauer, Niklas Beuster & Giovanni Del Galdo (2018) high precision measurement of sine and pulse reference signals has been carried out. Spectrum sensing using eigen value method has been carried out in C. I. M. Althaf & S. C. Prema (2018). The capacity of the channel in cooperative environment is analysed using USRP in Shujaat Ali Khan Tanoli, Mubashir Rehman, Muhammad Bilal Khan, Ihtesham Jadoon, Farman Ali Khan, et al. (2018). The presence of the primary user is detected using energy detection method and eigen value method in A. Kumar, A. S. Khan, N. Modanwal & S. Saha (2019). Instead of considering minimum eigen value average eigen value has been considered for decision making. In Nagarjuna Telagam, S. Lakshmi & K. Nehru (2019) digital audio signal has been transmitted and received using generalised frequency division multiplexing technique. A simple digital communication system with Gaussian Minimum Shift Keying (GMSK) as the modulation scheme has been developed in J. Muslimin, A. L. Asnawi, A. F. Ismail & A. Z. Jusoh (2016) using GNU radio. After transmitting and receiving the signal, the power spectral density has been plotted and analysed. Frequency modulated transmitter and receiver has been designed and an audio signal has been transmitted in Devidas Kushnure, Murtaza Jiniyawala, Sushama Molawade & Snehal Patil (2017). Simulated signals proved that that the transmitted signal is similar to the received signal. In addition to USRP receiver the audio signal is received through mobile phone. The LTE framework has been modified according to the real time scenario in Fei Peng, Shunqing Zhang, Shan Cao & Shugong Xu (2018) and it has been concluded that 4dB back off is need to support reliable vehicle to vehicle communications.

In Padmapriya Praveenkumar, P. Catherine Priya, J. Avila1, K. Thenmozhi, ohn Bosco Balaguru Rayappan et al. (2017) the image is encrypted to protect it from intruders and the encrypted image is transmitted via USRP with the medium as air. At the receiving end the original image has been retrieved. The authors have mainly focussed on the encryption algorithm. This manuscript mainly focusses on USRP based data transmission.

PROPOSED METHODOLOGY

Huffman coding is one of the lossless compression techniques (Arshad, Saleem, Khan, 2016). Huffman encoding has been employed post scrambling using Hadamard matrix. The output of this scrambler unit, which is a scrambled set of pixel values, is written into a file. The histogram of these values (i.e., the symbol values), is computed and written into a file. This histogram will give us the unique pixel values that the image comprises of. The probability of occurrence of each pixel is calculated by dividing each pixel's occurrence by the total number of pixels present in the input image and written into a file. The encoded values are written into a file which is read by the Permute block for further processing. the receiver end, decompressing is done post descrambling. The output of this decoder is written into a file for further stages of processing.

Permutation

The Huffman encoded input bits are given as input to the MT Permute block. This block changes the position of input data elements based on values specified in the permutation array parameter. The permutation array parameter is an array of user-specified elements which act as a key for encryption at both the end. Greater the shuffling up, more secure is the encryption. Also, the level of encryption might be increased with the increase in the number of array elements in the permutation array parameter and also the number of permuters used. At the receiver end, decryption is performed by entering the same permutation array parameter as the input to the MT depermute block. This will rearrange the received data as per the position of the elements of the permutation array.

Channel Coding

Channel coding has been performed using the MT BCH encoder (Mathew, Augustine, G. & Devis, 2014) and MT BCH decoder blocks. In this system, BCH encoder and decoder has been employed where (n, k, t) = (7, 4, 1). This encoding scheme takes in a bit data word of k bits and produces a code word of n bits. Post BCH encoding, the encoded data is converted to Boolean and sent ahead for bit-to-word conversion.

Data Hiding Using Hadamard Matrix

Let H be a Hadamard matrix of order n. The construction of the Hadamard matrix is as follows:

$$H_{2^k} = \begin{bmatrix} H_{2^{k-1}} & H_{2^{k-1}} \\ H_{2^{k-1}} & -H_{2^{k-1}} \end{bmatrix} = H_2 \otimes H_{2^{k-1}} \tag{1}$$

Where 2^k denotes the order of the Hadamard matrix. All the elements of the first row and column are 1. The pixel matrix is multiplied with the 256*256 Hadamard matrix to give rise to a scrambled output image. Similar to the procedure at the transmitter, the received pixel values have to be descrambled at the receiver end. Since the Hadamard matrix equals its inverse according to the above-mentioned properties, the scrambled 2-Dimensional array is again multiplied by the same Hadamard matrix of order 256 to regenerate the input image.

FFT and IFFT

The Fourier transform is a powerful tool to analyse the signals and construct them to and from their frequency components. The Inverse Fourier Transform is used to convert the signal from the frequency domain to the time domain. At the transmitter side the OFDM symbol is constructed in the frequency domain by mapping the input bits of the QPSK symbols and then ordering them in a sequence with specific length according to the number of subcarriers in the OFDM symbol. That is, by the mapping and ordering process, one constructs the frequency components of the OFDM symbol. To transmit them, the signal must be represented in time domain. This is accomplished by the Inverse Fast Fourier Transform (IFFT). In the receiver part of the OFDM system, Fast Fourier transform has been used. The Fast Fourier transform is used to convert the received signal back from the time domain to the frequency domain in order to process the signal in the rest of the system.

$$X(n) = \frac{1}{N} * \sum_{k=0}^{N-1} X(k) * e^{i*2*pi*n*k/N} \tag{2}$$

$$X(k) = \sum_{n=0}^{N-1} X(n) * e^{-i*2*pi*n*k/N} \tag{3}$$

Here,

$X(k)$ is the frequency domain sample
$X(n)$ is the time domain sample
K ranges from 0 to (N-1)
N is the FFT size

Image Reconstruction

At the receiver end, the processed pixel values need to be reconstructed. The pixel values are received in the format of a 1-dimensional array. To depict as a picture, the 1- dimensional array has to be converted into 2 dimensional. Thus, the reshape array block from the array palette is used where both the row and column dimensions are stated as 256. Thus, the 2D representation is obtained back. These pixels are flattened using the Flatten pixmap block from graphics and Sound palette. The corresponding colour chart for 8-bit grayscale image is also given as an input. The output can be written into a file or displayed using an indicator. Incorporating the above discussed block the transmitter and receiver block diagram of the proposed method is shown in figure 1a and figure 1b.

USRP Transmission

USRP is universally accepted prototype for wireless system. The experimental set up is shown in figure 2. Two USRP's are utilized. One USRP functions as transmitter and another fas receiver. The experiment is conducted indoor with air as the medium. The image to be transmitted into one dimensional array and transmitter. At the receiving end the reverse process is carried out and the image has been retrieved.

Figure 1a. Transmitter- block diagram

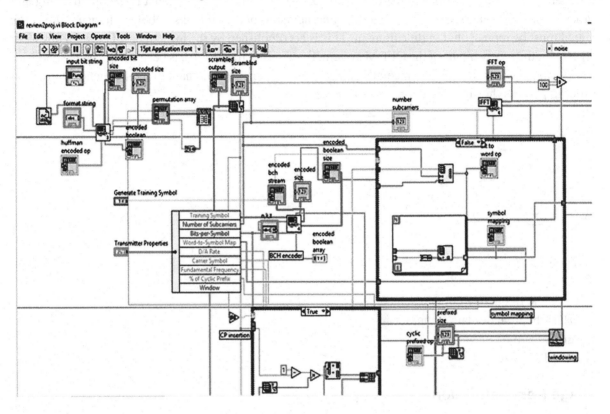

Figure 1b. Receiver block diagram

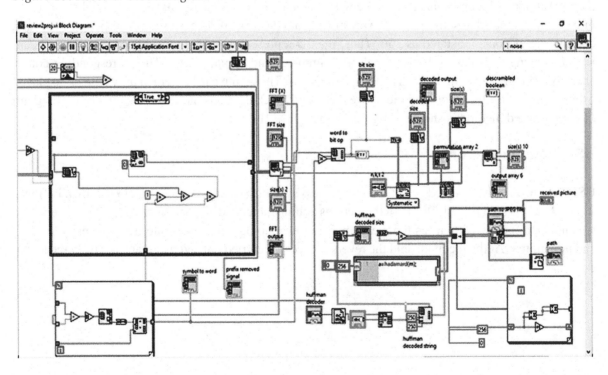

Figure 2. Experimental setup

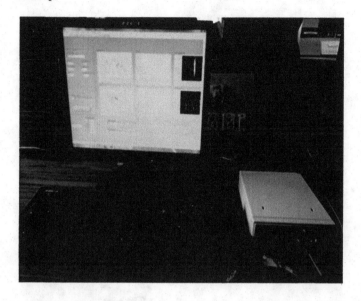

RESULTS AND DISCUSSION

Software simulation involves appreciable transmission and reception of the input 256*256 grayscale image and its proper reconstruction at the receiver end through a simulated AWGN Noise Channel model. The software simulation results incorporating the above obtained parameter values are tested on the LabVIEW platform. The proposed methodologies include the addition of modules in the given ordered series of low-level encryption using Hadamard matrix, BCH encoder, Permuter, symbol mapping, IFFT block, Cyclic prefix insertion and windowing in the transmitter section. The above modules are constructed using different modules present in various signal processing and RF Communication palettes present in LabVIEW. The simulated results obtained are illustrated in a closer view as below in the block diagram window and front panel window.

The image to be transmitted is acquired using image acquisition blocks present in the vision toolkit of LabVIEW and it is shown in figure 3. The image fom the input file path is read andusing the block IMAQ Image to Pixel, every pixel value is obtained in a 2 Dimensional array. These pixel values are further processed and sent for low level encryption with Hadamard matrix. Meanwhile the transmitter properties inputs are also entered which comprises of parameters like number of bits, number of subcarriers, word to symbol mapping, D/A rate, fundamental frequency, percentage of cyclic prefix and type of windowing method opted.

The 2-Dimensional array of pixels is multiplied with a 256 order Hadamard matrix to scramble the pixels. This image on further encryption using the permutation matrix gives rise to an appreciable amount of data hiding and it is shown in figure 4a and 4b respectively.

Post low level encryption with Hadamard matrix and permuter, the pixels are converted into unsigned 8-bit binary values which are concatenated to each other to form the input bit stream. Then, the input bits are Huffman encoded as part of source coding and BCH encoded as part of channel coding. Since the addition of Hadamard matrix processing and channel coding increases the bandwidth usage it is of

Figure 3. Image acquisition

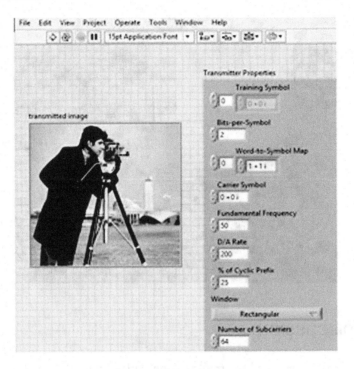

Figure 4a. Post hadamard

Figure 4b. Post permuter

utmost importance to nullify this effect with lossless compression. Huffman encoding, a variable length encoding scheme is used. Figure 5 shows the front panel of source coded and channel coded data.

Figure 5. Source and channel coding front panel

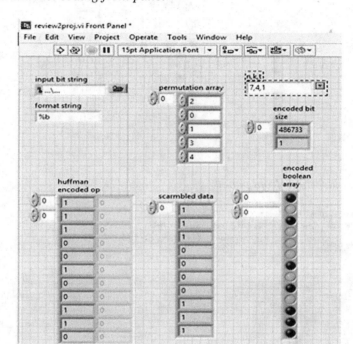

The output serial bits need to be converted from bit to word and from word to symbol to employ symbol mapping. Bit to word conversion can be employed by using reshape array and slit 1D array block from the array palette. Here number of bits per symbol is taken as 2. For software simulation QPSK mapping is employed. Further analysis can be employed for different modulation schemes like 4- and 16- QAM. The constellation positions of the appropriate symbols are given in the word to symbol mapping input parameter in the transmitter properties. The panel window is as shown in figure 6.

IFFT processing is done to acquire and maintain orthogonality and for transformation of domains. Emulating the characteristic specifications of 802.11a, the size of FFT is fixed as 64. Post IFFT the signal is sent for cyclic prefix insertion. 25% of signal in the end is appended to the beginning with the help of array functions. The last step in the transmitter side is windowing and the signal is sent through the channel modelled as an AWGN Noise channel model. The front panel of cyclic prefix insertion is as shown in figure 7.

The front panel window of the entire transmitter section is as shown in figure 8.

The transmitted signal after passing through a modelled AWGN noise channel reaches the receiver for cyclic prefix removal, FFT processing with size 64 and symbol to bit conversion. The converted bit stream is further decoded and the image is reconstructed. The removal of cyclic prefix is shown in figure 9 and source decoding is shown in figure 10.

The front panel of USRP as shown in figure 11a and figure 11b .

Figure 6. Symbol mapping –front panel

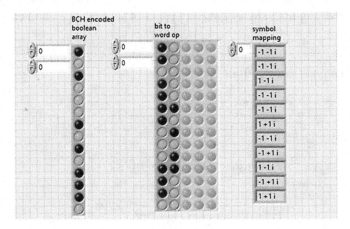

Figure 7. Cyclic prefix insertion- front panel

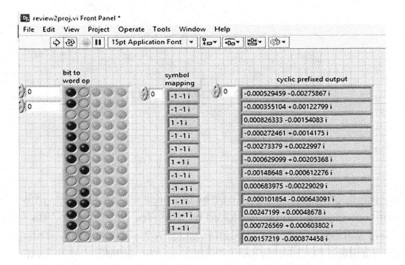

PERFORMANCE METRICES

The performance metric considered in this work are Mean-Squared Error (MSE) (Romi Singh, Shipra Sharma & Shikha Singh,2014) and Peak Signal-to-Noise Ratio. The MSE between two images can be calculated as:

$$MSE = \frac{1}{MN} \sum_{n=1}^{M} \sum_{m=1}^{N} \left[\hat{g}(x,y) - g(x,y) \right] \char`\^ 2$$

Peak Signal-to-Noise Ratio (PSNR) is given by

Figure 8. transmitter- front panel

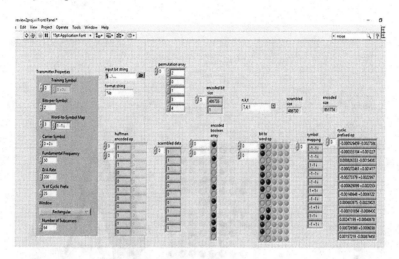

$$PSNR = -10 \log_{10} \frac{eMSE}{S^2}$$

The results have been obtained to find the optimum value of BCH encoder parameters (n, k, t). All the results have been obtained by the assumption of the permutation array being [2 0 1 3 4].

From the results in Table 1, it could be seen that the maximum PSNR is obtained for the encoder (n, k, t) values of (7, 4, 1), (15, 5, 3) and (63,51, 2). Here the optimum value is found by considering the trade off with respect to number of encoded bits also. The lesser the number of encoded bits, the lesser the number of symbols and therefore the lesser is the number of subcarriers required to transmit them

Figure 9. Cyclic prefix removal- front panel

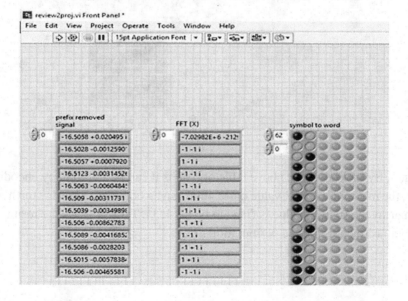

Figure 10. Source and channel decoding with depermuter and image reconstruction

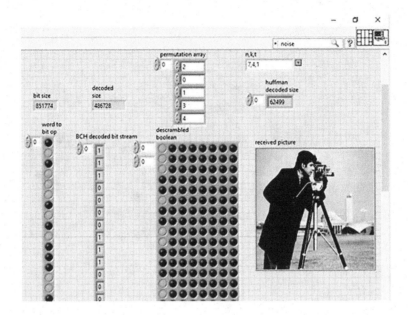

Figure 11a. USRP transmitter- front panel

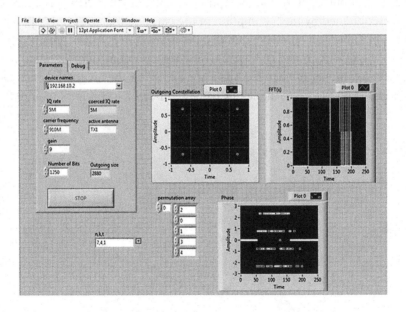

across the channel. By looking at the above table of results it can be said that by encoding with parameters of (7, 4, 1), the maximum PSNR value of 42.4006 can be obtained. Thus for further testing, to find the permutation array the (n, k, t) value is fixed to be (7, 4, 1). Table 2 gives the result of the MSE and PSNR values obtained by altering the permutation arrays.

Figure 11b. USRP receiver – front panel

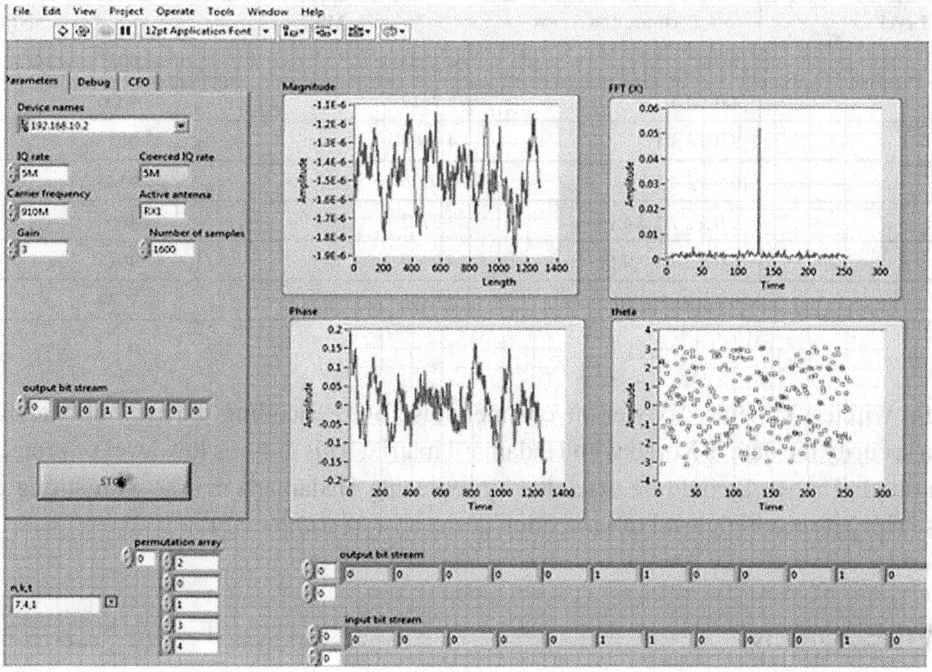

Table 1. MSE and PSNR values for different (n,k,t) of BCH coding blocks

S. No	BCH (n, k, t)	BCH Encoded Bits	Number of Words	(MSE)	(PSNR)
1	(7,4,1)	875000	437500	3.7412	42.4006
2	(15,11,1)	681810	340905	4.4806	41.617
3	(15,7,2)	1071420	535710	4.1003	42.0027
4	(15,5,3)	1500000	750000	3.7412	42.4006
5	(31,26,1)	596130	298065	5.0051	41.13
6	(31,16,3)	968750	484375	3.7412	42.4006
7	(63,51,2)	617589	308795	6.3971	40.0710
8	(63,36,5)	874944	437472	5.6426	40.6160

On analysing the Table 2, it is seen that the permutation array of [2 0 1 3 4] has given the maximum PSNR value and thus these parameter values of (n, k, t) and permutation array can be fixed for employing along with the hardware component of Universal Software Radio Peripheral (USRP- 2920).

CONCLUSION

This work focusses on developing OFDM based transceiver using LabVIEW tool and transmit the data using OFDM transceiver. This is achieved with the aid of USRP because it is universally accepted

Table 2. MSE and PSNR for different permutation arrays

Level	Permutation Array	MSE	PSNR
1.	[2 0 1]	4.1003	42.0037
2.	[2 0 1 3 4]	3.7412	42.4006
3.	[3 0 5 2 4 1]	4.1003	42.0027
4.	[6 0 5 2 4 1 3]	4.0516	42.0545
5.	[6 0 5 2 7 1 3 4]	3.3712	42.4006
6.	[6 0 8 2 7 1 3 4 5]	4.7078	41.4026
7.	[6 9 10 2 7 1 3 4 5 0 8]	4.9396	41.1939

prototype for wireless systems. To over the channel noise BCH encoding scheme has been utilized. To ensure data security the data is Xored with Hadamard matrix. This assures low level of protection to the data transmitted. The work could be extended by replacing Hadamard matrix with strong encryption algorithms. This ensures high level of protection at the cost of complexity.

ACKNOWLEDGMENT

The Authors would like to express their sincere thanks to SASTRA Deemed University, for the grant received under R&M fund (R&M / 0027 / SEEE – 010 / 2012 – 13) to carry out this research work.

REFERENCES

Althaf, C. I. M., & Prema, S. C. (2018). Covariance and eigenvalue-based spectrum sensing using USRP in real environment. *10th International Conference on Communication Systems & Networks (COMS-NETS)*, 414-417. 10.1109/COMSNETS.2018.8328231

Andrich, C., Ihlow, A., Bauer, J., Beuster, N., & Del Galdo, G. (2018). High-Precision Measurement of Sine and Pulse Reference Signals Using Software-Defined Radio. *IEEE Transactions on Instrumentation and Measurement, 67*(5), 1132–1141. doi:10.1109/TIM.2018.2794940

Arshad, R., Saleem, A., & Khan, D. (2016). Performance comparison of Huffman coding and double Huffman coding. *Proceedings Sixth International Conference on Innovative Computing Technology*, 361-364. 10.1109/INTECH.2016.7845058

Balouch, Z. A., Aslam, M. I., & Ahmed, I. (2017). Energy efficient image encryption algorithm. *Proceedings International Conference on Innovations in Electrical Engineering and Computational Technologies (ICIEECT)*, 1-6.

Bartalwar, S., & Deepa, T. (2017). Design and implementation of OFDM signal transmission for Visible light communication. *International Journal of Engineering Sciences & Research Technology, 6*, 577–583.

Chen, J., Zhang, S., Wang, H., & Zhang, X. (2013). Practicing a Record-and-Replay System on USRP. *Proceedings of the second workshop on Software radio implementation forum*, 61-64. 10.1145/2491246.2491257

Gouda, M, Hussien, M., Ragab, M.R., Anwar, A.M., & Gouda, A.F. (2017). USRP Implementation of PTS Technique for PAPR Reduction in OFDM Using LABVIEW. *Advances is Wireless Communications and Networks*, 2, 15-24.

Kumar, A., Khan, A. S., Modanwal, N., & Saha, S. (2019). Experimental Studies on Energy / Eigenvalue based Spectrum Sensing Algorithms using USRP Devices in OFDM Systems. *URSI Asia-Pacific Radio Science Conference (AP-RASC)*, 1-4. 10.23919/URSIAP-RASC.2019.8738506

Kushnure, D., Jiniyawala, M., Molawade, S., & Patil, S. (2017). Implementation of FM Transceiver using Software Defined Radio (SDR). *International Journal of Engineering Development and Research*, 5, 225–233.

Lee, M. H., Shahab, M. B., Kader, M. F., & Shin, S. Y. (2016). Spatial multiplexing using walsh-hadamard transform. *Proceedings International Conference on Smart Green Technology in Electrical and Information Systems (ICSGTEIS)*, 43-46. Academic Press.

Mathew, P., Augustine, L., & Devis, T. (2014). Hardware Implementation of (63, 51) BCH Encoder and Decoder For WBAN Using LFSR and BMA. *International Journal on Information Theory*, 3(3), 1–11. doi:10.5121/ijit.2014.3301

Muslimin, J., Asnawi, A. L., Ismail, A. F., & Jusoh, A. Z. (2016). SDR-Based Transceiver of Digital Communication System Using USRP and GNU Radio. *International Conference on Computer and Communication Engineering (ICCCE)*, 449-453. 10.1109/ICCCE.2016.100

Nafkha, A., Naoues, M., Cichon, K., & Kliks, A. (2014). Experimental spectrum sensing measurements using USRP Software Radio platform and GNU-radio. *Proceedings 9th International Conference on Cognitive Radio Oriented Wireless Networks and Communications*, 429-434. 10.4108/icst.crowncom.2014.255415

Peng, F., Zhang, S., Cao, S., & Xu, S. (2018). A Prototype Performance Analysis for V2V Communications using USRP-based Software Defined Radio Platform. *Proceedings 6th IEEE Global Conference on Signal and Information Processing*, 1-5.

Praveenkumar, P., Priya, P. C., Avila, J., Thenmozhi, K., Rayappan, J. B. B., & Amirtharajan, R. (2017). Tamper Proong Identification and Authenticated DICOM Image Transmission Using Wireless Channels and CR Network. *Wireless Personal Communications*, 97, 5573-5595.

Rupali, B. (2018). Patil, K., Kulat, D., & Gandhi, A. S. (2018). SDR Based Energy Detection Spectrum Sensing in Cognitive Radio for Real Time Video Transmission. *Modelling and Simulation in Engineering*, 1–10.

Salwa, M., & Eldin, S. (2017). Encrypted gray image transmission over OFDM channel for TV cloud computing. *International Journal of Speech Technology*, 20(3), 431–442. doi:10.100710772-017-9415-3

Saravanan. (2010). Color Image to Grayscale Image Conversion. *Proceedings Second International Conference on Computer Engineering and Applications*, 96-199. Academic Press.

Serkin, F. B., & Vazhenin, N. A. (2013). USRP platform for communication systems research. *Proceedings 2013 15th International Conference on Transparent Optical Networks (ICTON)*, 1-4. Academic Press.

Shujaat, A. K. T., Rehman, M., Khan, M. B., Jadoon, I., Khan, F. A., Nawaz, F., ... Nasir, A. A. (2018). An Experimental Channel Capacity Analysis of Cooperative Networks Using Universal Software Radio Peripheral (USRP). *Sustainability*, *10*, 1–13. PMID:30607262

Singh, R., Sharma, S., & Singh, S. (2014). Image Encryption Using Block Scrambling Technique. *International Journal of Computer Technology and Applications*, *5*, 963–966.

Sklar, B., & Ray, P. K. (2001). *Digital communication-Fundamentals and applications* (2nd ed.). Pearson Education.

Telagam, N., Lakshmi, S., & Nehru, K. (2019). Digital Audio Broadcasting Based Gfdm Transceiver Using Software Defined Radio. *International Journal of Innovative Technology and Exploring Engineering*, *8*, 273–281.

Telagam, N., Reddy, S., Nanjundan, M., & Nehru, K. (2018). USRP 2901 Based MIMO-OFDM Transceiver in Virtual and Remote Laboratory. *International Journal on Computer Science and Engineering*, *6*, 1033–1040.

Chapter 13
Continuous User Authentication on Touchscreen Using Behavioral Biometrics Utilizing Machine Learning Approaches

Amany Sarhan

Department of Computers and Control Engineering, Faculty of Engineering, Tanta University, Egypt

Ahmed Ramadan

Department of Computer and Control Engineering, Faculty of Engineering, Tanta University, Egypt

ABSTRACT

Nowadays, touchscreen mobile devices make up a larger share in the market, necessitating effective and robust methods to continuously authenticate touch-based device users. A classification framework is proposed that learns the touch behavior of a user and is able afterwards to authenticate users by monitoring their behavior in performing input touch actions. Two models of features are built; the low-level features (stoke-level) model or the high-level abstracted features (session-level) model. In building these models, two different methods for features selection and data classification were weighted features and PCA. Two classification algorithms were used; ANN and SVM. The experimental results indicate the possibility of continuous authentication for touch-input users with higher promises for session-level features than stroke-level features. Authors found out that using weighted features method and artificial neural networks in building the session-level model yields the most efficient and accurate behavioral biometric continuous user authentication.

INTRODUCTION

With the increasing popularity of mobile computing devices and their applications that access secure services such as banking and other transactions, protecting user data on mobile devices is becoming more and more important day after day. Digital technology is now just a part of life. From online shop-

DOI: 10.4018/978-1-7998-2701-6.ch013

ping to net banking, government transactions and business infrastructure, securing this large amount of data plays a vital role. Data can be secured using various hardware and software technologies (Karnan et al.'s, 2011), (Ouaguid et al.'s, 2018) and (Olakanmi & Dada, A. 2019).

Some common tools are antivirus, encryption, firewalls, two-factor authentication, software patches, updates, etc. Many people have a common misconception that data security is important only for big organizations, governments and businesses and they are only the target of data attackers. Data security is not just important for businesses or governments. Your computer, tablet, and mobile devices could be the next target. Usually, common users get targeted by attackers for their sensitive information, such as their credit card details, banking details, passwords, etc. All the previous lead to the existence of the most famous authentication scheme to protect user data and privacy that is password scheme (Mahfouz et al., 2017, Feng et al., 2012, Zhao et al., 2014, Jouini & Rabai, 2016).

Current applications maintain the privacy of user sensitive data by supporting user authentication at every login. Most mobile device applications today enforce security using traditional text-based password schemes to authenticate a user. However, users often choose weak passwords to make the login process more easy and quick (Jain et al., 2004). This is especially true with touch devices that are rapidly becoming ubiquitous. Findlater et al. (2011) have shown that the speed of typing on fiash glass is 31% slower than a physical keyboard. This typically leads to a shorter password chosen by users to shorten their login time. Choosing the appropriate password puts the user in a dilemma between using an easy-to-remember password and, at the same time, safe password so, most users sacrifice security to guarantee easy and quick login process which is the most frequent action done by touch input mobile devices so there was an urgent need to find other alternative authentication methods to solve this dilemma and give the user a more quick and easy login experience and at the same time doesn't make the user to sacrifice security (Frank et al., 2013).

Other authentication methods that could be better alternatives to a password authentication scheme, such as graphical patterns are most encouraging, but also are vulnerable to attacks, such as trying to discover the residues left on the touchscreen of the device after entering the same pattern many times. In addition to the previously mentioned, the main limitation of traditional security systems is that the user is only authenticated once at the beginning of the session. This authentication process is not performed until the next time the device needs to be unlocked (Karnan et al., 2011). All these problems and limitations lead to using some type of implicit and continuous authentication method to overcome these limitations. According to that, the authentication method needs to be continuous to overcome any attempt to access secured data illegally (Gianni et al., 2017). These methods are not valid in many situations like authentication of a student in an online exam.

In addition to being continuous, the authentication process should be implicit and transparent so that it cannot affect the user activity. In this context several academic and industrial research groups have proposed different solutions to monitor user activity and authenticate him along the time he is using his device. Continuous authentication can be the primary authentication method or an auxiliary fraud detection for higher assurance. It adds an extra reliability to the system and enhances the usability (Eberz and Rasmussen, 2017). Continuous authentication can be implemented using different methods according to hardware and software requirements. For example, we can implement it by setting session time out and ask the user to perform the authentication process which is very annoying to the user. Another method is to record data about how the user uses the device, and make a frequent comparison between this data and the previously recorded data of the same user. This solution is more applicable when we deal with behavioral biometric authentication methods which will be discussed later.

From a usability point of view, the traditional authentication schemes, i.e. password, pin code or graphical pattern, are inconvenient because users must focus on the authentication step every time they begin interacting with their devices. Such inconvenience becomes a significant problem when we consider mobile devices, since they are frequently accessed, and each use is typically shorter.

Another significant problem is that users mostly choose easy-to-remember password, as we mentioned before, which can be stolen easily. Even the most powerful password can be stolen by dictionary attacks, shoulder attacks, brute force attacks or recently social engineering in addition it can be forgotten. This led researchers to the biometrics such as fingerprint, iris scanning, face recognition and voice recognition as more convenient and secured authentication methods, but this brings another problem that is many of biometric-based authentication methods are either highly costed, inconvenient or complex to implement. To solve the previously mentioned problems, most of the studies like Mahfouz et al. (2017), Fierrez et al. (2018), Yampolskiy and Govindaraju (2008), and Song Fierrez et al. (2017) introduced behavioral biometric authentication methods which considered the inherence factor i.e. something that users are. These methods depend on monitoring users' behaviors while they are interacting with their devices using input peripherals like mouse, keyboard and touchscreen.

This paper is concerned with touchscreen input actions as a behavioral biometric authentication method to identify users through monitoring and analyzing how they interact with touchscreen mobile devices. Monitoring interaction data of the touchscreen can be applied at the level of the simplest gesture that the user can perform by touching the screen down then release his finger up which called stroke. The stroke is the trajectory made by the user when he puts his finger on the screen then releases it (Eljetlawi, 2010). Each stroke consists of several touch actions according to the sample rate that these actions are recorded. The other monitoring level is the session level in which many strokes can be recorded and processed as one unit, called touch session, which is different from the previous stroke level in which every single stroke is processed as a single unit of information.

Major researches concentrated on stroke-level as an information unit (Frank et al., 2013 and Fierrez et al., 2018) which can simplify system implementation, however, it ignores the correlation between all these single strokes that can hold a lot of important information about the user identity. Few researches, like O'connell and Walker (2017), and Karnan et al. (2011), have introduced session-level authentication, which we are going to apply in our thesis besides applying stroke-level monitoring. Previous studies have proposed applicable solutions in different manners to the problems defined before, therefore, we are going to make use of these solutions to propose a more efficient and accurate solution. We will use both single-touch stroke and multi-touch stroke that modern touchscreens technology support, as in our point of view, multi-touch stroke holds important information about user identity specially his hand geometry than single-touch. The main contribution of this paper is to propose a behavioral biometric-based authentication framework that concentrates on analyzing the touchscreen input actions from two different perspectives, i.e. we propose two different feature extraction models; stroke-level features model and session-level features model. We compare the performance of the two models using a combination between two different classification algorithms and two different features selection methods to decide which model is more accurate and effective in authentication process.

The paper methodology to introduce its contribution can be listed in points as:

- Introducing a user authentication framework that serves as a proof-of-concept for considering session-level information about the user input actions on touchscreen obtains more accurate and efficient authentication method.

- Using artificial neural networks and support vector machine as a classification algorithm in the two models to choose the classification algorithm.
- Introducing a new features selection method by searching features discrimination and feature consistency and using weighted features method according to their importance.
- Using PCA as an alternative method for feature selection instead of using weighted features method to choose the feature selection method.
- We also combined single touch strokes and multi-touch strokes into one model to make use of all modern touchscreen capabilities and to maximize the overall accuracy and efficiency of the authentication system.

This paper is organized as follows. In addition to the present section, section 2 focuses on some background knowledge that are related to behavioral biometrics specially touchscreen input behavior to help us understand touchscreen based behavioral biometric authentication scheme. It also shows in some detail the previous related work contributions in this field of study. Section 3 comes to introduce a proposed method to select the most appropriate features that are extracted from raw data of users' touch actions and describes the concepts behind it in detail then shows how we develop this framework to be flexible for future improvements. Section 4 shows the stages of the experiment that was held to build and evaluate this authentication framework and also presents the results of all experiments we carried out to evaluate our proposed framework and analyze these results to evaluate the proposed framework performance. Finally, section 5 comes to conclude this thesis and give us the features of the road map for future work.

BIOMETRICS AUTHENTICATION

Any biometric recognition system (see Figure 1) is bounded to automatically identify a person by examining some already enrolled physical and/or behavioral characteristics with its corresponding query characteristics submitted by that person. Ideal biometrics is supposed to have "zero" false acceptance and false rejection rates, and should satisfy some properties, such as universality, uniqueness, permanence, acceptability, and should be robust against possible attacks. Figure 1 depicts the block diagram of a biometric system with four components, defined below (Jain et al., 2004):

- **Data Source:** This block deals with the biometric data captured from an individual. It includes both the hardware and software. It may also incorporate an additional "Quality Checker" component to ensure data quality.
- **Feature Extractor:** This block deals with the extraction of discriminatory features from the captured biometric sample in order to profile the most relevant user information in the database.
- **Database:** This block deals with the storage and management of the biometric template generated from the user's data.
- **Matcher/Comparator**: This block matches the claimed or query pattern with the earlier stored pattern(s), and decides the acceptance/rejection. For verification, it performs the one-to-one match, and for identification it matches the input query pattern with all the stored patterns of all the classes (1: N), after which the user is identified based on the highest achieved score.

Figure 1. Generalized biometric recognition system

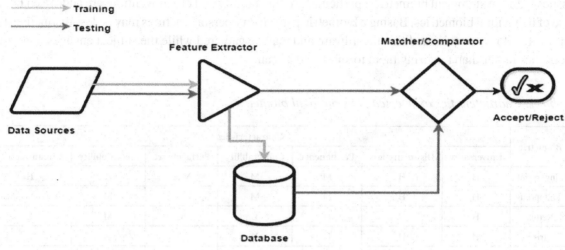

The choice of biometric modality(ies) depends upon various issues besides their recognition performance. The literature considers seven factors for determining the suitability of these traits as discussed below (Jain et al., 2011):

1. **Universality**: Every user needs to have that biometric modality. This factor helps in determining (Failure to Enroll Rate (FTER)) of biometric recognition system.
2. **Uniqueness**: The given modality should be sufficiently different across individuals in a set of population.
3. **Consistency**: The given modality should be consistent over a certain time period.
4. **Measurability**: The possibility to acquire and digitize the biometric modality with best devices without causing any inconvenience to the user.
5. **Performance**: Besides recognition accuracy, the throughput of the biometric system should also cope with the constraints imposed by the application.
6. **Acceptability**: It reflects the ease and comfort with which users provide their traits to the system.
7. **Circumvention**: It refers the ease with which the modality of other participants is copied, imitated or modified to gain illegitimate access of the system.

The physiological biometrics generally require a method of obtaining them such as a scanner or camera, and a method of converting them from a detailed scan to a concise feature vector that represents the most salient (i.e., distinctive) parts. Each of these biometrics has strengths and weaknesses and the selection of which to use depends on the needs of the application that will deploy it. Examples of physiological biometrics include: fingerprint, Palmprints, Iris and Retina scans and facial recognition.

Table 1 shows how each of these biometrics meets biometric characteristics. For each biometric, a determination for its adherence to the characteristic in question has been made. The determinations are High (H), Medium (M) and Low (L), and have been selected by the author. For example, a determination of H for fingerprint universality implies that most people can be authenticated via a fingerprint scan. A determination of L for retina collectability means that there are issues surrounding collecting retina scans that stop it from being more highly collectable (Yampolskiy and Govindaraju, 2008). Some of the issues with physiological biometrics, particularly collectability and circumvention, are addressed by the use of behavioral biometrics. Basing a biometric pattern on a person's actions may be less distinctive, but they often do not require additional hardware and may be gathered while the subject engages in normal activities rather than requiring them to submit to a scan.

Table 1. Characteristics of selected physiological biometrics.

Biometric	Characteristics						
	Universality	Distinctiveness	Permanence	Collectability	Performance	Acceptability	Circumvention
Fingerprint	H	H	M	M	M-L	H	H
Palmprint	H	H	M	M	M	M	M
Retina	H	H	H	L	M	M	L
Iris	H	H	H	H	H	M	L
Face	H	M	M	M	M	M	L

Behavioral Biometrics

Physiological biometrics can be limiting, particularly in a mobile device environment, because they can require additional hardware to gather the biometric. Behavioral biometrics are known to be less distinctive than physiological biometrics (Yampolskiy and Govindaraju, 2008), but have several benefits over physiological systems. They are easy to gather while the subject goes about other tasks and thus are ideal for transparent authentication. Their collection does not usually require special hardware and thus may be more cost effective. Much research has been undertaken into various possibilities, including keystroke dynamics (Clarke and Furnell, 2007), speaker verification (Bimbot et al., 2004 and Kenny et al., 2004), touch screen interaction patterns (Khan et al., 2014) and device use patterns (Gamboa and A. Fred 2004, Yampolskiy and Govindaraju, 2008). The list below briefly describes key behavioral biometrics.

1. **Signature**: It is the distinctive way in which a person signs their name. Signature metrics include the writing instrument pressure (electronic signatures only), shape of letters and other additions such as dots and flourishes. It has long been accepted as a method of identification and verification by government and legal bodies as well as by the general public. It requires use of a writing instrument and either a paper or electronic surface upon which to sign, which are relatively low-cost. Signatures are highly susceptible to forgery, although signature verification by a person or improved pattern matching algorithms can improve these methods (Fierrez et al., 2018). Signatures can be highly variable and thus require acceptance within certain tolerances rather than exact matches.

2. **Gait**: It is the characteristic way in which a person walks. Gait is a complex biometric because it combines spatial and temporal issues, in that both movement in a 3D space as well as the timing of each movement must be measured. It uses hardware such as accelerometers and gyroscopes for measurement (Mantyjarvi et al., 2005), which are common in mobile devices, as well as 3D cameras. Issues with gait include limited universality since those who cannot walk are immediately exempt, which includes young children, the elderly and infirm and people in wheelchairs. Gait may also

vary depending on the subject's weight, age and mental state, among others, and thus is not highly invariant (Gafurov et al., 2006). It is computationally-intensive both in feature vector creation and matching due to the complexity of the data gathered.

3. **Device Use**: It attempts to gather patterns in how subjects use devices such as desktop and laptop computers and mobile phones. Examples of device use include sequences of events, use of shortcuts versus menu items, and routes taken while walking or driving (Mazhelis and Puuro, 2007). These patterns, which can be gathered from such things as browser history and application notifications, are expected to be moderately distinctive, and require a relatively long training period (Shi et al., 2011). They are subject to variability due to device changes (i.e., if the subject begins to use a new mobile phone), and changes to the functionality of the device (i.e., new software or programs on the computer). This sort of monitoring may be cause for concern in subjects due to its similarity to eavesdropping.

4. **Typing**: The way a person types is expected to be distinctive and is known as keystroke dynamics (Karnan et al., 2011). Measurements of the speed, frequency of characters and n-grams as well as the pressure with which keys are pressed are gathered and combined into a distinctive pattern (Clarke and Furnell, 2007, and Eberz and Rasmussen, 2017). It is considered discriminatory for verification but not identification (Jain et al., 2004). This biometric is highly variable due to mental state, subject position (i.e., standing, sitting or walking) and keyboard familiarity. It can be gathered using a standard keyboard while the subject goes about other tasks. Keystroke dynamics may be subject to replay and imitation attacks, although the latter may be more difficult.

5. **Voice**: It is both a physiological and a behavioral biometric. The physiological aspects include measurements of voice features that change due to the distinctive shape of the subject's features such as larynx, glottal folds, mouth and lips (Jain et al., 2004). The behavioral aspects include pronunciation, word frequency and use and accent. The physiological aspects are relatively invariant over a person's life, but the behavioral aspects may be affected by mood, state of mind, age and medical conditions such as the common cold. Voice biometrics are not very distinctive and unsuitable for large-scale deployment due to issues with contamination from other noise during recording (Bonastre et al., 2003). It is subject to misuse due to recording and replaying a subject's voice, and it can be gathered without the subject's knowledge.

Table 2 shows the biometrics described above in relation to Jain's seven biometric characteristics. As with the physiological biometrics discussed in the previous section, a determination of High (H), Medium (M) or Low (L) denotes how well the biometric adheres the characteristic. The individual determinations are based on the author's opinions and knowledge of biometrics Yampolskiy and Govindaraju, 2008).

Table 2. Characteristics of selected behavioral biometrics.

Biometric	Characteristics						
	Universality	**Distinctiveness**	**Permanence**	**Collectability**	**Performance**	**Acceptability**	**Circumvention**
Signature	H	M	L	H	M	H	M
Gait	L	M	L	H	M	H	L
Device Use	L	M	L	H	M	L	L
Typing	H	M	L	H	M	M	M
Voice	H	M	M	H	M	H	M

Multi-Modal Biometrics

Recent years have witnessed a significant increase in accuracy and reliability in biometric authentication. However, mostly evaluated and tested advance biometric systems also have some limitations; some of these limitations are related with type of data, and some are related with methodology. More specifically, performance of the biometrics systems suffers a lot due to the presence of noise in input data, inter-class variations, non-universality, and other possible factors that may affect the performance, security and usability of those systems (Ross et al., 2008).

A multimodal biometric system is a newer way to address some of the problems associated with unimodal biometric systems. It incorporates the consolidation of data presented by multiple information sources such as combining data that comes from fingerprint scanner and iris scanner in addition to that collect data from input dynamics of mouse and keyboard. This kind of combination improves recognition performance and efficiency. Multimodal systems can significantly improve recognition performance along with increase in population coverage (thus reducing FTER), prevents spoof attacks, and increase the degree of freedom. Although these systems require more storage, take higher processing time, and involve more computational cost as compared to unimodal biometric systems, the above-mentioned advantages are compelling for their deployment in large scale authentication systems (Clancy et al., 2003).

Performance Metrics of Biometric Authentication Systems

The most commonly used metrics to evaluate the performance of a keystroke biometric system or any other biometric system are False Rejection Rate (FRR) and False Acceptance Rate (FAR) (AbdelDayem et al. (2017). FRR is the percentage of legitimate users who are labeled as imposters and denied access. It is defined as (Kumar et al. (2016), and AbdelDayem et al. (2017)):

$$FRR = \frac{Number\ of\ False\ Rejects}{Total\ Number\ of\ Legitimate\ Match\ Attempts}$$

where *False Rejects* is the number of legitimate users that are denied access.

FAR is the percentage of imposters (posing as legitimate users) who are allowed access to the system. It is defined as (Kumar et al. (2016), and AbdelDayem et al. (2017)):

$$FAR = \frac{Number\ of\ False\ Accepts}{Total\ Number\ of\ Imposter\ Match\ Attempts}$$

where *False Accepts* is the number of imposters that are allowed access.

In statistics, FRR is referred to as a Type I error. It denotes the system's specificity. FAR is referred to as a Type II error. It denotes the system's sensitivity. Both error rates should ideally be 0%. From a security point of view, type II errors should be minimized that is no chance for an unauthorized user to login. However, type I errors should also be infrequent because valid users get annoyed if the system rejects them incorrectly. The relationship between FAR and FRR is inversely proportional; when one decreases, the other increases. Thus, both metrics cannot be improved for an authentication system at the same time. Higher FAR is generally preferred in systems where security is not of prime importance, whereas higher FRR is preferred in high security applications (AbdelDayem et al., 2016).

One of the most common measures of biometric systems is the rate at which both FAR and FRR are equal. This is known as the Equal Error Rate (EER), or the Cross-Over Error Rate (CER) (Jain et al., 2004). The value indicates that the proportion of false acceptances is equal to the proportion of false rejections. The lower the EER value, the better the biometric system is.

CONTINUOUS AUTHENTICATION METHODS AND APPROACHES

Authentication is a common measure to improve the security of mobile devices. In the authentication process, the user identity is verified according to different sources of information which provided directly or indirectly by the user. Authentication process can be categorized into knowledge-based approaches such as passwords, PIN codes and graphical patterns and biometric-based approaches.

Knowledge-based approaches have been used since the appearance of this technology in the market and they are used widely despite their weaknesses and drawbacks. Biometric-based authentication approaches are considered more reliable and secure and the recent integrating of many new sensors in recent mobile devices provide more opportunities to develop new systems. Most of the biometric approaches operate as one-time authentication method, where the user is validated at the beginning of the used session on the device leaving it vulnerable to unauthorized access during the rest of the session.

As a result of the previously mentioned problem, continuous authentication methods have been proposed. The few number of continuous biometric authentication approaches proposed so far are based on machine learning techniques such as k-nearest neighbor, support vector machines and artificial neural networks. These methods allow for automatic detection of fraud users, but not always achieve sufficiently effectiveness results in all situations. In the next section, we will provide some of the previous research approaches.

Using touchscreens in authentication grew in the last decade. Many researches were directed towards either merging it with other biometrics in authentication or to verify its viability to stand alone as a method of authentication. Zhao et al. (2017) used multimodal biometrics composed of voice, face, and signature data for authentication on mobile phones. The goal is to enable legal binding contracts to be signed. While the face verification shows very high Equal Error Rate (EER), around 28%, the EER of voice and signature are around 5% and 8%, respectively. The fusion of the three biometrics enhanced the system by decreasing the EER to 2%. The problem with such a system is the highly intrusive authentication procedure where the user needs to read, sign, and enter a PIN code. In addition, there are several studies concerning employing graphic-based password instead of the text-based password for authentication. Rachna and Adrian (2000) studied the use of the graphic-based password and compared it with the traditional password and the PIN authentication. The result showed that the graphic-based password is better under the situations that the text-based password is hard for frequently access.

Another study by Wei et al. (2010) compared many types of passwords. The study confirmed that the graphical password supported a better memorability than the text-based password. Moreover, the graphical password also has much difficulty to be broken when using a traditional attack method such as brute-force, dictionary attack, etc.

A one-finger touch swipe gesture, or simply a swipe, is considered to be a touch gesture in which the user places one finger on a touchscreen and quickly moves it horizontally or vertically, typically for scrolling purposes. Despite the fact that swipes are not the only touch signals adequate for mobile biometrics (e.g., one may also use fiing, press, or pinch signals), most, if not all works in touch biometrics so far, have demonstrated the best results using one-finger swipe gestures. We will, therefore, concentrate in swipe signals, using the terms swipe biometrics and touch biometrics interchangeably in the rest of the paper.

Existing literature on swipe biometrics may be categorized into two main groups. The first one uses swipes made on the entry-point, i.e. a secret pattern, to authenticate the subject. Thus, the authentication is not being continuously performed. The second type of approaches explores the active authentication methods, where swipes made on the screen during the normal interaction with the device are continuously exploited for authentication. Since, as presented in the introduction, the main focus of the article is the use of swipe biometrics for active authentication, in this section we will review some of the existing methods belonging to this type of technology. Other related work comparing image-based features and exploring factors such as experience, gender, and age, have been published, respectively, in (Zhao et al's, 2014 and Antal et al's, 2015).

Pioneer authentication methods for smartphones were based on touchscreen analytics. Feng et al's (2012) introduced FAST (Finger-gestures Authentication System using Touchscreen), a novel touchscreen-based authentication approach on mobile devices. Besides extracting touch data from touchscreen equipped smartphones, FAST complements and validates this data using a digital sensor glove that we have built using off-the-shelf components. FAST leverages state-of-the-art classification algorithms to provide transparent and continuous mobile system protection. A notable feature is FAST's continuous, user transparent post-login authentication. They use touch data collected from 40 users to show that FAST achieves a False Accept Rate (FAR) of 4.66% and False Reject Rate of 0.13% for the continuous post-login user authentication. The low FAR and FRR values indicate that FAST provides excellent post-login access security, without disturbing the honest mobile users.

Lin et al's (2013) proposed an approach based on the weighted k-nearest neighbor algorithm. Experiments in a controlled environment showed an EER of 3.5% when the re-authentication time was set up to ten minutes. Decreasing the re-authentication time gives considerably worse results, thus limiting the practicality of the approach on real scenarios being the average smartphone session duration 72 seconds, as a recent study by Budiu (2015) suggests. Additionally, an obvious limitation of touch recognition for continuous authentication is the requirement of continuous input from the user. The smartphone activity usage is very diverse, and some of the most popular activities involve few typing. With the embedding of sensors such as an accelerometer, magnetometer and gyroscope, motion authentication for smartphones became a subject of an increasing number of studies. Some of the recent literature is focused on identifying users based on their holding patterns (Conti et al., 2011). Since motion data on smartphones can be continuously collected, a similar methodology can be used to implement continuous biometric authentication systems, although the literature in this area is very sparse (Lin et al., 2013).

Neverova et al's (2016) proposed a continuous motion recognition system based on the accelerometer and gyroscope data. The method is applied in two phases. In the first phase, they transform the observations in a new set of features and estimated their general distribution using a Gaussian mixture model. When a new user joins the scheme, they perform maximum posterior adaptation of the mean vectors of the general data model to build a client-specific model. Then, both models are used to produce a verification score for each new observation. The authors obtained an ERR of 18.2% in real-world scenarios.

Song Fierrez et al. (2017) introduced a multi-modal approach, including accelerometer, gyroscope and touch-screen observations. The authors use a one-class SVM model to classify the samples as either belonging to the owner or a guest/attacker. They tested the approach with a dataset collected in a controlled environment where users were asked to type a text when sitting and when walking. They obtained an EER of 7.16% when the user was walking and 10.05% when the user was sitting. The authors deferred the evaluation of the approach on real-world scenarios to future studies.

Touchscreen technology has been improved to cope with more complex input needs. Instead of supporting only one finger to perform gestures needed, modern touchscreens now support up to ten fingers touch actions in one gesture, this leads to perform more complex gestures and provide more information about user-hand geometry which can be very useful when it comes to behavioral biometric authentication.

Jain et al., 2011 used 22 different multi-touch gestures to authenticate 34 users on an iPad. The authors reported EERs of 7%–15% if the users performed one gesture, 2.6%–3.9% if two gestures were combined, and 3% with one unique gesture for each user. There are at least two significant differences concerning the problem setting in these two papers and our work. While Buriro et al's (2016), required a defined entry-point for the user to authenticate, they aim at an implicit and continuous scenario. Second, in their authentication scheme, the users can interact with the screen as they like, while in Jain et al., (2011) and Buriro et al. (2016), touch trajectories are compared with a particular (secret) gesture.

Frank et al. (2013) is one of the first and most comprehensive works using touch data for continuous authentication. They studied 41 subjects who provided data from single touch operations while comparing images and reading texts. Intra and inter-session authentication is studied, obtaining less than 4.0% Equal Error Rate (EER) using Support Vector Machines (SVM) with Radial-Basis Functions (RBF) and k-Nearest Neighbors (kNN). The classifier achieves a median equal error rate of 0% for intra-session authentication, 2%–3% for inter-session authentication, and below 4% when the authentication test was carried out after one week from the enrollment phase. In addition, it was observed that combining blocks of strokes for authentication results in better performance, conclusion also reached in other works, such as Serwadda et al. (2013) and Shen et al. (2016).

In Serwadda et al. (2013), a benchmark of the best suited algorithms for active authentication using swipe biometrics was generated using a large dataset with touch data operations, acquired across two different sessions for 190 subjects. Extracting a 28-feature vector, they reported that the best performance, around 15% EER, was obtained using logistic regression, SVM and random forests.

Shen et al. (2016) studied SVM, kNNs, neural networks and random forest classifiers for different applications (e.g. document reading or picture viewing), as well as with free tasks. They analyzed four types of touch operations (up, down, left and right) and different feature sets were extracted in each of them. They concluded that: 1) swipes with a smaller active area (horizontal gestures) are more stable and discriminative; and 2) better results are obtained with specific tasks (1% EER) than free ones (5% EER) following the same methodology.

In Zhang et al. (2015), SVM and dictionaries based on sparse representations were compared for three datasets, two of them public (Frank et al., 2013, 14], reporting that dictionaries perform slightly better than SVM, with EER ranging from 0.4% to 23.8%.

Mahbub et al. (2016) studied touch data authentication over a dataset with a large number of samples per subject obtained with a more realistic application that allowed free interaction. kNN, SVM, random forest and Gradient Boosting Model (GBM) were exploited for authentication, resulting in EER ranging from 22% to 38%.

Additionally, fusion of single touch operations with other biometrics have been studied in Xu et al. (2014) (keystroke, swipe, pinch), Kumar et al. (2018) (keystroke, swipe, phone movement) and Sitov´a et al. (2016) (hand movement, orientation, grasp, tap, keystroke features). The first one reported accuracies above 90% with SVM, whilst the second obtained 10% EER with kNN and random forest, using only swipe data for authentication. Finally, in the third one they compared the EER obtained while the user was walking and sitting, reporting a 7.16% and 10.05% EER, respectively, when they combined all the mentioned features.

Most of the literature summarized above assume the availability of both genuine and impostor samples for training. However, some applications impose restrictions that make difficult or even impractical the use of impostor samples for training. In order to deal with those cases, researchers have explored the use of one-class classifiers and anomaly detection techniques. Murmuria et al. (2015) proposed Strangeness-based Outlier Detection (StrOUD) to monitor the user behavior based on power consumption, touch gestures, and physical movement. Those algorithms demonstrated competitive performance with EER under 7% when sufficient data is available to model each user (only genuine samples).

Kumar et al. (2018) analyzed three one-class classifiers for continuous authentication including one-class Support Vector Machines, Elliptic Envelop, and Local Outlier Factor algorithms. The results obtained suggest that it is possible to achieve comparable performance only with genuine data compared to using both genuine and impostor data for training. Anomaly detection methods have been also applied for continuous authentication based on touchscreen interaction. Perera and Patel (2018) proposed different quick intrusion detection methods for mobile active user authentication. Their results show that it is possible to detect a high percentage of intrusions with a relatively small number of gestures. Similarly, in Mondal and Bours (2015) proposed a trust model based on Counter Propagation Artificial Neural Networks.

Kin et al. (2017) have proposed a user-adaptive feature extraction method for novelty detection algorithms to improve the performance of keystroke dynamics-based user authentication based on freely typed texts. Inspired by the fact that an individual user's typing behavior is represented by their keystroke data, they adjusted digraph assignments adaptively to eight features by considering the average typing speed of all digraph pairs. Then, five novelty detection algorithms were trained to build an authentication model. To verify the proposed user-adaptive feature extraction method, they collected keystroke data from 150 participants who each provided more than 13,000 keystrokes. The effectiveness of the proposed method was supported by the experimental results obtained under various conditions, i.e., two languages with 25 different combinations of training and test keystroke lengths. Performance improvement was noticeable when the length of the test keystrokes was relatively short and when users were typing a more familiar language. When the length of the training and test keystrokes was 1,000, the EER of the proposed method was 0.44% on average, which is considered acceptable for practical implementation.

AbdelDayem et al. (2017) proposed a statistical method for short-text authentication while a k-nearest neighbor algorithm is used for long-text authentication. Two sets of experiments were carried out to test the authentication performance of the system. The results of their work show that for short-text authentication, the system had a FRR of 0% for both sets of users, which means that no user who knows his login data (username/password combination) will be denied access to the system. Moreover, FAR of 12.5% and 27.5% for the two sets of users mean that some imposter tries could be accepted. Since keystroke dynamics is not the only mechanism for authentication, but is integrated with password typing, so an imposter needs to know the user's password and try to simulate his typing pattern too to gain access into the system.

For long-text authentication, FAR of 2.08% and 1.28% for the two sets of users mean that very few imposter tries would be allowed to gain access to the system. Using the same long-text for training and testing has very low FRR (0% and 3.84% for the two sets of users) which enhances the system's performance. However, making the users type the same long-text each time can cause inconvenience and that's why they needed to test the system performance when using different long-text data for training and testing. The system then had higher FRR values, especially for the second set of users. The reason for the high rejection rate for the large set of users is the inconsistent and erratic typing patterns of some of our users when they have to copy a long-text they are not familiar with.

Fridman and Weber (2016) proposed a parallel binary decision-level fusion architecture for classifiers based on four biometric modalities: text, application usage, web browsing, and location. Using this fusion method, they addressed the problem of active authentication and characterized its performance on a real-world dataset of 200 subjects, each using their personal Android mobile device for a period of at least 30 days. The authentication system achieved an equal error rate (ERR) of 0.05 (5%) after 1 minute of user interaction with the device, and an EER of 0.01 (1%) after 30 minutes. They showed the performance of each individual classifier and its contribution to the fused global decision. The location-based classifier, while having the lowest firing rate, contributes the most to the performance of the fusion system

CONTINUOUS USER AUTHENTICATION FRAMEWORK BASED ON TOUCHSCREEN ACTIONS

In the context of this work, implicit authentication is defined as verifying the identity of the mobile device user without explicitly interrupt his activity or require him any extra effort. The implication is that the data upon which to base an authentication decision is found in how a user uses the device to perform his regular tasks (Gianni et al., 2017). The proposed framework aims at providing an implicit continuous authentication scheme, where the users can use their mobile devices as they used to do while an implicit authentication process is performed continuously. First, a model is built for the user during the offline learning stage. Then, during his casual usage of the device, the authentication will be performed as a background process (Eljetlawi, 2010).

Previous studies like (Eljetlawi, 2010), (Nakamura et al., 2012), (Jeanjaitrong and Bhattarakoso, 2013) and (Eberz and Rasmussen, 2017) concentrated on simple features related to user behavior in each touch stroke as a single independent vector without considering all touch strokes within the same touch session. Touch strokes data within the same session could contain correlated information about user behavior which could be more benefit information in user authentication than information which we could get from single touch stroke. In this study, we build two user behavioral models: stroke-level model and session-level model. We compare the performance of the two models searching for a model that results in an efficient authentication process.

Android MotionEvent Overview

Motion events describe the movements in terms of an action code and a set of axis values. The action code specifies the occurred state change, such as a pointer going down or up. The axis values describe the position and other movement properties. For example, when the user touches the screen for the first time, the system delivers a touch event to the appropriate view with the action code ACTION_DOWN and a set of axis values that include the X and Y coordinates of the touch, and information about the pressure, size and orientation of the contact area (Android Developer, 2018).

Some devices can report multiple movement traces at the same time. Multi-touch screens emit one movement trace for each finger. The individual fingers or other objects that generate movement traces are referred to as pointers. Motion events contain information about all of the pointers that are currently active even if some of them have not moved since the last event was delivered. The number of pointers only ever changes by one as individual pointers go up and down, except when the gesture is canceled (Android Developer, 2018).

Each pointer has a unique id that is assigned when it first goes down (indicated by ACTION_DOWN or ACTION_POINTER_DOWN). A pointer id remains valid until the pointer eventually goes up (indicated by ACTION_UP or ACTION_POINTER_UP) or when the gesture is canceled (indicated by ACTION_CANCEL i.e. when the pointer leaves the boundaries of the child view towards parent view). The MotionEvent class provides many methods to query the position and other properties of pointers, such as getX(int), getY(int), getAxisValue(int), getPointerId(int), getToolType(int), and many others. Most of these methods accept the pointer index as a parameter rather than the pointer id. The pointer index of each pointer in the event ranges from 0 to one less than the value returned by getPointerCount() (Android Developer, 2018). The order in which individual pointers appear within a motion event is undefined. Thus the pointer index of a pointer can change from one event to the next, but the pointer id is guaranteed to remain constant as long as the pointer remains active. We use the getPointerId(int) method to obtain the pointer id to track it across all the subsequent motion events in a gesture. Then for successive motion events, we use the findPointerIndex(int) method to obtain the pointer index for a given pointer id in that motion event.

Mouse and stylus buttons can be retrieved using getButtonState(). It is a good idea to check the button state while handling ACTION_DOWN as part of a touch event. The application may choose to perform some different action, if the touch event starts due to a secondary button click, such as presenting a context menu (Android Developer, 2018). For efficiency, motion events with ACTION_MOVE may batch together multiple movement samples within a single object. The most current pointer coordinates are available using getX(int) and getY(int). Earlier coordinates within the batch are accessed using getHistoricalX(int, int) and getHistoricalY(int, int) functions. The coordinates are "historical" as they are older than the current coordinates in the batch; however, they are still distinct from any other coordinates reported in prior motion events. To process all the coordinates in the batch in time order, we first consume the historical coordinates, then consume the current coordinates (Android Developer, 2018).

For a touch screen or touch pad, it reports the approximate pressure applied to the surface with a finger or any other tool. The value is normalized to a range from 0 (no pressure at all) to 1 (normal pressure), although values higher than 1 may be generated depending on the calibration of the input device. For a touch screen or touch pad, it reports the approximate size of the contact area in relation to the maximum detectable size for the device. This value is also normalized to a range from 0 (smallest detectable size) to 1 (largest detectable size), although it is not a linear scale. This value is of limited use. To obtain the calibrated size information, we use AXIS_TOUCH_MAJOR or AXIS_TOOL_MAJOR (Android Developer, 2018).

Single-touch and Multi-touch Stroke

A stroke is a sequence of touch data that begins with touching the screen and ends with lifting the finger. A stroke "s" is a trajectory encoded as a sequence of touch strokes vectors in the format of:

$$s_i = \left(x_i, y_i, t_i, P_i, A_i \right), i \in \left\{ 1, 2, 3, ..., N \right\} \tag{1}$$

with the location x_i, y_i, the timestamp t_i, the pressure on screen P_i and the area covered by the finger A_i. All touch gestures composite from number of strokes; single touch strokes or multi-touch strokes where single stroke in

Figure 2 (a) has only one trajectory with only one ACTION_DOWN action, one ACTION_UP action and variable number of ACTION_MOVE actions according to sample rate that Android system uses to generate and consume motion event objects. On the other hand, a multi-touch stroke, as shown in Figure 2 (b), contains more than one single touch stroke up to 10 strokes in one gesture. Multi-touch gestures are used to perform complex touch operations such as zooming and rotating on screen objects in many Android applications.

Figure 2. (a) Single-touch and (b) multi-touch strokes

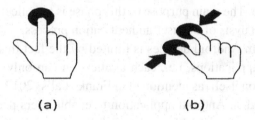

(a)　　　　**(b)**

The Proposed Framework

Figure 3 shows the proposed user authentication framework. Here we want to emphasis that our main purpose is to identify the user on his own touchscreen mobile device not to verify multiple users, but we designed the experiment in that manner to simplify our study.

Figure 3. The Proposed Touch Stroke-Level/Session-Level Authentication Framework

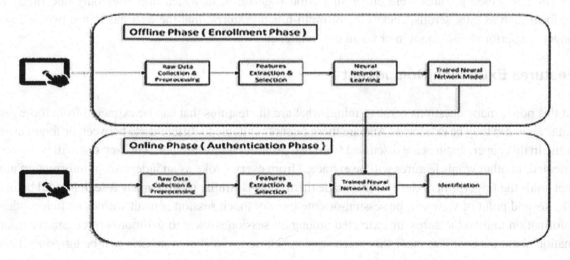

Offline Phase

At this phase, a trained neural network model is built that represents every user profile which will be used later in the online phase to authenticate users. This phase is divided into four stages, as depicted in Figure 4; which starts with the raw data collection performed using Android operating system APIs via an application developed for this purpose. The features of these raw data are then extracted, selected and used to train a neural network model producing a trained model for each user. This model represents his behavior in touching the device screen.

Raw Data Collection and Preprocessing Component

The raw data in our framework are collected using APIs found in the operating system. In our work, we rely on the events' data provided by the Android operating system of the mobile device. In the raw data collection phase, the user is asked to perform specific single-touch and multi-touch gestures that are commonly used in all mobile device applications. This is actually via an application designed and implemented for that purpose. The main purpose of this phase is to collect raw touch data that represent every user to make further analysis of the user authentication process.

Collecting touch data from Android devices is limited by the fact that Android prohibits access to touch data across different applications, i.e., each application can only read touch data produced by interacting with the application itself as mentioned in Frank et al's (2013). According to the previously mentioned fact, we developed an Android application to enable users perform specific touch gestures and record raw touch data in a structured form. In the following sections, we illustrate the design and implementation of the application.

Choosing the Gestures

In our application, the user was asked to perform the most used gestures among all Android applications in order to simulate the user real experience when she/he uses any Android application (see Figure 4). Therefore, we choose the following gestures: Tap - Long Tap - Scroll Up - Scroll Down - Scroll Left - Scroll Right – Rotate - Zoom in - Zoom out – Flick.

The performed gestures were either single-touch gestures, in which user uses only one finger to perform such as taps, scrolls, flicks etc., or multi-touch gestures, that the user has to use two or more fingers to perform; like zoom in or zoom out, rotate, etc.

Features Extraction Component

At this point, many questions come to mind; what are the features that can be extracted from these raw data? How can they be extracted? And are these features suitable to differentiate between different users well? In this paper, features are discussed from two different points of view. The first one will be stroke-oriented, in other words features will be extracted from every stroke as an independent information unit that holds the fingerprint of the user that made them. This is similar to what many researches did before. The second point of view will be session-oriented; every touch session is dealt with as an independent information unit and features are extracted among all session strokes to get more representative information about the user that made this touch session. These two different models will be introduced and

Figure 4. List of the Used Touch Gestures

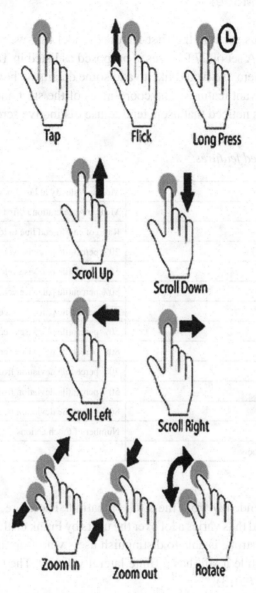

a complete comparison between the two models will be provided to choose which of these models is more accurate and efficient in the authentication process. In the following sections, we will deeply dive into the details of the features extraction and the features selection processes.

Previous researches introduced a lot of features that can be extracted from raw touch data. We put these features into consideration and in addition to that, we will introduce other features that we thought they would be more useful in our models by well representing user behavior on touchscreen input device. We try to cover almost the most mentioned features in the previous researches related to touch such as: coordinates, time, area covered, velocity, acceleration and pressing pressure. We also used more complex features that, we think, will give better results in the next stage (i.e. classification and identification) which will be discussed later in this chapter.

Stroke-level Features Model

As mentioned in the previous section, the first features model that we are going to implement is the stroke-level features model. A set of 27 features is proposed as listed in Table 3. Most of them are self-explained, but for some of them, we would like to add some details on how they are computed and why we believe that they are relevant features. The coordinates of the start and the end points of the stroke have been selected since it is noticed that users tend to use distinctive screen areas for their strokes.

Table 3. Stroke-level proposed features.

Start-X Coordinate	Median Velocity at last 3 points
Start-Y Coordinate	Median Acceleration at first 5 points
End-X Coordinate	Ratio of end-to-end line to length of Trajectory
End-Y Coordinate	20% percentile pairwise velocity
Average Velocity	50% percentile pairwise velocity
Average Direction	80% percentile pairwise velocity
Stroke Duration	20% percentile pairwise acceleration
Mid-Stroke Pressure	50% percentile pairwise acceleration
Mid-Stroke Area Covered	80% percentile pairwise acceleration
Direct end-to-end distance	20% percentile deviation from end-to-end line
Direction of end-to-end line	50% percentile deviation from end-to-end line
Length of Trajectory	80% percentile deviation from end-to-end line
Mean Resultant Length	Number of touch actions
Largest Deviation from end-to-end line	

The device reacts independently from the stroke location. Therefore, the choice of this location is completely left to the user and thus varies a lot over the users by Frank et al's (2013). The median velocity of the last five points of the stroke is able to distinguish users who stop the finger before lifting it from those that lift their finger while it still has a finite lateral velocity. They might have distinct throwing velocities as in Frank et al's (2013).

An important factor in touch analysis is the time. Some users steadily and slowly scroll while reading. Others quickly scroll to a new position and read on the still screen. This can be detected by stroke duration. It is an informative data about the reading speed which is supposedly different for different users (Frank et al's, 2013). All the formulas that we used to extract these features from raw data will be mentioned in Appendix A at the end of this thesis. Every feature of the previously mentioned features represents user behavior in somehow, for example, the average velocity of the stroke tells us if the user writes quickly or slowly, and so on for the other features.

Session-level Features Model

The second features model is the session-level features model in which session is taken as an information unit. By this way, more generalized informative data are collected that will give a wider view of the touchscreen device user behavior. Most of the session-level features are extracted from the aggregation of the stroke-level features to give the use general view. Here, a set of 35 features is proposed as listed in Table 4.

Table 4. Session-level proposed features.

Average Tap Pressure	Scroll right Average Velocity
Rotation Average Pressure At Focal Point	Scroll up Average Distance
Scroll left Average Velocity At Last 3 Points	Long Tap Average Pressure
Scroll up Average Velocity At Last 3 Points	Rotation Average Radius
Scroll left Average Distance	Scroll down Average Distance
Scroll up Average Direction	Scroll down Average Velocity At Last 3 Points
Zoom-in Distance Between Lifting Points	Scroll right Average Velocity At Last 3 Points
Scroll left Average Velocity	Zoom-in Two Lifting Latency
Tap Time	Zoom-out Distance Between Lifting Points
Flicking Average Direction	Tap Max Distance
Scroll up Average Velocity	Zoom-out Distance Between Landing Points
Scroll right Average Distance	Scroll left Average Direction
Scroll down Average Velocity	Average Tap Area
Scroll down Average Direction	Zoom-out Two Landing Latency
Zoom-out Zooming Time	Flicking Average Velocity
Zoom-in Zooming Time	Zoom-out Two Lifting Latency
Scroll right Average Direction	Zoom-in Two Landing Latency
Zoom-in Distance Between Landing Points	

Features Selection

Now we have all features data, but the big number of features leads to complex classification and identification models. We have to select the best features from all proposed features list. This leads to another question; what are the best features and how can we select them? In the following sections, we will introduce an answer to this question by providing two different features selection methods; the first one uses the discrimination and consistency values while the second one uses the principal component analysis. Before that, we would like to give a clearer view about the importance of selecting the features.

The main purpose of the features selection stage is to select the features that discriminate between all users in an efficient manner. The optimal situation in this stage will be reached if the selected features always have different values for each user among all touch sessions and constant value for the feature among different user sessions. In other words, the best features are the features that have the best discrimination value and the best consistency value at the same time.

In the next sections, we will search the user-feature consistency between touch sessions and the feature discriminately between the different users. Then, we will apply this method to the stroke-level features model and the session-level features model.

Features Data Normalization

Before we can deal with the features data, we must denote that they come in different value ranges. The following is a sample of features data vector for the stroke-level features model:

```
[2176.875 1247.65625 2138.125 742.578125 128 506.5624096 6.135431403
-1.647367132 -1.328851684 508.1420725 0.996891297 8.63E-16 4.667189765
12.38841707 5.125475014 3.969859941 -0.302622586 0.066943557 0.87611035
0.07316436 18.16903201 -3.63E-07 5.95685666 16.69311958 0.074509807 0.003921569
8]
```

We have to normalize all the features data so that searching the discrimination and consistency becomes more flexible. We normalize all the features values, to get scaled values for each feature from 0 to 1 according to Equation (2):

$$z_i = \frac{x_i - \min(x)}{\max(x) - \min(x)} \tag{2}$$

where x = (x_1, ..., x_n) and z_i are the ith normalized data, min and max are the minimum and maximum data values for this data.

Discrimination and Consistency

The variance of each feature set per user is calculated using Equation (3).

$$Variance(f) = \frac{\sum_{i=1}^{n}(x_i - \mu)^2}{N} \tag{3}$$

The summation of variances for all users per feature is computed using Equation (4):

$$Sum\ of\ Variances(f) = \sum_{i=0}^{m} Variance(f) \tag{4}$$

We can determine which features are more consistent than the other by arranging the summation of variances in an ascending order. The most first features are the most user-feature consistency between sessions, i.e. the most desirable features. Feature discriminately is to find which features would discriminate the different users better than any other features. We calculate the variance of each feature among all sessions of all users, then determine the most desirable features by arranging these resulted variances in a descending order. The most first features are the most discriminant between the different users.

Principal Component Analysis

Principal component analysis (PCA) simplifies the complexity in high- dimensional data while retaining trends and patterns. It does this by transforming the data into fewer dimensions, which act as summaries of features. High-dimensional data are very common in biology and arise when multiple features, such as expression of many genes, are measured for each sample. This type of data presents several challenges that PCA mitigates: computational expense and an increased error rate due to multiple test correction when testing each feature for association with an outcome (Lever et al's, 2017).

PCA is an unsupervised learning method and is similar to clustering —it finds patterns without reference to prior knowledge about whether the samples come from different treatment groups or have phenotypic differences. PCA reduces data by geometrically projecting them onto lower dimensions called principal components (PCs), with the goal of finding the best summary of the data using a limited number of PCs (Lever et al's, 2017).

ANN & SVM Learning (Classification Phase)

The core of the authentication process is data classification which is the most important and critical stage in user authentication. It represents the decision-making stage in which the system decides which features data belong to which class (i.e. the classification system classifies every set of features data to the user that they belong to) (Matlab guide (2019)).

The classification algorithms can follow three different learning approaches: supervised, unsupervised, or semi-supervised. In supervised learning, the algorithm works with a set of examples whose labels are known. The labels can be nominal values in the case of the classification task, or numerical values in the case of the regression task. In unsupervised learning, in contrast, the labels of the examples in the dataset are unknown, and the algorithm typically aims at grouping examples according to the similarity of their attribute values, characterizing a clustering task. While semi-supervised learning is usually used when a small subset of labeled examples is available, together with a large number of unlabeled examples (Matlab guide (2019)).

The classification task can be seen as a supervised technique where each instance belongs to a class, which is indicated by the value of a special goal attribute or simply the class attribute. The goal attribute can take on categorical values, each of them corresponding to a class. Each example consists of two parts, namely a set of predictor attribute values and a goal attribute value. The former is used to predict the value of the latter. The predictor attributes should be relevant for predicting the class of an instance. In the classification task the set of examples being mined is divided into two mutually exclusive and exhaustive sets, called the training set and the test set (Matlab guide (2019)) and Shen et al. (2016).

The classification process is correspondingly divided into two phases: training, when a classification model is built from the training set, and testing, when the model is evaluated on the test set. In the training phase, the algorithm has access to the values of both predictor attributes and the goal attribute for all examples of the training set, and it uses that information to build a classification model. This model represents classification knowledge – essentially, a relationship between predictor attribute values and classes – that allows the prediction of the class of an example given its predictor attribute values (Matlab guide (2019)).

In the testing phase, only after a prediction is made, the algorithm is allowed to see the actual class of the just-classified example. One of the major goals of a classification algorithm is to maximize the predictive accuracy obtained by the classification model when classifying examples in the test set unseen during training. The knowledge discovered by a classification algorithm can be expressed in many different ways like rules, decision trees, Bayesian network etc. (Mondal and Bours, 2015). For classification in our research, we will use Artificial Neural Networks and Support Vector Machines as a classification algorithm to build the decision making component of our authentication framework.

ANN & SVM are used as a classifier to classify the extracted data features into its corresponding classes (i.e. assigning every feature vector to its corresponding user) as neural network classifier provides the ability to be adapted using a learning algorithm to produce a trained model that can discriminate between the different users. The user features vectors are taken as input while the output is determining the user that the input features belong to. In the next subsection, an overview about how the ANN & SVM work is given. In our work, the performances of the two different classifiers are compared to find the best classifier for the authentication framework.

Online Phase

In this phase, we walkthrough almost all the stages as in the offline phase except that in the online phase, we use the previously trained model of every single user to identify if the new features data which didn't participate in the training offline phase belong to the user, then we use its trained model as a user profile or not.

Identification Component

The identification component uses the previously trained and adapted model of the desired user, produced in the offline phase, and tests it against new untrained feature vectors to verify to what extent the trained model can really discriminate the touch actions of the device owner over an imposter touch actions.

EXPERIMENT DESIGN, RESULTS AND PERFORMANCE EVALUATION

In this section, the proposed continuous touchscreen authentication framework is validated. At the start, we are going to introduce the experiment carried out to prove that concept from the two different points of view; the level of stroke and the level of touch sessions. The experimental results are given, and the performance of the two different models is evaluated to decide which is more representative and satisfies the user authentication needs.

Raw Data Mobile Application Design

The raw data collector mobile application is designed in a simple way, as mentioned before, we couldn't use the system service to listen to all touch data among all running applications on the mobile device due to security issues. The Android operating system is designed to pass every touch action to its process only, so we have designed a simple application that asks the user to perform the previously mentioned single-touch and multi-touch gestures.

Data Collected Through the Application

Some basic information about the developed application are given in this subsection to fully comprehend its details and the data extracted through it. Every stroke performed by the user is stored in memory in a stroke object that has a list of touch actions which contains the following data fields:

- **ActionType**: This field stores an integer value that determines the user's action type, i.e. ACTION_DOWN, ACTION_MOVE or ACTION_UP, which points to the start and the end of any single-touch stroke. There are also ACTION_POINTER_DOWN and ACTION_POINTER_UP fields which point to the start and the end of any multi-touch stroke.
- **xPosition & yPosition**: These two fields store the position of the user's finger in 2D according to an origin point measured in pixels.
- **Size**: this field stores the size of the pointer that relays on the touch screen.
- **Pressure**: this field stores the value of the pressure that the user applied on the touch screen using his finger.
- **TimeStamp**: This field stores the timestamp which we use to compute the duration of every stroke.

A touch session object is then created that contains a list of single-touch strokes and multi-touch strokes, accompanied by the user information; name, session start time and session end time. The way we transfer these raw data from the client mobile device to the server, where we manipulate them to extract data features used the classification and identification models, will be discussed next.

In this stage, we have faced two problems; the first was how to collect the raw data from the users in an efficient way during the duration of the experiment as we had to collect the data over a long duration of time (to overcome users' adaptation to the experiment). The second problem was how to collect more data during more the touch sessions if we need? It will be so difficult to achieve that. To overcome these two problems, we come to design a Windows Communication Foundation (WCF) web service to accept the raw data from our mobile application and store them in a database for further analysis.

Windows Communication Foundation (WCF) is a framework for building service-oriented applications. Using WCF, you can send data as asynchronous messages from one service endpoint to another. A service endpoint can be part of a continuously available service hosted by IIS, or it can be a service hosted in an application. An endpoint can be a client of a service that requests data from a service endpoint. The messages can be as simple as a single character or word sent as XML, JSON Objects, or as complex as a stream of binary data (What Is Windows Communication Foundation, 2017). WCF is designed to offer a manageable approach to create Web services and Web services clients.

JSON (JavaScript Object Notation) is a lightweight data-interchange format. It is easy for humans to read and write, and it is easy for machines to parse and generate. JSON is a text format that is completely language independent, but uses conventions that are familiar to programmers of the C-family of languages, including C, C++, C#, Java, JavaScript, Perl, Python, and many others. These properties make JSON an ideal data-interchange language (Introducing JSON, 2018).

In our experiment, the in-memory objects (i.e. session objects, stroke objects and touch action objects) are converted into serialized JSON objects so that they can be transferred across the Internet from the Android client device to the database server using a web service for further data analysis. Here, JSON objects are preferred over XML messages as JSON is less resource consumption than XML messages and supported by almost all programming languages in addition to that it is less complex than the other choice (i.e. XML messages).

Experiment Setup

Ten mobile device users, aged from 24 to 60 years, 4 females and 6 males, right-handed were selected to perform specific touch actions; a combination of single-touch and multi-touch gestures. The used device is Samsung Galaxy Note 10.1 Tablet which has 2560 x 1600 pixel, 299 ppi density super clear LCD display operating on Android version 4.4 system.

From our review of the literature, most researchers like AbdelDayem et al's, (2016), Fridman and Weber (2016), and Ali et al's, (2016) have designed their experiment scenario with guidelines that guide the user throughout the experiment in order to keep the collected raw data in a suitable region and reduce its roughness. However, in our experiment scenario, we did not put any restrictions on how the user performs the touch gestures. In our scenario, the user was free to perform the gestures as if he was using a real mobile application and performing a list of touch gestures. In our opinion, this is more realistic and gives us results that reflect a robust applicable model than most researches have done in their experiment scenarios.

We developed an Android application to enable the users to perform specific touch gestures, and to record the raw touch data in a structured form. Every user made around 10 touch sessions over a period of time spanning 2 months to avoid user adaptation to the experimental tasks. Users were to perform specific touch actions which we consider the most common touch gestures used in most of the mobile device applications. Users are asked to perform the following touch gestures: Tap, Flick, Long Press, Scroll Up, Scroll Down, Scroll Left, Scroll Right, Zoon in, Zoon out and Rotate. Figure Error*! No text of specified style in document.*5 shows a snapshot of the application used in our experiment that simulates user input actions. The performed gestures were either single-touch gestures, in which user uses only one finger to perform such as taps, scrolls, flicks etc., or multi-touch gestures, that the user has to use two or more fingers, like zoom in or zoom out, rotating etc.

Figure 5. Experiment mobile application sample snapshot

During the experiment, the tablet device recorded the users' touch raw data that represent several raw features: an event code (e.g., finger up, finger down, finger move, multi-touch), the absolute event time in milliseconds, and the device orientation. For each touching finger, we record the following data:

$$S_i = \{x_i, y_i, P_i, A_i, Oi\} \qquad (5)$$

where x_i, y_i are the finger position as x-and y-coordinates, P_i is the finger pressure on the touchscreen, A_i is the area of the touchscreen covered by the finger, and Oi is the screen orientation. All these are raw features that the Android system provides from its standard API.

The collected raw data is submitted to a database server to be analyzed and to extract the required features for our study in the next step. In the next sections, we will present the results of the experiments categorized into two directions. The stroke-level approach results are given first followed by the session-level approach results. Finally, we make a conclusion of both approaches. In each group of experiments, the features selection method and the classifier are varied.

Stroke-Level Model Feature Selection Results

The experiment results in the stroke-level model are divided into two parts; the first one presents the results of the features selection analysis to search the most effective features that can be used in the second part, which is the classification results part, where MATLAB ANN Toolbox is used to train the model according to the extracted features in the first part.

Table 5 shows the resulted data of applying the previously mentioned method in section 3.4.9 of selecting the most desirable features in stroke-level features which are extracted at the low level of single stroke. In that table, the absolute value of the sum of variances of each feature value of all users among all sessions are given that can be considered as the consistency value of the feature.

The second column shows the variance value of each feature among all sessions which can be considered as discrimination value of the feature. The other two columns represent the same information, but in a normalized form to be in the same range to create an overall view of these data.

Table 5 shows the overall view of summation of variances of each feature among all users' sessions in which smaller value means better feature consistency. Finally, we need to select the most desirable features which have an acceptable value of consistency and discrimination at the same time. The features that are more consistent than the other features are determined from these data by arranging the summation of variances in an ascending order. The most first features are the most consistence user features between the sessions, i.e. the most desirable features.

In our study, we found out that the best features in stroke-level features, according to the weighted features selection method, were the features related to the coordinates of the user touch actions, and the shape of the touch stroke trajectory such as: X-Coordinates, Y-Coordinates, Average Direction and Ratio of end-to-end line to length of trajectory. This behavior may be related to the size of the experiment device screen which gives every user the freedom to use the most suitable part of the screen.

However, in our study, we used all the 27 features shown in the table, but we assign a weight value ranged from 0 to 1 to each feature, according to its consistency and discrimination. This is achieved by computing the average value of the feature consistency and discrimination values to compute the weight of this feature according to Equation 6.

$$W_i = \frac{D_i + C_i}{2} \qquad (6)$$

Table 5. Stroke-level consistency discrimination values

Feature Description	Sum of Variances (Consistency)	Variance (Discrimination)	Normalized Sum of Variances	Normalized Variance
50% deviation from end-to-end line	0.08597607866	0.0017443867795	0	0.01892669
50% pairwise acceleration	0.12191647153	0.0035294891894	0.054216727	0.04306106
Mean Resultant Length	0.12521411032	0.0073703514352	0.059191274	0.094989056
80% deviation from end-to-end line	0.13456069189	0.0046514209368	0.07329076	0.058229443
20% pairwise acceleration	0.14206934727	0.0035347693435	0.084617701	0.043132447
20% deviation from end-to-end line	0.16722562492	0.0033399277953	0.122566396	0.040498213
Median Acceleration at first 5 points	0.19261333971	0.0034226791721	0.160864219	0.041617002
Stroke Duration	0.21250147927	0.0039212026484	0.190865834	0.048356979
Length of Trajectory	0.21683257970	0.0079892614752	0.197399376	0.103356646
No. of touch actions	0.22354377488	0.0044499277322	0.207523334	0.055505279
Median Velocity at last 3 points	0.22649064052	0.0069118974813	0.211968734	0.088790814
Average Velocity	0.26149607620	0.0003444712366	0.264775061	0
Mid-Stroke Pressure	0.27124661640	0.0172294676278	0.279483925	0.228283123
Largest Deviation from end-to-end line	0.28940424229	0.0094406059292	0.306875029	0.122978649
80% pairwise velocity	0.32438135857	0.0091010604295	0.359638636	0.118388034
80% pairwise acceleration	0.32438135857	0.0045256348739	0.359638636	0.05652883
Direct end-to-end distance	0.37424064676	0.0322362243687	0.434852266	0.431172672
50% pairwise velocity	0.41225286236	0.0177240850101	0.492194374	0.234970291
20% pairwise velocity	0.43066194058	0.0265467575918	0.519964798	0.354251765
Start-Y Coordinate	0.50603138353	0.0250682819510	0.633660953	0.334262952
Start-X Coordinate	0.51352087609	0.0426363109063	0.644958987	0.571780593
Mid-Stroke Area Covered	0.55119801564	0.0350609514825	0.701795627	0.469362644
End-X Coordinate	0.56432637849	0.0448502027826	0.721599997	0.601712145
End-Y Coordinate	0.64400412646	0.0322282084201	0.841795308	0.431064298
Average Direction	0.65768638319	0.0658071238084	0.862435237	0.885047201
Ratio of end-to-end line to length of Trajectory	0.70491614020	0.0703418607344	0.933682172	0.946356299
Direction of end-to-end line	0.74887838122	0.0743096253077	1	1

where W_i is the resulted weight of feature i, D_i is the discrimination normalized value of feature i and C_i is the consistency normalized value of feature i.

As an alternative, one can select a range of features according to the required model complexity, or use any suitable criteria to choose the features according to the application needs. Using principal component analysis (PCA) in dimensionality reduction results in choosing only 13 dimensions from the 27 dimensions of all the features.

STROKE-LEVEL CLASSIFICATION

In this section, we will consider two different classification algorithms; artificial neural network (ANN) and support vector machine (SVM).

Artificial Neural Network

In this section, we will dive deeply into the details of how we use the ANN tool to model our stroke-level and session-level classifiers and how we use the generated model in the identification process. We will also discuss the performance evaluation parameters.

We use an artificial neural network classifier to classify about 2903 input samples of 27 input features belonging to 10 mobile device users as we mentioned before. Our ANN consists of an input layer, a hidden layer and an output layer with sigmoid activation function (Activation Functions in Neural Networks, 2017) as shown in Figure6.

$$f(x) = \frac{1}{1 + e^{-x}} \tag{7}$$

Figure 6. The Artificial Neural Network Classifier Construction

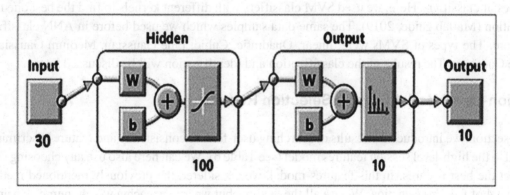

We used this kind of activation function as it has the property to be similar to the step function, but with the addition of a region of uncertainty. Sigmoid function is also very similar to the input/output relationship of biological neurons so it is used in most neural network applications. The main reason why we use sigmoid function is because it exists between (0 to 1). Therefore, it is especially used for models where we have to predict the probability as an output. Since the probability of anything exists only between the range of 0 and 1, sigmoid is the right choice.

We divide the input samples into three sets:

- 50% of the samples are used for training.
- 25% of the samples are used for validation to measure the network generalization, and to halt training when generalization stops improving.

- 25% for testing, which has no effect on training and so provides an independent measure of network performance during and after training.

A Scaled Conjugate Gradient (SCG) Backpropagation learning algorithm was used in the artificial neural network learning process. This algorithm provides the best performance and is fast convergence over other algorithms such as Levenberg Marquardt algorithm which consumes computing resources greedily (Matlab guide (2019)). In our work, we have tested different learning algorithms, however, the SCG backpropagation algorithm results were the best in performance and speed considering our experiment specifications and conditions.

We used ready built ANN Modeling tool presented by MATLAB MathWorks. We used a PC laptop equipped with Intel core i5 processor, 6GB of RAM and Nvidia Geforce 520m GPU with MATLAB 2017a version. It saves a lot of time implementing ANN, training and deploying. Neural Network toolbox in MATLAB presents an application with a graphical user interface in which every user can provide input samples and desired output samples easily by following some sequential steps to provide inputs, outputs, learning algorithm, and number of hidden neurons and also an activation function that is needed for activating every single neuron in the neural network.

Support Vector Machine

MATLAB MathWorks also provides a graphical user interface application to classify data using different types of classifiers. Here, we used SVM classifiers with different kernels to find the best one for our application (Matlab guide, 2019). The same data samples which we used before in ANN classifier are used here. The types of SVMs were: linear, Quadratic, Cubic, Fine Gaussian, Medium Gaussian and Coarse Gaussian. The results of the classification and identification will be discussed later.

Session-Level Model Feature Selection Results

In this section, we introduce the results of searching user-feature consistency and feature-discrimination applied to the high-level session features model (see Table 6). We can here also use any choosing criteria to select the best features. In this features model, we considered the previously mentioned method in section 4.4 of features selection. We use all the features but we assign each a weight number to amplify the effect of the best features and damp the effect of the worst features in the classification stage.

In session-level model, the best features were related to the user behavior in multi-touch strokes mainly Zoom-in and Zoom-out timing. Also, flicking speed was the best feature. This behavior may be due to the different hand geometry between the different users in our experiment. When we used principal component analysis in MATLAB, these 35 features were reduced to 21 features; in other words, PCA algorithms transferred data of 35 dimensions to new 21 dimensions or spaces to reduce complexity and remove redundant information in these features.

Session-Level Classification

An artificial neural network classifier was also employed to classify the input samples of all the touch sessions. The same ANN construction shown in Figure 6 was used with 35 input features instead of 27 input features. The input samples were divided randomly into:

Table 6. Session-level consistency discrimination values

Feature	Sum of Variances (Consistency)	Variance (Discrimination)	Normalized Sum of Variances	Normalized Variance
AverageTapPressure	0.935454918	0.0317629	0	0.370576219
RotationAvragePressureAtFocalPoint	0.941972536	0.030645399	0.016246158	0.352349274
ScrllftAverageVelocityAtLast3Points	0.970368406	0.022546893	0.087027202	0.220258995
ScrlupAverageVelocityAtLast3Points	0.972349357	0.018102023	0.091965025	0.147761164
ScrllftAverageDistance	0.976429909	0.03102865	0.102136424	0.35860027
ScrlupAverageDirection	0.9782688	0.036290528	0.106720141	0.44442387
ZinDistanceBetweenLiftingPoints	0.982755983	0.03430992	0.11790513	0.412119261
ScrllftAverageVelocity	0.988857071	0.032667095	0.133113024	0.385324046
TapTime	1.000697871	0.037244976	0.162628027	0.459991346
FlickingAverageDirection	1.007975099	0.023170917	0.180767629	0.230437107
ScrlupAverageVelocity	1.008596165	0.028823075	0.182315731	0.322626349
ScrlrghtAverageDistance	1.012578397	0.038585207	0.192242053	0.481851117
ScrldwnAverageVelocity	1.018875299	0.009639019	0.207938043	0.009725758
ScrldwnAverageDirection	1.021380252	0.016335433	0.214182021	0.118947286
ZoutZoomingTime	1.024730234	0.043670717	0.222532363	0.564798075
ZinZoomingTime	1.03930496	0.031730664	0.258862093	0.370050435
ScrlrghtAverageDirection	1.04155984	0.009042729	0.264482726	0
ZinDistanceBetweenLandingPoints	1.050980586	0.029852361	0.287965375	0.339414467
ScrlrghtAverageVelocity	1.052226046	0.039409691	0.291069874	0.495298823
ScrlupAverageDistance	1.055615215	0.027538978	0.299517896	0.301682149
LongTapAveragePressure	1.056163214	0.024239621	0.300883867	0.247868151
RotationAverageRadius	1.06462446	0.033319379	0.321974815	0.395963092
ScrldwnAverageDistance	1.079791013	0.021464011	0.359779765	0.202596702
ScrldwnAverageVelocityAtLast3Points	1.099246635	0.020324903	0.408275875	0.184017338
ScrlrghtAverageVelocityAtLast3Points	1.104491914	0.026062204	0.421350534	0.2775953
ZinTwoLeftingLatency	1.11474821	0.021940877	0.446915919	0.210374601
ZoutDistanceBetweenLiftingPoints	1.122617174	0.035174115	0.466530513	0.426214671
TapMaxDistance	1.125634365	0.043033319	0.474051323	0.554401827
ZoutDistanceBetweenLandingPoints	1.142329203	0.045892838	0.515665757	0.601041869
ScrllftAverageDirection	1.184228311	0.070353115	0.620105684	1
AverageTapArea	1.199902944	0.054531073	0.659177101	0.741935371
ZoutTwoLandingLatency	1.233478428	0.013970284	0.742869124	0.080370641
FlickingAverageVelocity	1.240893604	0.027310432	0.761352583	0.297954461
ZoutTwoLeftingLatency	1.253710473	0.052696271	0.793300586	0.712008925
ZinTwoLandingLatency	1.336633942	0.048222567	1	0.639040798

- 65% for training.
- 15% for validation
- 20% for testing.

We have divided the data samples in this manner because we have a few number of samples in the session level model.

PERFORMANCE EVALUATION AND RESULTS DISCUSSION

In this section, we introduce the results of our experiments using both classification and identification algorithms; ANN and SVM with both features selection methods: weighted features using discrimination and consistency values and principal component analysis (PCA) method.

Artificial Neural Network

Figure 7. Histogram of Session-Level Classification Error

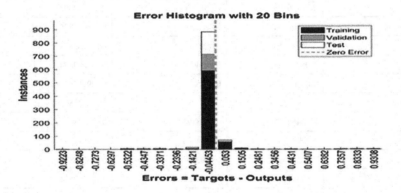

After performing 10 training sessions in the stroke-level features model, we have obtained 14% - 16% misclassification error of training samples and 25% - 30% misclassification error of testing samples, while in the session-level features model, we have obtained 0% misclassification error of training samples and 16% - 20% misclassification error of testing samples. Using this session-level features model, we got more efficient classifier than we had in the stroke-level features model.

Figure 7 shows the error histogram of the classifier training of session-level model. This figure shows the number of samples that result in a specific error value.

According to Figure 7, the training error of samples majority is about 0.04 and overall accuracy about 93% according to the confusion matrix shown in Figure 8. Confusion Matrix that shows the target class of every training sample and the actual resulted output class the classifier provides the diagonal of the matrix shows the number of the correctly classified samples in the training session.

As seen from Figure 8, the session-level features give better classification accuracy according to the values of the diagonal cells in the confusion matrix. It also can be seen that the classifier reached its best validation performance 0.003 at training epoch 31 which means that the classifier training algorithm converges well, see Figure which shows the relation between the number of epochs and the validation performance of the three sets of data: training, test and validation. Generally, the error reduces after more epochs of training, but might start to increase on the validation dataset as the network starts overfitting the training data. In the default setup, the training stops after six consecutive increases in validation error, and the best performance is taken from the epoch with the lowest validation error.

Figure 8. Confusion Matrix of Session-level Classifier for 10 Users

In the context of learning, backpropagation is commonly used by the gradient descent optimization algorithm to adjust the weight of neurons by calculating the gradient of the loss function. The magnitude of the gradient and the number of validation checks in Figure are used to terminate the training. The gradient will become very small as the training reaches the minimum performance while the number of validation checks represents the number of successive iterations that the validation performance fails to decrease. Accordingly, from this figure, it can be seen that we obtained the most accurate classifier considering our experiment specifications.

Figure 9. Validation Performance

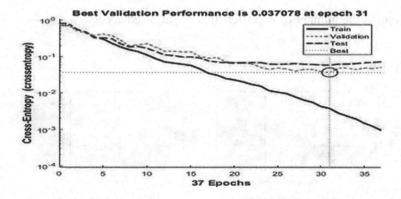

Figure 10. Validation checks

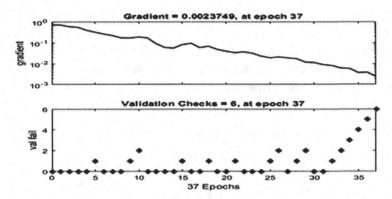

The most commonly used metrics to evaluate the performance of a touch-based biometrics system or any other biometrics system are False Rejection Rate (FRR) and False Acceptance Rate (FAR) (Abdel-Dayem et al's, 2017). FRR is the percentage of legitimate users who are labeled as imposters and denied access. FRR denotes the system's specificity. FAR is the percentage of imposters who are allowed access to the system. FAR denotes the system's sensitivity. The following formulas are used to calculate FAR and FRR (AbdelDayem et al's, 2017).

$$FRR = \frac{Number\ of\ False\ Rejects}{Total\ Number\ of\ Legitimate\ Match\ Attempts} \tag{8}$$

where *False Rejects* is the number of legitimate users that are denied access.

$$FAR = \frac{Number\ of\ False\ Accepts}{Total\ Number\ of\ Imposter\ Match\ Attempts} \tag{9}$$

where *False Accepts* is the number of imposters that are allowed access.

Figure 11. Example of identification confusion matrix

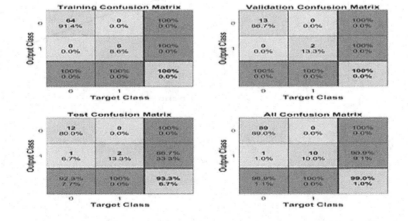

Figure 11 shows the confusion matrices of one of the users. FAR is computed by dividing the number of "0" class samples that was verified that "1" class by the total number of "0" class samples. Using the same way, we can compute FRR by dividing the number of "1" class samples that was verified as "0" class by the total number of "1" class samples.

Support Vector Machine

A support vector machine (SVM) classifier was used in both stroke-level and session-level models. The accuracy values are summarized in Table 7. From the table, we can notice that the cubic SVM gives the best accuracy in case of the stroke-level model, but in the session-level model the quadratic SVM gives the highest accuracy value.

Table 7. Support vector machine classifier accuracy.

SVM	Accuracy	
	Stroke-Level	Session-Level
Linear	56.1%	69%
Quadratic	73.3%	75%
Cubic	75.2%	69%
Fine Gaussian	65.3%	27%
Medium Gaussian	67.3%	70%
Coarse Gaussian	47.2%	57%

It has been found, through the experiments of the two proposed models, that the stroke-level and session-level models resulted in FAR about 0.8% and 0%; respectively and as we think these results reflect more secured model. However, in terms of FRR, the session-level model gives us better rate than the stroke-level model. In the session-level model, FRR is about 5% where in the stroke-level model it reached 40% considering the ANN classifier.

Table 8. Overall results summary.

Results Summary							
	ANN				SVM		
Features No.	Stroke-Level		Session-Level		Stroke-Level		Session-Level	
	(27/27)	PCA (13/27)	(35/35)	PCA (21/35)	(27/27)	PCA (13/27)	(35/35)	PCA (21/35)
Classification Accuracy	70-85%	72.6-76.5%	90-94%	83-94%	75%	72%	74%	63%
Identification Accuracy	92.25%	94.57%	97%	98.1%	95.8%	94.23%	95.3%	93.2%
FAR	0.85%	1.22%	0%	0.88%	2.22%	3.2%	3.31%	2.7%
FRR	57.13%	43.18%	5%	11%	36.22%	53.4%	44%	42%

On the other side, considering SVM classifier, the stroke-level and session-level models resulted in FAR equal to 2% and 3% respectively, while the FRR was 36% and 44%, respectively. But when we used PCA in both models; stroke-level and session-level, we obtained a higher FRR value about 53% and 43% in stroke-level and session-level, respectively. All these results are summarized in Table 8.

CONCLUSION AND FUTURE WORK

In this paper, we have presented a framework for continuous user authentication on touchscreen with the aim to identify any misuse of the machine by an imposter. Our study proved that using session-level features model, that can be extracted at touch session-level, is more efficient to use in classifying the touch device users using the ANN classifier. We have obtained better performance and identification accuracy considering our experiment conditions and specifications. In addition to that, in stroke-level features model the imposter user could simulate the stroke behavior in somehow, however, he can't simulate all the strokes among all touch session as it lasts for a long time of work on the device. So, this model is strongly recommended especially when we have large number of training samples, where the accuracy of classification will be very satisfying.

The results of using SVM classifier are not satisfying due to the small number of samples in session-level model. According to using PCA in both features model using ANN and SVM classification algorithms, we found that reducing features could affect positively the model complexity and dimensionality reduction, but it had a negative effect on the classification accuracy and FRR.

Different operating systems and different touchscreen sizes with different resolutions and pixel density can be considered in the future work to converge the concept to be applicable in all devices with satisfied performance and efficiently. Also, other machine learning algorithms and tools such as deep learning, k-Nearest Neighbor, Native Bayes or decision trees can be used to obtain better performance and higher accuracy. New trends in mobile application development framework like Xamarin cross platform and Cordova framework can be used to build authentication framework.

REFERENCES

AbdelDayem, M., Hemeda, H., & Sarhan, A. (2016). Enhanced User Authentication through Keystroke Biometrics for Short-Text and Long-Text Inputs. Artificial Intelligence and Machine Learning Journal, ICGST LLC, Delaware, USA, 16(1).

Activation Functions in Neural Networks. (2017). Retrieved from https://towardsdatascience.com/activation-functions-neural-networks-1cbd9f8d91d6

Ali, L., Monaco, J. V., Tappert, C. C., & Qiu, M. (2016). Keystroke Biometric Systems for User Authentication. *Journal of Signal Processing Systems, Springer, 86*(2-3), 175–190. doi:10.100711265-016-1114-9

Android Developer. (2018). Retrieved from https://developer.android.com/reference/android/view/

Antal, M., Bokor, Z., & Szab'o, L. Z. (2015). Information Revealed from Scrolling Interactions on Mobile Devices. *Pattern Recognition Letters, 56*, 7–13. doi:10.1016/j.patrec.2015.01.011

Bimbot, F., Bonastre, J. F., Fredouille, C., Gravier, G., Magrin-Chagnolleau, I., Meignier, S., ... Reynolds, D. A. (2004). A Tutorial on Text-Independent Speaker Verification. *EURASIP Journal on Applied Signal Processing*, 430–451.

Bonastre, J. F., Bimbot, F., Boe, L. J., Cambell, J. P., Reynolds, D. A., & Magrin-Chagnolleau, I. (2003). Person Authentication by Voice: A Need for Caution. *Proceedings of Eurospeech*.

Budiu, R. (2015). Mobile User Experience: Limitations and Strengths. Retrieved from https://www.nngroup.com/articles/mobile-ux/

Buriro, A., Crispo, B., Del Frari, F., Klardie, J., & Wrona, K. (2016). Itsme: Multi-modal and Unobtrusive Behavioural User Authentication for Smartphones. *Proceedings of the 9th Conference on passwords (PASSWORDS 2015)*, Springer, 45–61. 10.1007/978-3-319-29938-9_4

Clancy, T. C., Kiyavash, N., & Lin, D. J. (2003). Secure Smartcard Based Fingerprint Authentication. *Proceedings of the 2003 ACM SIGMM workshop on Biometrics methods and applications*, 45–52. 10.1145/982507.982516

Conti, M., Zachia-Zlatea, I., & Crispo, B. (2011). Mind How You Answer Me! Transparently Authenticating the User of a Smartphone When Answering or Placing A Call. *Proceedings of the 6th ACM Symposium on Information, Computer and Communications Security*, 249-259. Hong Kong, China.

Eberz, S., & Rasmussen, K. B. (2017). Evaluating Behavioral Biometrics for Continuous Authentication: Challenges and Metrics. *Proceedings of the 2017 ACM on Asia Conference on Computer and Communications Security*, 386-399. Abu Dhabi, United Arab Emirates. 10.1145/3052973.3053032

Eljetlawi, M. (2010). Graphical Password: Existing Recognition Based Graphical Password Usability. *Proceedings of the IEEE 6th Conference on Networked Computing (INC)*. IEEE.

Feng, T., Liu, Z., Kwon, K. A., Shi, W., Carbunar, B., Jiang, Y., & Nguyen, N. (2012). Continuous Mobile Authentication Using Touchscreen Gestures. *Proceedings of the 2012 IEEE International Conference on Technologies for Homeland Security (HST 2012)*, Waltham, MA, 451–456. 10.1109/THS.2012.6459891

Fierrez, J., Morales, A., Vera-Rodriguez, R., & Camacho, D. (2018). Multiple Classifiers in Biometrics. Part 2: Trends and Challenges. *Information Fusion, 44*, 103–112. doi:10.1016/j.inffus.2017.12.005

Fierrez, J., Pozo, A., Martinez-Diaz, M., Galbally, J., & Morales, A. (2018). Benchmarking Touchscreen Biometrics for mobile Authentication. *IEEE Transactions on Information Forensics and Security, 13*(11), 1556–6013. doi:10.1109/TIFS.2018.2833042

Findlater, L., Wobbrock, J. O., & Wigdor, D. (2011). Typing on fiat Glass: Examining Ten-finger Expert Typing Patterns on Touch Surfaces. *Proceedings of the 2011 Annual Conference on Human Factors in computing systems, CHI '11*, 2453–2462. New York, NY. ACM. 10.1145/1978942.1979301

Frank, M., Biedert, R., Ma, E., Martinovic, I., & Song, D. (2013). Touchalytics: On the Applicability of Touchscreen Input as a Behavioral Biometric for Continuous Authentication. *IEEE Transactions on Information Forensics and Security, 8*(1), 136–148. doi:10.1109/TIFS.2012.2225048

Fridman, L., & Weber, S. (2016). Active Authentication on Mobile Devices via Stylometry Application Usage, Web Browsing, and GPS Location. *IEEE Systems Journal*, 513–521.

Gafurov, D., Snekkenes, E., & Buvarp, T. E. (2006). Robustness of Biometric Gait Authentication Against Impersonation Attacks. *Proceedings of the Workshop on the Move to Meaningful Internet Systems, ser. Lecture Notes in Computer Science, 4277/2006*, 479–488. 10.1007/11915034_71

Gianni, F., Mirko, M., & Ludovico, B. (2017). A Multi-Biometric System for Continuous Student Authentication in E-learning Platforms. *Pattern Recognition Letters, Elsevier, 113*, 83–92.

Hu, W., Wu, X., & Wei, G. (2010). The Security Analysis of Graphical Passwords. *Proceedings of the IEEE International Conference on Communications and Intelligence Information Security (ICCIIS)*, China. IEEE.

Introducing, J. S. O. N. (2018). Retrieved from https://www.json.org/

Jain, A., Ross, A., & Nandakumar, K. (2011). *Introduction to Biometrics*. Springer Science & Business Media. doi:10.1007/978-0-387-77326-1

Jain, A., Ross, A., & Pankanti, S. (2006). A Tool for Information Security. *IEEE Transactions on Information Forensics and Security, 1*(2), 125–143. doi:10.1109/TIFS.2006.873653

Jain, A., Ross, A., & Prabhakar, S. (2004). An Introduction to Biometric Recognition. *IEEE Transactions on Circuits and Systems for Video Technology, 14*(1), 4–20. doi:10.1109/TCSVT.2003.818349

Jeanjaitrong, N., & Bhattarakoso, P. (2013). Feasibility Study on authentication Based Keystroke Dynamics over Touch-Screen Devices. *Proceedings of the International Symposium on Communications and Information Technology (ISCIT)*. 10.1109/ISCIT.2013.6645856

Jouini, M., & Rabai, L. (2016). A Security Framework for Secure Cloud Computing Environments. *International Journal of Cloud Applications and Computing, 6*(3), 32–44. doi:10.4018/IJCAC.2016070103

Karnan, M., Akila, M., & Krishnaraj, N. (2011). Biometric Personal Authentication Using Keystroke Dynamics: A Review. *Applied Soft Computing, 11*(2), 1565–1573. doi:10.1016/j.asoc.2010.08.003

Kenny, P., Ouellet, P., Dehak, N., Gupta, V., & Dumouchel, P. (2008). A Study of Inter-Speaker Variability in Speaker Verification. *IEEE Transactions on Audio, Speech, and Language Processing, 16*(5), 980–988. doi:10.1109/TASL.2008.925147

Khan, H., Atwater, A., & Hengartner, U. (2014). Itus: An Implicit Authentication Framework for Android. *Proceedings of the 20th Annual International Conference on Mobile computing and networking*, 507–518. ACM. 10.1145/2639108.2639141

Kim, J., Kim, H., & Kang, P. (2017). Keystroke Dynamics-Based User Authentication Using Freely Typed Text Based on User-Adaptive Feature Extraction and Novelty Detection. *Applied Soft Computing*.

Kumar, R., Kundu, P. P., & Phoha, V. V. (2018). Continuous Authentication Using One-Class Classifiers and Their Fusion. *Proceedings of the IEEE International Conference on Identity, Security, and Behavior Analysis*. 10.1109/ISBA.2018.8311467

Kumar, R., Phoha, V. V., & Serwadda, A. (2016). Continuous Authentication of Smartphone Users by Fusing Typing Swiping and Phone Movement Patterns. *Proceedings of the IEEE International Conference on Biometrics: Theory, Applications, and Systems (BTAS)*, 1–8. 10.1109/BTAS.2016.7791164

Lever, J., Krzywinski, M., & Altman, N. (2017). Principal Component Analysis. *Nature Methods*, *14*(7), 641–642. doi:10.1038/nmeth.4346

Lin, C. C., Chang, C. C., & Liang, D. (2013). A Novel Non-Intrusive User Authentication Method Based on touchscreen of Smartphones. *Proceedings of the 2013 IEEE International Symposium on Biometrics and Security Technologies*, 212–216. 10.1109/ISBAST.2013.37

Mahbub, U., Sarkar, S., Patel, V. M., & Chellappa, R. (2016). Active User Authentication for Smartphones: A Challenge Data Set and Benchmark Results. *Proceedings of the IEEE International Conference on Biometrics: Theory, Applications and Systems (BTAS)*. 10.1109/BTAS.2016.7791155

Mahfouz, A., Mahmoud, T. M., & Sharaf Eldin, A. (2017). A Survey on Behavioral Biometric Authentication on Smartphones. *Journal of Information Security and Applications, Elsevier*, *37*, 28–37. doi:10.1016/j.jisa.2017.10.002

Mantyjarvi, J., Lindholm, M., Vildjiounaite, E., Makela, S. M., & Allisto, H. (2005). Identifying Users of Portable Devices from Gait Pattern with Accelerometers. *Proceedings of the IEEE International Conference on Acoustics, Speech, and Signal Processing*, *2*, 973–976.

Mazhelis, O., & Puuronen, S. (2007). A Framework for Behavior-Based Detection of User Substitution in a Mobile Context. *Computers & Security*, *26*(2), 154–176. doi:10.1016/j.cose.2006.08.010

Mondal, S., & Bours, P. (2015). Swipe Gesture Based Continuous Authentication for Mobile Devices. *Proceedings of the IAPR International Conference on Biometrics*. 10.1109/ICB.2015.7139110

Murmuria, R., Stavrou, A., Barbara, D., & Fleck, D. (2015). Continuous Authentication on Mobile Devices Using Power Consumption, Touch Gestures and Physical Movement of Users. *Proceedings of the International Workshop on Recent Advances in Intrusion Detection*, 405–424. Springer. 10.1007/978-3-319-26362-5_19

Nakamura, K., Kono, K., Ito, Y., & Babaguchi, N. (2012). Tablet Owner Authentication Based on Behavioral Characteristics of Multi-touch Actions. *Proceedings of the IEEE 21st International Conference on Pattern Recognition*, Tsukuba, Japan. IEEE.

Neverova, N., Wolf, C., Lacey, G., Fridma, L., Chandaran, D., Barbello, B., & Taylor, G. (2016). Learning Human Identity from Motion Patterns. *IEEE Access: Practical Innovations, Open Solutions*, *4*, 1810–1820. doi:10.1109/ACCESS.2016.2557846

O'Connell, B. M., & Walker, K. R. (2017). User - Touchscreen Interaction Analysis Authentication System. *US Patent 9,817,963*.

Olakanmi, O. O., & Dada, A. (2019). An Efficient Privacy-preserving Approach for Secure Verifiable Outsourced Computing on Untrusted Platforms. *International Journal of Cloud Applications and Computing*, *9*(2), 79–98. doi:10.4018/IJCAC.2019040105

Ouaguid, A., Abghour, N., & Ouzzif, M. (2018). A Novel Security Framework for Managing Android Permissions Using Blockchain Technology. *International Journal of Cloud Applications and Computing*, *8*(1), 55–79. doi:10.4018/IJCAC.2018010103

Perera, P., & Patel, V. M. (2018). Efficient and Low Latency Detection of Intruders in Mobile Active Authentication. *IEEE Transactions on Information Forensics and Security, 13*(6), 1392–1405. doi:10.1109/TIFS.2017.2787995

Ross, A., Nandakumar, K., & Jain, A. K. (2008). Introduction to Multibiometrics. Handbook of Biometrics, Springer, 271–292.

Serwadda, A., Phoha, V. V., & Wang, Z. (2013). Which Verifiers Work? A Benchmark Evaluation of Touch-based Authentication Algorithms. *Proceedings of the 6th IEEE International Conference on Biometrics: Theory, Applications and Systems (BTAS)*, 1–8. 10.1109/BTAS.2013.6712758

Shen, C., Zhang, Y., Guan, X., & Maxion, R. A. (2016). Performance Analysis of Touch-interaction Behavior for Active Smartphone Authentication. *IEEE Transactions on Information Forensics and Security, 11*(3), 498–513. doi:10.1109/TIFS.2015.2503258

Shi, E., Niu, Y., Jakobsson, M., & Chow, R. (2011). Implicit Authentication Through Learning User Behavior. *Proceedings of the Information Security Conference, Lecture Notes in Computer Science*, 99–113. Berlin, Germany: Springer, 6531.

Sitova, Z., Sedenka, J. J., Yang, J., Peng, G., Zhou, G., Gasti, P., & Balagani, K. (2016). Hmog: New Behavioral Biometric Features for Continuous Authentication of Smartphone Users, Information Forensics and Security. *IEEE Transactions on Information Forensics and Security, 11*(5), 877–892. doi:10.1109/TIFS.2015.2506542

What is Windows Communication Foundation. (2017). Retrieved from https://docs.microsoft.com/en-us/dotnet/framework/wcf/whats-wcf

Xu, H., Zhou, Y., & Lyu, M. R. (2014). Towards Continuous and Passive Authentication via Touch Biometrics: An Experimental Study on Smartphones. *Proceedings of the International Symposium on Usable Privacy and Security (SOUPS)*, 187–198. Menlo Park, CA.

Yampolskiy, R. V., & Govindaraju, V. (2008). Behavioural Biometrics: A Survey and Classification. *International Journal of Biometrics, 1*(1), 81–113. doi:10.1504/IJBM.2008.018665

Zhang, H., Patel, V. M., Fathy, M., & Chellappa, R. (2015). Touch Gesture-based Active User Authentication Using Dictionaries. *Proceedings of the IEEE Winter Conference on Applications of Computer Vision*, 207–214. 10.1109/WACV.2015.35

Zhao, X., Feng, T., Shi, W., & Kakadiaris, I. A. (2014). Mobile user authentication using statistical touch dynamics images. *IEEE Transactions on Information Forensics and Security, 9*(11), 1780–1789. doi:10.1109/TIFS.2014.2350916

ADDITIONAL READING

Buchoux, A., & Clarke, N. (2008). Deployment of Keystroke Analysis on a Smartphone. *Proceedings of the 6th Australian Information Security Management Conference*, 40 – 47.

Centeno, M. P., Guan, Y., & Van Moorse, A. (2018). Mobile Based Continuous Authentication Using Deep Features. *Proceedings of the 2nd International ACM Workshop on Embedded and Mobile Deep Learning*, 19-24. Munich, Germany. 10.1145/3212725.3212732

Clarke, N., & Furnell, S. (2007). Authenticating Mobile Phone Users Using Keystroke Analysis. *International Journal of Information Security*, 6(1), 1–14. doi:10.100710207-006-0006-6

De Luca, A., Hang, A., Von Zezschwitz, E., & Hussmann, H. (2015). I Feel Like I'm Taking Selfies All Day!: Towards Understanding Biometric Authentication on Smartphones. *Proceedings of the 33rd Annual ACM Conference on Human Factors in Computing Systems*, 1411–1414. 10.1145/2702123.2702141

Li, Y., Hu, H., Zhou, G., & Deng, S. (2018). Sensor-Based Continuous Authentication Using Cost-Effective Kernel Ridge Regression. *IEEE Access: Practical Innovations, Open Solutions*, 6, 32554–32565. doi:10.1109/ACCESS.2018.2841347

Neguyen, T. V., Sae-Bae, N., & Memon, N. (2017). Authentication Using Finger Drawn Pen on Touch Devices. *Computers & Security*, 66, 115–128. doi:10.1016/j.cose.2017.01.008

Quirk, A. J., Chao, C. Y., Lingerfelt, D. D. L., & Whitt, W. D. (2018). Continuous monitoring of fingerprint signature on a mobile touchscreen for identity management. *US Patent 9,985,787, 2018*.

Song, Y., Cai, Z., & Zhang, Z. L. (2017). Multi-touch Authentication Using Hand Geometry and Behavioral Information. *Proceedings of the IEEE International Symposium on Security and Privacy*. 10.1109/SP.2017.54

Suthaharan, S. (2016). Machine Learning Models and Algorithms for Big Data Classification. *Integrated Series in Information Systems*, 36.

KEY TERMS AND DEFINITIONS

Keystroke: A keystroke means the pressing of a key either on a keyboard or on a touchscreen.

Keystroke Dynamics: Measurements of the speed, frequency of characters, other data related to pressing a key.

Principal component analysis (PCA): It is an algorithm to simplify the complexity in high- dimensional data while retaining trends and patterns by transforming the data into fewer dimensions, which act as summaries of features.

Single-touch and Multi-touch Stroke: A stroke is a sequence of touch data that begins with touching the screen and ends with lifting the finger. A single-touch means touching a single point on the touchscreen. A multi-touch means touching multiple points on the touchscreen to achieve a task.

Traditional authentication schemes: Conventional methods of verification of the legitimacy of the system user, i.e. password, pin code or graphical.

Chapter 14
Design and Implementation of Visual Blockchain With Merkle Tree

Rui Hu

https://orcid.org/0000-0003-0266-4348
Auckland University of Technology, New Zealand

Wei Qi Yan
Auckland University of Technology, New Zealand

ABSTRACT

Although our communities are paying extensive attention to the blockchain technology, it is still far away from realistic applications. Thus, this red-hot technology could be understood and employed for visual applications. Authors focus on online videos that collect sufficient user clicks owning to the high demand every day. When people watch the videos of TV drama episodes in an online website, they often need to exactly organise the playlists in ascending or descending order. However, video websites such as YouTube can't provide this service due to multiple reasons. This chapter creates a private blockchain for these video websites and applies Merkle tree to store the sorted videos in the chain. A sorted playlist has been created in the video website. Getting out of the box of video search so as to provide a quick video ranking solution is authors' main task. Sorting results are evaluated by using edit distance.

INTRODUCTION

With virus popularity of the Internet, it has brought much convenience to people in eliminating geographical restrictions and improving efficiency. Internet users have gradually formed a network-based life circle (Li, et al., 2018). The users spent at least one third of their daytime online, we have the observations that in various mainstream online video websites, the users have the following intentions amid watching videos (Wang, et al., 2018). First, they would like to question the authenticity of the video, suspect the falsification; they need to repeat the search for multiple times to get the target video; third, while playing

DOI: 10.4018/978-1-7998-2701-6.ch014

the current video, if there is not video episode to be played in the playlist or if they desire to go back to the previous episode, they will consume too much time repeating the same operation.

On the other hand, the decentralized ledger, blockchain, was invented by Satoshi Nakamoto which can effectively figure out the public's predicaments related to these existing issues of video search (Aste, Tasca & Matteo, 2017). At present, the research work of online video search mainly focuses on the follows:

- Comprehensive analysis based on preferences, habits, and frequency from the operators who would like to watch online videos. All statistical data is not only obtained from a single video platform, but also aggregated from the cross-platform ones (Zhou, et al., 2018).
- Online video streaming supplies users with the service including sorted advertisements, games, and others; these are results based on the users' behaviors (Hasan, Jha, & Liu, 2018) . Meanwhile, a user who frequently browses online videos will be recommended to watch special videos based on accurate analysis of this user's preferences (Tan, et al., 2018).
- As the Internet covers these growing fields, online video platforms are not only limited in a PC system, they have been already transferred to mobile device systems; the statistics of energy consumption are calculated by using the changes (Zhang, et al., 2018).

In this paper, we will present the related work and our design. Our experiments and resultant analysis as well as the discussions will be followed. Our conclusion and future work will be remarked at the end of this paper.

RELATED WORK

Nowadays, YouTube for video indexing is mainly divided into two parts, recall and sorting. As shown in Figure 1, the first green block represents the recall algorithm, which can help the recommendation system to filter hundreds of videos from millions of video resources. Additionally, other recall sources can be added except the recall algorithm used with deep learning; these resources will be transferred to the next part (Wang, et al., 2015). Probably due to the large amount of computation, it is impossible and hardly inevitable to use all features of the recall algorithm; thus, the recall algorithm only takes use of users behavior and scene characteristics (Sedhain, et al., 2015). The ranking algorithm takes advantage of more features, calculates a score for each candidate video, and ranks the scores from high to low. In this way, dozens of objects will be filtered from hundreds of videos (Davidson, et al. 2010). The offline indicator and the online AB test were applied to evaluate the algorithm, AB test was set as the main evaluation index.

The research outcomes based on blockchain show it is mainly concentrated on the following two directions:

- The development of cryptocurrency platform depends on blockchain generates such a forum to enlarge the influence of this cryptocurrency and eventually escalate the real value of this cryptocurrency (Kugler, 2018) .
- A variety of applications related to blockchain are developed, the ranges of these applications are widely employed in game, finance, auction, and bidding etc. (Rosa & Rothenberg, 2018).

Figure 1. Recommendation system architecture

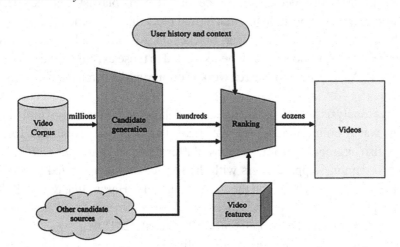

We have noticed that research work related to online video streaming mainly focuses on big data analysis and sorts the users with the purpose of recommending advertisements or videos. In this paper, we combine blockchain with traditional online video systems, deal with the problem of disordered playlist during video playing with online video websites.

OUR DESIGN

For the purpose of saving costs and improving efficiency, this paper will adopt the method of creating a private chain for testing. Although the demand for block expansion is huge, there are a multitude of organizations in the world conducting relevant research, there is not much progress, because everyone considers that expanding the capacity of the block itself will delay the transaction rate. There is a delay in the entire blockchain (Dai, et al., 2018).

In this paper, we fully take account of the data written into the blockchain while considering the transaction of the blockchain. We need to introduce the idea of Merkle tree; if it exceeds this capacity, it is cut to ensure that the maximum size of each data does not exceed the space, then we hash the two, form a root hash value, and write the root hash value into the block to achieve permanent storage on the data chain (Badra, Borghol, 2018).

Figure 2 illustrates the design method, there are also a lot of original files that need to be stored in the chain. Therefore, one of the files is split into eight parts and hashed separately to generate the leaf nodes of Merkle tree. According to the data structure, a unique root is finally generated. The root hash is produced correspondingly and saved on the chain. Once the root hash is corrupted, its data will be permanently saved and cannot be tampered. This ensures that uniqueness of the original data.

At the same time, unlike the idea of preliminary design, we no longer store the original data locally, but instead put the eight pieces of data after it has been split into a P2P network (Li, Wu, & Chen, 2018). Each node can be chosen to save one or more pieces of data, we assume that each node can only be saved individually (Chen, Li, Li, & Zhang, 2017).

Figure 2. Our designed method

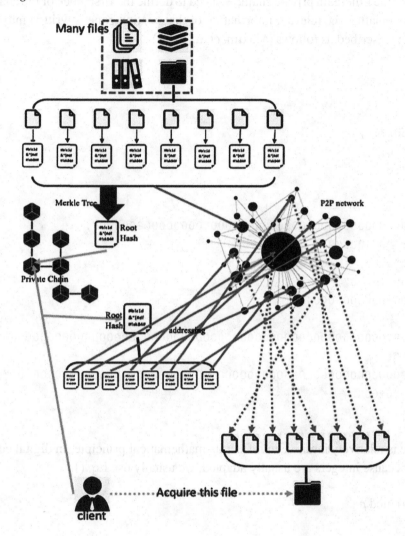

When a consumer needs to retrieve the document after a period, the following operations are performed. The client queries private chain for the related root hash stored at that time; the root hash branches downward obtain the hash value of the leaf node corresponding to the original file and then utilize its addressing attribute to index the P2P network. Because the hash value has a one-to-one correspondence with the file, the split file of the original file is found; finally, the full file can be composed.

EXPERIMENTS

In this paper, considering the incompleteness of the underlying technology of Bitcoin, we will optimize the current relatively wide-ranging and Turing-complete Ethereum to build a private chain for the purpose of installation and debugging (Gramoli & Staples, 2018).

Before running the Ethereum private chain, we need to define the first block of the chain, which is the genesis block. Hereinafter, the relevant information of the creation zone is written into a JSON format configuration file, described as follows (Maxim, et al., 2018).

```
{
"config":{
"chainID":1234,
"homesteadBlock":0,
"eip155Blcok":0,
"eip158Block":0
}
"alloc": {},
"coinbase":"0x0000000000000000000000000000000000000000",
"difficulty": "0x4000",
"extraData": "0x0",
"gasLimit":"0x2fefd8",
"nonce":"0x0000000000000042",
"mixhash":
"0x0000000000000000000000000000000000000000000000000000000000000000",
"parentHash":"
0x0000000000000000000000000000000000000000000000000000000000000000",
"timestamp": "0x00"
}
```

Elliptic curve is relatively intuitive to reflect its mathematical principle. In digital currency encryption algorithm, because integers are usually adapted, we usually use Eq. (1)

$$y^2 = (x^3 + ax + b) \bmod p \tag{1}$$

where $(0, p)$ is the interval of y^2.

Compared to DSA based on RSA cryptography, the length of public key required in digital signatures can be greatly reduced (Wang, He & Ji, 2017). As an example, we propose a digital signature with a security level of 80 bits, the public key length based on ECDSA is almost twice of the security level, the length of required public key of the RSA under the same security level is at least 1024. The length of the signature generated by the algorithm based on either ECDSA or RSA is 320 bits; thus, the advantage of ECDSA related to RSA is obvious.

We will apply this technology to tackle video data as shown in Figure 3. We parse the video data, considering that the nature of videos is composed of one frame in the order of time sequence and ensure the efficiency of transmission and the quality of transmission, we split the video in equal duration. The original video data is equally divided by its size, we set the last one which cannot reach the standard size as the remaining part. Then, the hash values are computed from each video, we save these hash values and the corresponding video data into the distributed database IPFS (Liu, et al., 2015).

Figure 3. Merkle tree for video data

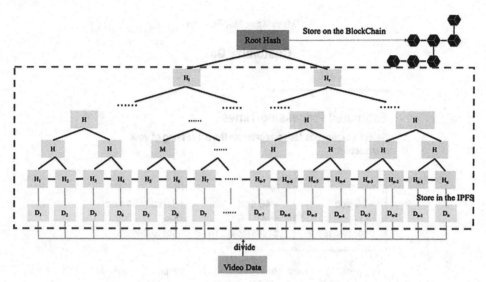

Next, we utilize the hash values obtained from the previous round and calculate the hash values obtained in this round again. Repeated these steps, finally we will get two hash values, the root hash value of this video file will be generated after this round. We save the root hash to the blockchain.

The data stored in the blockchain is charged in bytes. In our experiment, the principle of Merkle tree is adopted, the original video data is split into many parts, the divided video data is hashed multiple times, a root hash containing all the data of the video is generated, and finally stored in the chain. We only save the string on the blockchain; thus, we finally store 42-byte string including the entire video data. There is no cost in executing the transaction itself shown as shown in Figure 4.

In blockchain, the time it costs for data to be written into the block is determined by the miners, who are one of the crucial maintainers of the system. At the beginning of development, Bitcoins set up only two ways: one is mining, the other is to record the transfer transaction and confirm it. With the rise of various digital currencies, this discipline has been gradually changed, developers began to occupy a portion of the initially issued currency, but the constant is that recording and confirmation still reward for obtaining digital currency.

The main reason affecting the miners' recording and confirmation is the transaction fee. According to our experiment, the fastest one is less than 36 seconds, the slow one can be 18 minutes or more. This difference is overwhelmingly large, but the cost of both is only 12 points. Therefore, we choose the highest efficiency in this project.

This experiment is taken into consideration of the limitations of blockchain capacity with a view related to transaction efficiency issues. Hereby, we introduce the concept of IPFS, a distributed storage system. The system allows files to be shared on client computers and integrated into the global file system. This technology is based on the BitTorrent protocol and the Distributed Hash Table.

Therefore, anyone can upload any files to the system, it is content addressable. Hence, it is impossible to tamper a file with a given address. Based on this hypopaper, we ensure that the security of this file is achieved through quickly verifying the BitTorrent protocol. We can freely upload and download

Figure 4. Expenditure of storage

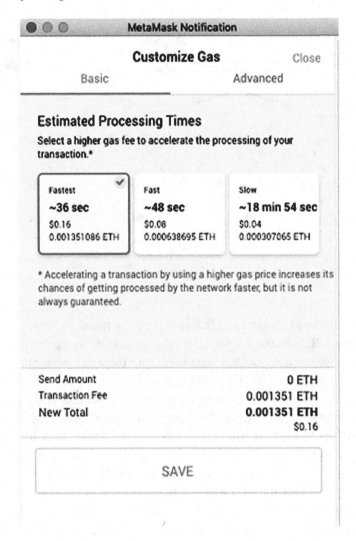

the files we need; the data can be confirmed by using the same address. In other word, we can create a database with infinite storage.

RESULTANT ANALYSIS AND DISCUSSIONS

In this section, we assume that all the data in the chain could be sorted in ascending or descending order. In this experiment, we upload the videos in the order of "American Best Dance Crew season 7 Week 1" to "Week 10", the default order is to store the videos according to the temporal order on the chain.

As shown in Figure 5, when the currently playing video is Episode 4, Episode 5 is ready to be played at the first rank in the playlist; the subsequent ones are 6, 7, 8, 9, 10, which give us potential guidance to watch the videos. It provides convenience for us when we watch TV drama series.

Figure 5. The re-ordered playlist

When we randomly select any episode in the playlist, in the refreshed webpage, the playlist will be recombined according to the currently playing episode, finally presented in order.

We simplify our search results (Figure 6 shows an example). The left list demonstrates the playlist on YouTube, the middle one is the target object, and the right is the playlist generated from our experiment. We find that some mismatched items in the left list, which are marked by using character "X".

In order to calculate the distance between the two lists, we introduce the "edit distance" which may also be referred to Levenshtein distance (Yujian, Bo, 2007) as shown in Eq (2).

$$
lev_{a,b}(i,j) = \begin{cases} \max(i,j) & if \min(i,j) = 0 \\ \min \begin{cases} lev_{a,b}(i-1,j)+1 \\ lev_{a,b}(i,j-1)+1 \\ lev_{a,b}(i-1,j-1)+1(a_i \neq b_j) \end{cases} & otherwise \end{cases} \tag{2}
$$

We convert Eq. (2) into a matrix and make it more intuitive, Figure 7 illustrates the example, (Wachter-Zeh, & Antonia, 2018). The first row represents the YouTube list, the first column stands for the target list. We can follow the following steps to get the result:

Step 1: A matrix is initialized.

Step 2: The matrix could be filled by obeying the rule from the left row to the right row and from top to bottom.

Step 3: Each horizontal or vertical jump corresponding to an insertion or a deletion, respectively.

Step 4: The cost of each jump is set to 1.

Step 5: Each cell is filled with the minimum value. If the two diagonal jumping objects in the row and line will cost 1, else 0.

Step 6: The number in the lower right corner in the matrix is the Levenshtein distance between two objects.

Figure 6. The simplified sequences

	YouTube		Target		Experiment	
row1	ABDC7 week1	1	ABDC7 week1	1	ABDC7 week1	1
row2	ABDC7 week2	2	ABDC7 week2	2	ABDC7 week2	2
row3	ABDC7 week8	8	ABDC7 week3	3	ABDC7 week3	3
row4	distracters	X	ABDC7 week4	4	ABDC7 week4	4
row5	ABDC7 week7	7	ABDC7 week5	5	ABDC7 week5	5
row6	ABDC7 week9	9	ABDC7 week6	6	ABDC7 week6	6
row7	ABDC7 week5	5	ABDC7 week7	7	ABDC7 week7	7
row8	ABDC7 week10	10	ABDC7 week8	8	ABDC7 week8	8
row9	distracters	X	ABDC7 week9	9	ABDC7 week9	9
row10	ABDC7 week3	3	ABDC7 week10	10	ABDC7 week10	10
	distracters	X				
	distracters	X				
	ABDC7 week4	4				
	ABDC7 week6	6				

The number at the lower right corner is 11, which means the distance between YouTube list and Target list is 11. We searched a variety of key words and compared these data with our experiment as follows.

Figure 7. The matrix used to calculate the edit distance

Search for "ABDC7"   YouTube List

		1	2	8	X	7	9	5	10	X	3	X	X	4	6
	0	1	2	3	4	5	6	7	8	9	10	11	12	13	14
1	1	0	1	2	3	4	5	6	7	8	9	10	11	12	13
2	2	1	0	1	2	3	4	5	6	7	8	9	10	11	12
3	3	2	1	1	2	3	4	5	6	7	7	8	9	10	11
4	4	3	2	2	2	3	4	5	6	7	8	8	9	9	10
5	5	4	3	3	3	3	4	4	5	6	7	8	9	10	10
6	6	5	4	4	4	4	4	5	5	6	7	8	9	10	10
7	7	6	5	5	5	4	5	5	6	6	7	8	9	10	11
8	8	7	6	5	6	5	5	6	6	7	7	8	9	10	11
9	9	8	7	6	6	6	5	6	7	7	8	8	9	10	11
10	10	9	8	7	7	7	6	6	6	7	8	9	9	10	11

Target List (row labels 1–10)

Figure 8. Search for "ABDC2"

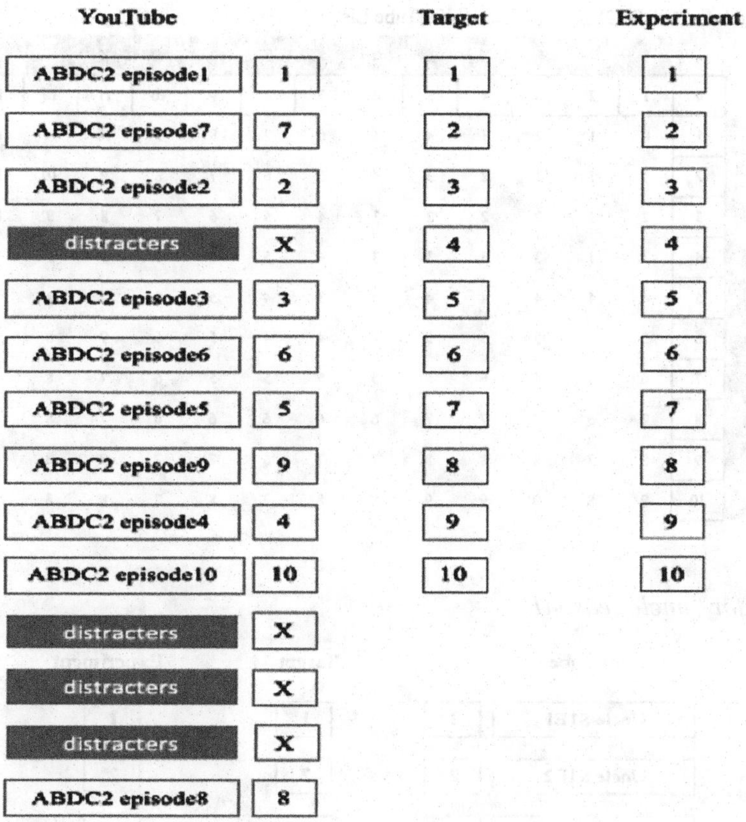

When we search for "ABDC2" both in YouTube and our experiment, the result is shown in Figure 8.

The distance between YouTube list and Target list is shown in Figure 9. When we change the key words to "Uncle Season1" the results show as Figure 10. The distance between YouTube list and Target list is shown in Figure 11.

As shown in Figure 12, the number of distracters reduces the number of target decreases, the distance also presents the trend. Through comparing the results, it is obvious that not only the cost of big data uplink storage is saved, but also the transaction time of the winding is stored in our experiments. We utilized blockchain as a database to ensure the robustness and immutability of video data; on the one hand, the playlists are sorted in right order, which saves the retrieval time of video browsing and improves the efficiency of video sites.

CONCLUSION

We consider the data stored in each block is re-sorted in chronological order by using the timestamp feature. In this paper, we have created a private chain that used as a database to store video data; there is one more point, another function of this database stores videos in the blockchain by using timestamps. Combining these features leads the playlist to be organized in an ascending or descending order; we

Figure 9. The Matrix used to calculate the edit distance

Search for "ABDC2"   YouTube List

Target List

		1	7	2	X	3	6	5	9	4	10	X	X	X	8
	0	1	2	3	4	5	6	7	8	9	10	11	12	13	14
1	1	0	1	2	3	4	5	6	7	8	9	10	11	12	13
2	2	1	1	1	2	3	4	5	6	7	8	9	10	11	12
3	3	2	2	2	2	2	3	4	5	6	7	8	9	10	11
4	4	3	3	3	3	3	3	4	5	5	6	7	8	9	10
5	5	4	4	4	4	4	4	3	4	5	6	7	8	9	10
6	6	5	5	5	5	5	4	4	4	5	6	7	8	9	10
7	7	6	5	6	6	6	5	5	5	5	6	7	8	9	10
8	8	7	6	7	7	7	6	6	6	6	6	7	8	9	9
9	9	8	7	8	8	8	7	7	6	7	7	7	8	9	10
10	10	9	8	9	9	9	8	8	7	8	7	8	8	9	10

Figure 10. Search for "uncle season1"

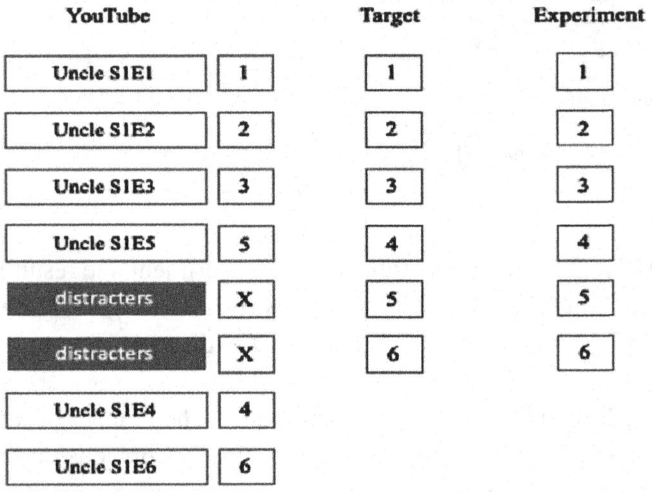

YouTube		Target	Experiment
Uncle S1E1	1	1	1
Uncle S1E2	2	2	2
Uncle S1E3	3	3	3
Uncle S1E5	5	4	4
distracters	X	5	5
distracters	X	6	6
Uncle S1E4	4		
Uncle S1E6	6		

thus save a lot of time when we browser these online websites with the help of visual blockchain. The updated playlist is still in an order and the following episode is the next one of the current playing video when we click on any icon of the playlist.

In our experiment, we created a private blockchain locally and all the data is based on the private network. Our experiment has achieved the expected results based on theory or in an ideal environment. In future, we will try to connect to the main network and synchronize the corresponding video data.

Figure 11. The matrix after calculated the edit distance

Search for "Uncle Season1"   YouTube List

Target List		1	2	3	5	X	X	4	6
	0	1	2	3	4	5	6	7	8
1	1	0	1	2	3	4	5	6	7
2	2	1	0	1	2	3	4	5	6
3	3	2	1	0	1	2	3	4	5
4	4	3	2	1	1	2	3	3	4
5	5	4	3	2	1	2	3	4	4
6	6	5	4	3	2	2	3	4	4

Table 1. Comparison between YouTube and our experiment with same searching words

Search Key Words	Distance (YouTube)	Distance (Experiment)
ABDC7	11	0
ABDC2	10	0
Uncle Season1	4	0

Figure 12. Results comparison

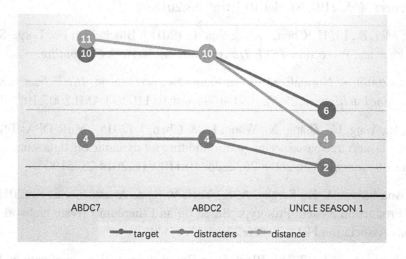

293

REFERENCES

Aste, T., Tasca, P., & Di Matteo, T. (2017). Blockchain Technologies: The Foreseeable Impact on Society and Industry. *Computer, 50*(9), 18–28. doi:10.1109/MC.2017.3571064

Badra, M., Borghol, R. (2018) Long-term integrity and non-repudiation protocol for multiple entities. Sustainable cities and society, 40, 189-193.

Chen, Y., Li, H., Li, K., & Zhang, J. (2017) An improved P2P file system scheme based on IPFS and Blockchain. IEEE International Conference on Big Data, pp. 2652-2657.

Dai, M., Zhang, S., Wang, H., & Jin, S. (2018). A Low Storage Room Requirement Framework for Distributed Ledger in Blockchain. *IEEE Access: Practical Innovations, Open Solutions, 6*, 22970–22975. doi:10.1109/ACCESS.2018.2814624

Davidson, J., Liebald, B., Liu, J., Nandy, P., Van Vleet, T., Gargi, U., ... Sampath, D. (2010) The YouTube video recommendation system. *Proceedings of the Fourth ACM Conference on Recommender Systems*, pp. 293–296. 10.1145/1864708.1864770

Gramoli, V., & Staples, M. (2018). Blockchain Standard: Can We Reach Consensus? *Communications Standards Magazine, IEEE, 2*(3), 16–21. doi:10.1109/MCOMSTD.2018.1800022

Hasan, M. R., Jha, A. K., & Liu, Y. (2018). Excessive use of online video streaming services: Impact of recommender system use, psychological factors, and motives. *Computers in Human Behavior, 80*, 220–228. doi:10.1016/j.chb.2017.11.020

Kugler, L. (2018). Why cryptocurrencies use so much energy--and what to do about it. *Communications of the ACM, 61*(7), 15–17. doi:10.1145/3213762

Li, J., Wu, J., & Chen, L. (2018). Block-Secure: Blockchain based scheme for secure P2P cloud storage. *Information Sciences, 465*, 219–231. doi:10.1016/j.ins.2018.06.071

Li, R., Song, T., Mei, B., Li, H., Cheng, X., & Sun, L. (2018). Blockchain For Large-Scale Internet of Things Data Storage and Protection. *IEEE Transactions on Services Computing*.

Li, Y., & Bo, L. (2007). A Normalized Levenshtein Distance Metric. *IEEE Transactions on Pattern Analysis and Machine Intelligence, 29*(6), 1091–1095. doi:10.1109/TPAMI.2007.1078 PMID:17431306

Liu, C., Ranjan, R., Yang, C., Zhang, X., Wang, L., & Chen, J. (2015). MuR-DPA: Top-down levelled multi-replica Merkle hash tree based secure public auditing for dynamic big data storage on cloud. *IEEE Transactions on Computers, 64*(9), 2609–2622. doi:10.1109/TC.2014.2375190

Maxim, Y. A., Anastasiya, A. K., Sergey, A. S., Yuri, V. F., & Anastasiia, S. S. (2018). A Design of Cyber-physical Production System Prototype Based on an Ethereum Private Network. Conference of Open Innovations Association FRUCT, 426(22), 3-11.

Rosa, R., & Rothenberg, C. E. (2018). Blockchain-Based decentralized applications for multiple administrative domain networking. *Communications Standards, IEEE, 2*(3), 29–37. doi:10.1109/MCOMSTD.2018.1800015

Sedhain, S., Menon, A. K., Sanner, S., & Xie, L. (2015). AutoRec: Autoencoders meet collaborative filtering. *Proceedings International Conference on World Wide Web*, pp. 111–112.

Tan, X., Guo, Y., Chen, Y., & Zhu, W. (2018). Accurate inference of user popularity preference in a large-scale online video streaming system. *Science China. Information Sciences*, *61*(1). doi:10.100711432-016-9078-0

Wachter-Zeh, A. (2018). List Decoding of Insertions and Deletions. *IEEE Transactions on Information Theory*, *64*(9), 6297–6304. doi:10.1109/TIT.2017.2777471

Wang, H., He, D., & Ji, Y. (2017). Designated-verifier proof of assets for bitcoin exchange using elliptic curve cryptography. *Future Generation Computer Systems*. doi:10.1016/j.future.2017.06.028

Wang, H., Wang, N., & Yeung, D.-Y. (2015). Collaborative deep learning for recommender systems. *Proceedings ACM SIGKDD International Conference on Knowledge Discovery and Data Mining*, pp. 1235–1244. 10.1145/2783258.2783273

Wang, S., Zhang, Y., & Zhang, Y. (2018). A blockchain-based framework for data sharing with fine-grained access control in decentralized storage systems. *IEEE Access: Practical Innovations, Open Solutions*, *6*(6), 38437–38450. doi:10.1109/ACCESS.2018.2851611

Zhang, J., Wang, Z., Quan, Z., Yin, J., Chen, Y., & Guo, M. (2018). Optimizing power consumption of mobile devices for video streaming over 4G LTE networks. *Peer-to-Peer Networking and Applications*, *11*(5), 1101–1114. doi:10.100712083-017-0580-6

Zhou, Y., Gu, X., Wu, D., Chen, M., Chan, T. H., & Ho, S. W. (2018). Statistical study of view preferences for online videos with cross-platform Information. *IEEE Transactions on Multimedia*, *20*(6), 1512–1524. doi:10.1109/TMM.2017.2769807

Chapter 15
Multiple Flames Recognition Using Deep Learning

Chen Xin
Auckland University of Technology, New Zealand

Minh Nguyen
Auckland University of Technology, New Zealand

Wei Qi Yan
Auckland University of Technology, New Zealand

ABSTRACT

Identifying fire flames is based on object recognition which has valuable applications in intelligent surveillance. This chapter focuses on flame recognition using deep learning and its evaluations. For achieving this goal, authors design a Multi-Flame Detection scheme (MFD) which utilises Convolutional Neural Networks (CNNs). Authors take use of TensorFlow in deep learning with an NVIDIA GPU to train an image dataset and constructed a model for flame recognition. The contributions of this book chapter are: (1) data augmentation for flame recognition, (2) model construction for deep learning, and (3) result evaluations for flame recognition using deep learning.

INTRODUCTION

Nowadays, flame identification has become one of the most popular topics in the field of visual object recognition (Jiao, et al., 2011; Wang, et al., 2018; Ren, et al., 2018; Wang, et al., 2017; Lu, et al., 2017; Gu, et al., 2017). It has a myriad of valuable applications in monitoring and surveillance for public security and safety. In this book chapter, we aim to develop a computational tool that could detect various types of flames automatically and classify the flames from input visual data. A reliable recognition requires a well-designed deep neural network. Our human visual system recognizes objects based on long-term training from our ordinary life. When the visual object is relatively complicated, we usually infer it based on our human experience (Yan, 2017).

DOI: 10.4018/978-1-7998-2701-6.ch015

For object classification, the output usually is class categories. In real scenarios, because of various reasons, our human vision sometimes even finds it is hard to recognize flames correctly (Gupta, Agrawal, Yamaguchi, 2018). If we use a computer to classify the flames quickly, the recognition rate by using machine learning algorithms will be low and could not achieve the expected goal of flame recognition.

The experimental results of traditional machine learning are mostly based on well-prepared and specific image datasets (Jiao, et al., 2011). Lighting/shielding variations of flames are much less than the ones in real scenarios. Moreover, appearance or shape of a flame is continuously changing, images of the same flame at different viewing angles are quite distinct. Therefore, the accuracy of flame recognition is rather lower than that we expect (Erhan, et al., 2014).

Hence, in this chapter, we propose the model: SSD (Liu, et al., 2016). Flame detection can be considered as a subject of flame recognition. We split our task of flame recognition into two categories (1) flame classification, (2) flame detection and locating. The feature maps firstly are extracted from input images using CNN operations, which are used as the input of deep neural networks for classification and identification. Using deep learning (LeCun, et al., 2015), the recognition accuracy will be greatly improved; it can enhance the robustness of flame recognition tremendously (Erhan, et al., 2014).

Since LeCun et al. have designed and trained a ConvNets (LeCun, Huang & Bottou, 2004) which used an error gradient-based algorithm (LeCun, et al, 1989); much excellent performance has been achieved in the field of pattern recognition. Also, the convolutional network has been proved to be effective (Luo, et al., 2017). At present, deep learning is successfully applied to various applications, such as document analysis, face detection, voice detection, license plate recognition, digital handwriting recognition, human motion recognition, and human face recognition (Zheng, et al., 2018).

In this chapter, we adopt CNN model to create a new neural network so as to recognize fire flames in depth. Also, this method could avoid the complexity that the traditional methods have. Our algorithm for flame recognition is implemented in the primary method CNN. We train the model with our image dataset assisted by using the GPU-based platform TensorFlow. We employ NVIDIA GTX 980M GPU to accelerate the computations of our experiments. Training with GPU is much efficient. By cropping flame regions from each frame in a recorded video, we collect these images and used them as our dataset. Also, we manually labeled the images having the flame regions.

This chapter is organized as follow. Related work is presented at Section 2, our method is described in Section 3. Our results and analysis are demonstrated in Section 4, the conclusion will be drawn in Section 5.

RELATED WORK

The performance of flame recognition primely depends on the flame classifiers (Jiao, et al., 2011). Thus, we require a classifier having high accuracy and low false alarm ratio. Most of video-based fire detection techniques devoted to flame detection so as to provide an early fire alarm. Traditional ultraviolet and infrared fire detection has a great deal of disadvantages. With too many influencing factors, an errant alert or false alarm is easily to be generated. At the same time, location, size, and growth rate of fire flames may also be wrong.

Due to these problems, a technology has been developed for video capturing and fire flame detection automatically by analyzing the streaming visual data. This algorithm is based on spectral, spatial, and temporal features of fire flame (Healey, et al., 1993). In 1994, digital image processing was used for fire detection in tunnels (Phillips, et al., 2000). The image processing methods were reviewed by using infrared cameras. Traffic flow maps were extracted in the event of a fire; then, flame detection is conducted by comparing grayscale intensities of the images (Healey, et al., 1993).

Flickering flames were captured by using a CCD camera and the data of flames in temporal sequence were processed in real time. The method can eliminate the interference of irrelevant information by using data mining to satisfy the robustness requirement of an inspection system (Yamagishi & Yamaguchi, 1999). Spectrum-based machine vision has been applied to detect hydrocarbon fires. Because luminance, color, spectrum, and flicker frequencies are unique characteristics of a flame, these characteristics are often employed to distinguish the flames from background. Fire alarm systems usually need to classify flames swiftly so as to prevent fire disasters.

Based on machine vision methods for early fire detection, the appearance of flames is considered by calculating whether the two sequential video images exceed the preset threshold, specifically when the difference between histograms of two video frames compare with a set of statistics based on the performance of real-time data (Foo, 2000; Healey, et al., 1993).

In 2016, a deep learning method was proposed for forest fire detection through neural networks (Shen, et al., 2018). The fire detection was performed in a cascade manner; that is, the full image was first tested by a global classifier. If there is a flame, a fine-grained classifier will be used for accurate fire location detection. The fire spot detectors achieved the accuracy above 90% by using the well-prepared datasets (Zhang, et al., 2014). A Convolutional Neural Network (CNN or ConvNet) was proposed to identify fire flames in videos. The CNN performed well in the field of object classification within the same architecture. Tested on real videos, the CNN-based method achieved excellent performance of classification and shew the results are very promising (Frizzi, et al., 2016).

YOLO (Redmon, et al. 2016) is one of the great object classification approaches which is completely different from other approaches (Shen, et al., 2018), such as F-FCN (Dai, et al., 2016), R-CNN (Zhang, et al., 2014), Fast R-CNN (Girshick, 2015), and Faster R-CNN (Ren, et al., 2015). YOLO (Redmon, et al., 2016; Redmon & Farhadi, 2017) (You Only Look Once) also illustrates how this method tackles digital images using neural networks. The architecture of YOLO was inspired by the GoogLeNet model for image classification. The network has 24 convolutional layers, followed by 2 fully connected layers. A 1×1 reduction layer is employed and then a 3×3 convolutional layer is followed instead of the initial module used by GoogLeNet. When an input image enters the neural network of YOLO, the image only is analyzed once, which is different from a conventional classifier like R-CNN (Girshick, 2015).

The network in YOLO splits the input image into a grid of 13×13, and each grid will predict five bounding boxes. These bounding boxes elaborate the rectangle that encloses an object; that means, those bounding boxes not only reveal whether there is an object but also describe what kind the object is. The prediction result is based on confidence score, which shows us how good the bounding box encloses an object. The confidence scores reflect whether the shape of the box is good or not, instead of what kind of objects are in the box. For each bounding box, the grid also predicts a class; it gives a probability distribution on all the possible classes. YOLO network also shows that adding convolutional and connection layers to pretrained networks can improve performance.

R-FCN (Dai, et al., 2016) is a state-of-the-art detector for object detection or recognition. It modified the traditional Faster R-CNN structure (Ren, et al., 2015) by moving the convolution operation to the front of RoI layer and used a position-sensitive feature map to evaluate the probability of each category. The RoI pool function has been used for all object detection methods. It converts an input rectangular region of any size into a fixed-size feature. This approach can achieve higher accuracy of position and tremendously increase the speed of object detection. The fundamental problem that R-FCN has to solve is the slow detection of Faster R-CNN. The reason why it is slow is that different proposals do not share their structure behind the RoI layer.

METHODOLOGY

The flame detection can be considered as one step of flame recognition. We split the task of flame recognition into two parts: classification and detection of fire flames. The images firstly are imported to extract high-level features (Girshick, et al., 2014); then, the features are used as the input of the networks. Considering the massive scale of the network model (Karpathy, et al., 2014), complexity of flame identification is also lower than that of the general object recognition (Szegedy, Toshev & Erhan, 2013).

For an n-class classification problem, we generally set a probability vector $p = (p_1, p_2, ..., p_n)$ as the output data. The probability $p_i \in [0, 1]$ indicates that the input image belongs to the i-th category. We set the labels $q = (q_1, q_2, ..., q_n)$ for the training samples. Therefore, if a training sample belongs to i-th class, then $q_i = 1$ and $q_j = 0$ $(i \neq j)$. The object classification problem uses cross entropy as the loss function.

For $p_i \in [0, 1]$, $\Sigma^p_{k=1} p_k = 1$, we normalize the output $f_{\text{loc}} = (y_1, y_2, ..., y_n)$ from Deep Neural Networks (DNNs) by using the softmax function

$$p_i = \frac{\exp\left(y_i\right)}{\sum_{k=1}^{n} \exp\left(y_k\right)} \tag{1}$$

On the other hand, we treat the flame positioning problem using regression. We set the output of location regression as f_{loc}, b is used as the bias of bounding boxes of the training samples. So, the loss function of positioning problem is

$$L_{loc} = l_{loc}\left(f_{loc} - b\right) \tag{2}$$

In this chapter, our work is different from the existing ones. Our contributions are to use data augmentation for the preprocessing, we adjust the YOLOv3 structures in our proposed model. f_{loc} and b are also suitable for the bounding box. In box encoding, we design the code as $[x_c/w, y_c/h, w_b/w, h_b/h]$, w and h denote width and height of the input image, $(x_{\min}, x_{\max})$ and $(y_{\min}, y_{\max})$ are the coordinates of the upper left corner and the lower right corner of the bounding box, respectively.

We also indicate the coordinates of the bounding box center as

$$x_c = \frac{x_{\max} + x_{\min}}{2}, y_c \frac{y_{\max} + y_{\min}}{2} \tag{3}$$

where w_b and h_b respectively indicate width and height of the bounding box, satisfying

$$w_b = x_{\max} - x_{\min} \,;\, h_b = y_{\max} - x_{\min} \tag{4}$$

We select L_1 function as the loss function l_{loc},

$$L = L_{loc} + \alpha \cdot L_{cls} \tag{5}$$

where α is a factor. Minimizing the above loss function, we can achieve flame recognition by using deep learning. Our model mainly consists of two types of layers: convolutional layers and fully connected layers. For the convolutional layer, its structure is

$$y = \sigma\left(W \cdot x + b\right) \tag{6}$$

where x denotes the input layer, y represents the output layer, W stands for the convolution template; b is the basis. The dimension of x in our model is $[N, M, N, C]$. N is the batch size in training, which is the number of the input samples in only one step of training. $M{\times}N$ indicates the size of the input feature, C indicates the number of input features. The dimension of convolutional template W is $[m, n, C, D]$, $m{\times}n$ refers to the size of the convolution template, C is the number of input features, D is the number of output features. Moreover, $\delta\,(\bullet)$ is an activation function. After convolutional processing, dimension of the output y goes to be $[N, M, N, D]$.

Pertaining to the activation function, there are also many choices, like Sigmoid, ReLU, and Leaky ReLU. We compare these functions and select the most suitable one. From those functions, Sigmoid is the oldest activation function. However, the problem of gradient vanishing is easy to occur, which makes the model difficult to be trained. ReLU function solves the problem of gradient vanishing, we choose Leaky ReLU as the new activation function.

After the convolutional layer, max pooling always is followed. In each pooling, its size is $m{\times}n$, the output data is the most significant value in that pooling operation. If the input data feature is in the size of $[N, M, N, C]$, then the size of the output data will become $[N, \lfloor M/m \rfloor, \lfloor N/n \rfloor, C]$.

In addition, avoiding the overfitting problem, we can add a dropout layer so that only a number of the nodes are trained. Based on this structure, we construct the model as shown in Table 1.

The input image comes into the $input_{process}$ layer, and the layer normalizes the pixel intensity within $[0, 255]$ to a floating-point number in $[-1, 1]$. In the CNN training, the box of training samples will be encoded in this layer at the same time. There are six layers in the CNN; these layers extract the high-level features from the original image. The structure is expanded as shown in Figure 1.

After the six layers of CNN, a layer named $flatten_{dropout}$ is followed. We expand the output of CNN and add a dropout operation to overcome the problem of overfitting. Then, the result of $flatten_{dropout}$ will be imported into the cls_{output} and loc_{output} layers for flame classification and positioning. Both cls_{output} and loc_{output} are equivalent to a two-layer MLP, which is composed of two sublayers. We use the nonlinear activation function in the output layer. The predict layer gives the final output by dealing with the output of the cls_{output} and loc_{output} layers, the final output is presented as $[classID, conf, x_{min}, x_{max}, y_{min}, y_{max}]$, where *classID* stands for the label of the class to which the object belongs, *conf* refers to the probability of belonging to this class. The rest of output $[x_{min}, x_{max}, y_{min}, y_{max}]$ is the coordinates of the bounding box.

Figure 1. The architecture of our proposed model

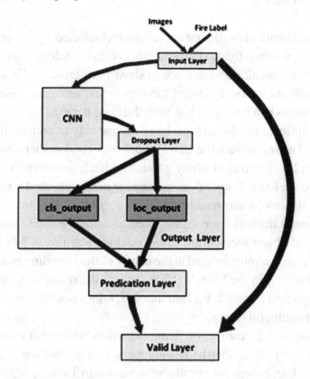

Table 1. The structure of our proposed neural network

Layer	Filters	Size	Output
Input Process			448 × 448
Con_1	16	5 × 5	
Max Pooling		2 × 2	244 × 244
Con_2	32	3 × 3	
Max Pooling		2 × 2	112 × 112
Con_3	64	3 × 3	
Max Pooling		2 × 2	56 × 56
Con_4	128	3 × 3	
Max Pooling		2 × 2	28 × 28
Con_5	256	3 × 3	
Max Pooling		2 × 2	14 × 14
Con_6	512	3 × 3	
Max Pooling		2 × 2	7 × 7
Con_6	1024	3 × 3	
Max Pooling		2 × 2	14 × 14
Con_6	512	3 × 3	
Max Pooling		2 × 2	7 × 7
Dropout			
Fully Connect Layers			

EXPERIMENTAL RESULTS

The classification is the most critical step in our experiment which directly influences the results of flame recognition. In this chapter, we investigate six flame categories including campfire, candle fire, gas fire, blowtorch fire, gas tank fire, and alcohol fireplace as shown in Figure 2. When a flame appears before our camera, our model will automatically detect the region and recognize one of these five classes of flames. We restrain the flames in a bounding box with the class name of flames and use the accuracy for classification. The convolutional neural network has a unique way to convert the color layer of a video frame to a digital matrix. The result from the CNN model is as good as that which uses color model, the accuracy of the bounding box locating is pretty good. The background in these pictures where shows very similar color and texture to the flames does not appear in our detected bounding boxes. The results of our experiments with six groups showcase the highest accuracy (98.6%).

Before running the neural networks, we do not need to extract features from the image. Therefore, compared to the traditional object recognition using machine learning, CNN has a significant performance. We see that the flame is almost located at the center of the bounding box. The flames of different burning materials are all sitting in the bounding box, except the result of a candle flame. Fortunately, from the last image as shown in Figure 2, we find that CNN does not recognize the reflection of candle flames on the wall as a meaningful case.

With regard to the positioning problem of flame detection, we treat it as a general regression. The predicted location f_{loc} and excepted location b in locating loss function are also suitable for the box. Hence, we tried the parameters of four groups for our model as shown in Table 3, where MFD2 is equivalent to a linear transformation of MFD1, the difference is that MFD2 normalizes the values within the interval [0, 1]. MFD3 and MFD4 aim to improve the location results of the models for small objects. Because MFD1 and MFD2 are based on absolute measurement of positioning errors, the deviation between large and small objects is treated equally. For example, a 10-pixel deviation may be treated as a large object, but it can be quite large for a small object.

After tested on these models with the same dataset, we have obtained the results in Table 2. We see that amongst these results, our MFD 1 got the best performance regarding overall accuracy. Because our tests were carried out based on an NVIDIA GTX 950M GPU and MFD 1 worked very well, we conducted the same training using our CPU. The accuracy of our results is 93.5% which also indicates that performance is very well; but the time used on CPU is almost doubled than that on the GPU; therefore, GPU significantly reduces the training time of our experiment.

Table 2. Comparisons of multiple models for flame recognition(%)

Name	Time	Hardware	Campfire	Candle Fire	Gas Oven Fire	Blowtorch Fire	Gas Tank Fire	Alcohol Fireplace	Average Accuracy
MFD_1	23hours	GPU	**100**	90.2	**100**	93.7	**95.1**	95.3	**98.6**
MFD_1	48hours	CPU	98.7	**95.3**	97.9	83.5	89.3	92.4	93.5
MFD_2	24hours	GPU	89.8	80.7	88.3	79.8	81.5	82.6	82.6
MFD_3	25hours	GPU	81.9	76.3	78.6	69.9	72.3	77.2	80.5
MFD_4	25hours	GPU	87.3	81.5	84.9	77.4	78.7	83.9	86.6
YOLO	20hours	GPU	95	88.9	94.9	87.3	89.6	89.3	93.1
R-FCN	23hours	GPU	97.3	91.9	89.7	**95.5**	92.6	**95.6**	95.4

Figure 2a. Motion pictures for single flame detection: Kindle fire detection

Figure 2b. Motion pictures for single flame detection: Camp fire detection

YOLO and R-FCN achieved 93.1% and 95.4% accuracy on the training results respectively, though they did not exceed our designed MFD 1 model. Regarding time-consuming, we see from Table 2 that using the same hardware and dataset to train the model, YOLO only spent 20 hours, which is the fastest one of all models. From the perspective of individual flame types, the accuracies of recognizing campfire, gas stove fire, and gas tank fire are the highest one based on MFD 1; the candlelight performs the best on MFD 2. At the same time, R-FCN has the best performance in the recognition of blowtorch flames and alcohol flames.

In general, the MFD 1 model performs the best in our flame recognition. The outstanding accuracy is shown not only for the recognition but also for the locating no matter the object is large or small. In our comparisons, YOLO does not perform well for small objects because it predicts two boxes in a grid and only falls into one category. Due to the selection of loss function, positioning error is the main reason that affects the detection efficiency, especially in the treatment of over large or small objects. Because of the complex structure, R-FCN performs better than YOLO in flame recognition.

Figure 3. Motion pictures for multiple flames detection

Table 3. Four groups of parameters for the proposed MFD models

Model	Box Encoding
MFD_1	$\{x_{min}, x_{max}, y_{min}, y_{max}\}$
MFD_2	$\{x_c/w, y_c/h, w_b/w, h_b/h\}$
MFD_3	$\{x_c/w, y_c/h, \sqrt{(w_b/w)}, \sqrt{(h_b/h)}\}$
MFD_4	$\{x_c/w, y_c/h, \log(w_b/w), \log(h_b/h)\}$

CONCLUSION

In this chapter, we used a convolutional neural network in deep learning to train a valuable model for recognizing and detecting the occurrences of fire flames automatically. Various elements of the convolutional neural networks and the relevant vital functions were introduced and examined based on our own dataset.

In the experimentation, we designed a relatively simplified neural network to achieve our goal of flame recognition. We collected six types of flames to augment our dataset. In the end, we received a 96% average accuracy. Also, we detected the flame regions and evaluated the corresponding accuracy. From where we found that when a flame occupies a large portion of the video frame, the recognition accuracy will be significantly improved.

In future, we will work towards the detection and recognition of multiple flames. Also, more complex flames from forest fire, building fire, etc. will be added into the project. Due to the complex and diverse environments in real scenes, there will be more uncontrolled factors that may affect our flame recognition. In future, dynamic characteristics of video sources such as incandescent lamps, fluorescent lamps, etc. will be taken into consideration.

REFERENCES

Borji, A., Cheng, M., Jiang, H., & Li, J. (2015). Salient object detection: A benchmark. *IEEE Transactions on Image Processing*, *24*(12), 5706–5722. doi:10.1109/TIP.2015.2487833 PMID:26452281

Dai, J., He, K., Li, Y., Ren, S., & Sun, J. (2016). *Instance-sensitive fully convolutional networks.* Proceedings *ECCV*, pp. 534–549.

Dai, J., Li, Y., He, K., & Sun, J. (2016). R-FCN: Object detection via region-based fully convolutional networks. Proceedings NIPS, pp. 379-387.

Erhan, D., Szegedy, C., Toshev, A., & Anguelov, D. (2014). Scalable object detection using deep neural networks. Proceedings IEEE CVPR, pp. 2147-2154. doi:10.1109/CVPR.2014.276

Foo, S. (2000). A machine vision approach to detect and categorize hydrocarbon fires in aircraft dry bays and engine compartments. *IEEE Transactions on Industry Applications*, *36*(2), 459–466. doi:10.1109/28.833762

Frizzi, S., Kaabi, R., Bouchouicha, M., Ginoux, J., Moreau, E., & Fnaiech, F. (2016). Convolutional neural network for video fire and smoke detection. *Proceedings Annual Conference of the IEEE Industrial Electronics Society*, pp. 877-882 10.1109/IECON.2016.7793196

Girshick, R. (2015). *Fast R-CNN*. Proceedings *IEEE ICCV*, pp. 1440–1448.

Girshick, R., Donahue, J., Darrell, T., & Malik, J. (2014). Rich feature hierarchies for accurate object detection and semantic segmentation. Proceedings IEEE CVPR, pp. 580-587 doi:10.1109/CVPR.2014.81

Gu, Q., Yang, J., Yan, W., & Klette, R. (2017). Integrated multi-scale event verification in an augmented foreground motion space. *Proceedings Pacific-Rim Symposium on Image and Video Technology*, pp. 488-500.

Gupta, B., Agrawal, D., & Yamaguchi, S. (2018). Deep learning models for human centered computing in fog and mobile edge networks (pp. 1–5). Academic Press.

Healey, G., Slater, D., Lin, T., Drda, B., & Goedeke, A. (1993). A system for real-time fire detection. Proceedings IEEE CVPR, pp. 605-606. doi:10.1109/CVPR.1993.341064

Jiao, Y., Weir, J., & Yan, W. (2011). Flame detection in surveillance. *Journal of Multimedia*, *6*(1), 22–32. doi:10.4304/jmm.6.1.22-32

Karpathy, A., Toderici, G., & Shetty, S. abd R., Sukthankar, T. L., & Li, F. (2014) Large-scale video classification with convolutional neural networks. Proceedings IEEE CVPR, pp. 1725-1732.

LeCun, Y., Bengio, Y., & Hinton, G. (2015). Deep learning. *Nature*, *521*(7553), 436–444. doi:10.1038/nature14539 PMID:26017442

LeCun, Y., Boser, B., Denker, J., Henderson, D., Howard, R., Hubbard, W., & Jackel, L. D. (1989). Backpropagation applied to handwritten zip code recognition. *Neural Computation*, *1*(4), 541–551. doi:10.1162/neco.1989.1.4.541

LeCun, Y., Huang, F., & Bottou, L. (2004). Learning methods for generic object recognition with invariance to pose and lighting. Proceedings IEEE CVPR. doi:10.1109/CVPR.2004.1315150

Liu, W., Anguelov, D., Erhan, D., Szegedy, C., Reed, S., Fu, C. Y., & Berg, A. C. (2016). SSD: Single shot multibox detector. Proceedings ECCV, pp. 21-37.

Lu, J., Shen, J., Yan, W., & Bacic, B. (2017). An empirical study for human behavior analysis. *International Journal of Digital Crime and Forensics*, *9*(3), 11–27. doi:10.4018/IJDCF.2017070102

Luo, H., Xu, L., Hui, B., & Chang, Z. (2017). Status and prospect of target tracking based on deep learning. *Infrared and Laser Engineering 46*(5).

Phillips, W., Shah, W., & Lobo, N. (2000). Flame recognition in video. *Proceedings IEEE Workshop on Applications of Computer Vision*, pp. 224-229. 10.1109/WACV.2000.895426

Redmon, J., Divvala, S., Girshick, R., & Farhadi, A. (2016). *You only look once: Unified, real-time object detection*. Proceedings *IEEE CVPR*.

Redmon, J., & Farhadi, A. (2017). *YOLO9000 (2017) Better, faster, stronger*. Proceedings *IEEE CVPR*. pp. 6517–6525.

Ren, S., He, K., Girshick, R., & Sun, J. (2015). Faster R-CNN: Towards real-time object detection with region proposal networks. *IEEE Transactions on Pattern Analysis and Machine Intelligence*, *39*(6), 1137–1149. doi:10.1109/TPAMI.2016.2577031 PMID:27295650

Ren, Y., Nguyen, M., & Yan, W. (2018). Real-time recognition of series seven New Zealand banknotes. *International Journal of Digital Crime and Forensics*, *10*(3), 50–65. doi:10.4018/IJDCF.2018070105

Shen, D., Chen, X., Nguyen, M., & Yan, W. (2018). Flame detection using deep learning. *Proceedings International Conference on Control, Automation and Robotics*, pp. 416-420.

Szegedy, C., Toshev, A., & Erhan, D. (2013). Deep neural networks for object detection. *Proceedings International Conference on Neural Information Processing Systems,* pp. 2553-2561.

Wang, J., Bacic, B., & Yan, W. (2018). An effective method for plate number recognition. *Multimedia Tools and Applications*, *77*(2), 1679–1692. doi:10.100711042-017-4356-z

Wang, J., Ngueyn, M., & Yan, W. (2017). A framework of event-driven traffic ticketing system. *International Journal of Digital Crime and Forensics*, *9*(1), 39–50. doi:10.4018/IJDCF.2017010103

Yamagishi, H., & Yamaguchi, J. (1999) Fire flame detection algorithm using a color camera. *Proceedings International Symposium on Micromechatronics and Human Science*, pp. 255-260 10.1109/MHS.1999.820014

Yan, W. (2017). *Introduction to Intelligent Surveillance: Surveillance Data Capture, Transmission, and Analytics*. Springer. doi:10.1007/978-3-319-60228-8

Zhang, N., Donahue, J., Girshick, R., & Darrell, T. (2014). Part-based R-CNNs for fine-grained category detection. *Proceedings European Conference on Computer Vision*, pp. 834-849.

Zheng, K., Yan, W., & Nand, P. (2018). *Video dynamics detection using deep neural networks*. IEEE Transactions on Emerging Topics in Computational Intelligence, 2(3), pp. 224–234.

Chapter 16
Network–Based Detection of Mirai Botnet Using Machine Learning and Feature Selection Methods

Ahmad Al-Qerem
Zarqa University, Jordan

Bushra Mohammed Abutahoun
Princess Sumaya University for Technology, Jordan

Shadi Ismail Nashwan
https://orcid.org/0000-0002-1476-4162
Computer Science Department, Jouf University, Saudi Arabia

Shatha Shakhatreh
Princess Sumaya University for Technology, Jordan

Mohammad Alauthman
https://orcid.org/0000-0003-0319-1968
Zarqa University, Jordan

Ammar Almomani
https://orcid.org/0000-0002-8808-6114
Department of Information Technology, Al-Huson University College, Al-Balqa Applied University, Jordan

ABSTRACT

The spread of IoT devices is significantly increasing worldwide with a low design security that makes it more easily compromised than desktop computers. This gives rise to the phenomenon of IoT-based botnet attacks such as Mirai botnet, which have recently emerged as a high-profile threat that contin-

DOI: 10.4018/978-1-7998-2701-6.ch016

ues. Accurate and timely detection methods are required to identify these attacks and mitigate these new threats. To do so, this chapter will implement a network-based anomaly detection approach for the Mirai botnet using various machine learning and feature selection algorithms. Authors use Multiphase Genetic Algorithm section methods and PSO to select the best subfield of features capable of producing good overall classification results, and with this Feature Selection Algorithm, Random forest algorithm can detect all anomaly behavior with 100% accuracy.

INTRODUCTION

Internet of things (IoT)' is a platform where everyday devices become smarter, every day processing becomes intelligent, and every day communication becomes informative'(Ray, 2018). As the IoT devices contribute to everything and its number increasing very fast with the lake of security, which creates disaster attacks, the need for timely detection methods of IoT attacks becomes very important to promote IoT network security and prevent attacks from spreading. IoT is a new paradigm that looks forward to linking all the components of the physical world within the digital world under the idea of merging the 'things' that represent the world into software applications and the internet, making them communicating and benefit from the world's context information(Alauthman et al., 2019; Alauthman et al., 2020; Atzori et al., 2010; Gonzalez et al., 2008; Sterling, 2005). IoT technology is developing rapidly, it becomes the focus of the modern cities, and huge enterprises, and many applications have been built recently. As a new technology, it is facing a lot of challenges, and one of them is very important and crucial, which is security (Alauthaman et al., 2018; Xia et al., 2012).

IoT devices and systems are suffering from security and privacy issues that are the heart of everything (Lee & Kim, 2017) and have very high-risk vulnerabilities. They are spreading in the market with little consideration of basic security and privacy protections 'Insecurity by design'. Therefore, the proliferation and increasing popularity of the internet of things with its insecure large number of devices with high computational power and resources make them an easy, attractive, and powerful target for attackers seeking to compromise these devices and use them to make large-scale botnets. Botnets are robot networks of compromised or infected machines of malicious software that become controlled by a third party (Attacker); it uses the command-control infrastructure to accomplish different bad attacks like email spam delivery, identity theft and distributed denial of service attack (DDOS).DDOS attack crowd a huge number of machines (bots) to overwhelming the target website with many requests. Therefore, the target website will not be able to serve requests by actual and legitimate users. The weakness of security in IoT devices promotes such attacks and support them to be larger and more dangerous (Bertino & Islam, 2017).

Figure 1 shows the DDOS attack. In 2016, a website of computer security consultant Brian Krebs was hit with 620 Gbps of traffic; another attack happened after it attacks hundreds of websites including Twitter, Netflix, Reddit, and GitHub; In February 2017, DDOS attack happened against a US college and stayed 54 hours long and other dangerous attacks. Analyzing these massive DDOS attacks considered that IoT devices are contributing to these attacks, and that is the reason why it is so huge. They called this type of DDOS attack (Mirai) stands for the future(Shoemaker, 2017). This attack showed the importance of security, which has been missed in the IoT devices and causes disaster attacks. Mirai attack is taking the place of the hugest most dangerous effectively DDOS attacks which reaches an unprecedented level(Kolias et al., 2017).

Figure 1. DDOS attack using botnet, Shoemaker
(Shoemaker, 2017).

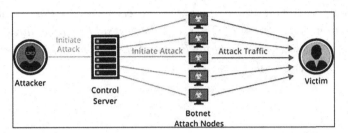

These types of IoT botnet attacks ensure the need of timely detection methods that promote network security. Thus real-time botnet detection is one of the most important research topics nowadays, it becomes essential for mitigating the risk associated with these attacks by detecting real-time anomaly behavior of infected machines to stop botnet from propagating and prevent further outbound attack traffic (Kamal et al., 2020; Meidan et al., 2018). Different deep learning and machine learning algorithms contribute to detecting the anomaly behavior of infected machines to alert about the attack before happening. The motivation of this paper is to propose a novel Mirai botnet detection technique using multi-stage feature selection algorithms of genetics and particle swarm optimization to prove that fewer features can achieve great results and efficiently detect anomaly behavior, then comparing the effects of different machine learning algorithms in classifying the network traffic behavior.

The paper is organized as follows: Related works are discussed in Section 2. The Description of the data set is presented in Section 3. Afterward, the proposed approach is described in Section 4. Then, the Experiment and results will be discussed in section 5. Finally, Section 6 summarizes and concludes the findings of this paper.

BACKGROUND

There are several botnets detection methods suggested, it depends on its categorization on the detection approach and the operational steps to be detected. In (Alieyan et al., 2019), they proposed a network-based detection of IoT attacks which are Bashlite and Mirai attack, to evaluate their approach they studied the behavior of nine commercial IoT devices and monitored the behavior of the packets by taking snapshots from five-time windows of the most recent 100ms to 1min then extracting 115 statistical features 23 per window. They used deep autoencoder as an unsupervised learning algorithm to detect anomaly behavior of the network. They trained auto-encoder for each device on the humid behavior, this gives the auto-encoder the ability to identify any anomaly behavior, and their proposed approach succeed to detect all anomaly behavior of miraias and bashlite with 100% accuracy.

In (Özçelik et al., 2017), they worked on the operational steps of detecting IoT botnets and focused at most on the early steps of infection and propagation and the communication with the c&c server. They used emulated IoT nodes, simulated data set, and used dynamic updating of flow rules to detect Mirai- infected IoT devices search for more devices. As in (Summerville et al., 2015) they used deep packet anomaly detection on two real devices as a detection approach of worm propagation, tunneling, and code injection attack. Detecting the attack by monitoring organizational network flow for identifying the early steps of infection in insufficient.

In (Sedjelmaci et al., 2016), they proposed to use the Hybrid detection method, which is signature-based and anomaly detection (BPN), in detecting devices that are compromised by a DDOS attack simulated on wireless sensor networks. As in (Bostani & Sheikhan, 2017), they also used the Hybrid detection method, which is specification-based and anomaly detection (OFPC), using simulation on 6LoWPAN WSN representing a smart city to detect routing attack (selective-forwarding and sinkhole).

In (Midi et al., 2017) they introduced Kalis, a knowledge-driven self-adapting intrusion detection system. They used real devices, simulated data on ZigBee,6LoWPAN, XBee, WIFI and BT to detect different attacks like ICMP flood, smurf, TCP SYN flood, wormhole, data modification, selective forwarding, hello jamming and replication using knowledge-driven anomaly detection. This approach does not affect the performance of the application on the IoT devices and does not require any change in the software.

Between these suggested botnets detection methods, there is an essential difference in the deployment level that each technique applied; the first is the host-based detection method in (Sedjelmaci et al., 2016; Summerville et al., 2015), and the second is network-based detection (Bostani & Sheikhan, 2017; Butun et al., 2015; Midi et al., 2017; Özçelik et al., 2017). The methods that depend on the host-based detection considered to be less realistic in detecting the infected devices in IoT because we can't guarantee in the software installation on the devices because some of them are wearable; we cant also rely on the manufacturers to install anomaly detectors on their devices. Moreover, the resource and the computational power of the tools differ and reflect the performance when installing anomaly detection algorithms, which can affect their primary functionality, so a single non-distributed solution is better.

In (Raza et al., 2013), they introduced SVELTE, an intrusion detection system for the Internet of things. They used simulated data on 6LoWPAN to detect selective-forwarding, sinkhole, and routing attacks like altered information or spoofed using hybrid signature-based and anomaly detection. This approach does not affect the energy and memory capacity of the application on the IoT devices and detects all launched malicious nodes.

In conclusion, this paper differs from the previous studies as it focuses on the feature selection algorithms that can select the most related features to the problem and reduce the number of the overall features for real-time detection problems which save time and computational power and become more efficient to depend on a small amount of features to detect real-time anomaly behavior, then using them to train a random forest machine-learning algorithm to recognize anomaly behavior.

PROPOSED APPROACH

In this section, we introduce the procedure that we followed for detecting the Mirai attack by studying the anomaly behavior of the network traffic generated by the infected machines. The efficient detecting of the Mirai attack will help to stop the attack in an early stage and prevent infection of other machines. We used multi-stage feature selection algorithms and different machine learning algorithms. Fig.2 shows the general approach, and every phase will be described in detail below.

Dataset

We used a data set called N-BALOT, this data set collected by capturing the raw network traffic data (in PCAP format) using port mirroring on the switch, then recording the traffic data using wire shark packet analyzer through which the organizational traffic usually flows. To ensure that the training data is clean of malicious behaviors, the regular traffic of an IoT is collected immediately following its installation in the network. They took behavioral snapshots of the hosts and protocols over several temporal time windows of the most recent 100ms, 500ms, 1.5sec, 10sec, and 1min and extracted 23 feature per window by calculating different traffic statistical measurements like mean and variance of the packet size, aggregated into four categories (1) packets generated from the same IP (2) packets generated from both the same IP address and the same source media access control layer, (3) packets have been sent between the source and destination IPs (channel) and (4) packets has been sent between the source to destination TCP/UDP sockets .the final data set consists of 115 feature and a target label with values of malicious behavior or benign (Meidan et al., 2018).

Data Pre-Processing and Feature Selection

N-BALOT data set is clean and has no missing values. So, there is no need to apply any missing values handling techniques. The feature selection phase comes after, which is considered the essential phase in building machine-learning models When the data set has hundreds of thousands of attributes. Its results affect the whole process and improve the performance of classification. This process concise in selecting the features that are related to the target variable and can contribute to the predicted results values.

Feature selection methods are divided into wrapper and filter methods. Filtering methods choose the subset independently from the predictor as a pre-processing step, while wrapper methods use search algorithms and learning machines to select the subset of the variables based on their predictive powers(Guyon & Elisseeff, 2003).

Our contribution in this paper focuses mainly on reducing the number of features to detect the anomaly behavior of Mirai botnet. We will make an experimental evaluation to prove that fewer features can achieve great results and efficiently identify anomaly behavior. We focused on the wrapper methods and applied two optimization search algorithms to select the best subset of features; we studied the double impact of the Genetic Algorithm, then particle swarm optimization (PSO). Feature wrapper methods require two stages: subset evaluation and search strategy.

Subset evaluation: It is a step to evaluate the subsets that are determined by the search algorithm, and to choose the best subset solution, we decided Correlation-based feature selection (CFS) to evaluate subsets. It works as finding the correlation between attributes together and against the target variable, and then the chosen subset would be the one with a low relationship between the characteristics together and the higher correlation against the target variable (Hall, 1999).

Search strategy: In this stage, any search algorithm can be applied to search for the optimal solution (a subset of variables) between multiple solutions and in our experiment to find the optimal subset we benefit from the impact of two of the most known meta-heuristic search algorithms which are Genetics and PSO (Leardi, 1996).

Figure 2. The main steps in the proposed approach

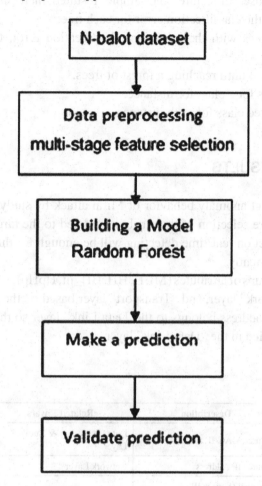

Modeling

After feature selection, the new filtered data set with the chosen suitable features become ready to feed it to a model to learn and become capable of detecting the anomaly behavior. The Random Forest Algorithm (RF) proposed by (Breiman, 2001) in 2001 will be used as a classification algorithm to classify observations into anomaly or benign classes. RF shows its efficiency recently in achieving high accuracy due to the nature of its work of combining several randomization trees (forest of trees) where the number of variables is much larger than the number of observations and then taking the average of their results has shown excellent performance Biau and Scorned.

Here is a description of how the "Random Forest algorithm works:

- Random subset with the replacement of samples k' generated from the original set k (samples bagging), where k' < k.
- After that attribute bagging applied on each subset where the chosen number of attributes is the square root of the total number of attributes n.

- Randomly generated subsets of features and samples resulted, then building a decision tree of each subgroup and compute the classification error for each tree.
- Choose the decision trees with the minimum classification error, to participate in the voting process.
- Repeat the steps from 2-4 until reaching a forest of trees.
- Each decision tree votes for a class for instance.
- Return the most predicted class for each instance.

EXPERIMENT AND RESULTS

Our goal is to correctly detect anomaly behavior of Mirai attack by studying the network traffic; our experiment focuses on feature selection of the attributes related to the target class to prove that fewer numbers of features to extract on real-time detecting will be enough for the prediction model to detect anomaly behavior more efficiently.

Table 1 illustrates five groups of attributes (MI, H, HH, HH_jit, HpHp); those groups were categorized to "Data Link" layer, "Network" layer, and "Transport" layer based on the captured attributes on those groups. For example, MAC address belongs to the"Data Link" layer so that all attributes that contain MAC addresses were classified in the "Data Link" layer.

Table 1. Groups of attributes

Attribute Header	Description	Related Layers	Number of Attributes
MI	Source MAC-IP addresses	Data Link Layer & Network Layer	15
H	Source IP Address	Network Layer	15
HH	Channel (Source IP - Destination IP)	Network Layer	35
HH_jit	Channel jitter (Source IP - Destination IP)	Delay (Time) - Related to the Network Layer	15
HpHp	Socket (Source IP: Port - Destination IP: Port)	Network layer & Transport Layer	35

Other attributes followed the same approach. Besides categorizing the data set into three categories, we perform a feature selection method to reduce the number of features in each category. We used particle swarm optimization to select the best features. Table 2 shows the number of elements of each category before and after selection.

After that, we used the Random Forest classification algorithm because it gave the best results in the experiment. We applied the random forest on the three categories to see which category of packet layers contributes the most in detecting the attack and have the higher effect and better accuracy, we also applied the random forest on the selected features of each category to check how the accuracy will change, getting minimum number of features with high efficiency will be the best solution.

Table 2. The number of features in each category after applying feature selection algorithm

Data Category	Number of Attributes	Number of Features After Selection
Network layer	65	9
Network and Transport layer	35	9
Network and Data Link layer	15	4

Experiment 1. At first, to accomplish our contribution in detecting Mirai attack with minimum features, we proposed to use two of the most common meta-heuristic search algorithms that are Genetics and PSO separately to check their efficiency in choosing the best subset of features after searching among multiple solutions. Genetics algorithm selects 18 features from 116 elements, and particle swarm optimization selects 12 elements.

After that, we applied three classification algorithms, which are (Naive Bayes, J48, and Random Forest) to build a model that can detect the malicious behavior of Mirai botnet in the network traffic to see which one gives the best results. We tested our model using 10-fold cross-validation and evaluate our results using different measures like accuracy, precision and recall, and F1-measure, Table 3 shows the results of applying Genetics and PSO separately on the data set and see the performance of these classification algorithms. Random forest algorithm gives the best results in both feature selection algorithms with an accuracy of 99.53% in genetics and 99.81% in PSO. The previous work on this data set achieved 100% accuracy (Meidan et al., 2018). So we thought of a way that can achieve better accuracy, by the experiment of applying genetics algorithm then PSO achieved the desirable results, this approach chose only 8 features that proved to be enough for detecting anomaly behavior of Mirai botnet with 100% accuracy. Table 4 shows the result after this experiment, a random forest algorithm with this double impact of feature selection algorithm also gave the best results of accuracy 100%.

Table 3. The results of the two subsets of network layers with the Random Forest algorithm

Subset of Data	Accuracy Before Feature Selection	Accuracy After Feature Selection
Network layer	100%	99.98
Network layer and Transport layer	99.96%	99.95%
Network and Data Link layer	100%	100%

Table 4 shows the results of applying Genetics and PSO separately on the data set and the evaluation results of different machine learning algorithms-Random Forest shows the best results in both

Table 5 shows the results of applying multi-stage Feature selection of Genetics, then PSO on the data set, and the evaluation results of different machine learning algorithms-Random Forest shows the best results of 100 accuracies.

Table 4. Results of applying genetics and PSO

	Genetic Algorithm			Particle Swarm Optimization		
	Naive Bayes	**J84**	**Random Forest**	**Naive Bayes**	**J84**	**Random Forest**
Accuracy	98.10%	96.3%	99.53%	98.00%	95.73%	99.81%
Precision	0.880	0.962	1.00	0.981	0.952	1.00
Recall	0.880	0.974	1.00	0.981	0.975	1.00
F1-Measure	0.880	0.967	1.00	0.981	0.963	1.00

Table 5. Results of applying multi-stage Feature selection

	Genetics and PSO		
	Naive Bayes	**J48**	**Random Forest**
Accuracy	99.99%	98.99%	100%
Precision	1.00	.989	1.00
Recall	1.00	1.00	1.00
F1-measure	1.00	0.994	1.00

CONCLUSION AND FUTURE WORK

An approach that applied multi-stage feature selection algorithms of Genetics and particle swarm optimization and Random Forest ensemble machine learning algorithms was used to build a classification model with the minimum number of features to detect network-based Mirai's anomaly behavior. A comparison made between three classification algorithms (Naive Bayes, j48, and Random Forest gave the best result as it succeeds in detecting all the anomaly behavior of 100% accuracy. For future work, we will try to focus on the characteristics of transport layer only (TCP/UDP sockets) and its effect on detecting anomaly traffic behavior to get a better results and accuracy and prove that it is enough to look at this layer and calculate its statistics in the real-time to detect Mirai's anomaly behavior.

REFERENCES

Alauthaman, M., Aslam, N., Zhang, L., Alasem, R., & Hossain, M. A. (2018). A P2P Botnet detection scheme based on decision tree and adaptive multilayer neural networks. *Neural Computing & Applications*, *29*(11), 991–1004. doi:10.100700521-016-2564-5 PMID:29769759

Alauthman, M., Almomani, A., Alweshah, M., Omoushd, W., & Alieyane, K. (2019). Machine Learning for phishing Detection and Mitigation. *Machine Learning for Computer and Cyber Security: Principle, Algorithms, and Practices*, 26.

Alauthman, M., Aslam, N., Al-kasassbeh, M., Khan, S., Al-Qerem, A., & Raymond Choo, K.-K. (2020). An efficient reinforcement learning-based Botnet detection approach. *Journal of Network and Computer Applications*, *150*, 102479. doi:10.1016/j.jnca.2019.102479

Alieyan, K., Almomani, A., Anbar, M., Alauthman, M., Abdullah, R., & Gupta, B. B. (2019). DNS rule-based schema to botnet detection. *Enterprise Information Systems*, 1–20. doi:10.1080/17517575.2019.1644673

Atzori, L., Iera, A., & Morabito, G. (2010). The internet of things: A survey. *Computer Networks*, *54*(15), 2787–2805. doi:10.1016/j.comnet.2010.05.010

Bertino, E., & Islam, N. (2017). Botnets and internet of things security. *Computer*, *50*(2), 76–79. doi:10.1109/MC.2017.62

Bostani, H., & Sheikhan, M. (2017). Hybrid of anomaly-based and specification-based IDS for Internet of Things using unsupervised OPF based on MapReduce approach. *Computer Communications*, *98*, 52–71. doi:10.1016/j.comcom.2016.12.001

Breiman, L. (2001). Random forests. *Machine Learning*, *45*(1), 5–32. doi:10.1023/A:1010933404324

Butun, I., Kantarci, B., & Erol-Kantarci, M. (2015). Anomaly detection and privacy preservation in cloud-centric Internet of Things. *Proceedings 2015 IEEE International Conference on Communication Workshop (ICCW)*. 10.1109/ICCW.2015.7247572

Gonzalez, G. R., Organero, M. M., & Kloos, C. D. (2008). Early infrastructure of an internet of things in spaces for learning. *Proceedings 2008 Eighth IEEE International Conference on Advanced Learning Technologies*. 10.1109/ICALT.2008.210

Guyon, I., & Elisseeff, A. (2003). An introduction to variable and feature selection. *Journal of Machine Learning Research*, *3*(Mar), 1157–1182.

Hall, M. A. (1999). Correlation-based feature selection for machine learning.

Kamal, A., Ammar, A., Rosni, A., Badr, A., & Mohammad, A. (2020). *Botnet and Internet of Things (IoTs): A Definition, Taxonomy, Challenges, and Future Directions. In Security, Privacy, and Forensics Issues in Big Data* (pp. 304–316). Hershey, PA: IGI Global.

Kolias, C., Kambourakis, G., Stavrou, A., & Voas, J. (2017). DDoS in the IoT: Mirai and other botnets. *Computer*, *50*(7), 80–84. doi:10.1109/MC.2017.201

Leardi, R. (1996). *Genetic algorithms in feature selection Genetic algorithms in molecular modeling* (pp. 67–86). Elsevier. doi:10.1016/B978-012213810-2/50004-9

Lee, J.-H., & Kim, H. (2017). Security and privacy challenges in the internet of things [security and privacy matters]. *IEEE Consumer Electronics Magazine*, *6*(3), 134–136. doi:10.1109/MCE.2017.2685019

Meidan, Y., Bohadana, M., Mathov, Y., Mirsky, Y., Shabtai, A., Breitenbacher, D., & Elovici, Y. (2018). N-BaIoT—Network-based detection of IoT botnet attacks using deep autoencoders. *IEEE Pervasive Computing*, *17*(3), 12–22. doi:10.1109/MPRV.2018.03367731

Midi, D., Rullo, A., Mudgerikar, A., & Bertino, E. (2017). Kalis—A system for knowledge-driven adaptable intrusion detection for the Internet of Things. *Proceedings 2017 IEEE 37th International Conference on Distributed Computing Systems (ICDCS)*. 10.1109/ICDCS.2017.104

Özçelik, M., Chalabianloo, N., & Gür, G. (2017). Software-defined edge defense against IoT-based DDoS. *Proceedings 2017 IEEE International Conference on Computer and Information Technology (CIT)*. 10.1109/CIT.2017.61

Ray, P. P. (2018). A survey on Internet of Things architectures. *Journal of King Saud University-Computer and Information Sciences, 30*(3), 291–319. doi:10.1016/j.jksuci.2016.10.003

Raza, S., Wallgren, L., & Voigt, T. (2013). SVELTE: Real-time intrusion detection in the Internet of Things. *Ad Hoc Networks, 11*(8), 2661–2674. doi:10.1016/j.adhoc.2013.04.014

Sedjelmaci, H., Senouci, S. M., & Al-Bahri, M. (2016). A lightweight anomaly detection technique for low-resource IoT devices: A game-theoretic methodology. *Proceedings 2016 IEEE International Conference on Communications (ICC)*. 10.1109/ICC.2016.7510811

Shoemaker, A. (2017). *How to Identify a Mirai-Style DDoS Attack. 2020.* Retrieved from https://www.imperva.com/blog/author/andrewshoemaker/

Sterling, B. (2005). *Shaping things*.

Summerville, D. H., Zach, K. M., & Chen, Y. (2015). Ultra-lightweight deep packet anomaly detection for Internet of Things devices. *Proceedings 2015 IEEE 34th international performance computing and communications conference (IPCCC)*. 10.1109/PCCC.2015.7410342

Xia, F., Yang, L. T., Wang, L., & Vinel, A. (2012). Internet of things. *International Journal of Communication Systems, 25*(9), 1101–1102. doi:10.1002/dac.2417

Chapter 17
The Cost Perspective of Password Security

Leandros Maglaras

https://orcid.org/0000-0001-5360-9782

De Montfort University, UK

Helge Janicke

Cyber Security Cooperative Research Centre, Edith Cowan University, Australia

Mohamed Amine Ferrag

https://orcid.org/0000-0002-0632-3172

Guelma University, Algeria

ABSTRACT

This study technically analyses the maximum number of combinations for common passwords up to 12 characters long. A maximum storage size necessary for the creation of a data base that holds all possible passwords up to 12 characters is also presented along with a comparison against the publicized cost of storage from popular cloud storage providers and the national budget for intelligence and defense activities of a nation. Authors prove that it is technically possible that any password could be computed within seconds with nothing more than currently commercially available components. The study concludes that it is possible that nation states or even combined nation states working in collaboration could or already have bought private citizens' and businesses' passwords revealing that it may already be an age where the password may not be a legitimate defense for privacy anymore.

INTRODUCTION

As Critical National Infrastructures are becoming more vulnerable to cyber attacks, their protection becomes a significant issue for any organization as well as a nation Moreover the synergy between the Industrial Control Systems and the Internet of Things (IoT) has emerged bringing new security challenges (Maglaras et al., 2018) making the deployment of an overlapping strategy based on security tools,

DOI: 10.4018/978-1-7998-2701-6.ch017

people, and processes a necessity. Traditional security mechanisms are both appropriate and effective means to defend the boundaries of an organisation or a nation. Firewall architectures, email scanning, DPI, VPNs, HIDS, NIDS are all established ways by which an organisation can reduce the opportunities for the ingress of malicious software into their environments. As a complimentary measure, the practice of locking-down unused ports, USB devices, use of access controls through corporate directories and the enforcement of least-privilege access all reduce the insider threat. One of the basic but important security measures that any organization must have in place is a password policy (Gupta et al., 2018) along with other defense mechanisms (Jiang et al., 2018, Almomani et al., 2013).

Without delving into the historical or philosophical descriptions of what a password is and purely concentrating on the modern-day scientific definition of a password, in business and computing terms, according to the Cambridge dictionary under "*Password" in Business English*" it states "*a secret word or combination of letters and numbers that you use to prove who you are when you use a computer, website, etc.:*" (Cambridge Dictionary, 2019). Obviously, this is inaccurate as it excludes special characters that are now commonplace in most corporate password policies. To this end, in this chapter when a password is mentioned, its definition will be 'a group of characters chosen by a user from the available character sets of modern computing hardware and software for the purposes of authentication'. Innately there are many variables with passwords, as they themselves are extracted out of our complex languages in all their forms, even if not representative of a definable word.

There are many complex and interesting theories surrounding passwords and this has sparked much discussion and interesting content such as the journal "Password Security as a Game of Entropies" (Rass et al, 2018) as well as initiating some truly inspiring mathematics. Also, we are witnessing an evolution in the art of the possible with emergence of Quantum Computing that is brings advancements in our understanding of physics. Quantum computing presents incredible opportunity for industry to potentially compute complex issues at an exponentially increased speed. However, it has been long since it was speculated that this dramatic increase in computing power could spell the death of the password and similar security defences that rely on complexity. This is well described in the paper "*Global catastrophic risk and security implications of quantum computers" (Major et al, 2015)*, and this view is supported by the authors. In this paper however, the authors are questioning the possible of the present, utilising only commercially of the shelf equipment available to everyone today.

Figure 1. Passwords rules

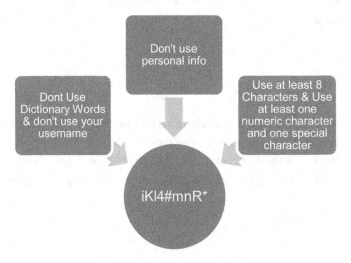

To question this efficiently the authors of this chapter, would like to look at the most basic elements of the password before the introduction of mathematical theories to increase possibilities of successful guessing. At this stage, it is a reasonable question to ask "Why would we not want to increase the probability of a match being found?" The answer would most probably be, we do. However, there are elements of our modern-day society that consider chance and possibility, dirty words that should be eliminated wherever possible such as the intelligence community, health and financial sectors. To that end, this chapter aims to approximate the cost of storage of every possible password combination that could be in use by anyone within reasonable constraints and alternatives to this.

In that this chapter we will not look into passwords longer than twelve characters long and will concentrate on the UK keyboard configuration. Further investigation without these constraints is interesting and should be followed up, however, to keep this chapter realistic and easy to follow, these constraints seem reasonable to prove the theory in its most basic form.

Figure 2. Passwords and hash functions

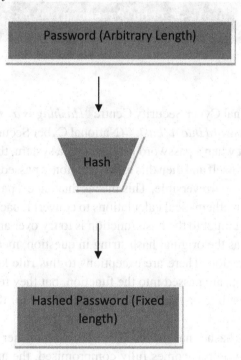

This chapter will question, how are passwords commonly stored, how long are common passwords, where and how are they stored, what is the maximum entropy of interest, what would this look like in storage size, what is the associated cost with this hypothetical storage, is this affordable, is there a better way and finally, what inferences can be drawn?

PASSWORDS AND HASH FUNCTIONS

A password could, of course, be stored as plain text in a computing system. This is to say, when a computer asks you to set a password, be it on a website, a remote server or even your local desktop, it would store it in the form you have typed it into the system, i.e. password you typed in = 'Password1', password stored by the system ='Password1'. However, this is not modern-day best practice or common for systems to be designed like this.

If a system becomes compromised, it is a trivial task to read the password if it is stored in plain text. Passwords are actually mostly stored in modern computing systems as values that are the output of a hash function. Below is an example of the string 'Password1' being hashed by a function known as the Message Digest 5 (MD5), you can see the output of the function bears no resemblance to the original text:

Figure 3. Example MD5

```
root@Local:~# echo Password1 | md5sum
b1345a0ce47f743bc94c5e32cf547ac0   -
```

According to the UK National Cyber Security Centre *"Hashing is a one-way cryptographic function which converts a plain text password into a 'hash'"*(National Cyber Security Centre (2016). Essentially, hashing a password means that when a password is typed into a system, the password is converted into a mathematical representation of itself and then this representation is passed through a one-way mathematical function that is designed to be irreversible. This means that once a password is hashed, it should not be possible to perform further mathematical calculations to convert it back to its original form. The only way to know the original string input to the hash function is to try over and over again inputting strings, until the same output appears as the original hash string in question, meaning this must be the original input string used for authentication. There are exceptions to this rule known as clashes or collisions, this is where two separate inputs are passed into the function, but they result in the same output. These clashes are relatively rare depending on the hash function used and for the purposes of this chapter are considered to be out of scope.

Having passwords stored as hashes has the benefits of being a further layer of defence for passwords (Gupta et al., 2015), as, if a system becomes fully compromised, the attacker can steal the password hashes (Gupta et al., May 2015) but then has the further job of cracking the hash to reveal the original password (assuming they are not utilising 'pass the hash' (SANS 2010) techniques that sit outside the scope of this chapter). The user's original password is never stored in the system, only the mathematical output from a hash function that represents it is, which is then more difficult for the attacker to utilise. Each time the user logs in post registration, the password is typed in, is hashed again and the output is compared to the stored hash from the registration stage, if they match, this means the correct password has been entered. This is represented in the following simplistic diagram:

One of the key benefits of hash functions is that the output of the hash function always produces the same string format and length regardless of what is input. This is demonstrated in the three following images utilising the MD5 hash function again:

Figure 4. Password registration and further authentications

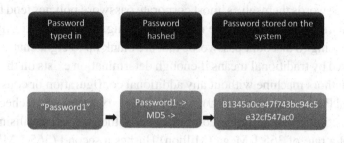

Initial Registration:

| Password typed in | Password hashed | Password stored on the system |

| "Password1" | Password1 -> MD5 -> | B1345a0ce47f743bc94c5e32cf547ac0 |

Authentication:

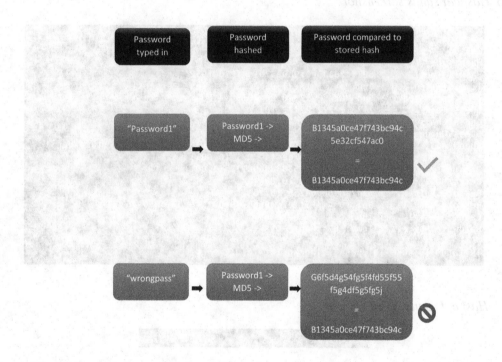

| Password typed in | Password hashed | Password compared to stored hash |

| "Password1" | Password1 -> MD5 -> | B1345a0ce47f743bc94c5e32cf547ac0 = B1345a0ce47f743bc94c | ✓ |

| "wrongpass" | Password1 -> MD5 -> | G6f5d4g54fg5f4fd55f55f5g4df5g5fg5j = B1345a0ce47f743bc94c | 🚫 |

Figure 5. MD5 length examples

```
root@Local:~# echo Password1 | md5sum
b1345a0ce47f743bc94c5e32cf547ac0
root@Local:~# echo two | md5sum
c193497a1a06b2c72230e6146ff47080  -
root@Local:~# echo Three333333333333333333333333333333333333333Three | md5sum
3e5ff6b7291707a23b780147bbf29d50
root@Local:~#
```

Notice how the output for each hash is the same length and format, although the input is different in length and format. There are many hash function types as can be seen on the Hashcat website. This will be a useful consideration later in this chapter.

Moving back to passwords themselves, most corporate password policies tend to be twelve characters or less in length for normal users. This is the reason for setting the limit arbitrarily at twelve characters. The authors are also going to discount passwords that are blank up to eight characters long, as these can be brute forced cracked by traditional means if enough determination exists on the behalf of the attacker. As an example, the authors machine without any additional configuration or consideration is capable of utilising its Graphical Processing Unit (GPU), which is now six years old, to check for the correct input to the MD5 hash function for all possible combinations of the password utilising the Hashcat default input character set at a rate of 365.1 Mega (Million) Hashes a second (365.1 MH/s) as can be seen in the below two images:

Figure 6. Hashcat status screenshot

```
Session..........: hashcat
Status...........: Running
Hash.Type........: MD5
Hash.Target......: 5217c28135c0f9b0a47d1d6f2266f952
Time.Started.....: Sun Mar  3 13:31:05 2019 (2 mins, 29 secs)
Time.Estimated...: Sun Mar  3 17:40:20 2019 (4 hours, 6 mins)
Guess.Mask.......: ?1?2?2?2?2?2?2?3 [8]
Guess.Charset....: -1 ?l?d?u, -2 ?l?d, -3 ?l?d*!$@, -4 Undefined
Guess.Queue......: 1/8 (12.50%)
Speed.#1.........:   370.0 MH/s (10.60ms) @ Accel:64 Loops:16 Thr:1024 Vec:1
Recovered........: 0/1 (0.00%) Digests, 0/1 (0.00%) Salts
Progress.........: 55146708992/5533380698112 (1.00%)
Rejected.........: 0/55146708992 (0.00%)
Restore.Point....: 524288/68864256 (0.76%)
Restore.Sub.#1...: Salt:0 Amplifier:49664-49680 Iteration:0-16
Candidates.#1....: 16p3ccck -> fhdk6x69
Hardware.Mon.#1..: Temp: 67c Fan:  0%

[s]tatus [p]ause [b]ypass [c]heckpoint [q]uit => p
```

Figure 7. Hashcat status speed value

```
Speed.#1.........:   370.0 MH/s
```

The above shows that even a dated and untuned system utilising an old GPU (NVIDIA Corporation GK106M [GeForce GTX 765M]) was able to check 55,146,708,992 passwords in 2 minutes, 29 seconds. Its total completion time could be measured in hours.

Even an old system with just one old GPU was capable of guessing all possible combinations in a very small-time scale given the task. The recent developments in crypto mining have driven advancements in hash cracking technology, this can be seen in the commercially available Antminer S15-28TH/s

(Britain 2019) which advertises itself as capable of achieving up to 28 Trillion Hash checks per second (28 TH/s). This shows that, if it were possible to tune this technology to check MD5 hashes, such as in our scenario where we had 5,533,380,698,112 (circa 5.5 trillion) possible combinations to check, the Antminer S15 would have completed checking all possible combinations in 0.198 seconds at a rate of 28TH/s. It is for this reason the authors felt that passwords of eight characters or less are no longer of academic interest. However, the technology of purpose-built hash mining software is pertinent.

A best practice for many organisations is to have nine or more characters for a password since the discovery of the weaknesses in Microsoft's LM hash function.

The LanMan (LM) hash function was found to have a flaw that showed that the password was actually split into two parts and then hashed, meaning a password could be brute forced by effectively guessing a four-character password twice. Worse still, one of these characters was a checksum for the others, making the two halves only four and three characters long. NTLM hashes are the replacement for LM hashes. The LM weakness can be seen referred to by Microsoft themselves in Microsoft's article "How to prevent Windows from storing a LAN manager hash of your password in Active Directory and local SAM databases". This is all relatively irrelevant for the purposes of this chapter, except to further justify why we are only looking at passwords that are specifically nine to twelve charters long as this is a social and cultural norm that perhaps has been caused by a technical finding.

The user's password or hash is normally stored on the system it was registered with or pushed to another system to be stored such as a database server. Regardless of where it is stored, it is this system or its communication links bearing the password that must be compromised for an attacker to steal the password or hash. Alternatively, if the system the attacker is attempting to break into is not rate limited (the amount of password attempts allowed is not restricted) then the rate of password attempts is limited by the system's capacity to process these attempts. This is known as an online brute force attack. Moreover Cross Site Scripting (XSS) attack is one of such attacks against the web applications in which a user has to compromise its browser's resources and hashing can be used in order to make the system robust to such attacks (Gupta et al., 2017).

So, what are the maximum possible password combinations, of a password that was created utilising a UK keyboard? Below is the character set generated for this chapter based on a UK Keyboard, based on the ASCII Printable Charters:

- **Numbers**: 0123456789
- **Lower case**: abcdefghijklmnopqrstuvwxyz
- **Upper case**: ABCDEFGHIJKLMNOPQRSTUVWXYZ
- **Special characters**: `~!@#$%^&*()-_=+[]\{ }|;':",./<>?£

If you include the space character, that is a total of ninety-six possible characters. There are ways to get a higher number than this, but this was deemed sufficient by the authors and would cover the majority of the population's usage. Using Crunch[1], a password generation tool included in the Kali Linux penetration testing operating system, we can see the calculated output statistics for the plain text results of every possible combination as seen in the below image:

We note here that the character set was edited prior to running this command to append additional characters that ensured it reflected the above ninety-six characters.

Figure 8. Crunch memory usage example

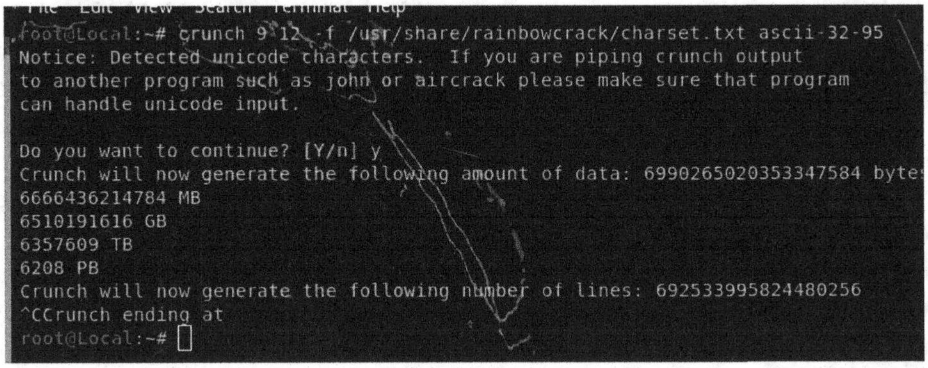

Even with the possibilities of passwords from 0 – 8 characters long not included, it is possible to see there are still 692,533,995,824,480,256 possibilities. Also, we can see that the total storage capacity needed for a wordlist like this without any compression is 6208 Peta-Bytes just in plain text.

PASSWORDS AND COST

According to Microsoft's published price list for Azure Data Lake Storage (Microsoft 2019) which at time of authoring this chapter was £0.001/GB per month, the storage cost for this list would be £6,510,191.62 rounded to the nearest penny, making an annual cost of £78,122,299.44. Obviously, this kind of figure is beyond the means of most entities, however, let's consider this figure in the context of the UK's Defence budget.

According to *"UK Defence in Numbers"* (Ministry of Defence UK, 2017) the UK's expenditure was £35.3bn for the 2016/17 financial year which was the 5th biggest defence budget in the world. This is before you combine the shared vested interest of defence with the budget allocation of the intelligence community and law enforcement. So, could a country similar to the UK afford to have a database of every possible password from nine to twelve characters long? Yes, they could, even in its most basic rudimentary form, in fact, they could probably afford to cater for a password database that considers passwords longer than twelve characters with relative ease.

So, the following question arises - would they? Well, this can be easily answered by looking at the technical side of this with the answer being no. This is of course because no degree of compression has been applied, meaning you are spending more money than is required. Just by applying basic zip file compression you would be able to greatly reduce this overall cost. Also, we know that it is not actually a list of all possible passwords that would be of interest, as these passwords are actually in most cases stored as hashes. So, to be useful each entry of this data set would need the corresponding MD5 hash if we are applying it to our above-worked example. An MD5 hash has 32 characters, assuming a one-byte to one-character mapping, this adds 32 bytes to every entry in our dataset. Our dataset was 692533995824480256 lines long, and so ((692533995824480256*32 = 2.2161088e+19) (2.2161088e+19 bytes converted to GB = 22161088000) (22161088000 GBs converted into PBs = 22161.088PB) an additional 22162 Peta-bytes is required. Again, based on Microsoft's published Azure data lake prices this would constitute an additional £22,161,088 per month or £265,933,056 a year before compression. Considering this is just the cost of one hash type alone, this is a significant increment in the cost.

So, how many other hash types are there and how would this affect our figures? Looking at the Hashcat website under example hashes it is easy to see there are many different types of hash know to Hashcat as seen in the below image:

Figure 9. Example hashes

Generic hash types

Hash-Mode	Hash-Name	Example
0	MD5	8743b52063cd84097a65d1633f5c74f5
10	md5($pass.$salt)	01dfae6e5d4d90d9892622325959afbe:7050461
20	md5($salt.$pass)	f0fda58630310a6dd91a7d8f0a4ceda2:4225637426
30	md5(utf16le($pass).$salt)	b31d032cfdcf47a399990a71e43c5d2a:144816
40	md5($salt.utf16le($pass))	d63d0e21fdc05f618d55ef306c54af82:13288442151473
50	HMAC-MD5 (key = $pass)	fc741db0a2968c39d9c2a5cc75b05370:1234
60	HMAC-MD5 (key = $salt)	bfd280436f45fa38eaacac3b00518f29:1234
100	SHA1	b89eaac7e61417341b710b727768294d0e6a277b
110	sha1($pass.$salt)	2fc5a684737ce1bf7b3b239df432416e0dd07357:2014
120	sha1($salt.$pass)	cac35ec206d868b7d7cb0b55f31d9425b075082b:5363620024
130	sha1(utf16le($pass).$salt)	c57f6ac1b71f45a07dbd91a59fa47c23abcd87c2:631225
140	sha1($salt.utf16le($pass))	5db61e4cd8776c7969cfd62456da639a4c87683a:8763434884872
150	HMAC-SHA1 (key = $pass)	c898896f3f70f61bc3fb19bef222aa860e5ea717:1234
160	HMAC-SHA1 (key = $salt)	d89c92b4400b15c39e462a8caa939ab40c3aeeea:1234
200	MySQL323	7196759210defdc0
300	MySQL4.1/MySQL5	fcf7c1b8749cf99d88e5f34271d636178fb5d130

When we study this page closely, we also can no longer avoid the topic of salts. A good practice when storing a password is to introduce a Salt into the hash function. A salt is a random value introduced to the mathematics to increase the complexity and make it harder for an attacker to brute force the answer. Sticking to our worked example, there are seven hash mode variants listed for an MD5 hash. We have already seen the cost of all possible MD5 hashes if stored in a public cloud environment as worked out above and represented in the below table:

Looking at the next entry in Hashcat example shows an example MD5 and its associated Salt as "01dfae6e5d4d90d9892622325959afbe:7050461", the key numbers being after the colon "7050461". This number is the Salt and, in this format, the maximum number it could be is 9,999,999. This means then, for each line in our original password list we would need to store a further 9,999,999 32-byte MD5 hashes. Making the cost of a database (without compression) approximately £2,659 trillion. Without doing any further mathematics it is obviously beyond the budget of a single nation and in fact most likely beyond the budget of any group of countries when you consider all the different hash types and formats as shown below only for MD5 hash types:

Table 1. MD5 hash storage costs

Mode	Hash Type	Example Hash	Cost per Year
0	MD5	8743b52063cd84097a65d1633f5c74f5	£265,933,056 + £78,122,299.44

Table 2. Hash storage costs

Mode	Hash Type	Example Hash	Cost per Year
0	MD5	8743b52063cd84097a65d1633f5c74f5	£265,933,056 + £78,122,299.44
10	md5($pass.$salt)	01dfae6e5d4d90d9892622325959afbe:7050461	£2,659 trillion+ £78,122,299.44
20	md5($salt.$pass)	f0fda58630310a6dd91a7d8f0a4ceda2:4225637426	> £2,659 trillion
30	md5(utf16le ($pass).$salt)	b31d032cfdcf47a399990a71e43c5d2a:144816	< £2,659 trillion
40	md5($salt. utf16le($pass))	d63d0e21fdc05f618d55ef306c54af82:13288442151473	> £2,659 trillion

SUMMARY AND CONCLUSION

In conclusion, is it likely that anyone has a database of every type of password in the world pre-computed? The answer is quite obviously no. This would be a pointless and futile exercise. The sheer volume of possibilities is incredible and the costs associated with it are astronomical. However, as seen earlier in the chapter, the advancement from GPU cracking to purpose-built cryptocurrency mining machines may actually be accelerating the extinction of the password. A far more practical approach to this problem is to look at the time it would take for a customised version of the Antminer S15-28TH/s or similar purposely built technology to solve the problem. This device currently retails for £772.14 ($1020) at the time this chapter was authored. Assuming the maker of the product has added a profit margin on this price enough for it to be worth their time, we could perhaps round this figure down to an estimated of £500 production cost when made on bulk. As this was an estimate, if we double this cost per unit to account for the estimation and the customisation costs of it to be able to look at multiple hash types and required associated cabling for it to be able to be linked into a network of such machines operated as one, this would give a unit price of circa £1000 for each node.

Now let's take another look at the defence budget context we considered earlier in the chapter. It would be fair to say that a one-hundred-million-pound project hardware cost would not be unreasonable to expect for a project that will be capitalised over three to five years if the correct business case were to be presented. This would mean a country could afford to create one-hundred-thousand of these devices based on the previously estimated unit price, each unit (or node) potentially checking up to 28 trillion hashes per a second dependant on the hash type. At this stage, the mathematical questions around technical possibilities seem to have been solved in that it would be feasible to check all possible combinations in a reasonable time frame. In fact, what would be more of a technical challenge at this scale and capability would power consumption and associated power costs.

Given all of this, is it technically possible that your password could be computed within seconds with nothing more than currently commercially available components? In short, yes. In fact, unless there is something significant and abnormally long and complex about it, this is a trivial matter for those entities with the time, resources and expertise.

REFRENCES

Almomani, A., Gupta, B. B., Wan, T. C., Altaher, A., & Manickam, S. (2013). Phishing dynamic evolving neural fuzzy framework for online detection zero-day phishing email.

Britain. (2019). Antminer S15-28TH/s. Retrieved from https://shop.bitmain.com/product/detail?pid=0 00201902221704359964U2e2qb490657

Dictionary, C. (2019). Meaning of password in English. [Online] Cambridge Dictionary. Retrieved from https://dictionary.cambridge.org/dictionary/english/password?q=Password

Gupta, B. B. (Ed.). (2018). *Computer and cyber security: principles, algorithm, applications, and perspectives*. CRC Press.

Gupta, B. B., Gupta, S., & Chaudhary, P. (2017). Enhancing the browser-side context-aware sanitization of suspicious HTML5 code for halting the DOM-based XSS vulnerabilities in cloud. [IJCAC]. *International Journal of Cloud Applications and Computing*, 7(1), 1–31. doi:10.4018/IJCAC.2017010101

Gupta, S., & Gupta, B. B. (2015). BDS: browser dependent XSS sanitizer. In Handbook of Research on Securing Cloud-Based Databases with Biometric Applications (pp. 174-191). IGI Global. doi:10.4018/978-1-4666-6559-0.ch008

Gupta, S., & Gupta, B. B. (2015, May). PHP-sensor: a prototype method to discover workflow violation and XSS vulnerabilities in PHP web applications. *Proceedings of the 12th ACM International Conference on Computing Frontiers* (p. 59). ACM. 10.1145/2742854.2745719

Hashcat. (n.d.). Advanced password recovery. Retrieved from https://hashcat.net/wiki/doku.php?id=example_hashes

Hashcat. (n.d.). Example hashes. Retrieved from https://hashcat.net/wiki/doku.php?id=example_hashes

Jiang, F., Fu, Y., Gupta, B. B., Lou, F., Rho, S., Meng, F., & Tian, Z. (2018). Deep learning based multi-channel intelligent attack detection for data security. *IEEE Transactions on Sustainable Computing*.

Kali. (2019) Crunch package description. Retrieved from https://tools.kali.org/password-attacks/crunch

Maglaras, L. A., Kim, K.-H., Janicke, H., Ferrag, M. A., Rallis, S., Fragkou, P., ... Cruz, T. J. (2018). Cyber security of critical infrastructures. *ICT Express*, 4(1), 42–45. doi:10.1016/j.icte.2018.02.001

Major, A., & Yampoiskiy, R. (2015) Global catastrophic risk and security implications of quantum computers. Elsevier, 72, pp. 17-26.

Microsoft. (2017) How to prevent Windows from storing a LAN manager hash of your password in Active Directory and local SAM databases. Retrieved from https://support.microsoft.com/en-us/help/299656/how-to-prevent-windows-from-storing-a-lan-manager-hash-of-your-passwor

Microsoft. (2019) Azure storage overview pricing. Retrieved from https://azure.microsoft.com/en-gb/pricing/details/storage/

Ministry of Defence UK. (2017) UK Defence in Numbers. [Online] Developed by DP and A. Retrieved from https://assets.publishing.service.gov.uk/government/uploads/system/uploads/attachment_data/file/652915/UK_Defence_in_Numbers_2017_-_Update_17_Oct.pdf

National Cyber Security Centre. (2016) Password Guidance. Simplifying Your Approach. Retrieved from https://www.ncsc.gov.uk/guidance/password-guidance-simplifying-your-approach

Rass, S., & König, S. (2018). Password Security as a Game of Entropies. *Entropy (Basel, Switzerland)*, *20*(5), 312. doi:10.3390/e20050312

SANS. (2010) Pass-the-hash attacks: Tools and Mitigation. Retrieved from https://www.sans.org/reading-room/whitepapers/testing/pass-the-hash-attacks-tools-mitigation-33283

ENDNOTE

[1]   Kali. (2019). Crunch package description. Retrieved from https://tools.kali.org/password-attacks/crunch

Compilation of References

(2018). Ogundoyin, Sunday Oyinlola. (2018). An autonomous lightweight conditional privacy-preserving authentication scheme with provable security for vehicular ad-hoc networks. *International Journal of Computers and Applications*, 1–16.

AbdelDayem, M., Hemeda, H., & Sarhan, A. (2016). Enhanced User Authentication through Keystroke Biometrics for Short-Text and Long-Text Inputs. Artificial Intelligence and Machine Learning Journal, ICGST LLC, Delaware, USA, 16(1).

Abdiansah, A., & Wardoyo, R. (2015). Time complexity analysis of support vector machines (SVM) in LibSVM. *International Journal of Computers and Applications*, *128*(3).

Abraham, J., & Paul, V. (2016). An imperceptible spatial domain color image watermarking scheme. *Journal of King Saud University-Computer and Information Sciences*.

Activation Functions in Neural Networks. (2017). Retrieved from https://towardsdatascience.com/activation-functions-neural-networks-1cbd9f8d91d6

Adeli, H. (1999). Machine Learning-Neural Networks, Genetic Algorithms and Fuzzy Systems. *Kybernetes*, *28*(3), 317–318. doi:10.1108/k.1999.28.3.317.5

Advith, J., Varun, K. R., & Manikantan, K. (2016, February). Novel digital image watermarking using DWT-DFT-SVD in YCbCr color space. *Proceedings International Conference on Emerging Trends in Engineering, Technology, and Science,* (pp. 1-6). IEEE. 10.1109/ICETETS.2016.7603032

Agarwal, S., & Sureka, A. (2015). Using knn and svm based one-class classifier for detecting online radicalization on twitter. *Proceedings International Conference on Distributed Computing and Internet Technology*, 431-442. 10.1007/978-3-319-14977-6_47

Aggarwal, J. K., & Cai, Q. (1997) Human motion analysis: A review. *Nonrigid and Articulated Motion Workshop*, pp. 99-102.

Aggarwal, J. K., Cai, Q., Liao, W., & Sabata, B. (1997). Nonrigid motion analysis: Articulated and elastic motion. *Computer Vision and Image Understanding*, 142–156.

Ahmed, R., Islam, M., & Uddin, J. (2018). Optimizing Apple Lossless Audio Codec Algorithm using NVIDIA CUDA Architecture. *International Journal of Electrical & Computer Engineering (2088-8708), 8*(1).

Ahonen, T., Hadid, A., & Pietikainen, M. (2006). Face description with local binary patterns: Application to face recognition. *IEEE Transactions on Pattern Analysis and Machine Intelligence*, *28*(12), 2037–2041. doi:10.1109/TPAMI.2006.244 PMID:17108377

Akiyama, T., Motoyoshi, F., Uchida, O., & Nakanishi, S. (2006). Hybrid digital watermarking for color images based on wavelet transform. Retrieved from https://www.researchgate.net/publication/267818801_HYBRID_DIGITAL_WATERMARKING_FOR_COLOR_IMAGES_BASED_ON_WAVELET_TRANSFORM

Alauthaman, M., Aslam, N., Zhang, L., Alasem, R., & Hossain, M. A. (2018). A P2P Botnet detection scheme based on decision tree and adaptive multilayer neural networks. *Neural Computing & Applications*, *29*(11), 991–1004. doi:10.100700521-016-2564-5 PMID:29769759

Alauthman, M., Almomani, A., Alweshah, M., Omoushd, W., & Alieyane, K. (2019). Machine Learning for phishing Detection and Mitigation. *Machine Learning for Computer and Cyber Security: Principle, Algorithms, and Practices*, 26.

Alauthman, M., Aslam, N., Al-kasassbeh, M., Khan, S., Al-Qerem, A., & Raymond Choo, K.-K. (2020). An efficient reinforcement learning-based Botnet detection approach. *Journal of Network and Computer Applications*, *150*, 102479. doi:10.1016/j.jnca.2019.102479

Alghoniemy, M., & Tewfik, A. H. (2000, May). Geometric distortion correction in image watermarking. In Security and Watermarking of Multimedia Contents II (Vol. 3971, pp. 82-89). International Society for Optics and Photonics.

Alghoniemy, M., & Tewfik, A. H. (2006). Progressive quantized projection approach to data hiding. *IEEE Transactions on Image Processing*, *15*(2), 459–472. doi:10.1109/TIP.2005.860318 PMID:16479816

Alieyan, K., Almomani, A., Anbar, M., Alauthman, M., Abdullah, R., & Gupta, B. B. (2019). DNS rule-based schema to botnet detection. *Enterprise Information Systems*, 1–20. doi:10.1080/17517575.2019.1644673

Ali, L., Monaco, J. V., Tappert, C. C., & Qiu, M. (2016). Keystroke Biometric Systems for User Authentication. *Journal of Signal Processing Systems, Springer*, *86*(2-3), 175–190. doi:10.100711265-016-1114-9

Almomani, A., Gupta, B. B., Wan, T. C., Altaher, A., & Manickam, S. (2013). Phishing dynamic evolving neural fuzzy framework for online detection zero-day phishing email.

Almomani, A., Gupta, B. B., Wan, T. C., Altaher, A., & Manickam, S. (2013). Phishing dynamic evolving neural fuzzy framework for online detection zero-day phishing email. *arXiv preprint arXiv:1302.0629*.

Almuairfi, S., Veeraraghavan, P., & Chilamkurti, N. (2011). IPAS: Implicit Password Authentication System. *Proceedings 2011 IEEE Workshops of International Conference Advanced Information Networking and Applications (WAINA)*, pp. 430-435, March 22-25, 2011 doi: 10.1109/WAINA.2011.36

Althaf, C. I. M., & Prema, S. C. (2018). Covariance and eigenvalue-based spectrum sensing using USRP in real environment. *10th International Conference on Communication Systems & Networks (COMSNETS)*, 414-417. 10.1109/COMSNETS.2018.8328231

Álvarez-Rodríguez, M., & Pérez-González, F. (2002). Analysis of pilot-based synchronization algorithms for watermarking of still images. *Signal Processing Image Communication*, *17*(8), 611–633. doi:10.1016/S0923-5965(02)00057-7

Alvi, S. A., Afzal, B., Shah, G. A., Atzori, L., & Mahmood, W. (2015). Internet of multimedia things: Vision and challenges. *Ad Hoc Networks*, *33*, 87–111. doi:10.1016/j.adhoc.2015.04.006

AlZu'bi, S., Hawashin, B., Mujahed, M., Jararweh, Y., & Gupta, B. B. (2019). An efficient employment of internet of multimedia things in smart and future agriculture. *Multimedia Tools and Applications*, 1–25.

Amato, F., Cozzolino, G., Mazzeo, A., & Romano, S. (2018). Intelligent medical record management: A diagnosis support system. *International Journal of High-Performance Computing and Networking*, *12*(4), 391–399. doi:10.1504/IJHPCN.2018.096726

Andrich, C., Ihlow, A., Bauer, J., Beuster, N., & Del Galdo, G. (2018). High-Precision Measurement of Sine and Pulse Reference Signals Using Software-Defined Radio. *IEEE Transactions on Instrumentation and Measurement, 67*(5), 1132–1141. doi:10.1109/TIM.2018.2794940

Android Developer. (2018). Retrieved from https://developer.android.com/reference/android/view/

Angelopoulou, O. (2010). *Analysis of Digital Evidence in Identity Theft Investigations* (Doctoral dissertation). Available from the University of Hertfordshire Research database (5061154).

Ansari, R., Devanalamath, M. M., Manikantan, K., & Ramachandran, S. (2012, October). Robust digital image watermarking algorithm in DWT-DFT-SVD domain for color images. In 2012 International Conference on Communication, Information, & Computing Technology, (pp. 1-6). IEEE. 10.1109/ICCICT.2012.6398160

Ansari, I. A., & Pant, M. (2017). Multipurpose image watermarking in the domain of DWT based on SVD and ABC. *Pattern Recognition Letters, 94*, 228–236. doi:10.1016/j.patrec.2016.12.010

Antal, M., Bokor, Z., & Szab'o, L. Z. (2015). Information Revealed from Scrolling Interactions on Mobile Devices. *Pattern Recognition Letters, 56*, 7–13. doi:10.1016/j.patrec.2015.01.011

Arshad, R., Saleem, A., & Khan, D. (2016). Performance comparison of Huffman coding and double Huffman coding. *Proceedings Sixth International Conference on Innovative Computing Technology*, 361-364. 10.1109/INTECH.2016.7845058

Aslantas, V. (2008). A singular-value decomposition-based image watermarking using genetic algorithm. *AEÜ. International Journal of Electronics and Communications, 62*(5), 386–394. doi:10.1016/j.aeue.2007.02.010

Assefi, M., Behravesh, E., Liu, G., & Tafti, A. P. (2018). Big data machine learning using apache spark MLlib. *Proceedings - 2017 IEEE International Conference on Big Data, Big Data 2017*. 10.1109/BigData.2017.8258338

Aste, T., Tasca, P., & Di Matteo, T. (2017). Blockchain Technologies: The Foreseeable Impact on Society and Industry. *Computer, 50*(9), 18–28. doi:10.1109/MC.2017.3571064

Atzori, L., Iera, A., & Morabito, G. (2010). The internet of things: A survey. *Computer Networks, 54*(15), 2787–2805. doi:10.1016/j.comnet.2010.05.010

Aware, Inc. (2019). Biometrics Software Solutions. - Fingerprint, Face, Iris, Keystroke Recognition. Retrieved October 29, 2019, from http://aware.com/biometrics-software-solutions/authentication-and-payments

Aydin, V. A., & Foroosh, H. (2017, September). Motion compensation using critically sampled dwt subbands for low-bitrate video coding. *Proceedings 2017 IEEE International Conference on Image Processing (ICIP)* (pp. 21-25). IEEE. 10.1109/ICIP.2017.8296235

Bachmann, J. P. (2019). The SuperM-Tree: Indexing metric spaces with sized objects. *ArXiv*, 1–14. Retrieved from http://arxiv.org/abs/1901.11453

Badra, M., Borghol, R. (2018) Long-term integrity and non-repudiation protocol for multiple entities. Sustainable cities and society, 40, 189-193.

Bala, J. D. (2017). *Application of Machine Learning in Feature Selection for Continuous Authentication*. Tennessee Tech University.

Balan, S., & Rege, J. (2017). Mining for social media: Usage patterns of small businesses. *Business Systems Research Journal: International Journal of the Society for Advancing Business & Information Technology (BIT), 8*(1), 43-50.

Balouch, Z. A., Aslam, M. I., & Ahmed, I. (2017). Energy efficient image encryption algorithm. *Proceedings International Conference on Innovations in Electrical Engineering and Computational Technologies (ICIEECT)*, 1-6.

Baraniuk, R. G., Goldstein, T., Sankaranarayanan, A. C., Studer, C., Veeraraghavan, A., & Wakin, M. B. (2017). Compressive video sensing: Algorithms, architectures, and applications. *IEEE Signal Processing Magazine, 34*(1), 52–66. doi:10.1109/MSP.2016.2602099

Baroňák, I., Čuba, M., Chen, C. M., & Beháň, L. (2017, November). Traffic Management by Admission Control in IMS Networks. *Proceedings of the 3rd Czech-China Scientific Conference 2017.* IntechOpen.

Bartalwar, S., & Deepa, T. (2017). Design and implementation of OFDM signal transmission for Visible light communication. *International Journal of Engineering Sciences & Research Technology, 6,* 577–583.

Bas, P., Chassery, J. M., & Macq, B. (2002). Geometrically invariant watermarking using feature points. *IEEE Transactions on Image Processing, 11*(9), 1014–1028. doi:10.1109/TIP.2002.801587 PMID:18249723

Batubara, H. H., & Ariani, D. N. (2016). Pemanfaatan Video sebagai Media Pembelajaran Matematika SD/MI. *Muallimuna, 2*(1), 47–66. doi:10.31602/muallimuna.v2i1.741

Beebe, N. (2009). Digital Forensic Research: The Good, the Bad and the Unaddressed. In *Advances in Digital Forensics V Digital Forensics 2009. IFIP Advances in Information and Communication Technology.* Berlin, Germany: Springer. doi:10.1007/978-3-642-04155-6_2

Begg, R. K., Palaniswami, M., & Owen, B. (2005). Support vector machines for automated gait classification. *IEEE Transactions on Biomedical Engineering, 52*(5), 828–838. doi:10.1109/TBME.2005.845241 PMID:15887532

BehavioSec, Inc. (2019). Continuous Authentication through Passive Behavioral Biometrics. Retrieved October 29, 2019, from http://behaviosec.com

Ben-Gal, I., Ruggeri, F., Faltin, F., & Kenett, R. (2007). Bayesian Network.

Bennett, D. (2012). The Challenges Facing Computer Forensics Investigators in obtaining the criminal investigation's information from the mobile devices. *Information Security Journal: A Global Perspective, 21*(3), 159-168.

Bernstein, D. (2014). Containers and cloud: From lxc to docker to kubernetes. *IEEE Cloud Computing, 1*(3), 81–84. doi:10.1109/MCC.2014.51

Berres, A. S., Turton, T. L., Petersen, M., Rogers, D. H., Ahrens, J. P., Rink, K., ... Bujack, R. (2017, June). Video compression for ocean simulation image databases. In *Workshop on Visualisation in Environmental Sciences (EnvirVis).*

Bertino, E., & Islam, N. (2017). Botnets and internet of things security. *Computer, 50*(2), 76–79. doi:10.1109/MC.2017.62

Bhatt, C. M. (2017). Data Protection and Security Issues in Social Media. In C. Bhatt, & S. Peddoju (Eds.), *Cloud Computing Systems and Applications in Healthcare* (pp. 135–162). Hershey, PA: IGI Global. doi:10.4018/978-1-5225-1002-4.ch008

Bianchi, T., & Piva, A. (2013). Secure watermarking for multimedia content protection: A review of its benefits and open issues. *IEEE Signal Processing Magazine, 30*(2), 87–96. doi:10.1109/MSP.2012.2228342

Bimbot, F., Bonastre, J. F., Fredouille, C., Gravier, G., Magrin-Chagnolleau, I., Meignier, S., ... Reynolds, D. A. (2004). A Tutorial on Text-Independent Speaker Verification. *EURASIP Journal on Applied Signal Processing,* 430–451.

Birget, J. C., Hong; D., & Memon, N. (2006). Graphical passwords based on robust discretization, *Information Forensics and Security. IEEE Transactions, 1*(3), 395–399.

Bo, C., Zhang, L., Li, X. Y., Huang, Q., & Wang, Y. (2013). SilentSense: Silent User's identification Via Touch and Movement Behavioral Biometrics. *Proceedings 19th Annual International Conference on Mobile Computing & Networking,* 187-190. 10.1145/2500423.2504572

Bonastre, J. F., Bimbot, F., Boe, L. J., Cambell, J. P., Reynolds, D. A., & Magrin-Chagnolleau, I. (2003). Person Authentication by Voice: A Need for Caution. *Proceedings of Eurospeech.*

Borji, A., Cheng, M., Jiang, H., & Li, J. (2015). Salient object detection: A benchmark. *IEEE Transactions on Image Processing*, 24(12), 5706–5722. doi:10.1109/TIP.2015.2487833 PMID:26452281

Bostani, H., & Sheikhan, M. (2017). Hybrid of anomaly-based and specification-based IDS for Internet of Things using unsupervised OPF based on MapReduce approach. *Computer Communications*, 98, 52–71. doi:10.1016/j.comcom.2016.12.001

Bovik, A. C. (2010). *Handbook of image and video processing.* Academic Press.

Bovik, A. L. (2000). *Handbook of Image and Video Processing. Academic Press* (pp. 99–69120). Canada: Library of Congress Catalog Number.

Boykov, Y. Y., & Jolly, M. P. (2001). Interactive graph cuts for optimal boundary & region segmentation of objects in ND images. *Proceedings IEEE International Conference on Computer Vision.* (Vol. 1, pp. 105-112). Academic Press.

Bregonzio, M., Gong, S., & Xiang, T. (2009). Recognizing action as clouds of space-time interest points. *CVPR*, 1948–1955.

Breiman, L. (2001). Random forests. *Machine Learning*, 45(1), 5–32. doi:10.1023/A:1010933404324

Britain. (2019). Antminer S15-28TH/s. Retrieved from https://shop.bitmain.com/product/detail?pid=00020190222170435964U2e2qb490657

Britanak, V., & Rao, K. R. (2018). Audio Coding Standards, (Proprietary) Audio Compression Algorithms, and Broadcasting/Speech/Data Communication Codecs: Overview of Adopted Filter Banks. In *Cosine-/Sine-Modulated Filter Banks* (pp. 13–37). Cham, Switzerland: Springer. doi:10.1007/978-3-319-61080-1_2

Budiu, R. (2015). Mobile User Experience: Limitations and Strengths. Retrieved from https://www.nngroup.com/articles/mobile-ux/

Bulat, A., & Tzimiropoulos, G. (2016). Human pose estimation via convolutional part heatmap regression. *Proceedings European Conference on Computer Vision* (pp. 717-732). Springer. 10.1007/978-3-319-46478-7_44

Buriro, A., Crispo, B., Del Frari, F., Klardie, J., & Wrona, K. (2016). Itsme: Multi-modal and Unobtrusive Behavioural User Authentication for Smartphones. *Proceedings of the 9th Conference on passwords (PASSWORDS 2015)*, Springer, 45–61. 10.1007/978-3-319-29938-9_4

Burroughs, B. (2019). A cultural lineage of streaming. *Internet Histories*, 3(2), 147–161. doi:10.1080/24701475.2019.1576425

Butun, I., Kantarci, B., & Erol-Kantarci, M. (2015). Anomaly detection and privacy preservation in cloud-centric Internet of Things. *Proceedings 2015 IEEE International Conference on Communication Workshop (ICCW).* 10.1109/ICCW.2015.7247572

Cai, H., Zheng, V. W., & Chang, K. C. C. (2018). A Comprehensive Survey of Graph Embedding: Problems, Techniques, and Applications. *IEEE Transactions on Knowledge and Data Engineering*, 30(9), 1616–1637. doi:10.1109/TKDE.2018.2807452

Cao, Z., Simon, T., Wei, S. E., & Sheikh, Y. (2017). Realtime multi-person 2D pose estimation using part affinity fields. *Proceedings IEEE Conference on Computer Vision and Pattern Recognition* (pp. 7291-7299). 10.1109/CVPR.2017.143

Cardozo, D., Campo, S., Manjarres, J., & Percybrooks, W. (2018, November). Sub-band coding for audio signals using Matlab. [IOP Publishing.]. *Journal of Physics: Conference Series*, 1126(1). doi:10.1088/1742-6596/1126/1/012029

Carmona, E. (2014). *Tutorial sobre Máquinas de Vectores Soporte (SVM)*. Department of Intelligence Artificial, Universidad Nacional de Educación a Distancia. Spain: UNED.

Cato, A. (2015). A Bit of Bytes: The Anatomy of Size and Memory. *Austl. L. Libr.*, *23*, 33.

Centeno, M. P., van Moorsel, A., & Castruccio, S. (2017). Smartphone continuous authentication using deep learning autoencoders. *Proceedings 15th Annual Conference on Privacy, Security and Trust (PST)*, 147-1478. 10.1109/PST.2017.00026

Chalmers, A., Campisi, P., Shirley, P., & Olaizola, I. G. (Eds.). (2016). *High dynamic range video: concepts, technologies, and applications*. Academic Press.

Chan, E. M. (2011*). Philosophy in Computer Science* (Doctoral dissertation). Available from the University of Illinois at Urbana Champaign theses database (24365).

Chaudhary, P., Gupta, S., & Gupta, B. B. (2016). Auditing defense against XSS worms in online social network-based web applications. In *Handbook of research on modern cryptographic solutions for computer and cyber security* (pp. 216–245). IGI Global. doi:10.4018/978-1-5225-0105-3.ch010

Chen, Y., Li, H., Li, K., & Zhang, J. (2017) An improved P2P file system scheme based on IPFS and Blockchain. IEEE International Conference on Big Data, pp. 2652-2657.

Chen, C., Liang, J., Zhao, H., Hu, H., & Tian, J. (2009). Frame difference energy image for gait recognition with incomplete silhouettes. *Pattern Recognition Letters*, *30*(11), 977–984. doi:10.1016/j.patrec.2009.04.012

Cheng, L. M., Cheng, L. L., Chan, C. K., & Ng, K. W. (2004, December). Digital watermarking based on frequency random position insertion. *Proceedings ICARCV 2004 8th Control, Automation, Robotics, and Vision Conference* (Vol. 2, pp. 977-982). IEEE. 10.1109/ICARCV.2004.1468975

Chen, J., Zhang, S., Wang, H., & Zhang, X. (2013). Practicing a Record-and-Replay System on USRP. *Proceedings of the second workshop on Software radio implementation forum*, 61-64. 10.1145/2491246.2491257

Cheong, C. W. V. (2008). *Data acquisition from volatile memory: A memory acquisition tool for Microsoft Windows Vista* (Doctoral dissertation). Available from the Naval Postgraduate School theses Archive Calhoun (10945/3795).

Chion, M. (2019). *Audio-vision: sound on screen*. Columbia University Press. doi:10.7312/chio18588

Chui, C. K. (2016). *An introduction to wavelets*. Elsevier.

Chu, W. C. (2003). DCT-based image watermarking using subsampling. *IEEE Transactions on Multimedia*, *5*(1), 34–38. doi:10.1109/TMM.2003.808816

Ciaccia, P., Patella, M., & Zezula, P. (1997). M-tree: An efficient access method for similarity search in metric spaces. *Proceedings of the 23rd International Conference on Very Large Databases, VLD*. Academic Press.

Ciresan, D., Giusti, A., Gambardella, L. M., & Schmidhuber, J. (2012). Deep neural networks segment neuronal membranes in electron microscopy images. *Advances in Neural Information Processing Systems*, 2843–2851.

Clancy, T. C., Kiyavash, N., & Lin, D. J. (2003). Secure Smartcard Based Fingerprint Authentication. *Proceedings of the 2003 ACM SIGMM workshop on Biometrics methods and applications*, 45–52. 10.1145/982507.982516

Coatrieux, G., Lamard, M., Lamard, W., Puentes, J., & Roux, C. (2005). A Low Distortion and Reversible Watermark: Application to Angiographic Images of the Retina. *Proceedings of the 27th IEEE Annual Conference on Engineering in Medicine and Biology*, pp. 1-4. Shanghai, China.

Coatrieux, G., Maitre, H., Sankur, B., Rolland, Y., & Collorec, R. (2000). Relevance of Watermarking in Medical Imaging. *Proceedings of the IEEE International Conference on Information Technology Applications in Biomedicine,* Arlington, TX, pp. 250-255, November 2000. 10.1109/ITAB.2000.892396

Cole, E. (2003). *Hiding in Plain Sight: Steganography and Art of Covert Communications.* USA: Wiley Publishing

Coltuc, D., & Bolon, P. (1999). Robust watermarking by histogram specification. *Proceedings of 1999 International Conference on Image Processing,* 236-239. 10.1109/ICIP.1999.822891

Containerd. (n.d.). Retrieved from https://containerd.io

Conti, M., Zachia-Zlatea, I., & Crispo, B. (2011). Mind How You Answer Me! Transparently Authenticating the User of a Smartphone When Answering or Placing A Call. *Proceedings of the 6th ACM Symposium on Information, Computer and Communications Security,* 249-259. Hong Kong, China.

Cox, I., Miller, M., Linnartz, J. P., & Kalker, T. (1999). A Review of Watermarking Principles and Practices. In K. K. Parhi, & T. Nishitani (Eds.), Digital Signal Processing in Multimedia Systems, pp. 461-485. Marcell Dekker Inc. doi:10.1201/9781482276046-17

CRI-O. (n.d.). Retrieved from http://cri-o.io

Cui, Y., Ahmad, S., & Hawkins, J. (2016). Continuous online sequence learning with an unsupervised neural network model. *Neural Computation, 28*(11), 2474–2504. doi:10.1162/NECO_a_00893 PMID:27626963

Cunado, D., Nixon, M. S., & Carter, J. N. (1997). Using gait as a biometric, via phase-weighted magnitude spectra. *Proceedings International Conference on Audio-and Video-Based Biometric Person Authentication* (pp. 93-102). Berlin, Germany: Springer. 10.1007/BFb0015984

Cutler, R., & Davis, L. S. (2000). Robust real-time periodic motion detection, analysis, and applications. *IEEE Transactions on Pattern Analysis and Machine Intelligence, 22*(8), 781–796. doi:10.1109/34.868681

Dabas, P., & Khanna, K. (2013). A study on spatial and transform domain watermarking techniques. *International Journal of Computers and Applications, 71*(14).

Dai, J., Li, Y., He, K., & Sun, J. (2016). R-FCN: Object detection via region-based fully convolutional networks. Proceedings NIPS, pp. 379-387.

Dai, J., He, K., Li, Y., Ren, S., & Sun, J. (2016). *Instance-sensitive fully convolutional networks.* Proceedings *ECCV,* pp. 534–549.

Dai, M., Zhang, S., Wang, H., & Jin, S. (2018). A Low Storage Room Requirement Framework for Distributed Ledger in Blockchain. *IEEE Access: Practical Innovations, Open Solutions, 6,* 22970–22975. doi:10.1109/ACCESS.2018.2814624

Dalal, N., & Triggs, B. (2005). Histograms of oriented gradients for human detection. *Proceedings International Conference on Computer Vision & Pattern Recognition, 1,* 886–893. IEEE.

Davidson, J., Liebald, B., Liu, J., Nandy, P., Van Vleet, T., Gargi, U., ... Sampath, D. (2010) The YouTube video recommendation system. *Proceedings of the Fourth ACM Conference on Recommender Systems,* pp. 293–296. 10.1145/1864708.1864770

Delannay, D., & Macq, B. (2000). Generalized 2-D cyclic patterns for secret watermark generation. *Proceedings of 2000 International Conference on Image Processing,* 77-79. Academic Press.

DelValle, R., Rattihalli, G., Beltre, A., Govindaraju, M., & Lewis, M. J. (2016, June). Exploring the Design Space for Optimizations with Apache Aurora and Mesos. In *2016 IEEE 9th International Conference on Cloud Computing (CLOUD)* (pp. 537-544). IEEE.

Deng, C., Gao, X., Li, X., & Tao, D. (2009). A local Tchebichef moments-based robust image watermarking. *Signal Processing*, *89*(8), 1531–1539. doi:10.1016/j.sigpro.2009.02.005

Derlatka, M., & Bogdan, M. (2015). Fusion of static and dynamic parameters at decision level in human gait recognition. *Proceedings International Conference on Pattern Recognition and Machine Intelligence* (pp. 515-524). Springer. 10.1007/978-3-319-19941-2_49

Developers, A. (2019). Distribution Dashboard. Retrieved October 29, 2019, from https://developer.android.com/about/dashboards/

Devi, H. S., & Singh, K. M. (2017). A Novel, Efficient, Robust, and Blind Imperceptible 3D Anaglyph Image Watermarking. *Arabian Journal for Science and Engineering*, *42*(8), 3521–3533. doi:10.100713369-017-2531-1

Deyan, G. (2019, March 28). 60+ Smartphone. *Stat, 2019.* Retrieved from https://techjury.net/stats-about/smartphone-usage/

Dictionary, C. (2019). Meaning of password in English. [Online] Cambridge Dictionary. Retrieved from https://dictionary.cambridge.org/dictionary/english/password?q=Password

Ding, H. Y. (2016). Novel Efficient Image Watermark Algorithm Based on DFT Transform. International Journal of Signal Processing. *Image Processing and Pattern Recognition*, *9*(10), 297–312.

Dirik, A. E., Memon, N., & Birget, J. C. (2007, July). Modeling user choice in the PassPoints graphical password scheme. *Proceedings of the 3rd symposium on Usable privacy and security* (pp. 20-28). Pittsburgh, PA: ACM.

Dittmar, T. (2017). *Audio Engineering 101: A Beginner's Guide to Music Production.* Routledge. doi:10.4324/9781315618173

Docker. (n.d). Retrieved from https://www.docker.com

Domingos, P. (2012). A Few Useful Things to Know about Machine Learning. *Communications of the ACM*, *55*(10), 78–87. doi:10.1145/2347736.2347755

Dong, P., & Galatsanos, N. P. (2002). Affine transformation resistant watermarking based on image normalization. *Proceedings of the International Conference on Image Processing*, 489-492. 10.1109/ICIP.2002.1039014

Dougherty, G. (2009). *Digital image processing for medical applications.* Cambridge University Press. doi:10.1017/CBO9780511609657

Dubin, R., Hadar, O., Dvir, A., & Pele, O. (2018). Video quality representation classification of encrypted http adaptive video streaming. *TIIS*, *12*(8), 3804–3819.

Dutta, M. K., Singh, A., Singh, A., Burget, R., & Prinosil, J. (2015). Digital identification tags for medical fundus images for teleophthalmology applications. *Proceedings 2015 38th International Conference on Telecommunications and Signal Processing.* pp. 781-784. Prague, Czech Republic. DOI: 10.1109/TSP.2015.7296372

Eberz, S., & Rasmussen, K. B. (2017). Evaluating Behavioral Biometrics for Continuous Authentication: Challenges and Metrics. *Proceedings of the 2017 ACM on Asia Conference on Computer and Communications Security*, 386-399. Abu Dhabi, United Arab Emirates. 10.1145/3052973.3053032

Ehatisham-ul-Haq, M., Azam, M. A., Loo, J., Shuang, K., Islam, S., Naeem, U., & Amin, Y. (2017). Authentication of Smartphone Users Based on Activity Recognition and Mobile Sensing. *Sensors (Basel)*, *17*(9), 2043. doi:10.339017092043 PMID:28878177

Elbafisi, E. (2012). Robust mpeg watermarking in dwt four bands. *Journal of Applied Research and Technology*, *10*(2), 87–93.

Eliseo, M. A., & Silva, L (2016). Desenvolvimento de Jogos em Ultra-Alta Definição (UHD-4K).

Eljetlawi, M. (2010). Graphical Password: Existing Recognition Based Graphical Password Usability. *Proceedings of the IEEE 6th Conference on Networked Computing (INC)*. IEEE.

Erhan, D., Szegedy, C., Toshev, A., & Anguelov, D. (2014). Scalable object detection using deep neural networks. Proceedings IEEE CVPR, pp. 2147-2154. doi:10.1109/CVPR.2014.276

Etcd. (n.d.). Retrieved from https://coreos.com/etcd

Farabet, C., Couprie, C., Najman, L., & LeCun, Y. (2013). Learning hierarchical features for scene labeling. *IEEE Transactions on Pattern Analysis and Machine Intelligence*, *35*(8), 1915–1929. doi:10.1109/TPAMI.2012.231

Feng, T., Liu, Z., Kwon, K. A., Shi, W., Carbunar, B., Jiang, Y., & Nguyen, N. (2012). Continuous Mobile Authentication Using Touchscreen Gestures. *Proceedings of the 2012 IEEE International Conference on Technologies for Homeland Security (HST 2012)*, Waltham, MA, 451–456. 10.1109/THS.2012.6459891

Fierrez, J., Morales, A., Vera-Rodriguez, R., & Camacho, D. (2018). Multiple Classifiers in Biometrics. Part 2: Trends and Challenges. *Information Fusion*, *44*, 103–112. doi:10.1016/j.inffus.2017.12.005

Fierrez, J., Pozo, A., Martinez-Diaz, M., Galbally, J., & Morales, A. (2018). Benchmarking Touchscreen Biometrics for mobile Authentication. *IEEE Transactions on Information Forensics and Security*, *13*(11), 1556–6013. doi:10.1109/TIFS.2018.2833042

Findlater, L., Wobbrock, J. O., & Wigdor, D. (2011). Typing on fiat Glass: Examining Ten-finger Expert Typing Patterns on Touch Surfaces. *Proceedings of the 2011 Annual Conference on Human Factors in computing systems, CHI '11*, 2453–2462. New York, NY. ACM. 10.1145/1978942.1979301

Firmansah, L., & Setiawan, E. B. (2016, May). Data audio compression lossless FLAC format to lossy audio MP3 format with Huffman shift coding algorithm. *Proceedings 2016 4th International Conference on Information and Communication Technology (ICoICT)* (pp. 1-5). IEEE. 10.1109/ICoICT.2016.7571951

Foo, S. (2000). A machine vision approach to detect and categorize hydrocarbon fires in aircraft dry bays and engine compartments. *IEEE Transactions on Industry Applications*, *36*(2), 459–466. doi:10.1109/28.833762

Foresti, G. L. (1999). Object recognition and tracking for remote video surveillance. *IEEE Transactions on Circuits and Systems for Video Technology*, *9*(7), 1045–1062. doi:10.1109/76.795058

Fowler, S. (2011). An *Overview of small-scale digital forensics*. Available from the Eastern Michigan University Theses & Projects database (274).

Frakti. (n.d.). Retrieved from https://github.com/kubernetes/frakti

Frank, M., Biedert, R., Ma, E., Martinovic, I., & Song, D. (2013). Touchalytics: On the Applicability of Touchscreen Input as a Behavioral Biometric for Continuous Authentication. *IEEE Transactions on Information Forensics and Security*, *8*(1), 136–148. doi:10.1109/TIFS.2012.2225048

Fridman, L., & Weber, S. (2016). Active Authentication on Mobile Devices via Stylometry Application Usage, Web Browsing, and GPS Location. *IEEE Systems Journal*, 513–521.

Fridman, L., Weber, S., Greenstadt, R., & Kam, M. (2017). Active Authentication on Mobile Devices via Stylometry, Application Usage, Web Browsing, and GPS Location. *IEEE Systems Journal, 11*(2), 513–521. doi:10.1109/JSYST.2015.2472579

Frizzi, S., Kaabi, R., Bouchouicha, M., Ginoux, J., Moreau, E., & Fnaiech, F. (2016). Convolutional neural network for video fire and smoke detection. *Proceedings Annual Conference of the IEEE Industrial Electronics Society*, pp. 877-882 10.1109/IECON.2016.7793196

Fujiyoshi, H., Lipton, A. J., & Kanade, T. (2004). Real-time human motion analysis by image skeltonization. *IEICE Transactions on Information and Systems*, 113–120.

Gafurov, D., Snekkenes, E., & Buvarp, T. E. (2006). Robustness of Biometric Gait Authentication Against Impersonation Attacks. *Proceedings of the Workshop on the Move to Meaningful Internet Systems, ser. Lecture Notes in Computer Science*, 4277/2006, 479–488. 10.1007/11915034_71

Ganic, E., & Eskicioglu, A. M. (2004). Robust DWT-SVD domain image watermarking: embedding data in all frequencies. *Proceedings of 6th workshop on Multimedia & Security, MM & Sec*, p. 166-174.

Garcia-Gasulla, D., Béjar, J., Cortés, U., Ayguadé, E., & Labarta, J. (2015). Extracting Visual Patterns from Deep Learning Representations. *ArXiv:1507.08818 [Cs]*.

Geir, M. K. (2013, October). Privacy enhanced mutual authentication in LTE. *Proceedings 2013 IEEE 9th International Conference on Wireless and Mobile Computing, Networking and Communications (WiMob)* (pp. 614-621). IEEE.

Gianni, F., Mirko, M., & Ludovico, B. (2017). A Multi-Biometric System for Continuous Student Authentication in E-learning Platforms. *Pattern Recognition Letters, Elsevier, 113*, 83–92.

Gibson, J. (2016). Speech compression. *Information, 7*(2), 32. doi:10.3390/info7020032

Gilles, L. (2014). *Understanding Random Forest from Theory to Practice*. University of Liège.

Girshick, R., Donahue, J., Darrell, T., & Malik, J. (2014). Rich feature hierarchies for accurate object detection and semantic segmentation. Proceedings IEEE CVPR, pp. 580-587 doi:10.1109/CVPR.2014.81

Girshick, R. (2015). *Fast R-CNN*. Proceedings *IEEE ICCV*, pp. 1440–1448.

Girshick, R., Donahue, J., Darrell, T., & Malik, J. (2014). Rich feature hierarchies for accurate object detection and semantic segmentation. *CVPR, 14*, 580–587.

Giustini, G. (2009). Open Source Live Distributions for Computer Forensics. In E. Huebner, & S. Zanero (Eds.), *Open source software for Digital* (pp. 69–82). US: Springer.

Goldstein, M., & Uchida, S. (2016). A comparative evaluation of unsupervised anomaly detection algorithms for multivariate data. *PLoS One, 11*(4). doi:10.1371/journal.pone.0152173 PMID:27093601

Gonzalez, R. C., & Woods, R. E. (2002). Digital Image Processing (2nd Ed.), Prentice-Hall Publishers, Upper Saddle River, NJ 07458.

Gonzalez, G. R., Organero, M. M., & Kloos, C. D. (2008). Early infrastructure of an internet of things in spaces for learning. *Proceedings 2008 Eighth IEEE International Conference on Advanced Learning Technologies*. 10.1109/ICALT.2008.210

Gouda, M, Hussien, M., Ragab, M.R., Anwar, A.M., & Gouda, A.F. (2017). USRP Implementation of PTS Technique for PAPR Reduction in OFDM Using LABVIEW. *Advances is Wireless Communications and Networks, 2*, 15-24.

Gramoli, V., & Staples, M. (2018). Blockchain Standard: Can We Reach Consensus? *Communications Standards Magazine, IEEE, 2*(3), 16–21. doi:10.1109/MCOMSTD.2018.1800022

Gregor, K., Besse, F., Rezende, D. J., Danihelka, I., & Wierstra, D. (2016). Towards conceptual compression. In Advances In Neural Information Processing Systems (pp. 3549-3557).

Guerrero, C., Lera, I., & Juiz, C. (2018). Genetic algorithm for multi-objective optimization of container allocation in cloud architecture. *Journal of Grid Computing, 16*(1), 113–135. doi:10.100710723-017-9419-x

Guo, C. (2013). Design and implementation of a multimedia database application system. *Journal of Theoretical and Applied Information Technology, 47(3).*

Guo, Y., Ding, G., & Han, J. (2017). Robust quantization for general similarity search. *IEEE Transactions on Image Processing, 27*(2), 949–963. doi:10.1109/TIP.2017.2766445 PMID:29757738

Guo, Y., Xu, G., & Tsuji, S. (1994). Tracking human body motion based on a stick figure model. *Journal of Visual Communication and Image Representation, 5*(1), 1–9. doi:10.1006/jvci.1994.1001

Gupta, B. B. (2018). Computer and cyber security: principles, algorithm, applications, and perspectives. Boca Raton, FL: CRC Press.

Gupta, B. B. (Ed.). (2018). Computer and cyber security: principles, algorithm, applications, and perspectives. Boca Raton, FL: CRC Press.

Gupta, B., Agrawal, D., & Yamaguchi, S. (2018). Deep learning models for human centered computing in fog and mobile edge networks (pp. 1–5). Academic Press.

Gupta, B. B. (Ed.). (2018). *Computer and cyber security: principles, algorithm, applications, and perspectives.* CRC Press.

Gupta, B. B., & Agrawal, D. P. (Eds.). (2019). *Handbook of Research on Cloud Computing and Big Data Applications in IoT.* IGI Global. doi:10.4018/978-1-5225-8407-0

Gupta, B. B., Gupta, S., & Chaudhary, P. (2017). Enhancing the browser-side context-aware sanitization of suspicious HTML5 code for halting the DOM-based XSS vulnerabilities in cloud. [IJCAC]. *International Journal of Cloud Applications and Computing, 7*(1), 1–31. doi:10.4018/IJCAC.2017010101

Gupta, B. B., Yamaguchi, S., & Agrawal, D. P. (2018). Advances in security and privacy of multimedia big data in mobile and cloud computing. *Multimedia Tools and Applications, 77*(7), 9203–9208. doi:10.100711042-017-5301-x

Gupta, B., Agrawal, D. P., & Yamaguchi, S. (Eds.). (2016). *Handbook of research on modern cryptographic solutions for computer and cyber security.* IGI Global. doi:10.4018/978-1-5225-0105-3

Gupta, R., Kumar, M., & Bathla, R. (2016). Data Compression-Lossless and Lossy Techniques. *International Journal of Application or Innovation in Engineering & Management, 5*(7), 120–125.

Gupta, S., & Gupta, B. B. (2015). BDS: browser dependent XSS sanitizer. In *Handbook of Research on Securing Cloud-Based Databases with Biometric Applications* (pp. 174–191). IGI Global. doi:10.4018/978-1-4666-6559-0.ch008

Gupta, S., & Gupta, B. B. (2015, May). PHP-sensor: a prototype method to discover workflow violation and XSS vulnerabilities in PHP web applications. *Proceedings of the 12th ACM International Conference on Computing Frontiers* (p. 59). ACM. 10.1145/2742854.2745719

Gu, Q., Yang, J., Yan, W., & Klette, R. (2017). Integrated multi-scale event verification in an augmented foreground motion space. *Proceedings Pacific-Rim Symposium on Image and Video Technology*, pp. 488-500.

Guyon, I., & Elisseeff, A. (2003). An introduction to variable and feature selection. *Journal of Machine Learning Research*, *3*(Mar), 1157–1182.

Haddad, Z. J., Taha, S., & Saroit, I. A. (2017). Anonymous authentication and location privacy, preserving schemes for LTE-A networks. *Egyptian Informatics Journal*, *18*(3), 193–203. doi:10.1016/j.eij.2017.01.002

Hai, H., Qing, X. D., & Ke, Q. (2018). A watermarking-based authentication and image restoration in multimedia sensor networks. *International Journal of High Performance Computing and Networking*, *12*(1), 65–73. doi:10.1504/IJHPCN.2018.093846

Hall, M. A. (1999). Correlation-based feature selection for machine learning.

Hamandi, K., Sarji, I., Chehab, A., Elhajj, I. H., & Kayssi, A. (2013, March). Privacy enhanced and computationally efficient HSK-AKA LTE scheme. *Proceedings 2013 27th International Conference on Advanced Information Networking and Applications Workshops*. (pp. 929-934). IEEE.

Hameed, M. A., Aly, S., & Hassaballah, M. (2017). An efficient data hiding method based on adaptive directional pixel value differencing (ADPVD). *Multimedia Tools and Applications*, 1–19.

Hamidi, M., El Haziti, M., Cherifi, H., & Aboutajdine, D. (2015, November). A blind robust image watermarking approach exploiting the DFT magnitude. *Proceedings 2015 IEEE/ACS 12th International Conference of Computer Systems and Applications* (pp. 1-6). IEEE. 10.1109/AICCSA.2015.7507124

Han, J., & Bhanu, B. (2005). Individual recognition using gait energy image. *IEEE Transactions on Pattern Analysis and Machine Intelligence*, *28*(2), 316–322. doi:10.1109/TPAMI.2006.38 PMID:16468626

Hanjalic, A. (2017). Multimedia Research: What Is the Right Approach? *IEEE MultiMedia*, *24*(2), 4–6. doi:10.1109/MMUL.2017.31

Han, X. (2010). *Gait recognition considering walking direction*. USA: University of Rochester.

Hasan, M. R., Jha, A. K., & Liu, Y. (2018). Excessive use of online video streaming services: Impact of recommender system use, psychological factors, and motives. *Computers in Human Behavior*, *80*, 220–228. doi:10.1016/j.chb.2017.11.020

Hashcat. (n.d.). Advanced password recovery. Retrieved from https://hashcat.net/wiki/doku.php?id=example_hashes

Hashcat. (n.d.). Example hashes. Retrieved from https://hashcat.net/wiki/doku.php?id=example_hashes

Hashem, I. A. T., Yaqoob, I., Anuar, N. B., Mokhtar, S., Gani, A., & Khan, S. U. (2015). The rise of "big data" on cloud computing: Review and open research issues. *Information Systems*, *47*, 98–115. doi:10.1016/j.is.2014.07.006

Healey, G., Slater, D., Lin, T., Drda, B., & Goedeke, A. (1993). A system for real-time fire detection. Proceedings IEEE CVPR, pp. 605-606. doi:10.1109/CVPR.1993.341064

He, K., Gkioxari, G., Dollár, P., & Girshick, R. (2017). Mask R-CNN. *Proceedings IEEE International Conference on Computer Vision* (pp. 2961-2969). IEEE.

He, K., Zhang, X., Ren, S., & Sun, J. (2015). Spatial pyramid pooling in deep convolutional networks for visual recognition. *IEEE Transactions on Pattern Analysis and Machine Intelligence*, *37*(9), 1904–1916. doi:10.1109/TPAMI.2015.2389824

He, K., Zhang, X., Ren, S., & Sun, J. (2016). *Deep residual learning for image recognition* (pp. 770–778). CVPR.

Hennequin, R., Royo-Letelier, J., & Moussallam, M. (2017, March). Codec independent lossy audio compression detection. In *2017 IEEE International Conference on Acoustics, Speech and Signal Processing (ICASSP)* (pp. 726-730). IEEE. 10.1109/ICASSP.2017.7952251

Herrigel, A., Voloshynovskiy, S. V., & Rytsar, Y. B. (2001). Watermark template attack. In Security and Watermarking of Multimedia Contents III (Vol. 4314, pp. 394-405). International Society for Optics and Photonics.

Herrigel, A., Perrig, A., & Ruanaidh, J. Ó. (1997). *A Copyright Protection Environment for Digital Images* (pp. 1–16). Berlin, Germany: Springer. doi:10.1007/978-3-322-86842-8_1

Hidayat, T., Zakaria, M. H., Pee, A. N. C., & Naim, A. (2018). Comparison of Lossless Compression Schemes for WAV Audio Data 16-Bit between Huffman and Coding Arithmetic. *International Journal of Simulation-Systems, Science & Technology, 19*(6).

Hightower, K., Burns, B., & Beda, J. (2017). *Kubernetes: up and running: dive into the future of infrastructure.* O'Reilly Media.

Hindman, B., Konwinski, A., Zaharia, M., Ghodsi, A., Joseph, A. D., Katz, R. H., . . . Stoica, I. (2011, March). Mesos: A platform for fine-grained resource sharing in the data center. In NSDI (Vol. 11, No. 2011, pp. 22-22).

Hinton, G. E., & Salakhutdinov, R. R. (2006). Reducing the dimensionality of data with neural networks. *Science, 313*(5786), 504–507. doi:10.1126cience.1127647

Hinton, G., Osindero, S., & Teh, Y. (2006). A fast learning algorithm for deep belief nets. *Neural Computation, 18*(7), 1527–1554. doi:10.1162/neco.2006.18.7.1527

Homepage, Y. A. G. O. (n.d.). Retrieved January 21, 2019, from https://www.mpi-inf.mpg.de/departments/databases-and-information-systems/research/yago-naga/yago

Hu, S. H., Li, Y., & Li, B. (2016). Video2vec: Learning semantic spatio-temporal embeddings for video representation. *Proceedings - International Conference on Pattern Recognition.* 10.1109/ICPR.2016.7899735

Hu, Z., Guo, X., Hu, X., Chen, X., & Wang, Z. (2005). The Identification and Recognition Based on Ocular Fundus, Springer Link Lecture Notes in Computer Science, 3832, pp. 770-776.

Huang, P. S., Chiang, C. S., Chang, C. P., & Tu, T. M. (2005). Robust spatial watermarking technique for colour images via direct saturation adjustment. *IEE Proceedings Vision Image and Signal Processing, 152*(5), 561–574. doi:10.1049/ip-vis:20041081

Huebner, E., Bem, D., & Cheung, H. (2010). Computer Forensics Education–the Open Source Approach. In *Open Source Software for Digital Forensics* (pp. 9–23). Boston, MA: Springer.

Huertas, A., García, F. J., Gil, M., & Martínez, G. (2016). SeCoMan: A Semantic-Aware Policy Framework for Developing Privacy-Preserving and Context-Aware Smart Applications. *IEEE Systems Journal, 10*(3), 111–1124.

Huertas, A., Gil, M., García, F. J., & Martínez, G. (2014a). Precise: Privacy-aware recommender based on context information for cloud service environments. *IEEE Communications Magazine, 52*(8), 90–96. doi:10.1109/MCOM.2014.6871675

Huertas, A., Gil, M., García, F. J., & Martínez, G. (2014b). *What Private Information Are You Disclosing? A Privacy-Preserving System Supervised by Yourself* (pp. 1221–1228). Paris, France: IEEE Intl Conf on High Performance Computing and Communications.

Huertas, A., Gil, M., García, F. J., & Martínez, G. (2016). MASTERY: A multicontext-aware system that preserves the users' privacy. *NOMS IEEE/IFIP Network Operations and Management Symposium*, 523-528.

Huertas, A., Gil, M., García, F. J., & Martínez, G. (2017). Preserving patients' privacy in health scenarios through a multicontext-aware system. *Annales des Télécommunications, 72*(9-10), 577–587. doi:10.100712243-017-0582-7

Hu, W., Wu, X., & Wei, G. (2010). The Security Analysis of Graphical Passwords. *Proceedings of the IEEE International Conference on Communications and Intelligence Information Security (ICCIIS)*, China. IEEE.

Hu, Y., Wang, Z., Liu, H., & Guo, G. (2011). A Geometric Distortion Resilient Image Watermark Algorithm Based on DWT-DFT. *JSW*, *6*(9), 1805–1812. doi:10.4304/jsw.6.9.1805-1812

Hyperplane, W. (2019). Retrieved October 29, 2019, from https://en.wikipedia.org/wiki/Hyperplane

Introducing, J. S. O. N. (2018). Retrieved from https://www.json.org/

Islam, A., Por, L. Y., Othman, F., & Ku, C. S. (2019). A Review on Recognition-Based Graphical Password Techniques. Proceedings *Computational Science and Technology* (pp. 503–512). Singapore: Springer. doi:10.1007/978-981-13-2622-6_49

Ivanov, Y. A., & Bobick, A. F. (2000). Recognition of visual activities and interactions by stochastic parsing. *IEEE Transactions on Pattern Analysis and Machine Intelligence*, *22*(8), 852–872. doi:10.1109/34.868686

Jagadeesh, B., Patil, C. M. (2019). Video based human activity detection, recognition and classification of actions using SVM. Transactions on Machine Learning and Artificial Intelligence, 22-34.

Jain, A., Ross, A., & Nandakumar, K. (2011). *Introduction to Biometrics*. Springer Science & Business Media. doi:10.1007/978-0-387-77326-1

Jain, A., Ross, A., & Pankanti, S. (2006). A Tool for Information Security. *IEEE Transactions on Information Forensics and Security*, *1*(2), 125–143. doi:10.1109/TIFS.2006.873653

Jain, A., Ross, A., & Prabhakar, S. (2004). An Introduction to Biometric Recognition. *IEEE Transactions on Circuits and Systems for Video Technology*, *14*(1), 4–20. doi:10.1109/TCSVT.2003.818349

Jararweh, Y., Alsmirat, M., Al-Ayyoub, M., Benkhelifa, E., Darabseh, A., Gupta, B., & Doulat, A. (2017). Software-defined system support for enabling ubiquitous mobile edge computing. *The Computer Journal*, *60*(10), 1443–1457. doi:10.1093/comjnl/bxx019

Jeanjaitrong, N., & Bhattarakoso, P. (2013). Feasibility Study on authentication Based Keystroke Dynamics over Touch-Screen Devices. *Proceedings of the International Symposium on Communications and Information Technology (ISCIT)*. 10.1109/ISCIT.2013.6645856

Jeevan, M., Jain, N., Hanmandlu, M., & Chetty, G. (2013). Gait recognition based on gait pal and pal entropy image. *Proceedings IEEE International Conference on Image Processing* (pp. 4195-4199). IEEE. 10.1109/ICIP.2013.6738864

Jeschke, S., Brecher, C., Meisen, T., Özdemir, D., & Eschert, T. (2017). Industrial internet of things and cyber manufacturing systems. In *Industrial Internet of Things* (pp. 3–19). Cham, Switzerland: Springer. doi:10.1007/978-3-319-42559-7_1

Jiang, F., Fu, Y., Gupta, B. B., Lou, F., Rho, S., Meng, F., & Tian, Z. (2018). Deep learning based multi-channel intelligent attack detection for data security. *IEEE transactions on Sustainable Computing*.

Jiang, F., Fu, Y., Gupta, B. B., Lou, F., Rho, S., Meng, F., & Tian, Z. (2018). Deep learning based multi-channel intelligent attack detection for data security. *IEEE Transactions on Sustainable Computing*.

Jiao, Y., Weir, J., & Yan, W. (2011). Flame detection in surveillance. *Journal of Multimedia*, *6*(1), 22–32. doi:10.4304/jmm.6.1.22-32

Ji, S., Xu, W., Yang, M., & Yu, K. (2013). 3D convolutional neural networks for human action recognition. *IEEE Transactions on Pattern Analysis and Machine Intelligence*, *35*(1), 221–231. doi:10.1109/TPAMI.2012.59

Johansson, G. (1973). Visual perception of biological motion and a model for its analysis. *Perception & Psychophysics*, *14*(2), 201–211. doi:10.3758/BF03212378

Jorquera, J. M., Sánchez, P. M., Fernández, L., Huertas, A., Arjona, M., De Los Santos, S., & Martínez, G. (2018). Improving the Security and QoE in Mobile Devices through an Intelligent and Adaptive Continuous Authentication System. *Sensors (Basel)*, *18*(11), 3769. doi:10.339018113769 PMID:30400377

Joshi, G., Soljanin, E., & Wornell, G. (2017). Efficient redundancy techniques for latency reduction in cloud systems. *ACM Transactions on Modeling and Performance Evaluation of Computing Systems*, *2*(2), 12. doi:10.1145/3055281

Jouini, M., & Rabai, L. (2016). A Security Framework for Secure Cloud Computing Environments. *International Journal of Cloud Applications and Computing*, *6*(3), 32–44. doi:10.4018/IJCAC.2016070103

Kaae, J. (2017). Theoretical approaches to composing dynamic music for video games. In *From pac-man to pop music* (pp. 75–91). Routledge. doi:10.4324/9781351217743-6

Kaewkasi, C., & Chuenmuneewong, K. (2017, February). Improvement of container scheduling for docker using ant colony optimization. *Proceedings 2017 9th international conference on knowledge and smart technology (KST)* (pp. 254-259). IEEE. 10.1109/KST.2017.7886112

Kali. (2019) Crunch package description. Retrieved from https://tools.kali.org/password-attacks/crunch

Kamal, A., Ammar, A., Rosni, A., Badr, A., & Mohammad, A. (2020). *Botnet and Internet of Things (IoTs): A Definition, Taxonomy, Challenges, and Future Directions. In Security, Privacy, and Forensics Issues in Big Data* (pp. 304–316). Hershey, PA: IGI Global.

Kang, X., Huang, J., Shi, Y. Q., & Lin, Y. (2003). A DWT-DFT composite watermarking scheme robust to both affine transform and JPEG compression. *IEEE Transactions on Circuits and Systems for Video Technology*, *13*(8), 776–786. doi:10.1109/TCSVT.2003.815957

Kaplan, A. M., & Haenlein, M. (2014). Users of the world, unite! The challenges and opportunities of Social Media. *Business Horizons*, *53*(1), 59–68. doi:10.1016/j.bushor.2009.09.003

Karmakar, R., & Basu, A. (2019). Implementation of a Reversible Watermarking Technique for Medical Images. In S. Bhattacharyya (Ed.), *Intelligent Innovations in Multimedia Data Engineering and Management* (pp. 1–37). Hershey, PA: IGI Global. doi:10.4018/978-1-5225-7107-0.ch001

Karnan, M., Akila, M., & Krishnaraj, N. (2011). Biometric Personal Authentication Using Keystroke Dynamics: A Review. *Applied Soft Computing*, *11*(2), 1565–1573. doi:10.1016/j.asoc.2010.08.003

Karpathy, A., Toderici, G., & Shetty, S. abd R., Sukthankar, T. L., & Li, F. (2014) Large-scale video classification with convolutional neural networks. Proceedings IEEE CVPR, pp. 1725-1732.

Kaur, R., & Choudhary, P. (2016). A Review of Image Compression Techniques. *International Journal of Computers and Applications*, *975*, 8887.

Kehrer, S., & Blochinger, W. (2018). TOSCA-based container orchestration on Mesos. *Computer Science-Research and Development*, *33*(3-4), 305–316. doi:10.100700450-017-0385-0

Kenny, P., Ouellet, P., Dehak, N., Gupta, V., & Dumouchel, P. (2008). A Study of Inter-Speaker Variability in Speaker Verification. *IEEE Transactions on Audio, Speech, and Language Processing*, *16*(5), 980–988. doi:10.1109/TASL.2008.925147

Khan, H., Atwater, A., & Hengartner, U. (2014). Itus: An Implicit Authentication Framework for Android. *Proceedings of the 20th Annual International Conference on Mobile computing and networking*, 507–518. ACM. 10.1145/2639108.2639141

Khan, M. U. K., Shafique, M., & Henkel, J. (2017). *Energy Efficient Embedded Video Processing Systems: A Hardware-Software Collaborative Approach*. Springer.

Kim, B., & Rafii, Z. (2018, September). Lossy audio compression identification. *Proceedings 2018 26th European Signal Processing Conference (EUSIPCO)* (pp. 2459-2463). IEEE. 10.23919/EUSIPCO.2018.8553611

Kim, J., Kim, H., & Kang, P. (2017). Keystroke Dynamics-Based User Authentication Using Freely Typed Text Based on User-Adaptive Feature Extraction and Novelty Detection. *Applied Soft Computing*.

Kimpan, S., Lasakul, A., & Chitwong, S. (2004, October). Variable block size based adaptive watermarking in spatial domain. *Proceedings IEEE International Symposium on Communications and Information Technology* (Vol. 1, pp. 374-377). IEEE. 10.1109/ISCIT.2004.1412871

Kok, J. N., Boers, E. J., Kosters, W. A., Van der Putten, P., & Poel, M. (2009). Artificial intelligence: Definition, trends, techniques, and cases. *Artificial Intelligence*, 1.

Kolias, C., Kambourakis, G., Stavrou, A., & Voas, J. (2017). DDoS in the IoT: Mirai and other botnets. *Computer*, *50*(7), 80–84. doi:10.1109/MC.2017.201

Kothari, A. M., & Dwivedi, V. V. (2013). Video Watermarking-Combination of Discrete Wavelet & Cosine Transform to Achieve Extra Robustness. *International Journal of Image Graphics and Signal Processing*, *5*(3), 36–41. doi:10.5815/ijigsp.2013.03.05

Kouahla, Z. (2011). Exploring intersection trees for indexing metric spaces. *CEUR Workshop Proceedings*.

Krizhevsky, A., Sutskever, I., & Hinton, G. E. (2012). ImageNet classification with deep convolutional neural networks. *Advances in Neural Information Processing Systems*, 1097–1105.

Kubernetes. (2019, June 12). Building Large Clusters. Retrieved from https://kubernetes.io/docs/setup/best-practices/cluster-large/

Kugler, L. (2018). Why cryptocurrencies use so much energy--and what to do about it. *Communications of the ACM*, *61*(7), 15–17. doi:10.1145/3213762

Kumar, S., & Dutta, A. (2016, February). Performance analysis of spatial domain digital watermarking techniques. *Proceedings 2016 International Conference on Information Communication and Embedded Systems* (pp. 1-4). IEEE. 10.1109/ICICES.2016.7518910

Kumar, A., Khan, A. S., Modanwal, N., & Saha, S. (2019). Experimental Studies on Energy / Eigenvalue based Spectrum Sensing Algorithms using USRP Devices in OFDM Systems. *URSI Asia-Pacific Radio Science Conference (AP-RASC)*, 1-4. 10.23919/URSIAP-RASC.2019.8738506

Kumar, C., Singh, A. K., & Kumar, P. (2018). A recent survey on image watermarking techniques and its application in e-governance. *Multimedia Tools and Applications*, *77*(3), 3597–3622. doi:10.100711042-017-5222-8

Kumar, R., Kundu, P. P., & Phoha, V. V. (2018). Continuous Authentication Using One-Class Classifiers and Their Fusion. *Proceedings of the IEEE International Conference on Identity, Security, and Behavior Analysis*. 10.1109/ISBA.2018.8311467

Kumar, R., Phoha, V. V., & Serwadda, A. (2016). Continuous Authentication of Smartphone Users by Fusing Typing Swiping and Phone Movement Patterns. *Proceedings of the IEEE International Conference on Biometrics: Theory, Applications, and Systems (BTAS)*, 1–8. 10.1109/BTAS.2016.7791164

Kusakunniran, W. (2014). Attribute-based learning for gait recognition using spatio-temporal interest points. *Image and Vision Computing, 32*(12), 1117–1126. doi:10.1016/j.imavis.2014.10.004

Kushnure, D., Jiniyawala, M., Molawade, S., & Patil, S. (2017). Implementation of FM Transceiver using Software Defined Radio (SDR). *International Journal of Engineering Development and Research, 5,* 225–233.

Kutter, M. (1999). Watermarking resistance to translation, rotation, and scaling. Proceedings Multimedia Systems and Applications (Vol. 3528, pp. 423-431). International Society for Optics and Photonics.

Kutter, M., Jordan, F. D., & Bossen, F. (1998). Digital watermarking of color images using amplitude modulation. *Journal of Electronic Imaging, 7*(2), 326–333. doi:10.1117/1.482648

Lam, T. H., Cheung, K. H., & Liu, J. N. (2011). Gait flow image: A silhouette-based gait representation for human identification. *Pattern Recognition, 44*(4), 973–987. doi:10.1016/j.patcog.2010.10.011

Laptev, I., & Lindeberg, T. (2004). Local descriptors for spatio-temporal recognition. *International Workshop on Spatial Coherence for Visual Motion Analysis*, pp. 91-103. Academic Press.

Lashkari, A. H., Saleh, R., Towhidi, F., & Farmand, S. (2009, December). A complete comparison on pure and cued recall-based graphical user authentication algorithms. *Proceedings 2009 Second International Conference on Computer and Electrical Engineering* (Vol. 1, pp. 527-532). IEEE.

Leardi, R. (1996). *Genetic algorithms in feature selection Genetic algorithms in molecular modeling* (pp. 67–86). Elsevier. doi:10.1016/B978-012213810-2/50004-9

LeCun, Y., & Bengio, Y. (1995). Convolutional networks for images, speech, and time series. The Handbook of Brain Theory and Neural Networks.

LeCun, Y., Huang, F. J., & Bottou, L. (2004). Learning methods for generic object recognition with invariance to pose and lighting. *Proceedings of the 2004 IEEE Computer Society Conference on Computer Vision and Pattern Recognition.* (Vol. 2, pp. II-104). IEEE.

LeCun, Y., Huang, F., & Bottou, L. (2004). Learning methods for generic object recognition with invariance to pose and lighting. Proceedings IEEE CVPR. doi:10.1109/CVPR.2004.1315150

LeCun, Y., Bengio, Y., & Hinton, G. (2015). Deep learning. *Nature, 521*(7553), 436–444. doi:10.1038/nature14539 PMID:26017442

LeCun, Y., Boser, B., Denker, J., Henderson, D., Howard, R., Hubbard, W., & Jackel, L. D. (1989). Backpropagation applied to handwritten zip code recognition. *Neural Computation, 1*(4), 541–551. doi:10.1162/neco.1989.1.4.541

LeCun, Y., Bottou, L., Bengio, Y., & Haffner, P. (1998). Gradient-based learning applied to document recognition. *Proceedings of the IEEE, 86*(11), 2278–2324.

Lee, M. H., Shahab, M. B., Kader, M. F., & Shin, S. Y. (2016). Spatial multiplexing using walsh-hadamard transform. *Proceedings International Conference on Smart Green Technology in Electrical and Information Systems (ICSGTEIS),* 43-46. Academic Press.

Lee, H. Y., Kim, H., & Lee, H. K. (2006). Robust image watermarking using local in variant features. *Optical Engineering (Redondo Beach, Calif.), 45*(3). doi:10.1117/1.2181887

Lee, H., Grosse, R., Ranganath, R., & Ng, A. Y. (2009). Convolutional deep belief networks for scalable unsupervised learning of hierarchical representations. *Proceedings ACM Annual International Conference on Machine Learning* (pp. 609-616). 10.1145/1553374.1553453

Lee, J.-H., & Kim, H. (2017). Security and privacy challenges in the internet of things [security and privacy matters]. *IEEE Consumer Electronics Magazine, 6*(3), 134–136. doi:10.1109/MCE.2017.2685019

Lee, L., & Grimson, W. E. L. (2002). Gait analysis for recognition and classification. *Proceedings IEEE International Conference on Automatic Face Gesture Recognition* (pp. 155-162). IEEE. 10.1109/AFGR.2002.1004148

Lever, J., Krzywinski, M., & Altman, N. (2017). Principal Component Analysis. *Nature Methods, 14*(7), 641–642. doi:10.1038/nmeth.4346

Li, C., Zhang, Z., & Zhang, L. (2018). A Novel Authorization Scheme for Multimedia Social Networks Under Cloud Storage Method by Using MA-CP-ABE. *International Journal of Cloud Applications and Computing, 8*(3), 32–47. doi:10.4018/IJCAC.2018070103

Lichtenauer, J. F., Setyawan, I., Kalker, T., & Lagendijk, R. L. (2003). Exhaustive geometrical search and the false positive watermark detection probability. In Security and Watermarking of Multimedia Contents V (Vol. 5020, pp. 203-214). International Society for Optics and Photonics.

Li, D., Deng, L., Gupta, B. B., Wang, H., & Choi, C. (2019). A novel CNN-based security guaranteed image watermarking generation scenario for smart city applications. *Information Sciences, 479*, 432–447. doi:10.1016/j.ins.2018.02.060

Li, F., Clarke, N., Papadaki, M., & Dowland, P. (2011). Behaviour Profiling for Transparent Authentication for Mobile Devices. *Proceedings 10th European Conference on Information Warfare and Security, (pp. 307-314).*

Li, J., Wu, J., & Chen, L. (2018). Block-Secure: Blockchain based scheme for secure P2P cloud storage. *Information Sciences, 465*, 219–231. doi:10.1016/j.ins.2018.06.071

Li, J., Yu, C., Gupta, B. B., & Ren, X. (2018). Color image watermarking scheme based on quaternion Hadamard transform and Schur decomposition. *Multimedia Tools and Applications, 77*(4), 4545–4561. doi:10.100711042-017-4452-0

Li, L. D., & Guo, B. L. (2009). Localized image watermarking in spatial domain resistant to geometric attacks. *AEÜ. International Journal of Electronics and Communications, 63*(2), 123–131. doi:10.1016/j.aeue.2007.11.007

Lin, C. C., Chang, C. C., & Liang, D. (2013). A Novel Non-Intrusive User Authentication Method Based on touchscreen of Smartphones. *Proceedings of the 2013 IEEE International Symposium on Biometrics and Security Technologies*, 212–216. 10.1109/ISBAST.2013.37

Lin, C. Y., Wu, M., Bloom, J. A., Cox, I. J., Miller, M. L., & Lui, Y. M. (2001). Rotation-, scale-, and translation-resilient public watermarking for images. *IEEE Transactions on Image Processing, 10*(5), 767–782. doi:10.1109/83.918569 PMID:18249666

Lin, F., & Brandt, R. D. (1993). Towards absolute invariants of images under translation, rotation, and dilation. *Pattern Recognition Letters, 14*(5), 369–379. doi:10.1016/0167-8655(93)90114-S

Lin, S. D., Shie, S. C., & Guo, J. Y. (2010). Improving the robustness of DCT-based image watermarking against JPEG compression. *Computer Standards & Interfaces, 32*(1-2), 54–60. doi:10.1016/j.csi.2009.06.004

Li, R., Song, T., Mei, B., Li, H., Cheng, X., & Sun, L. (2018). Blockchain For Large-Scale Internet of Things Data Storage and Protection. *IEEE Transactions on Services Computing.*

Little, J., & Boyd, J. (1998). Recognizing people by their gait: The shape of motion. *Journal of Computer Vision Research, 1*(2), 1–32.

Liu, F., & Ming, K., & Zhou, Z.-H. (2008). Isolation forest. *Proceedings Eighth IEEE International Conference on Data Mining (ICDM)*, 413–422. Academic Press.

Liu, W., Anguelov, D., Erhan, D., Szegedy, C., Reed, S., Fu, C. Y., & Berg, A. C. (2016). SSD: Single shot multibox detector. Proceedings ECCV, pp. 21-37.

Liu, C., Ranjan, R., Yang, C., Zhang, X., Wang, L., & Chen, J. (2015). MuR-DPA: Top-down levelled multi-replica Merkle hash tree based secure public auditing for dynamic big data storage on cloud. *IEEE Transactions on Computers*, *64*(9), 2609–2622. doi:10.1109/TC.2014.2375190

Liu, W., Anguelov, D., Erhan, D., Szegedy, C., Reed, S., Fu, C.-Y., & Berg, A. C. (2016). SSD: Single shot multibox detector. *ECCV*, 21–37.

Liu, X., & Payandeh, S. (2018). A study of chained stochastic tracking in RGB and depth sensing. *Journal of Control Science and Engineering*, 2018.

Li, Y., & Bo, L. (2007). A Normalized Levenshtein Distance Metric. *IEEE Transactions on Pattern Analysis and Machine Intelligence*, *29*(6), 1091–1095. doi:10.1109/TPAMI.2007.1078 PMID:17431306

Loukhaoukha, K., Nabti, M., & Zebbiche, K. (2014). A robust SVD-based image watermarking using a multi-objective particle swarm optimization. *Opto-Electronics Review*, *22*(1), 45–54. doi:10.247811772-014-0177-z

Lowe, D. G. (2004). Distinctive image features from scale-invariant keypoints. *International Journal of Computer Vision*, *60*(2), 91–110. doi:10.1023/B:VISI.0000029664.99615.94

Lu, C. S., Huang, S. K., Sze, C. J., & Liao, H. Y. M. (2000). Cocktail watermarking for digital image protection. *IEEE Transactions on Multimedia*, *2*(4), 209–224. doi:10.1109/6046.890056

Lu, J., Shen, J., Yan, W., & Bacic, B. (2017). An empirical study for human behavior analysis. *International Journal of Digital Crime and Forensics*, *9*(3), 11–27. doi:10.4018/IJDCF.2017070102

Luo, H., Xu, L., Hui, B., & Chang, Z. (2017). Status and prospect of target tracking based on deep learning. *Infrared and Laser Engineering* 46(5).

Lu, W., Lu, H., & Chung, F. L. (2006). Feature based watermarking using watermark template match. *Applied Mathematics and Computation*, *177*(1), 377–386. doi:10.1016/j.amc.2005.11.015

Lu, W., Lu, H., & Chung, F. L. (2006). Robust digital image watermarking based on subsampling. *Applied Mathematics and Computation*, *181*(2), 886–893. doi:10.1016/j.amc.2006.02.012

Maglaras, L. A., Kim, K.-H., Janicke, H., Ferrag, M. A., Rallis, S., Fragkou, P., ... Cruz, T. J. (2018). Cyber security of critical infrastructures. *ICT Express*, *4*(1), 42–45. doi:10.1016/j.icte.2018.02.001

Mahbub, U., Sarkar, S., Patel, V. M., & Chellappa, R. (2016). Active User Authentication for Smartphones: A Challenge Data Set and Benchmark Results. *Proceedings of the IEEE International Conference on Biometrics: Theory, Applications and Systems (BTAS)*. 10.1109/BTAS.2016.7791155

Mahfouz, A., Mahmoud, T. M., & Sharaf Eldin, A. (2017). A Survey on Behavioral Biometric Authentication on Smartphones. *Journal of Information Security and Applications, Elsevier, 37*, 28–37. doi:10.1016/j.jisa.2017.10.002

Major, A., & Yampoiskiy, R. (2015) Global catastrophic risk and security implications of quantum computers. Elsevier, 72, pp. 17-26.

Mantyjarvi, J., Lindholm, M., Vildjiounaite, E., Makela, S. M., & Allisto, H. (2005). Identifying Users of Portable Devices from Gait Pattern with Accelerometers. *Proceedings of the IEEE International Conference on Acoustics, Speech, and Signal Processing, 2*, 973–976.

Marathon. (n.d.). Retrieved from https://mesosphere.github.io/marathon

Masrom, M., Towhidi, F., & Lashkari, A. H. (2009, October). Pure and cued recall-based graphical user authentication. *Proceedings 2009 International Conference on Application of Information and Communication Technologies* (pp. 1-6). IEEE.

Mathew, P., Augustine, L., & Devis, T. (2014). Hardware Implementation of (63, 51) BCH Encoder and Decoder For WBAN Using LFSR and BMA. *International Journal on Information Theory*, 3(3), 1–11. doi:10.5121/ijit.2014.3301

Mathon, B., Cayre, F., Bas, P., & Macq, B. (2014). Optimal transport for secure spread-spectrum watermarking of still images. *IEEE Transactions on Image Processing*, 23(4), 1694–1705. doi:10.1109/TIP.2014.2305873 PMID:24808340

Maxim, Y. A., Anastasiya, A. K., Sergey, A. S., Yuri, V. F., & Anastasiia, S. S. (2018). A Design of Cyber-physical Production System Prototype Based on an Ethereum Private Network. Conference of Open Innovations Association FRUCT, 426(22), 3-11.

Mazhelis, O., & Puuronen, S. (2007). A Framework for Behavior-Based Detection of User Substitution in a Mobile Context. *Computers & Security*, 26(2), 154–176. doi:10.1016/j.cose.2006.08.010

Medel, V., Rana, O., Bañares, J. Á., & Arronategui, U. (2016, December). Modelling performance & resource management in kubernetes. *Proceedings 2016 IEEE/ACM 9th International Conference on Utility and Cloud Computing (UCC)* (pp. 257-262). IEEE. 10.1145/2996890.3007869

Meidan, Y., Bohadana, M., Mathov, Y., Mirsky, Y., Shabtai, A., Breitenbacher, D., & Elovici, Y. (2018). N-BaIoT—Network-based detection of IoT botnet attacks using deep autoencoders. *IEEE Pervasive Computing*, 17(3), 12–22. doi:10.1109/MPRV.2018.03367731

Melkemi, K., & Golea, N. E. H. (2017). ROI-based fragile watermarking for medical image tamper detection. *International Journal of High-Performance Computing and Networking.*, 1(1), 1. doi:10.1504/IJHPCN.2017.10013846

Merch, E. E., & White, M. D. (2003). A taxonomy of relationships between images and text. *The Journal of Documentation*, 59(6), 647–672. doi:10.1108/00220410310506303

Microsoft. (2017) How to prevent Windows from storing a LAN manager hash of your password in Active Directory and local SAM databases. Retrieved from https://support.microsoft.com/en-us/help/299656/how-to-prevent-windows-from-storing-a-lan-manager-hash-of-your-passwor

Microsoft. (2019) Azure storage overview pricing. Retrieved from https://azure.microsoft.com/en-gb/pricing/details/storage/

Midi, D., Rullo, A., Mudgerikar, A., & Bertino, E. (2017). Kalis—A system for knowledge-driven adaptable intrusion detection for the Internet of Things. *Proceedings 2017 IEEE 37th International Conference on Distributed Computing Systems (ICDCS)*. 10.1109/ICDCS.2017.104

Mikolajczyk, K., & Schmid, C. (2002). An Affine Invariant Interest Point Detector. In A. Heyden, G. Sparr, M. Nielsen, & P. Johansen (Eds.), Lecture Notes in Computer Science: Vol. 2350. *Computer Vision — ECCV 2002. ECCV 2002.* Berlin, Germany: Springer. doi:10.1007/3-540-47969-4_9

Mikolov, T., Chen, K., Corrado, G., & Dean, J. (2013). Efficient Estimation of Word Representations in Vector Space. *ArXiv*, 1–12. Retrieved from http://arxiv.org/abs/1301.3781

Ministry of Defence UK. (2017) UK Defence in Numbers. [Online] Developed by DP and A. Retrieved from https://assets.publishing.service.gov.uk/government/uploads/system/uploads/attachment_data/file/652915/UK_Defence_in_Numbers_2017_-_Update_17_Oct.pdf

Mondal, S., & Bours, P. (2015). Swipe Gesture Based Continuous Authentication for Mobile Devices. *Proceedings of the IAPR International Conference on Biometrics.* 10.1109/ICB.2015.7139110

M-Tree Wikipedia. (n.d.). Retrieved March 15, 2019, from https://en.wikipedia.org/wiki/M-tree

Muharemagic, E., & Furht, B. (2004). Survey of Watermarking Techniques and Applications, Department of Computer Science and Engineering Florida Atlantic University, 777 Glades Road, Boca Raton, FL 33431-0991, USA.

Murase, H., & Sakai, R. (1996). Moving object recognition in eigenspace representation: Gait analysis and lip reading. *Pattern Recognition Letters, 17*(2), 155–162. doi:10.1016/0167-8655(95)00109-3

Murmuria, R., Stavrou, A., Barbara, D., & Fleck, D. (2015). Continuous Authentication on Mobile Devices Using Power Consumption, Touch Gestures and Physical Movement of Users. *Proceedings of the International Workshop on Recent Advances in Intrusion Detection*, 405–424. Springer. 10.1007/978-3-319-26362-5_19

Muslimin, J., Asnawi, A. L., Ismail, A. F., & Jusoh, A. Z. (2016). SDR-Based Transceiver of Digital Communication System Using USRP and GNU Radio. *International Conference on Computer and Communication Engineering (ICCCE)*, 449-453. 10.1109/ICCCE.2016.100

Nafkha, A., Naoues, M., Cichon, K., & Kliks, A. (2014). Experimental spectrum sensing measurements using USRP Software Radio platform and GNU-radio. *Proceedings 9th International Conference on Cognitive Radio Oriented Wireless Networks and Communications*, 429-434. 10.4108/icst.crowncom.2014.255415

Naik, N. (2016, October). Building a virtual system of systems using Docker Swarm in multiple clouds. *Proceedings 2016 IEEE International Symposium on Systems Engineering (ISSE)* (pp. 1-3). IEEE. 10.1109/SysEng.2016.7753148

Nakamura, K., Kono, K., Ito, Y., & Babaguchi, N. (2012). Tablet Owner Authentication Based on Behavioral Characteristics of Multi-touch Actions. *Proceedings of the IEEE 21st International Conference on Pattern Recognition*, Tsukuba, Japan. IEEE.

Nammer, N., & Emman, E. L. (2007). Hiding a Large Amount of Data with High Security using Steganography Algorithm. *Journal of Computer Science, 3*(4). pp. 223-232.

Nasir, I., Weng, Y., & Jiang, J. (2007, December). A new robust watermarking scheme for color image in spatial domain. *Proceedings Third International IEEE Conference on Signal-Image Technologies and Internet-Based System* (pp. 942-947). IEEE. 10.1109/SITIS.2007.67

National Cyber Security Centre. (2016) Password Guidance. Simplifying Your Approach. Retrieved from https://www.ncsc.gov.uk/guidance/password-guidance-simplifying-your-approach

Nectar. (n.d.) Retrieved from https://nectar.org.au/

Neeta, D., Snehal, K., & Jacobs, D. (2006). Implementation of LSB steganography and its evaluation for various bits. *Proceedings of 1st International Conference on Digital Information Management*, 173-178.

Nespoli, P., Zago, M., Huertas, A., Gil, M., Gómez, F., & García, F. J. (2018). A Dynamic Continuous Authentication Framework in IoT-Enabled Environments. *IoTSMS'18: Proceedings of the 5th International Conference on Internet of Things: Systems, Management, and Security*, Valencia (Spain). 10.1109/IoTSMS.2018.8554389

Nespoli, P., Zago, M., Huertas, A., Gil, M., Gómez, F., & García, F. J. (2019). PALOT: Profiling and Authenticating Users Leveraging Internet of Things. *Sensors. Special Issue on Sensor Systems for Internet of Things, 19*(12), 2832.

Neverova, N., Wolf, C., Lacey, G., Fridma, L., Chandaran, D., Barbello, B., & Taylor, G. (2016). Learning Human Identity from Motion Patterns. *IEEE Access: Practical Innovations, Open Solutions, 4*, 1810–1820. doi:10.1109/ACCESS.2016.2557846

Ng, A. Y. (2003). Support Vector Machines. CS229 Lecture notes, 5, 45-69.

Niebles, J. C., Wang, H., Li, F. (2008). Unsupervised learning of human action categories using spatial-temporal words. IJCV, 299-318.

Niyogi, S. A., & Adelson, E. H. (1994). Analyzing gait with spatiotemporal surfaces. *Proceedings IEEE Workshop on Motion of Non-rigid and Articulated Objects* (pp. 64-69). IEEE.

Novelty and Outlier detection. Scikit-learn documentation. Retrieved October 29, 2019, from http://scikit-learn.org/stable/modules/outlier_detection.html

O'Connell, B. M., & Walker, K. R. (2017). User - Touchscreen Interaction Analysis Authentication *System. US Patent* 9,817,963.

Ohm, J. R. (2015). *Multimedia signal coding and transmission.* Springer. doi:10.1007/978-3-662-46691-9

Olakanmi, O. O., & Dada, A. (2019). An Efficient Privacy-preserving Approach for Secure Verifiable Outsourced Computing on Untrusted Platforms. *International Journal of Cloud Applications and Computing, 9*(2), 79–98. doi:10.4018/IJCAC.2019040105

Ömer Cengiz, Ç. E. L. E. B. İ. (2019). *Neural Networks and Pattern Recognition Using MATLAB.* Non-Parametric Techniques. Retrieved from http://www.byclb.com/TR/Tutorials/neural_networks/ch11_1.htm

Onggosanusi, E., Li, Y., Rahman, M. S., Nam, Y. H., Zhang, J., Seol, J. Y., & Kim, T. (2015, June). Reduced space channel feedback for FD-MIMO. *Proceedings 2015 IEEE International Conference on Communications (ICC)* (pp. 3873-3878). IEEE. 10.1109/ICC.2015.7248928

O'Ruanaidh, J. J., Dowling, W. J., & Boland, F. M. (1996). Phase watermarking of digital images.

Ouaguid, A., Abghour, N., & Ouzzif, M. (2018). A Novel Security Framework for Managing Android Permissions Using Blockchain Technology. *International Journal of Cloud Applications and Computing, 8*(1), 55–79. doi:10.4018/IJCAC.2018010103

Owens, J. (2017). *Video production handbook.* Routledge. doi:10.4324/9781315530574

Özçelik, M., Chalabianloo, N., & Gür, G. (2017). Software-defined edge defense against IoT-based DDoS. *Proceedings 2017 IEEE International Conference on Computer and Information Technology (CIT).* 10.1109/CIT.2017.61

Pagès, G. (2015). Introduction to vector quantization and its applications for numerics. *ESAIM: proceedings and surveys, 48,* 29-79.

Paikray, B., Mallick, C., Sundaram, R. M., Sharma, R., Sengupta, S., Mishra, S. S., ... & Pradhan, D. C. (2018). *Introduction to Multimedia.* Academic Press.

Panjanathan, R., & Ramachandran, G. (2017). Enhanced low latency queuing algorithm with active queue management for multimedia applications in wireless networks. *International Journal of High Performance Computing and Networking, 10*(1-2), 23–33. doi:10.1504/IJHPCN.2017.083197

Parne, B. L., Gupta, S., & Chaudhari, N. S. (2019). PSE-AKA: Performance and security enhanced authentication key agreement protocol for IoT enabled LTE/LTE-A networks. *Peer-to-Peer Networking and Applications, 12*(5), 1156–1177. doi:10.100712083-019-00785-5

Parreño, M., Moorsel, A., & Castruccio, S. (2017). Smartphone Continuous Authentication Using Deep Learning Autoencoders. *Proceedings 15th International Conference on Privacy, Security and Trust,* 147-1478.

Pasupuleti, S. K. (2019). Privacy-Preserving Public Auditing and Data Dynamics for Secure Cloud Storage Based on Exact Regenerated Code. *International Journal of Cloud Applications and Computing, 9*(4), 1–20. doi:10.4018/IJCAC.2019100101

Patel, M., Sajja, P. S., & Sheth, R. K. (2013). Analysis and Survey of Digital Watermarking Techniques. *International Journal of Advanced Research in Computer Science and Software Engineering, 3*(10), 203–210.

Patel, S. B., Mehta, T. B., & Pradhan, S. N. (2011). A unified technique for robust digital watermarking of colour images using data mining and DCT. *International Journal of Internet Technology and Secured Transactions, 3*(1), 81–96. doi:10.1504/IJITST.2011.039680

Patel, V. M., Chellappa, R., Chandra, D., & Barbello, B. (2016). Continuous User's authentication on Mobile Devices: Recent Progress and Remaining Challenges. *IEEE Signal Processing Magazine, 33*(4), 49–61. doi:10.1109/MSP.2016.2555335

Peng, F., Zhang, S., Cao, S., & Xu, S. (2018). A Prototype Performance Analysis for V2V Communications using USRP-based Software Defined Radio Platform. *Proceedings 6th IEEE Global Conference on Signal and Information Processing*, 1-5.

Peng, T., Liu, Q., Meng, D., & Wang, G. (2017). Collaborative trajectory privacy preserving scheme in location-based services. *Information Sciences, 387*, 165–179. doi:10.1016/j.ins.2016.08.010

Perera, P., & Patel, V. M. (2018). Efficient and Low Latency Detection of Intruders in Mobile Active Authentication. *IEEE Transactions on Information Forensics and Security, 13*(6), 1392–1405. doi:10.1109/TIFS.2017.2787995

Peterson, L. E. (2009). K-nearest neighbor. *Scholarpedia, 4*(2), 1883. doi:10.4249cholarpedia.1883

Petrushin, V. A. (2005). Mining rare and frequent events in multi-camera surveillance video using self-organizing maps. *ACM Conference on Knowledge Discovery in Data Mining*, pp. 794-800. 10.1145/1081870.1081975

Phillips, W., Shah, W., & Lobo, N. (2000). Flame recognition in video. *Proceedings IEEE Workshop on Applications of Computer Vision*, pp. 224-229. 10.1109/WACV.2000.895426

Pierce, J. D., Wells, J. G., Warren, M. J., & Mackay, D. R. (2005). A Conceptual Model for Graphical Authentication. Paper presented in First Australian Information Security Management Conference. Perth, Australia, Sep. paper 16.

Poisel, R., & Tjoa, S. (2012). Discussion on the Challenges and Opportunities of Cloud Forensics. *Proceedings of the International Cross-Domain Conference and Workshop on Availability, Reliability, and Security (CDARES)*, Prague, Czech Republic. 10.1007/978-3-642-32498-7_45

Poonkuntran, S., & Rajesh, R. S. (2014). Chaotic model-based semi-fragile watermarking using integer transforms for digital fundus image authentication. *Multimedia Tools and Applications, 68*. doi:10.100711042-012-1227-5

Poonkuntran, S., Rajesh, R. S., & Eswaran, P. (2009a). Reversible, Multilayered Watermarking Scheme for Fundus Images Using Intra-Plane Difference Expanding. *Proceedings of the IEEE International Advance Computing Conference*, pp. 2583-2587, Patiala, India.

Poonkuntran, S., Rajesh, R. S., & Eswaran, P. (2009b). Wavetree Watermarking: An Authentication Scheme for Fundus Images. *Proceedings of the IEEE Sponsored International Conference on Emerging Trends in Computing*, pp. 507-511. India.

Poonkuntran, S., Rajesh, R. S., & Eswaran, P. (2009d). Imperceptible Watermarking Scheme for Fundus Images Using Intra-Plane Difference Expanding. *International Journal on Computer and Electrical Engineering, 1*(4). 1793-8198.

Poonkuntran, S., Rajesh, R. S., & Eswaran, P. (2009e). Analysis of Difference Expanding Method for Medical Image Watermarking. *Proceedings of 2009 International Symposium on Computing, Communication, and Control*, pp. 30-34. Singapore.

Poonkuntran, S., Rajesh, R. S., & Eswaran, P. (2009c). A Robust Watermarking Scheme for Fundus Images Using Intra-Plane Difference Expanding. *Proceedings of the IEEE Sponsored International Conference on Emerging Trends in Computing. pp.* 433-436. India.

Praveenkumar, P., Priya, P. C., Avila, J., Thenmozhi, K., Rayappan, J. B. B., & Amirtharajan, R. (2017). Tamper Proong Identification and Authenticated DICOM Image Transmission Using Wireless Channels and CR Network. *Wireless Personal Communication*s, 97, 5573-5595.

Quinlan, J. R. (1986). *Machine Learning. Springer, 1*(1), 81–106.

Rai, R., & Sathuvalli, S. (2017). Five Key Criteria for Choosing the Right Audio Codec Implementation.

Rasch, J., Kolehmainen, V., Nivajärvi, R., Kettunen, M., Gröhn, O., Burger, M., & Brinkmann, E. M. (2018). Dynamic MRI reconstruction from undersampled data with an anatomical prescan. *Inverse Problems, 34*(7), 074001. doi:10.1088/1361-6420/aac3af

Rass, S., & König, S. (2018). Password Security as a Game of Entropies. *Entropy (Basel, Switzerland), 20*(5), 312. doi:10.3390/e20050312

Ray, P. P. (2018). A survey on Internet of Things architectures. *Journal of King Saud University-Computer and Information Sciences, 30*(3), 291–319. doi:10.1016/j.jksuci.2016.10.003

Raza, S., Wallgren, L., & Voigt, T. (2013). SVELTE: Real-time intrusion detection in the Internet of Things. *Ad Hoc Networks, 11*(8), 2661–2674. doi:10.1016/j.adhoc.2013.04.014

Reddy, A. A., & Chatterji, B. N. (2005). A new wavelet-based, logo-watermarking scheme. *Pattern Recognition Letters, 26*(7), 1019–1027. doi:10.1016/j.patrec.2004.09.047

Redi, J., D'Acunto, L., & Niamut, O. (2015, June). Interactive UHDTV at the Commonwealth Games: An Explorative Evaluation. *Proceedings of the ACM International Conference on Interactive Experiences for TV and Online Video* (pp. 43-52). ACM. 10.1145/2745197.2745203

Redmon, J., Divvala, S., Girshick, R., & Farhadi, A. (2016). You only look once: Unified, real-time object detection. *CVPR, 2016*, 779–788.

Redmon, J., Divvala, S., Girshick, R., & Farhadi, A. (2016). *You only look once: Unified, real-time object detection.* Proceedings *IEEE CVPR.*

Redmon, J., & Farhadi, A. (2017). *YOLO9000 (2017) Better, faster, stronger.* Proceedings *IEEE CVPR.* pp. 6517–6525.

Redmon, J., & Farhadi, A. (2017). YOLO9000: Better, faster, stronger. *CVPR, 2017*, 7263–7271.

Renaud, K. (2009). On user involvement in production of images used in visual authentication. *Journal of Visual Languages and Computing, 20*(1), 1–15. doi:10.1016/j.jvlc.2008.04.001

Ren, S., He, K., Girshick, R., & Sun, J. (2017). Faster R-CNN: Towards real-time object detection with region proposal networks. *IEEE Transactions on Pattern Analysis and Machine Intelligence, 39*(6), 1137–1149. doi:10.1109/TPAMI.2016.2577031

Ren, Y., Nguyen, M., & Yan, W. (2018). Real-time recognition of series seven New Zealand banknotes. *International Journal of Digital Crime and Forensics, 10*(3), 50–65. doi:10.4018/IJDCF.2018070105

Riaz, A., Ashraf, I., & Aslam, G. (2014). A Review On Multimedia Databases. *International Journal of Scientific & Technology Research*, *3*(10), 186–191.

Rida, I., Boubchir, L., Al-Maadeed, N., Al-Maadeed, S., & Bouridane, A. (2016). Robust model-free gait recognition by statistical dependency feature selection and Globality-Locality Preserving Projections. *Proceedings International Conference on Telecommunications and Signal Processing* (TSP) (pp. 652-655). 10.1109/TSP.2016.7760963

Rocha, A. (2011). Current trends and challenges in digital image and video forensics. *ACM Computing Surveys*, *25*(1), 111–116.

Rodriguez, M. A., & Buyya, R. (2019). Container-based cluster orchestration systems: A taxonomy and future directions. *Software, Practice, & Experience*, *49*(5), 698–719. doi:10.1002pe.2660

Romero, J. J., Dafonte, C., Gómez, A., & Penousal, F. (2007). Inteligencia artificial y computación avanzada. Santiago de Compostela: Fundación Alfredo Brañas, 10-15.

Rosa, R., & Rothenberg, C. E. (2018). Blockchain-Based decentralized applications for multiple administrative domain networking. *Communications Standards, IEEE*, *2*(3), 29–37. doi:10.1109/MCOMSTD.2018.1800015

Ross, A., Nandakumar, K., & Jain, A. K. (2008). Introduction to Multibiometrics. Handbook of Biometrics, Springer, 271–292.

Rousseeuw, P. J., & Driessen, K. V. (1999). A fast algorithm for the minimum covariance determinant estimator. *Technometrics*, *41*(3), 212–223. doi:10.1080/00401706.1999.10485670

Ruanaidh, J. J. O., & Pun, T. (1998). Rotation, scale and translation invariant spread spectrum digital image watermarking. *Signal Processing*, *66*(3), 303–317. doi:10.1016/S0165-1684(98)00012-7

Rui, Y., & Anandan, P. (2000). Segmenting visual actions based on spatio-temporal motion patterns. *CVPR*, *2000*, 111–118.

Runc. (n.d.). Retrieved from https://github.com/opencontainers/runc

Rupali, B. (2018). Patil, K., Kulat, D., & Gandhi, A. S. (2018). SDR Based Energy Detection Spectrum Sensing in Cognitive Radio for Real Time Video Transmission. *Modelling and Simulation in Engineering*, 1–10.

Sahoo, S. R., & Gupta, B. B. (2018). Security Issues and Challenges in Online Social Networks (OSNs) Based on User Perspective. In Computer and Cyber Security (pp. 591-606). Auerbach Publications.

Sahoo, S. R., & Gupta, B. B. (2019). Classification of various attacks and their defence mechanism in online social networks: A survey. *Enterprise Information Systems*, *13*(6), 832–864. doi:10.1080/17517575.2019.1605542

Sahoo, S. R., & Gupta, B. B. (2019). Hybrid approach for detection of malicious profiles in twitter. *Computers & Electrical Engineering*, *76*, 65–81. doi:10.1016/j.compeleceng.2019.03.003

Sahoo, S. R., & Gupta, B. B. (2020). Popularity-Based Detection of Malicious Content in Facebook Using Machine Learning Approach. *Proceedings First International Conference on Sustainable Technologies for Computational Intelligence* (pp. 163-176). Springer, Singapore. 10.1007/978-981-15-0029-9_13

Salwa, M., & Eldin, S. (2017). Encrypted gray image transmission over OFDM channel for TV cloud computing. *International Journal of Speech Technology*, *20*(3), 431–442. doi:10.100710772-017-9415-3

Sánchez, P., Huertas, A., Fernández, L., Martínez, G., & Wang, G. (2019). Securing Smart Offices through an Intelligent and Multi-device Continuous Authentication System. *Proceedings of the 7th International Conference on Smart City and Informatization.* Guangzhou, China: Springer Computer Science Proceedings.

Sande, K., Uijlings, J., Gevers, T., Smeulders, A. (2011). Segmentation as selective search for object recognition. *ICCV 2011*, pp. 1879-1886.

Sanders, A. (2017). *Multimedia Signals: Image, Audio, and Video Processing*. NY: Research Press.

SANS. (2010) Pass-the-hash attacks: Tools and Mitigation. Retrieved from https://www.sans.org/reading-room/white-papers/testing/pass-the-hash-attacks-tools-mitigation-33283

Saravanan. (2010). Color Image to Grayscale Image Conversion. *Proceedings Second International Conference on Computer Engineering and Applications*, 96-199. Academic Press.

Sarkar, S., Phillips, P. J., Liu, Z., Vega, I. R., Grother, P., & Bowyer, K. W. (2005). The humanid gait challenge problem: Data sets, performance, and analysis. *IEEE Transactions on Pattern Analysis and Machine Intelligence*, 27(2), 162–177. doi:10.1109/TPAMI.2005.39 PMID:15688555

Sayood, K. (2017). *Introduction to data compression*. Morgan Kaufmann.

Schwarzkopf, M., Konwinski, A., Abd-El-Malek, M., & Wilkes, J. (2013). Omega: flexible, scalable schedulers for large compute clusters.

Scikit-learn developers. (2019). Scikit-learn: machine learning in Python. Retrieved October 1, 2019, from http://scikit-learn.org/stable/index.html

Sedhain, S., Menon, A. K., Sanner, S., & Xie, L. (2015). AutoRec: Autoencoders meet collaborative filtering. *Proceedings International Conference on World Wide Web*, pp. 111–112.

Sedjelmaci, H., Senouci, S. M., & Al-Bahri, M. (2016). A lightweight anomaly detection technique for low-resource IoT devices: A game-theoretic methodology. *Proceedings 2016 IEEE International Conference on Communications (ICC)*. 10.1109/ICC.2016.7510811

Seo, J. S., & Yoo, C. D. (2004). Localized image watermarking based on feature points of scale-space representation. *Pattern Recognition*, 37(7), 1365–1375. doi:10.1016/j.patcog.2003.12.013

Seo, J. S., & Yoo, C. D. (2006). Image watermarking based on invariant regions of scale-space representation. *IEEE Transactions on Signal Processing*, 54(4), 1537–1549. doi:10.1109/TSP.2006.870581

Serkin, F. B., & Vazhenin, N. A. (2013). USRP platform for communication systems research. *Proceedings 2013 15th International Conference on Transparent Optical Networks (ICTON)*, 1-4. Academic Press.

Serwadda, A., Phoha, V. V., & Wang, Z. (2013). Which Verifiers Work? A Benchmark Evaluation of Touch-based Authentication Algorithms. *Proceedings of the 6th IEEE International Conference on Biometrics: Theory, Applications and Systems (BTAS)*, 1–8. 10.1109/BTAS.2013.6712758

Shanahan, J. G., & Dai, L. (2019). Large scale distributed data science from scratch using apache spark 2.0. *Proceedings 26th International World Wide Web Conference 2017, WWW 2017 Companion*. 10.1145/3041021.3051108

Shanmugam, P., Rajesh, R. S., & Perumal, E. (2008). A Reversible Watermarking With Low Warping: An Application to Digital Fundus Images. *Proceedings of the IEEE International Conference on Computer and Communication Engineering*, pp. 472-477.

Shen, C., Zhang, Y., Guan, X., & Maxion, R. A. (2016). Performance Analysis of Touch-interaction Behavior for Active Smartphone Authentication. *IEEE Transactions on Information Forensics and Security*, 11(3), 498–513. doi:10.1109/TIFS.2015.2503258

Shen, D., Chen, X., Nguyen, M., & Yan, W. (2018). Flame detection using deep learning. *Proceedings International Conference on Control, Automation and Robotics*, pp. 416-420.

Sherekar, S., Thakare, V., & Jain, S. (2011). Attacks and countermeasures on digital watermarks: Classification, implications, benchmarks. *International Journal of Computer Science and Applications, 4*(2), 32–45.

Shi, E., Niu, Y., Jakobsson, M., & Chow, R. (2011). Implicit Authentication Through Learning User Behavior. *Proceedings of the Information Security Conference, Lecture Notes in Computer Science*, 99–113. Berlin, Germany: Springer, 6531.

Shi, W., Yang, J., Jiang, Y., Yang, F., & Xiong, Y. (2011). SenGuard: Passive user identification on smartphones using multiple sensors. *Proceedings IEEE 7th International Conference on Wireless and Mobile Computing, Networking, and Communications (WiMob)*, 141-148.

Shin, J., Kim, S., Kang, S., Lee, S. W., Paik, J., Abidi, B., & Abidi, M. (2005). Optical flow-based real-time object tracking using non-prior training active feature model. *Real-Time Imaging, 11*(3), 204–218. doi:10.1016/j.rti.2005.03.006

Shiraga, K., Makihara, Y., Muramatsu, D., Echigo, T., & Yagi, Y. (2016). Geinet: View-invariant gait recognition using a convolutional neural network. *Proceedings International Conference on Biometrics* (ICB) (pp. 1-8). IEEE. 10.1109/ICB.2016.7550060

Shoemaker, A. (2017). *How to Identify a Mirai-Style DDoS Attack. 2020*. Retrieved from https://www.imperva.com/blog/author/andrewshoemaker/

Shree, M. (2016). *Zoom Detection in Video Sequences* (Doctoral dissertation).

Shujaat, A. K. T., Rehman, M., Khan, M. B., Jadoon, I., Khan, F. A., Nawaz, F., ... Nasir, A. A. (2018). An Experimental Channel Capacity Analysis of Cooperative Networks Using Universal Software Radio Peripheral (USRP). *Sustainability, 10*, 1–13. PMID:30607262

Siegert, I., Lotz, A. F., Duong, L. L., & Wendemuth, A. (2016). Measuring the impact of audio compression on the spectral quality of speech data. *Elektronische Sprachsignalverarbeitung, 81*, 229–236.

Sikora, T. (2018). MPEG digital video coding standards. In Compressed Video over Networks (pp. 45–88). Boca Raton, FL: CRC Press.

Singh, A. K., Dave, M., & Mohan, A. (2014). Wavelet based image watermarking: futuristic concepts in information security. *Proceedings of the National Academy of Sciences, India Section A: Physical Sciences, 84*(3), 345-359. 10.100740010-014-0140-x

Singh, A. K. (2017). Improved hybrid algorithm for robust and imperceptible multiple watermarking using digital images. *Multimedia Tools and Applications, 76*(6), 8881–8900. doi:10.100711042-016-3514-z

Singh, A. K., Kumar, B., Singh, G., & Mohan, A. (2017). *Medical image watermarking: techniques and applications*. Cham, Switzerland: Springer. doi:10.1007/978-3-319-57699-2

Singh, A. K., Sharma, N., Dave, M., & Mohan, A. (2012). A novel technique for digital image watermarking in spatial domain. *Proceedings of 2nd IEEE International Conference on Parallel, Distributed, and Grid Computing*, 497-501. 10.1109/PDGC.2012.6449871

Singh, R., Sharma, S., & Singh, S. (2014). Image Encryption Using Block Scrambling Technique. *International Journal of Computer Technology and Applications, 5*, 963–966.

Sitova, Z., Sedenka, J. J., Yang, J., Peng, G., Zhou, G., Gasti, P., & Balagani, K. (2016). Hmog: New Behavioral Biometric Features for Continuous Authentication of Smartphone Users, Information Forensics and Security. *IEEE Transactions on Information Forensics and Security, 11*(5), 877–892. doi:10.1109/TIFS.2015.2506542

Sivapalan, S., Chen, D., Denman, S., Sridharan, S., & Fookes, C. (2013). Histogram of weighted local directions for gait recognition. *Proceedings IEEE Conference on Computer Vision and Pattern Recognition Workshops* (pp. 125-130). 10.1109/CVPRW.2013.26

Sklar, B., & Ray, P. K. (2001). *Digital communication-Fundamentals and applications* (2nd ed.). Pearson Education.

Sliwa, J. (2019). Assessing complex evolving cyber-physical systems (case study: Smart medical devices). *International Journal of High-Performance Computing and Networking, 13*(3), 294–303. doi:10.1504/IJHPCN.2019.098570

Solachidis, V., & Pitas, I. (2000). Self-similar ring-shaped watermark embedding in 2-DDFT domain. *Proceedings of 10th European Signal Processing Conference*, pp. 1-4. Academic Press.

Sruthi, N., Sheetal, A. V., & Elamaran, V. (2014, April). Spatial and spectral digital watermarking with robustness evaluation. *Proceedings 2014 International Conference on Computation of Power, Energy, Information, and Communication* (pp. 500-505). IEEE. 10.1109/ICCPEIC.2014.6915415

Stankovic, S., Djurovic, I., & Pitas, I. (2001). Watermarking in the space/spatial-frequency domain using two-dimensional Radon-Wigner distribution. *IEEE Transactions on Image Processing, 10*(4), 650–658. doi:10.1109/83.913599 PMID:18249654

Stearns, S. D., & Hush, D. R. (2016). Digital signal processing with examples in MATLAb. Boca Raton, FL: CRC Press. doi:10.1201/9781439837832

Sterling, B. (2005). *Shaping things*.

Summerville, D. H., Zach, K. M., & Chen, Y. (2015). Ultra-lightweight deep packet anomaly detection for Internet of Things devices. *Proceedings 2015 IEEE 34th international performance computing and communications conference (IPCCC)*. 10.1109/PCCC.2015.7410342

Suo, X., Zhu, Y., & Owen, G. S. (2005, December). Graphical passwords: A survey. In 21st Annual Computer Security Applications Conference (ACSAC'05) (pp. 10-pp). IEEE.

Su, Q., & Chen, B. (2018). Robust color image watermarking technique in the spatial domain. *Soft Computing, 22*(1), 91–106. doi:10.100700500-017-2489-7

Sutton, O. (2012). Introduction to k Nearest Neighbour Classification and Condensed Nearest Neighbour Data Reduction. 10.

Svetnik, V., Andy, L., Christopher, T., Culberson, J., Sheridan, R., & Bradley, F. (2003). A Classification and Regression Tool for Compound Classification and QSAR Modeling. *Journal of Chemical Information and Computer Sciences, 43*(6), 1947–1958. doi:10.1021/ci034160g PMID:14632445

Szegedy, C., Toshev, A., & Erhan, D. (2013). Deep neural networks for object detection. *Proceedings International Conference on Neural Information Processing Systems*, pp. 2553-2561.

Szegedy, C., Toshev, A., & Erhan, D. (2013). Deep neural networks for object detection. In Advances in Neural Information Processing Systems (pp. 2553-2561).

Takada, T., & Koike, H. (2003). *Awase-E: Image-Based Authentication for Mobile Phones Using User's Favourite Images. Human-Computer Interaction with Mobile Devices and Services* (Vol. 2795, pp. 347–351). Berlin, Germany: Springer. doi:10.1007/978-3-540-45233-1_26

Tan, D., Huang, K., Yu, S., & Tan, T. (2006). Efficient night gait recognition based on template matching. *Proceedings International Conference on Pattern Recognition* (Vol. 3, pp. 1000-1003).

Tang, C. W., & Hang, H. M. (2003). A feature-based robust digital image watermarking scheme. *IEEE Transactions on Signal Processing, 51*(4), 950–959. doi:10.1109/TSP.2003.809367

Tan, X., Guo, Y., Chen, Y., & Zhu, W. (2018). Accurate inference of user popularity preference in a large-scale online video streaming system. *Science China. Information Sciences, 61*(1). doi:10.100711432-016-9078-0

Tao, P., & Eskicioglu, A. M. (2004). A robust multiple watermarking scheme in the discrete wavelet transform domain. Proceedings of 5601 International Society for Optics and Photonics, 133-144. doi:10.1117/12.569641

Tao, D., Li, X., Wu, X., & Maybank, S. J. (2007). General tensor discriminant analysis and gabor features for gait recognition. *IEEE Transactions on Pattern Analysis and Machine Intelligence, 29*(10), 1700–1715. doi:10.1109/TPAMI.2007.1096 PMID:17699917

Telagam, N., Lakshmi, S., & Nehru, K. (2019). Digital Audio Broadcasting Based Gfdm Transceiver Using Software Defined Radio. *International Journal of Innovative Technology and Exploring Engineering, 8,* 273–281.

Telagam, N., Reddy, S., Nanjundan, M., & Nehru, K. (2018). USRP 2901 Based MIMO-OFDM Transceiver in Virtual and Remote Laboratory. *International Journal on Computer Science and Engineering, 6,* 1033–1040.

Terplan, K., & Morreale, P. A. (2018). Video Communications. In The Telecommunications Handbook (pp. 344-411). Boca Raton, FL: CRC Press.

Thompson, D. M. (2018). *Understanding audio: getting the most out of your project or professional recording studio.* Hal Leonard Corporation.

Tian, J. (2003). Reversible Data Embedding using a Difference Expansion. *IEEE Transactions on Circuits and Systems for Video Technology, 13*(8), pp. 890-893.

Tian, F., Shang, F., & Sun, N. (2019). Multimedia auto-annotation via label correlation mining. *International Journal of High Performance Computing and Networking, 13*(4), 427–435. doi:10.1504/IJHPCN.2019.099266

Tian, J. (2002). Reversible Watermarking by Difference Expansion. *Proceedings of Workshop on Multimedia and Security: Authentication, Secrecy, and Steganalysis, pp.* 19-22.

Tran, D., Bourdev, L., Fergus, R., Torresani, L., & Paluri, M. (2015). Learning spatiotemporal features with 3D convolutional networks. *Proceedings of the IEEE International Conference on Computer Vision,* pp. 4489-4497.

Tsai, H. H., Jhuang, Y. J., & Lai, Y. S. (2012). An SVD-based image watermarking in wavelet domain using SVR and PSO. *Applied Soft Computing, 12*(8), 2442–2453. doi:10.1016/j.asoc.2012.02.021

Tsai, J. S., Huang, W. B., Kuo, Y. H., & Horng, M. F. (2012). Joint robustness and security enhancement for feature-based image watermarking using invariant feature regions. *Signal Processing, 92*(6), 1431–1445. doi:10.1016/j.sigpro.2011.11.033

Tsui, T. K., Zhang, X. P., & Androutsos, D. (2008). Color image watermarking using multidimensional Fourier transforms. *IEEE Transactions on Information Forensics and Security, 3*(1), 16–28. doi:10.1109/TIFS.2007.916275

Tyagi, S., Singh, H. V., Agarwal, R., & Gangwar, S. K. (2016, March). Digital watermarking techniques for security applications. *Proceedings International Conference on Emerging Trends in Electrical Electronics & Sustainable Energy Systems* (pp. 379-382). IEEE. 10.1109/ICETEESES.2016.7581413

Uijlings, J., Sande, K., Gevers, T., & Smeulders, A. (2013). Selective search for object recognition. *International Journal of Computer Vision, 104*(2), 154-171.

Uthayakumar, J., Vengattaraman, T., & Dhavachelvan, P. (2018). A survey on data compression techniques: From the perspective of data quality, coding schemes, data type and applications. *Journal of King Saud University-Computer and Information Sciences.*

Vallabha, V. (2003). Multiresolution watermark based on wavelet transform for digital images. Retrieved from https://www.mathworks.com/matlabcentral/mlc-downloads/downloads/submissions/3508/versions/1/download/pdf

Vavilapalli, V. K., Murthy, A. C., Douglas, C., Agarwal, S., Konar, M., Evans, R., ... Saha, B. (2013, October). Apache hadoop yarn: Yet another resource negotiator. *Proceedings of the 4th annual Symposium on Cloud Computing* (p. 5). ACM. 10.1145/2523616.2523633

Veridium Ltd. (2019). Biometric Authentication Technology - Fingerprint, Face, Camera, Sensors. Retrieved October 29, 2019, from http://veridiumid.com/biometric-authentication-technology/mobile-authentication

Verma, A., Pedrosa, L., Korupolu, M., Oppenheimer, D., Tune, E., & Wilkes, J. (2015, April). Large-scale cluster management at Google with Borg. *Proceedings of the Tenth European Conference on Computer Systems* (p. 18). ACM. 10.1145/2741948.2741964

Verma, B., Jain, S., Agarwal, D. P., & Phadikar, A. (2006). A New color image watermarking scheme. *INFOCOMP, 5*(3), 37–42.

Viola, P., Jones, M. J., & Snow, D. (2005). Detecting pedestrians using patterns of motion and appearance. *International Journal of Computer Vision, 63*(2), 153–161. doi:10.100711263-005-6644-8

Vlachou, A., Doulkeridis, C., & Kotidis, Y. (2010). *Peer-to-peer similarity search based on M-Tree indexing.* Lecture Notes in Computer Science Including Subseries Lecture Notes in Artificial Intelligence and Lecture Notes in Bioinformatics. doi:10.1007/978-3-642-12098-5_21

Vlasveld, R. (2013). Introduction to One-class Support Vector Machines. Retrieved October 29, 2019, from http://rvlasveld.github.io/blog/2013/07/12/introduction-to-one-class-support-vector-machines

Voloshynovskiy, S., Pereira, S., Pun, T., Eggers, J. J., & Su, J. K. (2001). Attacks on digital watermarks: Classification, estimation-based attacks, and benchmarks. *IEEE Communications Magazine, 39*(8), 118–126. doi:10.1109/35.940053

Wachter-Zeh, A. (2018). List Decoding of Insertions and Deletions. *IEEE Transactions on Information Theory, 64*(9), 6297–6304. doi:10.1109/TIT.2017.2777471

Wang, C., Zheng, W., Ji, S., Liu, Q., & Wang, A. (2018). Identity-based fast authentication scheme for smart mobile devices in body area networks. *Wireless Communications and Mobile Computing, 2018.*

Wang, B., Ding, Q., & Gu, X. (2019). A secure reversible chaining watermark scheme with hidden group delimiter for WSNs. *International Journal of High-Performance Computing and Networking, 14*(3). doi:10.1504/IJHPCN.2019.102126

Wang, H., He, D., & Ji, Y. (2017). Designated-verifier proof of assets for bitcoin exchange using elliptic curve cryptography. *Future Generation Computer Systems.* doi:10.1016/j.future.2017.06.028

Wang, H., Wang, N., & Yeung, D.-Y. (2015). Collaborative deep learning for recommender systems. *Proceedings ACM SIGKDD International Conference on Knowledge Discovery and Data Mining*, pp. 1235–1244. 10.1145/2783258.2783273

Wang, H., & Yao, X. (2016). Objective reduction based on nonlinear correlation information entropy. *Soft Computing*, *20*(6), 2393–2407. doi:10.100700500-015-1648-y

Wang, J., Bacic, B., & Yan, W. (2018). An effective method for plate number recognition. *Multimedia Tools and Applications*, *77*(2), 1679–1692. doi:10.100711042-017-4356-z

Wang, J., Ngueyn, M., & Yan, W. (2017). A framework of event-driven traffic ticketing system. *International Journal of Digital Crime and Forensics*, *9*(1), 39–50. doi:10.4018/IJDCF.2017010103

Wang, L., Ning, H., Tan, T., & Hu, W. (2004). Fusion of static and dynamic body biometrics for gait recognition. *IEEE Transactions on Circuits and Systems for Video Technology*, *14*(2), 149–158. doi:10.1109/TCSVT.2003.821972

Wang, L., Tan, T., Ning, H., & Hu, W. (2003). Silhouette analysis-based gait recognition for human identification. *IEEE Transactions on Pattern Analysis and Machine Intelligence*, *25*(12), 1505–1518. doi:10.1109/TPAMI.2003.1251144

Wang, S., Zhang, Y., & Zhang, Y. (2018). A blockchain-based framework for data sharing with fine-grained access control in decentralized storage systems. *IEEE Access: Practical Innovations, Open Solutions*, *6*(6), 38437–38450. doi:10.1109/ACCESS.2018.2851611

Wang, T., Zeng, J., Bhuiyan, M. Z. A., Tian, H., Cai, Y., Chen, Y., & Zhong, B. (2017). Trajectory privacy preservation based on a fog structure for cloud location services. *IEEE Access: Practical Innovations, Open Solutions*, *5*, 7692–7701. doi:10.1109/ACCESS.2017.2698078

Wang, Y. G., Xie, D., & Gupta, B. B. (2018). A study on the collusion security of LUT-based client-side watermark embedding. *IEEE Access: Practical Innovations, Open Solutions*, *6*, 15816–15822. doi:10.1109/ACCESS.2018.2802928

Wei-Chi, K., & Maw-Jinn, T. (2005). A Remote User Authentication Scheme Using Strong Graphical Passwords. *Local Computer Networks, 30th Anniversary.*

Weka 3. (2019) Data Mining Software in Java. Retrieved October 1, 2019, from https://www.cs.waikato.ac.nz/ml/weka/

Wells, J., Hutchinson, D., & Pierce, J. (2006). Enhanced Security for Preventing Man-in-the-Middle Attacks in Authentication, Data Entry and Transaction Verification. *Proceedings of the 6th Australian Information Security Conference.* [Online]. Edith Cowan University, Perth, Australia.

What is Windows Communication Foundation. (2017). Retrieved from https://docs.microsoft.com/en-us/dotnet/framework/wcf/whats-wcf

Wiedenbeck, S., Waters, J., Birget, J. C., Brodskiy, A., & Memon, N. (2006). Authentication using graphical passwords: Effects of tolerance and image choice. *Symposium on Usable Privacy and Security (SOUPS)*, Carnegie-Mellon University, USA.

Wiedenbeck, S., Waters, J., Birget, J. C., Brodskiy, A., & Memon, N. (2005). PassPoints: Design and longitudinal evaluation of a graphical password system. [Special Issue on HCI Research in Privacy and Security]. *International Journal of Human-Computer Studies*, *63*(1-2), 102–127. doi:10.1016/j.ijhcs.2005.04.010

Wien, M. (2015). High efficiency video coding. Coding Tools and specification, 133-160.

Winer, E. (2017). *The audio expert: everything you need to know about audio*. Routledge. doi:10.4324/9781315223162

Wu, H. R., & Rao, K. R. (Eds.). (2017). Digital video image quality and perceptual coding. Boca Raton, FL: CRC Press. doi:10.1201/9781420027822

Wu, M., & Liu, B. (2003). Data Hiding in Image and Video. I. Fundamental Issues and Solutions, *IEEE Transactions on Image Processing, 12*(6), pp. 685-695.

Wu, C. Y., Singhal, N., & Krahenbuhl, P. (2018). Video compression through image interpolation. *Proceedings of the European Conference on Computer Vision (ECCV)* (pp. 416-431).

Wu, C. Y., Zaheer, M., Hu, H., Manmatha, R., Smola, A. J., & Krähenbühl, P. (2018). Compressed video action recognition. *Proceedings of the IEEE Conference on Computer Vision and Pattern Recognition* (pp. 6026-6035).

Wu, H., Miao, Z., Wang, Y., Chen, J., Ma, C., & Zhou, T. (2015). Image completion with multi-image based on entropy reduction. *Neurocomputing, 159*, 157–171. doi:10.1016/j.neucom.2014.12.088

Wu, M. L., Fahn, C. S., & Chen, Y. F. (2017). Image-format-independent tampered image detection based on overlapping concurrent directional patterns and neural networks. *Applied Intelligence, 47*(2), 347–361. doi:10.100710489-017-0893-4

Xia, F., Yang, L. T., Wang, L., & Vinel, A. (2012). Internet of things. *International Journal of Communication Systems, 25*(9), 1101–1102. doi:10.1002/dac.2417

Xiang, T., Gong, S. (2005) Video behavior profiling and abnormality detection without manual labelling. *Proceedings of the IEEE International Conference on Computer Vision*, pp. 1238-1245.

Xianglin, C. R. W. Y. L. (2006). An Adaptive DFT Domain Digital Watermarking Scheme [J]. Computer Engineering and Applications, 10, 022.

Xia, Y., Chen, W., Liu, X., Zhang, L., Li, X., & Xiang, Y. (2017). Adaptive multimedia data forwarding for privacy preservation in vehicular ad-hoc networks. *IEEE Transactions on Intelligent Transportation Systems, 18*(10), 2629–2641. doi:10.1109/TITS.2017.2653103

Xia, Z., Wang, X., Zhang, L., Qin, Z., Sun, X., & Ren, K. (2016). A privacy-preserving and copy-deterrence content-based image retrieval scheme in cloud computing. *IEEE Transactions on Information Forensics and Security, 11*(11), 2594–2608. doi:10.1109/TIFS.2016.2590944

Xiong, L., & Shi, Y. (2018). On the privacy-preserving outsourcing scheme of reversible data hiding over encrypted image data in cloud computing. *Computers, Materials, & Continua, 55*(3), 523–539.

Xu, X., Yu, H., & Pei, X. (2014, December). A novel resource scheduling approach in container based clouds. *Proceedings 2014 IEEE 17th International Conference on Computational Science and Engineering* (pp. 257-264). IEEE. 10.1109/CSE.2014.77

Xu, D., Huang, Y., Zeng, Z., & Xu, X. (2011). Human gait recognition using patch distribution feature and locality-constrained group sparse representation. *IEEE Transactions on Image Processing, 21*(1), 316–326. doi:10.1109/TIP.2011.2160956 PMID:21724511

Xu, H., Zhou, Y., & Lyu, M. R. (2014). Towards Continuous and Passive Authentication via Touch Biometrics: An Experimental Study on Smartphones. *Proceedings of the International Symposium on Usable Privacy and Security (SOUPS)*, 187–198. Menlo Park, CA.

Xu, M., Toosi, A. N., & Buyya, R. (2018). ibrownout: An integrated approach for managing energy and brownout in container-based clouds. *IEEE Transactions on Sustainable Computing, 4*(1), 53–66. doi:10.1109/TSUSC.2018.2808493

YAGO. (database) Wikipedia. (n.d.). Retrieved January 21, 2019, from https://en.wikipedia.org/wiki/YAGO_(database)

Yamagishi, H., & Yamaguchi, J. (1999) Fire flame detection algorithm using a color camera. *Proceedings International Symposium on Micromechatronics and Human Science*, pp. 255-260 10.1109/MHS.1999.820014

Yampolskiy, R. V., & Govindaraju, V. (2008). Behavioural Biometrics: A Survey and Classification. *International Journal of Biometrics*, *1*(1), 81–113. doi:10.1504/IJBM.2008.018665

Yan, C., Zhang, B., & Coenen, F. (2015). Multi-attributes gait identification by convolutional neural networks. *Proceedings International Congress on Image and Signal Processing* (pp. 642-647). IEEE. 10.1109/CISP.2015.7407957

Yang, Z., Huang, Y., Li, X., Wang, W., Wu, F., Zhang, X., ... & Li, W. (2018). Efficient, secure data provenance scheme in multimedia outsourcing and sharing. *Computers, Materials, & Continua*, *56*(1), 1–17.

Yan, W. (2017). *Introduction to Intelligent Surveillance: Surveillance Data Capture, Transmission, and Analytics*. Springer. doi:10.1007/978-3-319-60228-8

Yin, L., Luo, J., & Luo, H. (2018). Tasks scheduling and resource allocation in fog computing based on containers for smart manufacturing. *IEEE Transactions on Industrial Informatics*, *14*(10), 4712–4721. doi:10.1109/TII.2018.2851241

Yu, S., Tan, D., & Tan, T. (2006). Modelling the effect of view angle variation on appearance-based gait recognition. *Proceedings Asian Conference on Computer Vision* (pp. 807-816). Berlin, Germany: Springer. 10.1007/11612032_81

Yu, Y., Lu, Z., Ling, H., & Zou, F. (2006). A robust blind image watermarking scheme based on feature points and RS-invariant domain. *Proceedings of the 8th international Conference on Signal Processing*. Academic Press.

Yuan, W., Ling, H., Lu, Z., Zou, F., & Yu, Y. (2006). Image Content-based Watermarking Resistant against Geometrical Distortions. Proceedings of the 8th international Conference on Signal Processing. Academic Press.

Yu, S., Tan, D., & Tan, T. (2006). A framework for evaluating the effect of view angle, clothing and carrying condition on gait recognition. *Proceedings International Conference on Pattern Recognition* (Vol. 4, pp. 441-444).

Yu, S., Tan, T., Huang, K., Jia, K., & Wu, X. (2009). A study on gait-based gender classification. *IEEE Transactions on Image Processing*, *18*(8), 1905–1910. doi:10.1109/TIP.2009.2020535 PMID:19447706

ZainEldin, H., Elhosseini, M. A., & Ali, H. A. (2015). Image compression algorithms in wireless multimedia sensor networks: A survey. *Ain Shams Engineering Journal, 6*(2), 481-490.

Zecevic, P., & Bonaci, M. (2017). *Spark in Action*. Manning Publications.

Zedan, S., & Miller, W. (2017). Using social network analysis to identify stakeholders' influence on energy efficiency of housing. *International Journal of Engineering Business Management*, *9*. doi:10.1177/1847979017712629

Zeimpekis, D., & Gallopoulos, E. (2006). TMG: A MATLAB toolbox for generating term-document matrices from text collections. In *Grouping multidimensional data* (pp. 187–210). Berlin, Germany: Springer. doi:10.1007/3-540-28349-8_7

Zeki, A. M., Abdul Manaf, A., & Mahmod, S. S. (2011). High watermarking capacity based on spatial domain technique. *Information Technology Journal, 10*(7), 1367-1373.

Zeki, A. M., Manaf, A. A., Ibrahim, A. A., & Zamani, M. (2011). A robust watermark embedding in smooth areas. *Research Journal of Information Technology, 3*(2), 123–131. doi:10.3923/rjit.2011.123.131

Zhang, H., Ma, H., Fu, G., Yang, X., Jiang, Z., & Gao, Y. (2016, June). Container based video surveillance cloud service with fine-grained resource provisioning. *Proceedings 2016 IEEE 9th International Conference on Cloud Computing (CLOUD)* (pp. 758-765). IEEE. 10.1109/CLOUD.2016.0105

Zhang, J., Sun, J., Zhang, R., Zhang, Y., & Hu, X. (2018, April). Privacy-preserving social media data outsourcing. *Proceedings IEEE INFOCOM 2018-IEEE Conference on Computer Communications* (pp. 1106-1114). IEEE. 10.1109/INFOCOM.2018.8486242

Zhang, H., Patel, V. M., Fathy, M., & Chellappa, R. (2015). Touch Gesture-based Active User Authentication Using Dictionaries. *Proceedings of the IEEE Winter Conference on Applications of Computer Vision*, 207–214. 10.1109/WACV.2015.35

Zhang, J., Wang, Z., Quan, Z., Yin, J., Chen, Y., & Guo, M. (2018). Optimizing power consumption of mobile devices for video streaming over 4G LTE networks. *Peer-to-Peer Networking and Applications*, *11*(5), 1101–1114. doi:10.100712083-017-0580-6

Zhang, N., Donahue, J., Girshick, R., & Darrell, T. (2014). Part-based R-CNNs for fine-grained category detection. *Proceedings European Conference on Computer Vision,* pp. 834-849.

Zhang, T., & Mao, S. (2019). An Overview of Emerging Video Coding Standards. GetMobile. *Mobile Computing and Communications*, *22*(4), 13–20.

Zhang, Z., & Gupta, B. B. (2018). Social media security and trustworthiness: Overview and new direction. *Future Generation Computer Systems*, *86*, 914–925. doi:10.1016/j.future.2016.10.007

Zhang, Z., Li, C., Gupta, B. B., & Niu, D. (2018). Efficient compressed ciphertext length scheme using multi-authority CP-ABE for hierarchical attributes. *IEEE Access: Practical Innovations, Open Solutions*, *6*, 38273–38284. doi:10.1109/ACCESS.2018.2854600

Zhang, Z., Sun, R., Zhao, C., Wang, J., Chang, C. K., & Gupta, B. B. (2017). CyVOD: A novel trinity multimedia social network scheme. *Multimedia Tools and Applications*, *76*(18), 18513–18529. doi:10.100711042-016-4162-z

Zhao, N., Zhang, L., Du, B., Zhang, L., Tao, D., & You, J. (2016). Sparse tensor discriminative locality alignment for gait recognition. *Proceedings International Joint Conference on Neural Networks* (pp. 4489-4495). 10.1109/IJCNN.2016.7727787

Zhao, X., Feng, T., Shi, W., & Kakadiaris, I. A. (2014). Mobile user authentication using statistical touch dynamics images. *IEEE Transactions on Information Forensics and Security*, *9*(11), 1780–1789. doi:10.1109/TIFS.2014.2350916

Zheng, D., Liu, Y., Zhao, J., & Saddik, A. E. (2007). A survey of RST invariant image watermarking algorithms. *ACM Computing Surveys*, *39*(2), 5. doi:10.1145/1242471.1242473

Zheng, K., Yan, W., & Nand, P. (2018). *Video dynamics detection using deep neural networks*. IEEE Transactions on Emerging Topics in Computational Intelligence, 2(3), pp. 224–234.

Zheng, S., Zhang, J., Huang, K., He, R., & Tan, T. (2011). Robust view transformation model for gait recognition. *Proceedings IEEE International Conference on Image Processing* (pp. 2073-2076). 10.1109/ICIP.2011.6115889

Zhou, Y., Gu, X., Wu, D., Chen, M., Chan, T. H., & Ho, S. W. (2018). Statistical study of view preferences for online videos with cross-platform Information. *IEEE Transactions on Multimedia*, *20*(6), 1512–1524. doi:10.1109/TMM.2017.2769807

Zhu, F., Yang, J., Gao, C., Xu, S., Ye, N., & Yin, T. (2016). A weighted one-class support vector machine. *Neurocomputing*, *189*, 1–10. doi:10.1016/j.neucom.2015.10.097

Zhu, J. (2018). *Machine Learning Decision Tree*. University of Wisconsin.

Zighra. (2019). Smart Identity Defense. AI-Powered Continuous Authentication and Fraud Detection. Retrieved October 29, 2019, from https://zighra.com/

About the Contributors

B. B. Gupta received PhD degree from Indian Institute of Technology Roorkee, India in the area of Information and Cyber Security. In 2009, he was selected for Canadian Commonwealth Scholarship award by Government of Canada. He has published more than 200 research papers in International Journals and Conferences of high repute including IEEE, Elsevier, ACM, Springer, Wiley, Taylor & Francis, Inderscience, etc. He has visited several countries, i.e. Canada, Japan, Australia, China, Spain, Hong-Kong, Italy, Malaysia, Macau, etc. to present his research work. His biography was selected and published in the 30th Edition of Marquis Who's Who in the World, 2012. In addition, he has been selected to receive 2017 Albert Nelson Marquis Lifetime Achievement Award' by Marquis Who's Who in the World, USA. Dr. Gupta also received Sir Visvesvaraya Young Faculty Research Fellowship Award in 2017 from Ministry of Electronics and Information Technology, government of India. Moreover, he has been awarded with Best Faculty Award in year 2018 and 2019 from National Institute of Technology Kurukshetra, India. He is also working as principal investigator of various R&D projects sponsored by various government of India funding agencies. He is serving as Associate editor of IEEE Transactions on Industrial Informatics, IEEE Access, and Executive editor of IJITCA, Inderscience, respectively. Moreover, Dr. Gupta is also leading International Journal of Cloud Applications and Computing (IJ-CAC), IGI Global, USA as Editor-in-Chief. He is also serving as reviewer for various Journals of IEEE, Springer, Wiley, Taylor & Francis, etc. He also served as TPC Chair of 2018 IEEE INFOCOM: CCSNA, USA. Moreover, he served as publicity chair of 10th NSS 2016, 17th IFSA-SCIS 2017 which were held in Taiwan and Japan, respectively. He is also founder chair of FISP and ISCW workshops which organize in different countries every year. Dr. Gupta is serving as organizing Chair of Special Session on Recent Advancements in Cyber Security (SS-CBS) in IEEE Global Conference on Consumer Electronics (GCCE), Japan every year since 2014. Dr. Gupta received outstanding paper awards in both regular and student categories in 5th IEEE Global Conference on Consumer Electronics (GCCE) in Kyoto, Japan during Oct. 7-10, 2016. Dr. Gupta is Senior member of IEEE, Member ACM, SIGCOMM, SDIWC, Internet Society, Institute of Nanotechnology, Life Member, International Association of Engineers (IAENG), Life Member, International Association of Computer Science and Information Technology (IACSIT). He was also visiting researcher with Yamaguchi University, Japan, with Deakin University, Australia and with Swinburne University of Technology, Australia during 2015 and 2018, 2017, and 2018, respectively. At present, Dr. Gupta is working as Assistant Professor in the Department of Computer Engineering, National Institute of Technology Kurukshetra India. His research interest includes Information security, Cyber Security, Mobile/Smartphone, Cloud Computing, Web security, Intrusion detection, Computer networks and Phishing.

Deepak Gupta received his Master of Science degree from Illinois Institute of Technology, Chicago, USA, in the area of Computer Forensics and Cyber Security with a specialization in Voice Over Internet Protocol (VOIP). As an undergraduate student, he became certified on the major networking platforms, first as a CCNA (Cisco Certified Network Administrator) and then as a MCP (Microsoft Certified Professional) which would come to serve him well in his professional life. As a graduate student, Deepak continued to challenge himself by working on a number of research papers and projects related to Computer Network Security and Forensics Research, including the topics of multi-boot computer systems with change of boot loader and MP3 steganography. He also developed and furthered his interest in VOIP technology by working on and leading research projects with Bell Labs, a prominent VOIP research lab based in Chicago. Deepak also wrote research papers in this field on the topics of P2P communication and SIP protocols which won him the best student VOIP project award in 2007. Over the last 10 years of professional experience, Deepak has gained a broad range of experience in computer security and technology that spans multiple fields and industries. After graduating with distinction with a MS in Computer Science, Deepak went on to work for Sageworks, a financial software company based in Raleigh, NC. There, among other things, he developed a centralized integration process for core banking platforms that would allow customers to easily port and map their data to the central banking database. Deepak is a product visionary who founded a web agency and two other startups as a software entrepreneur to help businesses to simplify their user communication. It was during this time that Deepak's passion for innovation and entrepreneurship led him to found LoginRadius, a cloud identity and access management (cIAM) SaaS platform that helps businesses improve and optimize their customer experience by creating unified digital identities across multiple touch points, where he remains today as co-founder and CTO. At LoginRadius, Deepak makes use of his expertise in security and forensics to innovate and improve how identity services are delivered and secured in the cloud identity space and helps businesses deliver social media integrations by a simplified REST API. Currently, LoginRadius is a leading provider of cloud-based CIAM solutions for mid-to-large sized companies, and the platform serves over 3,000 businesses with a monthly reach of 850 million users worldwide. The company has been named as an industry leader in the cIAM space by Gartner, Forrester, Kuppingercole, and Computer Weekly. Deepak is also passionate about helping businesses improve and optimize their customer experience. He lives and breathes this topic with customers everyday by helping them think through questions such as how do users interact with their website, how to simplify the customer's experience (via single sign-on, one touch login, etc.), and how to keep the customer's data secure. Deepak is active member of IEEE, ACM, OpenID Foundation, Cloud Security Alliance (CSA), etc. tech communities. Deepak is doing his current research in Machine Learning, Artificial Intelligence and Blockchain Technologies. Web: www.guptadeepak.com, www.loginradius.com

***

Mohammad Alauthman received PhD degree from Northumbria University Newcastle, UK in 2016. He received a B.Sc. degree in Computer Science from Hashemite University, Jordan, in 2002, and received M.Sc. degrees in Computer Science from Amman Arab University, Jordan, in 2004. Currently, he is Assistant Professor and senior lecturer at Department of Computer Science, Zarqa University, Jordan. His main research areas cyber-security, Cyber Forensics, advanced machine learning and data science applications.

Mamdouh Alenezi is currently the Dean of Educational Services at Prince Sultan University. Dr. Alenezi received his MS and Ph.D. degrees from DePaul University and North Dakota State University in 2011 and 2014, respectively. He has extensive experience in data mining and machine learning where he applied several data mining techniques to solve several Software Engineering problems. He conducted several research areas and development of predictive models using machine learning to predict fault-prone classes, comprehend source code, and predict the appropriate developer to be assigned to a new bug.

Ammar Almomani received PhD degree from Universiti Sains Malaysia (USM) in 2013. He has published more than 60 research papers in International Journals and Conferences of high repute. Currently he is assistant professor and senior lecturer at Dept. of Information Technology, Al-Huson University College, Al-Balqa Applied University, Jordan. His research interest includes advanced Internet security and monitoring.

Sadiq Almuairfi is currently an E-Service director and a researcher at Security Engineering Lab in Prince Sultan University, Riyadh, Saudi Arabia. He received his PhD in Cyber-security from La Trobe University, Melbourne, Australia, in 2014 and his Master degree in Information Management from King Abdulaziz University, Jeddah, Saudi Arabia, in 2005 and his Bachelor degree in Computer Engineering from KFUPM, Dhahran, Saudi Arabia in 2001. His research interests include Cyber-security, Network Security, E-Commerce Security.

Ahmad Al-Qerem graduated in applied mathematics and MSc in Computer Science at the Jordan University of Science and Technology in 1997 and 2002, respectively. After that, he was appointed as full-time lecturer at the Zarqa University. Currently he is a visiting professor at Princess Sumaya University for Technology (PSUT). He obtained a PhD from Loughborough University, UK. His research interests are in performance and analytical modeling, mobile computing environments, protocol engineering, communication networks, transition to IPv6, and transaction processing. He has published several papers in various areas of computer science. Currently, he has a full academic post as associate professor and the head of the Department of Internet Technology at Zarqa University - Jordan.

Kirti Raj Bhatele is an Assistant Professor in the RJIT BSF Academy Tekanpur, an institute run by the Border Security. Currently he is pursuing PhD in the field of Computer Science engineering and information technology. He has done M.Tech in Information Technology and B.E. in Information Technology from the RGPV, university. He also has PG Diploma in Cyber Law from the National law institute University Bhopal. He has teaching experience of more than eight years and has published 20 research papers and eight chapters.

Xin Chen received a master's degree in computer science from Auckland University of Technology in 2018, his research interests include deep learning and intelligent surveillance.

Phuc Do is currently an Associate Professor of the University of Information Technology (UIT), VNU-HCM, Vietnam. His research interests include data mining, text mining, information network analysis, artificial intelligence and machine learning, big data analysis and applications.

Mohamed Amine Ferrag received the bachelor's, master's, and Ph.D. degrees from Badji Mokhtar–Annaba University, Algeria, in 2008, 2010, and 2014, respectively, all in computer science. Since 2014, he has been an Assistant Professor with the Department of Computer Science, Guelma University, Algeria. He has edited the book Security Solutions and Applied Cryptography in Smart Grid Communications (IGI Global). His research interests include wireless network security, network coding security, and applied cryptography. He is currently serving in various editorial positions such as Editorial Board Member with Computer Security Journals like the International Journal of Information Security and Privacy (IGI Global), the International Journal of Internet Technology and Secured Transactions (Inderscience Publishers), and the EAI Endorsed Transactions on Security and Safety (EAI). He has served as an Organizing Committee Member (the Track Chair, the Co-Chair, the Publicty Chair, the Proceedings Editor, and the Web Chair) in numerous international conferences.

Reinaldo França graduated in Computer Engineering. He is currently a Ph.D. Candidate by the DECOM, Faculty of Electrical and Computer Engineering (FEEC) at UNICAMP, and a researcher at the Laboratory of Visual Communications (LCV). Has affinity in the area of technological and scientific research as well as knowledge in programming and development in C/C++, Python, Java, and .NET languages, with topics of interest in Simulation, Operating Systems, Wireless and Networking, Broadcasting, Telecommunications Systems, Digital Signal Processing, Digital Image Processing and Deep Learning.

Rui Hu is a Master student studying in the AUT.

Alberto Huertas Celdrán is an Irish Research Council Government of Ireland Postdoctoral research fellow associated with the TSSG, WIT. Huertas Celdr\'an received M.Sc. and Ph.D. degrees in Computer Science from the University of Murcia, Spain. His scientific interests include medical cyber-physical systems (MCPS), Brain-Computer Interfaces (BCI), cybersecurity, data privacy, continuous authentication, semantic technology, context-aware systems, and computer networks.

Prerana Jain is teaching assistant and pursuing her graduation from the Rustmaji Institute of Technology Border Security Force Academy in the Computer science Engineering discipline.

Shivangi Jain is an engineering graduate from the Rustamji Institute of Technology, BSF Academy Tekanpur, an institute run by the Border Security. She has work on various projects related to Cyber security and Machine Learning and represented college in the National Level competitions like Hackathon. She has written various articles and Blogs on Computer Programming and Cyber Security.

Avila Jayapalan received her B.E (ECE) from the V.M.K.V college of Engineering, M.Tech (Communication Engineering) from Vellore Institute Of Technology and Ph.D from SASTRA Deemed University, Thanjavur. Currently she is working as Senior Assistant Professor in the Department of ECE in SASTRA Deemed University, Thanjavur. She has a teaching experience of 15 years and she has published 35 Research articles in National & International journals. She has supervised many U.G and P.G projects. Her research area includes Wireless communication and Cognitive radio. She has published a book chapter in the book titled "Cognitive Radio in 4G/5G Wireless Communication Systems".

Manessa Jayaprakasam completed her B.E in CSE from Anna University, Trichy in 2011. She is having 2+ Years of Experience in IT. She is now working as a Freelance Trainer on Java Application Development and PHP. Her interest includes content security and multimedia applications.

José María Jorquera Valero is a PhD student working on Cybersecurity and Cyberdefence Research Lab at Murcia University. Jorquera Valero received BSc. and M.Sc. degrees in Computer Science from the University of Murcia, Spain. His scientific interests include computer networks, Machine Learning, cybersecurity, data privacy, and continuous authentication.

Abhishek Kataria is an engineering graduate from the Rustamji Institute of Technology, BSF Academy Tekanpur, an institute run by the Border Security. He has work on various projects related to Cyber security and Machine Learning and represented college in the National Level competitions like Hackathon. He has written various articles and Blogs on Computer Programming and Cyber Security.

Vinash Kaur - Research Area: IOT, Cloud Computing.

Gregorio Martinez Perez - Department of Information and Communication Engineering of the University of Murcia, Spain. His scientific activity is mainly devoted to cybersecurity, privacy and networking. Prof. Martinez Perez received M.Sc. and Ph.D. degrees in Computer Science from the University of Murcia. He has published more than 200 papers in national and international conference proceedings, magazines and journals. He has already supervised 10 PhD students, several of them recognized with honours.

Ana Carolina Monteiro graduated in Biomedicine, holds a Master's degree in Engineering, she is currently a Ph.D. Candidate by the DECOM, Faculty of Electrical and Computer Engineering (FEEC) at UNICAMP, and a researcher at the Laboratory of Visual Communications (LCV), developing research related to Digital Image Processing related to medical areas. Has affinity and expertise in Health and Clinical Analysis, with development in Matlab, C/C++, with topics of interest in Hematology, Medical Informatics, Cell Biology, Cell Pathology, Telecommunications, Broadcasting and Deep Learning

Shadi Nashwan was born in Amman, Jordan, 1978. He received the B.Sc. degree in Computer Science from Alazhar University, Palestine, 2001, the M.Sc. degree in Computer Science from University of Jordan, Jordan, 2003, and the Ph.D. degree in Computer and Network Security from Anglia Ruskin University, United Kingdom, 2009. After his Ph.D., he was assistant professor in Computer Science department, Al-Zaytoonah University, Amman, Jordan. In 2010 he joined as Assistant Professor in the Computer Science department, Jouf University, Saudi Arabia, where he became Associate Professor in Computer and Network Security, 2018. He is a publication chair of the annual International Conference on Computer and Information Sciences (ICCIS). Prof. Nashwan his research focuses on Cybersecurity, Authentication Protocol, Mobility Management, and Security of the Wireless Network such as NFC, RFID and WSNs. He has published several ISI and SCOPUS indexed papers in the area of authentication protocol, recovery techniques and mobility management.

Ser Minh Nguyen received his PhD degree in computer science from University of Auckland, New Zealand. His research interests include machine vision, deep learning and virtual reality.

Pedro Miguel Sánchez is a PhD student in Computer Science at the University of Murcia. Pedro Miguel Sánchez received M.Sc. and Bachelor degrees in Computer Science from the University of Murcia, Spain. His scientific interests include Machine learning, cybersecurity, data privacy, continuous authentication and computer networks.

Amany Sarhan received the B.Sc degree in Electronics Engineering, and M.Sc. in Computer Engineering from the Faculty of Engineering, Mansoura University, in 1990, and 1997, respectively. She awarded the Ph.D. degree as a joint research between Tanta Univ., Egypt and Univ. of Connecticut, USA. She is working now as a Full Prof. and head Computers and Control Dept., Tanta Univ., Egypt. Her interests are in the area of: Distributed Systems, Software Restructuring, Object-oriented Databases, and Image and video processing, GPU and Distributed Computations.

Shatha Shakhatreh is a lab instructor in the Network and Security Engineering department at Princess Sumaya University for technology (PSUT), Amman, Jordan. She received a Master's degree in Information System Security and Digital Criminology from PSUT. She has practical experience in Linux system administration. Her research interest includes threat hunting, malware analysis, privacy and digital forensics.

Poonkuntran Shanmugam received B.E in Information Technology from Bharathidasan University, Tiruchirapalli, India in 2003, M.Tech and Ph.D. in Computer and Information Technology from Manonmaniam Sundaranar University, Tirunelveli, India in 2005 and 2011 respectively. He is presently working as a Professor in Velammal College of Engineering and Technology, Madurai, Tamilnadu, India and executing three funded research grants from ISRO, India, DRDO, New Delhi and MNRE, New Delhi. He is having 15+ years of experience in teaching and research. He is a lifetime member of IACSIT, Singapore, CSI, India and ISTE, India. He has published papers in 4 national conferences, 43 international conferences, 1 national journal and 20 international journals on image processing, information security, and soft computing. He has written 6 books and 1 Chapter in Computer Science. He was the State Level Student Coordinator Position for Region VII, CSI, India in 2016-17. He received cognizant best faculty award for 2017-18. Presently he is working on Computer Vision for underwater autonomous vehicles and Information Security for Healthcare Information Systems. His areas of research interest include digital image processing, soft computing, energy aware computing, and computer vision.

Wei Qi Yan is an Associate Professor with the Auckland University of Technology (AUT), his expertise is in digital security, surveillance and forensics, he is leading the Computer and Communication Security (CCS) Research Group at AUT. Dr. Yan was an exchange Computer Scientist between the Royal Society of New Zealand (RSNZ) and the Chinese Academy of Sciences (CAS) China, he is Chair of the ACM Multimedia Chapter of New Zealand, a Member of the ACM, a Senior Member of the IEEE, TC members of the IEEE. Dr. Yan is a guest (adjunct) Professor with PhD supervision of the State Key Laboratory of Information Security (SKLOIS) China. A visiting Professor of the University of Auckland, New Zealand and the National University of Singapore, Singapore in computer science.

Index

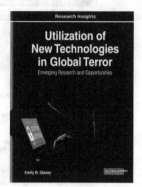

Ensure Quality Research is Introduced to the Academic Community

Become an IGI Global Reviewer for Authored Book Projects

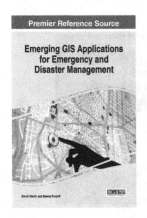

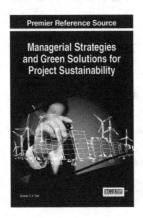

The overall success of an authored book project is dependent on quality and timely reviews.

In this competitive age of scholarly publishing, constructive and timely feedback significantly expedites the turnaround time of manuscripts from submission to acceptance, allowing the publication and discovery of forward-thinking research at a much more expeditious rate. Several IGI Global authored book projects are currently seeking highly-qualified experts in the field to fill vacancies on their respective editorial review boards:

Applications and Inquiries may be sent to:
development@igi-global.com

Applicants must have a doctorate (or an equivalent degree) as well as publishing and reviewing experience. Reviewers are asked to complete the open-ended evaluation questions with as much detail as possible in a timely, collegial, and constructive manner. All reviewers' tenures run for one-year terms on the editorial review boards and are expected to complete at least three reviews per term. Upon successful completion of this term, reviewers can be considered for an additional term.

If you have a colleague that may be interested in this opportunity,
we encourage you to share this information with them.

Printed in the United States
By Bookmasters